THE O'LEARY SERIES

COMPLETE EDITION

Microsoft®
Excel 2010:
A Case Approach

Timothy J. O'Leary

Professor Emeritus,
Arizona State University

Linda I. O'Leary

Connect
Learn
Succeed™

THE O'LEARY SERIES MICROSOFT® EXCEL 2010: A CASE APPROACH, COMPLETE EDITION

Published by McGraw-Hill, a business unit of The McGraw-Hill Companies, Inc., 1221 Avenue of the Americas, New York, NY, 10020. Copyright © 2011 by The McGraw-Hill Companies, Inc. All rights reserved. Printed in the United States of America. No part of this publication may be reproduced or distributed in any form or by any means, or stored in a database or retrieval system, without the prior written consent of The McGraw-Hill Companies, Inc., including, but not limited to, in any network or other electronic storage or transmission, or broadcast for distance learning.

Some ancillaries, including electronic and print components, may not be available to customers outside the United States.

This book is printed on acid-free paper.

1 2 3 4 5 6 7 8 9 0 RMN/RMN 1 0 9 8 7 6 5 4 3 2 1

ISBN   978-0-07-733136-8
MHID   0-07-733136-2

Vice president/Editor in chief: *Elizabeth Haefele*
Vice president/Director of marketing: *Alice Harra*
Publisher: *Scott Davidson*
Sponsoring editor: *Paul Altier*
Director, digital products: *Crystal Szewczyk*
Development editor II: *Alaina G. Tucker*
Development editor: *Alan Palmer*
Marketing manager: *Tiffany Russell*
Digital development editor: *Kevin White*
Director, Editing/Design/Production: *Jess Ann Kosic*
Project manager: *Marlena Pechan*
Senior buyer: *Michael R. McCormick*
Senior designer: *Srdjan Savanovic*
Senior photo research coordinator: *Jeremy Cheshareck*
Manager, digital production: *Janean A. Utley*
Media project manager: *Cathy L. Tepper*
Cover design: *Srdjan Savanovic*
Interior design: *Srdjan Savanovic*
Typeface: *10/12 New Aster LT STD*
Compositor: *Laserwords Private Limited*
Printer: *R. R. Donnelley*
Cover credit: © *Kjpargeter/Dreamstime.com*
Credits: The credits section for this book begins on page EXC.1 and is considered an extension of the copyright page.

Library of Congress Cataloging-in-Publication Data

O'Leary, Timothy J., 1947-
    Microsoft Excel 2010 : a case approach / Timothy J. O'Leary, Linda I. O'Leary.—1st ed.
      p. cm.—(The O'Leary series)
    Includes index.
    ISBN-13: 978-0-07-733136-8 (alk. paper)
    ISBN-10: 0-07-733136-2 (alk. paper)
    1. Microsoft Excel (Computer file) 2. Business—Computer programs. 3. Electronic spreadsheets. I. O'Leary, Linda I. II. Title. III. Series: O'Leary, Timothy J., 1947- O'Leary series.
HF5548.4.M523O354 2011
005.54—dc22   2011008995

The Internet addresses listed in the text were accurate at the time of publication. The inclusion of a Web site does not indicate an endorsement by the authors or McGraw-Hill, and McGraw-Hill does not guarantee the accuracy of the information presented at these sites.

www.mhhe.com

Brief Contents

Contents

LAB ② ENHANCING THE WORKSHEET WITH GRAPHICS AND CHARTS *EX2.1*

LAB 3 — MANAGING AND ANALYZING A WORKBOOK — EX3.1

WORKING TOGETHER 1: LINKING AND EMBEDDING BETWEEN WORD 2010 AND EXCEL 2010 — EXWT1.1

LAB 4 — USING SOLVER, CREATING TEMPLATES, AND EVALUATING SCENARIOS — EX4.1

LAB 5 USING DATA TABLES, USING LOOKUP AND IF FUNCTIONS, AND DESIGNING FORMS *EX5.1*

LAB 6 CREATING AND WORKING WITH TABLES *EX6.1*

Acknowledgments

We would like to extend our thanks to the professors who took time out of their busy schedules to provide us with the feedback necessary to develop the 2010 Edition of this text. The following professors offered valuable suggestions on revising the text:

Joan Albright
Greenville Technical College

Wilma Andrews
Virginia Commonwealth University

Robert M. Benavides
Collin College

Kim Cannon
Greenville Technical College

Paulette Comet
The Community College of Baltimore County

Michael Dunklebarger
Alamance Community College

Joel English
Centura College

Deb Fells
Mesa Community College

Tatyana Feofilaktova
ASA Institute

Sue Furnas
Collin College

Debbie Grande
The Community College of Rhode Island

Rachelle Hall
Glendale Community College

Katherine Herbert
Montclair State University

Terri Holly
Indian River State College

Mark W. Huber
University of Georgia

Joyce Kessel
Western International University

Hal P. Kingsley
Trocaire College

Diane Lending
James Madison University

Dr. Mo Manouchehripour
The Art Institute of Dallas

Sue McCrory
Missouri State University

Gary McFall
Purdue University

Margaret M. Menna
The Community College of Rhode Island

Philip H. Nielson
Salt Lake Community College

Craig Piercy
University of Georgia

Mark Renslow
Globe University/Minnesota School of Business

Ann Rowlette
Liberty University

Chakra Pani Sharma
ASA Institute

Eric Weinstein
Suffolk County Community College

Sheryl Wright
College of the Mainland

Laurie Zouharis
Suffolk University

We would like to thank those who took the time to help us develop the manuscript and ensure accuracy through painstaking edits: Brenda Nielsen of Mesa Community College–Red Mountain, Stephen J. Adams of Cleveland State University, Candice Spangler of Columbus State Community College, Kaari Busick, and Kate Scalzi.

Finally, we would like to thank team members from McGraw-Hill, whose renewed commitment, direction, and support have infused the team with the excitement of a new project. Leading the team from McGraw-Hill are Tiffany Russell, Marketing Manager, and Development Editor Alaina Tucker.

The production staff is headed by Marlena Pechan, Project Manager, whose planning and attention to detail have made it possible for us to successfully meet a very challenging schedule; Srdjan Savanovic, Designer; Michael McCormick, Production Supervisor; Kevin White, Digital Development Editor; Jeremy Cheshareck, Senior Photo Research Coordinator; and Betsy Blumenthal, copyeditor—team members on whom we can depend to do a great job.

Christy Parrish spent 20 years developing, designing, and delivering corporate training programs. She has contributed to several books on Microsoft Office and other productivity software packages. As a freelance author, she also has written a magazine series and numerous online articles on a wide variety of topics. Christy is also a member of her community artists' group and is recognized for her unique photographic skills that are on display at various galleries. She is married and has two sons that both share her love of writing and art.

Kaari Busick is a freelance technical writer and editor with over 15 years of experience in technical documentation, from end-user manuals to programmer training materials. After receiving a BA from Colby College, she went on to receive a certificate in Technical Communication from the University of Washington. She has co-authored two nonfiction books with VeloPress and Prima Publishing, as well as various articles and reviews. She lives in Chicago, and her Web site is at kaaribusick.com.

Preface

The 20th century brought us the dawn of the digital information age and unprecedented changes in information technology. There is no indication that this rapid rate of change will be slowing—it may even be increasing. As we begin the 21st century, computer literacy is undoubtedly becoming a prerequisite in whatever career you choose.

The goal of the O'Leary Series is to provide you with the necessary skills to efficiently use these applications. Equally important is the goal to provide a foundation for students to readily and easily learn to use future versions of this software. This series does this by providing detailed step-by-step instructions combined with careful selection and presentation of essential concepts.

Times are changing, technology is changing, and this text is changing too. As students of today, you are different from those of yesterday. You put much effort toward the things that interest you and the things that are relevant to you. Your efforts directed at learning application programs and exploring the Web seem, at times, limitless.

On the other hand, students often can be shortsighted, thinking that learning the skills to use the application is the only objective. The mission of the series is to build upon and extend this interest by not only teaching the specific application skills but by introducing the concepts that are common to all applications, providing students with the confidence, knowledge, and ability to easily learn the next generation of applications.

Instructor's Resource Center

The Online **Instructor's Resource Center** contains access to a computerized Test Bank, an Instructor's Manual, Solutions, and PowerPoint Presentation Slides. Features of the Instructor's Resource are described below.

- **Instructor's Manual** The Instructor's Manual, authored by the primary contributor, contains lab objectives, concepts, outlines, lecture notes, and command summaries. Also included are answers to all end-of-chapter material, tips for covering difficult materials, additional exercises, and a schedule showing how much time is required to cover text material.

- **Computerized Test Bank** The test bank, authored by the primary contributor, contains hundreds of multiple choice, true/false, and discussion questions. Each question will be accompanied by the correct answer, the level of learning difficulty, and corresponding page references. Our flexible EZ Test software allows you to easily generate custom exams.

- **PowerPoint Presentation Slides** The presentation slides, authored by the primary contributor, include lab objectives, concepts, outlines, text figures, and speaker's notes. Also included are bullets to illustrate key terms and FAQs.

Online Learning Center/Web Site

Found at **www.mhhe.com/oleary,** this site provides additional learning and instructional tools to enhance the comprehension of the text. The OLC/Web Site is divided into these three areas:

- **Information Center** Contains core information about the text, supplements, and the authors.

- **Instructor Center** Offers the aforementioned instructional materials, downloads, and other relevant links for professors.

- **Student Center** Contains data files, chapter competencies, chapter concepts, self-quizzes, additional Web links, and more.

Simnet Assessment for Office Applications

Simnet Assessment for Office Applications provides a way for you to test students' software skills in a simulated environment. Simnet is available for Microsoft Office 2010 and provides flexibility for you in your applications course by offering:

Pretesting options
Post-testing options
Course placement testing
Diagnostic capabilities to reinforce skills
Web delivery of tests
Certification preparation exams
Learning verification reports

For more information on skills assessment software, please contact your local sales representative, or visit us at **www.mhhe.com.**

O'Leary Series

The O'Leary Application Series for Microsoft Office is available separately or packaged with *Computing Essentials.* The O'Leary Application Series offers a step-by-step case-based approach to learning computer applications and is available in both introductory and complete versions.

Computing Concepts

Computing Essentials 2013 offers a unique, visual orientation that gives students a basic understanding of computing concepts. *Computing Essentials* encourages "active" learning with exercises, explorations, visual illustrations, and screen shots. While combining the "active" learning style with current topics and technology, this text provides an accurate snapshot of computing trends. When bundled with software application lab manuals, students are given a complete representation of the fundamental issues surrounding the personal computing environment.

About the Authors

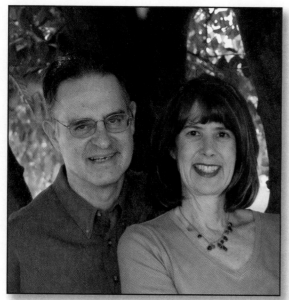

Tim and Linda O'Leary live in the American Southwest and spend much of their time engaging instructors and students in conversation about learning. In fact, they have been talking about learning for over 25 years. Something in those early conversations convinced them to write a book, to bring their interest in the learning process to the printed page. Today, they are as concerned as ever about learning, about technology, and about the challenges of presenting material in new ways, in terms of both content and method of delivery.

A powerful and creative team, Tim combines his 30 years of classroom teaching experience with Linda's background as a consultant and corporate trainer. Tim has taught courses at Stark Technical College in Canton, Ohio, and at Rochester Institute of Technology in upstate New York, and is currently a professor emeritus at Arizona State University in Tempe, Arizona. Linda offered her expertise at ASU for several years as an academic advisor. She also presented and developed materials for major corporations such as Motorola, Intel, Honeywell, and AT&T, as well as various community colleges in the Phoenix area.

Tim and Linda have talked to and taught numerous students, all of them with a desire to learn something about computers and applications that make their lives easier, more interesting, and more productive.

Each new edition of an O'Leary text, supplement, or learning aid has benefited from these students and their instructors who daily stand in front of them (or over their shoulders). The O'Leary Series is no exception.

Dedication

We dedicate this edition to our parents—Irene Perley Coats, Jean L. O'Leary, and Charles D. O'Leary—for all their support and love. We miss you.

Objectives

After completing the Introduction to Microsoft Office 2010, you should be able to:

1 Describe the Office 2010 applications.

2 Start an Office 2010 application.

3 Use the Ribbon, dialog boxes, and task panes.

4 Use menus, context menus, and shortcut keys.

5 Use Backstage view.

6 Open, close, and save files.

7 Navigate a document.

8 Enter, edit, and format text.

9 Select, copy, and move text.

10 Undo and redo changes.

11 Specify document properties.

12 Print a document.

13 Use Office 2010 Help.

14 Exit an Office 2010 application.

What Is Microsoft Office 2010?

Microsoft's Office 2010 is a comprehensive, integrated system of programs designed to solve a wide array of business needs. Although the programs can be used individually, they are designed to work together seamlessly, making it easy to connect people and organizations to information, business processes, and each other. The applications include tools used to create, discuss, communicate, and manage projects. If you share a lot of documents with other people, these features facilitate access to common documents. If you are away on business or do not have your PC with you, you can use Office 2010 Web applications, browser versions of Word, Excel, PowerPoint, and OneNote, to edit documents and collaborate with others.

Microsoft Office 2010 is packaged in several different combinations of programs or suites. The major programs and a brief description are provided in the following table.

Program	Description
Word 2010	Word processor program used to create text-based documents
Excel 2010	Spreadsheet program used to analyze numerical data
Access 2010	Database manager used to organize, manage, and display a database
PowerPoint 2010	Graphics presentation program used to create presentation materials
Outlook 2010	Desktop information manager and messaging client
InfoPath 2010	Used to create XML forms and documents
OneNote 2010	Note-taking and information organization tools
Publisher 2010	Tools to create and distribute publications for print, Web, and e-mail
Visio 2010	Diagramming and data visualization tools
SharePoint Designer 2010	Web site development and management for SharePoint servers
Project 2010	Project management tools

The four main components of Microsoft Office 2010—Word, Excel, Access, and PowerPoint—are the applications you will learn about in this series of labs. They are described in more detail in the following sections.

Word 2010

Word 2010 is a word processing software application whose purpose is to help you create text-based documents such as letters, memos, reports, e-mail messages, or any other type of correspondence. Word processors are one of the most flexible and widely used application software programs.

WORD 2010 FEATURES

The beauty of a word processor is that you can make changes or corrections as you are typing. Want to change a report from single spacing to double spacing? Alter the width of the margins? Delete some paragraphs and add others from yet another document? A word processor allows you to do all these things with ease.

Edit Content

Word 2010 excels in its ability to change or **edit** a document. Basic document editing involves correcting spelling, grammar, and sentence-structure errors and revising or updating existing text by inserting, deleting, and rearranging areas of text. For example, a document that lists prices can easily be updated to reflect new prices. A document that details procedures can be revised by deleting old procedures and inserting new ones. Many of these changes are made easily by cutting (removing) or copying (duplicating) selected text and then pasting (inserting) the cut or copied text in another location in the same or another document. Editing allows you to quickly revise a document, by changing only the parts that need to be modified.

To help you produce a perfect document, Word 2010 includes many additional editing support features. The AutoCorrect feature checks the spelling and grammar in a document as text is entered. Many common errors are corrected automatically for you. Others are identified and a correction suggested. A thesaurus can be used to display alternative words that have a meaning similar or opposite to a word you entered. The Find and Replace feature can be used to quickly locate specified text and replace it with other text throughout a document. In addition, Word 2010 includes a variety of tools that automate the process of many common tasks, such as creating tables, form letters, and columns.

Format Content

You also can easily control the appearance or **format** of the document. Perhaps the most noticeable formatting feature is the ability to apply different fonts (type styles and sizes) and text appearance changes such as bold, italics, and color to all or selected portions of the document. Additionally, you can add color shading behind individual pieces of text or entire paragraphs and pages to add emphasis. Other formatting features include changes to entire paragraphs, such as the line spacing and alignment of text between the margins. You also can format entire pages by displaying page numbers, changing margin settings, and applying backgrounds.

To make formatting even easier, Word 2010 includes Document Themes and Styles. Document Themes apply a consistent font, color, and line effect to an entire document. Styles apply the selected style design to a selection of text. Further, Word 2010 includes a variety of built-in preformatted content that helps you quickly produce modern-looking, professional documents. Among these are galleries of cover page designs, pull quotes, and header and footer designs. While selecting many of these design choices, a visual live preview is displayed, making it easy to see how the design would look in your document. In addition, you can select from a wide variety of templates to help you get started on creating many common types of documents such as flyers, calendars, faxes, newsletters, and memos.

Insert Illustrations

To further enhance your documents, you can insert many different types of graphic elements. These include drawing objects, SmartArt, charts, pictures, clip art, and screenshots. The drawing tools supplied with Word 2010 can be used to create your own drawings, or you can select from over 100 adjustable shapes and modify them to your needs. All drawings can be further enhanced with 3-D effects, shadows, colors, and textures. SmartArt graphics allow you to create a visual representation of your information. They include many different layouts such as a process or cycle that are designed to help you communicate an idea. Charts can be inserted to illustrate and compare data. Complex pictures can be inserted in documents by scanning your own, using supplied or purchased clip art, or downloading images from the World Wide Web. Additionally, you can produce fancy text effects using the WordArt tool. Finally, you can quickly capture and insert a picture, called a screenshot, from another application running on your computer into the current document.

Collaborate with Others

Group collaboration on projects is common in industry today. Word 2010 includes many features to help streamline how documents are developed and changed by group members. A discussion feature allows multiple people to insert remarks in the same document without having to route the document to each person or reconcile multiple reviewers' comments. You can easily consolidate all changes and comments from different reviewers in one simple step and accept or reject changes as needed.

Two documents you will produce in the first two Word 2010 labs, a letter and flyer, are shown here.

A letter containing a tabbed table, indented paragraphs, and text enhancements is quickly created using basic Word features

January 27, 2012

Dear Adventure Traveler:

Imagine camping under the stars in Africa, hiking and paddling your way through the rainforests of Costa Rica, or following in the footsteps of the ancient Inca as you backpack along the Inca trail to Machu Picchu. Turn these thoughts of adventure into memories you will cherish forever by joining Adventure Travel Tours on one of our four new adventure tours.

To tell you more about these exciting new advent[...] area. These presentations will focus on the features and c[...] of the places you will visit and activities you can participate[...] Plan to attend one of the following presentations:

Date	Time	Locati[...]
February 5	8:00 p.m.	Renaissan[...]
February 19	7:30 p.m.	Airport Pla[...]
March 8	8:00 p.m.	Crowne Co[...]

In appreciation of your past patronage, we are ple[...] of the new tour packages. You must book the trip at least[...] this letter to qualify for the discount.

Our vacation tours are professionally developed s[...] everything in the price of your tour while giving you the be[...] these features:

➤ All accommodations and meals
➤ All entrance fees, excursions, transfers and tips
➤ Professional tour manager and local guides

We hope you will join us this year on another spec[...] Travel Tours each day is an adventure. For reservations, pl[...] Travel Tours directly at 1-800-555-0004.

Be[...]

St[...]
Ad[...]

ADVENTURE TRAVEL TOURS

NEW ADVENTURES

Attention adventure travelers! Attend an Adventure Travel presentation to learn about some of the earth's greatest unspoiled habitats and find out how you can experience the adventure of a lifetime. This year Adventure Travel Tours is introducing four new tours that offer you a unique opportunity to combine many different outdoor activities while exploring the world.

Costa Rica Rivers and Rainforests

India Wildlife Adventure

Safari in Tanzania

Inca Trail to Machu Picchu

Presentation dates and times are January 5 at 7:00 p.m., February 3 at 7:30 p.m., and March 8 at 7:00 p.m. All presentations are held at convenient hotel locations. The hotels are located in downtown Los Angeles, in Santa Clara, and at the LAX airport.

Call Adventure Travel Tours at 1-800-555-0004 for presentation locations, a full color brochure, and itinerary information, costs, and trip dates. Student Name will gladly help with all of your questions.

A flyer incorporating many visual enhancements such as colored text, varied text styles, and graphic elements is both eye-catching and informative

IO.4   Introduction to Microsoft Office 2010

Excel 2010 is an electronic spreadsheet, or **worksheet**, that is used to organize, manipulate, and graph numeric data. Once used almost exclusively by accountants, worksheets are now widely used by nearly every profession. Nearly any job that uses rows and columns of numbers can be performed using an electronic spreadsheet. Once requiring hours of labor and/or costly accountants' fees, data analysis is now available almost instantly using electronic spreadsheets and has become a routine business procedure. This powerful business tool has revolutionized the business world. Typical uses include the creation of budgets and financial planning for both business and personal situations. Marketing professionals record and evaluate sales trends. Teachers record grades and calculate final grades. Personal trainers record the progress of their clients.

EXCEL 2010 FEATURES

Excel 2010 includes many features that not only help you create a well-designed worksheet, but one that produces accurate results. The features include the ability to quickly edit and format data, perform calculations, create charts, and print the spreadsheet. Using Excel 2010, you can quickly analyze and manage data and communicate your findings to others. The program not only makes it faster to create worksheets, but it also produces professional-appearing results.

Enter and Edit Data

The Microsoft Excel 2010 spreadsheet program uses a workbook file that contains one or more worksheets. Each worksheet can be used to organize different types of related information. The worksheet consists of rows and columns that create a grid of cells. You enter numeric data or descriptive text into a cell. These entries can then be erased, moved, copied, or edited.

Format Data

Like text in a Word document, the design and appearance of entries in a worksheet can be enhanced in many ways. For instance, you can change the font style and size and add special effects such as bold, italic, borders, boxes, drop shadows, and shading to selected cells. You also can use cell styles to quickly apply predefined combinations of these formats to selections. Additionally, you can select from different document themes, predefined combinations of colors, fonts, and effects, to give your workbooks a consistent, professional appearance.

Unlike the Word application, Excel includes many formatting features that are designed specifically for numeric data. For example, numeric entries can be displayed with commas, dollar signs, or a set number of decimal places. Special formatting, such as color bars, can be applied automatically to ranges of cells to emphasize data based on a set of criteria you establish and to highlight trends.

Analyze Data

The power of a spreadsheet application is its ability to perform calculations from very simple sums to the most complex financial and mathematical formulas. Formulas can be entered that perform calculations using data contained in specified cells. The results of the calculations are displayed in the cell containing the formula. Predefined formulas, called functions, can be used to quickly perform complex calculations such as calculating loan payments or statistical analysis of data.

Analysis of data in a spreadsheet once was too expensive and time-consuming. Now, using electronic worksheets, you can use what-if or sensitivity analysis by changing the values in selected cells and immediately observing the effect on related cells in the worksheet. Other analysis tools such as Solver and Scenarios allow you to see the effects of possible alternative courses of action to help forecast future outcomes.

Chart Data

Using Excel, you also can produce a visual display of numeric data in the form of graphs or charts. As the values in the worksheet change, charts referencing those values automatically adjust to reflect the changes. You also can enhance the appearance of a chart by using different type styles and sizes, adding three-dimensional effects, and including text and objects such as lines and arrows.

Two worksheets you will produce using Excel 2010 are shown below.

A worksheet showing the quarterly sales forecast containing a graphic, text enhancements, and a chart of the data is quickly created using basic Excel 2010 features

A large worksheet incorporating more complex formulas, visual enhancements such as colored text, varied text styles, and graphic elements is both informative and attractive

Access 2010 is a relational database management application that is used to create and analyze a database. A **database** is a collection of related data. **Tables** consist of columns (called **fields**) and rows (called **records**). Each row contains a record, which is all the information about one person, thing, or place. Each field is the smallest unit of information about a record.

In a relational database, the most widely used database structure, data is organized in linked tables. The tables are related or linked to one another by a common field. Relational databases allow you to create smaller and more manageable database tables, since you can combine and extract data between tables.

For example, a state's motor vehicle department database might have an address table. Each row (record) in the table would contain address information about one individual. Each column (field) would contain just one piece of information, for example, zip codes. The address table would be linked to other tables in the database by common fields. For example, the address table might be linked to a vehicle owner's table by name and linked to an outstanding citation table by license number (see example below).

Address Table

Name	License Number	Street Address	City	State	Zip
Aaron, Linda	FJ1987	10032 Park Lane	San Jose	CA	95127
Abar, John	D12372	1349 Oak St	Lakeville	CA	94128
Abell, Jack	LK3457	95874 State St	Stone	CA	95201
•	•	•	•	•	•
•	•	•	•	•	•
•	•	•	•	•	•

key fields linked   key fields linked

Owner's Table

Name	Plate Number
Abell, Jack	ABK241
Abrams, Sue	LMJ198
Abril, Pat	ZXA915
•	•
•	•
•	•

Outstanding Citation Table

License Number	Citation Code	Violation
T25476	00031	Speed
D98372	19001	Park
LK3457	89100	Speed
•	•	•
•	•	•
•	•	•

ACCESS 2010 FEATURES

Access 2010 is a powerful program with numerous easy-to-use features including the ability to quickly locate information; add, delete, modify, and sort records; analyze data; and produce professional-looking reports. Some of the basic Access 2010 features are described next.

Find Information

Once you enter data into the database table, you can quickly search the table to locate a specific record based on the data in a field. In a manual system, you can usually locate a record by knowing one key piece of information. For example, if the records are stored in a file cabinet alphabetically by last name, to quickly find a record, you must know the last name. In a computerized database, even if the records are sorted or organized by last name, you can still quickly locate a record using information in another field.

Add, Delete, and Modify Records

Using Access, it is also easy to add and delete records from the table. Once you locate a record, you can edit the contents of the fields to update the record or delete the record entirely from the table. You also can add new records to a table. When you enter a new record, it is automatically placed in the correct organizational location within the table. Creation of forms makes it easier to enter and edit data as well.

Sort and Filter Records

The capability to arrange or sort records in the table according to different fields can provide more meaningful information. You can organize records by name, department, pay, class, or any other category you need at a particular time. Sorting the records in different ways can provide information to different departments for different purposes.

Additionally, you can isolate and display a subset of records by specifying filter criteria. The criteria specify which records to display based on data in selected fields.

Analyze Data

Using Access, you can analyze the data in a table and perform calculations on different fields of data. Instead of pulling each record from a filing cabinet, recording the piece of data you want to use, and then performing the calculation on the recorded data, you can simply have the database program perform the calculation on all the values in the specified field. Additionally, you can ask questions or query the table to find only certain records that meet specific conditions to be used in the analysis. Information that was once costly and time-consuming to get is now quickly and readily available.

Generate Reports

Access includes many features that help you quickly produce reports ranging from simple listings to complex, professional-looking reports. You can create a simple report by asking for a listing of specified fields of data and restricting the listing to records meeting designated conditions. You can create a more complex professional report using the same restrictions or conditions as the simple report, but you can display the data in different layout styles, or with titles, headings, subtotals, or totals.

A database and a report that you will produce using Access 2010 are shown on the next page.

A relational database can be created and modified easily using basic Access 2010 features

Job Position Report
For Landis

Employee ID	First Name	Last Name	Position
12703	Jeff	Bader	Fitness Instructor
12389	Jennifer	Blackman	Sales Associate
05015	Scott	Briggs	Personal Trainer Director
12501	Elizabeth	DeLuca	Personal Trainer
12855	Kimberly	Fachet	Sales Associate
13484	Stephanie	Franklin	Food Service Server
12914	Alfonso	Gomez	Cleaning
22469	Ryan	Hogan	Personal Trainer
13303	Chris	Jensen	Greeter
13027	Kimberly	Kieken	Food Service Server
07650	Chris	Lamm	Sales Director
22085	Kristina	Lindau	Child Care Provider
13655	Juan	Martinez	Fitness Instructor
03225	Dan	Morgan	Food Service Director
99999	Student	Name	Human Resources Administrator
12420	Allison	Player	Maintenance
13005	Emily	Reilly	Assistant Manager
22297	Patricia	Rogondino	Greeter
07287	Anita	Roman	Child Care Director
12918	Carlos	Ruiz	Assistant Manager
00212	Chad	Schiff	Club Director
12583	Marie	Sullivan	Greeter
03890	Erona	Thi	Fitness Director
12380	Jessica	Thomas	Fitness Instructor

Saturday, December 01, 2012

Page 1 of 1

A professional-looking report can be quickly generated from information contained in a database

PowerPoint 2010 is a graphics presentation program designed to help you produce a high-quality presentation that is both interesting to the audience and effective in its ability to convey your message. A presentation can be as simple as overhead transparencies or as sophisticated as an on-screen electronic display. Graphics presentation programs can produce black-and-white or color overhead transparencies, 35 mm slides, onscreen electronic presentations called **slide shows**, Web pages for Web use, and support materials for both the speaker and the audience.

POWERPOINT 2010 FEATURES

Although creating an effective presentation is a complicated process, Power-Point 2010 helps simplify this process by providing assistance in the content development phase, as well as in the layout and design phase. PowerPoint includes features such as text handling, outlining, graphing, drawing, animation, clip art, and multimedia support. In addition, the programs suggest layouts for different types of presentations and offer professionally designed templates to help you produce a presentation that is sure to keep your audience's attention. In addition, you can quickly produce the support materials to be used when making a presentation to an audience.

Develop, Enter, and Edit Content

The content development phase includes deciding on the topic of your presentation, the organization of the content, and the ultimate message you want to convey to the audience. As an aid in this phase, PowerPoint 2010 helps you organize your thoughts based on the type of presentation you are making by providing both content and design templates. Based on the type of presentation, such as selling a product or suggesting a strategy, the template provides guidance by suggesting content ideas and organizational tips. For example, if you are making a presentation on the progress of a sales campaign, the program would suggest that you enter text on the background of the sales campaign as the first page, called a **slide**; the current status of the campaign as the next slide; and accomplishments, schedule, issues and problems, and where you are heading on subsequent slides.

Design Layouts

The layout for each slide is the next important decision. Again, PowerPoint 2010 helps you by suggesting text layout features such as title placement, bullets, and columns. You also can incorporate graphs of data, tables, organizational charts, clip art, and other special text effects in the slides.

PowerPoint 2010 also includes professionally designed themes to further enhance the appearance of your slides. These themes include features that standardize the appearance of all the slides in your presentation. Professionally selected combinations of text and background colors, common typefaces and sizes, borders, and other art designs take the worry out of much of the design layout.

Deliver Presentations

After you have written and designed the slides, you can use the slides in an onscreen electronic presentation or a Web page for use on the Web. An onscreen presentation uses the computer to display the slides on an overhead projection screen. As you prepare this type of presentation, you can use the rehearsal feature that allows you to practice and time your presentation. The length of time to display each slide can be set and your entire presentation can be completed within the allotted time. A presentation also can be modified to display on a Web site and run using a Web browser. Finally, you can package the presentation to a CD for distribution.

A presentation that you will produce using PowerPoint 2010 is shown below.

A presentation consists of a series of pages or "slides" presenting the information you want to convey in an organized and attractive manner

When running an on-screen presentation, each slide of the presentation is displayed full-screen on your computer monitor or projected onto a screen

As you follow the directions in the following hands-on section and in the application labs, you need to know the instructional conventions that are used. Hands-on instructions you are to perform appear as a sequence of numbered steps. Within each step, a series of bullets identifies the specific actions that must be performed. Step numbering begins over within each topic heading throughout the lab.

Three types of marginal notes appear throughout the labs. Another Method notes provide alternate ways of performing the same command. Having Trouble? notes provide advice or cautions for steps that may cause problems. Additional Information notes provide more information about a topic.

COMMANDS

Commands that are initiated using a command button and the mouse appear following the word "Click." The icon (and the icon name if the icon does not include text) is displayed following "Click." If there is another way to perform the same action, it appears in an Another Method margin note when the action is first introduced as shown in Example A.

When a feature has already been covered and you are more familiar with using the application, commands will appear as shown in Example B.

Example A

1

- Select the list of four tours.

- Open the Home tab.

- Click **B** Bold in the Font group.

Another Method

The keyboard shortcut is Ctrl + B.

Example B

1

- Select the list of four tours.

- Click **B** Bold in the Font group of the Home tab.

OR

1

- Bold the list of four tours.

Sometimes, clicking on an icon opens a drop-down list or a menu of commands. Commands that are to be selected follow the word "Select" and appear in black text. You can select an item by pointing to it using the mouse or by moving to it using the directional keys. When an option is selected, it appears highlighted; however, the action is not carried out. Commands that you are to complete appear following the word "Choose." You can choose a command by clicking on it using the mouse or by pressing the [Enter] key once it is selected. Initially these commands will appear as in Example A. Choosing a command carries out the associated action. As you become more familiar with the application, commands will appear as shown in Example B.

Example A

1

● Click [A ▼] **Font Color in the Font group of the Home tab.**

● **Select Green.**

● **Choose Dark Blue.**

Example B

1

● Click [A ▼] **Font Color and choose Dark Blue.**

FILE NAMES AND INFORMATION TO TYPE

Plain blue text identifies file names you need to select or enter. Information you are asked to type appears in blue and bold. (See Example C.)

Example C

1

● **Open the document** wd01_Flyer.

● **Type Adventure Travel presents four new trips**

Common Office 2010 Features

Now that you know a little about each of the applications in Microsoft Office 2010, you will take a look at some of the features that are common to all Office 2010 applications. In this hands-on section you will learn to use the common interface and application features to allow you to get a feel for how Office 2010 works. Although Word 2010 will be used to demonstrate how the features work, only features that are common to all the Office applications will be addressed.

COMMON INTERFACE FEATURES

All the Office 2010 applications have a common **user interface**, a set of graphical elements that are designed to help you interact with the program and provide instructions as to the actions you want to perform. These features include the use of the Ribbon, Quick Access Toolbar, task panes, menus, dialog boxes, and the File tab.

Starting an Office 2010 Application

To demonstrate the common features, you will start the Word 2010 application. There are several ways to start an Office 2010 application. The two most common methods are by clicking the ● Start button to see a menu of available programs or by clicking a desktop shortcut for the program if it is available.

Additional Information

The procedure to start Excel, Access, and PowerPoint is the same as starting Word, except that you must select the appropriate program name or shortcut.

1

● **Click** ● **Start to display the Start menu.**

● **Choose Microsoft Word 2010.**

Having Trouble?

If you do not see the program name on the Start menu, select All Programs, choose Microsoft Office, and then choose Microsoft Word 2010.

OR

1

● **Double-click the** ▣ **shortcut on the desktop.**

2

● **If necessary, click** ▣ **Maximize in the title bar to maximize the window.**

Your screen should be similar to Figure 1

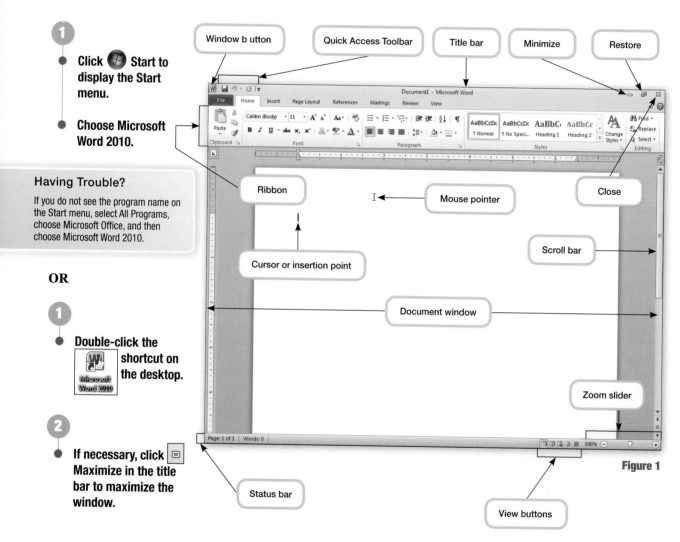

Figure 1

WWW.MHHE.COM/OLEARY

Additional Information

Application windows can be sized, moved, and otherwise manipulated like any other windows on the desktop.

Additional Information

You will learn about opening existing files shortly.

Additional Information

You will learn about other mouse pointer shapes and what they mean as you use the specific application programs.

The Word 2010 program is started and displayed in a window on the desktop. All application windows display a title bar at the top of the window that includes the file name followed by the program name, in this case Microsoft Word. They also include the ⬛ Minimize, ⬛ Restore Down, and ⬛ Close buttons at the right end of the title bar. **Buttons** are graphical elements that perform the associated action when you click on them using the mouse. At the left end of the title bar is the ⬛ Window button. Clicking this button opens a menu of commands that allow you to size, move, and close the window just as the buttons on the right end of the title bar. To the right of the ⬛ Window button is the **Quick Access Toolbar** (QAT), which provides quick access to frequently used commands. By default, it includes the ⬛ Save, ⬛ Undo, and ⬛ Redo buttons, commands that Microsoft considers to be crucial. It is always available and is a customizable toolbar to which you can add your own favorite buttons.

Below the title bar is the **Ribbon**, which provides a centralized location of commands that are used to work in your document. The Ribbon has the same basic structure and is found in all Office 2010 applications. However, many of the commands found in the Ribbon vary with the specific applications. You will learn how to use the Ribbon shortly.

The large center area of the program window is the **document window** where open application files are displayed. When you first start Word 2010, a new blank Word document named Document1 (shown in the title bar) automatically opens, ready for you to start creating a new document. In Excel, a new, blank workbook named Book1 would be opened and in PowerPoint a new, blank presentation file named Presentation1 would be opened. In Access, however, a new blank database file is not opened automatically. Instead, you must create and name a new database file or open an existing database file.

The **cursor**, also called the **insertion point**, is the blinking vertical bar that marks your location in the document and indicates where text you type will appear. Across all Office applications, the mouse pointer appears as I I-beam when it is used to position the insertion point when entering text and as a ⬛ when it can be used to select items. There are many other mouse pointer shapes that are both common to and specific to the different applications.

On the right of the document window is a vertical scroll bar. A **scroll bar** is used with a mouse to bring additional information into view in a window. The vertical scroll bar is used to move up or down. A horizontal scroll bar is also displayed when needed and moves side to side in the window. The scroll bar is a common feature to all Windows and Office 2010 applications; however, it may not appear in all applications until needed.

At the bottom of the application window is another common feature called the **status bar**. It displays information about the open file and features that help you view the file. It displays different information depending upon the application you are using. For example, the Word status bar displays information about the number of pages and words in the document, whereas the Excel status bar displays the mode of operation and the count, average, and sum of values in selected cells. All Office 2010 applications include **View buttons** that are used to change how the information in the document window is displayed. The View buttons are different for each application. Finally, a **Zoom Slider**, located at the far right end of the status bar, is used to change the amount of information displayed in the document window by "zooming in" to get a close-up view or "zooming out" to see more of the document at a reduced view.

Displaying ScreenTips

You are probably wondering how you would know what action the different buttons perform. To help you identify buttons, the Office applications display ScreenTips when you point to them.

1

Point to the 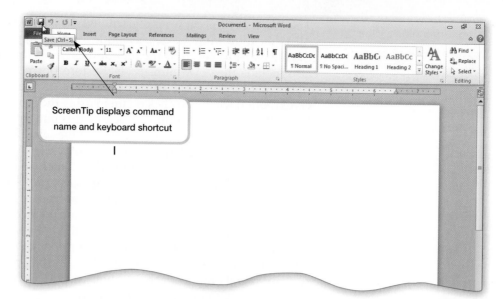 Save button in the Quick Access Toolbar.

Your screen should be similar to Figure 2

ScreenTip displays command name and keyboard shortcut

Figure 2

A **ScreenTip**, also called a **tooltip**, appears displaying the command name and the keyboard shortcut, Ctrl + S. A **keyboard shortcut** is a combination of keys that can be used to execute a command in place of clicking the button. In this case, if you hold down the Ctrl key while typing the letter S, you will access the command to save a file. ScreenTips also often include a brief description of the action a command performs.

Using Menus

Notice the small button at the end of the Quick Access Toolbar. Clicking this button opens a menu of commands that perform tasks associated with the Quick Access Toolbar.

1

Point to the ⏷ button at the end of the Quick Access Toolbar to display the ScreenTip.

Click ⏷ to open the menu.

Your screen should be similar to Figure 3

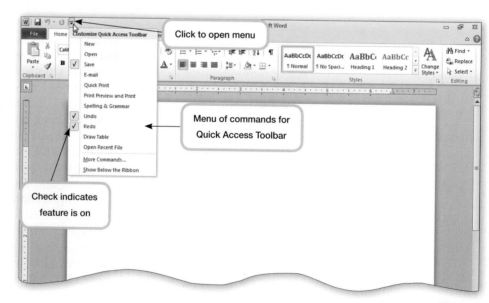

Click to open menu

Menu of commands for Quick Access Toolbar

Check indicates feature is on

Figure 3

The first 11 items in the menu allow you to quickly add a command button to or remove a command button from the Quick Access Toolbar. Those commands that are already displayed in the Quick Access Toolbar are preceded with a checkmark. The last two commands allow you to access other command features to customize the Quick Access Toolbar or change its location.

Once a menu is open, you can select a command from the menu by pointing to it. As you do the selected command appears highlighted. Like buttons, resting the mouse pointer over the menu command options will display a ScreenTip. Then to choose a selected command, you click on it. Choosing a command performs the action associated with the command or button. You will use several of these features next.

2

● **Point to the commands in the Quick Access Toolbar menu to select (highlight) them and see the ScreenTips.**

● **Click on the Open command to choose it and add it to the Quick Access Toolbar.**

Your screen should be similar to Figure 4

Figure 4

The command button to open a document has been added to the Quick Access Toolbar. Next, you will remove this button and then you will change the location of the Quick Access Toolbar. Another way to access some commands is to use a context menu. A **context menu**, also called a **shortcut menu**, is opened by right-clicking on an item on the screen. This menu is context sensitive, meaning it displays only those commands relevant to the item or screen location. For example, right-clicking on the Quick Access Toolbar will display the commands associated with using the Quick Access Toolbar and the Ribbon. You will use this method to remove the Open button and move the Quick Access Toolbar.

3 ● Point to the Open button on the Quick Access Toolbar and right-click.

● Click on the Remove from Quick Access Toolbar command to choose it.

● Right-click on any button in the Quick Access Toolbar again and choose the Show Quick Access Toolbar Below the Ribbon option.

Another Method

You also can type the underlined letter of a command to choose it or press [Enter] to choose a selected command.

Your screen should be similar to Figure 5

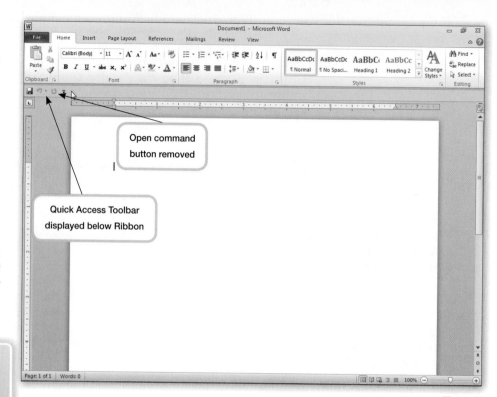

Figure 5

The Quick Access Toolbar is now displayed full size below the Ribbon. This is useful if you have many buttons on the toolbar; however, it takes up document viewing space. You will return it to its compact size.

4 ● Display the Quick Access Toolbar menu.

● Choose Show Above the Ribbon.

Your screen should be similar to Figure 6

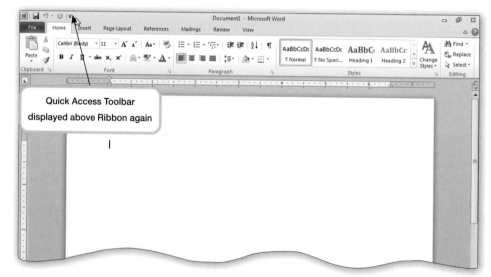

Figure 6

The Quick Access Toolbar is displayed above the Ribbon again.

Using the Ribbon

The Ribbon has three basic parts: tabs, groups, and commands (see Figure 7). **Tabs** are used to divide the Ribbon into major activity areas. Each tab is then organized into **groups** that contain related items. The related items are **commands** that consist of command buttons, a box to enter information, or a menu. Clicking on a command button performs the associated action or displays a list of additional options.

The Ribbon tabs, commands, and features vary with the different Office applications. For example, the Word Ribbon displays tabs and commands used to create a text document, whereas the Excel Ribbon displays tabs and commands used to create an electronic worksheet. Although the Ribbon commands are application specific, many are also common to all Office 2010 applications. In all applications, the Ribbon also can be customized by changing the built-in tabs or creating your own tabs and groups to personalize your workspace and provide faster access to the commands you use most.

Opening Tabs

The Word application displays the File tab and seven Ribbon tabs. The Home tab (shown in Figure 6), consisting of five groups, appears highlighted, indicating it is the open or active tab. This tab is available in all the Office 2010 applications and because it contains commands that are most frequently used when you first start an application or open a file, it is initially the open tab. In Word, the commands in the Home tab help you perform actions related to creating the text content of your document. In the other Office 2010 applications, the Home tab contains commands related to creating the associated type of document, such as a worksheet, presentation, or database. To open another tab you click on the tab name.

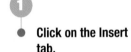

Click on the Insert tab.

Your screen should be similar to Figure 7

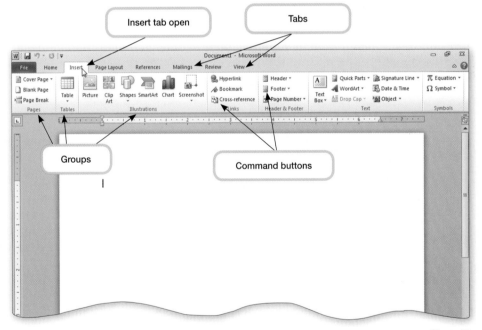

Figure 7

This Insert tab is now open and is the active tab. It contains seven groups whose commands have to do with inserting items into a document. As you use the Office applications, you will see that the Ribbon contains many of the same tabs, groups, and commands across the applications. For example, the Insert tab is available in all applications except Access. Others, such as the References tab in Word, are specific to the application. You also will see that many of the groups and commands in the common tabs, such as the Clipboard group of commands in the Home tab, contain all or many of the same commands across applications. Other groups in the common tabs contain commands that are specific to the application.

To save space, some tabs, called **contextual tabs** or **on-demand tabs**, are displayed only as needed. For example, when you are working with a picture, the Picture Tools tab appears. The contextual nature of this feature keeps the work area uncluttered when the feature is not needed and provides ready access to it when it is needed.

2

● Click on each of the other tabs, ending with the View tab, to see their groups and commands.

Your screen should be similar to Figure 8

Figure 8

Each tab relates to a type of activity; for example, the View tab commands perform activities related to viewing the document. Within each tab, similar commands are grouped together to make it easy to find the commands you want to use.

Displaying Enhanced ScreenTips

Although command buttons display graphic representations of the action they perform, often the graphic is not descriptive enough. As you have learned, pointing to a button displays the name of the button and the keyboard short-cut in a ScreenTip. To further help explain what a button does, many buttons in the Ribbon display **Enhanced ScreenTips**. For example, the Paste button in the Clipboard group of the Home tab is a two-part button. Clicking on the upper part will immediately perform an action, whereas clicking on the lower part will display additional options. You will use this feature next to see the Enhanced ScreenTips.

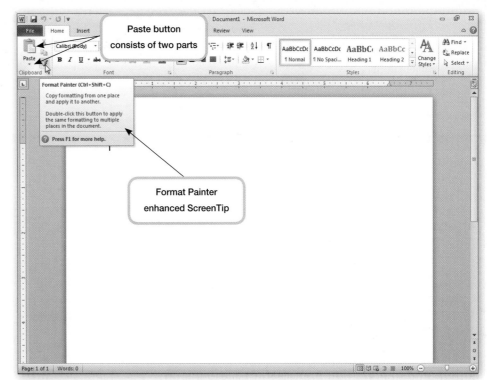

1

- Click on the Home tab to open it.

- Point to the upper part of the Paste button in the Clipboard group.

- Point to the lower part of the Paste button in the Clipboard group.

- Point to Format Painter in the Clipboard group.

Your screen should be similar to Figure 9

Figure 9

Additional Information

Not all commands have keyboard shortcuts.

Additional Information

You will learn about using Help shortly.

Because the Paste button is divided into two parts, both parts display separate Enhanced ScreenTips containing the button name; the keyboard shortcut key combination, Ctrl + V; and a brief description of what action will be performed when you click on that part of the button. Pointing to Format Painter displays an Enhanced ScreenTip that provides more detailed information about the command. Enhanced ScreenTips may even display information such as procedures or illustrations. You can find out what the feature does without having to look it up using Office Help, a built-in reference source. If a feature has a Help article, you can automatically access it by pressing F1 while the Enhanced ScreenTip is displayed.

Using Command Buttons

Clicking on most command buttons immediately performs the associated action. Many command buttons, however, include an arrow as part of the button that affects how the button works. If a button includes an arrow that is separated from the graphic with a line when you point to the button (as in Bullets), clicking the button performs the associated default action and clicking the arrow displays a menu of options. If a button displays an arrow that is not separated from the graphic with a line when you point to it (as in Line Spacing), clicking the button immediately displays a menu of options. To see an example of a drop-down menu, you will open the Bullets menu.

1

Click in the 📋▾ Bullets button.

Your screen should be similar to Figure 10

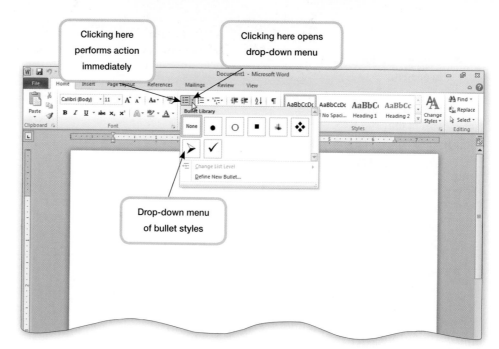

Figure 10

A drop-down menu of different bullet styles is displayed. The drop-down menu will disappear when you make a selection or click on any other area of the window.

2

Click outside the Bullet menu to clear it.

Click Line and Paragraph Spacing.

Your screen should be similar to Figure 11

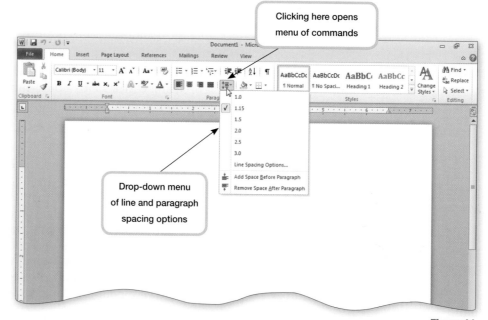

Figure 11

Another Method

You also can open tabs and choose Ribbon commands using the access key shortcuts. Press Alt or F10 to display the access key letters in KeyTips over each available feature. Then type the letter for the feature you want to use.

The menu of options opened automatically when you clicked Line and Paragraph Spacing.

Using the Dialog Box Launcher

Because there is not enough space, only the most used commands are displayed in the Ribbon. If more commands are available, a ⬜ button, called the **dialog box launcher**, is displayed in the lower-right corner of the group. Clicking ⬜ opens a dialog box or task pane of additional options.

1

- **Click outside the Line and Paragraph Spacing menu to clear it.**

- **Point to the ⬜ of the Paragraph group to see the ScreenTip.**

- **Click ⬜ of the Paragraph group.**

Your screen should be similar to Figure 12

Clicking dialog box launcher opens dialog box of commands

Dialog box of paragraph commands

Figure 12

The Paragraph dialog box appears. It provides access to the more advanced paragraph settings options. Selecting options from the dialog box and clicking OK will close the dialog box and apply the options as specified. To cancel the dialog box, you can click Cancel or ❌ Close in the dialog box title bar.

2

- **Click ❌ to close the dialog box.**

- **Click ⬜ in the Clipboard group.**

Your screen should be similar to Figure 13

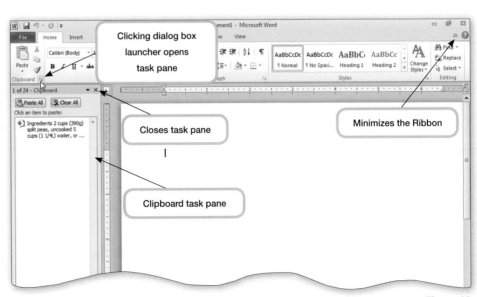

Clicking dialog box launcher opens task pane

Closes task pane

Minimizes the Ribbon

Clipboard task pane

Figure 13

A task pane is open that contains features associated with the Clipboard. Unlike a dialog box, a task pane is a separate window that can be sized and moved. Generally, task panes are attached or docked to one edge of the application window. Also, task panes remain open until you close them. This allows you to make multiple selections from the task pane while continuing to work on other areas of your document.

● Click ☒ Close in the upper-right corner of the task pane to close it.

Minimize and Expand the Ribbon

Sometimes you may not want to see the entire Ribbon so that more space is available in the document area. You can minimize the Ribbon by double-clicking the active tab.

● **Double-click the Home tab.**

Your screen should be similar to Figure 14

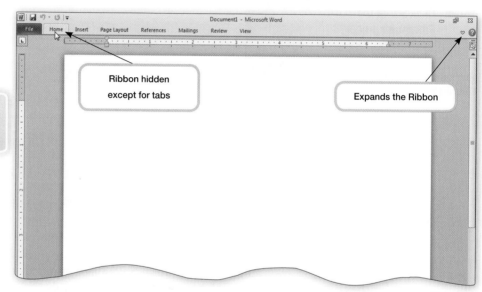

Ribbon hidden except for tabs

Expands the Ribbon

Figure 14

Now, the only part of the Ribbon that is visible is the tab area. Then, to expand the Ribbon, simply double click on the tab you want to make active. Another way to hide and redisplay the Ribbon is to click ⌃ Minimize the Ribbon or ⌄ Expand the Ribbon located at the far right end of the Ribbon tabs. You will unhide it using this feature.

● Click ⌄ Expand the Ribbon.

The full Ribbon reappears and the tab that was active when you minimized the Ribbon is active again.

Using Backstage View

To the left of the Home tab in the Ribbon is the File tab. Unlike the other tabs that display a Ribbon of commands, the File tab opens Backstage view. **Backstage view** contains commands that allow you to work *with* your document, unlike the Ribbon that allows you to work *in* your document.

Backstage view contains commands that apply to the entire document. For example, you will find commands to open, save, print, and manage your files and set your program options. This tab is common to all the Office 2010 applications, although the menu options may vary slightly.

1

● **Click the File tab to open Backstage view.**

Your screen should be similar to Figure 15

Command buttons

Tabs

Command buttons

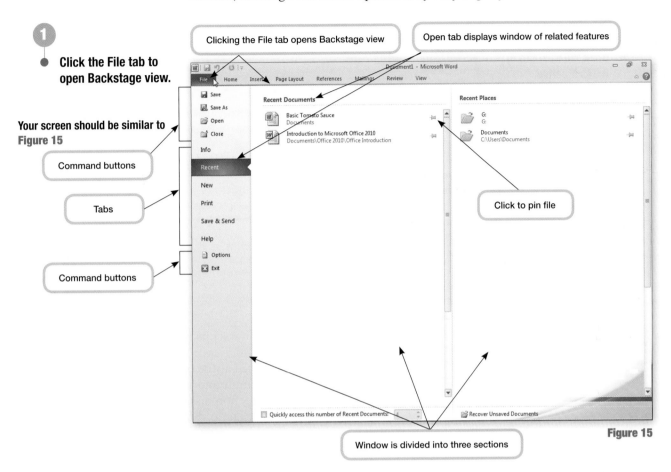

Clicking the File tab opens Backstage view

Open tab displays window of related features

Click to pin file

Window is divided into three sections

Figure 15

Another Method

You also can use the directional keys to move up, down, left, or right within Backstage view and press Enter to choose a selected command or tab.

The document window is hidden and the Backstage view window is open. The Backstage view window completely covers the document window and is divided into sections or panes. In all Office 2010 applications, the first (left) section always displays command buttons and tabs. You can select a tab or a button by pointing to it. As you do, the selected tab or button appears highlighted. Then to choose a selected tab or button, you click on it. Choosing a command button either opens a dialog box or immediately performs the associated action. Clicking a tab opens the tab and displays the related commands and features.

When you first open Backstage view and you have not yet opened a document or started to create a new document, the Recent tab is open. It displays a list of links to recently opened Word files in the second section, making it easy to quickly locate and resume using a file. The third section displays a list of folder locations that have been recently visited. In Excel, PowerPoint, and Access, the recently opened file list displays files for the associated application. The list of files and folders changes as you work to reflect only the most recent files and folder locations. The most recently used files and folder locations appear at the top of the list.

Next, you will try out some of these features by selecting and opening different tabs and command buttons.

Additional Information

A list of recent files also may appear above the Info tab if this option is selected.

Additional Information

Clicking [📌] next to a file name pins the file and permanently keeps the file name in the recently used list until it is unpinned.

2

Point to all the tabs and commands in the Backstage view menu.

Click the New tab to make it active.

Your screen should be similar to Figure 16

New tab displays links to template files that are used to create new documents

Preview of selected file

Icons representing folders containing template files on the Office.com Web site

Figure 16

The second section of the New tab displays icons representing links to available templates on your computer or on the Office.com Web site. A **template** is a professionally designed document that is used as the basis for a new document. The Blank document icon is selected by default and is used to create a new Word document file from scratch. The third section displays a preview of the selected file. Icons in the Office.com area are links to different categories of template files that are contained in folders. Clicking on a folder icon opens the folder and displays file icons. Double-clicking on a file icon opens the file in Word. Again, the available templates are specific to the Office application you are using.

3

Click the Info tab.

Your screen should be similar to Figure 17

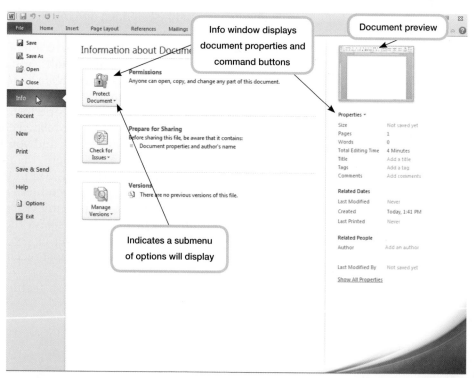

Info window displays document properties and command buttons

Document preview

Indicates a submenu of options will display

Figure 17

The Info tab displays information about your current document. The three buttons in the second section are used to define permissions, check for issues related to distribution, and manage document versions for the current document. A description of these buttons and the current document settings is shown to the right of the button. Notice that the buttons display a ▼. This indicates that a menu of commands will be displayed when you click the button. The third section displays a preview picture of the current document and a list of the settings, called **properties**, associated with the document. The current properties displayed in the Info window show the initial or **default** properties associated with a new blank document.

Additional Information

You will learn more about document properties shortly.

4

● Click to open the menu.

● Point to Restrict Permission by People.

Your screen should be similar to Figure 18

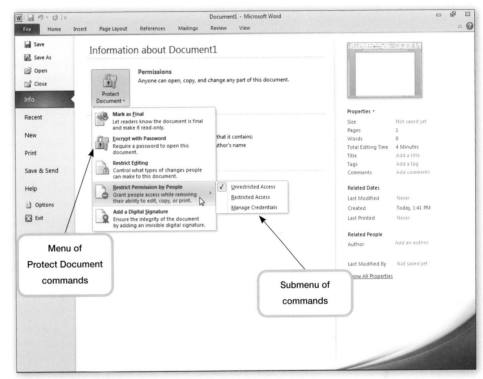

Figure 18

The Protect Document drop-down menu displays five commands. The highlighted command displays a submenu of additional commands. Next, you will clear the Protect Document menu and close Backstage view.

5

● Click again to clear the submenu.

● Click the Home tab to close Backstage view and open the Home tab again.

Another Method

You also can press Esc, click on the File tab or any other Ribbon tab, or click on the document preview in the Info screen to close the Backstage view window.

Common Office 2010 Features   **IO.27**

COMMON APPLICATION FEATURES

So far you have learned about using the Office 2010 user interface features. Next, you will learn about application features that are used to work in and modify documents and are the same or similar in all Office 2010 applications. These include how to open, close, and save files; navigate, scroll, and zoom a document; enter, select, edit, and format text; and document, preview, and print a file. To do this, you will open a Word document file and make a few changes to it. Then you will save and print the revised document. Once you have gained an understanding of the basic concepts of the common features using Word, you will be able to easily apply them in the other Office applications.

Opening a File

In all Office 2010 applications, you either need to create a new file using the blank document file or open an existing file. Opening a file retrieves a file that is stored on your computer hard drive or an external storage device and places it in RAM (random access memory) of your computer so it can be read and modified. There are two main methods that can be used to open an existing file. One is to select the file to be opened from the list of recently opened documents. If you have not recently opened the file you want to use, then you use the Open command in Backstage view.

- **Click** the File tab to open Backstage view.

- **Click** 📂 Open .

Your screen should be similar to Figure 19

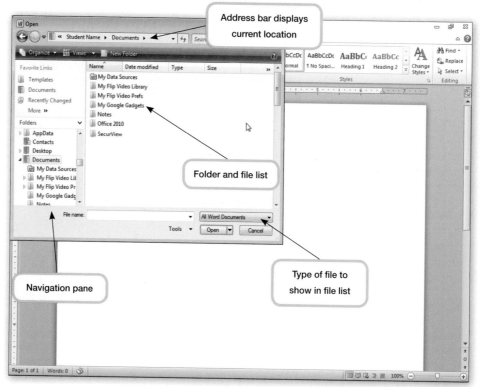

Figure 19

Additional Information

The Open dialog box is common to all programs using the Windows operating system. Your dialog box may look slightly different depending on the version of Windows on your computer.

The Open dialog box is displayed in which you specify the location where the file you want to open is stored and the file name. The location consists of identifying the hard drive of your computer or an external storage device or a remote computer followed by folders and subfolders within that location. The Address bar displays the default folder as the location to open the file. The file list displays folder names as well as the names of any Word documents in the current location. Only Word documents are listed because All Word Documents is the specified file type in the File Type list box. In Excel and PowerPoint, only files of that application's file type would be displayed.

Additional Information

By default, the Open dialog box only lists files created in the application. You will learn about the different file types shortly.

Another Method

You also can navigate by clicking the ⊙ Back or ⊙ Forward buttons to the left of the Address bar to return to locations that were previously visited during this session.

First you need to change the location to where your data files for completing these labs are stored. The file location may be on a different drive, in an external storage device, or in a folder or subfolder. There are several methods that can be used to locate files. One is to use the Address bar to specify another location by either typing the complete folder name or path or by opening the drop-down list of previously accessed locations and clicking a new location. Another is to use the Favorite Links list in the Navigation pane, which provides shortcut links to specific folders on your computer. A third is to use the Folders list in the navigation pane to navigate through the hierarchical structure of drives and folders on your computer. Clicking a link or folder from the list displays files at that location in the file list. Then, from the file list, you can continue to select subfolders until the file you want to open is located.

- **Change to the location where your student data files for this lab are located.**

Your screen should be similar to Figure 20

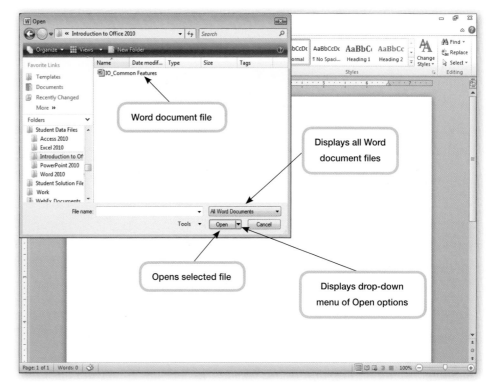

Figure 20

Now the file list displays the names of all Word files at that location. Next, you open the file by selecting it and clicking the [Open ▾] button. In addition, in the Office applications you can specify how you want to open a file by choosing from the [Open ▾] drop-down menu options described in the following table.

Open Options	Description
Open	Opens with all formatting and editing features enabled. This is the default setting.
Open Read-only	Opens file so it can be read or copied only, not modified in any way.
Open as Copy	Automatically creates a copy of the file and opens the copy with complete editing capabilities.
Open in Browser	Opens HTML type files in a Web browser.
Open with Transform	Opens certain types of documents and lets you change it into another type of document.
Open in Protected View	Opens files from potentially unsafe locations with editing functions disabled.
Open and Repair	Opens file and attempts to repair any damage.

Another Method

You could also press ⏎Enter⏎ to open a selected file or double-click on the file name.

You will open the file IO_Common Features. Clicking the [Open ▾] button opens the file using the default Open option so you can read and edit the file.

3

● **Select** IO_Common Features.

● **Click** [Open ▾].

Your screen should be similar to Figure 21

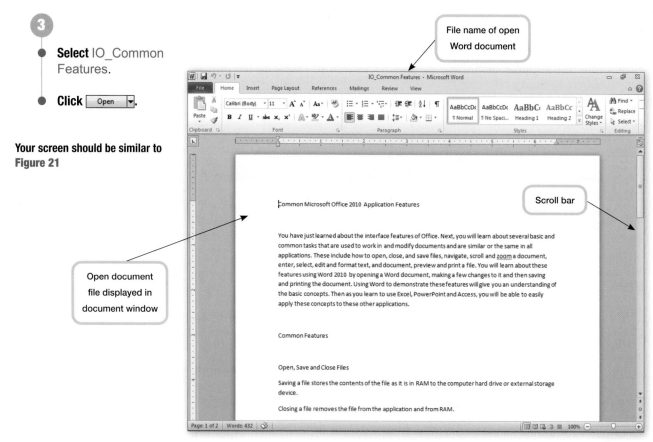

File name of open Word document

Open document file displayed in document window

Scroll bar

Figure 21

A Word document file describing the common Microsoft Office application features is displayed in the document window.

Scrolling the Document Window

As documents increase in size, they cannot be easily viewed in their entirety in the document window and much time can be spent moving to different locations in the document. All Office 2010 applications include features that make it easy to move around and view the information in a large document. The basic method is to scroll through a document using the scroll bar or keyboard. Both methods are useful, depending on what you are doing. For example, if you are entering text using the keyboard, using the keyboard method may be more efficient than using the mouse.

Additional Information

Scroll bars are also found in task panes and dialog boxes and operate similarly.

Additional Information

If you have a mouse with a scroll wheel, you can use it to scroll a document vertically.

The table below explains the basic mouse and keyboard techniques that can be used to vertically scroll a document in the Office 2010 applications. There are many other methods for navigating through documents that are unique to an application. They will be discussed in the specific application text.

Mouse or Key Action	Effect in:			
	Word	**Excel**	**PowerPoint**	**Access**
Click ▼ Or ↓	Moves down line by line.	Moves down row by row	Moves down slide by slide	Moves down record by record
Click ▲ Or ↑	Moves up line by line.	Moves up row by row	Moves up slide by slide	Moves up record by record
Click above/below scroll box Or Page Up / Page Down	Moves up/down window by window	Moves up/down window by window	Displays previous/next slide	Moves up/down window by window
Drag ▤ Scroll Box	Moves up/down line by line	Moves up/down row by row	Moves up/down slide by slide	Moves up/down record by record
Ctrl + Home	Moves to beginning of document	Moves to first cell in worksheet or beginning of cell entry	Moves to first slide in presentation or beginning of entry in placeholder	Moves to first record in table or beginning of field entry
Ctrl + End	Moves to end of document	Moves to last-used cell in worksheet or end of cell entry	Moves to last slide in presentation or to end of placeholder entry	Moves to last record in table or end of field entry

Additional Information

You also can scroll the document window horizontally using the horizontal scroll bar or the → and ← keys.

You will use the vertical scroll bar to view the text at the bottom of the Word document. When you use the scroll bar to scroll, the actual location in the document where you can work does not change, only the area you are viewing changes. For example, in Word, the cursor does not move and in Excel the cell you can work in does not change. To move the cursor or make another cell active, you must click in a location in the window. However, when you scroll using the keyboard, the actual location as identified by the position of the cursor in the document also changes. For example, in Word the cursor attempts to maintain its position in a line as you scroll up and down through the document. In Excel the cell you can work in changes as you move through a worksheet using the keyboard.

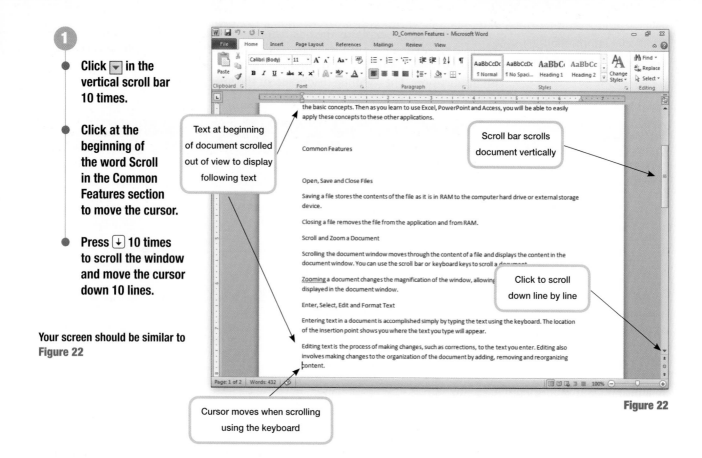

1

● Click ⯆ in the vertical scroll bar 10 times.

● Click at the beginning of the word Scroll in the Common Features section to move the cursor.

● Press ⯆ 10 times to scroll the window and move the cursor down 10 lines.

Your screen should be similar to Figure 22

Text at beginning of document scrolled out of view to display following text

Scroll bar scrolls document vertically

Click to scroll down line by line

Cursor moves when scrolling using the keyboard

Figure 22

Having Trouble?

If your screen scrolls differently, this is a function of the type of monitor you are using.

The text at the beginning of the document has scrolled line by line off the top of the document window, and the following text is now displayed. In a large document, scrolling line by line can take a while. You will now try out several additional mouse and keyboard scrolling features that move by larger increments through the document.

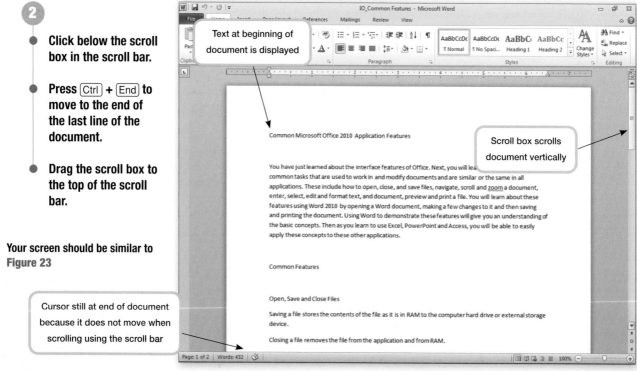

2

● Click below the scroll box in the scroll bar.

● Press Ctrl + End to move to the end of the last line of the document.

● Drag the scroll box to the top of the scroll bar.

Your screen should be similar to Figure 23

Text at beginning of document is displayed

Scroll box scrolls document vertically

Cursor still at end of document because it does not move when scrolling using the scroll bar

Figure 23

WWW.MHHE.COM/OLEARY

The document window displays the beginning of the document; however, the cursor is still at the end of the document. Using these features makes scrolling a large document much more efficient.

Using the Zoom Feature

Another way to see more or less of a document is to use the zoom feature. Although this feature is available in all Office 2010 applications, Excel and PowerPoint have fewer options than Word. In Access, the zoom feature is available only when specific features are used, such as viewing reports.

The Zoom Slider in the status bar is used to change the magnification. To use the Zoom Slider, click and drag the slider control. Dragging to the right zooms in on the document and increases the magnification whereas dragging to the left zooms out on the document and decreases the magnification. You also can change the zoom percentage by increments of 10 by clicking the ⊕ or ⊖ on each end of the slider control. In Word, the default display, 100 percent, shows the characters the same size they will be when printed. You can increase the onscreen character size up to five times the normal display (500 percent) or reduce the character size to 10 percent.

You will first "zoom out" on the document to get an overview of the file, and then you will "zoom in" to get a close-up look. When a document is zoomed, you can work in it as usual.

Additional Information

The degree of magnification varies with the different applications.

1

● **Click ⊖ in the Zoom Slider five times to decrease the zoom percentage to 50%.**

● **Press Ctrl + Home to move the cursor to the beginning of the document.**

● **Drag the Zoom Slider all the way to the right to increase the zoom to 500%.**

Your screen should be similar to Figure 24

Another Method

You can also hold down Ctrl while using the scroll wheel on your mouse to zoom a document.

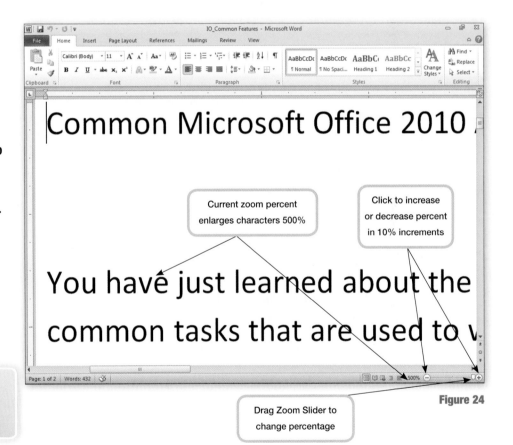

Figure 24

Another Method

You can also click on the zoom percentage in the status bar to open the Zoom dialog box.

Another way to change the magnification is to use the [Zoom] button in the View tab. This method opens the Zoom dialog box containing several preset zoom options, or an option that lets you set a precise percentage using the Percent scroll box. You will use this feature next to zoom the document. This method is available in Word only.

- Open the View tab.

- Click in the Zoom group.

- Click Whole Page and note that the percent value in the Percent text box and the preview area reflect the new percentage setting.

- Click the ▲ up scroll button in the Percent scroll box to increase the zoom percentage to 57.

Another Method

You could also type a value in the Percent text box to specify an exact percentage.

Your screen should be similar to Figure 25

Figure 25

The Zoom dialog box preview areas show how the document will appear on your screen at the specified zoom percent. Not until you complete the command by clicking [OK] will the zoom percent in the document actually change. You will complete the command to apply the 57% zoom setting. Then, you will use the [100%] button in the Zoom group to quickly return to the default zoom setting.

3

- Click [OK] to apply the 57% zoom setting.

- Click [100%] in the Zoom group of the View tab.

The document is again at 100% magnification.

Entering and Editing Text

Now that you are familiar with the entire document, you will make a few changes to it. The keyboard is used to enter information into a document. In all applications, the location of the cursor shows you where the text will appear as you type. After text is entered into a document, you need to know how to move around within the text to edit or make changes to the text. Again, the process is similar for all Office applications.

Currently, in this Word document, the cursor is positioned at the top of the document. You will type your name at this location. As you type, the cursor moves to the right and the characters will appear to the left of the cursor. Then you will press [Enter] to end the line following your name and press [Enter] again at the beginning of a line to insert a blank line.

Additional Information

The effect of pressing [Enter] varies in the different Office applications. For example, in Excel, it completes the entry and moves to another cell. You will learn about these differences in the individual application labs.

1

● Type your first and last name.

● Press [Enter] two times.

Your screen should be similar to Figure 26

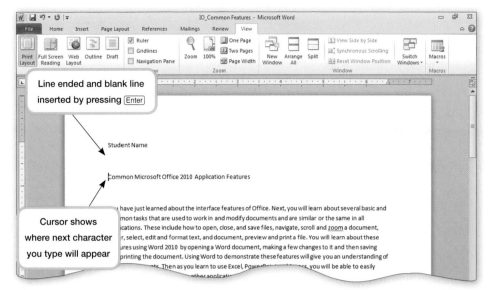

Line ended and blank line inserted by pressing [Enter]

Student Name

Common Microsoft Office 2010 Application Features

Cursor shows where next character you type will appear

...have just learned about the interface features of Office. Next, you will learn about several basic and ...mon tasks that are used to work in and modify documents and are similar or the same in all ...cations. These include how to open, close, and save files, navigate, scroll and zoom a document, ...r, select, edit and format text, and document, preview and print a file. You will learn about these ...ures using Word 2010 by opening a Word document, making a few changes to it and then saving ...printing the document. Using Word to demonstrate these features will give you an understanding of ...ts. Then as you learn to use Excel, PowerP... ...ss, you will be able to easily ...ther applicati...

Figure 26

Figure 26

Additional Information

You can use the directional keys on the numeric keypad or the dedicated directional keypad area. If using the numeric keypad, make sure the Num Lock feature is off; otherwise, numbers will be entered in the document. The Num Lock indicator light above the keypad is lit when on. Press [Num Lock] to turn it off.

Additional Information

The mouse pointer also has other shapes whose meaning varies with the different applications. These specific features will be described in the individual application labs.

As you typed your name, to make space for the text on the line, the existing text moved to the right. Then, when you pressed [Enter] the first time, all the text following your name moved down one line. A blank line was inserted after pressing [Enter] the second time.

Next, you want to add a word to the first line of the first paragraph. To do this, you first need to move the cursor to the location where you want to make the change. The keyboard or mouse can be used to move through the text in the document window. Depending on what you are doing, one method may be more efficient than another. For example, if your hands are already on the keyboard as you are entering text, it may be quicker to use the keyboard rather than take your hands off to use the mouse.

You use the mouse to move the cursor to a specific location in a document simply by clicking on the location. When you can use the mouse to move the cursor, the mouse pointer is shaped as an I I-beam. You use the arrow keys located on the numeric keypad or the directional keypad to move the cursor in a document. The keyboard directional keys are described in the following table.

Key	Word/PowerPoint	Excel	Access
→	Right one character	Right one cell	Right one field
←	Left one character	Left one cell	Left one field
↑	Up one line	Up one cell	Up one record
↓	Down one line	Down one cell	Down one record
[Ctrl] + →	Right one word	Last cell in row	One word to right in a field entry
[Ctrl] + ←	Left one word	First cell in row	One word to left in a field entry
[Home]	Beginning of line	First cell in row	First field of record
[End]	End of line		Last field of record

Additional Information

Many of the keyboard keys and key combinations have other effects depending on the mode of operation at the time they are used. You will learn about these differences in the specific application labs as they are used.

In the first line of the first paragraph, you want to add the word "common" before the word "interface" and the year "2010" after the word "Office." You will move to the correct locations using both the keyboard and the mouse and then enter the new text.

- Click at the beginning of the word You in the first paragraph.

- Press → four times to move to the beginning of the second word.

- Press Ctrl + → five times to move to the beginning of the seventh word.

Additional Information

Holding down a directional key or key combination moves quickly in the direction indicated, saving multiple presses of the key.

- Type **basic** and press Spacebar .

Having Trouble?

Do not be concerned if you make a typing error; you will learn how to correct them next.

- Position the I-beam between the e in Office and the period at the end of the first sentence and click.

- Press Spacebar and type **2010**

Your screen should be similar to Figure 27

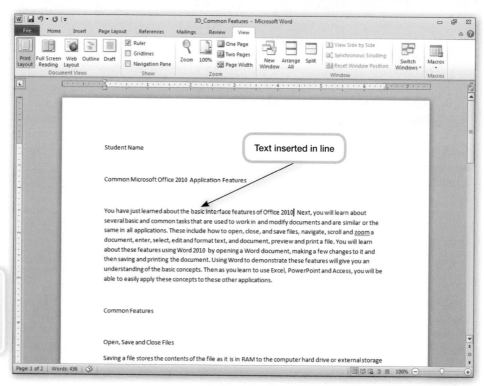

Figure 27

Next, you want to edit the text you just entered by changing the word "basic" to "common." Removing typing entries to change or correct them is one of the basic editing tasks. Corrections may be made in many ways. Two of the most basic editing keys that are common to the Office applications are the Backspace and Delete keys. The Backspace key removes a character or space to the left of the cursor. It is particularly useful when you are moving from right to left (backward) along a line of text. The Delete key removes the character or space to the right of the cursor and is most useful when moving from left to right along a line.

You will use these features as you make the correction.

3

- Move the cursor between the s and i in "basic" (in the first sentence).

- Press ⌈Del⌉ to remove the two characters to the right of the insertion point.

- Press ⌈Backspace⌉ three times to remove the three characters to the left of the cursor.

- Type **common**

- Correct any other typing errors you may have made using ⌈Backspace⌉ or ⌈Delete⌉.

Your screen should be similar to Figure 28

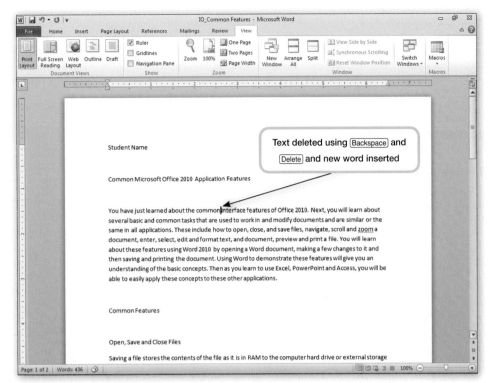

Figure 28

The word "basic" was deleted from the sentence and the word "common" was entered in its place.

Selecting Text

While editing and formatting a document, you will need to select text. Selecting highlights text and identifies the text that will be affected by your next action. To select text using the mouse, first move the cursor to the beginning or end of the text to be selected, and then drag to highlight the text you want selected. You can select as little as a single letter or as much as the entire document. You also can select text using keyboard features. The following table summarizes common mouse and keyboard techniques used to select text in Word.

To Select	Mouse	Keyboard
Next/previous space or character	Drag across space or character.	⌈Shift⌉ + →/⌈Shift⌉ + ←
Next/previous word	Double-click in the word.	⌈Ctrl⌉ + ⌈Shift⌉ + →/⌈Ctrl⌉ + ⌈Shift⌉ + ←
Sentence	Press ⌈Ctrl⌉ and click within the sentence.	
Line	Click to the left of a line when the mouse pointer is ⌐.	
Multiple lines	Drag up or down to the left of a line when the mouse pointer is ⌐.	
Text going backward to beginning of paragraph	Drag left and up to the beginning of the paragraph when the mouse pointer is ⌐.	⌈Ctrl⌉ + ⌈Shift⌉ + ↑
Text going forward to end of paragraph	Drag right and down to the end of the paragraph when the mouse pointer is ⌐.	⌈Ctrl⌉ + ⌈Shift⌉ + ↓
Paragraph	Triple-click on the paragraph or double-click to the left of the paragraph when the mouse pointer is ⌐.	
Multiple paragraphs	Drag to the left of the paragraphs when the mouse pointer is ⌐.	
Document	Triple-click or press ⌈Ctrl⌉ and click to the left of the text when the mouse pointer is ⌐.	⌈Ctrl⌉ + A

You want to change the word "tasks" in the next sentence to "application features". Although you could use ⬚Delete⬚ and ⬚Backspace⬚ to remove the unneeded text character by character, it will be faster to select and delete the word. First you will try out several of the keyboard techniques to select text. Then you will use several mouse features to select text and finally you will edit the sentence.

1

● Move the cursor to the beginning of the word "basic" in the second sentence.

● Press ⬚Shift⬚ + ⬚→⬚ five times to select the word basic.

● Press ⬚Shift⬚ + ⬚Ctrl⬚ + ⬚→⬚ to extend the selection word by word until the entire line is selected.

● Press ⬚Shift⬚ + ⬚Ctrl⬚ + ⬚↓⬚ to extend the selection to the end of the paragraph.

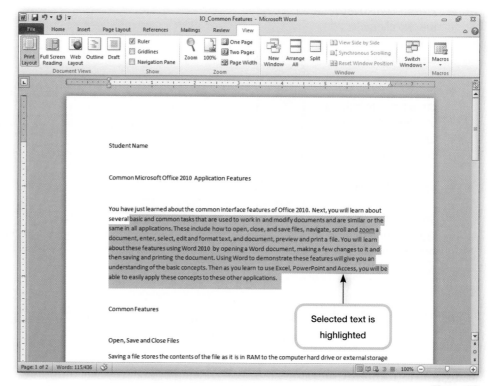

Figure 29

Your screen should be similar to Figure 29

The text from the cursor to the end of the paragraph is selected. Next, you will clear this selection and then use the mouse to select text.

2

- Click anywhere in the paragraph to clear the selection.

- Click at the beginning of the word "basic" and drag to the right to select the text to the end of the line.

- Click in the left margin to the left of the fourth line of the paragraph when the mouse pointer is to select the entire line.

- Double-click in the margin to the left of the paragraph when the mouse pointer is to select the paragraph.

Your screen should be similar to Figure 30

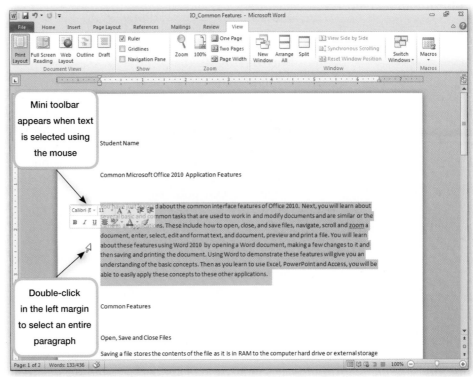

Figure 30

When you select text using the mouse, the **Mini toolbar** appears automatically in Word, Excel, and PowerPoint. You will learn about using this feature in the next section.

Text that is selected can be modified using many different features. In this case, you want to replace the word "tasks" in the second sentence with "application features".

3

- Double-click on the word "tasks" in the second sentence.

- Type **application features**

Your screen should be similar to Figure 31

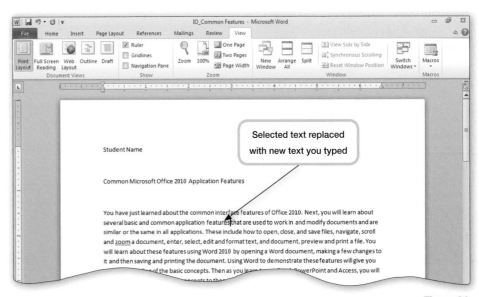

Figure 31

As soon as you began typing, the selected text was automatically deleted. The new text was inserted in the line just like any other text.

Formatting Text

An important aspect of all documents you create using Office 2010 is the appearance of the document. To improve the appearance you can apply many different formatting effects. The most common formatting features are font and character effects. A **font**, also commonly referred to as a **typeface**, is a set of characters with a specific design. The designs have names such as Times New Roman and Courier. Each font has one or more sizes. **Font size** is the height and width of the character and is commonly measured in points, abbreviated "pt." One point equals about 1/72 inch. **Character effects** are enhancements such as bold, italic, and color that are applied to selected text. Using font and character effects as design elements can add interest to your document and give readers visual cues to help them find information quickly.

First you want to change the font and increase the font size of the title of this document.

1

- Click in the left margin next to the title line when the mouse pointer is to select it.

- Open the Home tab.

- Open the Calibri (Body) ▾ Font drop-down menu in the Font group.

- Point to the Arial Black font option in the menu.

Your screen should be similar to Figure 32

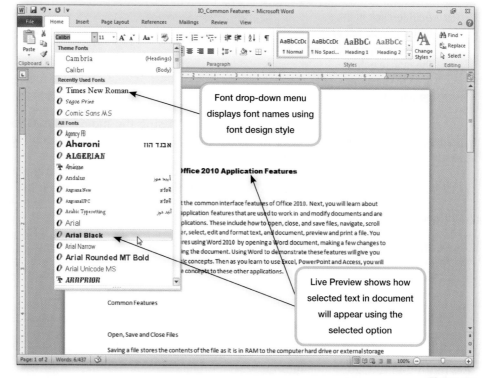

Figure 32

As you point to the font options, the **Live Preview** feature shows you how the selected text in the document will appear if this option is chosen.

②

● **Point to several different fonts in the menu to see the Live Preview.**

● **Scroll the menu and click Segoe Print to choose it.**

Additional Information

Font names are listed in alphabetical order.

Having Trouble?

If this font is not available on your computer, choose a similar font.

Your screen should be similar to Figure 33

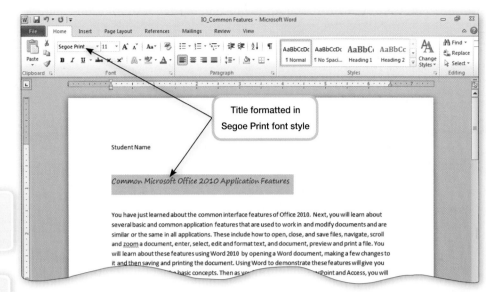

Title formatted in Segoe Print font style

Figure 33

The title appears in the selected font and the name of the font used in the selection is displayed in the [Segoe Print ▾] Font button. Next you want to increase the font size. The current (default) font size of 11 is displayed in the [11 ▾] Font Size button. You will increase the font size to 16 points.

③

● **Open the [11 ▾] Font Size drop-down menu in the Font group of the Home tab.**

● **Point to several different font sizes to see the Live Preview.**

● **Click 16 to choose it.**

Another Method

The keyboard shortcut is [Ctrl] + [Shift] + P.

Title font size increased to 16 points

Figure 34

Your screen should be similar to Figure 34

Now the title stands out much more from the other text in the document. Next you will use the Mini toolbar to add formatting to other areas of the document. As you saw earlier, the Mini toolbar appears automatically when you select text. Initially the Mini toolbar appears dimmed (semi-transparent) so that it does not interfere with what you are doing, but it changes to solid when you point at it. It displays command buttons for often-used commands from the Font and Paragraph groups that are used to format a document.

4

● Select the line "Common Features" and point to the Mini toolbar.

● Click $\boxed{11 \ \vee}$ Font Size and choose 14.

● Click $\boxed{\text{B}}$ Bold.

● Click $\boxed{\mathit{I}}$ Italic.

● Click $\boxed{\underline{\text{U}}}$ Underline.

Your screen should be similar to Figure 35

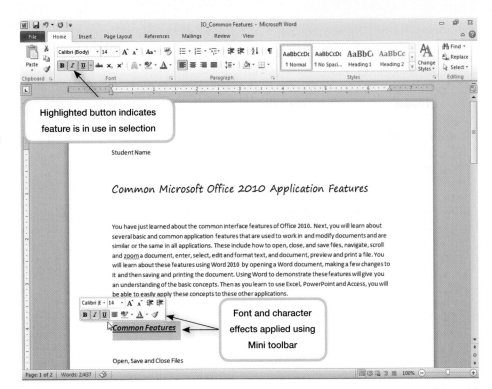

Highlighted button indicates feature is in use in selection

Student Name

Common Microsoft Office 2010 Application Features

You have just learned about the common interface features of Office 2010. Next, you will learn about several basic and common application features that are used to work in and modify documents and are similar or the same in all applications. These include how to open, close, and save files, navigate, scroll and zoom a document, enter, select, edit and format text, and document, preview and print a file. You will learn about these features using Word 2010 by opening a Word document, making a few changes to it and then saving and printing the document. Using Word to demonstrate these features will give you an understanding of the basic concepts. Then as you learn to use Excel, PowerPoint and Access, you will be able to easily apply these concepts to these other applications.

Common Features

Font and character effects applied using Mini toolbar

Open, Save and Close Files

Figure 35

The increase in font size as well as the text effects makes this topic head much more prominent. Notice the command button for each selected effect is highlighted, indicating the feature is in use in the selection.

Using the Mini toolbar is particularly useful when the Home tab is closed because you do not need to reopen the Home tab to access the commands. It remains available until you clear the selection or press [Esc]. If you do nothing with a selection for a while, the Mini toolbar will disappear. To redisplay it simply right-click on the selection again. This will also open the context menu.

You will remove the underline effect from the selection next.

5
- **Right-click on the selection to redisplay the Mini toolbar.**

- **Click [U] Underline on the Mini toolbar.**

Your screen should be similar to Figure 36

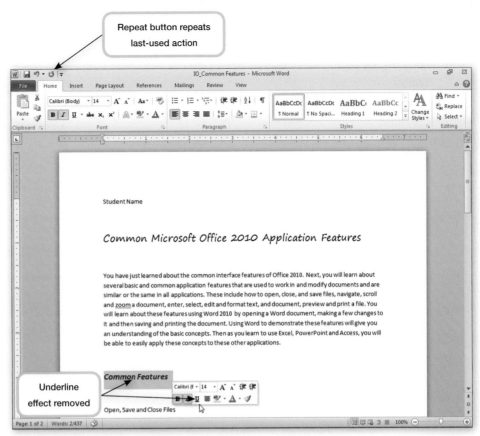

Figure 36

The context menu and Mini toolbar appeared when you right-clicked the selection. The context menu displayed a variety of commands that are quicker to access than locating the command on the Ribbon. The commands that appear on this menu change depending on what you are doing at the time. The context menu disappeared after you made a selection from the Mini toolbar. Both the Mini toolbar and context menus are designed to make it more efficient to execute commands.

Also notice that the [↻] Redo button in the Quick Access Toolbar has changed to a [↺] Repeat button. This feature allows you to quickly repeat the last-used command at another location in the document.

Undoing and Redoing Editing Changes

Instead of reselecting the [U] Underline command to remove the underline effect, you could have used [↩ ▾] Undo to reverse your last action or command. You will use this feature to restore the underline (your last action).

1

Click Undo in the Quick Access Toolbar.

Another Method

The keyboard shortcut is Ctrl + Z.

Your screen should be similar to Figure 37

Undo restores last-used action

Underline effect restored using Undo

Figure 37

Undo reversed the last action and the underline formatting effect was restored. Notice that the Undo button includes a drop-down menu button. Clicking this button displays a menu of the most recent actions that can be reversed, with the most-recent action at the top of the menu. When you select an action from the drop-down menu, you also undo all actions above it in the menu.

2

Open the Undo drop-down menu.

Choose Bold.

Your screen should be similar to Figure 38

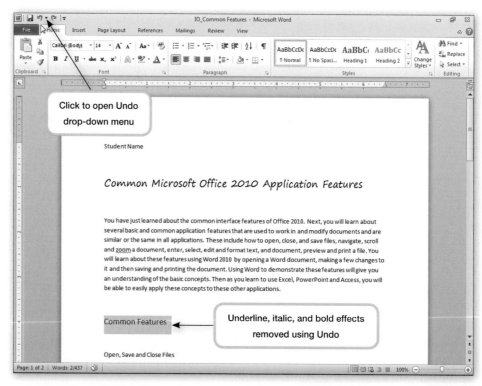

Click to open Undo drop-down menu

Underline, italic, and bold effects removed using Undo

Figure 38

The underline, italic, and bold effects were all removed. Immediately after you undo an action, the ↺ Repeat button changes to the ↻ Redo button and is available so you can restore the action you just undid. You will restore the last-removed format, bold.

● Click ↻ Redo.

Another Method

The keyboard shortcut is Ctrl + Y.

Copying and Moving Selections

Common to all Office applications is the capability to copy and move selections to new locations in a document or between documents, saving you time by not having to recreate the same information. A selection that is moved is cut from its original location, called the **source**, and inserted at a new location, called the **destination**. A selection that is copied leaves the original in the source and inserts a duplicate at the destination.

Additional Information

You will learn about using the Office Clipboard in the individual application texts.

When a selection is cut or copied, the selection is stored in the system **Clipboard**, a temporary Windows storage area in memory. It is also stored in the **Office Clipboard**. The system Clipboard holds only the last cut or copied item, whereas the Office Clipboard can store up to 24 items that have been cut or copied. This feature allows you to insert multiple items from various Office documents and paste all or part of the collection of items into another document.

First, you will copy the text "Office 2010" to two other locations in the first paragraph.

● Select the text "Office 2010" in the title line.

● Click 📋 Copy in the Clipboard group of the Home tab.

● Move to the beginning of the word "applications" (third line of first paragraph).

● Click 📋 Paste in the Clipboard group.

Another Method

The Copy keyboard shortcut is Ctrl + C.
The Paste keyboard shortcut is Ctrl + V.

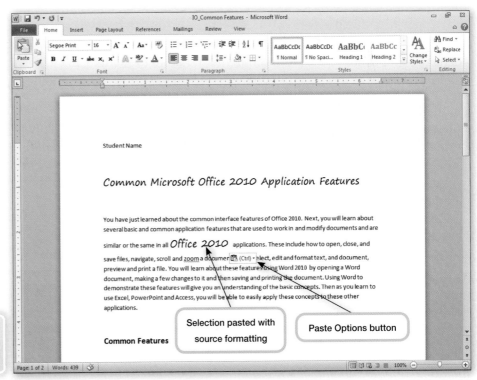

Figure 39

Your screen should be similar to
Figure 39

The copied selection is inserted at the location you specified with the same formatting as it has in the title. The (Ctrl) ▾ Paste Options button appears automatically whenever a selection is pasted. It is used to control the format of the pasted item.

2

● **Click the** **(Ctrl) ▾**
Paste Options button.

Your screen should be similar to
Figure 40

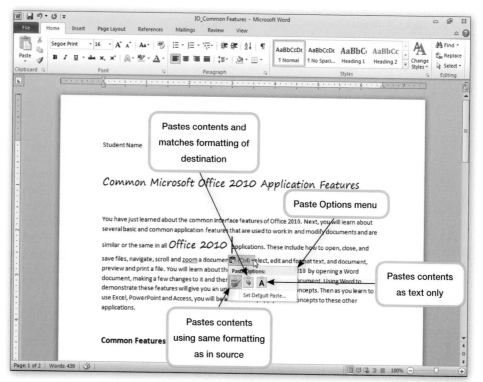

Figure 40

The Paste Options are used to specify whether to insert the item with the same formatting that it had in the source, to change it to the formatting of the surrounding destination text, or to insert text only (from a selection that is a combination of text and graphics). The default as you have seen is to keep the formatting from the source. You want to change it to the formatting of the surrounding text. As you point to a Paste Options button, a **Paste Preview** will show how that option will affect the selection. Then you will copy it again to a second location.

3

- Click 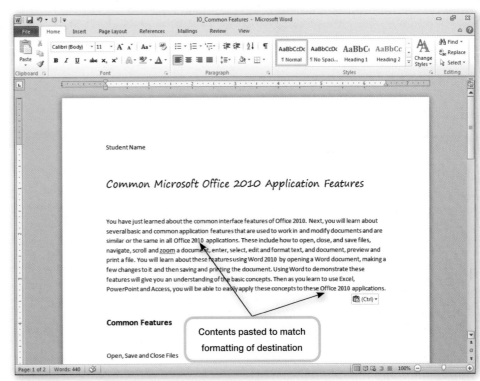 Merge Formatting.

- Select "other" in the last line of the first paragraph.

- Right-click on the selection and point to each of the Paste Options in the context menu to see the Paste Preview.

- Click Merge Formatting.

Your screen should be similar to Figure 41

Figure 41

The selected text was deleted and replaced with the contents of the system Clipboard. The system Clipboard contents remain in the Clipboard until another item is copied or cut, allowing you to paste the same item multiple times.

Now you will learn how to move a selection by rearranging several lines of text in the description of common features. You want to move the last sentence in the document, beginning with "Opening a file", to the top of the list. The Cut and Paste commands in the Clipboard group of the Home tab are used to move selections.

4

- Scroll to see the end of the document.

- Double-click in the left margin next to the last sentence in the document to select it.

- Click ✄ Cut in the Clipboard group.

Another Method

The Cut keyboard shortcut is Ctrl + X. You also can choose Cut from the context menu.

Your screen should be similar to Figure 42

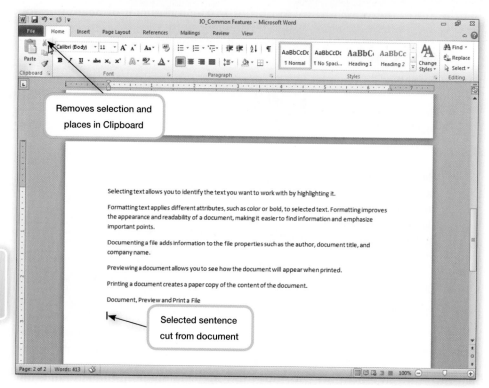

Removes selection and places in Clipboard

Selecting text allows you to identify the text you want to work with by highlighting it.

Formatting text applies different attributes, such as color or bold, to selected text. Formatting improves the appearance and readability of a document, making it easier to find information and emphasize important points.

Documenting a file adds information to the file properties such as the author, document title, and company name.

Previewing a document allows you to see how the document will appear when printed.

Printing a document creates a paper copy of the content of the document.

Document, Preview and Print a File

Selected sentence cut from document

Figure 42

The selected paragraph is removed from the source and copied to the Clipboard. Next, you need to move the cursor to the location where the text will be inserted and paste the text into the document from the Clipboard.

5

- Move to the beginning of the word "Saving" at the top of the Common Features list.

- Press Ctrl + V.

Your screen should be similar to Figure 43

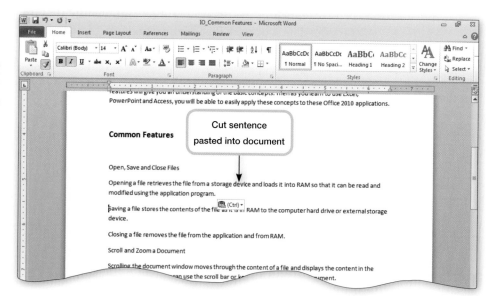

Features will give you an understanding of the basic concepts. Then as you learn to use Excel, PowerPoint and Access, you will be able to easily apply these concepts to these Office 2010 applications.

Common Features

Cut sentence pasted into document

Open, Save and Close Files

Opening a file retrieves the file from a storage device and loads it into RAM so that it can be read and modified using the application program.

Saving a file stores the contents of the file as it is in RAM to the computer hard drive or external storage device.

Closing a file removes the file from the application and from RAM.

Scroll and Zoom a Document

Scrolling the document window moves through the content of a file and displays the content in the ... can use the scroll bar or k... ...ment.

Figure 43

The cut sentence is reentered into the document at the cursor location. That was much quicker than retyping the whole sentence! Because the source has the same formatting as the text at the destination, the default setting to keep the source formatting is appropriate.

Specifying Document Properties

In addition to the content of the document that you create, all Office 2010 applications automatically include details about the document that describe or identify it called **metadata** or document **properties**. Document properties include details such as title, author name, subject, and keywords that identify the document's topic or contents (described below). Some of these properties are automatically generated. These include statistics such as the number of words in the file and general information such as the date the document was created and last modified. Others such as author name and tags or keywords are properties that you can specify. A **tag** or **keyword** is a descriptive word that is associated with the file and can be used to locate a file using a search.

By specifying relevant information as document properties, you can easily organize, identify, and search for your documents later.

Property	Action
Title	Enter the document title. This title can be longer and more descriptive than the file name.
Tags	Enter words that you associate with the presentation to make it easier to find using search tools.
Comments	Enter comments that you want others to see about the content of the document.
Categories	Enter the name of a higher-level category under which you can group similar types of presentations.
Author	Enter the name of the presentation's author. By default this is the name entered when the application was installed.

You will look at the document properties that are automatically included and add documentation to identify you as the author, and specify a document title and keywords to describe the document.

1

- Open the File tab.

- Click the "Show all properties" link at the bottom of the Properties panel in the Info window to display all properties.

Your screen should be similar to Figure 47

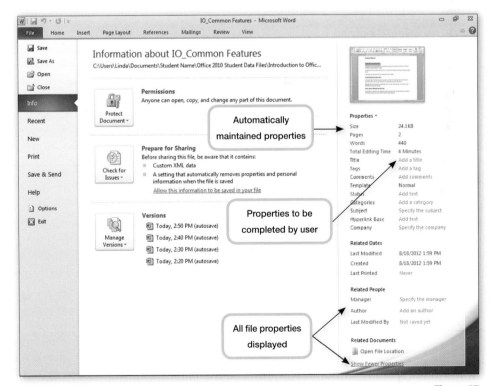

Figure 47

The Properties panel in the right section of the Info tab is divided into four groups and displays the properties associated with the document. Properties such as the document size, number of words, and number of pages are automatically maintained. Others such as the title and tag properties are blank waiting for you to specify your own information.

You will add a title, a tag, and your name as the author name.

2

● Click in the Title text box and type **Common Office Features**

● In the same manner, enter **common, features, interface** as the tags.

● Click in the Add an Author text box and enter your name.

Your screen should be similar to Figure 48

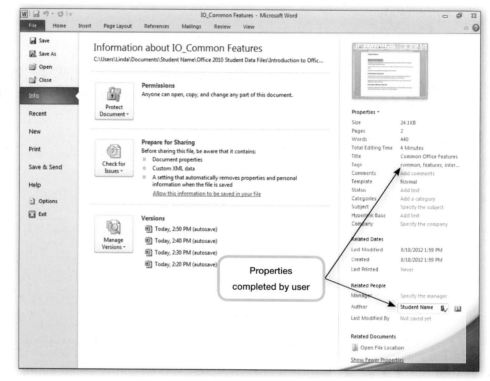

Figure 48

Once the document properties are specified, you can use them to identify and locate documents. You also can use the automatically updated properties for the same purpose. For example, you can search for all files created by a specified user or on a certain date.

Saving a File

As you enter and edit text to create a document in Word, Excel, and PowerPoint, the changes you make are immediately displayed onscreen and are stored in your computer's memory. However, they are not permanently stored until you save your work to a file on a disk. After a document has been saved as a file, it can be closed and opened again at a later time to be edited further. Unlike Word, Excel, and PowerPoint, where you start work on a new document and then save your changes, Access requires that you name the new database file first and create a table for your data. Then, it saves your changes to the data automatically as you work. This allows multiple users to have access to the most up-to-date data at all times.

As a backup against the accidental loss of work from power failure or other mishap, Word, Excel, and PowerPoint include an AutoRecover feature. When this feature is on, as you work you may see a pulsing disk icon briefly appear in the status bar. This icon indicates that the program is saving your work to a temporary recovery file. The time interval between automatic saving can be set to any period you specify; the default is every 10 minutes. After a problem has occurred, when you restart the program, the recovery file is automatically opened containing all changes you made up to the last time it was saved by AutoRecover. You then need to save the recovery file. If you do not save it, it is deleted when closed. AutoRecover is a great feature for recovering lost work but should not be used in place of regularly saving your work.

You will save the work you have done so far on the document. You use the Save or Save As commands to save files. The [💾 Save] command on the File tab or the 💾 Save button on the Quick Access Toolbar will save the active file using the same file name by replacing the contents of the existing disk file with the document as it appears on your screen. The [💾 Save As] command on the File tab is used to save a file using a new file name, to a new location, or as a different file type. This leaves the original file unchanged. When you create a new document, you can use either of the Save commands to save your work to a file on the disk. It is especially important to save a new document very soon after you create it because the AutoRecover feature does not work until a file name has been specified.

You will save this file using a new file name to your solution file location.

Additional Information

You can specify different AutoRecover settings by choosing Options/Save in Backstage view and specifying the AutoRecover settings of your choice.

Another Method

The keyboard shortcut for the Save command is [Ctrl] + S.

Additional Information

Saving a file is the same in all Office 2010 applications, except Access.

1

● **Click** [📄 Save As] **in the left section of Backstage view.**

Your screen should be similar to Figure 49

Specify location to save file

Enter new file name

Word 2010 file extension

Specify file type

Figure 49

The Save As dialog box is used to specify the location where you will save the file and the file name. The Address bar displays the folder location from which the file was opened and the File name text box displays the name of the open file. The file name is highlighted, ready for you to enter a new file name. The Save as type box displays "Word Document.docx" as the default format in which the file will be saved. Word 2010 documents are identified by the file extension .docx. The file type you select determines the file extension that will be automatically added to the file name when the file is saved. The file types and extensions for the four Office 2010 applications are described in the following table.

Extensions	File Type
Word 2010	
.docx	Word 2007-2010 document without macros or code
.dotx	Word 2007-2010 template without macros or code
.docm	Word 2007-2010 document that could contain macros or code
.xps	Word 2007-2010 shared document (see Note)
.doc	Word 95–2003 document
Excel 2010	
.xlsx	Excel 2007-2010 default workbook without macros or code
.xlsm	Excel 2007-2010 default workbook that could contain macros
.xltx	Excel 2007-2010 template without macros
.xltm	Excel 2007-2010 template that could contain macros
.xps	Excel 2007-2010 shared workbook (see Note)
.xls	Excel 97–2003 workbook
PowerPoint	
.pptx	PowerPoint 2007-2010 default presentation format
.pptm	PowerPoint 2007-2010 presentation with macros
.potx	PowerPoint 2007-2010 template without macros
.potm	PowerPoint 2007-2010 template that may contain macros
.ppam	PowerPoint 2007-2010 add-in that contains macros
.ppsx	PowerPoint 2007-2010 slide show without macros
.ppsm	PowerPoint 2007-2010 slide show that may contain macros
.thmx	PowerPoint 2007-2010 theme
.ppt	PowerPoint 2003 or earlier presentation
Access	
.accdb	Access 2007-2010 database
.mdb	Access 2003 or earlier database

NOTE XPS file format is a fixed-layout electronic file format that preserves document formatting and ensures that when the file is viewed online or printed, it retains exactly the format that you intended. It also makes it difficult to change the data in the file. To save as an XPS file format, you must have installed the free add-in.

Office 2007 and 2010 save Word, Excel, and PowerPoint files using the XML format (Extensible Markup Language) and a four-letter file extension. This format makes your documents safer by separating files that contain macros (small programs in a document that automate tasks) to make it easier for a virus checker to identify and block unwanted code or macros that could be dangerous to your computer. It also makes file sizes smaller by compressing the content upon saving and makes files less susceptible to damage. In addition, XML format makes it easier to open documents created with an Office application using another application.

Additional Information

Depending upon your Office 2010 setup, a prompt to check for compatibility may appear automatically when you save a file.

Additional Information

Using Save As in Access creates a copy of the open database file and then opens the copy. Access automatically closes the original database.

Previous versions of Word, Excel, and PowerPoint did not use XML and had a three-letter file extension. If you plan to share a file with someone using an Office 2003 or earlier version, you can save the document using the three-letter file type; however, some features may be lost. Otherwise, if you save it as a four-letter file type, the recipient may not be able to view all features. There also may be loss of features for users of Office 2007 (even though it has an XML file type) because the older version does not support several of the new features in Office 2010. Office 2010 includes a feature that checks for compatibility with previous versions and advises you what features in the document may be lost if opened by an Office 2007 user or if the document is saved in the 2003 format.

If you have an Office Access 2007 (.accdb) database that you want to save in an earlier Access file format (.mdb), you can do so as long as your .accdb database does not contain any multivalued lookup fields, offline data, or attachments. This is because older versions of Access do not support these new features. If you try to convert an .accdb database containing any of these elements to an .mdb file format, Access displays an error message.

First you may need to change the location to the location where the file will be saved. The same procedures you used to specify a location to open a file are used to specify the location to save a file. Then, you will change the file name to Common Features using the default Word document type (.docx).

2

● If necessary, select the location where you save your solution files.

● If necessary, triple-click or drag in the File Name text box to highlight the existing file name.

● Type **Common Features**

● Click ▢ Save ▮.

Your screen should be similar to Figure 50

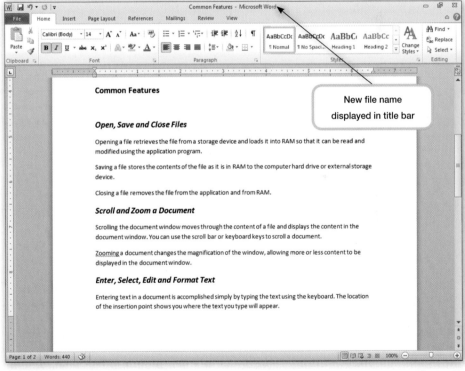

Figure 50

Additional Information

Windows files can have up to 256 characters in the file name. Names can contain letters, numbers, and spaces; however, the symbols \, /, ?, :, *, ", <, and > cannot be used. The file name can be entered in either uppercase or lowercase letters and will appear exactly as you type it.

The document is saved as Common Features.docx at the location you selected, and the new file name is displayed in the Word application window title bar.

Printing a Document

Once a document appears how you want, you may want to print a hard copy for your own reference or to give to others. All Office 2010 applications include the capability to print and have similar options. You will print this document next.

1

Open the File tab and choose Print.

Another Method

The keyboard shortcut for the Print command is Ctrl + P.

Your screen should be similar to Figure 51

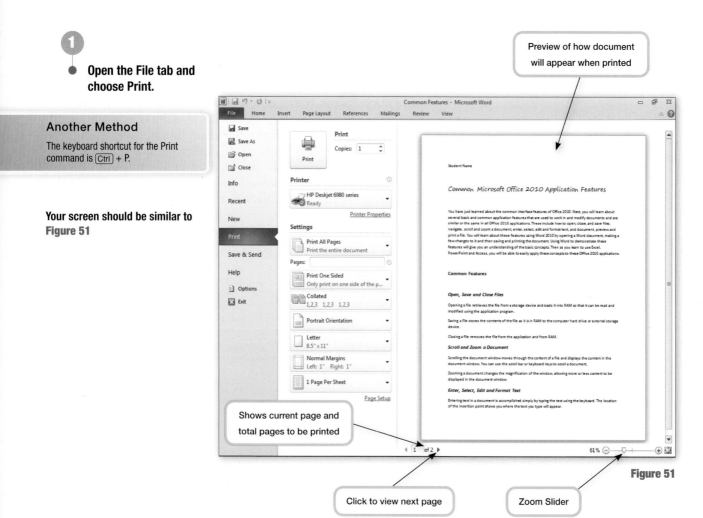

Preview of how document will appear when printed

Shows current page and total pages to be printed

Click to view next page

Zoom Slider

Figure 51

Having Trouble?

If necessary, use the Zoom Slider to change the preview zoom to 60%.

The right section of the Print window displays a preview of the current page of your document. To save time and unnecessary printing and paper waste, it is always a good idea to preview each page of your document before printing. Notice below the preview, the page scroll box shows the page number of the page you are currently viewing and the total number of pages. The scroll buttons on either side are used to scroll to the next and previous pages. Additionally, a Zoom Slider is available to adjust the size of the preview.

2

● Click ▶ to view the second page of the document.

● Increase the zoom to 70%.

Your screen should be similar to Figure 52

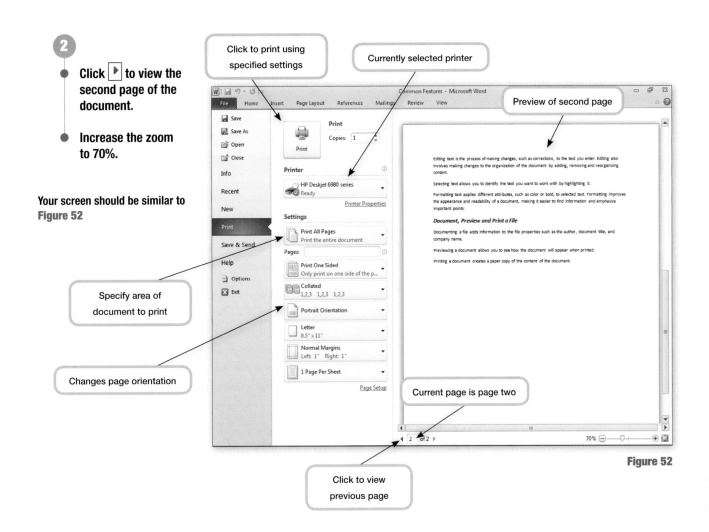

Click to print using specified settings

Currently selected printer

Preview of second page

Specify area of document to print

Changes page orientation

Current page is page two

Click to view previous page

Figure 52

If you see any changes you want to make to the document, you would need to close the File tab and make the changes. If the document looks good, you are ready to print.

The second section of the Print window is divided into three areas: Print, Printer, and Settings. In the Print section you specify the number of copies you want printed. The default is to print one copy. The Printer section is used to specify the printer you will use and the printer properties such as paper size and print quality. The name of the default printer on your computer appears in the list box. The Settings area is used to specify what part of the document you want to print, whether to print on one or both sides of the paper or to collate (sort) the printed output, the page orientation, paper size, margins, and sheet settings. The Word print setting options are explained in the following table. The Print settings will vary slightly with the different Office applications. For example, in Excel, the options to specify what to print are to print the entire worksheet, entire workbook, or a selection. The differences will be demonstrated in the individual labs.

Option	Setting	Action
Print what	All	Prints entire document (default)
	Current page	Prints selected page or page where the cursor is located.
	Pages	Prints pages you specify by typing page numbers in Pages text box
	Selection	Prints selected text only (default)
Sides	One	Prints on one side of the paper.
	Both (short)	Prints on both sides by flipping the page vertically using a duplex printer
	Both (long)	Prints on both sides by flipping the page horizontally using a duplex printer
	Manually both	Reload the paper when prompted to print on the other side
Collate	Collated	Prints all of specified document before printing second or multiple copies; for example, pages 1,2 then 1,2 again (default)
	Uncollated	Prints multiple copies of each specified page sequentially (for example, pages 1,1 then 2,2)
Orientation	Portrait	Prints across the width of the paper (default)
	Landscape	Prints across the length of the paper
Paper	Size	Select the paper size (8.5 × 11 is default)
	Envelope	Select an envelope size
Margins	Normal	One-inch margins all around (default)
	Narrow, Wide	Select alternative margin settings
Sheet	One Page Per Sheet	Prints each page of the document on a separate sheet (default)
	Multiple pages per sheet	Specify number of pages to print on a sheet

NOTE Please consult your instructor for printing procedures that may differ from the following directions.

You will specify several different print settings to see the effect on the preview, then you will print using the default print settings.

③

If you need to change the selected printer to another printer, open the Printer drop-down menu and choose the appropriate printer (your instructor will tell you which printer to select).

Click

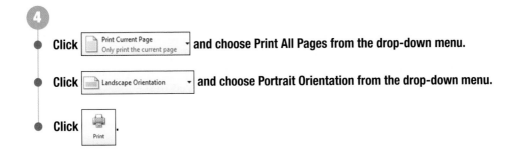

Print All Pages
Print the entire document

and choose **Print Current Page** from the drop-down menu.

Click

Portrait Orientation

and choose **Landscape Orientation** from the drop-down menu.

Your screen should be similar to Figure 53

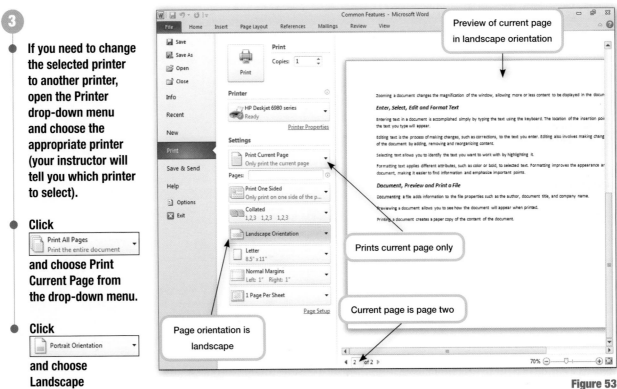

Preview of current page in landscape orientation

Prints current page only

Current page is page two

Page orientation is landscape

Figure 53

The preview window displays the current page in landscape orientation and the page indicator shows that page two of two will print. You will return these settings to their defaults and then print the document.

④

Click | Print Current Page / Only print the current page | and choose **Print All Pages** from the drop-down menu.

Click | Landscape Orientation | and choose **Portrait Orientation** from the drop-down menu.

Click | Print |.

Your printer should be printing the document.

Closing a File

Finally, you want to close the document.

1 **Open the File tab and click** 🗋 Close **.**

Another Method

The keyboard shortcut is Ctrl + F4 .

Your screen should be similar to Figure 54

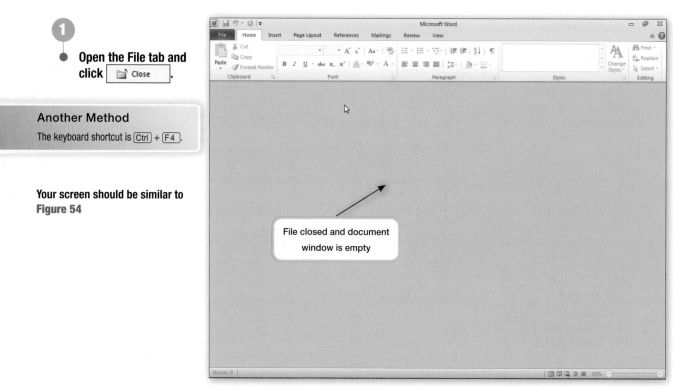

File closed and document window is empty

Figure 54

Additional Information

Do not click ⊠ Close in the window title bar as this closes the application.

Now the Word window displays an empty document window. Because you did not make any changes to the document since saving it, the document window closed immediately. If you had made additional changes, the program would ask whether you wanted to save the file before closing it. This prevents the accidental closing of a file that has not been saved first.

USING OFFICE HELP

Another Method

You also can press F1 to access Help.

Notice the 🔘 in the upper-right corner of the Ribbon. This button is used to access the Microsoft Help system. The Help button is always visible even when the Ribbon is hidden. Because you are using the Microsoft Word 2010 application, Word Help will be accessed.

Click ⊘ **Microsoft Word Help.**

If a Table of Contents pane is not displayed along the left side of the Help window, click ▦ **Show Table of Contents in the Help window toolbar to open it.**

Your screen should be similar to Figure 55

Additional Information

Click ▦ Hide Table of Contents in the Help window toolbar to hide the Table of Contents pane when it is open.

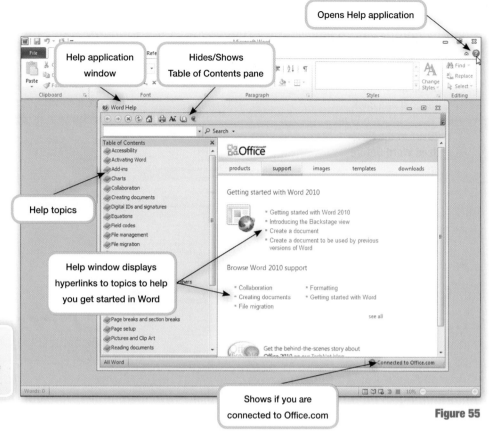

Figure 55

Additional Information

Because Help is an online feature, the information is frequently updated. Your screens may display slightly different information than those shown in the figures in this lab.

Additional Information

Depending on the size of your Help window, you may need to scroll the window to see all the Help information provided.

Having Trouble?

In addition to being connected to the Internet, the Help feature to show content from the Internet must be selected. If necessary, click

 at the bottom of

the Help window and choose Show content from Office.com.

The Word Help feature is a separate application and is opened and displayed in a separate window. The Help window on your screen will probably be a different size and arrangement than in Figure 56. A list of help topics is displayed in the Table of Contents pane along the left side of the window and the Help window on the right side displays several topics to help you get started using Word. If you are connected to the Internet, the Microsoft Office Online Web site, Office.com, is accessed and help information from this site is displayed in the window. If you are not connected, the offline help information that is provided with the application and stored on your computer is located and displayed. Generally, the listing of topics is similar but fewer in number.

Selecting Help Topics

There are several ways you can get help. The first is to select a topic from the listing displayed in the Help window. Each topic is a **hyperlink** or connection to the information located on the Office.com Web site or in Help on your computer. When you point to a hyperlink, it appears underlined and the mouse pointer appears as 🖑. Clicking the hyperlink accesses and displays the information associated with the hyperlink.

- Click "Getting started with Word 2010."

- Scroll the Help window and click "Basic tasks in Word 2010" in the Never Used Word Before area.

Your screen should be similar to Figure 56

Figure 56

An article containing information about basic features of Word 2010 is displayed and the table of contents has expanded and current topic is underlined to show your location in Help. A topic list appears at the top of the article. You can either scroll the article to read it, or you can jump to a specific location in the article by clicking on a topic link.

- Click "Create a new document."

Your screen should be similar to Figure 57

Figure 57

The information on the selected topic is displayed in the window. Notice, as you made selections in the Help window, that the Table of Contents pane shows your current location in Help.

Using the Help Table of Contents

Choosing a topic from the Table of Contents is another method of locating Help information. Using this method allows you to browse the entire list of Help topics to locate topics of interest to you. In this case, the Getting Started with Word topic has expanded to show the subtopics and the topic you are currently viewing is underlined, indicating it is selected. Notice the 📖 Open Book and 📘 Closed Book icons in the Table of Contents. The 📖 Open Book icon identifies those chapters that are open. Clicking on an item preceded with a 📘 Closed Book icon opens a chapter, which expands to display additional chapters or topics. Clicking on an item preceded with ❓ displays the specific Help information.

Additional Information

Pointing to a topic that is not fully displayed in the Table of Contents displays a ScreenTip of the entire topic heading.

1

- Click "Word for new users" in the Table of Contents list.

- Click "A tour of the Word user interface" in the Help window.

Your screen should be similar to Figure 58

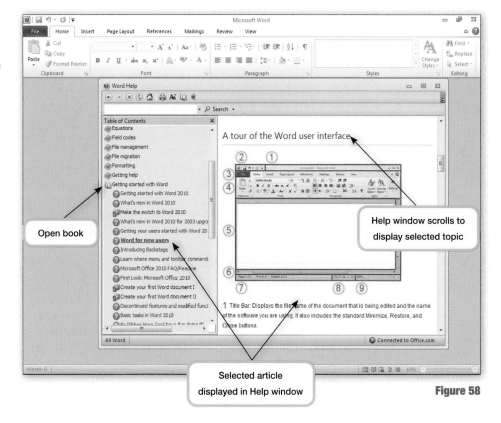

Figure 58

Now information about the user interface features of Word 2010 is displayed in the Help window. To move through previously viewed Help topics, you can use the ◀ Back and ▶ Forward buttons in the Help toolbar. You can quickly redisplay the opening Help window using 🏠 Home on the Help toolbar.

2

- Click ◀ Back to display the previous topic.

- Click 🏠 Home in the Help window toolbar.

- Click "Getting started with Word" in the Table of Contents pane to close this topic.

Your screen should be similar to Figure 59

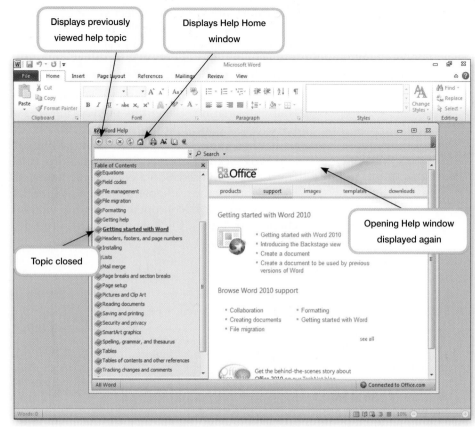

Displays previously viewed help topic

Displays Help Home window

Topic closed

Opening Help window displayed again

Figure 59

The opening Help window is displayed, the Table of Contents topic is closed, and the ▶ Forward button in the Help window toolbar is now available for use.

Searching Help Topics

Another method to find Help information is to conduct a search by entering a word or phrase you want help on in the Search text box. When searching, you can specify the scope of the search by selecting from the 🔎 Search ▾ drop-down menu. The broadest scope for a search, All Word under Content from Office .com, is preselected. You will use this feature to search for Help information about the Office user interface.

1

- **Click in the Search text box to display the cursor and type user interface**

Additional Information

The search is not case sensitive.

- **Click** 🔍 Search ▾ .

- **Scroll the Help window to see the search results.**

Additional Information

You also could press [Enter] to start the search.

Your screen should be similar to Figure 60

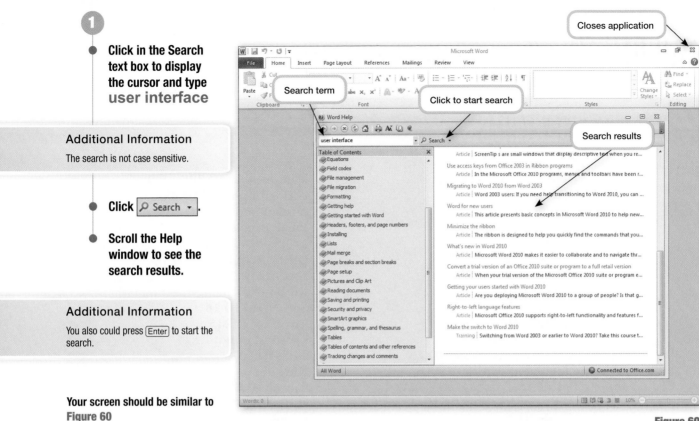

Figure 60

The Help window displays links to articles that contain both the words "user" and "interface." The results are shown in order of relevance, with the most likely matches at the top of the list.

EXITING AN OFFICE 2010 APPLICATION

Now you are ready to close the Help window and exit the Word program. The ⊠ Close button located on the right end of the window title bar can be used to exit most application windows. Alternatively, you can use the ⊠ Exit command on the File tab. If you attempt to close an application without first saving your document, a warning appears asking if you want to save your work. If you do not save your work and you exit the application, any changes you made since last saving it are lost.

1

- **Click** ⊠ **Close in the Help window title bar to close the Help window.**

- **Click** ⊠ **Close in the Word window title bar to exit Word.**

Another Method

The keyboard shortcut for the Exit command is [Alt] + [F4].

The program window is closed and the Windows desktop is visible again.

KEY TERMS

Backstage view IO.24
buttons IO.15
character effects IO.40
Clipboard IO.45
commands IO.18
context menu IO.17
contextual tabs IO.20
cursor IO.15
database IO.7
default IO.27
destination IO.45
dialog box launcher IO.23
document window IO.15
edit IO.3
Enhanced ScreenTip IO.20
fields IO.7
font IO.40
font size IO.40
format IO.3
groups IO.18
hyperlink IO.61
insertion point IO.15
keyboard shortcut IO.16
keyword IO.51
Live Preview IO.40
metadata IO.51

Mini toolbar IO.39
Office Clipboard IO.45
on-demand tabs IO.20
Paste Preview IO.46
properties IO.27, 51
Quick Access Toolbar IO.15
records IO.7
Ribbon IO.15
ScreenTip IO.16
scroll bar IO.15
shortcut menu IO.17
slide IO.10
slide shows IO.10
source IO.45
status bar IO.15
tables IO.7
tabs IO.18
tag IO.51
task pane IO.23
template IO.26
tooltip IO.16
typeface IO.40
user interface IO.14
View buttons IO.15
worksheet IO.5
Zoom Slider IO.15

COMMAND SUMMARY

Command/Button	Shortcut	Action
Quick Access Toolbar		
↺ ▾ Undo	Ctrl + Y	Restores last change
↻ Redo	Ctrl + Y	Restores last Undo action
↻ Repeat	Ctrl + Y	Repeats last action
❓ Microsoft Word Help	F1	Opens Microsoft Help

COMMAND SUMMARY (CONTINUED)

Command/Button	Shortcut	Action
File tab		
🖫 Save	Ctrl + S or 🖫	Saves document using same file name
🖫 Save As	F12	Saves document using a new file name, type, and/or location
📂 Open	Ctrl + O	Opens existing file
📁 Close	Ctrl + F4 or ⊠	Closes document
Info		Displays document properties
Print/🖨 Print	Ctrl + P	Prints document using specified settings
⊠ Exit	Alt + F4 or ⊠	Exits Office program
View tab		
Zoom group		
🔍 Zoom		Changes magnification of document
Home tab		
Clipboard group		
📋 Paste	Ctrl + V	Inserts copy of Clipboard at location of cursor
✂ Cut	Ctrl + X	Removes selection and copies to Clipboard
📄 Copy	Ctrl + C	Copies selection to Clipboard
🖌 Format Painter		Duplicates formats of selection to other locations
Font group		
Calibri (Body) ▾ Font	Ctrl + Shift + F	Changes typeface
11 ▾ Font Size	Ctrl + Shift + P	Changes font size
B Bold	Ctrl + B	Adds/removes bold effect
I Italic	Ctrl + I	Adds/removes italic effect
U Underline	Ctrl + U	Adds/removes underline effect

LAB EXERCISES | Hands-On Exercises

STEP-BY-STEP

EXPLORING EXCEL 2010

1. In this exercise you will explore the Excel 2010 application and use many of the same features you learned about while using Word 2010 in this lab.

   a. Use the Start menu or a shortcut icon on your desktop to start Office Excel 2010.

   b. What shape is the mouse pointer when positioned in the document window area? _____

   c. Excel has _____ tabs. Which tabs are not the same as in Word? _____

   d. Open the Formulas tab. How many groups are in the Formulas tab? _____

   e. Which tab contains the group to work with charts? _____

   f. From the Home tab, click the Number group dialog box launcher. What is the name of the dialog box that opens? _____ How many number categories are there? _____ Close the dialog box.

   g. Display ScreenTips for the following buttons located in the Alignment group of the Home tab and identify what action they perform.

   _____

   _____

   _____

   h. Open the Excel Help window. From the Help window choose "Getting started with Excel 2010" and then choose "Basic tasks in Excel 2010." Read this article and answer the following question: What is Excel used for? _____

   i. In the Table of Contents, open the "Worksheets" topic and then "Entering Data." Read the topic "Enter data manually in worksheet cells" and answer the following:

   • What is the definition of worksheet? Hint: Click on the grayed term "worksheet" to view a definition.

   _____

   • What four types of data can be entered in a worksheet? _____, _____, _____, _____

   j. Read the topic "Quick Start: Edit and enter data in a worksheet." If you have an Internet connection, click the Watch the video link and view the video. Close your browser window.

   k. Enter the term "formula" in the Search text box. Look at several articles and answer the following question: All formula entries begin with what symbol? _____

   l. Close the Help window. Exit Excel.

EXPLORING POWERPOINT 2010

2. In this exercise you will explore the PowerPoint 2010 application and use many of the same features you learned about while using Word 2010 in this lab.

    a. Use the Start menu or a shortcut icon on your desktop to start Office PowerPoint 2010.

    b. PowerPoint has _____ tabs. Which tabs are not the same as in Word?

    _____

    c. Open the Animations tab. How many groups are in this tab? _____

    d. Which tab contains the group to work with themes? _____

    e. Click on the text "Click to add title." Type your name. Select this text and change the font size to 60; add italic and bold. Cut this text. Click in the box containing "Click to add subtitle" and paste the cut selection. Use the Paste Options to keep the source formatting.

    f. Click on the text "Click to add title" and type the name of your school. Select the text and apply a font of your choice.

    g. Open the PowerPoint Help window. From the Help window, choose "Getting Started with PowerPoint 2010" and then choose "Basic tasks in PowerPoint 2010." Read the information in this article and answer the following questions:

    *   In the "What is PowerPoint?" topic, what is the primary use of PowerPoint?_____.

    *   In the "Save a presentation" topic, what is the default file format for a presentation?

        _____

    *   What is the first tip in the "Tips for creating an effective presentation" topic?

        _____

    h. Enter the term "placeholder" in the Search text box. Look at several articles and write the definition of this term. Hint: Click on a word in an article that appears in light gray to view a definition.

    _____

    i. In the Table of Contents, open the "Delivering your presentation" topic. Choose "Create and print notes pages" and answer the following questions:

    *   What are notes pages?

        _____

    *   What is the Green Idea?

        _____

    j. Close the Help window. Exit PowerPoint and do not save the changes you made to the presentation.

LAB EXERCISES

EXPLORING ACCESS 2010

3. As noted in this Introduction to Microsoft Office 2010, when you start Access 2010 you need to either open an existing database file or create and name a new database. Therefore, in this exercise, you simply explore the Access 2010 Help information without opening or creating a database file.

   a. Use the Start menu or a shortcut icon on your desktop to start Office Access 2010.

   b. Open the Help tab in Backstage view and choose Microsoft Office Help.

   c. From the Help window, choose "Basic tasks in Access 2010." Read the information in this article and answer the following questions:

   - In the "What is Access?" topic, what are the two locations where you can keep your data? _____ and _____.

   - In the "Create a Database from Scratch" topic, what are the two choices? _____ or _____.

   d. In the Table of Contents pane, open the "Access basics" topic. Choose "Database basics" and answer the following questions:

   - In the "What is a database?" topic, define "database."

     _____

   - In "The parts of an Access database" topic, what are the six main parts? _____, _____, _____, _____, _____, _____.

   - In "The parts of an Access database" topic, how is data in a table stored? _____ and _____.

   - In "The parts of an Access database" topic, each row in a table is referred to as a _____.

   e. Enter the term "field" in the Search text box. Look at several articles and write the definition of this term. Hint: Click on a word in an article that appears in light gray to view a definition.

     _____

   f. Close the Help window. Exit Access.

ON YOUR OWN

EXPLORING WORD HELP

1. In addition to the Help information you used in this lab, Office 2010 Help also includes many interactive tutorials. Selecting a Help topic that starts a tutorial will open the browser program on your computer. Both audio and written instructions are provided. You will use one of these tutorials to learn more about using Word 2010.

   Start Word 2010. Open Help and choose "Getting started with Word" from the Help window. Click on the training topic "Create your first Word document I." Follow the directions in your browser to run the tutorial. When you are done, close the browser window, close Help, and exit Word 2010.

Creating and Editing a Worksheet Lab 1

Objectives

After completing this lab, you will know how to:

1. Create new worksheets.

2. Enter and edit data.

3. Modify column widths and row heights.

4. Use proofing tools.

5. Copy and paste cell contents.

6. Create formulas.

7. Insert and delete rows and columns.

8. Format cells and cell content.

9. Hide and unhide rows and columns.

10. Create a basic chart.

11. Format values as a date.

12. Preview and print a worksheet.

13. Display and print formulas.

14. Change worksheet orientation and scale content.

Downtown Internet Café

You are excited about your new position as manager and financial planner for a local coffeehouse. Evan, the owner, has hired you as part of a larger effort to increase business at the former Downtown Café. Evan began this effort by completely renovating his coffeehouse and installing a wireless network. He plans to offer free Wi-Fi service for customers to use with their own laptop computers. In addition, he has set up several computer kiosks for customers to use who do not have laptops and has provided a printer and copier for all customers to use. He also has decided to rent an MP3 download kiosk for customers who may want to update the music on their iPods or PDAs. Finally, to reflect the new emphasis of the café, he has changed its name to the Downtown Internet Café.

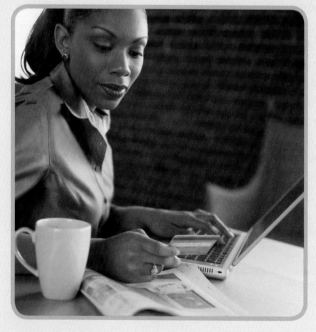

You and Evan expect to increase sales by attracting techno-savvy café-goers, who you hope will use the Downtown Internet Café as a place to meet, study, work, or download music for their iPods and PDAs. You also believe the rental computers will be a draw for vacationers who want to check e-mail during their travels.

Evan wants to create a forecast estimating sales and expenses for the first quarter. As part of a good business plan, you and Evan need a realistic set of financial estimates and goals.

In this lab, you will help with the first-quarter forecast by using Microsoft Office Excel 2010, a spreadsheet application that can store, manipulate, and display numeric data. You will learn to enter numbers, perform calculations, copy data, and label rows and columns as you create the basic structure of a worksheet for the Downtown Internet Café. You will then learn how to enhance the worksheet using formatting features and by adding color as shown here.

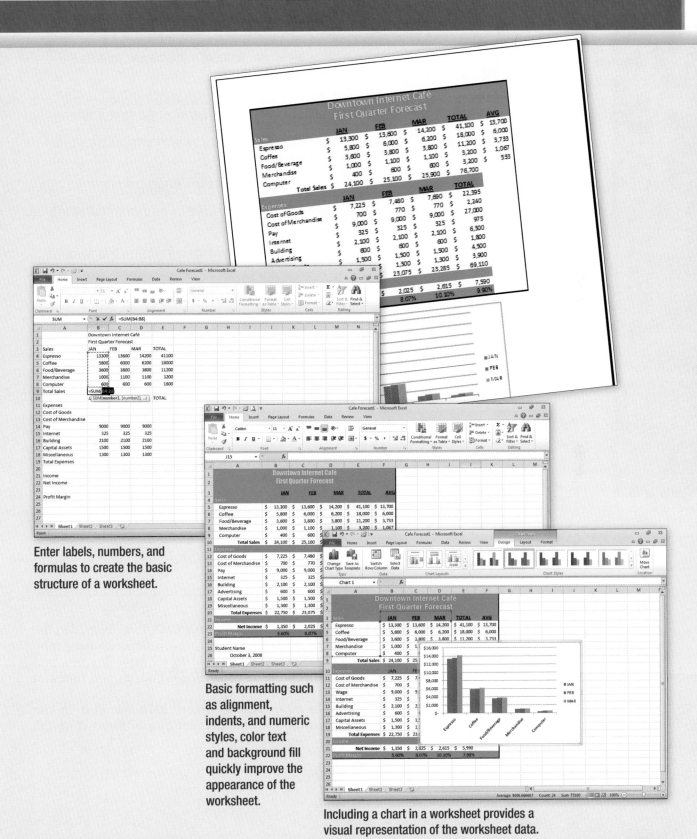

Enter labels, numbers, and formulas to create the basic structure of a worksheet.

Basic formatting such as alignment, indents, and numeric styles, color text and background fill quickly improve the appearance of the worksheet.

Including a chart in a worksheet provides a visual representation of the worksheet data.

EX1.3

The following concepts will be introduced in this lab:

1 Data The basic information or data you enter in a cell can be text or numbers.

2 AutoCorrect The AutoCorrect feature makes some basic assumptions about the text you are typing and, based on these assumptions, automatically corrects the entry.

3 Column Width The column width is the size or width of a column and controls the amount of information that can be displayed in a cell.

4 Spelling Checker The spelling checker locates misspelled words, duplicate words, and capitalization irregularities in the active worksheet and proposes the correct spelling.

5 Thesaurus The thesaurus is a reference tool that provides synonyms, antonyms, and related words for a selected word or phrase.

6 Range A selection consisting of two or more cells on a worksheet is a range.

7 Formula A formula is an equation that performs a calculation on data contained in a worksheet.

8 Relative Reference A relative reference is a cell or range reference in a formula whose location is interpreted in relation to the position of the cell that contains the formula.

9 Function A function is a prewritten formula that performs certain types of calculations automatically.

10 Recalculation When a number in a referenced cell in a formula changes, Excel automatically recalculates all formulas that are dependent upon the changed value.

11 Alignment Alignment settings allow you to change the horizontal and vertical placement and the orientation of an entry in a cell.

12 Row Height The row height is the size or height of a row measured in points.

13 Number Formats Number formats change the appearance of numbers onscreen and when printed, without changing the way the number is stored or used in calculations.

Creating a Workbook

As part of the renovation of the Downtown Internet Café, Evan upgraded the office computer with the latest version of the Microsoft Office System suite of applications, Office 2010. You are very excited to see how this new and powerful application can help you create professional budgets and financial forecasts for the Café.

You will use the spreadsheet application Excel 2010 included in the Microsoft Office 2010 System suite to create the first-quarter forecast for the Café.

1

● **Start Microsoft Excel 2010.**

● **If necessary, maximize the Excel application window.**

Having Trouble?

See "Common Office 2010 Features" page IO.13, for information on how to start the application and for a discussion of features common to all Microsoft Office 2010 applications.

Your screen should be similar to Figure 1.1

Title bar displays default file name

Excel Ribbon consists of seven tabs

Formula bar

Name box

Mouse pointer

Workbook window

Figure 1.1

Additional Information

Because the Ribbon can adapt to the screen resolution and orientation, your Ribbon may look slightly different. It also may display additional tabs if other application add-ins associated with Office 2010 are on.

Additional Information

You will learn all about using these features throughout these labs.

Having Trouble?

If the workbook is floating in the workbook window, the title bar displays the file name and the ☐ Minimize, ☐ Maximize, and ☒ Close buttons. Click ☐ to maximize the workbook window.

After a few moments, the Excel application window is displayed. Because Excel remembers many settings that were in use when the program was last closed, your screen might look slightly different.

The Excel application window title bar displays the default file name, Book1, and program name. The Ribbon below the title bar consists of seven tabs that provide access to the commands and features you will use to create and modify a worksheet.

Below the Ribbon is the formula bar. The **formula bar** displays entries as they are made and edited in the workbook window. The **Name box**, located at the left end of the formula bar, provides information about the selected item.

The large center area of the program window is the **workbook window**. A **workbook** is an Excel file that stores the information you enter using the program. You will learn more about the different parts of the workbook window shortly.

The mouse pointer can appear as many different shapes. The mouse pointer changes shape depending upon the task you are performing or where the pointer is located on the window. Most commonly it appears as a ⌖ or ⬍. When it appears as a ⬍, it is used to move to different locations in the workbook window; when it appears as a ⌖, it is used to choose items, such as commands from the Ribbon.

2

- Move the mouse pointer into the center of the workbook window to see it appear as ✛.

- Move the mouse pointer to the Ribbon to see it appear as �><.

Your screen should be similar to Figure 1.2

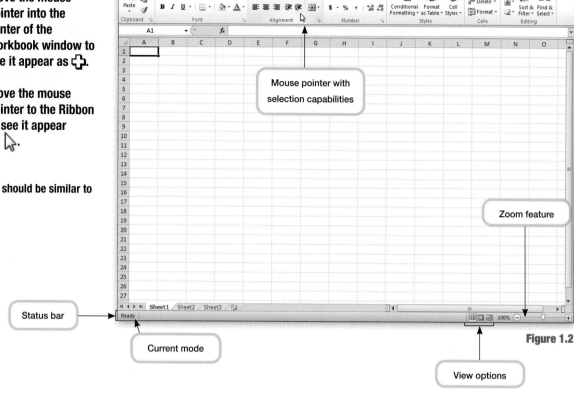

Mouse pointer with selection capabilities

Zoom feature

Status bar

Current mode

View options

Figure 1.2

The status bar at the bottom of the Excel window displays information about various Excel settings. The left side of the status bar displays the current mode or state of operation of the program, in this case, Ready. When Ready is displayed, you can move around the workbook, enter data, use the function keys, or choose a command. As you use the program, the status bar displays the current mode. The right side of the status bar contains buttons to change the view and a zoom feature.

Exploring the Workbook Window

Additional Information

See "Using Backstage View" in the Introduction to Microsoft Office 2010 to review these features.

When you first start Excel 2010, the workbook window displays a new blank workbook that includes many default settings. These default settings, are stored in the default workbook template file named Book.xltx.

The default workbook file includes three blank sheets. A **sheet** is used to display different types of information, such as financial data or charts. Whenever you open a new workbook, it displays a worksheet. A **worksheet**, also commonly referred to as a **spreadsheet**, is a rectangular grid of **rows** and **columns** used to enter data. It is always part of a workbook and is the primary type of sheet you will use in Excel. The worksheet is much larger than the part you are viewing in the window. The worksheet actually extends 16,384 columns to the right and 1,048,576 rows down.

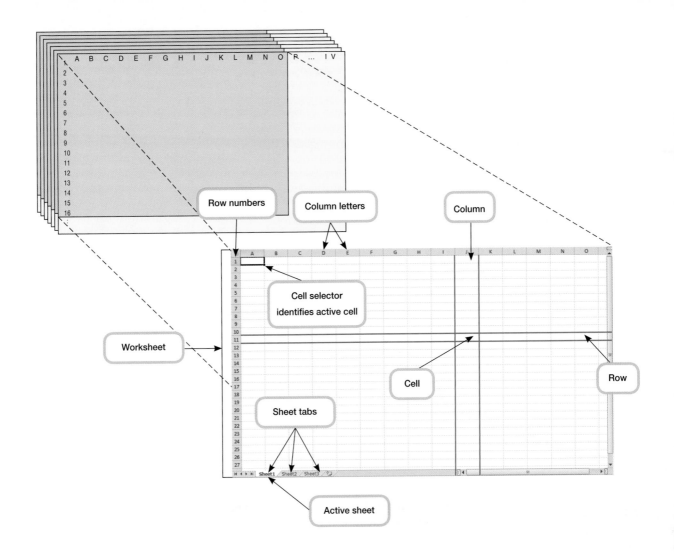

The **row numbers** along the left side and the **column letters** across the top of the workbook window identify each worksheet row and column. The intersection of a row and column creates a **cell**. Notice the black border, called the **cell selector**, surrounding the cell located at the intersection of column A and row 1. This identifies the **active cell**, which is the cell your next entry or procedure affects. Additionally, the Name box in the formula bar displays the **cell reference**, consisting of the column letter and row number of the active cell. The reference of the active cell is A1.

Each sheet in a workbook is named. Initially, the sheets are named Sheet1, Sheet2, and so on, displayed on **sheet tabs** at the bottom of the workbook window. The name of the **active sheet**, which is the sheet you can work in, appears bold. The currently displayed worksheet in the workbook window, Sheet1, is the active sheet.

Additional Information

Columns are labeled A through Z, AA through ZZ, and so forth through the last column, XFD. There are 17,179,869,184 cells in a worksheet.

1 Click the Sheet2 tab.

Another Method

You also can press Ctrl + Page Down to move to the next sheet and Ctrl + Page Up to move to the previous sheet.

Your screen should be similar to Figure 1.3

Figure 1.3

Additional Information

Do not be concerned if your workbook window displays more or fewer column letters and row numbers than shown here. This is a function of your computer monitor settings.

An identical blank worksheet is displayed in the window. The Sheet2 tab letters are bold, the background is highlighted, and it appears in front of the other sheet tabs to show it is the active sheet.

The sheet tab area also contains **tab scroll buttons**, which are used to scroll tabs right or left when there are more sheet tabs than can be seen. You will learn about these features throughout the labs.

MOVING AROUND THE WORKSHEET

Additional Information

You can use the directional keys in the numeric keypad (with Num Lock off) or, if you have an extended keyboard, you can use the separate directional keypad area.

The mouse or keyboard commands can be used to move the cell selector from one cell to another in the worksheet. To move using a mouse, simply point to the cell you want to move to and click the mouse button. Depending upon what you are doing, using the mouse to move may not be as convenient as using the keyboard, in which case the directional keys can be used. You will make Sheet1 active again and use the mouse, then the keyboard, to move in the worksheet.

Click the Sheet1 tab to make it the active sheet again.

Click cell B3.

Press → (3 times).

Press ↓ (4 times).

Your screen should be similar to Figure 1.4

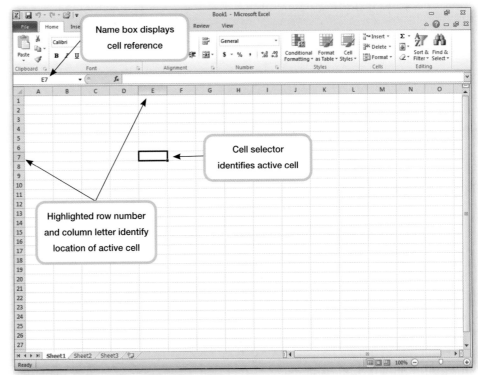

Figure 1.4

Cell E7 is outlined in black, indicating this cell is the active cell. The Name box displays the cell reference. In addition, the row number and column letter are gold to further identify the location of the active cell.

As you have learned, the worksheet is much larger than the part you are viewing in the window. To see an area of the worksheet that is not currently in view, you need to scroll the window. The keyboard procedures shown in the table that follows can be used to move around the worksheet.

Keyboard	Action
Alt + Page Down	Moves right one full window.
Alt + Page Up	Moves left one full window.
Home	Moves to beginning of row.
Ctrl + Home	Moves to upper-left corner cell of worksheet.
Ctrl + End	Moves to last-used cell of worksheet.
End →	Moves to last-used cell in row.
End ↓	Moves to last-used cell in column.

In addition, if you hold down the arrow keys, the Alt + Page Up or Alt + Page Down keys, or the Page Up or Page Down keys, you can quickly scroll through the worksheet. When you use the scroll bar, however, the active cell does not change until you click on a cell that is visible in the window.

You will scroll the worksheet to see the rows below row 27 and the columns to the right of column O.

Press [Page Down] **(3 times).**

Press [Alt] +
[Page Down] **(3 times).**

Your screen should be similar to Figure 1.5

Additional Information

If you have a mouse with a scroll wheel, rotating the wheel forward or back scrolls up or down a few rows at a time.

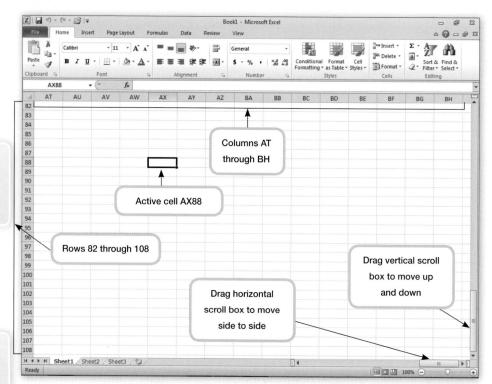

Columns AT through BH

Active cell AX88

Rows 82 through 108

Drag vertical scroll box to move up and down

Drag horizontal scroll box to move side to side

Figure 1.5

The worksheet scrolled downward and left three full windows, and the window displays rows 82 through 108 and columns AT through BH of the worksheet. The active cell is cell AX88. As you scroll the worksheet using the keyboard, the active cell also changes.

It is even more efficient to use the scroll bar to move long distances.

Slowly drag the vertical scroll box up the scroll bar until row 1 is displayed.

Slowly drag the horizontal scroll box left along the scroll bar until column A is displayed.

Additional Information

As you scroll, the scroll bar identifies the current row position at the top of the window or column position at the left side of the window in a ScreenTip.

Your screen should be similar to Figure 1.6

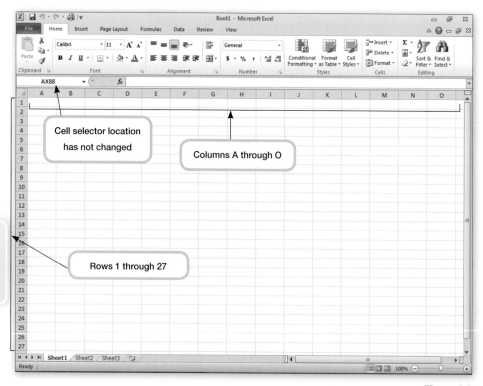

Cell selector location has not changed

Columns A through O

Rows 1 through 27

Figure 1.6

WWW.MHHE.COM/OLEARY

Rows 1 to 27 and columns A to O are displayed again. Notice that the Name box displays the active cell location as AX88. When you use the scroll bar to scroll the worksheet, the active cell does not change.

Another Method

You also can type a cell address in the Name box and press ←Enter to move to that location.

● **Practice moving around the worksheet using the keys presented in the table on page EX1.9.**

Additional Information

The Ctrl + End key presented in the table will not change the worksheet location until the worksheet contains data.

● **Press Ctrl + Home to move to cell A1.**

You can use the mouse or the keyboard with most of the exercises in these labs. As you use both the mouse and the keyboard, you will find that it is more efficient to use one or the other in specific situations.

DEVELOPING A WORKSHEET

Now that you are familiar with the parts of the workbook and with moving around the worksheet, you are ready to create a worksheet showing the forecast for the first three months of operation for the Downtown Internet Café.

Worksheet development consists of four steps: planning, entering and editing, testing, and formatting. The objective is to create well-designed worksheets that produce accurate results and are clearly understood, adaptable, and efficient.

Step	Description
1. Plan	Specify the purpose of the worksheet and how it should be organized. This means clearly identifying the data that will be input, the calculations that are needed to achieve the results, and the output that is desired. As part of the planning step, it is helpful to sketch out a design of the worksheet to organize the worksheet's structure. The design should include the worksheet title and row and column headings that identify the input and output. Additionally, sample data can be used to help determine the formulas needed to produce the output.
2. Enter and edit	Create the structure of the worksheet using Excel by entering the worksheet labels, data, and formulas. As you enter information, you are likely to make errors that need to be corrected or edited, or you will need to revise the content of what you have entered to clarify it or to add or delete information.
3. Test	Test the worksheet for errors. Use several sets of real or sample data as the input, and verify the resulting output. The input data should include a full range of possible values for each data item to ensure the worksheet can function successfully under all possible conditions.
4. Format	Enhance the appearance of the worksheet to make it more readable or attractive. This step is usually performed when the worksheet is near completion. It includes many features such as boldface text, italic, and color.

As the complexity of the worksheet increases, the importance of following the design process increases. Even for simple worksheets like the one you will create in this lab, the design process is important. You will find that you will generally follow these steps in the order listed above for your first draft of a worksheet. However, you will probably retrace steps such as editing and formatting as the final worksheet is developed.

During the planning phase, you have spoken with the Café manager, Evan, regarding the purpose of the worksheet and the content in general. The primary purpose is to develop a forecast for sales and expenses for the next year. First, Evan wants you to develop a worksheet for the first-quarter forecast and then extend it by quarters for the year. After reviewing past budgets and consulting with Evan, you have designed the basic layout for the first-quarter forecast for the Café, as shown below.

Entering and Editing Data

Now that you understand the purpose of the worksheet and have a general idea of the content, you are ready to begin entering the data. Each worksheet is like a blank piece of paper that already has many predefined settings. You will use the blank Sheet1 worksheet with the default settings to create the worksheet for the Café.

As you can see, the budget you designed above contains both descriptive text entries and numeric data. These are two types of data you can enter in a worksheet.

Concept Data

The basic information or **data** you enter in a cell can be text, numbers, dates, or times. **Text** entries can contain any combination of letters, numbers, spaces, and any other special characters. **Number** entries can include only the digits 0 to 9 and any of the special characters + − ( ) , . / $ % ? =. Number entries can be used in calculations.

Text and number entries generally appear in the cell exactly as they are entered. However, some entries such as formulas direct Excel to perform a calculation on values in the worksheet. In these cases, the result of the formula appears in the cell, not the formula itself. You will learn about formulas later in the lab.

Adding Text Entries

You enter data into a worksheet by moving to the cell where you want the data displayed and typing the entry using the keyboard. First, you will enter the worksheet headings. Row and column **headings** are entries that are used

WWW.MHHE.COM/OLEARY

to create the structure of the worksheet and describe other worksheet entries. Generally, headings are text entries. The column headings in this worksheet consist of the three months (January through March) and a total (sum of entries over three months) located in columns B through E. You will begin by entering the column heading for January in cell B2.

Click on cell B2 to move to it.

Type January

Having Trouble?

Do not be concerned if you make a typing error. You will learn how to correct it shortly.

Your screen should be similar to Figure 1.7

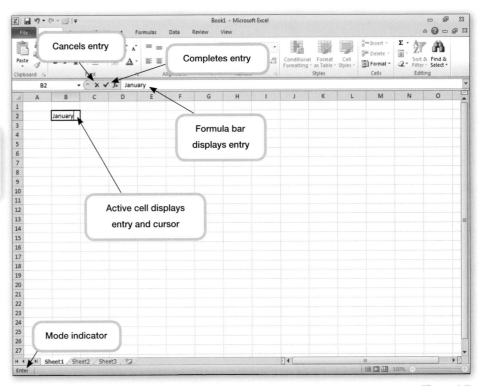

Figure 1.7

Several changes have occurred in the window. As you type, the entry is displayed both in the active cell and in the formula bar. The cursor appears in the active cell and marks your location in the entry. Two new buttons, ✖ and ✔, appear in the formula bar. They can be used with a mouse to cancel your entry or complete it.

Notice also that the mode displayed in the status bar has changed from Ready to Enter. This notifies you that the current mode of operation in the worksheet is entering data.

Although the entry is displayed in both the active cell and the formula bar, you need to press the ←Enter or Tab key, click ✔, or click on any other cell to complete your entry. If you press Esc or click ✖, the entry is cleared and nothing appears in the cell. Since your hands are already on the keyboard, it is quicker to press ←Enter or Tab than it is to use the mouse.

Press ⏎Enter.

Your screen should be similar to
Figure 1.8

Figure 1.8

Additional Information

Pressing ⇧Shift + ⏎Enter to
complete an entry moves up a cell, and
Ctrl + ⏎Enter completes the entry
without moving to another cell.

The entry January is displayed in cell B2, and the mode has returned to Ready. In addition, the active cell is cell B3. Whenever you use the ⏎Enter key to complete an entry, the cell selector moves down one cell.

Notice that the entry is positioned to the left side of the cell space. This is one of the worksheet default settings.

CLEARING AN ENTRY

After looking at the entry, you decide you want the column headings to be in row 3 rather than in row 2. This will leave more space above the column headings for a worksheet title. The Delete key can be used to clear the contents from a cell. You will remove the entry from cell B2 and enter it in cell B3.

Move to B2.

Press Delete.

Another Method

You also can use ✎ ▾ Clear/Clear
Contents in the Editing group of the
Home tab.

Move to B3.

Type January

Click ✓ Enter.

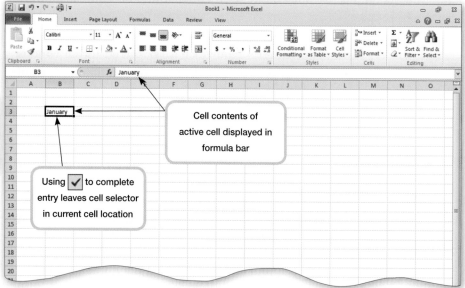

Figure 1.9

Your screen should be similar to
Figure 1.9

The active cell does not change when you click ✓ to complete an entry. Because the active cell contains an entry, the cell content is displayed in the formula bar.

EDITING AN ENTRY

Next, you decide to change the heading from January to JAN. An entry in a cell can be entirely changed in the Ready mode or partially changed or edited in the Edit mode. To use the Ready mode, you move to the cell you want to change and retype the entry the way you want it to appear. As soon as a new character is entered, the existing entry is cleared.

Generally, however, if you need to change only part of an entry, using the Edit mode is quicker. To change to Edit mode, double-click on the cell whose contents you want to edit.

1

● **Double-click B3.**

Having Trouble?

The mouse pointer must be when you double-click on the cell.

Another Method

Pressing the F2 key also will change to Edit mode. The cursor is positioned at the end of the entry.

Your screen should be similar to Figure 1.10

Figure 1.10

The status bar shows that the new mode of operation is Edit. The cursor appears at the location you clicked in the entry, and the mouse pointer changes to an I-beam when positioned on the cell. Now you can click again or use the directional keys to move the cursor within the cell entry to the location of the text you want to change.

After the cursor is appropriately positioned, you can edit the entry by removing the incorrect characters and typing the correct characters. To do this, you can use the Backspace and Delete keys to delete text character by character and enter the new text, or you can select the text to be changed and then type the correction. You will change this entry to JAN.

Having Trouble?

Refer to the "Entering and Editing Text" and "Selecting Text" sections of the Introduction to Office 2010 to review these features.

Additional Information

You also can use Ctrl + Delete to delete everything to the right of the cursor.

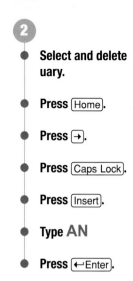

- ● Select and delete uary.
- ● Press [Home].
- ● Press [→].
- ● Press [Caps Lock].
- ● Press [Insert].
- ● Type AN
- ● Press [↵Enter].

Your screen should be similar to Figure 1.11

Figure 1.11

Additional Information

The Caps Lock indicator light on your keyboard is lit when this feature is on.

Additional Information

Overwrite is automatically turned off when you leave Edit mode or you press [Insert] again.

The four characters at the end of the entry were deleted. Turning on the Caps Lock feature produced the uppercase letters AN without having to hold down [⇧Shift]. Finally, by pressing Insert, the program switched from inserting text to overwriting text as you typed. When overwriting text is on, the cursor changes to a highlight to show that the character will be replaced with the new text you type.

The new heading JAN is entered into cell B3, replacing January. As you can see, editing will be particularly useful with long or complicated entries.

Next, you will enter the remaining three headings in row 3. Because you want to move to the right one cell to enter the next month label, you will complete the entries using [→] or [Tab⇥].

3

● Click on cell C3.

● Type FEB

● Press → or Tab⇥.

● Complete the column headings by entering MAR in cell D3 and TOTAL in cell E3.

Having Trouble?

Remember to press ←Enter, Tab⇥, or an arrow key or click in another cell to complete each entry.

● Press Caps Lock to turn off this feature.

Your screen should be similar to Figure 1.12

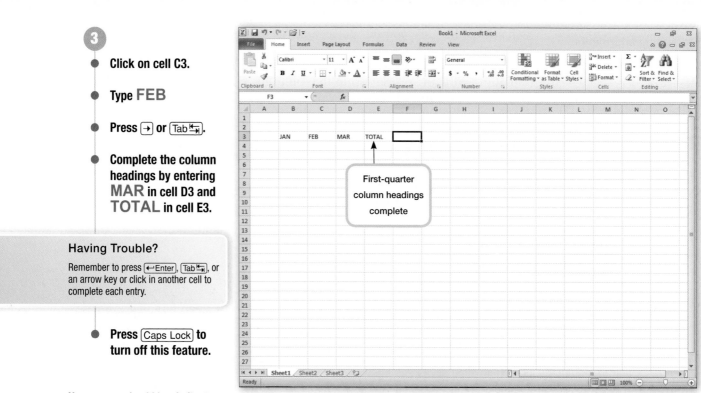

First-quarter column headings complete

Figure 1.12

The column headings are now complete for the first quarter. Above the column headings, you want to enter a title for the worksheet. The first title line will be the café name, Downtown Internet Café.

4

● Move to B1.

● Type Downtown Café and click ✓ Enter.

● Double-click on cell B1 to change to Edit mode.

● Move the cursor to the beginning of the word Café.

● Type Internet followed by a space.

● Press Ctrl + ←Enter.

Your screen should be similar to Figure 1.13

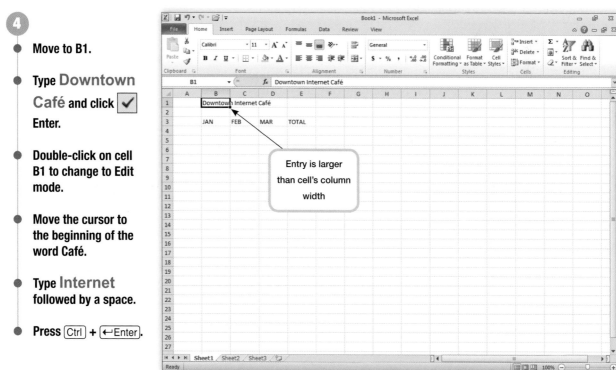

Entry is larger than cell's column width

Figure 1.13

This time, because you did not change to overwriting text as you edited the entry, the new text was inserted between the existing text. Inserting text while editing is the default setting. Also notice that the entry is longer than the cell's column width and overlaps into the cell to the right. As long as the cell to the right is empty, the whole entry will be displayed. If the cell to the right contains an entry, the overlapping part of the entry is not displayed.

USING AUTOCORRECT

Next, you will enter the second title line, First Quarter Report. As you enter text in a cell, Excel checks the entry for accuracy. This is part of the automatic correcting feature of Excel.

Concept 2 AutoCorrect

The **AutoCorrect** feature makes some basic assumptions about the text you are typing and, based on these assumptions, automatically corrects the entry. The AutoCorrect feature automatically inserts proper capitalization at the beginning of sentences and in the names of days of the week. It also will change to lowercase letters any words that were incorrectly capitalized because of the accidental use of the ⌈Caps Lock⌋ key. In addition, it also corrects many common typing and spelling errors automatically.

One way the program automatically makes corrections is by looking for certain types of errors. For example, if two capital letters appear at the beginning of a word, the second capital letter is changed to a lowercase letter. If a lowercase letter appears at the beginning of a sentence, the first letter of the first word is capitalized. If the name of a day begins with a lowercase letter, the first letter is capitalized.

Another way the program makes corrections is by checking all entries against a built-in list of words that are commonly spelled incorrectly or typed incorrectly. If it finds the entry on the list, the program automatically replaces the error with the correction. For example, the typing error "aboutthe" is automatically changed to "about the" because the error is on the AutoCorrect list. You also can add words that you want to be automatically corrected to the AutoCorrect list. Words you add are added to the list on the computer you are using and will be available to anyone who uses the machine later.

You will enter the second title line and will intentionally misspell two words to demonstrate how the AutoCorrect feature works.

● **Move to B2.**

● **Type** Firts Quater Forecast

● **Press** ⌈←Enter⌋.

Your screen should be similar to Figure 1.14

Typing errors automatically corrected

Figure 1.14

The two typing errors were automatically corrected as soon as you completed a word by pressing the spacebar. If the entry was a single word, it would be checked as soon as you completed the entry.

Next, the row headings need to be entered into column A of the worksheet. The row headings and what they represent are shown in the following table.

Heading	Description
Sales	
Espresso	Income from sales of espresso-based drinks
Coffee	Income from drip coffee sales
Food/Beverage	Income from sales of baked goods, sandwiches, salads, and other beverages
Merchandise	Income from sales of mugs, books, magazines, candy, etc.
Computer	Income from computer rental usage, printing, copier use, and MP3 downloads
Total Sales	Sum of all sales
Expenses	
Cost of Goods	Cost of espresso, coffee, and food items sold
Cost of Merchandise	Cost of merchandise other than food and beverage
Wages	Manager and labor costs
Internet	Wi-Fi access, MP3 kiosk rental, etc.
Building	Lease, insurance, electricity, water, etc.
Capital Assets	Equipment leases, interest, depreciation
Miscellaneous	Maintenance, phone, office supplies, outside services, taxes, etc.
Income	
Net Income	Total sales minus total expenses
Profit Margin	Net income divided by total sales

2

Complete the row headings for the Sales portion of the worksheet by entering the following headings in the indicated cells.

Cell	Heading
A3	Sales
A4	Espresso
A5	Coffee
A6	Food/Beverage
A7	Merchandise
A8	Computer
A9	Total Sales

Figure 1.15

Your screen should be similar to Figure 1.15

ADDING NUMBER ENTRIES

Next, you will enter the expected sales numbers for January into cells B4 through B8. As you learned earlier, number entries can include the digits 0 to 9 and any of these special characters: + – ( ) , . / $ % ? =. When entering numbers, it is not necessary to type the comma to separate thousands or the currency ($) symbol. You will learn about adding these symbols shortly.

- Move to B4.

- Type 13300 and press ⏎Enter.

- In the same manner, enter the January sales numbers for the remaining items using the values shown below.

Cell	Number
B5	5800
B6	3600
B7	1000
B8	600

Additional Information

You can use the number keys above the alphabetic keys or the numeric keypad area to enter numbers. If you use the numeric keypad, the Num Lock key must be on.

Your screen should be similar to Figure 1.16

Figure 1.16

Unlike text entries, Excel displays number entries right-aligned in the cell space by default. Also notice that the entries in cells A6 and A7 are no longer completely displayed. They contain long text entries and because the cells to the right now contain an entry, the overlapping part of the entry is shortened. However, the entire entry is fully displayed in the formula bar. Only the display of the entry in the cell has been shortened.

Modifying Column Widths

To allow the long text entries in column A to be fully displayed, you can increase the column's width.

Concept 3 — Column Width

The **column width** is the size or width of a column and controls the amount of information that can be displayed in a cell. A text entry that is larger than the column width will be fully displayed only if the cells to the right are blank. If the cells to the right contain data, the text is interrupted. On the other hand, when numbers are entered in a cell, the column width is automatically increased to fully display the entry.

The default column width setting is 8.43. The number represents the average number of digits that can be displayed in a cell using the standard type style. The column width can be any number from 0 to 255. If it is set to 0, the column is hidden.

When the worksheet is printed, it appears as it does currently on the screen. Therefore, you want to increase the column width to display the largest entry. Likewise, you can decrease the column width when the entries in a column are short.

There are several ways to change the column width. Using the mouse, you can change the width by dragging the boundary of the column heading. You also can set the column width to an exact value or to automatically fit the contents of the column.

DRAGGING THE COLUMN BOUNDARY

The column width can be quickly adjusted by dragging the boundary line located to the right of the column letter. Dragging it to the left decreases the column width, while dragging it to the right increases the width. As you drag, a temporary column reference line shows where the new column will appear and a ScreenTip displays the width of the column.

1

- Point to the boundary line to the right of the column letter A, and when the mouse pointer changes to ↔, click and drag the mouse pointer to the right.

- When the ScreenTip displays 24.00, release the mouse button.

Your screen should be similar to Figure 1.17

Figure 1.17

Now column A is more than wide enough to fully display all the row headings.

USING A SPECIFIED VALUE

Next, you will reduce the width of column A to 20.

1

- **Move to any cell in column A.**

- **Click** **in the Cells group and choose Column Width.**

- **Type 20 in the Column Width text box and click** OK .

Your screen should be similar to Figure 1.18

Figure 1.18

Although this is close, you would like to refine it a little more.

USING AUTOFIT

Another way to change the column width is to use the **AutoFit** feature to automatically adjust the width to fit the column contents. When using AutoFit, double-click the boundary to the right of the column heading of the column you want to fit to contents.

1

- **Double-click the right boundary line of column A.**

Your screen should be similar to Figure 1.19

Figure 1.19

The column width is sized to just slightly larger than the longest cell contents.

Having Trouble?

Refer to the section "Saving a File" in the Introduction to Office 2010 to review this feature.

You have a meeting you need to attend shortly, so you want to save the work you have completed so far on the workbook to a file and then close the file. You will name the file Cafe Forecast and use the default file type settings of Excel Workbook (*.xlsx). The file extension .xlsx identifies the file as an Excel 2007 or 2010 workbook. The default file type saves the workbook file in XML (Extensible Markup Language) format.

Excel 2003 and earlier versions used the .xls file extension. If you plan to share a file with someone using Excel 2003 or earlier, you can save the file using the .xls file type; however, some features may be lost. Otherwise, if you save it as an .xlsx file type, the recipient may not be able to view all the features.

1

- Click **Save in the Quick Access Toolbar.**

- **Select the location where you want to save your file.**

- **Click in the File Name text box to highlight the proposed file name, or if necessary triple-click on the file name to select it.**

- **Type Cafe Forecast**

- **Click** Save **or press** ←Enter.

Your screen should be similar to Figure 1.20

New file name

Figure 1.20

Additional Information

The file name in the title bar may display the workbook file extension, .xlsx, depending on your Windows Folder settings.

The new file name is displayed in the application window title bar. The worksheet data that was on your screen and in the computer's memory is now saved at the location you specified in a new file called Cafe Forecast.

You are now ready to close the workbook file.

2

- **Click the File tab to open Backstage view and click** Close.

Because you did not make any changes to the workbook after saving it, the workbook file is closed immediately and the Excel window displays an empty workbook window. If you had made changes to the file before closing it, you would have been prompted to save the file to prevent the accidental loss of data.

After attending your meeting, you continued working on the Café forecast. To see what has been done so far, you will open the workbook file named ex01_CafeForecast1.

3

● **Click the File tab to open Backstage view and click**

📂 Open .

Another Method

The keyboard shortcut is Ctrl + O.

● **Select the location containing your data files.**

● **Select** ex01_Cafe Forecast1.

● **Click** Open ▾ .

Another Method

You also could double-click the file name to both select it and choose

Open ▾ .

● **If necessary, maximize the workbook window.**

Figure 1.21

The workbook is opened and displayed in the workbook window. The workbook contains the additional sales values for February and March, the expense row headings, and several of the expense values for the month of January.

Your screen should be similar to Figure 1.21

Using Proofing Tools

When entering information into a worksheet, you are likely to make spelling and typing errors. To help locate and correct these errors, the spelling checker feature can be used. Additionally, you may find that the descriptive headings you have entered may not be exactly the word you want. The thesaurus can suggest better words to clarify the meaning of the worksheet.

CHECKING SPELLING

In your rush to get the row headings entered you realize you misspelled a few words. For example, the Expenses label is spelled "Espenses." Just to make sure there are no other spelling errors, you will check the spelling of all text entries in this worksheet.

Concept 4 Spelling Checker

The **spelling checker** locates misspelled words, duplicate words, and capitalization irregularities in the active worksheet and proposes the correct spelling. This feature works by comparing each word to a dictionary of words, called the **main dictionary**, that is supplied with the program. You also can create a **custom dictionary** to hold words you commonly use but that are not included in the main dictionary. If the word does not appear in the main dictionary or in a custom dictionary, it is identified as misspelled.

When you check spelling, the contents of all cell entries in the entire active sheet are checked. If you are in Edit mode when you check spelling, only the contents of the text in the cell are checked. The spelling checker does not check spelling in formulas or in text that results from formulas.

Excel begins checking all worksheet entries from the active cell forward.

1

- If necessary, move to A1.

- Open the Review tab.

- Click in the Proofing group.

Another Method

The keyboard shortcut is F7.

Your screen should be similar to Figure 1.22

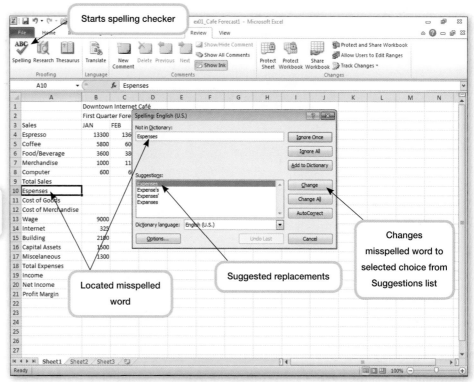

Figure 1.22

Additional Information

Spell-checking operates the same way in all Office 2010 programs. The dictionaries are shared between Office applications.

The spelling checker immediately begins checking the worksheet for words that it cannot locate in its main dictionary. The first cell containing a misspelled word, in this case Espenses, is now the active cell and the Spelling dialog box is displayed. The word it cannot locate in the dictionary is displayed in the Not in Dictionary text box. The Suggestions text box displays a list of possible replacements. If the selected replacement is not correct, you can select another choice from the suggestions list or type the correct word in the Not in Dictionary text box.

The option buttons shown in the table below have the following effects:

Option	Effect
Ignore Once	Leaves selected word unchanged.
Ignore All	Leaves this word and all identical words in worksheet unchanged.
Add to Dictionary	Adds selected word to a custom dictionary so Excel will not question this word during subsequent spell-checks.
Change	Changes selected word to word highlighted in Suggestions box.
Change All	Changes this word and all identical words in worksheet to word highlighted in Suggestions box.
AutoCorrect	Adds a word to the AutoCorrect list so the word will be corrected as you type.

You want to accept the suggested replacement, Expenses.

2

Click .

Your screen should be similar to Figure 1.23

Figure 1.23

The correction is made in the worksheet, and the program continues checking the worksheet and locates another error, Miscelaneous. You will make this correction. When no other errors are located, a dialog box is displayed, informing you that the entire worksheet has been checked.

3

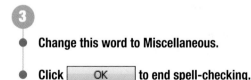

• **Change this word to Miscellaneous.**

• **Click** OK **to end spell-checking.**

The worksheet is now free of spelling errors.

USING THE THESAURUS

The next text change you want to make is to find a better word for "Wage" in cell A13. To help find a similar word, you will use the thesaurus tool.

Concept 5 Thesaurus

The **thesaurus** is a reference tool that provides synonyms, antonyms, and related words for a selected word or phrase. **Synonyms** are words with a similar meaning, such as "cheerful" and "happy." **Antonyms** are words with an opposite meaning, such as "cheerful" and "sad." Related words are words that are variations of the same word, such as "cheerful" and "cheer." The thesaurus can help to liven up your documents by adding interest and variety to your text.

To use the thesaurus, first move to the cell containing the word you want to change. If a cell contains multiple words, you need to select the individual word in the cell.

●1

● Move to A13.

● Click in the Proofing group.

Another Method

You also can hold down [Alt] while clicking on the cell containing the word you want looked up to access the thesaurus in the Research task pane.

Your screen should be similar to Figure 1.24

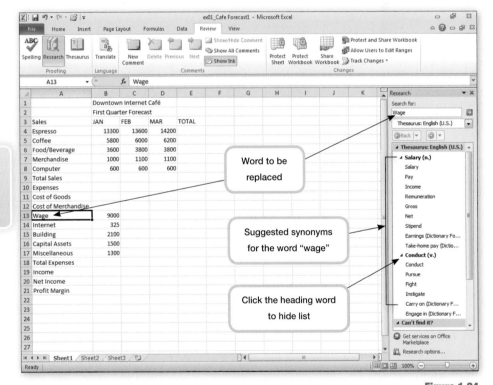

Figure 1.24

The Research task pane opens. The word in the active cell, Wage, is entered in the Search for text box and the list box displays words in the thesaurus that have similar meanings for this word. The list contains synonyms for "wage" used as a noun or as a verb. The first word at the top of each group is the group heading and is closest in meaning. It is preceded by a ▲ symbol, and the word is bold. The ▲ indicates the list of synonyms is displayed. Clicking the heading word will hide the list of synonyms.

Additional Information

Clicking on the word is the same as using the Lookup menu option.

When you point to a word in the list, a drop-down list of three menu options, Insert, Copy, and Lookup, becomes available. The Insert option inserts the word into the active cell. The Copy option is used to copy and then paste the word into any worksheet cell. The Lookup option displays additional related words for the current word. You decide to use the word "Pay" and will insert the word into cell A13 in place of "Wage."

2

- Point to "Pay" and click ▼ to display the menu.

- Choose Insert.

- Click ✖ in the title bar of the Research task pane to close it.

Your screen should be similar to Figure 1.25

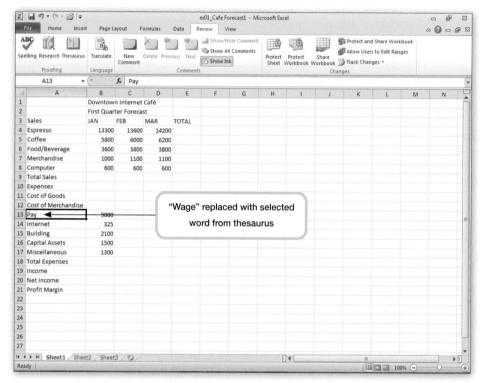

Figure 1.25

The word "Wage" is replaced with the selected word from the thesaurus. Notice the replacement word is capitalized correctly. This is because the replacement text follows the same capitalization as the word it replaces.

Copying and Pasting Cell Contents

Having Trouble?

Refer to the section "Copying and Moving Selections" in the Introduction to Microsoft Office 2010 to review this feature.

Next, you want to enter the estimated expenses for salary, computers, lease, and miscellaneous for February and March. They are the same as the January expense numbers. Because these values are the same, instead of entering the same number repeatedly into each cell you can quickly copy the contents of one cell to another. You also want to move information from one location in the worksheet to another.

COPYING AND PASTING DATA

To use the Copy command, you first must select the cell or cells in the source containing the data to be copied. This is called the **copy area**. You will copy the Pay value in cell B13 into cells C13 and D13.

1

- Move to B13.

- Open the Home tab.

- Click Copy in the Clipboard group.

Another Method

The shortcut key is Ctrl + C. Copy is also available on the context menu.

Your screen should be similar to Figure 1.26

Figure 1.26

A moving border identifies the copy area and indicates that the contents have been copied to the system Clipboard. The instructions displayed in the status bar tell you to select the destination, called the **paste area**, where you want the contents copied. You will copy them to cell C13.

2

- Move to C13.

- Click the top part of the Paste button.

Additional Information

The Paste button is a split button. Clicking the top part of the button pastes using the default settings. Clicking the lower part displays a menu of options.

Another Method

The shortcut key is Ctrl + V. Paste is also available on the context menu and on the Paste button's drop-down menu.

Your screen should be similar to Figure 1.27

Figure 1.27

The contents of the system Clipboard are inserted at the specified destination location. Each time the Paste command is used, the (Ctrl) ▾ Paste Options button is available. Clicking on the button opens the Paste Options menu that allows you to control how the information you are pasting is inserted. Be careful when pasting to the new location because any existing entries are replaced.

The moving border is still displayed, indicating the system Clipboard still contains the copied entry. Now you can complete the data for the Pay row by pasting the value again from the system Clipboard into cell D13. While the moving border is still displayed, you also can simply press ←Enter to paste. However, as this method clears the contents of the system Clipboard immediately, it can only be used once.

Additional Information

You will learn about the different Excel paste options in later labs.

3

● **Move to D13.**

● **Press** ←Enter.

Your screen should be similar to Figure 1.28

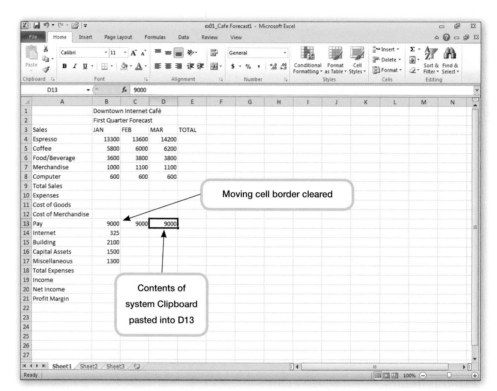

Figure 1.28

The contents of the system Clipboard are inserted at the specified destination location and the moving border is cleared, indicating the system Clipboard is empty.

Additional Information

You also can cancel a moving border and clear the system Clipboard contents by pressing Esc.

SELECTING A RANGE

Now you need to copy the Internet value in cell B14 to February and March. You could copy and paste the contents individually into each cell as you did with the Pay values. A quicker method, however, is to select a range and paste the contents to all cells in the range at once.

Concept 6 Range

A selection consisting of two or more cells on a worksheet is a **range**. The cells in a range can be adjacent or nonadjacent. An **adjacent range** is a rectangular block of adjoining cells. A **nonadjacent range** consists of two or more selected cells or ranges that are not adjoining. In the example shown below, the shaded areas show valid adjacent and nonadjacent ranges. A **range reference** identifies the cells in a range. A colon is used to separate the first and last cells of an adjacent range reference. For example, A2:C4 indicates the range consists of cells A2 through C4. Commas separate the cell references of a nonadjacent range. For example, A10,B12,C14 indicates the range consists of cells A10, B12, and C14 of a nonadjacent range.

You can select a range using the mouse procedures shown in the following table. You also can select using the keyboard by moving to the first cell of the range, holding down ⇧Shift or pressing F8 and using the navigational keys to expand the highlight. Using the F8 key turns on and off Extend mode. When this mode is on, Extend Selection appears in the status bar.

To Select	Mouse
A range	Click first cell of range and drag to the last cell.
A large range	Click first cell of range, hold down ⇧Shift, and click last cell of range.
All cells on worksheet	Click the ◢ All button located at the intersection of the row and column headings.
Nonadjacent cells or ranges	Select first cell or range, hold down Ctrl while selecting the other cell or range.
Entire row or column	Click the row number or column letter heading.
Adjacent rows or columns	Drag across the row number or column letter headings.
Nonadjacent rows or columns	Select first row or column, hold down Ctrl, and select the other rows or columns.

To complete the data for the Internet row, you want to copy the value in cell B14 to the system Clipboard and then copy the system Clipboard contents to the adjacent range of cells C14 through D14.

- Move to B14.

- Click Copy.

- Drag to select the range of cells C14 through D14.

- Click [Paste].

Your screen should be similar to Figure 1.29

Figure 1.29

The destination range is highlighted and identified by a dark border surrounding the selected cells. The source entry was copied from cell B14 and pasted into the selected destination range. Also notice the status bar now displays the average, count, and sum of values in the selected range.

Additional Information

The paste area does not have to be adjacent to the copy area.

USING THE FILL HANDLE

Next, you will copy the January Building expenses to cells C15 through D15, the Capital Assets expenses to cells C16 through D16, and the Miscellaneous expenses to cells C17 through D17. You can copy all values at the same time across the row by first specifying a range as the source. Another way to copy is to select the cells that contain the data you want to copy and drag the **fill handle**, the black box in the lower-right corner of a selection across or down the cells you want to fill.

1

- Press Esc to clear the moving border.

- Drag to select cells B15 through B17.

- Point to the fill handle and when the mouse pointer is a **+**, drag the mouse to extend the selection to cells D15 through D17.

| 2100 |
| 1500 |
| 1300 |

2100

- Release the mouse button.

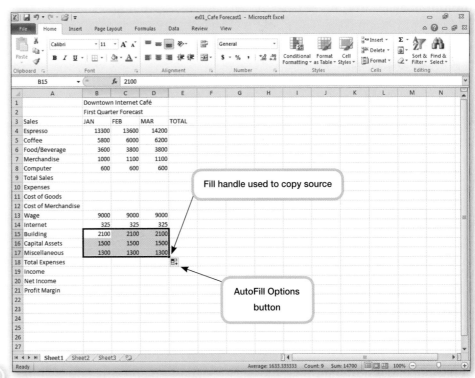

Figure 1.30

Another Method

You also can select the range B15:D17, click ⬇ ▼ Fill in the Editing group, and choose Right. The shortcut key is Ctrl + R.

Your screen should be similar to Figure 1.30

Additional Information

You will learn more about the AutoFill feature in later labs.

The range of cells to the right of the source is filled with the same values as in the source range. Using this method does not copy the source to the system Clipboard and therefore you cannot paste the source multiple times. When you copy by dragging the fill handle, the AutoFill Options button 🖳 appears. Its menu commands are used to modify how the fill operation was performed. It will disappear as soon as you make an entry in the worksheet.

INSERTING COPIED CELL CONTENT

You also decide to include another row of month headings above the expenses to make the worksheet data easier to read. To do this quickly, you can insert copied data between existing data. To indicate where to place the copied content, you move the cell selector to the upper-left cell of the area where you want the selection inserted.

The column headings you want to copy are in cells B3 through E3. You will also copy cell A3, and clear the text in column A of the new row when you paste the contents.

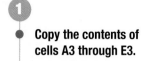

- **Copy the contents of cells A3 through E3.**

- **Move to A10.**

- **Click** Insert **in the Cells group.**

- **Select cell A10 and delete the word "Sales".**

Your screen should be similar to Figure 1.31

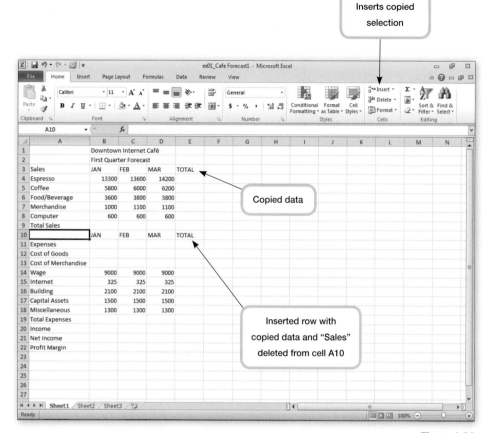

Figure 1.31

The copied data is inserted into the existing row (10) and all entries below are moved down one row.

CUTTING AND PASTING DATA

Next, you decide the Income, Net Income, and Profit Margin rows of data would stand out more if a blank row separated them from the expenses. Also, the Profit Margin row of data would be better separated from the Net Income row by a blank row. You will first remove the cell contents of the three cells using ✂ Cut and then paste the contents from the system Clipboard into the new location. The pasted content will copy over any existing content. You will use the keyboard shortcuts for these commands to complete this process.

Additional Information

You also can insert cut selections between existing cells by choosing Insert Cut Cells from the Insert drop-down menu.

1

- Select cells A20 through A22.

- Press Ctrl + X.

- Move to cell A21.

- Press Ctrl + V.

Another Method

You also can Click ✂ Cut followed by 📋 Paste in the Clipboard group. These commands are also available on the shortcut menu.

Your screen should be similar to Figure 1.32

Selected cells cut and then pasted to a new location

Figure 1.32

Additional Information

You also can hold down Ctrl and drag a selection to copy it to a new location. The mouse pointer appears as ⌖ as you drag when copying.

The contents of the three selected cells are copied to the system Clipboard. Then, when you paste, the cell contents are removed and inserted at the new location, copying over any existing content.

Another way you can cut and paste is to use drag and drop to move the cell contents. This method is quickest and most useful when the distance between cells is short and they are visible within the window, whereas cut and paste is best for long-distance moves. You will use this method to move the Profit Margin entry down one cell.

2

- Move to cell A23.

- Point to the border of the selection and when the mouse pointer shape is 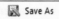, drag the selection down one row to cell A24 and release the mouse button.

- Open the File tab and click 📄 Save As .

- Save the changes you have made to the workbook as Cafe Forecast1 to your solution file location.

Your screen should be similar to Figure 1.33

Figure 1.33

The cell contents were moved into cell A24 and cleared from the original cell.

When you use the Copy and Cut commands, the contents are copied to the system Clipboard and can be copied to any location in the worksheet, another workbook, or a document in another application multiple times. When you use 📥 ▾ Fill or drag the fill handle, the destination must be in the same row or column as the source, and the source is not copied to the system Clipboard. Dragging the cell border to move or copy also does not copy the source to the system Clipboard.

NOTE If you are running short on lab time, this is an appropriate place to end your session. When you begin again, open the file Cafe Forecast1.

Working with Formulas

The remaining entries that need to be made in the worksheet are formula entries.

Concept ⑦ Formula

A **formula** is an equation that performs a calculation on data contained in a worksheet. A formula always begins with an equal sign (=) and uses arithmetic operators. An **operator** is a symbol that specifies the type of numeric operation to perform. Excel includes the following operators: + (addition), − (subtraction), / (division), * (multiplication), % (percent), and ^ (exponentiation). The calculated result from formulas is a **variable** value because it can change if the data it depends on changes. In contrast, a number entry is a **constant** value. It does not begin with an equal sign and does not change unless you change it directly by typing in another entry.

In a formula that contains more than one operator, Excel calculates the formula from left to right and performs the calculation in the following order: percent, exponentiation, multiplication and division, and addition and subtraction (see Example A). This is called the **order of precedence**. If a formula contains operators with the same precedence (for example, addition and subtraction), they are again evaluated from left to right. The order of precedence can be overridden by enclosing the operation you want performed first in parentheses (see Example B). When there are multiple sets of parentheses, Excel evaluates them working from the innermost set of parentheses out.

Example A: =5*4−3   Result is 17 (5 times 4 to get 20, and then subtract 3 for a total of 17)
Example B: =5*(4−3)   Result is 5 (4 minus 3 to get 1, and then 1 times 5 for a total of 5)

The values on which a numeric formula performs a calculation are called **operands**. Numbers or cell references can be operands in a formula. Usually cell references are used, and when the numeric entries in the referenced cell(s) change, the result of the formula is automatically recalculated.

ENTERING FORMULAS

The first formula you will enter will calculate the total Espresso sales for January through March (cell E4) by summing the numbers in cells B4 through D4. You will use cell references in the formula as the operands and the + arithmetic operator to specify addition. A formula is entered in the cell where you want the calculated value to be displayed. As you enter the formula, Excel helps you keep track of the cell references by identifying the referenced cell with a colored border and using the same color for the cell reference in the formula.

Move to E4.

Type =b

Your screen should be similar to Figure 1.34

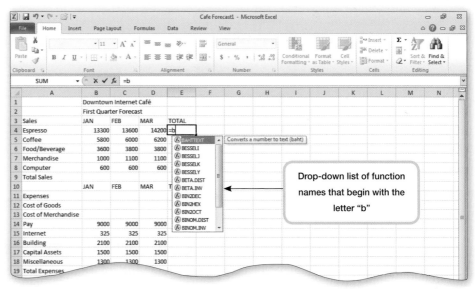

Figure 1.34

A drop-down list of function names that begin with the letter "b" is displayed. Functions are a type of formula entry that you will learn about shortly.

2

● **Type** 4+c4+d4

Your screen should be similar to Figure 1.35

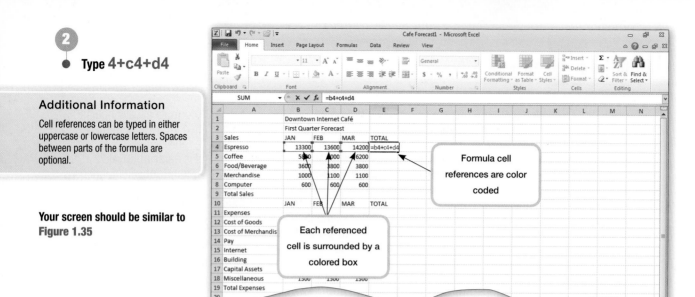

Figure 1.35

As you enter the formula, each cell that is referenced in the formula is surrounded by a colored box that matches the color of the cell reference in the formula.

3

● **Press** Ctrl + ←Enter
or click ✔ **Enter in the formula bar.**

Your screen should be similar to Figure 1.36

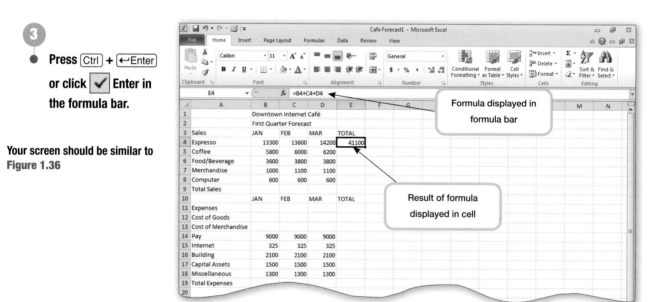

Figure 1.36

The number 41100 is displayed in cell E4, and the formula that calculates this value is displayed in the formula bar.

COPYING FORMULAS WITH RELATIVE REFERENCES

The formulas to calculate the total sales for rows 5 through 8 can be entered next. Just as you can with text and numeric entries, you can copy formulas from one cell to another.

Copy the formula in cell E4 to cells E5 through E8 using any of the copying methods.

Move to E5.

If necessary, press Esc to clear the moving border.

Your screen should be similar to Figure 1.37

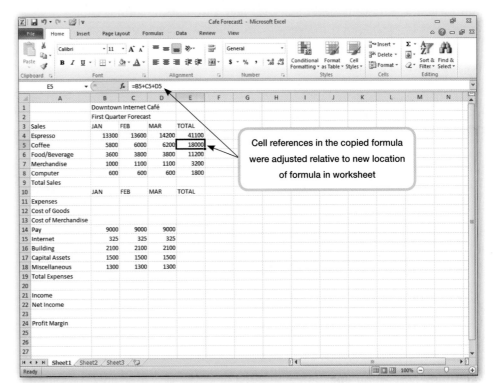

Figure 1.37

The calculated result, 18000, is displayed in the cell. The formula displayed in the formula bar is =B5+C5+D5. The formula to calculate the Coffee total sales is not an exact duplicate of the formula used to calculate the Espresso total sales (=B4+C4+D4). Instead, the cells referenced in the formula have been changed to reflect the new location of the formula in row 5. This is because the references in the formula are relative references.

Concept 8 Relative Reference

A **relative reference** is a cell or range reference in a formula whose location is interpreted by Excel in relation to the position of the cell that contains the formula. When a formula is copied, the referenced cells in the formula automatically adjust to reflect the new worksheet location. The relative relationship between the referenced cell and the new location is maintained. Because relative references automatically adjust for the new location, the relative references in a copied formula refer to different cells than the references in the original formula. The relationship between cells in both the copied and the pasted formulas is the same although the cell references are different.

For example, in the figure here, cell A1 references the value in cell A4 (in this case, 10). If the formula in A1 is copied to B2, the reference for B2 is adjusted to the value in cell B5 (in this case, 20).

	A	B
1	=A4	
2		=B5
3		
4	10	
5		20
6		

2 Move to cell E6, E7, and then to cell E8.

Your screen should be similar to Figure 1.38

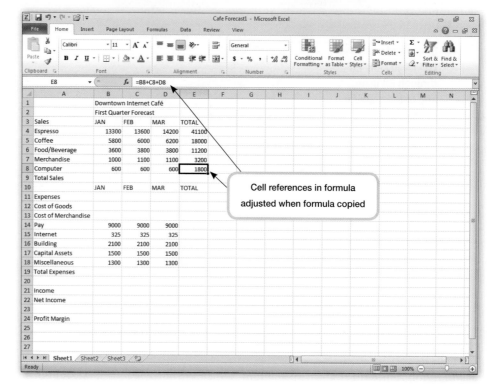

Figure 1.38

The formulas in these cells also have changed to reflect the new row location and to appropriately calculate the total based on the sales.

SUMMARIZING DATA

Next, you will calculate the monthly total sales. The formula to calculate the total sales for January needs to be entered in cell B9 and copied across the row. You could use a formula similar to the formula used to calculate the category sales in column E. The formula would be =B4+B5+B6+B7+B8. However, it is faster and more accurate to use a function.

Concept 9 Function

A **function** is a prewritten formula that performs certain types of calculations automatically. The **syntax** or rules of structure for entering all functions is as follows:

=Function name (argument1, argument2, . . .)

The function name identifies the type of calculation to be performed. Most functions require that you enter one or more arguments following the function name. An **argument** is the data the function uses to perform the calculation. The type of data the function requires depends upon the type of calculation being performed. Most commonly, the argument consists of numbers or references to cells that contain numbers. The argument is enclosed in parentheses, and commas separate multiple arguments. The beginning and ending cells of a range are separated with a colon.

Some functions, such as several of the date and time functions, do not require an argument. However, you still need to enter the opening and closing parentheses; for example, =NOW(). If a function starts the formula, enter an equal sign before the function name; for example, =SUM(D5:F5)/25.

Excel includes several hundred functions divided into 11 categories. Some common functions from each category and the results they calculate are shown in the following table.

Category	Function	Calculates
Financial	PMT	Calculates the payment for a loan based on constant payments and a constant interest rate.
	PV	Returns the present value of an investment—the total amount that a series of future payments is worth now.
	FV	Returns the future value of an investment—the total amount that a series of payments will be worth.
Date & Time	TODAY	Returns the serial number that represents today's date.
	DATE	Returns the serial number of a particular date.
	NOW	Returns the serial number of the current date and time.
Math & Trig	SUM	Adds all the numbers in a range of cells.
	ABS	Returns the absolute value of a number (a number without its sign).
Statistical	AVERAGE	Returns the average (arithmetic mean) of its arguments.
	MAX	Returns the largest value in a set of values; ignores logical values and text.
	MIN	Returns the smallest value in a set of values; ignores logical values and text.
	COUNT	Counts the number of cells in a range that contain numbers.
	COUNTA	Counts the number of cells in a range that are not empty.
	COLUMNS	Returns the number of columns in an array or reference.
Lookup & Reference	HLOOKUP	Looks for a value in the top row of a table and returns the value in the same column from a row you specify.
	VLOOKUP	Looks for a value in the leftmost column of a table and returns the value in the same row from a column you specify.
Database	DSUM	Adds the numbers in the field (column) or records in the database that match the conditions you specify.
	DAVERAGE	Averages the values in a column in a list or database that match conditions you specify.
Text	PROPER	Converts text to proper case in which the first letter of each word is capitalized.
	UPPER	Converts text to uppercase.
	LOWER	Converts text to lowercase.
	SUBSTITUTE	Replaces existing text with new text in a text string.
Logical	IF	Returns one value if a condition you specify evaluates to TRUE and another value if it evaluates to FALSE.
	AND	Returns TRUE if all its arguments are TRUE; returns FALSE if any arguments are FALSE.
	OR	Returns TRUE if any arguments are TRUE; returns FALSE if all arguments are FALSE.
	NOT	Changes FALSE to TRUE or TRUE to FALSE.
	IFERROR	Returns value-if-error if expression is an error and the value of the expression itself otherwise.
Information	ISLOGICAL	Returns TRUE if value is a logical value, either TRUE or FALSE.
	ISREF	Returns TRUE if value is a reference.
Engineering	BIN2DEC	Converts a binary number to decimal.
	CONVERT	Converts a number from one measurement system to another.
Cube	CUBESETCOUNT	Returns the number of items in a set.

You will use the SUM function to calculate the total sales for January. Because the SUM function is the most commonly used function, it has its own command button.

Move to B9.

Click $\boxed{\Sigma \;\cdot}$ **Sum in the Editing group.**

Another Method

Pressing $\boxed{\text{Alt}}$ + = is the keyboard shortcut for Sum. This function is also available on the Formulas tab.

Your screen should be similar to Figure 1.39

Additional Information

The $\boxed{\Sigma \;\cdot}$ Sum button also can calculate a grand total if the worksheet contains subtotals. Select a cell below or to the right of a cell that contains a subtotal and then click $\boxed{\Sigma \;\cdot}$ Sum.

Figure 1.39

Excel automatically proposes a range based upon the data above or to the left of the active cell. The formula bar displays the name of the function followed by the range argument enclosed in parentheses. You will accept the proposed range and enter the function.

Click ✔ **Enter.**

Your screen should be similar to Figure 1.40

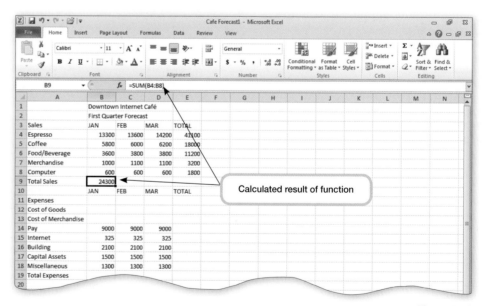

Figure 1.40

The result, 24300, calculated by the SUM function is displayed in cell B9. Next, you need to calculate the total sales for February and March and the Total column.

3

● Copy the function
from cell B9 to cells
C9 through E9.

● Move to C9.

**Your screen should be similar to
Figure 1.41**

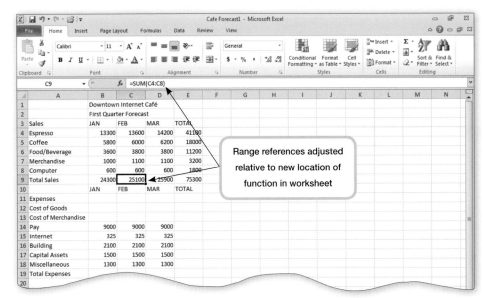

Figure 1.41

The result calculated by the function, 25100, is displayed in cell C9 and the copied function is displayed in the formula bar. The range reference in the function is adjusted relative to its new cell location because it is a relative reference.

You also decide to calculate the minimum, maximum, and average sales for each sales category. You will add appropriate column headings and enter the functions in columns F, G, and H. The ∑ ▾ Sum button also includes a drop-down menu from which you can select several other common functions. As you enter these functions, the proposed range will include the Total cell. Simply select another range to replace the proposed range.

4

● Enter MIN in cell F3,
MAX in cell G3, and
AVG in cell H3.

● Move to F4.

● Open the ∑ ▾ Sum
drop-down menu and
choose Min.

Having Trouble?
Click ▼ to the right of the button to
open the drop-down menu.

● Select the range B4
through D4 to specify
the January through
March sales values
and click ✔ Enter.

**Your screen should be similar to
Figure 1.42**

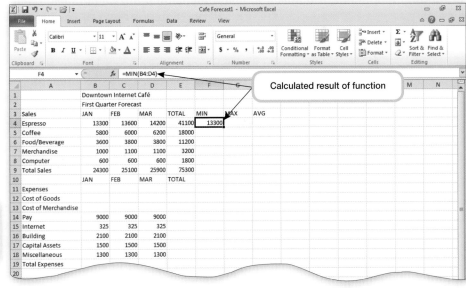

Figure 1.42

The MIN function correctly displays 13300, the smallest value in the range.

Next, you will enter the MAX and AVG values for the Espresso sales. Then you will copy the functions down the column through row 8.

Enter the MAX function in cell G4 and the AVG function in cell H4 to calculate the Espresso sales values for January through March.

Copy the functions in cells F4 through H4 to F5 through H8.

Move to H8.

Your screen should be similar to Figure 1.43

	A	B	C	D	E	F	G	H
1		Downtown Internet Café						
2		First Quarter Forecast						
3	Sales	JAN	FEB	MAR	TOTAL	MIN	MAX	AVG
4	Espresso	13300	13600	14200	41100	13300	14200	13700
5	Coffee	5800	6000	6200	18000	5800	6200	6000
6	Food/Beverage	3600	3800	3800	11200	3600	3800	3733.333
7	Merchandise	1000	1100	1100	3200	1000	1100	1066.667
8	Computer	600	600	600	1800	600	600	600
9	Total Sales	24300	25100	25900	75300			
10		JAN	FEB	MAR	TOTAL			
11	Expenses							
12	Cost of Goods							
13	Cost of Merchandise							
14	Pay	9000	9000	9000				
15	Internet	325	325	325				
16	Building	2100	2100	2100				
17	Capital Assets	1500	1500	1500				
18	Miscellaneous	1300	1300	1300				
19	Total Expenses							
20								
21	Income							
22	Net Income							
23								
24	Profit Margin							
25								
26								
27								

Cell references adjusted when functions copied

H8 | =AVERAGE(B8:D8)

Figure 1.43

The minimum, maximum, and average values for the five sales categories have been calculated. The Average column displays as many decimal places as cell space allows.

USING POINTING TO ENTER A FORMULA

Next, you will enter the formula to calculate the cost of goods for espresso, coffee, and food and beverages sold. These numbers are estimated by using a formula to calculate the number as a percent of sales. Evan suggested using estimated percents for this worksheet so he could get an idea of what to expect from the first three months after the remodel. He wants you to calculate espresso expenses at 25 percent of espresso sales, coffee expenses at 30 percent of coffee sales, and food and beverage expenses at 60 percent of food sales.

Rather than typing in the cell references for the formula, you will enter them by selecting the worksheet cells. In addition, to simplify the process of entering and copying entries, you can enter data into the first cell of a range and have it copied to all other cells in the range at the same time by using [Ctrl] + [←Enter] to complete the entry. You will use this feature to enter the formulas to calculate the beverage expenses for January through March. This formula needs to calculate the beverage cost of goods at 25 percent first and add it to the food cost of goods calculated at 50 percent.

1
- Select B12 through D12.
- Type **=**
- Click cell B4.

Additional Information

Even when a range is selected, you can still point to specify cells in the formula. You also can use the direction keys to move to the cell.

Your screen should be similar to Figure 1.44

Figure 1.44

Additional Information

While entering the formula in Point mode, if you make an error, edit the entry like any other error and then continue entering the remainder of the formula.

Notice that the status bar displays the current mode as Point. This tells you that the program is allowing you to select cells by highlighting them. The cell reference, B4, is entered following the equal sign. You will complete the formula by entering the percentage value to multiply by and adding the Food percentage to the formula.

2
- Type ***25%+**
- Click on B5.
- Type ***30%+**
- Click on B6.
- Type ***60%**
- Press Ctrl + ↩Enter.

Your screen should be similar to Figure 1.45

Figure 1.45

Having Trouble?

If you made an error in the formula, edit the entry in the formula bar and then press Ctrl + ↩Enter again to copy it to the selected range.

The formula to calculate the January Cost of Goods expenses was entered in cell B12 and copied to all cells of the selected range.

Now you will enter the Cost of Merchandise expenses by multiplying the value in B8 by 70%. Then you will calculate the total expenses in row 19 and column E. To do this quickly, you will preselect the range and use the Σ ▾ Sum button. Then you will enter the formula to calculate the net income. Net income is calculated by subtracting total expenses from total sales.

3

● Select cells B13 through D13.

● Type =

● Click on B7.

● Type *70%

● Press [Ctrl] + [←Enter].

● Select B12 through E19.

● Click Σ ▾ Sum.

● Select B22 through E22.

● Enter the formula **=B9-B19** and press [Ctrl] + [←Enter].

Your screen should be similar to Figure 1.46

Figure 1.46

The formulas were quickly entered into all cells of the specified ranges.

Finally, you will enter the formula to calculate the profit margin. Profit margin is calculated by dividing net income by total sales.

4

- Select B24 through E24.

- Enter the formula **=B22/B9** and press **Ctrl** + **←Enter**.

Your screen should be similar to Figure 1.47

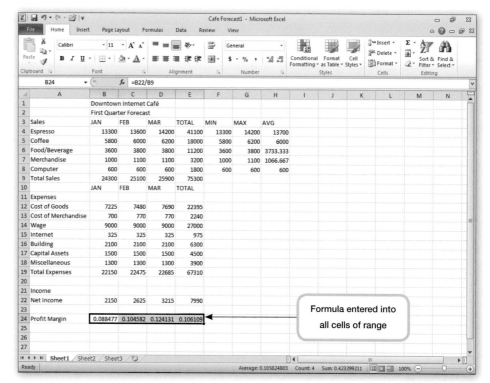

Figure 1.47

The net income and profit margins are calculated and displayed in the worksheet.

RECALCULATING THE WORKSHEET

Now that you have created the worksheet structure and entered some sample data for the forecasted sales for the first quarter, you want to test the formulas to verify that they are operating correctly. A simple way to do this is to use a calculator to verify that the correct result is displayed. You can then further test the worksheet by changing values and verifying that all cells containing formulas that reference the value are appropriately recalculated.

Concept 10 Recalculation

When a number in a referenced cell in a formula changes, Excel automatically **recalculates** all formulas that are dependent upon the changed value. Because only those formulas directly affected by a change in the data are recalculated, the time it takes to recalculate the workbook is reduced. Without this feature, in large worksheets it could take several minutes to recalculate all formulas each time a number is changed in the worksheet. Recalculation is one of the most powerful features of electronic worksheets.

After considering the sales estimates for the three months, you decide that the estimated sales generated from Computer usage for January are too high and you want to decrease this number from 600 to 400.

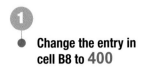

1
● **Change the entry in cell B8 to 400**

Your screen should be similar to Figure 1.48

Figure 1.48

The Computer total in cell E8 has been automatically recalculated. The number displayed is now 1600. The MIN and AVG values in cells F8 and H8 have been recalculated to 400 and 533.3333 respectively. Likewise, the January total in cell B9 of 24100 and the grand total in cell E9 of 75100 each decreased by 200 from the previous totals to reflect the change in cell B8. Finally, the Net Income and Profit Margin values also have adjusted appropriately.

The formulas in the worksheet are correctly calculating the desired result. The Sales portion of the worksheet is now complete.

Inserting and Deleting Rows and Columns

As you are developing a worksheet, you may realize you forgot to include information or decide that other information is not needed. To quickly add and remove entire rows and columns of information, you can insert and delete rows and columns. A new blank row is inserted above the active cell location and all rows below it shift down a row. Similarly, you can insert blank cells and columns in a worksheet. Blank cells are inserted above or to the left of the active cell, and blank columns are inserted to the left of the active cell. Likewise, you can quickly delete selected cells, rows, and columns, and all information in surrounding cells, rows, or columns automatically shifts appropriately to fill in the space.

Additionally, whenever you insert or delete cells, rows, or columns, all formula references to any affected cells adjust accordingly.

INSERTING ROWS

You realize that you forgot to include a row for the Advertising expenses. To add this data, you will insert a blank row above the Capital Assets row.

1

- Move to A17.

- Open the ⊟ Insert ▾ drop-down menu in the Cells group and choose Insert Sheet Rows.

Another Method

You also can choose Insert from the active cell's context menu.

- **Enter the heading Advertising** in cell A17 and the value **600** in cells B17 through D17.

- **Copy the function from cell E16 to E17 to calculate the total advertising expense.**

- **Move to cell B20.**

- **Click** 💾 **Save to save the workbook using the same file name.**

Your screen should be similar to Figure 1.49

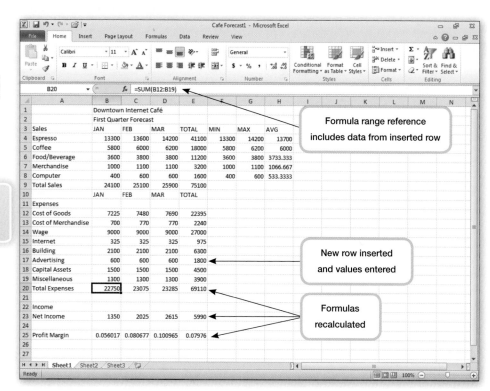

Figure 1.49

Additional Information

Click ⊟ Insert ▾ to insert blank cells, shifting existing cells down, and ⊟ Insert ▾ /Sheet Columns to insert blank columns, shifting existing columns right.

A blank row was inserted in the worksheet and the cell references in all formulas and functions below the inserted row adjusted appropriately. The range in the formula to calculate monthly total expenses in row 20 has been adjusted to include the data in the inserted row, and the total expense for the first quarter is 69110. Additionally, the net income in row 23 and the profit margin in row 25 have been recalculated to reflect the change in data.

DELETING COLUMNS

As you look at the worksheet data, you decide the minimum and maximum values are not very useful since this data is so easy to see in this small worksheet. You will delete these two columns from the worksheet to remove this information. To specify which column to delete, select any cell in the column.

1

● Select cells F20 and G20.

● Open the

Figure 1.50

Delete ▾

drop-down menu in the Cells group and choose Delete Sheet Columns.

Your screen should be similar to Figure 1.50

Additional Information

Select a cell or row and choose

Delete ▾ /Delete Cells or Delete Sheet Rows to delete it and shift the other cells or rows up or to the left.

The two columns have been removed and the columns to the right of the deleted columns automatically shifted to the left.

Formatting Cells and Cell Content

Now that the worksheet data is complete, you want to improve the appearance of the worksheet. Applying different formatting to text and numbers can greatly enhance the appearance of the document. In Excel, formats control how entries are displayed in a cell and include such features as the position of data in a cell, character font and color, and number formats such as commas and dollar signs.

You want to change the appearance of the row and column headings and apply formatting to the numbers. Applying different formats greatly improves both the appearance and the readability of the data in a worksheet.

CHANGING CELL ALIGNMENT

You decide the column headings would look better if they were right-aligned in their cell spaces, so that they would appear over the numbers in the column. Alignment is a basic format setting that is used in most worksheets.

 Concept **Alignment**

Alignment settings allow you to change the horizontal and vertical placement and the orientation of an entry in a cell.

Horizontal placement allows you to left-, right-, or center-align text and number entries in the cell space. Entries also can be indented within the cell space, centered across a selection, or justified. You also can fill a cell horizontally with a repeated entry.

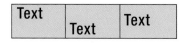

Vertical placement allows you to specify whether the cell contents are displayed at the top, the bottom, or the center of the vertical cell space or justified vertically.

You also can change the orientation or angle of text in a cell by varying the degrees of rotation.

The default workbook horizontal alignment settings left-align text entries and right-align number entries. The vertical alignment is set to Bottom for both types of entries, and the orientation is set to zero degrees rotation from the horizontal position. You want to change the horizontal alignment of the month headings in rows 3 and 10 to right-aligned.

The Alignment group contains commands to control the horizontal and vertical placement of entries in a cell. You can quickly apply formatting to a range of cells by selecting the range first. A quick way to select a range of filled cells is to hold down ⇧Shift and double-click on the edge of the active cell in the direction in which you want the range expanded. For example, to select the range to the right of the active cell, you would double-click the right border. You will use this method to select and right-align these entries.

Additional Information

If you do not hold down ⇧Shift while double-clicking on a cell border, the active cell moves to the last-used cell in the direction indicated.

1

- Move to B3.

- Hold down ⇧Shift and double-click the right cell border of cell B3.

Having Trouble?

The mouse pointer must be when you click the cell border.

- Click ≡ Align Text Right from the Alignment group.

- Select B10 through E10.

- Click ≡ Align Text Right.

Figure 1.51

Your screen should be similar to Figure 1.51

The entries in the selected ranges are right-aligned in their cell spaces. You notice the month labels do not stand out well and decide to try rotating them.

2

- Select cells B3 through F3.

- Click 🔣 Orientation and choose Angle Counterclockwise.

Your screen should be similar to Figure 1.52

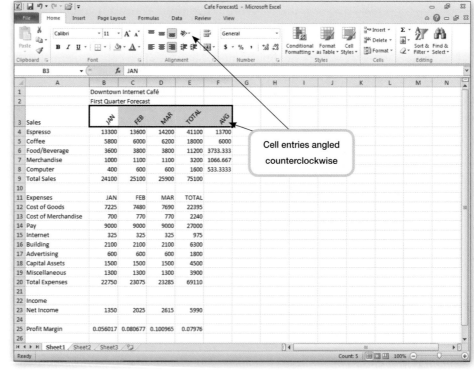

Figure 1.52

Notice how the row height increased automatically to accommodate the change in size.

CHANGING ROW HEIGHT

You don't like the way it looks rotated and decide to undo the change, add height to the row manually to help identify the month label row better, and center-align the labels. You also decide to move the month labels in row 10 down a row to match the first row of month labels.

Concept 12 Row Height

The **row height** is the size or height of a row measured in points. The default row height is 12.75 points which is slightly larger than the default font point size of 11. The row height can be any number from 0 to 409. If it is set to 0, the row is hidden. The row height automatically adjusts to changes in the character size, style and orientation.

The row height can also be changed manually using methods that are similar to those used to change the column width. The difference is that you drag or click the boundary below the row heading to adjust the row height.

1

- Click ↺ Undo.

- Move the entries in cells B10 through E10 into the same columns in row 11.

- Drag the bottom boundary of rows 3 and 11 to increase the row height to 22.5.

- Select the text in cells B3 through F3 and click ≣ Center.

- Do the same for cells B11 through E11.

Your screen should be similar to Figure 1.53

Figure 1.53

Increasing the row height of the month labels visually separates the labels from other worksheet entries.

INDENTING CELL CONTENT

Next, you would like to indent the row headings in cells A4 through A8 and A12 through A19 to show that the entries are subtopics below the Sales and Expense headings. You want to indent the headings in both ranges at the same time. To select nonadjacent cells or cell ranges, after selecting the first cell or range, hold down Ctrl while selecting each additional cell or range. You will select the cells and indent their contents.

Additional Information

You also can select entire nonadjacent rows or columns by holding down Ctrl while selecting the rows or columns.

Formatting Cells and Cell Content **EX1.53**

1

- Select A4 through A8.
- Hold down Ctrl.
- Select A12 through A19.
- Release Ctrl.
- Click 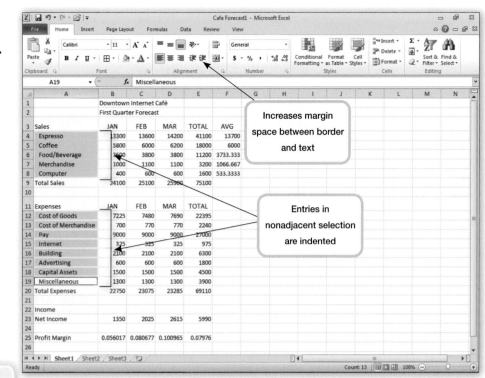 Increase Indent in the Alignment group.
- AutoFit the width of column A.

Your screen should be similar to Figure 1.54

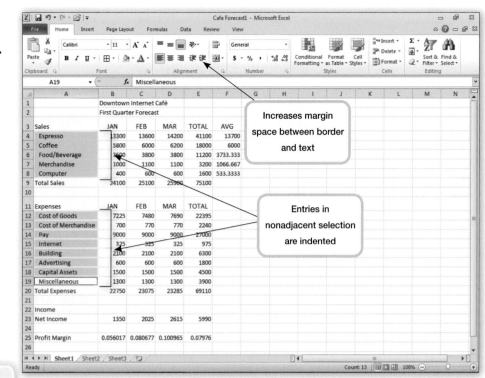

Figure 1.54

Each entry in the selected range is indented two spaces from the left edge of the cell. Finally, you want to right-align the Total Sales, Total Expenses, and Net Income headings.

2

- Select A9, A20, and A23.
- Click ▤ Align Text Right.

Your screen should be similar to Figure 1.55

Figure 1.55

MERGING CELLS

Next, you want to center the worksheet titles across columns A through F so they are centered over the worksheet data. To do this, you will merge or combine the cells in the range over the worksheet data (A1 through F1) into a single large **merged cell** and then center the contents of the range in the merged cell. This process is easily completed in one simple step using the Merge & Center command.

● Select A1 through F1.

● Click Merge & Center in the Alignment group.

Your screen should be similar to Figure 1.56

Figure 1.56

The six cells in the selection have been combined into a single large cell, and the entry that was in cell B1 is centered within the merged cell space. Only the contents of the first cell containing an entry in the upper-leftmost section of the selected range are centered in the merged cell. If other cells to the right of that cell contain data, it will be deleted. The cell reference for a merged cell is the upper-left cell in the original selected range, in this case A1.

● Merge and center the second title line across columns A through F.

Your screen should be similar to Figure 1.57

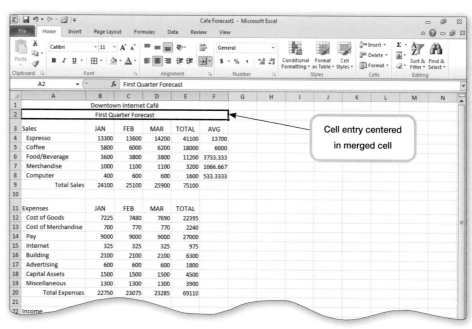

Figure 1.57

Formatting Cells and Cell Content **EX1.55**

You also can use the commands in the [icon] Merge & Center drop-down menu shown in the following table to control a merge. You can merge cells horizontally and vertically.

Merge Menu	Action
[icon] Merge & Center	Merges cells and centers entry
[icon] Merge Across	Merges cells horizontally
[icon] Merge Cells	Merges cells horizontally and vertically
[icon] Unmerge Cells	Splits cells that have been merged back into individual cells

CHANGING FONTS AND FONT SIZES

Having Trouble?

Refer to the section "Formatting Text" in the Introduction to Microsoft Office 2010 to review fonts.

Finally, you want to improve the worksheet appearance by enhancing the appearance of the title. One way to do this is to change the font and font size used in the title. There are two basic types of fonts: serif and sans serif. **Serif** fonts have a flare at the base of each letter that visually leads the reader to the next letter. Two common serif fonts are Roman and Times New Roman. Serif fonts generally are used in paragraphs. **Sans serif** fonts do not have a flare at the base of each letter. Arial and Helvetica are two common sans serif fonts. Because sans serif fonts have a clean look, they are often used for headings in documents. It is good practice to use only two types of fonts in a worksheet, one for text and one for headings. Too many styles can make your document look cluttered and unprofessional.

Here are several examples of the same text in various fonts and sizes.

Typeface	Font Size (12 pt/18 pt)
Calibri (Sans Serif)	This is 12 pt. This is 18 pt.
Times New Roman (Serif)	This is 12 pt. This is 18 pt.
Book Antiqua (Serif)	This is 12 pt. This is 18 pt.

Using fonts as a design element can add interest to your document and give readers visual cues to help them find information quickly. First you will try a different font for the title and a larger font size.

Select A1 and A2.

Open the

Calibri ▼

Font drop-down list box in the Font group.

Your screen should be similar to Figure 1.58

Selected font

Font names appear in font format

Indicates TrueType font

Figure 1.58

The Font drop-down list displays examples of the available fonts on your system in alphabetical order. The default worksheet font, Calibri, is highlighted. Notice the preceding the font name. This indicates the font is a TrueType font. TrueType fonts appear onscreen as they will appear when printed. They are installed when Windows is installed. Fonts that are preceded by a blank space are printer fonts. These fonts are supported by your printer and are displayed as closely as possible to how they will appear onscreen but may not match exactly when printed. You will change the font and increase the font size to 14. As you point to the font options, the Live Preview will show how it will appear if chosen.

2

Scroll the list and choose Lucida Sans.

Having Trouble?

You will not be able to see the Fonts Live Preview because the drop-down menu covers the selection to be formatted.

Open the `11` **Font Size drop-down list box.**

Point to several different font sizes in the list to see the Live Preview.

Choose 14.

Your screen should be similar to Figure 1.59

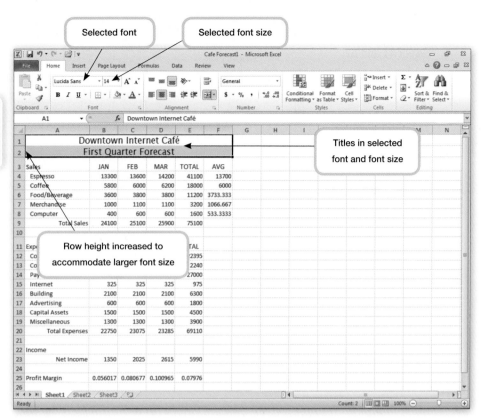

Figure 1.59

Another Method

The Font and Font Size commands are also available on the Mini toolbar.

The title appears in the selected typeface and size, and the Font and Font Size buttons display the name of the font and the size used in the active cell. Notice that the height of the row has increased to accommodate the larger font size of the heading.

APPLYING TEXT EFFECTS

Having Trouble?

Refer to the section "Formatting Text" in the Introduction to Microsoft Office 2010 to review text effects.

In addition to changing font and font size, you can apply different text effects to enhance the appearance of text. The table below describes some of the text effects and their uses.

Format	Example	Use
Bold	**Bold**	Adds emphasis.
Italic	*Italic*	Adds emphasis.
Underline	<u>Underline</u>	Adds emphasis.
Strikethrough	~~Strikethrough~~	Indicates words to be deleted.
Superscript	"To be or not to be."[1]	Used in footnotes and formulas.
Subscript	H_2O	Used in formulas.
Color	Color Color Color	Adds interest.

First you want to enhance the appearance of the column headings by increasing the font size and adding bold, italic, and underlines.

1

- Select B3 through F3.

- Increase the font size to 12.

- Click **B** Bold.

- Click **U** ▾ Underline.

Your screen should be similar to Figure 1.60

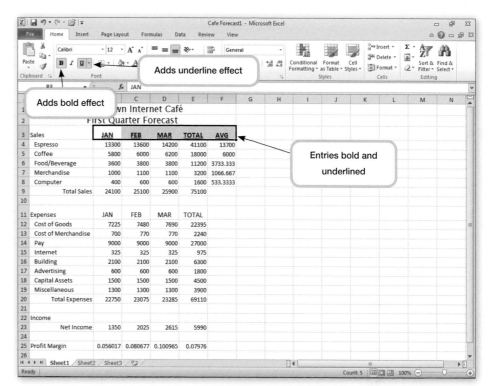

Figure 1.60

Having Trouble?

Refer to the section "Formatting Text" in the Introduction to Microsoft Office 2010 to review using the Mini toolbar.

Many of the formatting commands are also available on the Mini toolbar. In Excel, you must right-click on a cell to display the Mini toolbar and the shortcut menu. The selected formatting is applied to the entire cell contents. If you select text in a cell, the Mini toolbar appears automatically and the formatting is applied to the selected text only.

2

- Select A4 through A8.

- Right-click on the selection to display the Mini toolbar.

- Click **B** Bold.

- Click **I** Italic.

Another Method

The keyboard shortcut for bold is Ctrl + B; for italic, it is Ctrl + I; and for underline, it is Ctrl + U.

Your screen should be similar to Figure 1.61

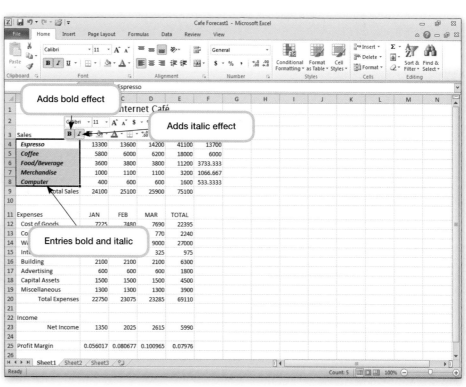

Figure 1.61

Formatting Cells and Cell Content   **EX1.59**

CLEARING FORMATS

Sometimes formatting changes you make do not have the expected result. In this case, you feel that the sales category names would look better without the formatting. One way to remove the format from cells is to use [Clear icon] Clear in the Editing group and choose Clear Formats. Because this will remove all formatting in the selected cells, you will need to redo the indenting in those cells.

1

- With cells A4 through A8 still selected, open the [Clear icon] Clear drop-down list in the Editing group.

- Choose Clear Formats.

- Click [icon] Increase Indent.

Another Method

You could also use [Undo icon] Undo to remove the formats by reversing your last actions.

Your screen should be similar to Figure 1.62

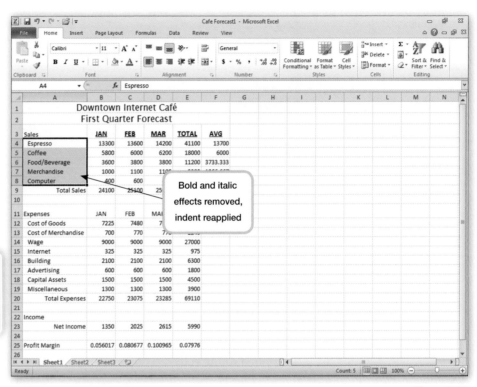

Figure 1.62

Bold and italic effects removed, indent reapplied

Additional Information

You can remove both formatting and content using [Clear icon] Clear/Clear All.

Having Trouble?

Refer to the section "Copying Formats" in the Introduction to Microsoft Office 2010 to review the Format Painter.

USING FORMAT PAINTER

You do think, however, that the Total Sales, Total Expenses, and Net Income headings would look good in bold. You will bold the entry in cell A9 and then copy the format from A9 to the other cells using Format Painter. You also will format the headings in row 11.

1

- Apply bold to cell A9.

- With cell A9 selected, double-click 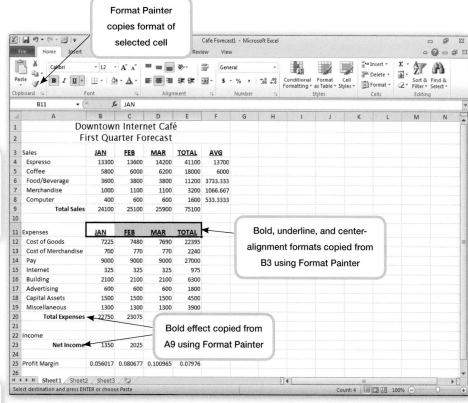 Format Painter in the Clipboard group.

Additional Information

When Format Painter is on, the mouse pointer appears as ⊞🖌 and the cell whose format will be copied appears with a moving border.

- Click A20.

- Click A23.

- Click 🖌 Format Painter to turn it off.

Another Method

You also can press [Esc] to turn off Format Painter.

- Use Format Painter to copy the format from cell B3 to cells B11 through E11.

Your screen should be similar to Figure 1.63

Figure 1.63

The formatting was quickly added to each cell or range as it was selected.

FORMATTING NUMBERS

You also want to improve the appearance of the numbers in the worksheet by changing their format.

Concept ⑬ Number Formats

Number formats change the appearance of numbers onscreen and when printed, without changing the way the number is stored or used in calculations. When a number is formatted, the formatting appears in the cell, while the value without the formatting is displayed in the formula bar.

The default number format setting in a worksheet is General. General format, in most cases, displays numbers just as you enter them, unformatted. Unformatted numbers are displayed without a thousands separator such as a comma, with negative values preceded by a – (minus sign), and with as many decimal place settings as cell space allows. If a number is too long to be fully displayed in the cell, the General format will round numbers with decimals and use scientific notation for large numbers.

First, you will change the number format of cells B4 through F9 to display as currency with dollar signs, commas, and decimal places.

1

- **Select cells B4 through F9.**

- **Open the**

General	▼

  Number Format drop-down list in the Number group.

- **Choose Currency.**

Your screen should be similar to Figure 1.64

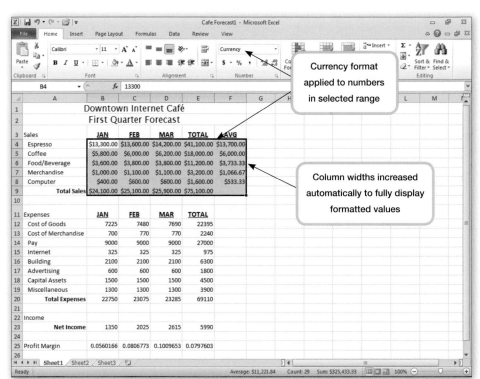

Figure 1.64

Another Method

Excel will also automatically apply a format to a cell based on the symbols you use when entering the number. For example, entering 10,000 in a cell formats the cell to Comma format, and entering $102.20 formats the cell to Currency with two decimal places.

The number entries in the selected range appear with a currency symbol, comma, and two decimal places. The column widths increased automatically to fully display the formatted values.

A second format category that displays numbers as currency is Accounting. You will try this format next on the same range. Additionally, you will specify zero as the number of decimal places because most of the values are whole values. To specify settings that are different than the default setting for a format, you can use the Format Cells dialog box.

2

- Make sure you still have cells B4 through F9 selected.

- Click [🖛] in the Number group to open the Format Cells: Number dialog box.

Another Method

The keyboard shortcut to open the Format Cells dialog box is Ctrl + 1.

- From the Category list box, choose Accounting.

- Reduce the decimal places to 0.

- Click [OK].

Your screen should be similar to Figure 1.65

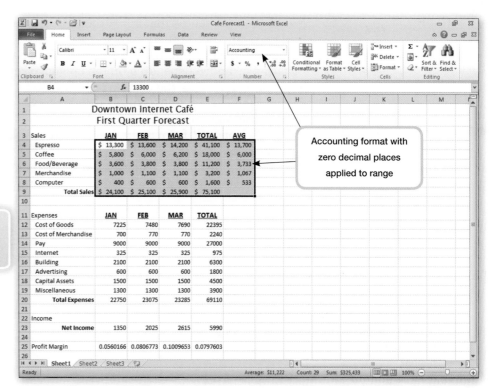

Figure 1.65

The numbers now appear in Accounting format. The primary difference between the Accounting and the Currency formats is that the Accounting format aligns numbers at the decimal place and places the dollar sign in a column at the left edge of the cell space. In addition, it does not allow you to select different ways of displaying negative numbers but displays them in black in parentheses.

You decide the Accounting format will make it easier to read the numbers in a column and you will use this format for the rest of the worksheet. An easier way to apply the Accounting format with 0 decimals is to use the commands in the Number group.

3

- Select the range B12 through E20.

- Click [$ ▼] Accounting Number Format in the Number group.

- Click [.00→] Decrease Decimal twice.

Your screen should be similar to Figure 1.66

Figure 1.66

Formatting Cells and Cell Content **EX1.63**

Notice the Number Format box displays Custom because you modified a copy of the existing Accounting number format code. The custom number format is added to the list of number format codes. Between 200 and 250 custom formats can be added depending on the language version of Excel you are using. You can then reapply the custom format by selecting it from the Custom category of the Format Cells: Number dialog box. This is useful for complicated formats, but not for formats that are easy to re-create.

Finally, you will format the Net Income values as Accounting with zero decimal places and the Profit Margin values as percentages with two decimal places. You will do this using the Mini toolbar. This feature is particularly helpful when working at the bottom of the worksheet window.

4

- Select B23 through E23.

- Click $ ▾ Accounting Number Format on the Mini toolbar.

Having Trouble

Right-click on the selection to display the Mini toolbar.

- Click .00→.0 Decrease Decimal twice on the Mini toolbar.

- Select B25 through E25.

- Click % Percent Style on the Mini toolbar.

- Click ←.0.00 Increase Decimal twice on the Mini toolbar.

Your screen should be similar to Figure 1.67

Figure 1.67

ADDING FONT COLOR

The last formatting change you would like to make to the worksheet is to add color to the text of selected cells. Font color can be applied to all the text in a selected cell or range or to selected words or characters in a cell.

1

- Select A1 through A2.

- Open the Font Color drop-down menu in the Font group.

Another Method

 Font Color is also available on the Mini toolbar.

Your screen should be similar to Figure 1.68

Font color palette

Figure 1.68

Additional Information

You will learn about using themes in Lab 2.

A palette of colors is displayed. Automatic is the default text color setting. This setting automatically determines when to use black or white text. Black text is used on a light background and white text on a dark background. The center area of the palette displays the theme colors. Theme colors are a set of colors that are associated with a **theme**, a predefined set of fonts, colors, and effects that can be applied to an entire worksheet. If you change the theme, the theme colors change. The Standard Colors bar displays 10 colors that are always the same.

As you point to a color, the entry in the selected cell changes color so you can preview how the selection would look. A ScreenTip displays the name of the standard color or the description of the theme color as you point to it.

2

- Choose Yellow from the Standard Colors bar.

- Click **B** Bold.

Your screen should be similar to Figure 1.69

Font color applied to selection

Figure 1.69

The font color of all the text in cells A1 and A2 has changed to the selected color and bold. The selected color appears in the button and can be applied again simply by clicking the button.

ADDING FILL COLOR

Next, you will change the cell background color, also called the fill color, behind the titles and in several other areas of the worksheet. Generally, when adding color to a worksheet, use a dark font color with a light fill color or a light font color with a dark fill color.

1

- Select cells A1 through F3.

- Open the ⬛ ▾ Fill Color drop-down color palette.

- Point to several colors to see a Live Preview.

- Select the Light Blue color from the Standard Colors bar.

- Select cells A11 through F11 and click ⬛ ▾ Fill Color to apply the last selected fill color.

- Apply the same fill color to A22 through F22 and A25 through F25.

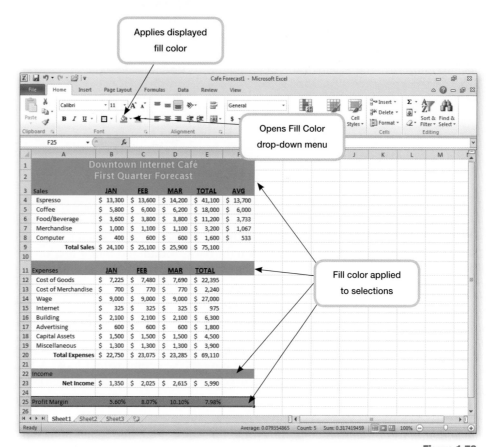

Figure 1.70

Your screen should be similar to Figure 1.70

The color highlight helps distinguish the different areas of the worksheet.

ADDING AND REMOVING CELL BORDERS

Finally, you decide to add a border around the entire worksheet area. Excel includes many predefined border styles that can be added to a single cell or to a range of cells. Then you will make several additional formatting changes to improve the appearance and readability of the worksheet.

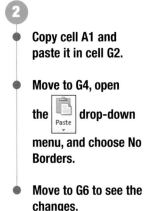

1

- Select the range A1 through F25.

- Open the ⊞ ▾ Borders drop-down menu in the Font group and choose the Thick Box Border style.

- Click outside the range to see the border.

Your screen should be similar to Figure 1.71

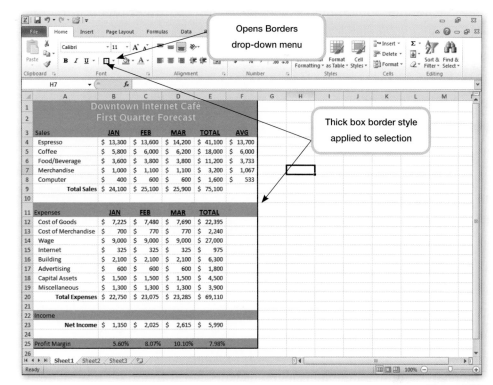

Figure 1.71

The range is considered a single block of cells, and the box border surrounds the entire worksheet selection.

When adding borders, the border also is applied to adjacent cells that share a bordered cell boundary. In this case, cells G1 through G25 acquired a left border and cells A26 through F26 acquired a top border. When pasting a cell that includes a cell border, the border is included unless you specify that the paste does not include the border. To see how this works, you will first copy a cell and its border, and then you will copy it again without the border.

2

- Copy cell A1 and paste it in cell G2.

- Move to G4, open the [Paste] drop-down menu, and choose No Borders.

- Move to G6 to see the changes.

Your screen should be similar to Figure 1.72

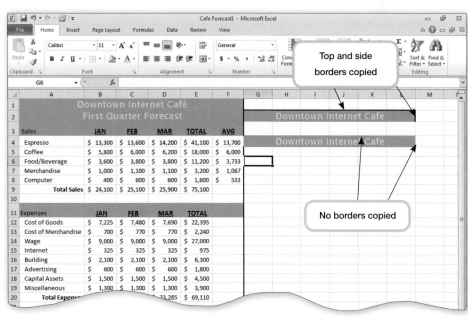

Figure 1.72

If you want to add additional borders or replace an existing border with another, select the range and then add the border. However, if you want to remove a border style from one area of a selection and add a border to another area, you need to remove all borders first and then apply the new border styles. You will try these features next on the entry in cell G2.

3

● Move to G2 and choose No Border from the Borders drop-down menu.

● Apply a Bottom Double Border to the selection.

● Move to G6 to see the changes.

Your screen should be similar to Figure 1.73

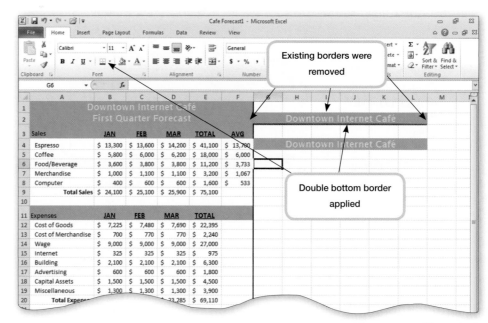

Figure 1.73

All existing borders were removed, including those that share a cell boundary, and the new double bottom border is applied to the selection. You will restore the worksheet to how it was prior to copying the title using Undo and then make some final adjustments to the worksheet.

4

● Undo your last four actions.

● Move to any cell in row 10 and choose Delete Sheet Rows from the

Delete ▼

drop-down menu in the Cells group.

● In the same manner, delete the blank rows 20 and 23.

● Add bold and yellow font color to cells A3, A10, A20, and A22.

● Click Save to save the worksheet changes.

Your screen should be similar to Figure 1.74

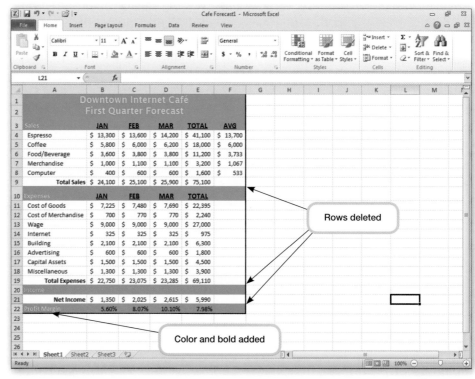

Figure 1.74

Now that the worksheet is nicely formatted, you want to focus on the data. One way to do this is to hide areas of data that you do not want to see in order to emphasize others. You will use this method to emphasize the total data.

1

Select columns B through D.

Additional Information

Any range of cells within the area you want to hide can be selected.

Open the

[Format ▾]

drop-down menu in the Cells group and select Hide & Unhide.

Choose Hide Columns.

Your screen should be similar to Figure 1.75

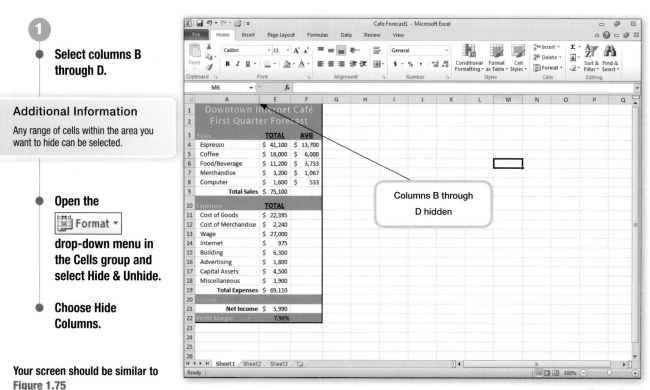

Columns B through D hidden

Figure 1.75

Another Method

You could also right-click on the selected columns and choose Hide from the context menu.

Now the worksheet focus is on the monthly total values, not the monthly values. The columns were hidden by reducing their column width to zero. Instead, you want to hide the rows.

2

● Click on column A and drag to select columns A and E.

● In the Cells group, click Format and select Hide & Unhide, and then choose Unhide Columns.

● Select any range of cells within rows 4 through 8.

● Open the Format drop-down menu, select Hide & Unhide, and then choose Hide Rows.

● Repeat to hide rows 11 through 18.

Figure 1.76

Notice how hiding the rows emphasizes the monthly totals by category.

Your screen should be similar to Figure 1.76

3

● Click ↶ Undo twice to unhide the rows.

Creating a Simple Chart

Another way to better understand the data in a worksheet is to create a chart. A **chart** is a visual representation of data that is used to convey information in an easy-to-understand and attractive manner. You decide to create a chart of the sales data for the three months.

SPECIFYING THE DATA TO CHART

To tell Excel what data to chart, you need to select the range containing the data you want to appear in the chart plus any row or column headings you want used in the chart.

1

● Select cells A3 through D8.

● Hold down the [Alt] key and press [F1].

Your screen should be similar to Figure 1.77

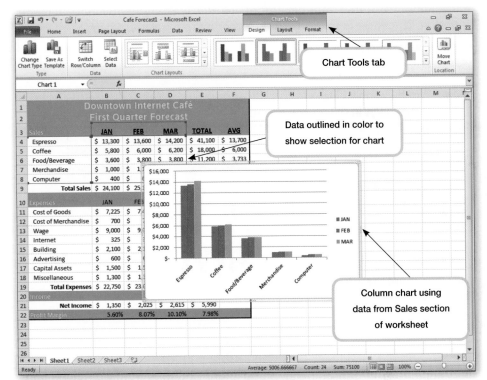

Figure 1.77

Additional Information

You will learn all about creating charts in Lab 2.

The information in the selected range was translated into a chart based on the shape and contents of the selection. A column chart showing the sales for the five items over three months was quickly created.

2

● Point to the edge of the chart object and drag to move it below the worksheet to cover rows 24 to 38.

● Click outside the chart object to deselect it.

Formatting Values as a Date

Now that the worksheet is complete, you want to include your name and the date in the worksheet as documentation. There are many ways to enter the date. For example, you could type the date using the format mm/dd/yy or as month dd, yyyy. When a date is entered as text, Excel converts the entry to a numeric entry that allows dates to be used in calculations. Excel stores all dates as **serial values** with each day numbered from the beginning of the 20th century. The date serial values are consecutively assigned beginning with 1, which corresponds to the date January 1, 1900, and ending with 2958465, which is December 31, 9999.

1

- Enter your first and last name in cell A40.

- Type the current date as mm/dd/yy in cell A41.

Another Method

You also could use the Today function, =Today(), to display the current date in the default date format, or you could use the keyboard shortcut Ctrl + ;.

Your screen should be similar to Figure 1.78

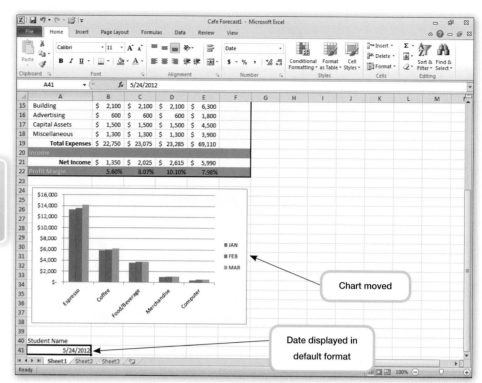

Figure 1.78

The date is displayed using the default date format, which is based on the settings in Windows. It is right-aligned in the cell because it is a numeric entry. You can change the date format in the worksheet without changing the Windows settings using the Format Cells: Number dialog box.

2

- If necessary, move to cell A41.

- Click 🔲 in the Number group to open the Format Cells dialog box.

- Choose the month xx, xxxx (March 14, 2001) date format from the Type list.

- Click [OK].

Your screen should be similar to Figure 1.79

Figure 1.79

The date appears in the specified format.

Documenting a Workbook

You are finished working on the worksheet for now and want to save the changes you have made to the file. In addition, you want to update the file properties to include your name as the author, a title, and keywords.

Having Trouble?

Refer to the section "Specifying Document Properties" in the Introduction to Microsoft Office 2010 to review this feature.

- **Open the File tab.**

- **In the Backstage view Info window, enter the following information in the appropriate boxes.**

Title	Downtown Internet Café
Tags	Sales Projections
Author	Your Name

Additional Information

The Author text box may be blank or may show your school or some other name. Clear the existing contents first if necessary.

Your screen should be similar to Figure 1.80

Figure 1.80

Previewing and Printing a Worksheet

Although you still plan to make more changes to the worksheet, you want to print a copy of the estimated first-quarter forecast for the owner to get feedback regarding the content and layout.

1

Choose Print and view the preview in the right pane.

Your screen should be similar to Figure 1.81

Figure 1.81

The preview displays the worksheet as it will appear on the printed page. Notice that the row and column gridlines are not displayed and will not print. This is one of the default worksheet print settings.

The preview of your worksheet may appear slightly different from that shown in Figure 1.81. This is because the way pages appear in the preview depends on the available fonts, the resolution of the printer, and the available colors. If your printer is configured to print in black and white, the preview will not display in color.

The Excel print settings let you specify how much of the worksheet you want printed. The options are described in the following table.

Option	Action
Print Active Sheets	Prints the active worksheet (default).
Print Entire Workbook	Prints all worksheets in the workbook.
Print Selection	Prints selected range only.
Pages	Prints pages you specify by typing page numbers in the text box.

The worksheet looks good and does not appear to need any further modifications immediately. Now you are ready to print the worksheet using the default print settings.

NOTE **Please consult your instructor for printing procedures that may differ from the following directions.**

2

- If necessary, make sure your printer is on and ready to print.

- If you need to change the selected printer to another printer, open the Printer drop-down list box and select the appropriate printer.

- Click [Print].

The printed copy should be similar to the document shown in the preview area.

When printing is complete, Backstage view is automatically closed. A dotted line may appear between columns G and H. This is the automatic page break line that shows where one printed page ends and the next begins.

DISPLAYING AND PRINTING FORMULAS

Often, when verifying the accuracy of the data in a worksheet, it is helpful to display all the formulas in a worksheet rather than the resulting values. This way you can quickly verify that the formulas are referencing the correct cells and ranges.

1

- Open the Formulas tab.

- Click [Show Formulas] in the Formula Auditing group.

Another Method

You also can use [Ctrl] + ` (accent grave is located to the left of the number 1 key) to toggle between values and formulas.

- Move to E8.

Your screen should be similar to Figure 1.82

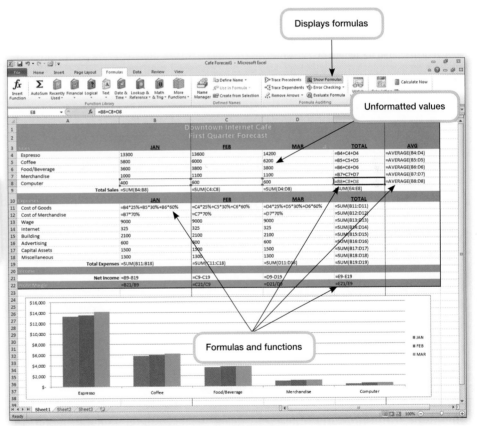

Figure 1.82

The display of the worksheet has changed to display unformatted values and the formulas and functions. It has automatically increased the column widths so the formulas and text do not overflow into the adjacent cells.

CHANGING WORKSHEET ORIENTATION AND SCALING CONTENT

Next, you will print the worksheet with formulas. Because the worksheet is so much wider, you will need to change the orientation to landscape, which prints across the length of the paper. Then you will reduce the scale of the worksheet so it fits on one page. The **scaling** feature will reduce or enlarge the worksheet contents by a percentage or to fit them to a specific number of pages by height and width. You want to scale the worksheet to fit on one page.

1

- Open the File tab and choose Print.

- Change the orientation setting to Landscape Orientation.

- Open the drop-down menu and choose Fit Sheet on One Page.

Your screen should be similar to Figure 1.83

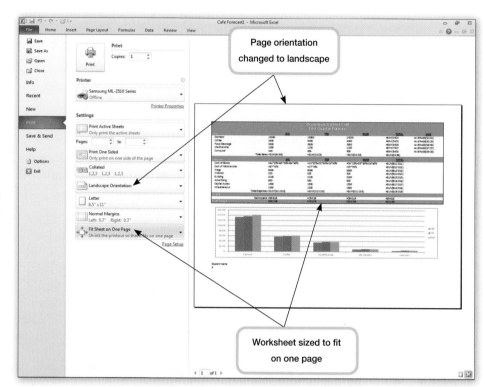

Figure 1.83

Another Method

You also can scale the worksheet using [Scale:] in the Scale to Fit group of the Page Layout tab and setting the scale percentage.

The entire worksheet will easily print across the length of the page when printed using landscape orientation and scaled to fit a single page.

2

- Print the worksheet.

- Press Ctrl + ` to return the display to values.

Having Trouble?

Refer to the "Closing a File" and "Exiting an Office 2010 Application" sections in the Introduction to Microsoft Office 2010 to review these features.

You are now ready to exit the Excel application. If you attempt to close the application without first saving the workbook, Excel displays a warning asking whether you want to save your work. If you do not save your work and you exit the application, all changes you made from the last time you saved will be lost.

1

● **Move to cell A1.**

● **Click** **Close (in the application window title bar).**

● **Click** Save **to resave the worksheet.**

Additional Information

Excel saves the file with the cell selector in the same cell location it is in at the time it is saved.

Because you added the date since last saving the worksheet, you were prompted to save it again before closing it.

FOCUS ON CAREERS

EXPLORE YOUR CAREER OPTIONS

Fan Coordinator

Did you know that 40 percent of the advertised positions in sports are for marketing and promotion? A marketing graduate hired as a basketball fan coordinator would use Excel to keep track of the income and expenses for coordinated halftime activities at professional sporting events. These worksheets would provide valuable information for promoting sponsors' products and services at games. A fan coordinator might start out as an unpaid intern, but after graduation could expect to earn from $25,000 to $45,000.

Lab 1 CONCEPT SUMMARY Creating and Editing a Worksheet

Data (EX1.12)

The basic information or data you enter in a cell can be text or numbers.

AutoCorrect (EX1.18)

The AutoCorrect feature makes some basic assumptions about the text you are typing and, based on these assumptions, automatically corrects the entry.

Column Width (EX1.21)

The column width is the size or width of a column and controls the amount of information that can be displayed in a cell.

Spelling Checker (EX1.25)

The spelling checker locates misspelled words, duplicate words, and capitalization irregularities in the active worksheet and proposes the correct spelling.

Thesaurus (EX1.27)

The thesaurus is a reference tool that provides synonyms, antonyms, and related words for a selected word or phrase.

Range (EX1.31)

A selection consisting of two or more cells on a worksheet is a range.

Formula (EX1.37)

A formula is an equation that performs a calculation on data contained in a worksheet.

Relative Reference (EX1.39)

A relative reference is a cell or range reference in a formula whose location is interpreted in relation to the position of the cell that contains the formula.

Function (EX1.40)

A function is a prewritten formula that performs certain types of calculations automatically.

Recalculation (EX1.47)

When a number in a referenced cell in a formula changes, Excel automatically recalculates all formulas that are dependent upon the changed value.

Alignment (EX1.51)

Alignment settings allow you to change the horizontal and vertical placement and the orientation of an entry in a cell.

Row Height (EX1.53)

The row height is the size or height of a row measured in points.

Number Formats (EX1.61)

Number formats change the appearance of numbers onscreen and when printed, without changing the way the number is stored or used in calculations.

KEY TERMS

active cell EX1.7
active sheet EX1.7
adjacent range EX1.31
alignment EX1.51
antonym EX1.27
argument EX1.40
AutoCorrect EX1.18
AutoFit EX1.22
cell EX1.7
cell reference EX1.7
cell selector EX1.7
chart EX1.70
column EX1.6
column letter EX1.7
column width EX1.21
constant EX1.37
copy area EX1.28
custom dictionary EX1.25
data EX1.12
fill handle EX1.32
formula EX1.37
formula bar EX1.5
function EX1.40
heading EX1.12
main dictionary EX1.25
merged cell EX1.55
Name box EX1.5
nonadjacent range EX1.31
number EX1.12

number formats EX1.61
operand EX1.37
operator EX1.37
order of precedence EX1.37
paste area EX1.29
range EX1.31
range reference EX1.31
recalculation EX1.47
relative reference EX1.39
row EX1.6
row number EX1.7
sans serif EX1.56
scaling EX1.76
serial value EX1.71
serif EX1.56
sheet EX1.6
sheet tab EX1.7
spelling checker EX1.25
spreadsheet EX1.6
synonym EX1.27
syntax EX1.40
tab scroll buttons EX1.8
text EX1.12
theme EX1.65
thesaurus EX1.27
variable EX1.37
workbook EX1.5
workbook window EX1.5
worksheet EX1.6

COMMAND SUMMARY

Command	Shortcut	Action
File		
📂 Open	Ctrl + O	Opens an existing workbook file
💾 **Save**	Ctrl + S	Saves file using same file name
📄 Save As	F12	Saves file using a new file name
📁 Close	Ctrl + F4	Closes open workbook file
New	Ctrl + N	Opens a new blank workbook
Print/ 🖨 Print	Ctrl + P	Prints a worksheet
Print/ No Scaling · Print sheets at their actual size /Fit sheet on one page		Scales worksheet to fit on a single page
☒ Exit	☒ or Alt + F4	Exits Excel program
Quick Access Toolbar		
💾 Save	Ctrl + S	Saves document using same file name
↩ Undo	Ctrl + Z	Reverses last editing or formatting change
↪ Redo	Ctrl + Y	Restores changes after using Undo
Home tab		
Clipboard group		
📋 Paste	Ctrl + V	Pastes selections stored in system Clipboard
✂ Cut	Ctrl + X	Cuts selected data from the worksheet
📋 Copy	Ctrl + C	Copies selected data to system Clipboard
🖌 Format Painter		Copies formatting from one place and applies it to another
Font group		
Calibri ▾ Font		Changes text font
11 ▾ Font Size		Changes text size
B Bold	Ctrl + B	Bolds selected text
I Italic	Ctrl + I	Italicizes selected text

LAB REVIEW

COMMAND SUMMARY (CONTINUED)

Command	Shortcut	Action
U ▾ Underline	Ctrl +U	Underlines selected text
▾ Borders		Adds border to specified area of cell or range
▾ Fill Color		Adds color to cell background
A ▾ Font Color		Adds color to text
Alignment group		
Align Text Left		Left-aligns entry in cell space
Center		Center-aligns entry in cell space
Align Text Right		Right-aligns entry in cell space
Increase Indent		Indents cell entry
Decrease Indent		Reduces the margin between the left cell border and cell entry
▾ Merge & Center		Combines selected cells into one cell and centers cell contents in new cell
Number group		
General ▾ Number Format		Applies selected number formatting to selection
$ ▾ Accounting Number Format		Applies Accounting number format to selection
% Percent Style		Applies Percent Style format to selection
Increase Decimal		Increases number of decimal places
Decrease Decimal		Decreases number of decimal places
Cells group		
Insert ▾ /Insert Cells		Inserts blank cells, shifting existing cells down
Insert ▾ /Insert Cut Cells		Inserts cut row of data into new worksheet row, shifting existing rows down
Insert ▾ /Insert Copied Cells		Inserts copied row into new worksheet row, shifting existing rows down
Insert ▾ /Insert Sheet Rows		Inserts blank rows, shifting existing rows down
Insert ▾ /Insert Sheet Columns		Inserts blank columns, shifting existing columns right
Delete ▾ /Delete Sheet Rows		Deletes selected rows, shifting existing rows up

COMMAND SUMMARY (CONTINUED)

Command	Shortcut	Action
Delete ▾ /Delete Sheet Columns		Deletes selected columns, shifting existing columns left
Format ▾ /Row Height		Changes height of selected row
Format ▾ /AutoFit Row Height		Changes row height to match the tallest cell entry
Format ▾ /Column Width		Changes width of selected column
Format ▾ /AutoFit Column Width		Changes column width to match widest cell entry
Format ▾ /Default Width		Returns column width to default width
Editing group		
Σ ▾ Sum		Calculates the sum of the values in the selected cells
Σ ▾ Sum/Average		Calculates the average of the values in the selected range
Σ ▾ Sum/Min		Returns the smallest of the values in the selected range
Σ ▾ Sum/Max		Returns the largest of the values in the selected range
▾ Fill/Right	Ctrl + R	Continues a pattern to adjacent cells to the right
▾ Clear		Removes both formats and contents from selected cells
▾ Clear/Clear Formats		Clears formats only from selected cells
▾ Clear/Clear Contents	Delete	Clears contents only from selected cells
Formulas tab		
Formula Auditing group		
Show Formulas	Ctrl + `	Displays and hides worksheet formulas
Review tab		
Proofing group		
ABC Spelling	F7	Spell-checks worksheet
Thesaurus		Opens the thesaurus for the selected word in the Research task pane

LAB EXERCISES

SCREEN IDENTIFICATION

1. In the following Excel 2010 screen, letters identify important elements. Enter the correct term for each screen element in the space provided.

Possible answers for the screen identification are:

Column	Workbook window	A. _____	I. _____
Status bar	Cell	B. _____	J. _____
Font color	Formula bar	C. _____	K. _____
Numeric entry	Active sheet	D. _____	L. _____
Fill color	Text label	E. _____	M. _____
Font	Cell reference	F. _____	N. _____
Range	Format Painter	G. _____	O. _____
Formula	View buttons	H. _____	P. _____
Row	Border		
Column labels	Sheet tabs		

MATCHING

Match the lettered item on the right with the numbered item on the left.

1. ▦   _____ a. an arithmetic operator
2. .xlsx   _____ b. changes the width of a column
3. ▢ ▾   _____ c. a graphic representation of data
4. chart   _____ d. Excel workbook file name extension
5. /   _____ e. two or more worksheet cells
6. ✔   _____ f. enters a SUM function
7. =C19*A21   _____ g. adds a cell border
8. D11   _____ h. merges cells and centers entry
9. range   _____ i. a formula multiplying the values in two cells
10. Σ ▾   _____ j. a cell reference
11. ↔   _____ K. Format Painter

TRUE/FALSE

Circle the correct answer to the following questions.

1. Number formats affect the way that numbers are used in calculations.	**True**	**False**
2. Charts are visual representations of the data in a worksheet.	**True**	**False**
3. A colon is used to separate cell references in nonadjacent ranges.	**True**	**False**
4. A function is a prewritten formula that performs a calculation.	**True**	**False**
5. The default column width setting is 10.12.	**True**	**False**
6. When a formula containing relative references is copied, the cell references in the copied formula refer to the same cells that are referenced in the original formula.	**True**	**False**
7. An adjacent range is two or more selected cells or ranges that are adjoining.	**True**	**False**
8. The spellingchecker can only find misspelled words if they are entered in the main dictionary.	**True**	**False**
9. Recalculation is one of the most powerful features of electronic worksheets.	**True**	**False**
10. Cell alignment allows you to change the horizontal and vertical placement and the orientation of an entry in a cell.	**True**	**False**

LAB EXERCISES

FILL-IN

Complete the following statements by filling in the blanks with the correct key terms.

1. Cells or ranges that are included in the same selection but are not located next to each other are part of a(n) _____.

2. _____ are integers assigned to the days from January 1, 1900, through December 31, 2099, that allow dates to be used in calculations.

3. The _____ displays the cell selector and will be affected by the next entry or procedure.

4. A(n) _____ window is used to display an open workbook file.

5. By default, text entries are _____-aligned and number entries are _____-aligned.

6. A(n) _____ entry is used to perform a calculation.

7. The _____ function automatically adds all the numbers in a range of cells.

8. A(n) _____ is a rectangular grid of rows and columns.

9. The _____ dictionary holds words the user enters that are not included in the main dictionary.

10. A(n) _____ cell is a cell made up of several selected cells combined into one.

MULTIPLE CHOICE

Circle the correct response to the questions below.

1. _____ entries can contain any combination of letters, numbers, spaces, and any other special characters.
   a. Number
   b. Variable
   c. Constant
   d. Text

2. The _____ is a small black square, located in the lower-right corner of the selection, used to create a series or copy to adjacent cells.
   a. sheet tab
   b. fill handle
   c. scroll box
   d. sizing handle

3. Rotating entries, using color, and using character effects are three ways to _____.
   a. emphasize information
   b. create reports
   c. perform calculations
   d. update spreadsheets

4. The amount of information that is displayed in a cell is determined by the _____.
   a. column size
   b. row size
   c. column width
   d. row height

5. Which of the following is a valid Excel formula?
   a. =(5 + 8)(2 + 1)
   b. 5 + 8*2 + 1
   c. =5 + 8(2 + 1)
   d. =(5 + 8)*(2 + 1)

6. Whenever a formula containing _____ references is copied, the referenced cells are automatically adjusted.
   a. relative
   b. automatic
   c. fixed
   d. variable

7. The _____ feature in Excel automatically inserts proper capitalization at the beginning of sentences and in the names of days of the week.
   a. AutoName
   b. AutoCorrect
   c. CorrectWords
   d. Word Wrap

8. The Currency number format can display _____.
   a. dollar signs
   b. commas
   c. decimal places
   d. all of the above

9. When a number in a referenced cell is changed, all the formulas that use the cell reference are _____.
   a. recalculated
   b. reformatted
   c. redefined
   d. left unchanged

10. The _____ is a reference tool that provides synonyms and related words for a selected word.
    a. synonym locator
    b. thesaurus
    c. spelling checker
    d. research book

STEP-BY-STEP

TEENAGE CELL PHONE USAGE DATA ANALYSIS ★

1. Mary Collins works for a cell phone company. She's been asked to analyze data gathered in a survey of teenage cell phone users to find possible service packages for the company to offer. After following the directions below to complete the worksheet, your solution will be similar to that shown here.

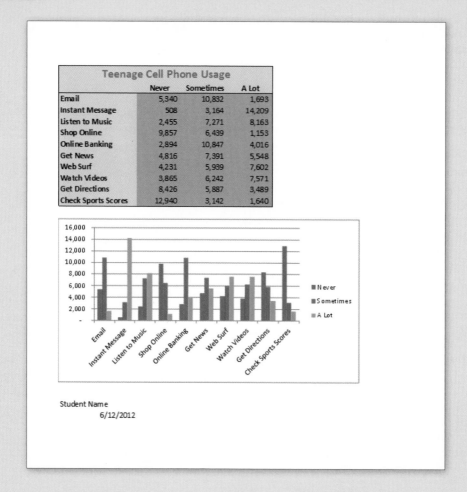

Teenage Cell Phone Usage	Never	Sometimes	A Lot
Email	5,340	10,832	1,693
Instant Message	508	3,164	14,209
Listen to Music	2,455	7,271	8,163
Shop Online	9,857	6,439	1,153
Online Banking	2,894	10,847	4,016
Get News	4,816	7,391	5,548
Web Surf	4,231	5,939	7,602
Watch Videos	3,865	6,242	7,571
Get Directions	8,426	5,887	3,489
Check Sports Scores	12,940	3,142	1,640

Student Name
6/12/2012

a. Open an Excel 2010 workbook.

b. Enter the data here into the spreadsheet.

Row	Col A	Col B	Col C	Col D
1		Never	Sometimes	A Lot
2	Email	5340	10832	1693
3	Instant Message	508	3164	14209
4	Listen to Music	2455	7271	8163
5	Shop Online	9857	6439	1153
6	Online Banking	2894	10847	4016
7	Get News	4816	7391	5548
8	Web Surf	4231	5939	7602
9	Watch Videos	3865	6242	7571
10	Get Directions	8426	5887	3489
11	Check Sports Scores	12940	3142	1640

c. AutoFit the width of column A. Insert a new row above row 1.

d. In cell A1, enter the worksheet title **Teenage Cell Phone Usage**

e. Merge and center the worksheet title over columns A through D.

f. Change the font in cell A1 to 16 points.

g. Bold the column labels in row 2 and the row labels in column A.

h. Add an outside border around A1 through D2, and another around A3 through D12.

i. Center the column headings and data in cells B2 through D12. AutoFit column C.

j. Apply the Comma number format with zero decimal places to the data in B3 through D12.

k. Add fill colors of your choice, using one color for rows 1 and 2 and the row labels in column A and a different color for cells B3 through D12. Change the text color for readability if needed. Add a font color of your choice and bold to the worksheet title.

l. Create a chart using the data in the worksheet, and move the chart to row 14.

m. Type your name in cell A30 and the date in cell A31.

n. Save the workbook as Teenage Cell Phone Usage to your solution file location. Print the worksheet.

LAB EXERCISES

ANIMAL RESCUE FOUNDATION ADOPTION ANALYSIS ★

2. Edward Corwin works for the Animal Rescue Foundation. One of his responsibilities is to collect and analyze data on the animals that enter the shelters. He has compiled a list of the cost of housing animals by the local shelters for the past four years. After following the directions below to complete the worksheet, your solution will be similar to that shown here.

   a. Open the workbook ex01_Animal Housing. Auto fit the column width of column A. Spell-check the worksheet and correct any misspelled words.

   b. Modify the title in cell B2 so the first letter of each word is capitalized. Increase the font size to 14 point and change the row height to 22.5. Merge and center both title lines across columns A through E.

   c. Bold and center the headings in row 5. Insert a blank row above row 6.

   d. In row 17, enter a function to total the data under the 2009 column and a function to total the data under the 2010 column.

   e. Format the numbers in rows 7 and 17 using the Accounting style with zero decimal places. Format the numbers in rows 8 through 16 using the Comma style with zero decimal places.

   f. Adjust the column widths so all the data is fully displayed. Insert a blank row above row 17.

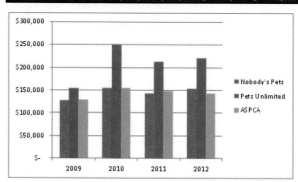

g. Edward has just received the information for the last two years. Enter the following data in the cells indicated.

Row	Col D	Col E
5	2011	2012
7	142600	152800
8	213500	220300
9	12500	14700
10	2200	4200
11	1400	1600
12	148500	142400
13	11700	10500
14	18900	25300
15	14200	13500
16	26700	29900

h. Format the column heads to match the style of the corresponding information in columns B and C.

i. Copy the Total function in cell B18 to calculate the total for each of the new years. Increase the indent in cell A18

j. Add font and fill colors to the worksheet as you like.

k. Add a thick box border around A1 through E18.

l. Move the row of ASPCA data to above the row of FOCAS data.

m. Delete the word "Shelter" in cell A5.

n. Next, you want to create a chart showing the annual data for the three largest shelter groups. Select the range A5 through E9 and create a chart displaying the data. Move the chart to cell A20.

o. Enter your name in cell A35 and the current date in cell A36. Format cell A36 to display the month, day, and year (March 14, 2001) date format.

p. Move to cell A1. Save the workbook as Animal Housing Analysis to your solution file location. Preview and print the worksheet.

q. Print the worksheet with formulas using landscape orientation so that it fits on one page.

LAB EXERCISES

HURRICANE ANALYSIS WORKSHEET ★

3. Mary Ellen is a manager for an insurance agency. One of her responsibilities is to collect and analyze data on weather conditions in geographical areas. She has compiled a list of hurricanes from the National Weather Service. After following the directions below to complete the worksheet, your solution will be similar to that shown here.

    a. Open the workbook ex01_US Hurricanes. Spell-check the worksheet and correct any misspelled words.

    b. Modify the title in cell A1 so the first letter of each word is capitalized, except "by." Merge and center the two worksheet titles across columns A through I. Increase the font size to 12 point. Bold the titles.

    c. Enter the heading **% Major to All** in cell I3 and increase the widths of columns H and I to fully display their headings.

    d. Merge and center cells A3 and A4. Merge and center cells I3 and I4.

    e. Adjust the width of column A so all the data is fully displayed.

    f. Insert new rows above row 1 and below row 3.

    g. Bold the labels in rows 5 and 6. Merge and center cells B5 through H5. Underline and center the labels in cells B6 through H6.

    h. Enter the formula **=H7/G7** in cell I7. Copy the formula down column I for the rest of the states. Format the numbers in column I as a percent with one decimal place.

    i. Center the data in cells B7 through I33.

    j. Add font and fill colors to the worksheet as you like.

    k. In the ALL column, locate the four states with the highest total number of major hurricanes and fill the cells with a different fill color.

    l. In cells K7 through K10, enter the names of the four states with the highest total number of major hurricanes. In cells L7 through L10, enter the corresponding numbers. Enter "Total Hurricanes" in cell L6. Add color to the cells to match the data.

    m. Create a chart using the data in the table you just created and move it to cell J12.

    n. Enter your name and the current date on separate rows just below the chart. Format the date to display the month, day, and year (March 14, 2001) date format.

    o. Move to cell A1. Save the workbook as US Hurricanes Analysis to your solution file location. Print the worksheet in landscape orientation on one page.

4. Terrence Lewis works for an employment agency and needs to provide information about salaries in different states for his clients. He has started a worksheet with data from the years 2006–2008. After following the directions below to complete the worksheet, the first page of your solution will be similar to that shown here.

a. Open the workbook ex01_Family Income. Spell-check the worksheet and correct any misspelled words.

b. Edit the title in cell A1 by capitalizing the first letter of each word except the word "by" and by deleting the comma following "income." Merge and center the title across columns A through F. Increase the font size to 12, and bold and apply a font color of your choice to the title.

c. Center-align and underline the column headings in row 2. Adjust the width of column A to fully display the labels. Insert blank rows above and below the title.

d. Right-align cells B5 through D56 and format the cells as Accounting with zero decimal places.

e. Enter the heading **Average** in cell E4. Center and underline the heading. Calculate the average income in cell E5 using the function =Average(B5:D5). Copy the formula to cells E6 through E56.

f. Next, you would like to calculate the percent of change from 2006 to 2008. Enter the heading **% Change** in cell F4. Center and underline the title. Enter the formula =(D5–B5)/D5 in cell F5. Format the cell as a percentage with two decimal places. Copy the formula to cells F6 through F56.

g. AutoFit columns B through F.

h. Add font and fill colors to the worksheet as you like. Locate the state with the highest positive % change and the state with the highest negative % change. Surround their entire rows with a box border and a different fill color.

i. Enter your name and the current date on separate rows just below the last lines. Format the date to day, month, year (14-Mar-01) date format.

LAB EXERCISES

   j. Move to cell A1. Save the workbook as Family Income to your solution file location. Change page size to legal to fit on one page, and print the worksheet.

   k. Print the worksheet again with formulas on one page using landscape orientation.

PECAN GROVES HOMEOWNERS ASSOCIATION ★ ★ ★

5. The Pecan Groves Homeowners Association is planning a large building project and wants to project how much there is likely to be in the cash budget after expenses. Using last year's final budget numbers, you will create a projected budget for 2012. After following the directions below to complete the worksheet, your solution will be similar to that shown here.

   a. Open the workbook file ex01_ Pecan Groves Budget. Spell-check the worksheet and correct any misspelled words.

   b. Change the font type, size, and color and fill color of the three worksheet title lines to a format of your choice. Merge and center the titles across columns A through E.

   c. Set the width of column A to 25. Insert a column between columns B and C. Merge and center cell B5 across columns B and C. Merge and center cell D5 across columns D and E. Set the fill color of cells B5 and D5 to match the fill color in the titles.

   d. Center the text in cell A6 and change the font color and fill color to a color of your choice. Apply the same formats to cell A13.

   e. Right-justify the text in cells A12 and A25. Indent the text in cells A19:A23. Indent the text in cell A23 again. Move the data in cells B14:B17 to C14:C17. Move the data in cell B24 to C24.

Pecan Groves
Homeowners Association
Projected Budget for 2012

	2011		2012	
Income				
Cash on hand	$	16,701	$	17,703
Funds		2,200		2,332
Member Dues		219,500		232,670
Transfer Fees		1,700		1,802
Interest - savings		1,200		1,272
Total Income		$ 241,301		$ 255,779
Expenditures				
Administration		$ 120,000		$ 134,400
Insurance		16,000		17,920
Audit & Tax Preparation		21,200		23,744
Lawyer		27,000		30,240
Maintenance				
Street Repair	$	2,700	$	3,105
Street Cleaning		1,582		1,819
Snow Removal		550		633
Street Signs		4,985		5,733
Total Maintenance		9,817		11,290
Miscellaneous		3,000		3,360
Total Expenditures		$ 197,017		$ 220,954
Ending Cash Balance		$ 44,284		$ 34,826

Student Name
7/6/2012

   f. In cell C12, sum the income data. In cell C23, sum the maintenance expenditure data. In cell C25, sum all the Expenditures items. In cell C27, enter a formula to calculate the ending cash balance (Hint: =C12-C25).

   g. Each of the 2012 Income items is projected to increase by 6 percent over the previous year. Enter a formula in cell D7 to calculate the increase in cash on hand (Hint: =B7*1.06). Copy this formula down column D to the other Income items. Enter the appropriate function into cell E12 to calculate the 2012 total income value.

h. Each of the 2012 expenditure items except for the maintenance expenditures is projected to increase by 12 percent over the previous year. Enter the appropriate formulas in column E to reflect this change. Each maintenance expense is projected to increase 15 percent. Enter the appropriate formulas in column D. Enter the appropriate function in cell E23 to calculate the total maintenance expenses. Use formulas to calculate the value for total expenditures and ending cash balance for 2012.

i. Format cells B7, B19, C12, C14, C25, C27, D7, D19, E12, E14, E25, and E27 as Accounting with zero decimal places. Format all other cells containing numbers except for B5 and D5 to Comma with zero decimal places. Set the column widths of columns B through E to 12. Fill the cells A27:E27 with the same fill color used for the titles. Delete column F. Surround the entire worksheet with a thick box border.

j. Enter your name and the current date on separate rows just below the worksheet.

k. Save the workbook file as Pecan Groves Budget to your solution file location. Print the worksheet.

l. Print the worksheet again with formulas using landscape orientation.

ON YOUR OWN

TRACKING YOUR CALORIES ★

1. A worksheet can be used to track your calories for the day. Design and create a worksheet to record the food you consume and the exercise you do on a daily basis. The worksheet should include your food consumption for all meals and snacks and the activities you performed for a week. Use the Web as a resource to find out the calorie values for the items you consumed (or refer to the calorie information on the product packaging) and to find out the caloric expenditure for the exercises you do. Include an appropriate title, row and column headings, and formulas to calculate your total calorie intake and expenditure on a daily basis. Include a formula to calculate the percent deviation from your recommended daily calorie intake. Format the worksheet appropriately using features presented in this lab. Enter real or sample data. Include your name and date above the worksheet. Spell-check the worksheet. Save the workbook as Calorie Tracking and print the worksheet.

LAB EXERCISES

CREATING A PERSONAL BUDGET ★

2. In a blank Excel 2010 workbook, create a personal three-month budget. Enter an appropriate title and use descriptive labels for your monthly expenses (food, rent, car payments, insurance, credit card payments, etc.). Spell-check your worksheet. Enter your monthly expenses (or, if you prefer, any reasonable sample data). Use formulas to calculate total expenses for each month and the average monthly expenditures for each expense item. Add a column for projection for the next year showing a 2.5 percent increase in the cost of living. Enhance the worksheet using features you learned in this lab. Enter your name and the current date on separate rows just below the worksheet. Save the workbook as Personal Budget. Preview and print the worksheet.

TRACKING PROJECT HOURS ★ ★

3. Samantha Johnson is the project manager for a small publishing company. She has four part-time employees (Melanie, Bob, Vanessa, and Rudy). Using the steps in the planning process, plan and create a worksheet for Samantha that can be used to record and analyze the hours each employee works per day during the month on two projects: magazine and brochure. Hours-worked data for each employee will be entered into the worksheet. Using that data, the worksheet will calculate the total number of hours for each person per project. Additionally, it will calculate the total weekly hours for each project. Write a short paragraph describing how you used each of the planning steps. Enter sample data in a worksheet. Include your name and the current date on separate rows just below the worksheet. Spell-check the worksheet. Save the workbook as Project Hours. Preview and print the worksheet.

MUSIC ANALYSIS ★ ★ ★

4. Use the library and/or the Web to locate information on trends in CD sales versus music downloads on the Internet. Create a worksheet to display information relating to the increasing usage by country, age group, or any other trend you locate. Calculate totals or averages based on your data. Enhance the worksheet using features you learned in this lab. Enter your name and the current date on separate rows just below the worksheet. Spell-check the worksheet. Save the workbook as Music Analysis. Preview and print the worksheet.

HOME ELECTRONICS ANALYSIS ★ ★ ★

5. A national electronics retailer wants to analyze the trend in home electronics sales and usage for the past three years. Design and create a worksheet to record the number of households (one-person, two-person, and four-person) that have computers, Internet access, televisions, and cable TV access. Include an appropriate title, row and column headings, and formulas to calculate average by category and by year. Include a formula to calculate the percent growth over the three years. Format the worksheet appropriately using features presented in this tutorial. Enter sample data for the three years. Include your name and date above the worksheet. Spell-check the worksheet. Save the workbook as Home Electronics Analysis and print the worksheet.

Enhancing the Worksheet with Graphics and Charts

Objectives

After completing this lab, you will know how to:

1. Apply and customize themes.

2. Use cell styles.

3. Insert and size a graphic.

4. Create a chart.

5. Move, size, and format a chart.

6. Change the type of chart.

7. Create, explode, and rotate a pie chart.

8. Apply patterns and color to a chart.

9. Document a workbook.

10. Size and align a sheet on a page.

11. Add predefined headers and footers.

Downtown Internet Café

Evan is impressed with how quickly you were able to create the first-quarter sales forecast for the Downtown Internet Café. He made several suggestions to improve the appearance of the worksheet, including applying different formats and adding a graphic. Evan also expressed concern that the sales values seem a little low and has asked you to contact several other Internet cafés to inquire about their start-up experiences.

While speaking with other Internet café managers, you heard many exciting success stories. Internet connections attract more customers, and the typical customer stays longer at an Internet café than at a regular café. As a result, they spend more money.

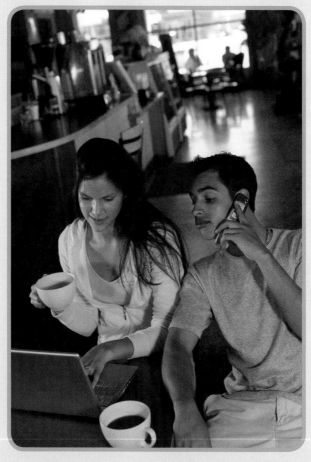

You would like to launch an aggressive advertising campaign to promote the new Internet aspect of the Café. The new Café features include free Wi-Fi connection, computer rentals, and printing and copying services. You believe that the campaign will lead to an increase in customers and subsequently to an increase in sales. To convince Evan, you need an effective way to illustrate the sales growth you are forecasting. You will use Excel 2010's chart-creating and formatting features to produce several different charts of your sales estimates, as shown on the following page.

Use of graphics and themes add visual interest to a worksheet.

Many different types of charts can be created and modified to visually represent worksheet data.

Features such as data labels, fill colors, textures, and shadows add a professional appearance to your charts.

The following concepts will be introduced in this lab:

1 Graphics A graphic is a nontext element or object such as a drawing or picture that can be added to a document.

2 Quick Style A quick style is a named group of formatting characteristics that allows you to quickly apply a whole group of formats to a selection in one simple step.

3 Theme A theme is a set of formatting choices that can be applied to an entire worksheet in one simple step. A theme consists of a set of theme colors, a set of theme fonts (including heading and body text fonts), and a set of theme effects (including line and fill effects).

4 Chart Elements Chart elements are the different parts of a chart that are used to graphically display the worksheet data.

5 Chart Types Different chart types are used to represent data in different ways. The type of chart you create depends on the type of data you are charting and the emphasis you want the chart to impart.

6 Chart Object A chart object is a graphic object that is created using charting features. An object can be inserted into a worksheet or into a special chart sheet.

7 Group A group is two or more objects that behave as a single object when moved or sized. A chart is a group that consists of many separate objects.

8 Data Labels Data labels provide additional information about a data point in the data series. They can consist of the value of the point, the name of the data series or category, a percent value, or a bubble size.

9 Headers and Footers Headers and footers provide information that typically appears at the top and bottom of each page and commonly include information such as the date and page number.

Inserting and Formatting Illustrations

To focus Evan's attention solely on the sales values for the Downtown Internet Café, you created a new worksheet containing only those values. Although you have added some formatting to the worksheet already, you still want to improve its appearance by adding a graphic, changing the theme, and applying different cell styles. Then you will create the charts to help Evan visualize the sales trends better.

INSERTING A PICTURE FROM FILES

You saved the sales portion of the worksheet in a new workbook file.

1

- Start Excel 2010.

- If necessary, maximize the Excel application window.

- Open the file ex02_ Cafe Sales.

Your screen should be similar to Figure 2.1

	A	B	C	D	E
4		Downtown Internet Café			
5		Sales Forecast			
6		First Quarter			
9		JAN	FEB	MAR	TOTAL
10	Espresso	$ 13,300	$ 13,600	$ 14,200	$ 41,100
11	Drip Coffee	$ 5,800	$ 6,000	$ 6,200	$ 18,000
12	Food/Beverage	$ 3,600	$ 3,800	$ 3,800	$ 11,200
13	Merchandise	$ 1,000	$ 1,100	$ 1,100	$ 3,200
14	Computer	$ 400	$ 600	$ 600	$ 1,600
15	Total Sales	$ 24,100	$ 25,100	$ 25,900	$ 75,100

Figure 2.1

First you want to add a graphic next to the worksheet title to add interest.

Concept **1** Graphics

A **graphic** is a nontext element or **object** such as a drawing or picture that can be added to a document. An object is an item that can be sized, moved, and manipulated.

A graphic can be a simple **drawing object** consisting of shapes, such as lines and boxes, that can be created using features on the Drawing toolbar. A drawing object is part of the Excel workbook. A **picture** is an illustration such as a graphic illustration or a scanned photograph. Pictures are graphics that were created from another program and are inserted in the worksheet as embedded objects. An **embedded object** becomes part of the Excel workbook and can be opened and edited using the **source program**, the program in which it was created. Any changes made to the embedded object are not made to the original picture file because they are independent. Several examples of drawing objects and pictures are shown below.

Drawing object

Graphic illustration

Photograph

Add graphics to your worksheets to help the reader understand concepts, to add interest, and to make your worksheet stand out from others.

Inserting and Formatting Illustrations **EX2.5**

Graphic files can be obtained from a variety of sources. Many simple drawings called **clip art** are available in the Clip Organizer, a Microsoft Office tool that arranges and catalogs clip art and other media files stored on the computer's hard disk. Additionally, you can access Microsoft's Clip Art and Media Web site for even more graphics.

Digital images created using a digital camera are one of the most common types of graphic files. You also can create graphic files using a scanner to convert any printed document, including photographs, to an electronic format. Most images that are scanned are stored as Windows bitmap files (.bmp). All types of graphics, including clip art, photographs, and other types of images, can be found on the Internet. These files are commonly stored as .jpg or .pcx files. Keep in mind that any images you locate on the Internet may be protected by copyright and should be used only with permission. You also can purchase CDs containing graphics for your use.

You want to insert a picture to the left of the title in the worksheet. You located a graphic of a coffee cup and coffee beans and saved a copy of the graphic as a file on your computer.

- **Open the Insert tab.**

- **Click** [Picture icon] **in the Illustrations group.**

- **Change to the location of your data files.**

- **Select** ex02_ Internet Cafe.bmp.

- **If a preview of the selected graphic is not displayed, click** [icon] ▼ **and choose Large Icons.**

Having Trouble?

Depending on the version of Windows on your computer, you may need to click [Views ▼] and choose Large Icons.

Figure 2.2

Only files that have a graphic file type are displayed in the file list. You think the selected picture illustrates the concept of a café and that it will look good in the worksheet.

Your screen should be similar to Figure 2.2

2

Click ▼.

Your screen should be similar to **Figure 2.3**

Figure 2.3

The picture is inserted in the worksheet at the location of the cell selector. The picture is surrounded by a **selection rectangle** and eight squares and circles, called **sizing handles**, indicating it is a selected object and can now be deleted, sized, moved, or modified. The Picture Tools Format tab is automatically displayed and can be used to modify the selected picture object.

SIZING A GRAPHIC

Usually, when a graphic is inserted, its size will need to be adjusted. To size a graphic, you select it and drag the sizing handles to increase or decrease the size of the object. The mouse pointer changes to ⬉ when pointing to a corner handle and ⬌ or ↕ when pointing to a side handle. The direction of the arrow indicates the direction in which you can drag to size the graphic. Dragging a corner handle maintains the scale of the picture by increasing both the width and length of the graphic equally. You also can move a graphic object by pointing to the graphic and dragging it to the new location. The mouse pointer changes to ⬌ when you can move the graphic.

Another Method

You also can size a picture to an exact measurement using commands in the Size group of the Picture Tools Format tab.

1

- Point to the lower-right corner sizing handle.

- With the pointer as a ⬉, drag the mouse inward to reduce the size of the graphic until the bottom of the graphic is even with row 6.

Additional Information

When you drag to size the graphic, the mouse pointer shape changes to a ✛.

- Point to the center of the graphic and, when the mouse pointer is ✛, drag the graphic to position it as in Figure 2.4.

Your screen should be similar to Figure 2.4

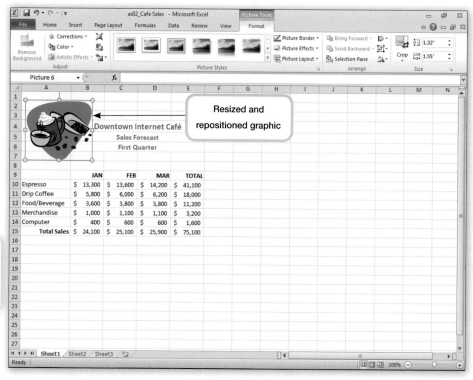

Figure 2.4

The graphic is smaller and moved to the left of the title as you want it.

INSERTING A PICTURE FROM THE CLIP ART GALLERY

Although you like the graphic, you decide to check the Clip Art gallery for pictures that show the use of a computer in a café environment.

1

- Move to cell F1 to deselect the graphic and choose the location where you want a new picture inserted.

- Open the Insert tab.

- Click Clip Art in the Illustrations group.

Your screen should be similar to Figure 2.5

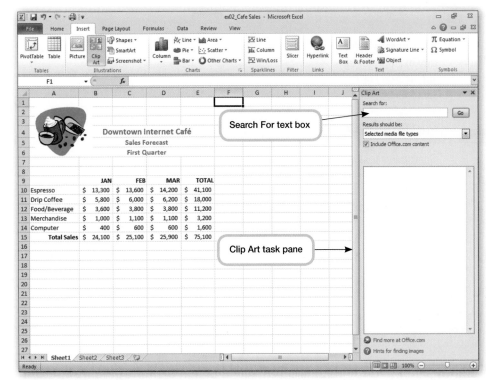

Figure 2.5

The Clip Art task pane appears in which you can enter a word or phrase that is representative of the type of picture you want to locate. You also can specify the locations to search and the type of media files, such as clip art, movies, photographs, or sound, to display in the results. You want to find photographs of computers and coffee.

2

- If necessary, select any existing text in the Search For text box.

- Type **computers, coffee** in the Search For text box.

- Open the Results Should Be drop-down menu, select Photographs, and deselect all other options.

Having Trouble?

Click the box next to an option to select or deselect (clear the checkmark).

- If necessary, select the Include Office.com content check box.

- Click **Go**.

Your screen should be similar to Figure 2.6

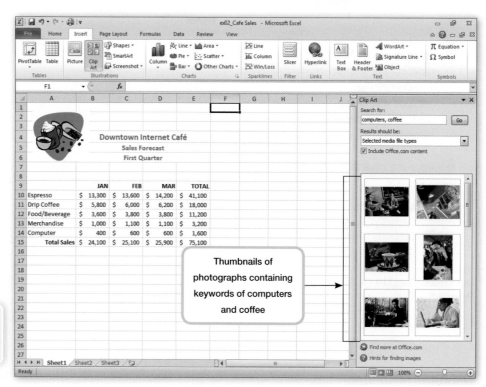

Figure 2.6

Having Trouble?

Your Clip Art task pane may display different pictures than those shown in Figure 2.6.

The program searches the Microsoft Clip Organizer on your computer and, if you have an Internet connection established, Microsoft's Office Online site for clip art and graphics that match your search terms. The Results area displays **thumbnails**, miniature representations of pictures, of all located graphics. The pictures stored on your computer in the Microsoft Clip Organizer appear first in the results list, followed by the Office Online clip art.

Pointing to a thumbnail displays a ScreenTip containing the **keywords** associated with the picture and information about the picture properties. It also displays a drop-down list bar that accesses the item's context menu.

3

- Scroll the list to view additional pictures.

- Point to the thumbnail shown in Figure 2.7 to see a ScreenTip.

Having Trouble?

If this graphic is not available, point to another of your choice.

Your screen should be similar to Figure 2.7

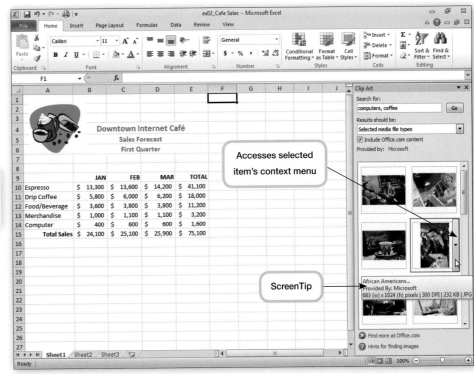

Figure 2.7

The ScreenTip displays the first keywords associated with the graphic as well as some basic information about the size and type of file. Additionally, because it is sometimes difficult to see the details in the graphic in the thumbnail, you can preview it in a larger size.

4

- Click ▾ next to the graphic to open the context menu.

- Choose Preview/ Properties.

Your screen should be similar to Figure 2.8

Figure 2.8

The Preview/Properties dialog box displays the selected graphic larger so it is easier to see. It also displays more information about the properties associated with the graphic, including all the keywords used to identify the graphic. You can now see that both keywords, "computer" and "coffee" appear in the list. You think this looks like a good choice and will insert it into the worksheet.

5

- Click [Close] to close the dialog box.

- Click on the graphic to insert it into the worksheet.

Another Method

You also could choose Insert from the thumbnail's context menu.

- Click [×] in the Clip Art task pane to close it.

Your screen should be similar to Figure 2.9

Figure 2.9

The picture is inserted in the worksheet at the location of the cell selector. You now have two graphic objects in the worksheet, a drawing and a photograph.

DELETING A GRAPHIC

You decide to use the drawing graphic and need to remove the photograph. To do this, you select the graphic and delete it.

1

If necessary, click on the photograph to select it.

Press [Delete].

Your screen should be similar to Figure 2.10

Figure 2.10

The photograph is deleted from the worksheet.

APPLYING AND MODIFYING A PICTURE QUICK STYLE

Next, you want to enhance the graphic by applying a quick style to it.

Concept 2 Quick Style

A **quick style** is a named group of formatting characteristics that allows you to quickly apply a whole group of formats to a selection in one simple step. The formatting options associated with the different quick styles vary depending upon the type of object. For example, a line quick style may consist of a combination of color, shadows, gradients, and three-dimensional (3-D) perspectives options, whereas a shape quick style may consist of a combination of fill color, line color, and line weight options.

Many quick styles are automatically applied when certain features, such as charts, are used. Others must be applied manually to the selected object. You also can create your own custom styles.

Quick styles are available for cell selections as well as many different types of objects. Some of the most common are described in the following table.

Type of Quick Style	Description
Cell style	Affects selected cells by applying effects such as fill color, text and number formatting, and bold and underline formats.
Shape style	Affects all aspects of a shape object's appearance, including fill color, outline color, and other effects.
Chart style	Provides a consistent look to charts by applying color, shading, line, and font effects.
Picture style	Adds a border around a graphic object that consists of combinations of line, shadow, color, and shape effects.

You will use a picture quick style to add a border around the picture to make it stand out more. You also can create your own picture style effects by selecting specific style elements such as borders and shadow individually using the Picture Layout ▾, Picture Border ▾, and Picture Effects ▾ commands.

1

- Select the graphic.

- Click ▾ More in the Picture Styles group of the Format tab to open the Picture Styles gallery.

- Point to several styles to see the Live Preview.

Your screen should be similar to Figure 2.11

Figure 2.11

When you point to a style, the style name appears in a ScreenTip and the Live Preview shows how the selected picture style will look with your graphic. As you can see, many are not appropriate. However, you decide that the rotated style with a white border will enhance the graphic and the worksheet.

2

- Choose Rotated, White.

- Size and position the graphic as in Figure 2.12.

- Click outside the graphic to deselect the object.

Your screen should be similar to Figure 2.12

Figure 2.12

After seeing how the graphic looks with the selected picture style, you decide to modify the quick style by adding color to and changing the weight of the border.

3

- Click on the graphic to select it again.

- Click [✎ Picture Border ▾] in the Picture Styles group of the Format tab.

- Choose the Red, Accent2 color from the Theme Colors category.

- Click [✎ Picture Border ▾], select Weight, and choose 6 pt.

- Click outside the graphic to deselect the object.

- Document the workbook by adding your name as author and the workbook title of Sales Forecast

- Save the revised workbook as Cafe Sales Forecast to your solution file location.

Your screen should be similar to Figure 2.13

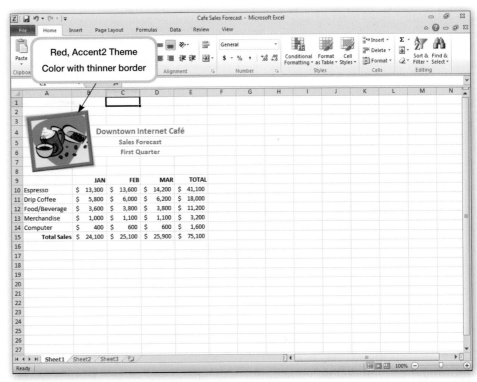

Figure 2.13

Using Themes

The addition of a graphic adds a nice touch to the worksheet title. Now, you want to continue to improve the worksheet appearance by selecting a different theme.

Concept **3** Theme

A **theme** is a set of formatting choices that can be applied to an entire workbook in one simple step. A theme consists of a set of theme colors, a set of theme fonts (including heading and body text fonts), and a set of theme effects (including line and fill effects). Excel includes 40 named built-in themes. Each theme includes three subsets of themes: colors, fonts, and effects. Each color theme consists of 12 colors that are applied to specific elements in a document. Each fonts theme includes different body and heading fonts. Each effects theme includes different line and fill effects. You also can create your own custom themes by modifying an existing document theme and saving it as a custom theme. The default workbook uses the Office theme. The font and fill colors and quick style effects that are available are determined by the current theme.

Using themes gives your documents a professional and modern look. Because themes are shared across Office 2010 applications, all your office documents can have the same uniform appearance.

APPLYING A THEME

You decide to see how the worksheet would look using a different theme.

1

Open the Page Layout tab.

Click [Aa] **from the Themes group.**

Your screen should be similar to Figure 2.14

Figure 2.14

A gallery of 40 built-in named themes is displayed. A sample shows the color and font effects included in each theme. The Office theme is highlighted because it is the default theme. Pointing to each theme will display a Live Preview of how it will appear in the worksheet.

2

- Point to several themes to preview them.

- Scroll through the selections and choose the Horizon theme.

Your screen should be similar to Figure 2.15

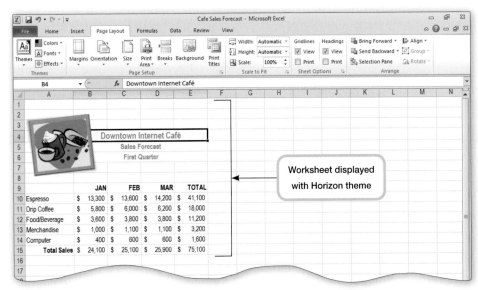

Figure 2.15

The formatting settings associated with the selected theme have been applied to the worksheet. Most noticeable is the color change of the picture border and titles. This is because the colors in the theme category have been updated to the Horizon theme colors. Consequently the available picture quick style colors and font colors have been updated to the new theme colors. Additionally, the font style used in the worksheet has changed from Calibri to Arial Narrow.

As you add other features to the worksheet, they will be formatted using the Horizon theme colors and effects. The same theme also has been applied to the other sheets in the workbook file.

CUSTOMIZING A THEME

Sometimes, you cannot find just the right combination of design elements in a built-in theme. To solve this problem, you can customize a theme by changing the color scheme, fonts, and effects. Although you like much of the Horizon theme design, you decide to try customizing the theme by changing the color scheme. Each theme has an associated set of colors that you can change by applying the colors from another theme to the selected theme.

1

- Click [icon] Colors ▾ Theme Colors in the Themes group.

Your screen should be similar to Figure 2.16

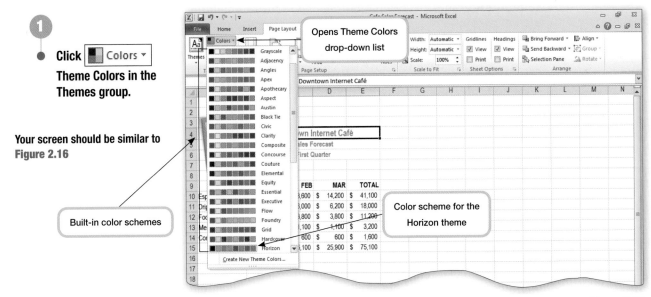

Figure 2.16

The colors used in each of the themes are displayed in the drop-down list. The set of eight colors that appears next to each theme color name represents the text, background, accent, and hyperlink colors. The Horizon color scheme is selected because it is the color scheme currently in use. Notice that the fourth color from the left in the Horizon color bar is the Accent2 color that is used in the picture border. Although you like that color, you think some of the other colors are drab. Instead, you want to see how the Metro color scheme would look.

2

• **Point to several color schemes to preview them.**

• **Choose the Metro theme color scheme.**

Your screen should be similar to Figure 2.17

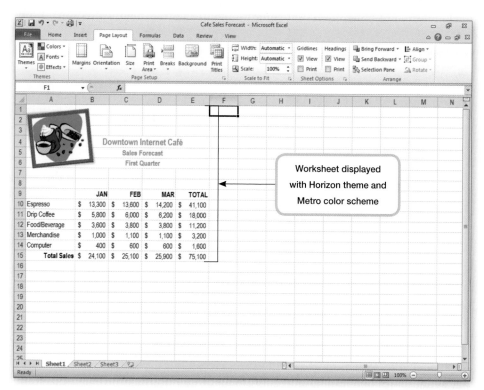

Figure 2.17

Additional Information

You can change the theme fonts and effects in a similar manner.

The new color scheme has been applied to the picture border and font color used in the worksheet titles. All other aspects of the Horizon theme are unchanged.

SAVING A CUSTOM THEME

Additional Information

Custom themes have the .thmx file extension, which identifies the file as an Office theme template file.

You decide to save the color change you have made to the Horizon theme as a custom theme. This will make it easy to reapply the same settings to another workbook in the future. Custom themes are saved in the Document Themes folder by default and are available in all Office applications that use themes.

1

Click .

Choose **Save Current Theme.**

Enter Horizon1 as the theme file name.

Click **Save**.

Having Trouble?

If an advisory message appears indicating this theme already exists, click **Yes** to replace it.

Click **Themes**.

Your screen should be similar to Figure 2.18

Figure 2.18

Additional Information

To remove a custom theme, choose Delete from the theme's shortcut menu.

The custom theme you created and saved appears at the top of the Themes gallery. Now you can quickly reapply this entire theme in one step to another workbook, just like the built-in themes, or to any other Office document.

Using Cell Styles

Next, you want to enhance the worksheet more by adding background cell shading to define areas of the worksheet, selecting heading styles for the title, and changing the format of the Food, Internet, and Merchandise values to display commas only, without dollar signs.

Although you could make these changes using individual formatting commands, a quicker way is to select a cell quick style. Excel includes 44 predefined cell styles, or you can create your own custom styles. Using cell styles allows you to apply several formats in one step and helps ensure that cells have consistent formatting. Cell styles are based on the theme that is applied to the entire workbook. When you switch to another theme, the cell styles are updated to match the new theme.

APPLYING THEMED CELL STYLES

First, you want to add background shading behind the entire worksheet.

- Select the range A1 through E15.

- Open the Home tab.

- Click 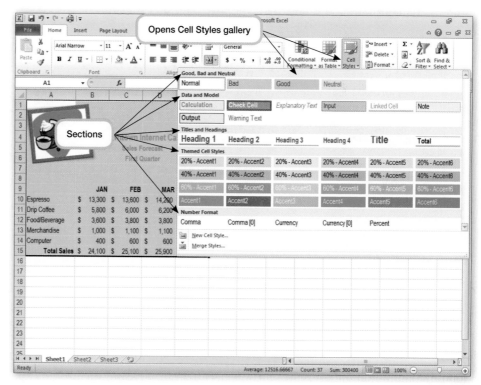 in the Styles group.

Your screen should be similar to Figure 2.19

Figure 2.19

The Cell Styles gallery is divided into five sections. The styles in each section are designed to identify different areas of a worksheet and types of cell entries, as explained in the following table:

Section	Identifies
Good, Bad and Neutral	Data trends or outcomes; for example, selecting Bad would be used to identify a bad outcome
Data and Model	Worksheet areas; for example, calculations and warning notes
Titles and Headings	Worksheet titles and headings
Themed Cell Styles	Basic worksheet data
Number Format	Number formats

You will use a cell style in the Themed Cell Styles section. These cell styles consist of background fill colors and either white or black text color. The colors are associated with the theme colors. Pointing to a cell style displays a Live Preview of the cell style.

2

- Point to several cell styles to see the Live Preview.

- Choose 40%—Accent3 in the Themed Cell Styles section.

- Click on the worksheet to clear the selection.

Your screen should be similar to Figure 2.20

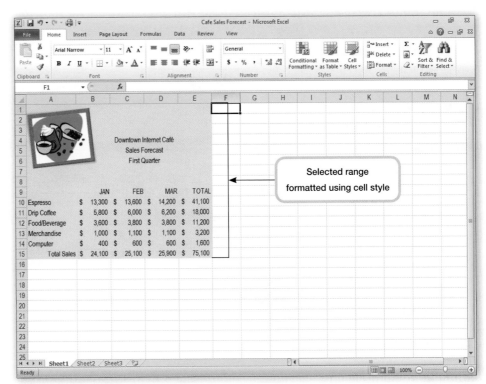

Figure 2.20

The selected range has been formatted using the selected cell style. It consists of a gold fill color for the cell background and black text in the theme font of Arial Narrow, 11 point. The green font color used in the titles was replaced with the font color associated with the cell style.

APPLYING HEADING AND TOTAL CELL STYLES

Next you will define the row headings area of the worksheet by selecting a different style from the Themed Cell Styles section. Then you will use two cell styles from the Titles and Headings section that will format the month column headings and the Total Sales row of data.

1

- Select A1 through A15.

- Click and choose the Accent1 style.

- Select cells A10 through A15 and make them bold.

- Select B9 through E9 and apply the Heading 3 cell style.

- Select A15 through E15 and apply the Total cell style.

- Click outside the selection to see the formatting changes.

Your screen should be similar to Figure 2.21

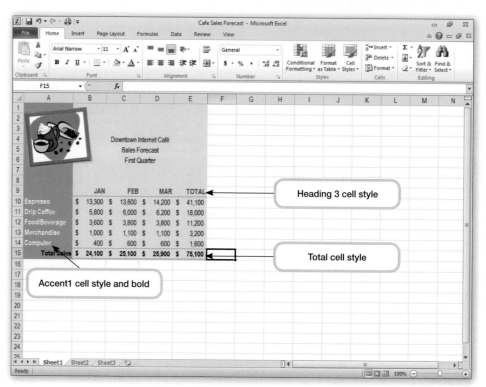

Figure 2.21

The Accent1 style uses a white font color with a green fill color. The Heading 3 style includes a gray font color and a bottom border. The Total cell style applies a black font color, bold text effect and a top and bottom border.

Next, you will add formatting to the worksheet titles by applying a Title style to the first title line, a Heading 1 style to the second line, and a Heading 2 style to the third line.

2

- Apply the Title cell style to cell B4.

- Apply the Heading 1 cell style to cell B5.

- Apply the Heading 2 cell style to cell B6.

- Click outside the selection to see the formatting changes.

- Resize and reposition the graphic as needed to show the full title text.

Your screen should be similar to Figure 2.22

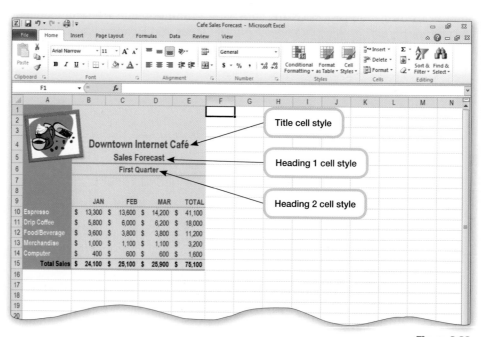

Figure 2.22

EX2.22   Lab 2: Enhancing the Worksheet with Graphics and Charts

WWW.MHHE.COM/OLEARY

MODIFYING CELL STYLES

Although you like the font size change and the colored bottom border line, you feel the titles could be improved by changing the font color to the same color as the fill color used in column A. Instead of changing the font color for each cell containing the titles, you will modify the cell styles so that the color changes to these styles will be easily available again.

1

- Click [Cell Styles] and right-click on the Title cell style.

- Choose Modify from the shortcut menu.

- Click [Format...] and open the Font tab.

- Open the Color gallery and choose Green, Accent1 from the Theme Colors category.

- Click [OK] twice.

- Modify the Heading 1 and Heading 2 cell styles in the same manner.

Your screen should be similar to Figure 2.23

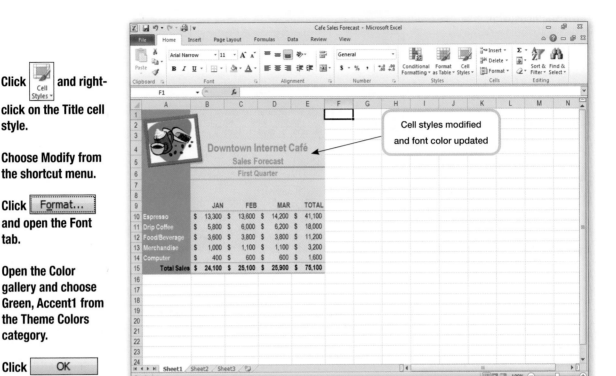

Figure 2.23

The three title lines have been updated to the new color associated with the three cell styles you modified. The changes to cell styles are saved with the current workbook file only.

APPLYING A NUMBER CELL STYLE

Additional Information

The Accounting number style with zero decimal places is the same as the Currency [0] cell style.

The final change you want to make is to change the format of some of the worksheet values. Currently all the values are formatted using the Accounting style with zero decimal places. The Cell Styles gallery also includes five predefined number format styles. Examples of the five predefined number styles are shown below.

Style	Example
Comma	89,522.00
Comma [0]	89,522
Currency	$ 89,522.00
Currency [0]	$ 89,522
Percent	89.52200%

You will use the Comma [0] style for the four middle rows of values.

1

- **Select B11 through E14.**
- **Open the Cell Styles gallery.**
- **Choose Comma [0].**
- **Clear the selection.**
- **Save the file.**

Additional Information

Using ⌐,⌐ Comma Style in the Number group applies the Comma number format with two decimal places.

Your screen should be similar to Figure 2.24

Figure 2.24

The Comma [0] style applies the Comma number format with zero decimal places and does not display a currency symbol. Using a style applies many formats in one easy step, making it quicker to apply formats to cells.

Creating Charts

Although the worksheet shows the sales data for each category, it is difficult to see how the different categories change over time. To make it easier to see the sales trends, you decide to create a chart of this data.

SELECTING THE CHART DATA

As you learned in Lab 1, a **chart** is a visual representation of data in a worksheet. Because all charts are drawn from data contained in a worksheet, the first step in creating a new chart is to select the worksheet range containing the data you want displayed as a chart plus any row or column headings you want used in the chart. Excel then translates the selected data into a chart based upon the shape and contents of the worksheet selection.

A chart consists of a number of parts or elements that are important to understand so that you can identify the appropriate data to select in the worksheet.

Chart elements are the different parts of a chart that are used to graphically display the worksheet data. The entire chart and all its elements is called the **chart area**.

The basic elements of a two-dimensional chart are described in the following table.

Element	Description
Plot area	Area within the X- and Y-axis boundaries where the chart data series appears.
Axis	The lines bordering the chart plot area used as a frame of reference for measurement. The **Y axis**, also called the **value axis**, is usually the vertical axis and contains data. The **X axis**, also called the **category axis**, is usually the horizontal axis and contains categories.
Data series	Related data points that are distinguished by different colors or patterns, called **data markers**, and displayed in the plot area.
Data labels	Labels that correspond to the data points that are plotted along the X axis.
Chart gridlines	Lines extending from the axis line across the plot area that make it easier to read the chart data.
Legend	A box that identifies the chart data series and data markers.
Chart title	A descriptive label displayed above the charted data that explains the contents of the chart.
Category-axis title	A descriptive label displayed along the X axis.
Value-axis title	A descriptive label displayed along the Y axis.

The basic parts of a two-dimensional chart are shown in the figure below.

3-D column, 3-D cone, or 3-D pyramid charts have a third axis, the **depth axis** (also known as the **series axis** or **Z axis**), so that data can be plotted along the depth of a chart. Radar charts do not have horizontal (category) axes, and pie and doughnut charts do not have any axes.

The first chart you want to create will show the total sales pattern over the three months. This chart will use the month headings in cells B9 through D9 to label the X axis. The numbers to be charted are in cells B15 through D15. In addition, the heading Total Sales in cell A15 will be used as the chart legend, making the entire range A15 through D15.

Notice that the two ranges, B9 through D9 and A14 through D14, are not adjacent and are not the same size. When plotting nonadjacent ranges in a chart, the selections must form a rectangular shape. To do this, you will include the blank cell A9 in the selection. You will specify the range and create the chart.

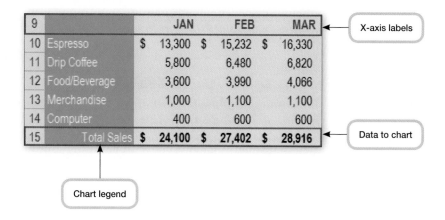

1
- Select cells A9 through D9.

- Hold down Ctrl.

- Select cells A15 through D15.

Your screen should be similar to Figure 2.25

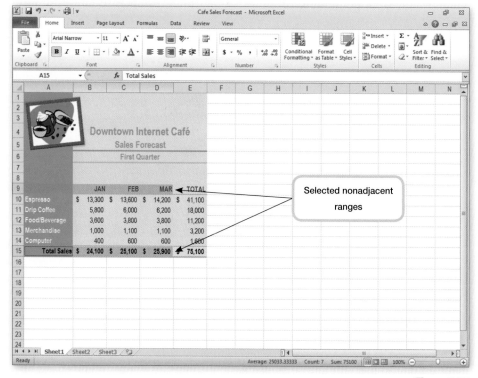

Figure 2.25

SELECTING THE CHART TYPE

The next step is to select the chart type. There are many different types of charts that can be used to convey the information in a worksheet in an attractive and easy-to-understand manner.

Concept 5 Chart Types

Different chart types are used to represent data in different ways. The type of chart you create depends on the type of data you are charting and the emphasis you want the chart to impart.

Excel 2010 can produce 14 standard types of graphs or charts, with many different subtypes for each standard type. In addition, Excel includes professionally designed, built-in custom charts that include additional formatting and chart refinements. The basic chart types and how they represent data are described in the following table.

Type	Description	Type	Description
	Area charts show the magnitude of change over time by emphasizing the area under the curve created by each data series.		**Radar charts** display a line or area chart wrapped around a central point. Each axis represents a set of data points.
	Bar charts display data as evenly spaced bars. The categories are displayed along the Y axis and the values are displayed horizontally, placing more emphasis on comparisons and less on time.		**XY (scatter) charts** are used to show the relationship between two ranges of numeric data.
	Column charts display data as evenly spaced bars. They are similar to bar charts, except that categories are organized horizontally and values vertically to emphasize variation over time.		**Surface charts** display values in a form similar to a rubber sheet stretched over a 3-D column chart. These are useful for finding the best combination between sets of data.
	Line charts display data along a line. They are used to show changes in data over time, emphasizing time and rate of change rather than the amount of change.		**Bubble charts** compare sets of three values. They are similar to a scatter chart with the third value displayed as the size of bubble markers.
	Pie charts display data as slices of a circle or pie. They show the relationship of each value in a data series to the series as a whole. Each slice of the pie represents a single value in the series.		**Stock charts** illustrate fluctuations in stock prices or scientific data. They require three to five data series that must be arranged in a specific order.
	Doughnut charts are similar to pie charts except that they can show more than one data series.		

Each type of chart includes many variations. The Charts group in the Insert tab contains commands to create the most commonly used types of charts. In addition, it includes the [Other Charts] button, which accesses the less commonly used charts. You also can open the Charts group dialog box to have access to all the available chart types. You think a column chart may best represent this data.

1

Open the Insert tab.

Click in the Charts group.

Your screen should be similar to Figure 2.26

Figure 2.26

Additional Information

3-D displays the data in a 3-D perspective. This is different from a 3-D chart that has a third axis.

The column chart gallery contains five categories of column charts. From within the categories you can choose clustered, stacked, 100% stacked, and 3-D. You decide to use the two-dimensional clustered column. An enhanced ScreenTip containing a description of the selected column chart type displays as you point to each chart type.

2

Click

Clustered Column from the 2-D Column category.

Your screen should be similar to Figure 2.27

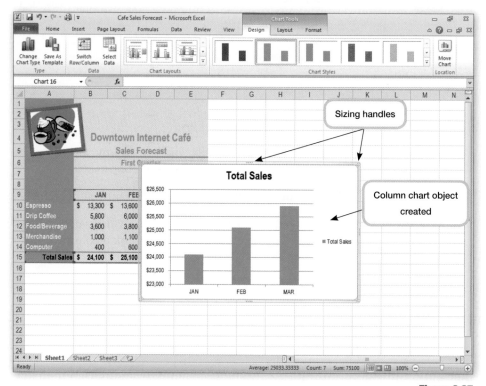

Figure 2.27

The column chart is created using the data from the worksheet and displayed as a chart object in the worksheet.

Concept 6 Chart Object

A **chart object** is a graphic object that is created using charting features. A chart object can be inserted into a worksheet or into a special chart sheet. By default, Excel inserts the chart object into the worksheet. Charts that are inserted into a worksheet are embedded objects. An **embedded chart** becomes part of the sheet in which it is inserted and is saved as part of the worksheet when you save the workbook file. Like all graphic objects, an embedded chart object can be sized and moved in a worksheet. A worksheet can contain multiple charts.

A chart that is inserted into a separate chart sheet also is saved with the workbook file. Only one chart can be added to a chart sheet, and it cannot be sized or moved.

Excel decides which data series to plot along the X and Y axes based on the type of chart selected and the number of rows and columns defined in the series. The worksheet data range that has the greater number of rows or columns appears along the X axis, and the smaller number is charted as the Y data series. When the data series is an equal number of rows and columns, as it is in this case, the default is to plot the rows. The first row defines the X-axis category labels and the second row the plotted data. The content of the first cell in the second row is used as the chart title and legend text.

MOVING AND SIZING A CHART

Notice that the new chart is on top of the worksheet data. As objects are added to the worksheet, they automatically **stack** in individual layers. The stacking order is apparent when objects overlap. Stacking allows you to create different effects by overlapping objects. Because you can rearrange the stacking order, you do not have to add or create the objects in the order in which you want them to appear.

First you want to move the chart so that it is displayed to the right of the worksheet data. In addition, you want to increase the size of the chart. A chart is moved by dragging the chart border and sized just like a graphic object. The sizing handles of a chart object are the dots that appear in the center and corners of the selected chart's border. If you hold down [Alt] while dragging to move and size a chart object, the chart automatically snaps into position or aligns with the closest worksheet cell when you release the mouse button. Release the mouse button before you release [Alt].

1

• **Point to the chart border and drag the chart object so the upper-left corner is in cell F1.**

• **Point to the bottom-center sizing handle, hold down Alt, and drag the chart border line down until it is even with the bottom of row 15.**

Your screen should be similar to Figure 2.28

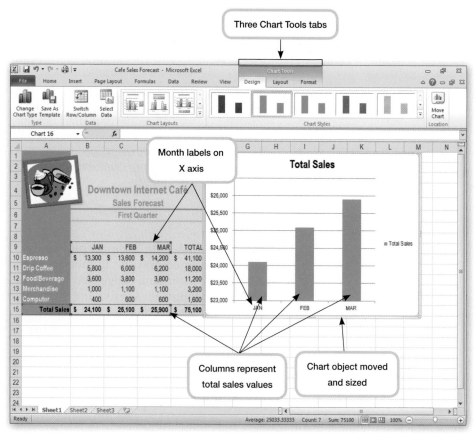

Three Chart Tools tabs

Month labels on X axis

Columns represent total sales values

Chart object moved and sized

Figure 2.28

Additional Information

Dragging a side handle does not maintain the scale.

It is now easy to see how the worksheet data you selected is represented in the chart. Each column represents a value or data point in the data series (row 15) and provides a visual representation of the total sales for each month. The month labels in row 9 have been used to label the X-axis category labels. The range or scale of values along the Y axis is determined from the data in the worksheet. The upper limit is the maximum value in the worksheet rounded upward to the next highest interval. The row label in cell A15 is the chart title.

Three new Chart Tools tabs appear on the Ribbon to help you modify the chart. The Design tab contains options to change the chart orientation, redefine the source data, and change the chart location or type. The Layout tab commands are used to change the display of chart elements by modifying or adding features such as chart titles, text boxes, callout lines, and pictures. The Format tab is used to add embellishments such as fill colors and special effects to the chart.

APPLYING CHART LAYOUTS

Next, you want to improve the appearance of the chart. To help you do this quickly, Excel includes many predefined chart layouts (also called quick layouts) and quick styles from which you can select. First, you want to change the chart layout. A **chart layout** is a predefined set of chart elements that can be quickly applied to a chart. The elements include chart titles, a legend, a data table, or data labels. These elements are displayed in a specific arrangement in the chart. Each chart type includes a variety of layouts. You can then modify or customize these layouts further to meet your needs. However, the custom layouts cannot be saved.

To see the different chart layouts for a column chart, you will open the chart layout gallery.

EX2.30   Lab 2: Enhancing the Worksheet with Graphics and Charts

WWW.MHHE.COM/OLEARY

Excel 2010

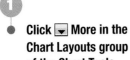

1

● Click ⏷ More in the
Chart Layouts group
of the Chart Tools
Design tab.

Additional Information

The three chart layouts shown in the
Ribbon are the most recently selected
chart layouts.

**Your screen should be similar to
Figure 2.29**

Layout 1 is default
column chart layout

Design tab is open

Figure 2.29

The chart layout gallery displays the 11 chart layouts for a column chart. The
default chart layout is Layout 1. Since this chart contains only three columns,
you decide to try Layout 10 because it shows a chart with wider columns and
data labels.

2

● Choose

Layout 10.

**Your screen should be similar to
Figure 2.30**

Chart Layout 10 applied

Default chart style

Data values displayed

Wider columns

Figure 2.30

The columns are now wider and include the data values.

APPLYING CHART STYLES

Next, you want to change the color of the columns to further enhance the chart. Although you could manually format the chart elements individually, it is quicker to use a chart quick style. The available chart styles are based on the document theme that has been applied. This ensures that the formats you apply to the chart will coordinate with the worksheet formatting. The chart styles use the same colors, fonts, line, and fill effects that are defined in the theme.

The default chart style is selected in the Chart Styles group in the Ribbon. You want to see all available choices.

● **Click ▾ More in the Chart Styles group.**

Your screen should be similar to Figure 2.31

Figure 2.31

The gallery of chart styles consists of 48 sample designs that include different color columns, background shadings, column shapes, and three-dimensional effects. You want to change the column color and add background shading to the plot area.

2

● Choose

Style 38.

Your screen should be similar to
Figure 2.32

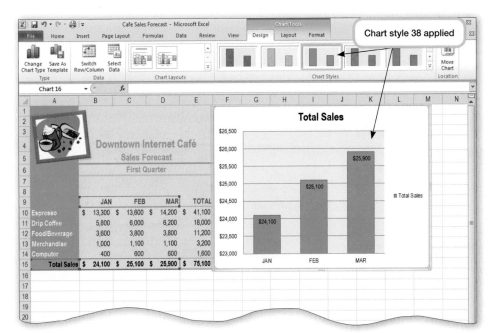

Figure 2.32

The columns are blue with a shaded background in the plot area.

ADDING AND REMOVING CHART LABELS

Finally, you want to clarify the data in the chart by adding labels along both
chart axes, removing the legend, and adding a more descriptive chart title. The
Labels group on the Layout tab contains options to add and remove chart labels.

You will start by adding titles along the X and Y axes. By default, the X- and
Y-axis titles do not display.

1

● Open the Chart Tools
Layout tab.

● In the Labels group,

click [Axis Titles].

● Select Primary
Horizontal Axis Title.

● Choose Title Below
Axis.

Your screen should be similar to
Figure 2.33

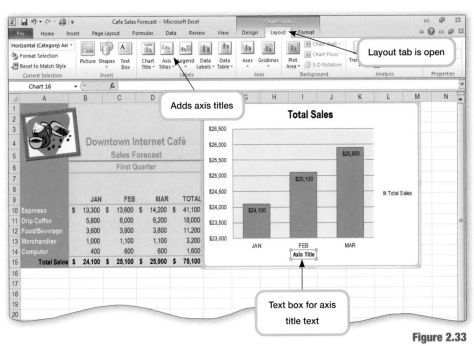

Figure 2.33

A title text box is inserted below the X-axis. It is a selected object and displays
the sample text, Axis Title. A **text box** is a graphic element that is a container
for specific types of information. In this case, it is designed to contain text for
the axis title. You will replace the sample text with the axis title.

To replace all the text in a text box, simply select the text box and type the new text. You also can edit text in a text box using the same features that are used to edit a cell entry.

2

Type Months

Click anywhere on the chart to deselect the text box.

Your screen should be similar to Figure 2.34

Figure 2.34

All the sample text in the text box was replaced by the text you typed. Next, you will add a title to the Y axis.

3

Click 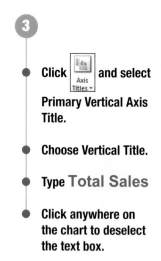 **and select Primary Vertical Axis Title.**

Choose Vertical Title.

Type Total Sales

Click anywhere on the chart to deselect the text box.

Your screen should be similar to Figure 2.35

Figure 2.35

You decide the Y-axis title text would look better if it were rotated.

4

● **Click** .

● **Select Primary Vertical Axis Title.**

● **Choose Rotated Title.**

Your screen should be similar to Figure 2.36

Title rotated

Figure 2.36

The titles clearly describe the information displayed in the chart. Now, because there is only one data range and the category title fully explains this data, you decide to remove the display of the legend.

5

● **Click** 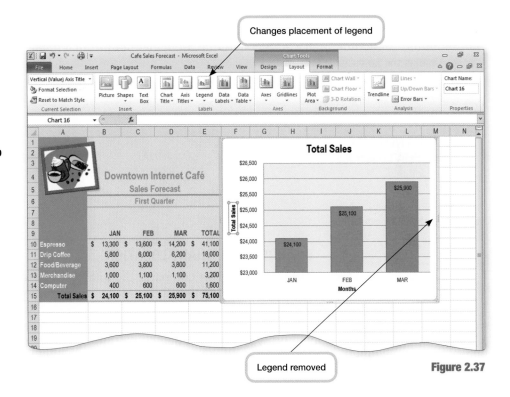 **and choose None.**

Your screen should be similar to Figure 2.37

Changes placement of legend

Legend removed

Figure 2.37

The legend is removed and the chart area resized to occupy the extra space. All chart labels can be removed in the same manner.

Finally, you want to add a more descriptive title to the chart and improve its appearance. The ⬚ button changes the location of the title on the chart, but the default selection of Above Chart works well. You just need to change the text, which you can do by editing and formatting the text in the text box. When you point to different areas in the chart, a chart ScreenTip appears that identifies the chart element that will be affected by your action.

6

- **Point to the chart title to see the ScreenTip.**

- **Click on the chart title to select it.**

- **Double click on the word "Total" to select it and type Downtown Internet Cafe**

- **Select all the text in the text box and point to the Mini toolbar.**

Additional Information

The Mini toolbar appears automatically when you select text and is dim until you point to it.

- **Change the font size to 16 and the font color to Turquoise, Accent 4.**

- **Click anywhere in the chart to clear the selection.**

Your screen should be similar to Figure 2.38

Figure 2.38

CHANGING THE CHART LOCATION

Although this chart compares the total sales for the three months, you decide you are more interested in seeing a comparison for the sales categories. You could delete this chart simply by pressing [Delete] while the chart area is selected. Instead, however, you will move it to a separate worksheet in case you want to refer to it again.

- Open the Chart Tools Design tab.

- Click 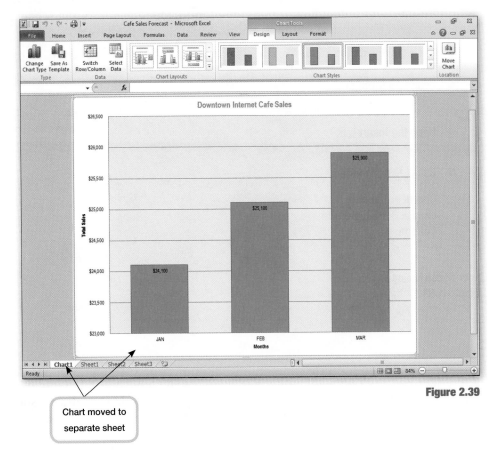 in the Location group.

- Choose New sheet.

- Click **OK**.

- Save the workbook.

Your screen should be similar to Figure 2.39

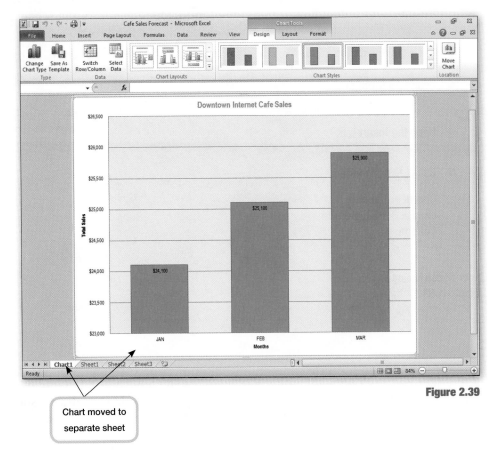

Chart moved to separate sheet

Figure 2.39

The column chart is now an object displayed in a separate chart sheet. Generally, you display a chart in a chart sheet when you want the chart displayed separately from the associated worksheet data. The chart is still automatically linked to the worksheet data from which it was created. The new chart sheet, named Chart1, was inserted to the left of the worksheet, Sheet1. The chart sheet is the active sheet, or the sheet in which you are currently working.

Additional Information

You also can create a chart using the default chart type (column) in a new chart sheet by selecting the data range and pressing F11.

Creating a Multiple Data Series Chart

Now you are ready to continue your analysis of sales trends. You want to create a second chart to display the sales data for each category for the three months. You could create a separate chart for each category and then compare the charts; however, to make the comparisons between the categories easier, you will display all the categories on a single chart.

The data for the three months for the four categories is in cells B10 through D14. The month headings (X-axis data series) are in cells B9 through D9, and the legend text is in the range A10 through A14.

1

● Click the **Sheet1** tab.

● Select **A9** through **D14**.

● Open the **Insert** tab.

● Click from the **Charts group** and choose **3-D Clustered Column.**

Your screen should be similar to Figure 2.40

Figure 2.40

A three-dimensional column chart is drawn showing the monthly sales for each category. A different column color identifies each data series, and the legend identifies the categories. When plotting the data for this chart, Excel plotted the three months as the data series because the data range has fewer columns than rows. This time, however, you want to change the data series so that the months are along the X axis.

2

● Click [Switch Row/Column] in the **Data group** of the **Chart Tools Design tab.**

Your screen should be similar to Figure 2.41

Figure 2.41

The chart is redrawn with the new orientation. The column chart now compares the sales by month rather than by category. The legend displays the names of the sales categories.

Next, you will specify the chart titles and finish the chart.

3

- Change the chart style to Style 18.

- Change the chart layout to Layout 9.

- Replace the axis and title text box sample text with the titles shown below:

Title	Entry
Chart title	Sales Forecast
Horizontal Axis	Months
Vertical Axis	Sales

- Move and size the chart until it covers cells F2 through L15.

Figure 2.42

Your screen should be similar to Figure 2.42

The column chart shows that sales in all categories are increasing, with the greatest increase occurring in espresso sales.

CHANGING THE DATA SOURCE

As you look at the chart, you see that the Merchandise and Computer sales values are inconsequential to the forecast because they are so small and do not change much. You will remove these data series from the chart.

1

● Click in the Data group.

Your screen should be similar to Figure 2.43

Opens Select Data Source dialog box

Removes selected data series

Current chart data series

Figure 2.43

In the Select Data Source dialog box, you can change the chart data range, switch the row and column orientation, and add, edit, and remove specific data series. You will remove the Merchandise and Computer data series.

2

● Select the Merchandise series name and click ✗ Remove.

● Select the Computer series name and click ✗ Remove.

● Click OK.

Your screen should be similar to Figure 2.44

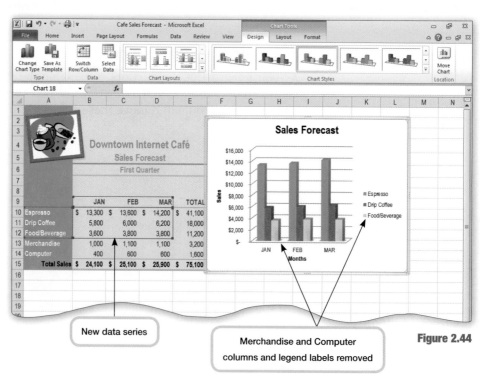

New data series

Merchandise and Computer columns and legend labels removed

Figure 2.44

The columns representing the Merchandise and Computer series were removed from the chart along with the legend labels. The new chart data series is identified in the worksheet.

CHANGING THE CHART TYPE: LINE, BAR, AREA, STACKED

Next, you would like to see how the same data displayed in the column chart would look as a line chart. A line chart displays data as a line and is commonly used to show trends over time. You can change the chart type easily using the button on the Design tab.

1

Click in the Type group.

Your screen should be similar to Figure 2.45

Figure 2.45

The Change Chart Type box displays all the available chart types. The current selection, Clustered Column, is highlighted. You want to change it to a line chart.

2

Choose Line with Markers.

Click **OK**.

Your screen should be similar to Figure 2.46

Figure 2.46

The line chart shows the sales trends from month to month. Notice the chart layouts and chart styles in the Ribbon reflect layouts and styles that are available for line charts.

You do not find this chart very interesting, so you will change it to a 3-D bar chart next.

3

Click 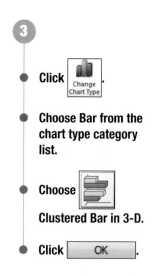.

Choose Bar from the chart type category list.

Choose [Clustered Bar in 3-D icon] Clustered Bar in 3-D.

Click [OK].

Your screen should be similar to Figure 2.47

Figure 2.47

The 3-D bar chart reverses the X and Y axes and displays the data series as three-dimensional bars. As you can see, it is very easy to change the chart type and format after the data series are specified. The same data can be displayed in many different ways. Depending upon the emphasis you want the chart to make, a different chart style can be selected.

Although the 3-D bar chart shows the sales trends for the three months for the sales categories, again it does not look very interesting. You decide to look at several other chart types to see whether you can improve the appearance. First you would like to see the data represented as an area chart. An area chart represents data the same way a line chart does, but, in addition, it shades the area below each line to emphasize the degree of change.

4

Click 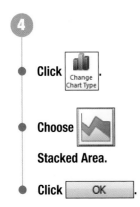.

Choose [icon] **Stacked Area.**

Click [OK].

Your screen should be similar to
Figure 2.48

Area chart layouts and styles

Y scale begins at 0

Area chart shows proportion each
category contributes to total sales

Figure 2.48

The Y-axis scale has changed to reflect the new range of data. The new Y-axis
range is the sum of the four categories or the same as the total number in the
worksheet. Using this chart type, you can see the magnitude of change that
each category contributes to the total sales each month.

Again, you decide that this is not the emphasis you want to show and will continue looking at other types of charts. You want to see how this data will look as
a stacked-column chart. You also can double-click a chart type to select it.

5

Click [Change Chart Type].

Double-click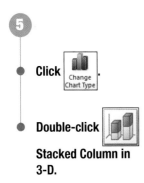
**Stacked Column in
3-D.**

Your screen should be similar to
Figure 2.49

Stacked column layouts and styles

Stacked column chart shows proportion of each
sales category to total sales for each month

Figure 2.49

The chart is redrawn showing the data as a **stacked-column chart**. This type of chart also shows the proportion of each sales category to the total sales.

Although this chart is interesting, you feel that the data is difficult to read and want to see how the data will be represented in several other chart types.

6

- Choose several other chart types to see how the data appears in the chart.

- Change the chart to Clustered Cylinder in the Column category.

Your screen should be similar to Figure 2.50

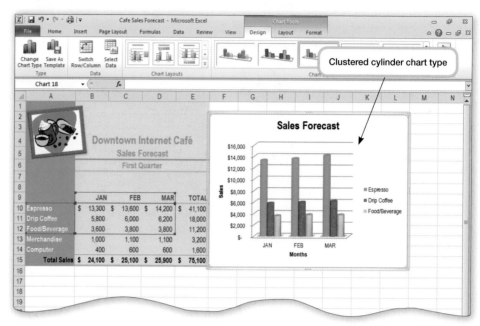

Figure 2.50

You like both the appearance of the clustered cylinders and how the data is represented.

MOVING THE LEGEND

While looking at the chart, you decide to move the legend below the X axis.

1

- Open the Chart Tools Layout tab.

- Click in the Labels group.

- Choose Show Legend at Bottom.

Your screen should be similar to Figure 2.51

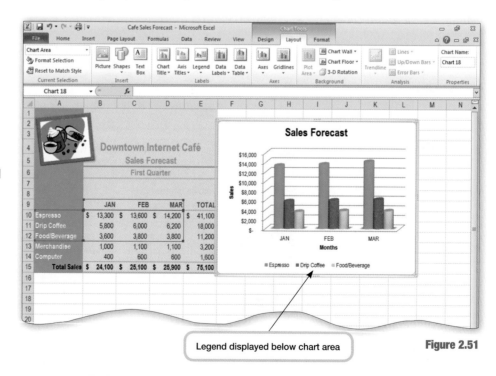

Legend displayed below chart area

Figure 2.51

The legend appears below the plot area of the chart.

FORMATTING CHART ELEMENTS

Next, you want to further improve the appearance of the chart by applying additional formatting to the chart titles. The chart is an object made up of many different objects or chart elements. Each element of a chart can be enhanced individually to create your own custom style chart. Because a chart consists of many separate objects, it is a group.

Concept **7** Group

A **group** is two or more objects that behave as a single object when moved or sized. A chart is a group that consists of many separate objects. For example, the chart title is a single object within the chart object. Some of the objects in a chart are also groups that consist of other objects. For example, the legend is a group object consisting of separate items, each identifying a different data series.

Other objects in a chart are the axis lines, a data series, a data marker, the entire plot area, or the entire chart.

There are several methods you can use to select chart elements. One as you have learned, is to click on the element. To help you select the correct chart element, the element name displays when you point to a chart element. Another method is to select the element from the [Chart Area ▾] drop-down list in the Format tab. Finally, you also can use the arrow keys located on the numeric keypad or the directional keypad to cycle from one element to another. The keyboard directional keys used to select chart elements are described in the following table.

Press	To
↓	Select the previous group of elements in a chart.
↑	Select the next group of elements in a chart.
→	Select the next element within a group.
←	Select the previous element within a group.
Esc	Cancel a selection.
Tab ⇄	Select the next object or shape in the chart.
Shift + Tab ⇄	Select the previous object or shape in the chart.

There are also several different methods you can use to format chart elements. These methods will be demonstrated as you add formatting to the chart.

The first formatting change you want to make is to increase the font size and add color to the chart title.

1

- **Right-click on the chart title to select it and open the shortcut menu.**

- **From the Mini toolbar, choose Tahoma as the font type.**

- **Change the font size to 20.**

- **Select the Gold, Accent 3, Darker 25% theme font color.**

Your screen should be similar to Figure 2.52

Figure 2.52

Your formatting selections were applied to all the text in the selected object.

Next, you want to add a subtitle below the main title. It will be in a smaller font size and italicized. You also can select individual sections of text in an object and apply formatting to them just as you would format any other text entry.

2

● Click at the end of the title to place the cursor.

● Press ⏎Enter.

● Type **First Quarter**

● Triple-click on the second title line to select it.

● Use the Mini toolbar to italicize the selection.

● Change the font size to 14.

● Apply the Gold, Accent 3, Darker 50% theme color to the subtitle.

● In a similar manner, apply the Gold, Accent 3, Darker 50% theme color to the axis titles.

● Click anywhere in the chart to clear the selection.

Your screen should be similar to Figure 2.53

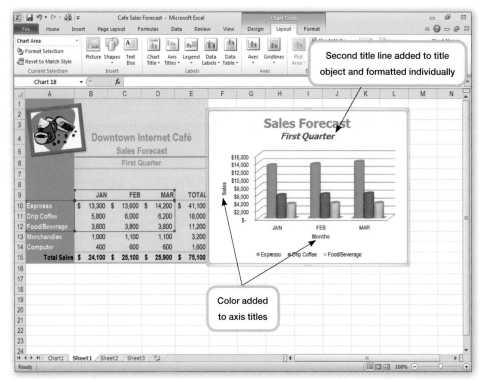

Figure 2.53

Next, you decide to add some formatting enhancements to the chart walls and floor.

③

● Open the

| Chart Area | ▼ |

Chart Elements drop-down list in the Current Selection group.

● **Choose Back Wall.**

● **Click**

| 🖌 Format Selection |

in the Current Selection group.

Your screen should be similar to Figure 2.54

Figure 2.54

From the Format Wall dialog box, you can change the wall fill colors, outside border, and style, and add shadow, 3-D format, and rotation effects. Fill is the currently selected category and shows that the fill colors use the default fill settings that were automatically set by Excel. You decide to add a gradient fill to the background and a solid line around the chart wall. A **gradient** is a gradual progression of colors and shades that can be from one color to another or from one shade to another of the same color. Excel includes several preset colors that include combinations of gradient fills.

- **Choose Gradient Fill.**

- **Open the Preset Colors gallery and choose Daybreak.**

- **Open the Direction gallery and choose** **Linear Diagonal—Top Right to Bottom Left (top row, option 3).**

- **Choose Border Color from the category list and choose Solid line.**

- **Click** Close .

Your screen should be similar to Figure 2.55

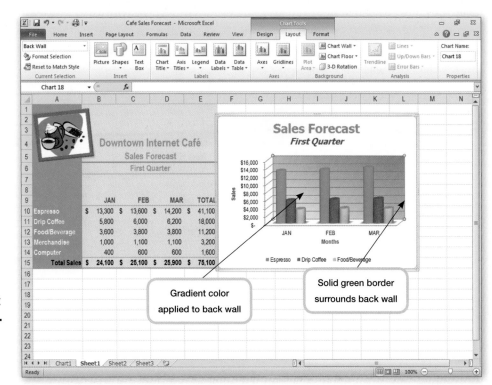

Figure 2.55

Another Method

You also could use in the Background group of the Layout tab and choose More Walls Options. This option formats both the back and side walls at the same time.

Next, you will format the side wall and floor using a solid fill color with a slight transparency.

5

● **Press ← to select the chart side wall.**

● **Click** 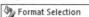 **.**

● **Choose Solid Fill, and select the Light Blue, Background 2, Darker 25% fill color.**

● **Increase the Transparency to 40%.**

● **Click on the chart floor to select it.**

● **Change the chart floor to the same color and transparency as the side wall.**

● **Click Close .**

Your screen should be similar to Figure 2.56

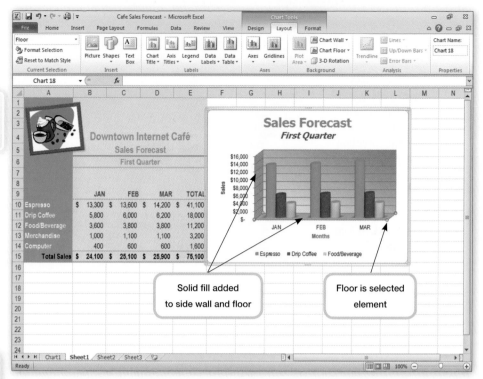

Figure 2.56

The last formatting change you will make is to modify the border line around the entire chart object.

6

● Click on the chart area (the white background) to select the entire chart.

● Open the Format tab.

● Click

[✏ Shape Outline ▼]

in the Shape Styles group.

● Select Weight and choose 2¼ points.

● Click

[✏ Shape Outline ▼]

and choose the Green, Accent 1, Darker 25% theme color.

● Click outside the chart to deselect it.

Your screen should be similar to Figure 2.57

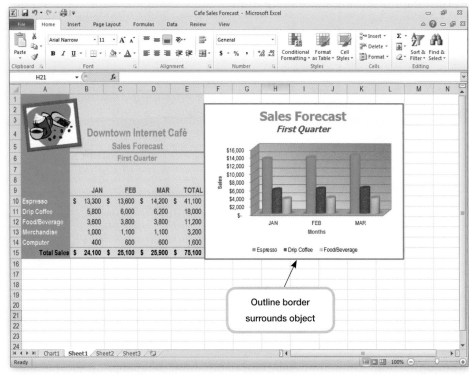

Figure 2.57

You have modified and enhanced many of the chart elements individually, creating a unique, professional-looking chart.

ADDING DATA LABELS

Finally, to make sure that Evan sees your projected increase in espresso and coffee sales, you will include data labels containing the actual numbers plotted on the column chart.

Concept ⑧ Data Labels

Data labels provide additional information about a data point in the data series. They can consist of the value of the point, the name of the data series or category, a percent value, or a bubble size. The different types of data labels that are available depend on the type of chart and the data that is plotted.

Value data labels are helpful when the values are large and you want to know the exact value for one data series. Data labels that display a name are helpful when the size of the chart is large and when the data point does not clearly identify the value. The percent data label is used when you want to display the percent of each series on charts that show parts of the whole. Bubble size is used on bubble charts to help the reader quickly see how the different bubbles vary in size.

You want to display the Espresso and Drip Coffee values as data labels for the three months.

1

● Click on any Espresso data column to select the series.

● Right-click the selection and choose **Add Data Labels**.

● Add data labels for the Drip Coffee sales.

Your screen should be similar to **Figure 2.58**

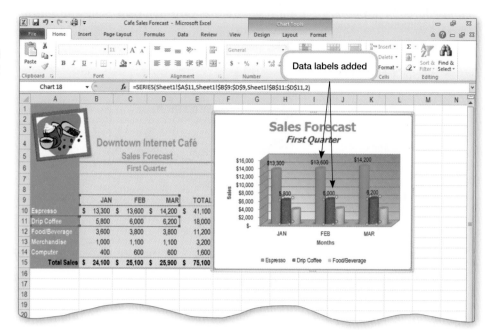

Figure 2.58

Another Method

You also could use [Data Labels] in the Chart Tools Layout tab to add data labels.

Data labels containing the actual values for Espresso and Drip Coffee sales are displayed above the appropriate sales columns on the chart. They use the same formatting as the values in the worksheet.

Data labels, like other chart elements, can be further enhanced by adding fill colors, shadows, 3-D effects, lines, and text orientation to the data label. You will use this feature to add the currency symbol to the Drip Coffee data label so the format matches the Espresso labels.

2

● Right-click on the Drip Coffee data labels and choose **Format Data Labels** from the shortcut menu.

● Select the Number category and choose **Accounting**.

● Reduce the decimal places to 0.

● Click [Close].

Your screen should be similar to **Figure 2.59**

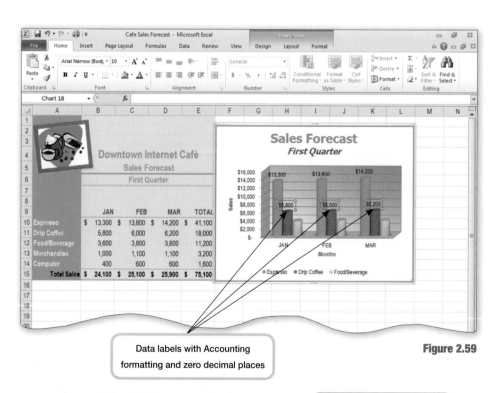

Data labels with Accounting formatting and zero decimal places

Figure 2.59

Next, you will reposition all the data labels so that they appear to the right of each column. Each data label needs to be selected and moved individually.

3

● **Click on the January Drip Coffee data label to select it and drag to position it as in Figure 2.60.**

Having Trouble?

To select an individual data label, first click on a data label to select the entire series, and then click on the individual label.

● **In the same manner, select the February and March Drip Coffee data labels and drag to position them as in Figure 2.60.**

● **Select each Espresso data label and drag to position it as in Figure 2.60.**

Your screen should be similar to Figure 2.60

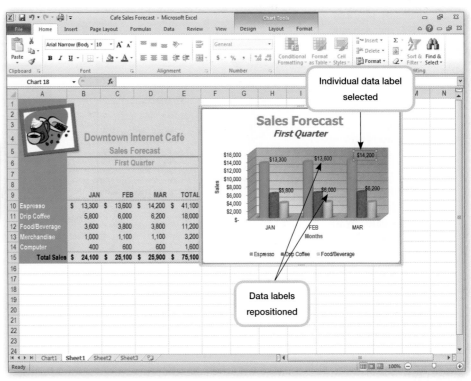

Figure 2.60

The data labels are positioned to the top right of each column.

Additional Information

You can delete individual data labels or the entire series by selecting the data label or series and pressing [Delete] or choosing Delete from the shortcut menu.

CHANGING WORKSHEET DATA

So far, the charts you have created reflect your original sales estimates for the quarter. You are planning to heavily promote the new Internet aspect of the Café and anticipate that Espresso, Drip Coffee, and Food/Beverage sales in February and March will increase dramatically and then level off in the following months. You want to change the worksheet to reflect these increases.

1 Increase the February and March Espresso sales by 12% and 15%, respectively.

Having Trouble?

Change the entry to a formula by inserting an = sign at the beginning of the entry and then multiply by 1 + increase; for example, a 12 percent increase in the February Espresso sales is =13600*1.12.

1 Increase the February and March Drip Coffee sales by 8% and 10%.

1 Increase the February and March Food/Beverage sales by 5% and 7%.

Figure 2.61

Your screen should be similar to Figure 2.61

The worksheet has been recalculated, and the chart columns that reference those worksheet cells have been redrawn to reflect the change in the sales data. Because the chart is linked to the source data, changes to the source data are automatically reflected in the chart. Likewise, the values in the data labels reflect the revised data.

2 Move the chart to its own chart sheet.

2 Make Sheet1 active again.

2 Save the workbook.

Creating and Formatting a Pie Chart

The last chart you will create will use the Total worksheet data in column E. You want to see what proportion each type of sales is of total sales for the quarter. The best chart for this purpose is a pie chart.

A pie chart compares parts to the whole in a similar manner to a stacked-column chart. However, pie charts have no axes. Instead, the worksheet data that is charted is displayed as slices in a circle or pie. Each slice is displayed as a percentage of the total.

SELECTING THE PIE CHART DATA

The use of X (category) and data series settings in a pie chart is different from their use in a column or line chart. The X series labels the slices of the pie rather than the X axis. The data series is used to create the slices in the pie. Only one data series can be specified in a pie chart.

The row labels in column A will label the slices, and the total values in column E will be used as the data series.

1

- Select A10 through A14 and E10 through E14.

Having Trouble?

Hold down Ctrl while selecting nonadjacent ranges.

- Open the Insert tab.

- Click and

- choose Pie in 3-D.

- Move and size the pie chart to be displayed over cells F1 through L15.

Additional Information

Hold down Alt while sizing to snap the chart to the cells.

Your screen should be similar to Figure 2.62

Figure 2.62

A three-dimensional pie chart is drawn in the worksheet. Each value in the data series is displayed as a slice of the pie chart. The size of the slice represents the proportion of total sales that each sales category represents.

ADDING TITLES AND DATA LABELS

To clarify the meaning of the chart, you need to add a chart title. In addition, you want to remove the legend and display data labels to label the slices of the pie instead. You will take a look at the predefined chart layouts to see if there is a layout that will accomplish all these things in one step.

● **Click** ⬇ **More in the Charts Layout group of the Design tab.**

● **Choose Layout 1.**

Your screen should be similar to Figure 2.63

Figure 2.63

The legend has been removed and replaced with data labels that display the category name and the percentage each category is of total sales. The data labels display the category name on a separate line from the value and, if needed, include a leader line to identify the associated wedge. Also, a chart title text box has been added to the pie chart.

Next, you will add a title and then you will improve the appearance of the data labels by adding a gradient fill to them.

2

- Enter the chart title **Total Sales by Category**

- Add the subtitle **First Quarter**

- Change the first title line to Tahoma with the Gold, Accent 3, Darker 25% color.

- Change the subtitle line to Tahoma, 14 pt, with the Gold, Accent 3, Darker 50% color, and italic.

- Click on one of the data labels to select the data label series.

- Choose Format Data Labels from the context menu.

- Uncheck the Show Leader Lines box in the Label Contains area.

- Choose the Fill category and choose Gradient Fill.

- Move the dialog box to see the chart.

Your screen should be similar to Figure 2.64

Figure 2.64

The default gradient fill has been added to each data label. You want to change the fill to a gradient fill composed of two colors. Currently the gradient fill consists of a range of light blue fading to white. The Gradient stops bar shows this gradient fill is made of four "**stops**," or specific points where the blending of two adjacent colors in the gradient ends. The Stop 1 fill color of blue is already correctly specified. You will change the Stop 2 color to green.

Click on Stop 2 on the Gradient stops bar.

• Click Color and choose Green, Accent 1, Lighter 60%.

• Click Close .

Your screen should be similar to Figure 2.65

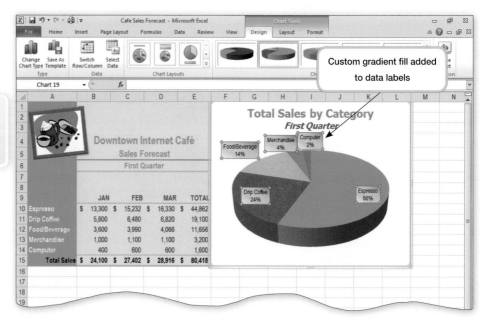

Figure 2.65

The data labels now include a gradient fill background that coordinates well with the chart colors.

The pie chart clearly shows the percent each category is of the total sales. The industry standard for a successful espresso café generates 60 percent of sales from espresso-based drinks. With your suggested advertising campaign, your sales forecast is very close to this standard.

EXPLODING AND ROTATING THE PIE

Next, you want to separate slightly or **explode** the slices of the pie to emphasize the data in the categories.

1

• **Right-click the pie chart and choose Change Series Chart Type.**

• **Choose** **Exploded Pie in 3-D.**

• **Click** OK .

Your screen should be similar to Figure 2.66

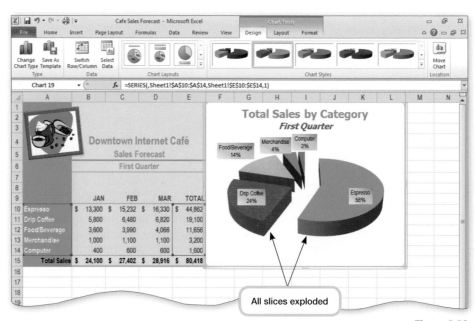

Figure 2.66

All slices are exploded from the center of the pie chart. However, you do not like how this looks. Instead, you decide you only want to explode the Espresso slice to give emphasis to the increase in sales in that category.

2

- Click 🔄 **Undo** to cancel your last action.

- Select the Espresso slice.

- Choose **Format Data Point** from the context menu.

Having Trouble?

If Format Data Point is not displayed, the slice is not selected. Double-click on the slice to select it and open the Format Data Point dialog box.

Your screen should be similar to Figure 2.67

Figure 2.67

Notice that the formula bar displays a **series formula**. A series formula links the chart object to the source worksheet, in this case, Sheet1. The formula contains four arguments: a reference to the cell that includes the data series name (used in the legend), references to the cells that contain the categories (X-axis numbers), references to the numbers plotted, and an integer that specifies the number of data series plotted.

The Format Data Point dialog box has options to rotate the pie and control the amount of explosion of the slices. You want to rotate the pie approximately 330 degrees so that the Espresso slice is more to the right side of the pie. When a pie chart is created, the first data point is placed to the right of the middle at the top of the chart. The rest of the data points are placed in order to the right until the circle is complete. To change the angle of the first slice, you rotate the pie chart. Then you will explode the Espresso slice.

• **Drag the slider to increase the Angle of first slice to 330 degrees.**

• **Increase the Point Explosion to 10%.**

• **Click** [Close].

Another Method

You also can drag a slice away from the pie to explode it.

Your screen should be similar to Figure 2.68

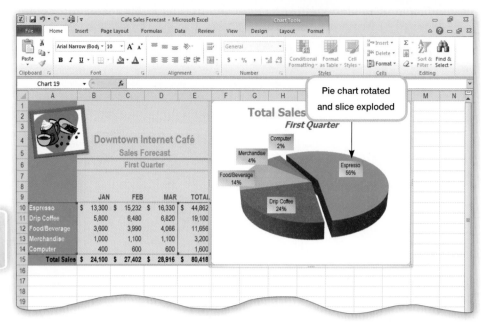

Figure 2.68

Even though the program tries to determine the best position for the data labels, many of the labels are close together and look crowded. You will fix this by changing the position of the data labels.

• **Select the data label series and choose Format Data Labels from the context menu.**

• **Choose Outside End from the Label Position area.**

• **Click** [Close].

• **Drag the Computer, Espresso, and Drip Coffee labels to the positions shown in Figure 2.69.**

Your screen should be similar to Figure 2.69

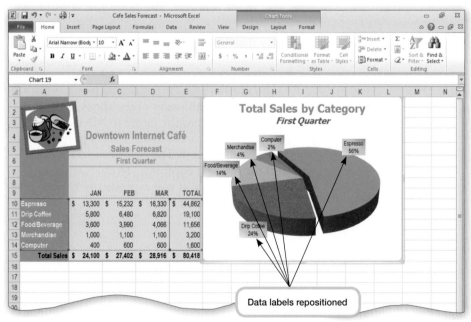

Figure 2.69

Now the labels are more evenly positioned on the pie chart.

APPLYING COLOR AND TEXTURE

The last change you would like to make is to change the color of the Drip Coffee slice and add a fill to the Espresso slice to make it stand out even further. First, you will enhance the Espresso slice by adding a texture.

1

- Select the Espresso slice.

- Choose **Format Data Point** from the context menu.

- Choose **Picture or texture fill** from the Fill category.

- Open the Texture gallery.

Your screen should be similar to Figure 2.70

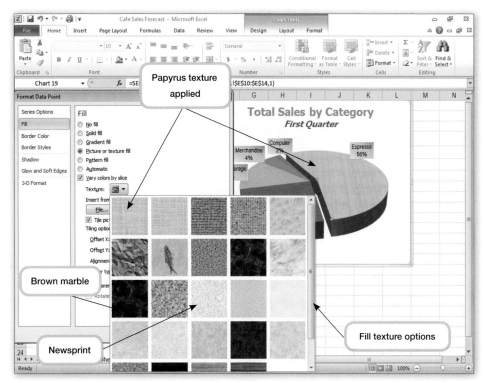

Figure 2.70

A variety of pictures and textures is displayed in the gallery. The Papyrus texture is applied by default. If none of the provided choices is suitable, you could use a picture from a file or clip art as the fill. Although you like how the Papyrus texture looks, you want to see how the brown marble texture would look instead.

2

- Choose several texture designs to see how they will look.

Having Trouble?

You will need to reopen the Texture gallery again after each selection.

- Choose the **Brown Marble** texture.

- Choose the **Papyrus** texture.

- Select the **Drip Coffee** slice.

- Choose **Gradient fill** from the Fill category.

- Click **Close**.

Your screen should be similar to Figure 2.71

Figure 2.71

The last-used gradient fill colors are automatically applied. You decide, however, that the gradient fill does not look good and instead will try using a shape style. Shape styles consist of predefined combinations of fills, outlines, and effects much like chart styles. Shape styles affect only the selected element.

3

- If necessary, select the Drip Coffee slice.

- Open the Format tab.

- Open the Shape Styles gallery in the Shape Styles group and point to several styles to see their effect on the slice.

- Choose the Subtle Effect—Green, Accent 1 Shape Style (4th row, 2nd column).

Your screen should be similar to Figure 2.72

Figure 2.72

Finally, you will add a colored outline border around the entire chart, like the one you used in the column chart. Then you will move the column chart from the chart sheet back into the worksheet.

● **Select the chart area.**

● **Click**

and increase the Weight to 2¼ points.

● **Click**

Shape Outline ▾

and change the line color to the Green, Accent 1, Darker 25% color.

● **Make the Chart2 sheet active.**

● **Click** [Move Chart] **in the Location group of the Design tab.**

● **Choose Object in and select Sheet1 from the drop-down menu.**

● **Click** OK .

● **Move and size the column chart to fit A17 through F33.**

● **Move and size the pie chart to fit A35 through F50.**

● **Deselect the chart.**

● **Save the workbook.**

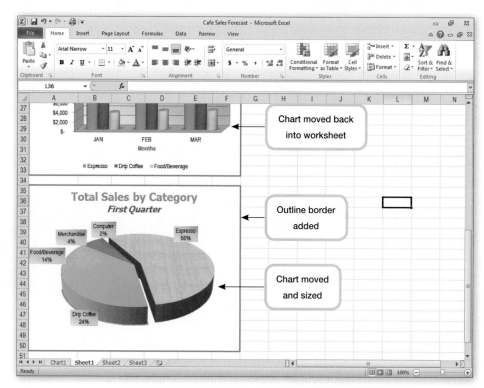

Figure 2.73

Your screen should be similar to Figure 2.73

The column chart was moved back into the sheet as an embedded object, and the chart sheet it occupied was deleted.

Before printing a large worksheet or a worksheet that contains charts, you can quickly fine-tune it in Page Layout view. Using this view, you can change the layout and format of data just as in Normal view, but, in addition, you can adjust the layout of the data on the page by changing the page orientation, page margins, scaling, and alignment. Additionally, you can easily add headers and footers.

SCALING THE WORKSHEET

Having Trouble?

Refer to the section "Using the Zoom Feature" in the Introduction to Microsoft Office 2010 for information on using this feature.

To get the worksheet ready for printing, you will first make several adjustments to the layout in Page Layout view. While in this view, you also will zoom out on the worksheet to see more information in the workbook window by adjusting the zoom percentage.

1

• Click 🖥 **Page Layout view (in the status bar).**

Another Method

You also can use 📄 Page Layout in the View tab.

• Click ⊖ **in the Zoom slider to reduce the zoom to 40%.**

• **Scroll the window up slightly to see the bottom of the pie chart.**

Your screen should be similar to Figure 2.74

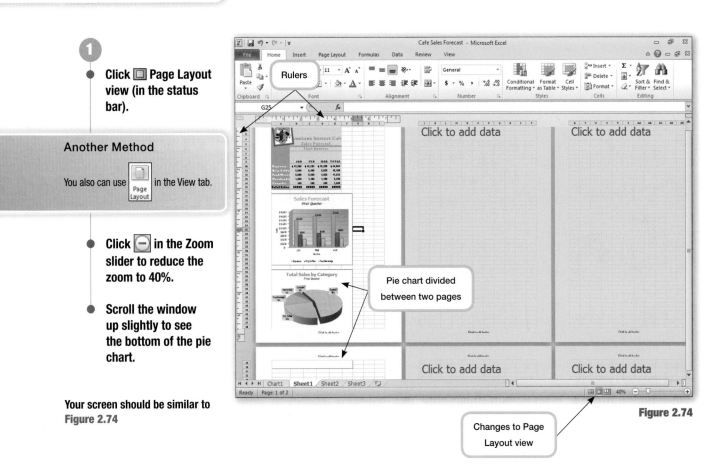

Pie chart divided between two pages

Changes to Page Layout view

Figure 2.74

This view shows how the data and charts lay out on each page of the work-sheet. Because you reduced the zoom, you can quickly see that the pie chart is divided between two pages. You also notice that the worksheet and charts are not centered on the page. In Page Layout view, horizontal and vertical rulers are displayed so you can make exact measurements of cells, ranges, and objects in the worksheet. You will make several changes to the layout of the page to correct these problems.

First you will reduce the scale of the worksheet until all the data fits on one page. Because the width is fine, you will only scale the height.

2

- Open the Page Layout tab.

- Open the 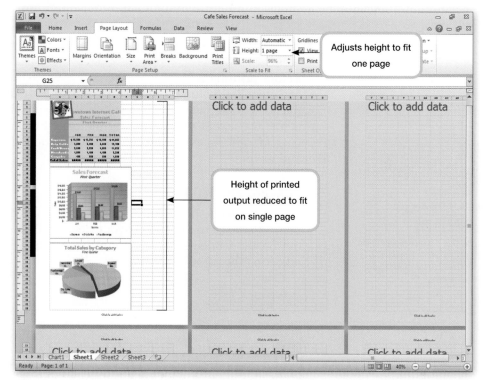 **Height: Automatic ▾** drop-down menu and choose 1 page.

Your screen should be similar to Figure 2.75

Figure 2.75

The height of the printed worksheet has been reduced to fit on a single page.

ADDING PREDEFINED HEADERS AND FOOTERS

Next, you want to include your name and the date in a header.

Concept ⑨ Headers and Footers

Headers and footers provide information that typically appears at the top and bottom of each page and commonly include information such as the date and page number. A **header** is a line or several lines of text that appear at the top of a page just above the top margin line. The header usually contains the file name or worksheet title. A **footer** is a line or several lines of text that appear at the bottom of a page just below the bottom margin line. The footer usually contains the page number and perhaps the date. Headers and footers also can contain graphics such as a company logo. Each worksheet in a workbook can have a different header and footer.

You can select from predefined header and footer text or enter your own custom text. The information contained in the predefined header and footer text is obtained from the file properties associated with the workbook and from the program and system settings.

Header and footer text can be formatted like any other text. In addition, you can control the placement of the header and footer text by specifying where it should appear: left-aligned, centered, or right-aligned in the header or footer space.

Additional Information

If the computer you are using has your name as the user name, you will not need to add your name as the author in the document properties.

You will add a predefined header to the worksheet that displays your name, the date, and page number. To have your name appear in a predefined header, you will need to first add your name as the author to the file properties.

2

● Click .

● Change to Normal view and move to cell A9 of Sheet1.

Additional Information

The dotted line between columns J and K shows the page margin.

● Exit Excel, saving the workbook again.

The page layout settings you specified have been saved with the workbook file.

FOCUS ON CAREERS

EXPLORE YOUR CAREER OPTIONS

Financial Advisor

With the stock market fluctuations in the last few years, investors are demanding more from their financial advisors than ever before. An advisor needs to promote the company's potential and growth in order to get investors to buy stock. One way to do this is to create a worksheet of vital information and to chart that information so the investor can see why the stock is a good investment. The position of Financial Advisor usually requires a college degree and commands salaries from $35,000 to $60,000, depending on experience.

Graphic (EX2.5)

A graphic is a nontext element or object, such as a drawing or picture, that can be added to a document.

Quick Style (EX2.13)

A quick style is a named group of formatting characteristics that allows you to quickly apply a whole group of formats to a selection in one simple step.

Theme (EX2.16)

A theme is a set of formatting choices that can be applied to an entire workbook in one simple step. A theme consists of a set of theme colors, a set of theme fonts (including heading and body text fonts), and a set of theme effects (including line and fill effects).

Chart Elements (EX2.25)

Chart elements are the different parts of a chart that are used to graphically display the worksheet data.

Chart Types (EX2.27)

Different chart types are used to represent data in different ways. The type of chart you create depends on the type of data you are charting and the emphasis you want the chart to impart.

Chart Object (EX2.29)

A chart object is a graphic object that is created using charting features. A chart object can be inserted into a worksheet or into a special chart sheet.

Group (EX2.45)

A group is two or more objects that behave as a single object when moved or sized. A chart is a group that consists of many separate objects.

Data Labels (EX2.51)

Data labels provide additional information about a data point in the data series. They can consist of the value of the point, the name of the data series or category, a percent value, or a bubble size.

Headers and Footers (EX2.66)

Headers and footers provide information that typically appears at the top and bottom of each page and commonly includes the date and page number.

KEY TERMS

area chart EX2.27
axis EX2.25
bar chart EX2.27
bubble chart EX2.27
category axis EX2.25
category-axis title EX2.25
cell style EX2.13
chart EX2.24
chart area EX2.25
chart elements EX2.25
chart gridlines EX2.25
chart layout EX2.30
chart object EX2.29
chart style EX2.13
chart title EX2.25
clip art EX2.6
column chart EX2.27
data label EX2.25, EX2.51
data marker EX2.25
data series EX2.25
depth axis EX2.25
doughnut chart EX2.27
drawing object EX2.5
embedded chart EX2.29
embedded object EX2.5
explode EX2.58
footer EX2.66
gradient EX2.48
graphic EX2.5
group EX2.45
header EX2.66

keyword EX2.10
legend EX2.25
line chart EX2.27
margin EX2.71
object EX2.5
picture EX2.5
picture style EX2.13
pie chart EX2.27
plot area EX2.25
quick style EX2.13
radar chart EX2.27
selection rectangle EX2.7
series axis EX2.25
series formula EX2.59
shape style EX2.13
sizing handle EX2.7
source program EX2.5
stack EX2.29
stacked-column chart EX2.44
stock chart EX2.27
stops (gradient stops) EX2.57
surface chart EX2.27
text box EX2.34
theme EX2.16
thumbnail EX2.10
value axis EX2.25
value-axis title EX2.25
X axis EX2.25
XY (scatter) chart EX2.27
Y axis EX2.25
Z axis EX2.25

COMMAND SUMMARY

Command	Action
File tab	
Print/Settings/ [Print Active Sheets / Only print the active sheets] / Print Entire Workbook	Prints all sheets in workbook file
Page Setup	Opens Page Setup dialog box
Home tab	
Styles group	
Cell Styles	Applies predefined combinations of colors, effects, and formats to selected cells
Cell Styles /Modify	Modifies existing cell style
Insert tab	
Illustrations group	
Picture	Inserts a picture from a file
Clip Art	Inserts a graphic from the Clip Organizer or from Office.com
Charts group	
Column	Inserts a column chart
Pie	Inserts a pie chart
Text group	
Header & Footer	Adds header or footer to worksheet
Page Layout tab	
Themes group	
Themes	Applies selected theme to worksheet

LAB REVIEW

COMMAND SUMMARY (CONTINUED)

Command	Action
[Themes icon] /Save Current Theme	Saves modified theme settings as a custom theme
[Colors icon] Colors ▾	Changes colors for the current theme
Scale to Fit group	
[Width icon] Width:	Scales worksheet width to specified number of pages
[Height icon] Height:	Scales worksheet height to specified number of pages
[Scale icon] Scale:	Scales worksheet by entering a percentage
Picture Tools Format tab	
Picture Styles group	
[Picture Layout icon] Picture Layout ▾	Converts selected picture to a SmartArt graphic
[Picture Border icon] Picture Border ▾	Specifies color, width, and line style for outline of shape
[Picture Effects icon] Picture Effects ▾	Adds glow, shadow, and other effects to pictures
Chart Tools Design tab	
Type group	
[Change Chart Type icon]	Changes to a different type of chart
Data group	
[Switch Row/Column icon]	Swap the data over the axes
[Select Data icon]	Change the data range included in chart
Location group	
[Move Chart icon]	Moves chart to another sheet in the workbook

COMMAND SUMMARY (CONTINUED)

Command	Action
Chart Tools Layout tab	
Labels group	
Chart Title ▾	Adds, removes, or positions the chart title
Axis Titles ▾	Adds, removes, or positions the axis titles
Legend ▾	Adds, removes, or positions the chart legend
Data Labels ▾	Adds, removes, or positions the data labels
Background group	
Chart Wall ▾	Formats chart walls
Chart Tools Format tab	
Current Selection group	
Chart Area ▾	Selects an element on the chart
🖑 Format Selection	Opens Format dialog box for selected element
Shape Styles group	
▾ More	Opens Shape Styles gallery
🖉 Shape Fill ▾	Adds selected fill to shape
🖉 Shape Outline ▾	Specifies color, weight, and type of outline
🖉 Shape Effects ▾	Adds selected effect to shape
View tab	
Zoom group	
🔍 Zoom	Changes the magnification of the worksheet

LAB EXERCISES

MATCHING

Match the lettered item on the right with the numbered item on the left.

1. plot area ____ a. bottom boundary line of the chart
2. value axis ____ b. identifies each number represented in a data series
3. explode ____ c. numbered scale along the left boundary line of the chart
4. theme ____ d. area of chart bounded by X and Y axes
5. legend ____ e. applies a set of colors, fonts, and effects
6. scaling ____ f. separate location that holds only one chart
7. gradient ____ g. a chart that displays data as vertical columns
8. X axis ____ h. identifies the chart data series and data markers
9. category ranges ____ i. to separate a slice slightly from other slices of the pie
10. column chart ____ j. identifies the data along the X axis
11. chart sheet ____ k. a gradual progression of colors and shades
12. data marker ____ l. adjusting print size to fit on the selected number of pages

TRUE/FALSE

Circle the correct answer to the following questions.

1. The chart title is visually displayed within the X- and Y-axis boundaries. **True** **False**
2. An object is an item that can be sized, moved, and manipulated. **True** **False**
3. A group is two or more objects that behave as a single object when moved or sized. **True** **False**
4. A line chart displays data commonly used to show trends over time. **True** **False**
5. The X-axis title line is called the category-axis title. **True** **False**
6. A chart style is a predefined set of chart formats that can be quickly applied to a chart. **True** **False**
7. A header is a line or several lines of text that appear at the bottom of each page just above the bottom margin. **True** **False**
8. A pie chart is best suited for data that compares parts to the whole. **True** **False**
9. A data series links the chart object to the source worksheet. **True** **False**
10. Exploding a slice of a pie chart emphasizes the data. **True** **False**

FILL-IN

Complete the following statements by filling in the blanks with the correct key terms.

1. A(n) _____ is a named combination of formats.
2. The small circles and squares that surround a selected object are called _____.
3. _____ is a collection of graphics that is usually bundled with a software application.
4. A(n) _____ is an object that contains other objects.
5. The axis of the chart that usually contains numerical values is called the _____ or _____.
6. A(n) _____ formula is a formula that links a chart object to the source worksheet.
7. _____ provide more information about a data marker.
8. The _____ is the part of the chart that gives a description of the symbols used in a chart.
9. _____ are combinations of formatting styles such as font, border, shadow, and shape effects that can be applied to a graphic.
10. The X axis of a chart is also called the _____ axis.

LAB EXERCISES

MULTIPLE CHOICE

Circle the correct response to the questions below.

1. A group is one or more _____ that behave as one when moved or sized.
   a. objects
   b. lines
   c. data markers
   d. symbols

2. A chart consists of a number of _____ that are used to graphically display the worksheet data.
   a. elements
   b. groups
   c. gridlines
   d. titles

3. 3-D charts have an additional axis called the _____.
   a. W axis
   b. X axis
   c. Y axis
   d. Z axis

4. A(n) _____ describes the symbols used within the chart to identify different data series.
   a. X axis
   b. legend
   c. Y axis
   d. chart title

5. Charts that are inserted into a worksheet are called _____.
   a. attached objects
   b. enabled objects
   c. embedded objects
   d. inserted objects

6. To change the appearance of the bars in a bar chart, select _____.
   a. format bars
   b. format data series
   c. format chart
   d. format data point

7. A visual representation of data in an easy-to-understand and attractive manner is called a(n)
   _____.
   a. object
   b. picture
   c. chart
   d. drawing

8. The _____ of a chart usually displays a number scale determined by the data in the worksheet.
   a. Z axis
   b. value axis
   c. X axis
   d. category axis

9. A _____ chart shows the relationship of each value in a data series to the series as a whole.
   a. line
   b. bar
   c. pie
   d. bubble

10. _____ provide additional information about information displayed in the chart.
   a. Data masks
   b. Data labels
   c. Headers
   d. Chart titles

STEP-BY-STEP

PATENTS BY REGION ★

1. Max's international studies paper is on patents. He has some data saved in a worksheet on how many computer technology patents are granted each year by region. He has asked you to help him chart the data and make the worksheet look more attractive. The completed worksheet with charts is shown here. (Your solution may look different depending upon the formatting selections you have made.)

   a. Open the workbook ex02_ Patent Data. Insert a graphic of your choice to the left of the worksheet data (or use ex02_ Computer Technology.bmp) and size it appropriately. Apply a picture style of your choice.

   b. Apply a theme of your choice. Use cell styles, cell fill color, and other formatting effects as needed.

   c. Document the workbook to include your name as the author. Save the workbook as Patents by Region to your solution file location.

   d. Create a Clustered Bar in 3-D chart and move it below the worksheet data.

   e. Apply the Layout 1 chart layout. Enter the chart title **Patents Granted**.

   f. Change the chart type to a Clustered Column. Switch the row and column orientation. Remove all except the top four data series.

   g. Select a chart style of your choice. Display the legend below the chart. Display data labels above the largest data series only.

   h. Add a second title line of **Top Four Regions**. Format the title appropriately.

   i. Size the chart to the same width as the worksheet. Increase the height of the chart to better show the data.

j. Preview the worksheet. Add a predefined footer to the worksheet that displays your name, page number, and date. Center the worksheet horizontally on the page. Print the worksheet.

k. Save the workbook again.

CAR COSTS ★★

2. Larissa works for the Department of Transportation. She is preparing a report on the costs of owning and operating a car as part of a program to analyze transportation costs. She has compiled some recent data for her report and wants to create several charts to highlight the data. (Your completed solution may be slightly different depending upon the formatting choices you make.)

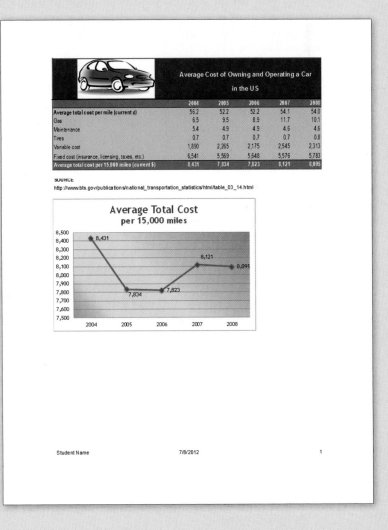

a. Open the file ex02_Vehicle Costs.

b. Apply a theme of your choice. Change the colors associated with the theme and save the theme as a custom theme. Use cell styles, font, and fill colors to enhance the worksheet as you like to improve its appearance.

c. Add a clip art image of your choice to the left of the title. If you do not have an Internet connection, you can use ex02_Car Costs.bmp.

d. Save the workbook as Vehicle Costs to your solution file location.

e. Create a column chart of the worksheet data in rows 8 and 9. Enter a chart title. Enhance the chart using features presented in the lab. Move the chart to a separate chart sheet.

LAB EXERCISES

f. Create a line chart with markers of the data in row 10. Include and format an appropriate title. Select a chart layout and style of your choice. Include data labels. Position the data labels appropriately. Do not display the legend. Format the chart plot area with a gradient color of your choice. Move the chart to below the worksheet data and size appropriately.

g. Document the workbook by adding your name as author. Preview the workbook. Add a predefined footer to the worksheet and chart sheet that displays your name, page number, and date. Scale the worksheet to fit all columns on the page. Print the workbook.

h. Save the workbook again.

MUSIC DOWNLOAD ANALYSIS ★★

3. The Downtown Internet Café is considering providing MP3 download kiosks in the café. To help with the decision, you have collected some data on the number of people who download music. You want to graph the data to get a better idea of the popularity of this activity. The completed worksheet with charts is shown here. (Your completed solution may be slightly different depending upon the formatting choices you make.)

   a. Open the workbook file ex02_Music Download Analysis.

   b. Insert a clip art image of your choice to the left of the data. Size the image as necessary. If you do not have an image, you can use ex02_MP3 Player.bmp.

   c. Change the theme to one of your choice. Apply cell styles and adjust column widths as needed.

   d. Create a line chart using the data in cells A5 through C9. Title the chart appropriately.

   e. Change the chart type to a bar chart of your choice. Apply a chart style of your choice. Adjust and format the chart title as needed and add a text color of your choice. Display the legend at the bottom of the chart.

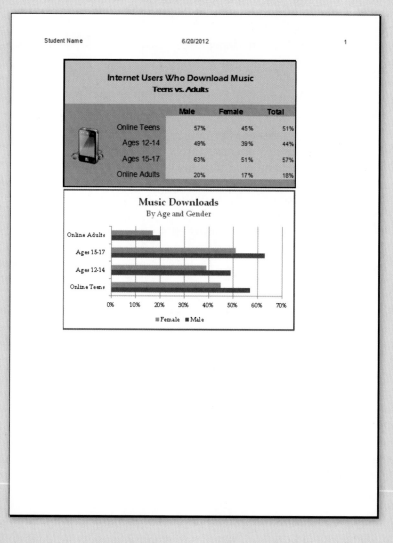

f. Position the chart below the worksheet data and size it appropriately. Add borders around the worksheet and chart.

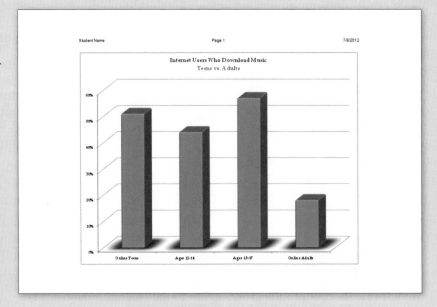

g. Save the workbook as Music Download Analysis to your solution file location.

h. Create a 3-D column chart showing the total percentage. Select the Style 27 chart style. Title the chart appropriately using font sizes and colors of your choice.

i. While reviewing the charts, you realize that the Male and Female columns of data were transposed. Correct the data using the table below.

	Male	Female
Online Teens	57	45
Ages 12–14	49	39
Ages 15–17	63	51
Online Adults	20	17

j. Move the chart to a separate chart sheet. Remove the legend.

k. Document the workbook file by adding your name as author.

l. Preview the workbook. Add a predefined header to the worksheet and chart sheet that displays your name, page number, and date. Center the worksheet horizontally on the page. Print the worksheet. Print the chart sheet.

m. Save the workbook again.

TRACKING ANIMAL ADOPTIONS ★ ★ ★

4. Richard Phillipe volunteers for Animal Angels, a volunteer group that supports the Animal Rescue Agency. He has compiled a worksheet of the number of adoptions in the downtown shelter for the last year. He would like to create a chart that shows how the adoptions differ by month and a chart that shows the total number of adoptions this year. The completed worksheet with charts is shown here. (Your completed solution may be slightly different depending upon the formatting choices you make.)

a. Open the file ex02_Adoptions.

b. Insert a clip art image of your choice in the top-left corner of the worksheet. Size and position the image as necessary. If you don't have an image, use ex02_Pets .bmp. (Hint: Use 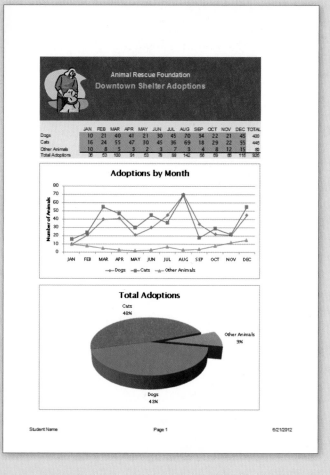 in the Adjust group and choose Set transparent color to change the picture background to transparent.)

c. Save the workbook as Adoption Tracking to your solution file location.

d. Chart the monthly data for the three animal categories as a column chart.

e. Enter the chart title **Adoptions by Month** and the value (Y) axis title **Number of Animals**. Display the legend below the chart.

f. Position the chart over cells A16 through N35.

g. Change the chart type to a line chart with markers.

h. Create a 3-D pie chart of the data in columns A11 through A13 and N11 through N13. Title the chart **Total Adoptions**. Turn off the legend and use the category names and percentages to label the data series.

i. Position the chart over cells A38 through N55. Add color and font refinements to the chart title as you like. Rotate the chart so the Dogs slice is at the front of the chart. Explode the Other Animals slice. Apply a chart style of your choice to the pie chart.

j. Richard found an error in the data. Change the value of Other Animals in June to **3** and Dogs to **22** in October.

k. Document the workbook file by adding your name as author.

l. Save the workbook.

m. Preview the worksheet. Scale the worksheet and charts to fit on one page. Add a predefined footer to the worksheet that displays your name, page number, and date. Center the worksheet horizontally on the page. Print the worksheet.

n. Save the workbook file again.

INTERNET EXPERIENCE ★ ★ ★

5. Wendy Murray teaches a class on Internet technology at a local community college. She has discovered some intriguing research that shows how people use the Internet. She would like to share this information with her students by creating several charts of the data.

 The completed worksheet with charts is shown here. (Your completed solution may be slightly different depending upon the formatting choices you make.)

LAB EXERCISES

a. Create a worksheet of the data in the table below.

Online Activities by Age (%)	18 to 29	30 to 49	50 to 64	65 years +
Email	57	62	53	46
Research	56	56	41	30
Get news	35	44	37	28
Check weather	31	38	29	27
Online banking	24	30	19	14
Watch video	36	17	10	10
Social networking	51	28	10	4
Instant messaging	20	12	4	3
Shopping	9	8	7	6
Job search	16	10	5	1
Journal or blog	5	3	2	2

b. Add a column at the right that averages the percentages. Show zero decimal places. Include an appropriate heading for the column.

c. Include a title above the worksheet data. Insert a clip art graphic of your choice to the left of the title. If you do not have an Internet connection, you can use ex02_Online Usage.bmp. (Hint: Use

[Color] in the Adjust group and choose Set transparent color to change the picture background to

transparent.) Apply a picture style of your choice to the graphic.

d. Apply a theme of your choice. Format the worksheet using the cell styles, fill color, and other formatting features you have learned. Add an outside border around the worksheet data. Save the workbook as **Online Activities**.

e. Create a bar chart for the activities by age group (excluding the average data). Increase the size of the chart to show all the data. Choose a chart layout that displays chart titles and axis titles. Include appropriate chart and axis titles. Move the legend to the bottom of the chart. Add a gradient fill to the chart area.

f. Remove the four categories with the lowest percentages from the chart: Instant messaging, Journal or blog, Job search, and Shopping. (Hint: You will need to switch orientation before removing data, and then switch the orientation back.)

g. Display the chart below the worksheet. Size the chart appropriately.

h. Create a pie chart of the average data for the top four activities. Include an appropriate title. Remove the legend and display data labels outside the slices for the category names and values. Format the data labels. Format the pie chart to be similar to the bar chart. Explode a slice of the pie. Rotate the pie to display the exploded slice at the right.

i. Move the chart below the bar chart. Size it appropriately.

j. Add colored borders around both charts.

k. Document the workbook file by adding your name as author.

l. Preview the worksheet. Add a predefined header to the worksheet that displays your name, page number, and date. Center the worksheet horizontally on the page. Scale the worksheet to fit on one page. Print the worksheet.

m. Save the workbook file again.

ON YOUR OWN

JOB MARKET SEMINAR ★

1. Nancy Fernandez is preparing for an upcoming job market seminar she is presenting. She has collected data comparing the mean hourly pay rate for several computer and mathematical jobs in the Midwest and Northeast to the U.S. average rates. Open the workbook ex02_Job Market. Calculate the percent difference between the Midwest states and U.S. average in column E. Calculate the percent difference between the Northeast states and U.S. average in column F. Add appropriate fill and font colors to the worksheet. Add a graphic to the top-left corner of the worksheet. Nancy thinks the information would be much more meaningful and have greater impact if it were presented in a chart. Create an appropriate chart of the average hourly wage for Computer Programmers, Computer Support Specialists, Computer Systems Analysts, and Database Administrators on a separate chart sheet. Include appropriate chart titles. Add a pattern to the data series and change the plot area fill color. Enhance the chart in other ways using different font sizes and font colors. Position the legend at the bottom of the chart. Add a predefined header to the chart sheet that displays your name, page number, and date. Save the workbook as Seminar and print the chart.

GRADE TRACKING ★

2. Create a worksheet that tracks your GPA for at least four semesters or quarters. (If necessary, use fictitious data to attain four grading periods.) Create a chart that best represents your GPA trends. Use the formatting techniques you have learned to change the appearance of the worksheet and the chart. Save the workbook as Grades. Include a header or footer that displays your name and the current date in the worksheet. Print the worksheet with the chart.

LAB EXERCISES

STOCK MARKET WORKBOOK ★★

3. You are interested in the stock market. Use Help to learn more about the Stock chart type. Pick five related mutual funds and enter data about their performance over a period of time. Create a stock chart of the data. Save the worksheet with the chart as Mutual Funds. Include a header or footer that displays your name and the current date in the worksheet. Print the worksheet and the chart.

GRADUATE SCHOOL DATA ★★★

4. Andrew Romine is considering graduate school at Ohio State and has gathered some data to present to his parents to make a case for paying part of his tuition and fees. Open the file ex02_Graduate School, which has two worksheets, one that shows Earnings and the other Payback data if Andrew chooses Ohio State. Using what you learned in the lab, create two charts from the data on the Earnings worksheet. One chart should represent the lifetime earning potential of people based on their level of education and the other should represent median earning by level. Create a pie chart on the Payback worksheet to represent the number of years after graduation that it will take Andrew to earn back what he paid for the higher education. Use the difference in salary as the data labels. Use the features you have learned to enhance the appearance of the worksheets and charts. Include a header on both worksheets that displays your name and the current date. Save the worksheet as Graduate School2. Print the worksheet with the charts.

INSURANCE COMPARISONS ★★★

5. Roberto Sanchez is thinking about purchasing a new car. However, he is concerned about the insurance rates. Before purchasing, he wants to find out the insurance rates on the cars he is evaluating. Select three different car manufacturers and models. Use the Web and select three different comparable insurance companies to get the insurance premium cost information for different amounts of coverage (minimum required). Use your own personal information as the basis for the insurance quotes. Create a worksheet that contains the cost of minimum coverage, cost of optional coverage, deductibles available, and insurance premium quotes for each vehicle. Create a chart of the data that shows the coverage and premiums. Enhance the chart appropriately. Add pictures of the cars. Include a header or footer that displays your name and the current date in the worksheet. Save the workbook as Insurance. Print the worksheet and chart.

Managing and Analyzing a Workbook

Lab 3

Objectives

After completing this lab, you will know how to:

1. Use absolute references.

2. Copy, move, name, and delete sheets.

3. Use AutoFill.

4. Reference multiple sheets.

5. Use Find and Replace.

6. Zoom the worksheet.

7. Split windows and freeze panes.

8. Use what-if analysis and Goal Seek.

9. Create Sparklines

10. Control page breaks.

11. Add custom headers and footers.

12. Print selected sheets and areas.

Downtown Internet Café

You presented your new, more-optimistic, first-quarter sales forecast for the Downtown Internet Café to Evan. He was impressed with the charts and the projected increase in sales if an aggressive advertising promotion is launched. However, because the Café's funds are low due to the cost of the recent renovations, he has decided to wait on launching the advertising campaign.

Evan wants you to continue working on the Café forecast using the original, more-conservative projected sales values for the first quarter. In addition, he asks you to include an average calculation and to extend the forecast for the next three quarters.

After discussing the future sales, you agree that the Café will likely make a small profit during the first quarter of operations. Then the Café should show increasing profitability. Evan stresses that the monthly profit margin should reach 20 percent in the second quarter.

As you develop the Café's financial forecast, the worksheet grows in size and complexity. You will learn about features of Office Excel 2010 that help you manage a large workbook efficiently. You also will learn how you can manipulate the data in a worksheet to reach a goal using the what-if analysis capabilities of Excel. The completed annual forecast is shown here.

Multiple sheets in a workbook make it easy to edit several sheets simultaneously and to perform calculations based on data from multiple sheets.

Forecasting values using Goal Seek to help perform what-if analysis and applying conditional formatting are powerful Excel features.

Conditional formatting allows you to quickly emphasize worksheet data based on specified conditions.

Concept Preview

The following concepts will be introduced in this lab:

1 **Absolute Reference** An absolute reference is a cell or range reference in a formula whose location does not change when the formula is copied.

2 **Sheet Name** Each sheet in a workbook can be assigned a descriptive sheet name to help identify the contents of the sheet.

3 **AutoFill** The AutoFill feature makes entering a series of headings easier by logically repeating and extending the series. AutoFill recognizes trends and automatically extends data and alphanumeric headings as far as you specify.

4 **Sheet and 3-D References** Sheet and 3-D references in formulas are used to refer to data from multiple sheets and to calculate new values based on this data.

5 **Find and Replace** The Find and Replace feature helps you quickly find specific information and automatically replace it with new information.

6 **Split Window** The split window feature allows you to divide a worksheet window into sections, making it easier to view different parts of the worksheet at the same time.

7 **Freeze Panes** Freezing panes prevents the data in the pane from scrolling as you move to different areas in a worksheet.

8 **What-If Analysis** What-if analysis is a technique used to evaluate the effects of changing selected factors in a worksheet.

9 **Goal Seek** The Goal Seek tool is used to find the value needed in one cell to attain a result you want in another cell.

10 **Conditional Formatting** Conditional formatting changes the appearance of a range of cells based on a condition that you specify.

Correcting Formulas

After talking with Evan, the owner of the Café, about the first-quarter forecast, you are ready to begin making the changes he suggested. Evan returned the workbook file to you containing several changes he made to the format of the worksheet.

1

- Start Excel 2010.

- Open the workbook
  ex03_First Quarter
  Forecast.

- If necessary,
  maximize the
  application and
  workbook windows.

Your screen should be similar to
Figure 3.1

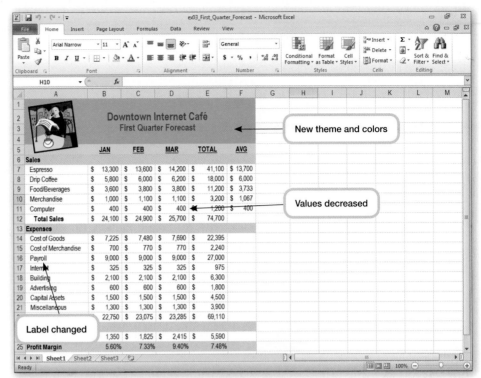

Figure 3.1

As you can see, Evan made several formatting changes to the worksheet. He added a graphic; changed the theme, fill, and text colors; and made several changes to the row headings. For example, the Pay heading has been changed to Payroll. Evan also decided to decrease the computer sales values to $400 for February and March.

IDENTIFYING FORMULA ERRORS

Now you are ready to enter the average formula for the expense values. To do this, you will copy the function down column F.

1

● Copy the function from cell F11 into cells F12 through F24.

● Move to cell F13.

Your screen should be similar to Figure 3.2

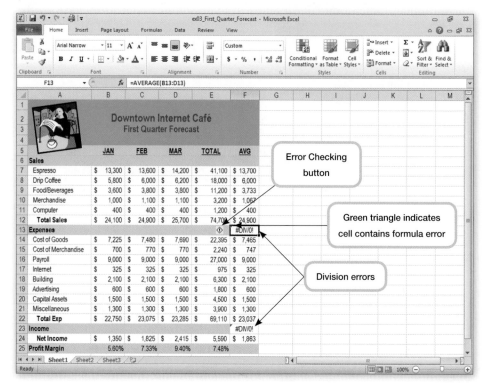

Figure 3.2

The average value has been correctly calculated for each row. Notice, however, that two cells display the error value #DIV/0!, indicating the cells contain a formula error. When a formula cannot properly calculate a result, an error value is displayed and a green triangle appears in the upper-left corner of the cell. In addition, the ◈ Error Checking button appears when you select a cell containing an error.

Each type of error value has a different cause, as described in the following table.

Error Value	Cause
#####	Column not wide enough to display result, or negative date or time is used
#VALUE!	Wrong type of argument or operand is used
#DIV/0!	Number is divided by zero
#NAME?	Text in formula not recognized
#N/A	Value not available
#REF!	Cell reference is not valid
#NUM!	Invalid number values
#NULL!	Intersection operator is not valid

Having Trouble?

If you don't see the green triangle or the ◈ Error Checking button when you click on a cell with a formula error, you may need to turn on background error checking. To do this, open the File tab, click ⊟ Options, choose Formulas, and choose Enable background error checking.

Excel 2010 includes several tools to help you find and correct errors in formula entries. These tools provide the capability to display the relationships between formulas and cells and to identify and suggest corrections to potential problems in formulas.

To correct this problem, you need to find out the cause of the error. Pointing to the ◈ Error Checking button displays a ScreenTip identifying the cause of the error. Clicking the ◈ Error Checking button displays a list of options for error checking the worksheet. In this case, the formula is attempting to divide by zero or empty cells.

2

• **Point to** ⬥ **Error Checking to see the ScreenTip.**

• **Click** ⬥ **Error Checking.**

• **Choose Edit in Formula Bar.**

Your screen should be similar to Figure 3.3

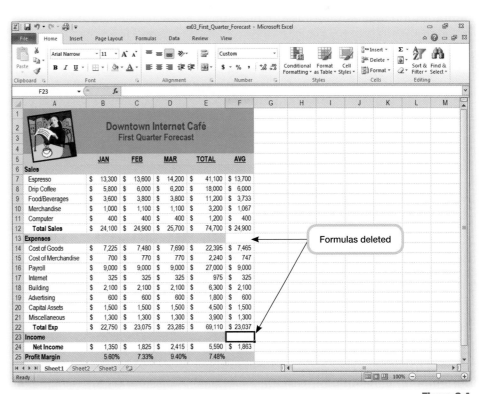

Figure 3.3

In Edit mode, the formula references are color coded to the referenced worksheet cells and you can now easily see the error is caused by references to blank cells when the function was copied.

Since you do not need this formula, you will delete it. Likewise, you need to delete the function that was copied into cell F23. You will clear the entry in this cell using the fill handle.

3

• **Press** Esc **to exit Edit mode.**

• **Press** Delete **.**

• **Move to cell F23.**

• **Point to the fill handle and when the mouse pointer changes to ✛, drag upward until the cell is gray.**

Your screen should be similar to Figure 3.4

Figure 3.4

While looking at the sales data in the worksheet, you decide it may be interesting to know what contribution each sales item makes to total sales. To find out, you will enter a formula to calculate the proportion of sales by each in column G. You will start by entering a new column heading in cell G5. Then you will enter the formula = Total Espresso Sales/Total Sales to calculate the proportion for Espresso sales in G7 and copy it to G8 to calculate the proportion for Drip Coffee sales.

4

- Enter the heading **Proportion** in cell G5.

- Enter the formula **=E7/E12** in cell G7.

- Drag the fill handle to copy the formula in cell G7 to G8.

Your screen should be similar to Figure 3.5

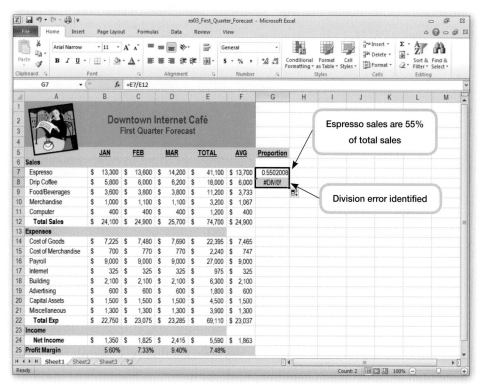

Figure 3.5

The value 0.5502008 is correctly displayed in cell G7. This shows that the Espresso sales are approximately 55 percent of Total Sales. However, a division by zero error has occurred in cell G8.

Another way to check a formula to locate errors or to confirm that the correct cell references are being used is to use the features in the Formula Auditing group of the Formulas tab.

5 ● Move to G8.

● Open the Formulas tab.

● Open the 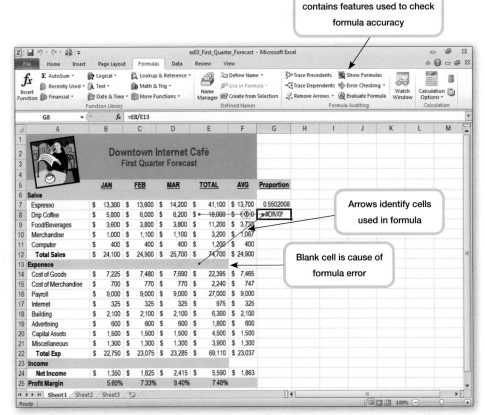 ◆ Error Checking ▾ menu in the Formula Auditing group and choose Trace Error.

Your screen should be similar to Figure 3.6

Excel displays arrows from each cell that affects the value in the current cell. You can now see the error occurred because the relative reference to cell E12 adjusted correctly to the new location when the formula was copied and now references cell E13, a blank cell.

USING ABSOLUTE REFERENCES

The formula in G7 needs to be entered so that the reference to the Total Sales value in cell E12 does not change when the formula is copied. To do this, you need to make the cell reference absolute.

Additional Information

You also can use

⊞₊ Trace Precedents or

◁₊ Trace Dependents to show relationships between formulas and cells.

Concept 1 Absolute Reference

An **absolute reference** is a cell or range reference in a formula whose location does not change when the formula is copied.

To stop the relative adjustment of cell references, enter a $ (dollar sign) character before the column letter and row number. This changes the cell reference to absolute. When a formula containing an absolute cell reference is copied to another row and column location in the worksheet, the cell reference does not change. It is an exact duplicate of the cell reference in the original formula.

A cell reference also can be a **mixed reference**. In this type of reference, either the column letter or the row number is preceded with the $. This makes only the row or column absolute. When a formula containing a mixed cell reference is copied to another location in the worksheet, only the part of the cell reference that is not absolute changes relative to its new location in the worksheet.

The table below shows examples of relative and absolute references and the results when a reference in cell G8 to cell E8 is copied to cell H9.

Cell Contents of G8	Copied to Cell H9	Type of Reference
E8	E8	Absolute reference
E$8	F$8	Mixed reference
$E8	$E9	Mixed reference
E8	F9	Relative reference

You will change the formula in cell G7 to include an absolute reference for cell E12. Then you will copy the formula to cells G8 through G10.

You can change a cell reference to absolute or mixed by typing in the dollar sign directly or by using the ABS (Absolute) key, [F4]. To use the ABS key, the program must be in Edit mode and the cell reference that you want to change must be selected. If you continue to press [F4], the cell reference will cycle through all possible combinations of cell reference types.

WWW.MHHE.COM/OLEARY

1

● Click Remove Arrows in the Formula Auditing group to remove the trace arrows.

● Move to G7.

● Click on the reference to E12 in the formula bar to enter Edit mode and select the reference.

● Press F4 four times to cycle through all reference types.

● Press F4 again to display an absolute reference.

Your screen should be similar to Figure 3.7

The cell reference now displays $ characters before the column letter and row number, making this cell reference absolute. Leaving the cell reference absolute, as it is now, will stop the relative adjustment of the cell reference when you copy it again.

Figure 3.7

2

● Click ✔ Enter or press ↵Enter.

● Copy the revised formula to cells G8 through G11.

● Move to G8 and click ⊡ Trace Precedents in the Formula Auditing group.

Your screen should be similar to Figure 3.8

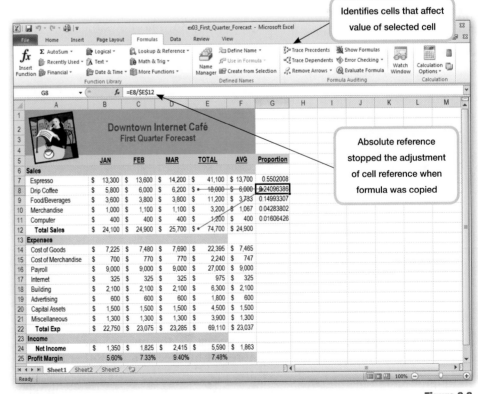

Figure 3.8

The trace arrows show that when the formula was copied it correctly adjusted the relative cell reference to Drip Coffee sales in cell E8 and did not adjust the reference to E12 because it is an absolute reference.

The last change you need to make to the proportion data is to format it to the Percent style.

3

- Click **Remove Arrows** in the Formula Auditing group.

- Select G7 through G11.

- Open the Home tab.

- Click **%** **Percent Style in the Number group.**

- Click **Increase Decimal (twice).**

- Extend the fill in the title area to column G.

Having Trouble?

Use Format Painter to copy the fill colors.

- Extend the fill in rows 6, 13, 23, and 25 to column G.

- Move to cell A6 and save the workbook as Forecast3 to your solution file location.

Your screen should be similar to Figure 3.9

Figure 3.9

The calculated proportion shows the same values that a pie chart of this data would show.

Creating a Second-Quarter Worksheet

Next, you want to add the second-quarter forecast to the workbook. You want this data in a separate sheet in the same workbook file. To make it easier to enter the forecast for the next quarter, you will copy the contents of the first-quarter forecast in Sheet1 into another sheet in the workbook. Then you will change the month headings, the title, and the number data for the second quarter. Finally, you want to include a formula to calculate a year-to-date total for the six months.

COPYING BETWEEN WORKSHEETS

You want to copy the worksheet data from Sheet1 to Sheet2. Copying between sheets is the same as copying within a sheet, except that you switch to the new sheet to specify the destination.

1

- **Select the worksheet range A1 through G25.**

Having Trouble?

A quick way to select this range is to move to cell A1, hold down (Shift), and click on cell G25.

- **Click** 📋 **Copy.**

- **Click on the Sheet2 tab.**

- **Click** 📋 **Paste .**

Your screen should be similar to Figure 3.10

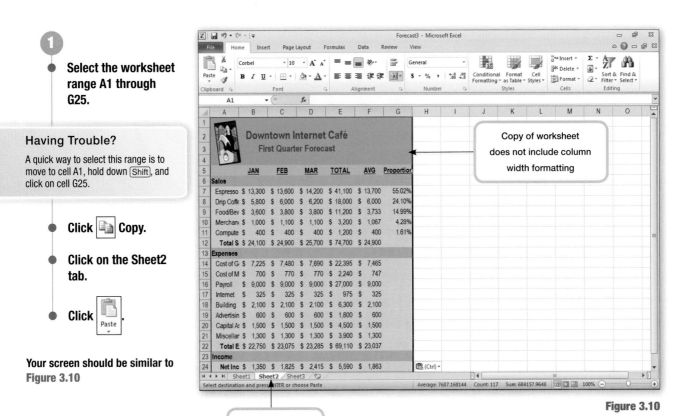

Copy of worksheet does not include column width formatting

Sheet 2 is active

Figure 3.10

All the worksheet data, graphic objects, and formatting, except for the column width, were copied into the existing Sheet2. You can change the column width settings by specifying that this feature be copied from the source. Notice that although the graphic was copied, it needs to be resized.

②

- **Open the** [Paste] **menu and choose Paste Special.**

- **Choose Column Widths.**

- **Click** [OK].

- **Appropriately size and position the graphic.**

- **Click outside the graphic to clear the selection.**

Your screen should be similar to Figure 3.11

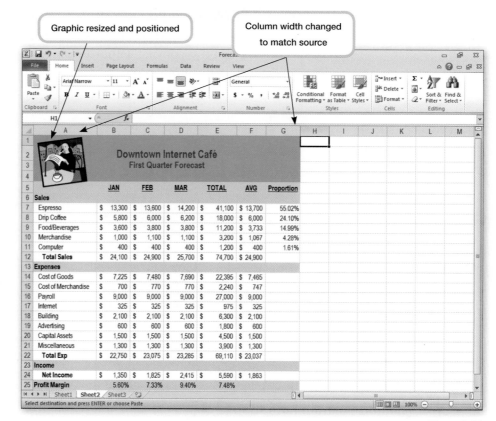

Figure 3.11

Another Method

You also can use [Format ▾] ✓

Move or Copy Sheet in the Cells group or hold down Ctrl while dragging the active sheet tab to copy an entire sheet. All formatting, including column widths, is copied into the destination sheet.

The column widths from the copied selection are pasted into the new sheet. Sheet2 now contains a duplicate of the first-quarter forecast in Sheet1.

RENAMING SHEETS AND COLORING SHEET TABS

As more sheets are added to a workbook, remembering what information is in each sheet becomes more difficult. To help clarify the contents of the sheets, you can rename the sheets.

Concept ② Sheet Name

Each sheet in a workbook can be assigned a descriptive **sheet name** to help identify the contents of the sheet. The following guidelines should be followed when naming a sheet. A sheet name

- Can be up to 31 characters.
- Can be entered in uppercase or lowercase letters or a combination (it will appear as entered).
- Can contain any combination of letters, numbers, and spaces.
- Cannot contain the characters : ? * / \.
- Cannot be enclosed in square brackets [ ].

Double-clicking the sheet tab makes the sheet active and highlights the existing sheet name in the tab. The existing name is cleared as soon as you begin to type the new name. You will change the name of Sheet1 to First Quarter and Sheet2 to Second Quarter.

1

- Double-click the Sheet1 tab.

- Type **First Quarter**

- Press ←Enter.

- Change the name of the Sheet2 tab to **Second Quarter**

Another Method

You also can use Format ▾ Rename Sheet in the Cells group of the Home tab.

Your screen should be similar to Figure 3.12

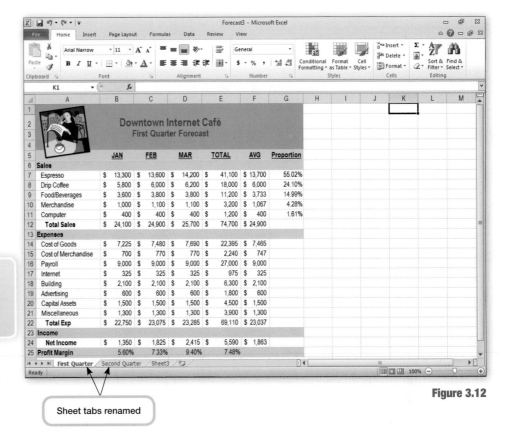

Sheet tabs renamed

Figure 3.12

To further differentiate the sheets, you can add color to the sheet tabs.

2

- Right-click on the First Quarter tab.

- Select Tab Color from the shortcut menu.

- Choose the Turquoise, Accent 4 theme color from the color palette.

- In the same manner, change the color of the Second Quarter sheet tab to the Pink, Accent 2 theme color.

Your screen should be similar to Figure 3.13

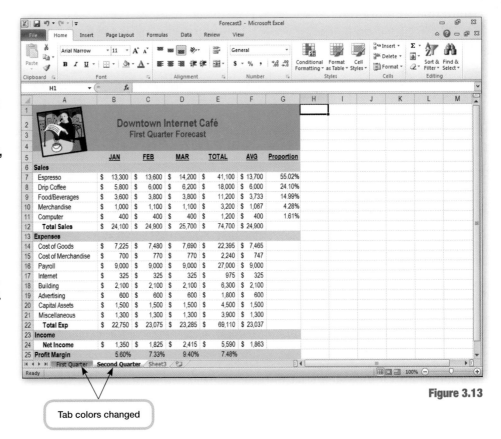

Tab colors changed

Figure 3.13

The sheet tab name of the selected sheet is underlined in the tab color of pink and the First Quarter sheet tab is turquoise. When a sheet is not selected, the sheet tab is displayed with the background color.

FILLING A SERIES

Now you can change the worksheet title and data in the Second Quarter sheet. First you will change the worksheet title to identify the worksheet contents as the second-quarter forecast. Then you will change the month headings to the three months that make up the second quarter: April, May, and June.

1

- **Change the title in cell B3 to** Second Quarter Forecast

- **Change the month heading in cell B5 to** APR.

Your screen should be similar to Figure 3.14

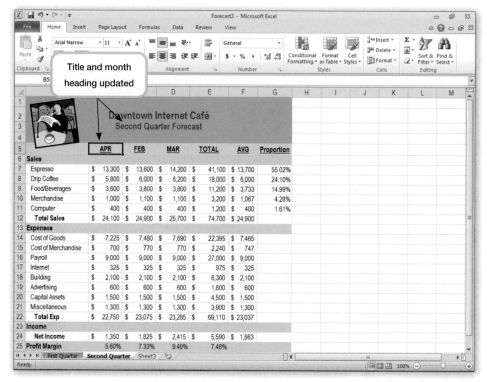

Figure 3.14

Now you need to change the remaining month headings to MAY and JUN. You will use the AutoFill feature to enter the month headings.

Concept 3 AutoFill

The **AutoFill** feature makes entering a series of numbers, numbers and text combinations, dates, or time periods easier by logically repeating and extending the series. AutoFill recognizes trends and automatically extends data and alphanumeric headings as far as you specify.

Dragging the fill handle activates the AutoFill feature if Excel recognizes the entry in the cell as an entry that can be incremented. When AutoFill extends the entries, it uses the same style as the original entry. For example, if you enter the heading for July as JUL (abbreviated with all letters uppercase), all the extended entries in the series will be abbreviated and uppercase. Dragging down or right increments in increasing order, and up or left increments in decreasing order. A linear series increases or decreases values by a constant value, and a growth series multiplies values by a constant factor. Examples of how AutoFill extends a series are shown in the table below.

Initial Selection	Extended Series
Qtr1	Qtr2, Qtr3, Qtr4
Mon	Tue, Wed, Thu
Jan, Apr	Jul, Oct, Jan

A starting value of a series may contain more than one item that can be incremented, such as JAN-02, in which both the month and year can increment. You can specify which value to increment by selecting the appropriate option from the 🔲 AutoFill Options menu.

The entry in cell B5, APR, is the starting value of a series of months. You will drag the fill handle to the right to increment the months. The mouse pointer displays the entry that will appear in each cell as you drag.

2

● **Drag the fill handle of cell B5 to extend the range from cell B5 through cell D5.**

● **Save the workbook.**

Your screen should be similar to Figure 3.15

Figure 3.15

The month headings now correctly reflect the three months for the second quarter. This is because the entry in cell B5 was a month that was recognized as an entry that can be incremented. Additionally, the months appear in upper-case characters, the same as the starting month. This is because AutoFill copies formatting when extending the series.

USING A 3-D REFERENCE

Finally, you need to update the forecast to reflect the April through June sales. You anticipate that sales will increase in all areas, except food and beverage sales, which will remain the same. Then you will enter a formula to calculate the year-to-date income total using data from both sheets.

1 ● Enter the following values in the specified cells.

Sales	Cell	Number
Espresso	B7	14400
	C7	15200
	D7	15500
Drip Coffee	B8	6200
	C8	6200
	D8	6200
Merchandise	B10	1500
	C10	1500
	D10	1500
Computer	B11	600
	C11	600
	D11	600

Your screen should be similar to Figure 3.16

Figure 3.16

The worksheet now contains the data for the second quarter and all dependent formulas have been recalculated.

Now you can enter the formula to calculate a year-to-date income total. The formula to make this calculation will sum the total income numbers from cell E24 in the First Quarter sheet and cell E24 in the Second Quarter sheet. To reference data in another sheet in the same workbook, you enter a formula that references cells in other worksheets.

Concept Sheet and 3-D References

Sheet and 3-D references in formulas are used to refer to data from multiple sheets and to calculate new values based on this data. A **sheet reference** in a formula consists of the name of the sheet, followed by an exclamation point and the cell or range reference. If the sheet name contains nonalphabetic characters, such as a space, the sheet name (or path) must be enclosed in single quotation marks.

If you want to use the same cell or range of cells on multiple sheets, you can use a **3-D reference**. A 3-D reference consists of the names of the beginning and ending sheets enclosed in quotes and separated by a colon. This is followed by an exclamation point and the cell or range reference. The cell or range reference is the same on each sheet in the specified sheet range. If a sheet is inserted or deleted, the range is automatically updated. 3-D references make it easy to analyze data in the same cell or range of cells on multiple worksheets.

Reference	Description
=Sheet2!B17	Displays the entry in cell B17 of Sheet2 in the active cell of the current sheet
=Sheet1!A1 + Sheet2!B2.	Sums the values in cell A1 of Sheet1 and B2 of Sheet2
=SUM(Sheet1:Sheet4!H6:K6)	Sums the values in cells H6 through K6 in Sheets 1, 2, 3, and 4
=SUM(Sheet1!H6:K6)	Sums the values in cells H6 through K6 in Sheet1
=SUM(Sheet1:Sheet4!H6)	Sums the values in cell H6 of Sheets 1, 2, 3, and 4

Just like a formula that references cells within a sheet, a formula that references cells in multiple sheets is automatically recalculated when data in a referenced cell changes.

You will enter a descriptive text entry in cell D26 and then use a 3-D reference in a SUM function to calculate the year-to-date total in cell E26.

The SUM function argument will consist of a 3-D reference to cell E24 in the First and Second Quarter sheets. Although a 3-D reference can be entered by typing it using the proper syntax, it is much easier to enter it by pointing to the cells on the sheets. To enter a 3-D reference, select the cell or range in the beginning sheet and then hold down ⇧Shift and click on the sheet tab of the last sheet in the range. This will include the indicated cell range on all sheets between and including the first and last sheets specified.

2

- In cell D26, enter and right-align the entry **Income Year-to-Date**

- Move to E26.

- Click **Σ ▾ Sum.**

- Click cell E24.

- Hold down **⇧Shift** and click the First Quarter tab.

- Release **⇧Shift**.

- Press **←Enter**.

- Move to E26.

Your screen should be similar to Figure 3.17

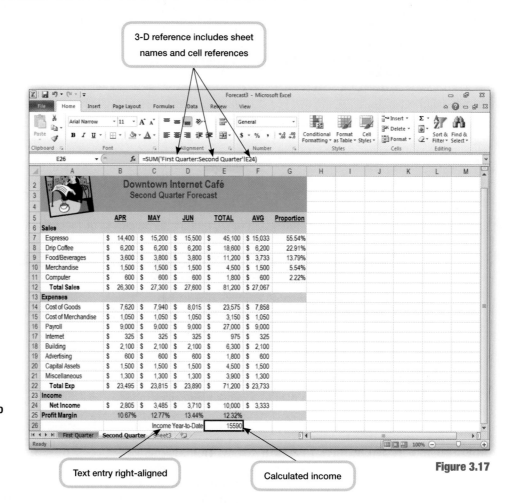

3-D reference includes sheet names and cell references

Text entry right-aligned

Calculated income

Figure 3.17

The calculated number 15,590 appears in cell E26, and the function containing a 3-D reference appears in the formula bar.

HIDING GRIDLINES AND HEADINGS

Just as you completed the forecast for the first half of the year, Evan, the Café owner, stopped in and you decide to show him the forecast. To simplify the screen display while showing Evan the worksheet, you will hide the gridlines and column and row headings.

1

- **Move to cell A1 and open the View tab.**

- **Choose** ☑ Gridlines **from the Show group to clear the selection.**

- **Choose** ☑ Headings **from the Show group to clear the selection.**

Your screen should be similar to Figure 3.18

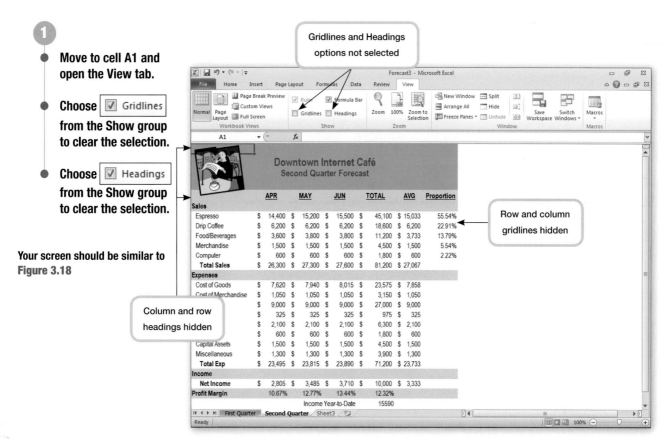

Gridlines and Headings options not selected

Row and column gridlines hidden

Column and row headings hidden

Figure 3.18

While these features are off, you will format the year-to-date income value to Accounting with zero decimal places. Rather than opening the Home tab to access these features, you will copy the format from another cell. The Paste Special menu option, Formatting, will do this quickly for you.

2

- **Select any cell that is formatted in the Accounting format and choose Copy from the context menu.**

- **Right-click on cell E26 and choose** 🔲 **Formatting from the Paste Options section of the context menu.**

Your screen should be similar to Figure 3.19

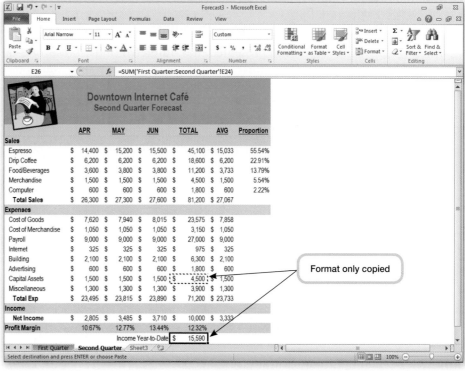

Format only copied

Figure 3.19

Hiding gridlines and headers is convenient for presenting the worksheet to others; however, it is not as easy to work in the sheet with these features off. You will turn them back on, add file documentation, and then print a copy of the workbook for Evan.

3

- Choose [Gridlines] from the Show group to select it.

- Choose [Headings] from the Show group to select it.

- Enter the following information in the workbook file properties:

Author	your name
Title	Downtown Internet Cafe
Subject	First and second quarter forecasts

Having Trouble?

Click Show All Properties to display the Subject box.

- Change the Print setting to print the entire workbook.

- Preview both worksheets.

- Add a predefined header containing your name, page number, and the date to both worksheets.

- Print the workbook.

- Move to cell A6 in both worksheets and save the workbook.

- Close the workbook.

DELETING AND MOVING WORKSHEETS

You presented the completed first- and second-quarter forecasts to Evan. He is very pleased with the results and now wants you to create worksheets for the third and fourth quarters and a combined annual forecast. Additionally, Evan has asked you to include a column chart of the data for each quarter. Finally, after looking at the forecast, Evan wants the forecast to show a profit margin of 15 percent for each month in the second quarter.

You have already made several of the changes requested and saved them as a workbook file. You will open this file to see the revised and expanded forecast.

1

● **Open the workbook file** ex03_Annual Forecast.

Your screen should be similar to Figure 3.20

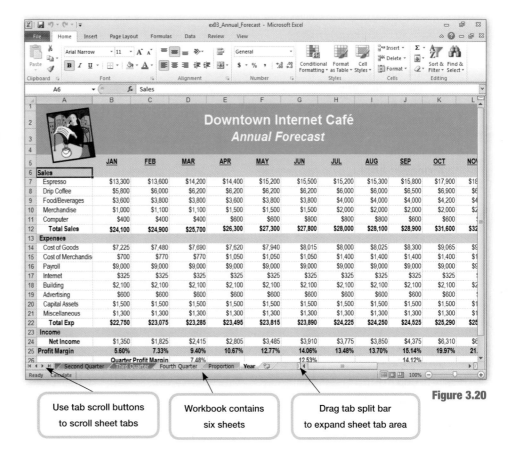

Figure 3.20

Use tab scroll buttons to scroll sheet tabs

Workbook contains six sheets

Drag tab split bar to expand sheet tab area

The workbook file now contains six sheets: First Quarter, Second Quarter, Third Quarter, Fourth Quarter, Proportion, and Year. The Proportion sheet contains the proportion of sales values from the first and second quarters. The Year sheet contains the forecast data for the entire 12 months. Each quarter sheet also includes a chart of the profit margin for that quarter.

Notice also that the First Quarter sheet tab is not entirely visible. This is because there is not enough space in the sheet tab area to display all the tabs. To see the tabs, you can drag the tab split bar located at the right edge of the sheet tab area to expand the area or use the sheet tab scroll buttons to scroll the tabs into view.

2

- Click on each of the Quarter sheet tabs to view the quarterly data and profit margin chart.

- Display the Proportion sheet.

Your screen should be similar to Figure 3.21

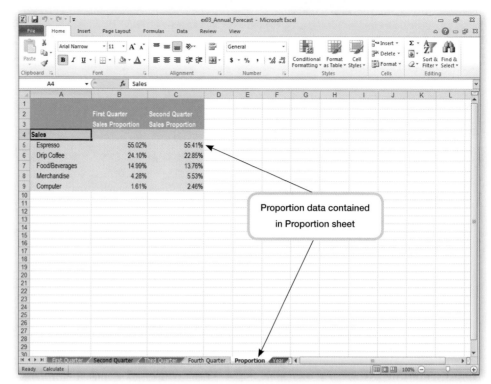

Proportion data contained in Proportion sheet

Figure 3.21

You decide this data, although interesting, is not needed in the forecast workbook and want to delete the entire sheet.

3

- In the Cells group of the Home tab, open the Delete menu and choose Delete Sheet.

- Click Delete to confirm that you want to permanently remove the sheet.

Another Method

You also can choose Delete from the sheet tab's shortcut menu to delete a sheet.

Your screen should be similar to Figure 3.22

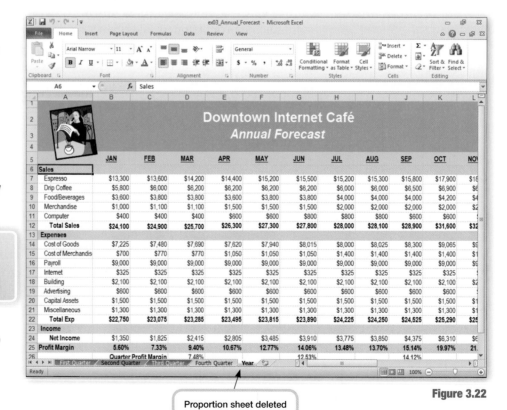

Proportion sheet deleted

Figure 3.22

Additional Information

You can insert a blank new sheet using Insert ▾ and choosing Insert Sheet. It is inserted to the left of the active sheet.

The entire sheet is deleted, and the Year sheet is now the active sheet. Next you want to move the Year sheet from the last position in the workbook to the first. You can quickly rearrange the order of sheets in a workbook by dragging the selected sheet tab along the row of sheet tabs to the new location.

④

● **Drag the Year tab to the left of the First Quarter tab.**

Additional Information

The mouse pointer appears as 🔲 and the symbol ▾ indicates the location where the sheet will be moved.

Another Method

You also can use Move or Copy from the sheet tab's shortcut menu to move a sheet to another location in the workbook.

Your screen should be similar to Figure 3.23

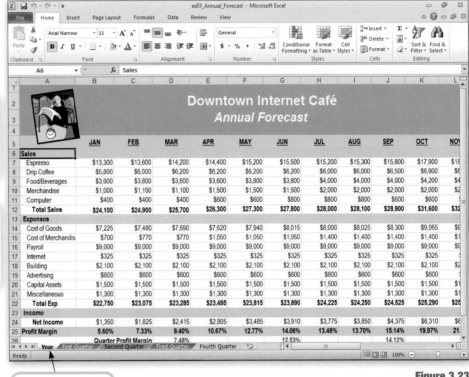

Sheet moved by dragging sheet tab

Figure 3.23

The Year sheet is now the first sheet in the workbook.

Finding and Replacing Information

As you look over the worksheets, you notice that the only abbreviation used in the entire workbook is for expenses in the Total Exp row heading. You want to change it to "Expenses" in all worksheets in the workbook.

You could change the word in each sheet by changing the text directly on the worksheet cells. However, the larger your workbook becomes, the more difficult it will be to find the data you want to modify. Therefore, you will use the Find and Replace feature to quickly locate the word and make the change.

Concept 5 Find and Replace

The **Find and Replace** feature helps you quickly find specific information and automatically replace it with new information. The Find command locates all occurrences of the text or numbers you specify. The Replace command is used with the Find command to locate the specified entries and replace the located occurrences with the replacement text you specify. You also can find cells that match a format you specify and replace the format with another. Finding and replacing data and formats is both fast and accurate, but you need to be careful when replacing that you do not replace unintended matches.

FINDING INFORMATION

First, you will locate and correct the abbreviation using the Find command. This command can be used to locate data in any type of worksheet.

● Click ![Find & Select] in the Editing group and choose Find.

● If necessary, click Options >> to display the additional search options.

Another Method

The keyboard shortcut is Ctrl + F.

Your screen should be similar to Figure 3.24

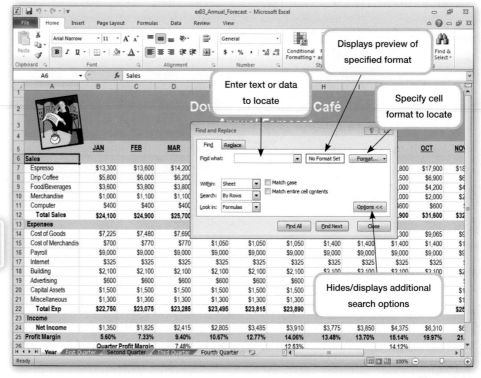

Figure 3.24

In the Find and Replace dialog box, you enter the information you want to locate in the Find what text box. It must be entered exactly as it appears in the worksheet. The additional options in the dialog box can be combined in many ways to help locate information. They are described in the table below.

Option	Effect
Within	Searches the active worksheet or workbook.
Search	Specifies the direction to search in the worksheet: By Columns searches down through columns and By Rows searches to the right across rows.
Look in	Looks for a match in the specified worksheet element: formulas, values, comments.
Match case	Finds words that have the same pattern of uppercase letters as entered in the Find what text box. Using this option makes the search case sensitive.
Match entire cell contents	Looks for an exact and complete match of the characters specified in the Find what text box.
Format	Used to specify a cell format to locate and replace. A sample of the selected format is displayed in the preview box.

You will enter the text to find, exp, and will search using the default options.

- Type **exp** in the Find what box.

- Click Options << to hide the additional search options.

- Click Find Next.

Additional Information

Because the Match Case option is not selected, Find looks for an exact match regardless of whether the characters are uppercase or lowercase.

Additional Information

Clicking Find All displays all text or format matches in a list. Selecting an item from the list moves the cell selector to the cell containing the entry.

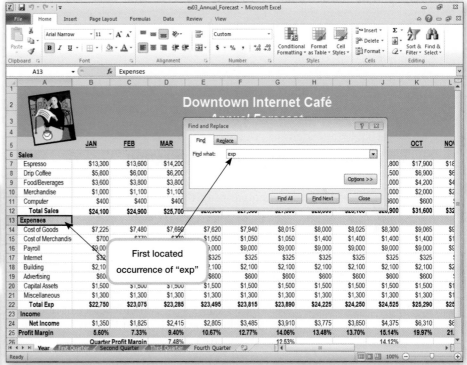

Figure 3.25

Your screen should be similar to Figure 3.25

The cell selector jumps to the first occurrence of "exp," in cell A13, which contains the word "Expenses." It located this word because the first three letters match. However, this is not the entry you are trying to locate. You will continue the search to locate the next occurrence. Then you will edit the cell to display the word "Expenses."

3

● Click [Find Next].

● Double-click on the selected cell.

● Change Exp to **Expenses**

● Click [✓] Enter or press [←Enter].

Your screen should be similar to Figure 3.26

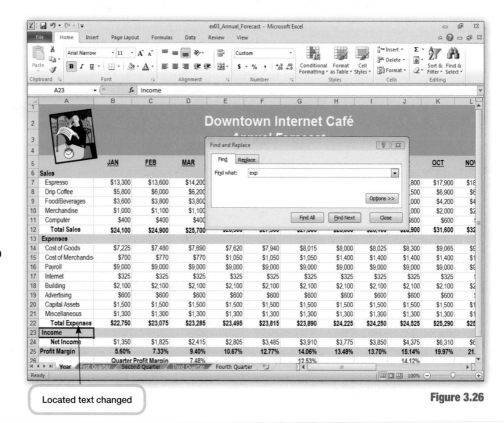

Located text changed

Figure 3.26

You manually made the correction to the label in cell A22. Next, you want to locate the word in all the other sheets and correct the entries.

REPLACING INFORMATION

You realize that "exp" will be located twice in every worksheet. Since you want to change only the Total Exp headings, you will refine your search term to locate only this heading and use the Replace command to make the correction automatically on the other sheets. The replacement text must be entered exactly as you want it to appear.

First, you will select all four quarter sheets as a group so that any changes you make are made to all selected sheets. To select two or more adjacent sheets, click on the tab for the first sheet and click on the last sheet tab while holding down [⇧Shift]. You can select nonadjacent sheets by holding down [Ctrl] while clicking on each sheet. The title bar displays "[Group]" whenever multiple sheets are selected.

Additional Information

You can select all sheets using Select All Sheets from the sheet tab shortcut menu.

Additional Information

The tabs of all sheets appear with a white top, indicating they are selected; the active sheet tab name is bold.

- Click on the First Quarter sheet tab, hold down ⬆Shift, and click on the Fourth Quarter tab.

- Change the entry in the Find What box to **total exp**

- Open the Replace tab.

- Type **Total Expenses** in the Replace with box.

- Click Find Next.

- Click Replace All.

Your screen should be similar to Figure 3.27

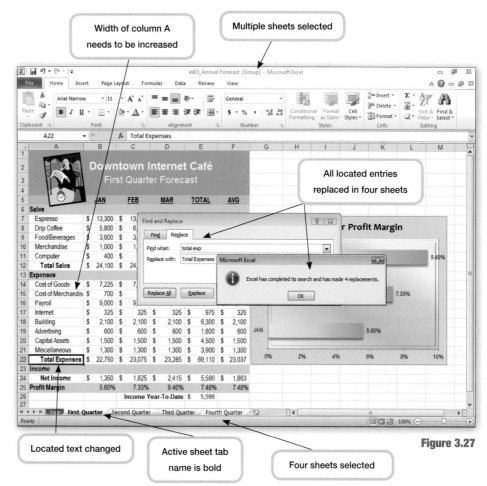

Width of column A needs to be increased

Multiple sheets selected

All located entries replaced in four sheets

Located text changed

Active sheet tab name is bold

Four sheets selected

Figure 3.27

Another Method

You also can use Find & Select/Replace; the keyboard shortcut is Ctrl + H.

Four replacements were made, indicating that the heading was corrected on all four sheets. It is much faster to use Replace All than to confirm each match separately. However, exercise care when using Replace All because the search text you specify might be part of another word and you may accidentally replace text you want to keep.

Now, you also notice that the labels in column A are not fully displayed, so you need to increase the column width. You will expand the group selection to include the Year sheet and adjust the width of column A on all worksheets at the same time.

- Click [OK].

- Click [Close].

- Hold down Ctrl and click on the Year tab to add it to the group.

- AutoFit column A.

Having Trouble?

Double-click on the column border of column A when the mouse pointer is a ↔.

- Right-click on the Second Quarter tab and choose Ungroup Sheets to cancel the group selection and make it the active sheet.

Another Method

You also can click on any unselected sheet tab to cancel a group selection.

Your screen should be similar to Figure 3.28

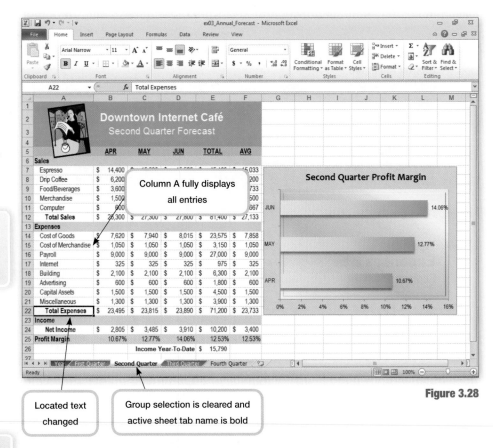

Located text changed

Group selection is cleared and active sheet tab name is bold

Figure 3.28

You can now see that the width of column A has been adjusted and that the Total Exp label has been replaced with Total Expenses, as it has in all other sheets. When multiple sheets are selected, be careful when making changes, as all selected sheets are affected.

Saving to a New Folder

You have made several changes to the workbook, and before continuing, you want to save it. Since the workbook is for projected forecasts, you decide to save it in a separate folder from the rest of the Café's financial workbooks. You will save the file to a new folder named Forecasts.

1

- Display the Year sheet.

- Open the File tab and choose Save As.

- If necessary, change the location to where you save your files.

- Enter **Annual Forecast** as the file name.

- Click [New folder] in the Save As dialog box.

Your screen should be similar to Figure 3.29

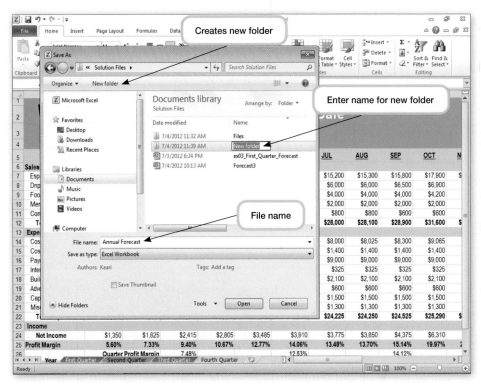

Figure 3.29

Having Trouble?

Your Save As dialog box may look slightly different depending upon the version of Windows you are using.

The file list displays a new folder with the default folder name, New Folder. You need to replace the default folder name with a descriptive folder name. Then you will open the new folder and save the file in it.

Additional Information

You also can rename an existing folder from the Save As dialog box by choosing Rename from the folder's shortcut menu and entering the new name.

- Type **Café Forecasts** in place of New Folder.

- Press ←Enter to complete the folder name.

- Double-click on the Café Forecasts folder to open it.

- Click [Save].

Additional Information

If you are running short on lab time, this is an appropriate place to end this session and begin again at a later time.

The Annual Forecast workbook is saved in the new Café Forecasts folder.

Now that the Year worksheet is much larger, you are finding that it takes a lot of time to scroll to different areas within the worksheet. To make managing large worksheets easier, you can zoom a worksheet, split the workbook window, and freeze panes.

The Year worksheet includes all of the quarterly data. The entire worksheet, however, is not visible in the window.

1

Reduce the zoom percentage to 80%.

Move to B7.

Another Method

You also can use Zoom in the Zoom group on the View tab or click the zoom percentage in the status bar to open the Zoom dialog box and set the magnification.

Your screen should be similar to Figure 3.30

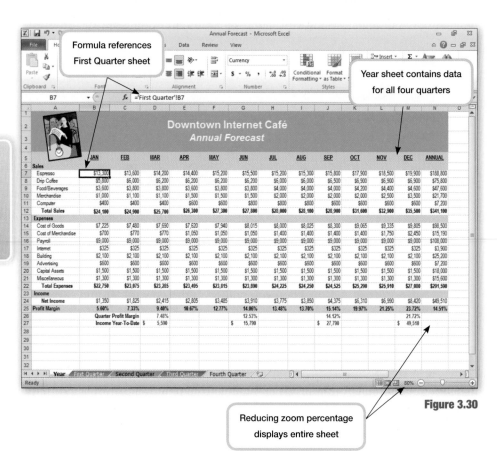

Figure 3.30

You can now see the entire worksheet. Most of the monthly values in the Year sheet, such as cell B7, contain linking formulas that reference the appropriate cells in the appropriate quarter sheets.

GOING TO A SPECIFIC CELL

The only formulas that do not reference cells outside the Year worksheet are those in the Annual column, N. Because you reduced the zoom, it is easy to see the values in column N and to move to a cell by clicking on the cell. However, when the worksheet is at 100 percent zoom, you would need to scroll the worksheet first. You will return the zoom to 100 percent and then use the Go To feature to quickly move to a cell that is not currently visible in the window.

Return the zoom to 100%.

Additional Information

Click on the vertical line in the center of the zoom scale to jump to 100%.

Click in the Name box and type N16

Having Trouble?

The Name box is located at the left end of the formula bar.

Press ⏎Enter.

Another Method

You also can use [Find & Select ▾] and choose

Go To or the keyboard shortcut Ctrl + G.

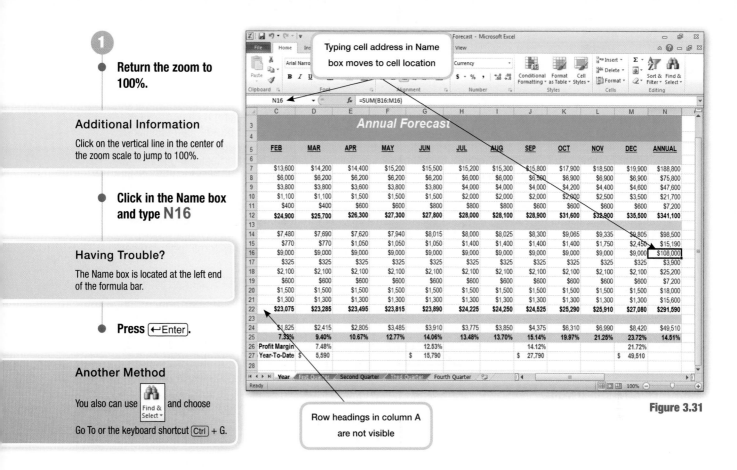

Typing cell address in Name box moves to cell location

Row headings in column A are not visible

Figure 3.31

Your screen should be similar to Figure 3.31

The cell selector jumps directly to cell N16 in the Annual column. The formula in this cell calculates the total of the values in row 16 and does not reference another sheet. However, it is difficult to know what the numbers represent in this row because the row headings are not visible. For example, is this number the total for the lease expenses, advertising expenses, or miscellaneous expenses? Without scrolling back to see the row headings, it is difficult to know.

SPLITTING WINDOWS

Whenever you scroll a large worksheet, you will find that information you may need to view in one area scrolls out of view as you move to another area. Although you could reduce the zoom percent to view more of a worksheet in the window, you still may not be able to see the entire worksheet if it is very large. And as you saw, continuing to reduce the zoom makes the worksheet difficult to read. To view different areas of the same worksheet at the same time, you can split the window.

Concept **6** Split Window

The **split window** feature allows you to divide a worksheet window into sections, making it easier to view different parts of the worksheet at the same time. The sections of the window, called **panes**, can consist of any number of columns or rows along the top or left edge of the window. You can divide the worksheet into two panes either horizontally or vertically, or into four panes if you split the window both vertically and horizontally.

Each pane can be scrolled independently to display different areas of the worksheet. When split vertically, the panes scroll together when you scroll vertically, but scroll independently when you scroll horizontally. Horizontal panes scroll together when you scroll horizontally, but independently when you scroll vertically.

Panes are most useful for viewing a worksheet that consists of different areas or sections. Creating panes allows you to display the different sections of the worksheet in separate panes and then to quickly switch between panes to access the data in the different sections without having to repeatedly scroll to the areas.

Two vertical panes

Two horizontal panes

Four panes

Dragging the split box at the top of the vertical scroll bar downward creates a horizontal split, and dragging the split box at the right end of the horizontal scroll bar leftward creates a vertical split.

You will split the window into two vertical panes. This will allow you to view the headings in column A at the same time as you are viewing data in column N.

Point to the vertical split box in the horizontal scroll bar.

Drag the split box to the left and position the bar between columns D and E.

Your screen should be similar to Figure 3.32

Figure 3.32

There are now two vertical panes with two separate horizontal scroll bars. The highlighted cell selector is visible in the right pane. The left pane also has a cell selector in cell N16, but it is not visible because that area of the worksheet is not displayed in the pane. When the same area of a worksheet is visible in multiple panes, the cell selector in the panes that are not active is highlighted whereas the cell selector in the active pane is clear. The active pane will be affected by your movement horizontally. The cell selector moves in both panes, but only the active pane scrolls.

You will scroll the left pane horizontally to display the month headings in column A.

2

Click C16 in the left pane to display the active cell selector in the pane.

Press ← twice.

Your screen should be similar to Figure 3.33

Left pane active and scrolled

Right pane not active and remained fixed

Figure 3.33

The right pane did not scroll when you moved horizontally through the left pane to display the row headings. The cell selector in the right pane is in the same cell location as in the left pane (A16), although it is not visible. You want to change the location of the split so that you can view an entire quarter in the left pane in order to more easily compare quarters.

3

Drag the split bar to the right three columns.

Click cell E16 in the right pane.

Press End →.

Press → (four times).

Your screen should be similar to Figure 3.34

Split windows make comparing distant areas of a large worksheet easier

Figure 3.34

Now you can easily compare the first-quarter data to the last-quarter data. As you can see, creating panes is helpful when you want to display and access distant areas of a worksheet quickly. After scrolling the data in the panes to display the appropriate worksheet area, you can then quickly switch between panes to make changes to the data that is visible in the pane. This saves you the time of scrolling to the area each time you want to view it or make changes to it. You will clear the vertical split from the window.

Another Method

You also can use Split in the Window group on the View tab to clear the split.

4
- **Double-click anywhere on the split bar.**
- **Scroll to the top of the window.**

Your screen should be similar to Figure 3.35

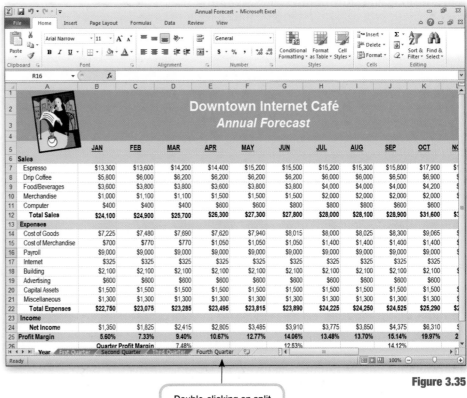

Double-clicking on split bar removes vertical split

Figure 3.35

FREEZING PANES

Another way to manage a large worksheet is to freeze panes.

Concept 7 Freeze Panes

Freezing panes prevents the data in the pane from scrolling as you move to different areas in a worksheet. You can freeze the information in the top and left panes of a window only. This feature is most useful when your worksheet is organized using row and column headings. It allows you to keep the titles on the top and left edge of your worksheet in view as you scroll horizontally and vertically through the worksheet data.

You want to keep the month headings in row 5 and the row headings in column A visible in the window at all times while looking at the Income and Profit Margin data beginning in row 22. To do this, you will create four panes with the upper and left panes frozen.

When creating frozen panes, first position the worksheet in the window to display the information you want to appear in the top and left panes. This is because data in the frozen panes cannot be scrolled like data in regular panes. Then move to the location specified in the following table before using the ⊞ Freeze Panes ▾ command in the Window group on the View tab to create and freeze panes.

To Create	Cell Selector Location	Example
Two horizontal panes with the top pane frozen	Move to the leftmost column in the window and to the row below where you want the split to appear.	
Two vertical panes with the left pane frozen	Move to the top row of the window and to the column to the right of where you want the split to appear.	
Four panes with the top and left panes frozen	Move to the cell below and to the right of where you want the split to appear.	

	A	B	C
13	**Expenses**		
20	Capital Assets	$ 1,500	$ 1,500
21	Miscellaneous	$ 1,300	$ 1,300
22	**Total Expenses**	$ 22,750	$ 23,075
23	**Income**		
24	Net Income	$ 1,350	$ 1,825
25	**Profit Margin**	5.60%	7.33%

Top pane frozen

	A	D	E
13	**Expenses**		
14	Cost of Goods	$ 9,805	$ 28,205
15	Cost of Merchandise	$ 2,450	$ 5,600
16	Payroll	$ 9,000	$ 27,000
17	Internet	$ 325	$ 975

Left pane frozen

	A	B	E
13	**Expenses**		
14	Cost of Goods	$ 9,065	$ 28,205
19	Advertising	$ 600	$ 1,800
20	Capital Assets	$ 1,500	$ 4,500
21	Miscellaneous	$ 1,300	$ 3,900
22	**Total Expenses**	$ 25,290	$ 78,280

Top and left panes frozen

You want to split the window into four panes with the month column headings at the top of the window and the row headings in column A at the left side of the window.

1

- Move to B6.

- Open the View tab.

- Click **Freeze Panes** in the Window group and choose Freeze Panes.

Your screen should be similar to Figure 3.36

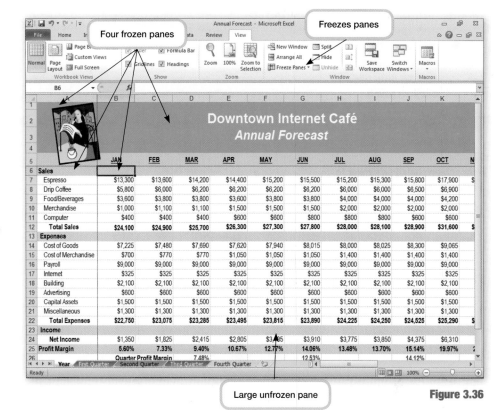

Figure 3.36

The window is divided into four panes at the cell selector location. Only one set of scroll bars is displayed because the only pane that can be scrolled is the larger lower-right pane. You can move the cell selector into a frozen pane, but the data in the frozen panes will not scroll. As you move the cell selector within the worksheet it moves from one pane to another over the pane divider, making it unnecessary to click on a pane to make it active before moving the cell selector into that pane.

Because Evan has asked you to adjust the Profit Margin values, you want to view this area of the worksheet only.

2

- Use the vertical scroll bar to scroll the window until row 25 is below row 5.

- Move to cell G25.

Your screen should be similar to Figure 3.37

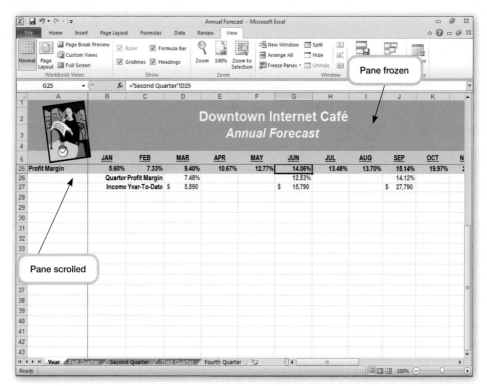

Figure 3.37

Now the Income and Profit Margin data are displayed immediately below the month headings in row 5. The data in rows 6 through 24 is no longer visible, allowing you to concentrate on this area of the worksheet.

WATCHING CELLS

While using a workbook with large worksheets and/or multiple sheets, you may want to keep an eye on how changes you make to values in one area affect cells in another. For example, if you change a value in one sheet that is referenced in a formula in another, you can view the effect on the calculated value using the Watch Window toolbar.

You will be changing values in the Second Quarter sheet next and want to be able to see the effect on the second-quarter profit margin (G26) and annual profit margin (N25) in the Year sheet at the same time.

1

- Select cells G26 and N25.

- Open the Formulas tab.

- Click in the Formula Auditing group.

- If the Watch Window toolbar is docked along an edge of the window, drag it into the workbook window area.

- Click

  🔍 Add Watch...

  from the Watch Window toolbar.

Your screen should be similar to Figure 3.38

Figure 3.38

The Add Watch dialog box is used to specify the cells you want to see in the Watch Window toolbar. The currently selected cells are identified with a moving border. You will add these cells to the Watch Window.

2

- Click [Add].

- If necessary, move the Watch Window toolbar to the upper-right corner of the worksheet window below the column headings.

Your screen should be similar to Figure 3.39

Figure 3.39

Additional Information

You also can watch linked cells in other open workbooks.

The values in the selected cells as well as the formula and location information are displayed in the Watch Window toolbar. The Watch Window toolbar will remain open on top of the worksheet as you move from one sheet to another.

Forecasting Values

Evan has asked you to adjust the forecast for the second quarter to show a profit margin of at least 15 percent for each month. After some consideration, you decide you can most easily reduce monthly payroll expenses by carefully scheduling the hours employees work during these three months. Reducing the monthly expense will increase the profit margin for the quarter. You want to find out what the maximum payroll value you can spend during that period is for each month to accomplish this goal. The process of evaluating what effect changing the payroll expenses will have on the profit margin is called what-if analysis.

Concept 8 What-If Analysis

What-if analysis is a technique used to evaluate the effects of changing selected factors in a worksheet. This technique is a common accounting function that has been made much easier with the introduction of spreadsheet programs. By substituting different values in cells that are referenced by formulas, you can quickly see the effect of the changes when the formulas are recalculated.

You can perform what-if analysis by manually substituting values or by using one of the what-if analysis tools included with Excel.

PERFORMING WHAT-IF ANALYSIS MANUALLY

To do this, you will enter different payroll expense values for each month and see what the effect is on that month's profit margin. You will adjust the April payroll value first.

- **Display the Second Quarter sheet.**

- **Type 7000 in cell B16.**

- **Press ←Enter.**

Your screen should be similar to Figure 3.40

Values in linked cells of Year sheet updated

Chart shows change in profit margin

Reducing Payroll expenses increases Profit Margin

Figure 3.40

Now by looking in cell B25, you can see that decreasing the payroll expenses has increased the profit margin for the month to 18.27 percent. This is more than you need. Also notice the chart has changed to reflect the change in April's profit margin. The Watch Window shows that the values in the two linked cells in the Year sheet were updated accordingly.

You will continue to enter payroll values until the profit margin reaches the goal.

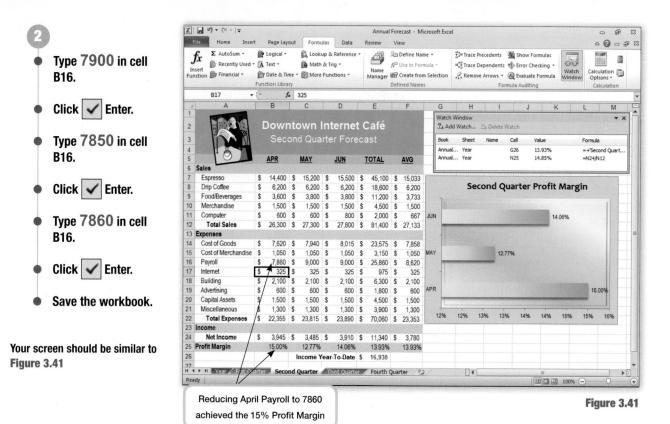

2
- Type **7900** in cell B16.
- Click ✔ **Enter.**
- Type **7850** in cell B16.
- Click ✔ **Enter.**
- Type **7860** in cell B16.
- Click ✔ **Enter.**
- Save the workbook.

Your screen should be similar to Figure 3.41

Reducing April Payroll to 7860 achieved the 15% Profit Margin

Figure 3.41

That's it! Reducing the payroll value from 9000 to 7860 will achieve the 15 percent profit margin goal for the month. Also notice that the column chart reflects the change in the April profit margin.

USING GOAL SEEK

It usually takes several tries to find the appropriate value when manually performing what-if analysis. A quicker way is to use the what-if analysis Goal Seek tool provided with Excel.

Concept ⑨ Goal Seek

The **Goal Seek** tool is used to find the value needed in one cell to attain a result you want in another cell. Goal Seek varies the value in the cell you specify until a formula that is dependent on that cell returns the desired result. The value of only one cell can be changed.

You will use this method to find the payroll value for May that will produce a 15 percent profit margin for that month. The current profit margin value is 12.77 percent in cell C25.

1

- Move to C25.

- Open the Data tab.

- Click
  What-If Analysis ▾
  in the Data Tools
  group.

- Choose Goal Seek.

Your screen should be similar to
Figure 3.42

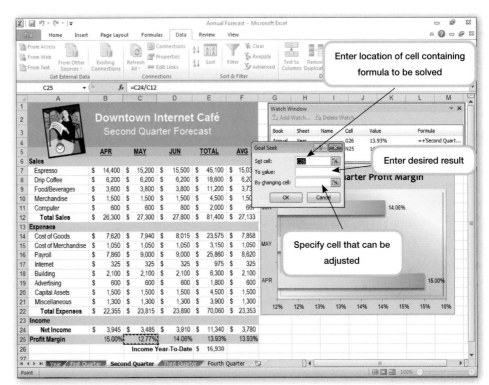

Figure 3.42

In the Goal Seek dialog box, you need to specify the location of the cell containing the formula to be solved, the desired calculated value, and the cell containing the number that can be adjusted to achieve the result. You want the formula in cell C25 to calculate a result of 15 percent by changing the payroll number in cell C16. The Set cell text box correctly displays the current cell as the location of the formula to be solved. You will enter the information needed in the Goal Seek dialog box.

2

- Click in the To value
  text box and enter
  15.00%

- Click in the By
  changing cell text
  box and then click
  on cell C16 in the
  worksheet to enter
  the cell reference.

- Click OK .

Your screen should be similar to
Figure 3.43

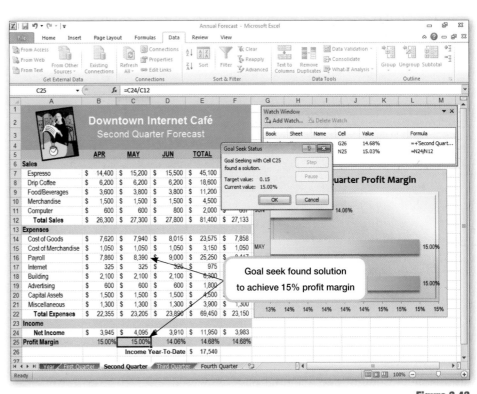

Figure 3.43

The Goal Seek dialog box tells you it found a solution that will achieve the 15 percent profit margin. The payroll value of 8390 that will achieve the desired result has been temporarily entered in the worksheet. You can reject the solution and restore the original value by choosing . In this case, however, you want to accept the solution.

3

● **Click** [OK].

Your screen should be similar to Figure 3.44

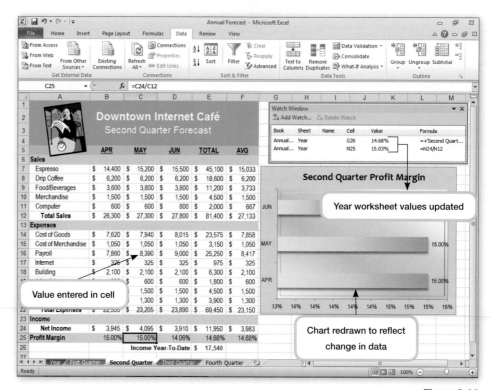

Figure 3.44

The payroll value is permanently updated and the chart redrawn to reflect the change in the May profit margin. Finally, you will adjust the June payroll value. When you are finished, you will close the Watch Window and unfreeze the Year sheet window.

4

- In a similar manner, use Goal Seek to adjust the June payroll value to achieve a 15% profit margin.

- Select both watch cell entries in the Watch Window and click .

- Click ✕ Close to close the Watch Window toolbar.

- Make the Year sheet active to further verify that the profit margin values for the second quarter were updated.

- Open the View tab.

- Click in the Window group and choose Unfreeze Panes.

- Save the workbook file again.

Your screen should be similar to Figure 3.45

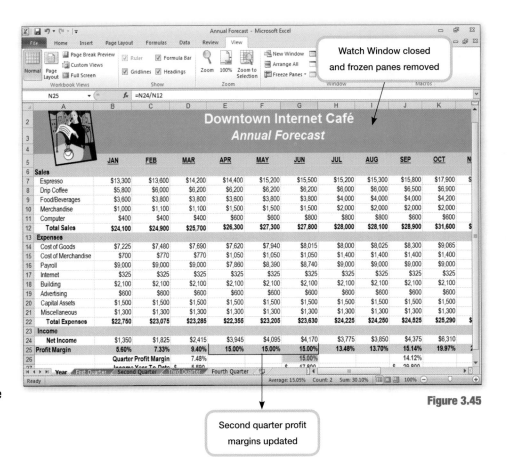

Figure 3.45

The second-quarter values are now at the 15 percent profit margin objective.

Using Conditional Formatting

Next, you want to highlight or emphasize certain values in the worksheet to help visualize the data and quickly analyze information in a worksheet. To do this, you can use conditional formatting.

Conditional formatting changes the appearance of a range of cells based on a condition that you specify. If the cells in the range meet the conditions (the condition is true), they are formatted. If they do not meet the conditions (the condition is false), they remain unformatted. There are several different ways you can apply conditional formatting as described in the following table.

Conditional Formatting	Description
Highlight Cells Rules	Highlights cells based on rules you specify, such as greater than or less than, between, or equal to. It also can highlight cells that contain certain text, dates, and duplicate values.
Top/Bottom Rules	Highlights the highest and lowest values in a range by number, percent, or average based on a cutoff value that you specify.
Data Bars	Displays a color bar in a cell to help you see the value of a cell relative to other cells. The length of the bar represents the value in the cell. A longer bar is a higher value and a shorter bar, a lower value.
Color Scales	Applies a two- or three-color graduated scale to compare values in a range. A two-color scale uses two different colors to represent high or low values and a three-color scale uses three colors to represent high, mid, and low values.
Icon Sets	Displays different color icons in the cell to classify data into three to five categories. Each icon represents a range of values.

CREATING CELL RULES

You will use the cell rules conditional formatting to highlight the payroll values that are less than $9,000 a month.

- Select cells B16 through M16.

- Open the Home tab.

- Click in the Styles group.

- Select Highlight Cells Rules.

- Choose Less Than.

Your screen should be similar to Figure 3.46

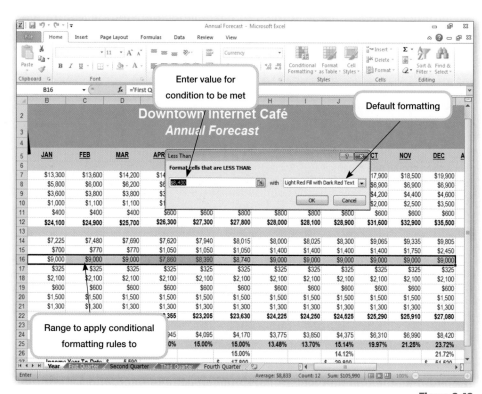

Figure 3.46

In the Less Than dialog box, you enter the value that will be used to determine which cells to highlight. In this case, you will enter the value 9000 so that all values below this amount in the selected range will be highlighted. It also lets you select the formatting to apply to those cells meeting the condition. The default formatting, a light red fill with dark red text, is acceptable.

● Type **9000** in the Less Than box.

● Click [OK].

● Click cell H16 to clear the selection.

Your screen should be similar to Figure 3.47

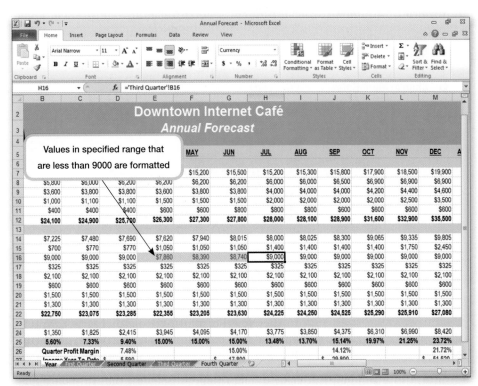

Figure 3.47

Only those cells in the Payroll row whose value is less than 9,000 are formatted using the light-red highlight and dark-red font color.

APPLYING TOP/BOTTOM RULES, DATA BARS, COLOR SCALES, AND ICON SETS CONDITIONAL FORMATTING

Next, you want to emphasize the Net Income values using the Top/Bottom Rules conditional formatting. This formatting identifies the highest and lowest values in a range of cells that are above or below a cutoff value you specify. You want to identify the net income values that are in the top 50% of the values in the range.

1

- Select the Net Income data in cells B24 through M24.

- Click and select Top/Bottom Rules.

- Choose More Rules

Your screen should be similar to Figure 3.48

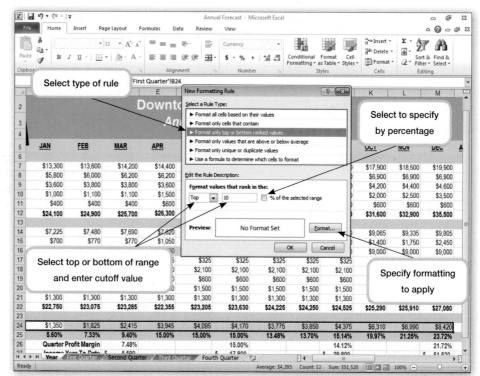

Figure 3.48

In the New Formatting Rule dialog box, you select the type of rule to apply and the rule conditions. The current type of rule is already correctly specified. In the Edit the Rule Description you will specify to format values that are in the top 50% of values in the range using red font color.

2

- Enter **50** in the value text box.

- Click in the check box for % of the selected range to select it.

- Click and choose red for the font color.

- Click OK twice to exit the dialog box.

Your screen should be similar to Figure 3.49

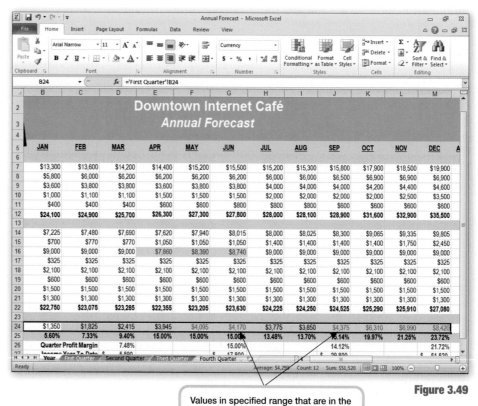

Values in specified range that are in the top 50% are shown in red

Figure 3.49

The net income values that are in the top 50% of values in the selection are now shown in red. Although this is interesting, it does not really provide much additional information. Instead, you decide to undo this formatting and see if applying data bars conditional formatting to the profit margin values is more informative. This option displays colored bars similar to a bar chart within each cell to show the relative values of the cell.

- Click Undo.

- Click **Conditional Formatting**.

- Select **Data Bars** and point to the different data bar colors to see the live preview.

- Choose **Light Blue Data Bar** from the **Solid Fill** section.

Your screen should be similar to Figure 3.50

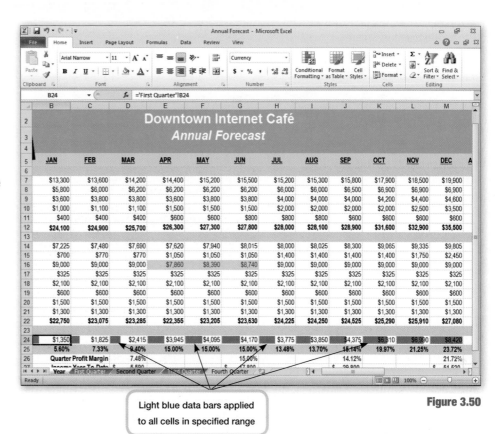

Light blue data bars applied to all cells in specified range

Figure 3.50

Color bars appear in each cell containing a number. The size of the number determines the length of the bar; the larger the value, the longer the bar. Again, you do not feel this adds much to the worksheet and will undo this formatting. Instead, you decide to try the Color Scales conditional formatting, which applies a scale consisting of a gradation of two colors to cells in a range. The shade of the color represents higher or lower values.

4

- Click 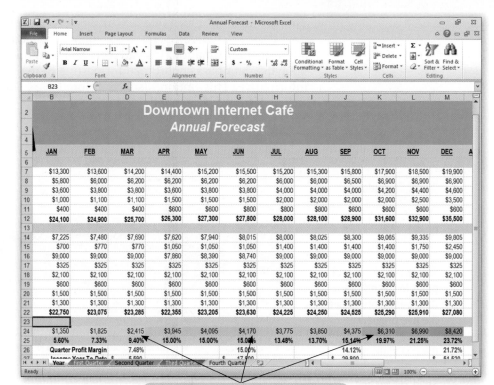 Undo.

- Click [Conditional Formatting] and select Color Scales.

- Choose the Green–Yellow Color Scale (3rd row, 3rd option).

- Move to cell A23 to clear the selection.

Your screen should be similar to Figure 3.51

Green–Yellow Color Scale rule identifies low values in yellow, midrange values in light green, and high values in dark green.

Figure 3.51

This formatting applies a color scale to the data in those cells, with yellow highlight identifying the lowest values, light green the middle values, and dark green the highest values.

Next, you decide to add icons as a visual indicator to the profit margin values.

5

- Select cells B25 through M25.

- Click .

- Select Icon Sets and point to the different icon sets to see the live preview.

- Choose 3 Traffic Lights (Rimmed) in the Shapes group.

Your screen should be similar to Figure 3.52

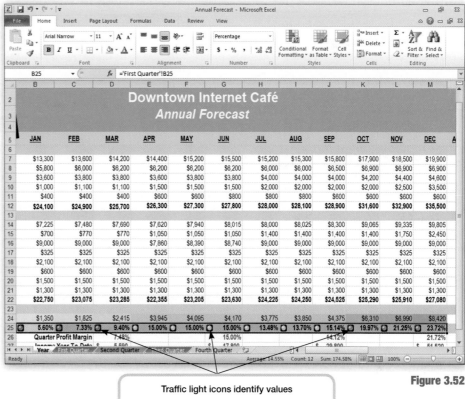

Traffic light icons identify values
in the lower third in red, middle third in yellow,
and upper third in green.

Figure 3.52

The icons give a better indication of which months had a higher or lower profit margin. Red shows where the profit margin value was in the lower third, yellow indicates a profit margin in the middle third, and green shows values in the upper third. These icons reflect the same trends as the color scale used in the net income row of data.

CLEARING CONDITIONAL FORMATTING

Because the icon set formatting really duplicates the information provided by the conditional formatting in the Net Income row, you decide to just keep the Profit Margin formatting. This time you cannot use Undo to remove the conditional formatting from the Net Income row because it also would remove the formatting from the Profit Margin row. To remove conditional formatting, you will need to clear the rules from the range.

1

- **Select B24 through M24.**

- **Click** [Conditional Formatting] **and select Clear Rules.**

- **Choose Clear Rules from Selected Cells.**

Your screen should be similar to Figure 3.53

	B	C	D	E	F	G	H	I	J	K	L	M	A
2				**Downtown Internet Café**									
3				**Annual Forecast**									
4													
5	JAN	FEB	MAR	APR	MAY	JUN	JUL	AUG	SEP	OCT	NOV	DEC	
6													
7	$13,300	$13,600	$14,200	$14,400	$15,200	$15,500	$15,200	$15,300	$15,800	$17,900	$18,500	$19,900	
8	$5,800	$6,000	$6,200	$6,200	$6,200	$6,200	$6,000	$6,000	$6,500	$6,900	$6,900	$6,900	
9	$3,600	$3,800	$3,800	$3,600	$3,800	$3,800	$4,000	$4,000	$4,000	$4,200	$4,400	$4,600	
10	$1,000	$1,100	$1,100	$1,500	$1,500	$1,500	$2,000	$2,000	$2,000	$2,000	$2,500	$3,500	
11	$400	$400	$400	$600	$600	$800	$800	$800	$600	$600	$600	$600	
12	$24,100	$24,900	$25,700	$26,300	$27,300	$27,800	$28,000	$28,100	$28,900	$31,600	$32,900	$35,500	
13													
14	$7,225	$7,480	$7,690	$7,620	$7,94				$8,300	$9,065	$9,335	$9,805	
15	$700	$770	$770	$1,050	$1,05				$1,400	$1,400	$1,750	$2,450	
16	$9,000	$9,000	$9,000	$7,860	$8,39				$9,000	$9,000	$9,000	$9,000	
17	$325	$325	$325	$325	$32				$325	$325	$325	$325	
18	$2,100	$2,100	$2,100	$2,100	$2,10				$2,100	$2,100	$2,100	$2,100	
19	$600	$600	$600	$600	$600	$600	$600	$600	$600	$600	$600	$600	
20	$1,500	$1,500	$1,500	$1,500	$1,500	$1,500	$1,500	$1,500	$1,500	$1,500	$1,500	$1,500	
21	$1,300	$1,300	$1,300	$1,300	$1,300	$1,300	$1,300	$1,300	$1,300	$1,300	$1,300	$1,300	
22	$22,750	$23,075	$23,285	$22,355	$23,205	$23,630	$24,225	$24,250	$24,525	$25,290	$25,910	$27,080	
23													
24	$1,350	$1,825	$2,415	$3,945	$4,095	$4,170	$3,775	$3,850	$4,375	$6,310	$6,990	$8,420	
25	5.60%	7.33%	9.40%	15.00%	15.00%	15.00%	13.48%	13.70%	15.14%	19.97%	21.25%	23.72%	
26	Quarter Profit Margin		7.48%				15.00%			14.12%		21.72%	

Color scale conditional formatting removed

Figure 3.53

The conditional formatting rules for the specified range were cleared and the formatting removed.

Using Sparklines

Although the icon set conditional formatting in the profit margin row identifies variances in a range, the trend is not entirely obvious. To show the data trends more clearly, you decide to create a sparkline. A **sparkline** is a tiny chart of worksheet data contained in the background of a single cell. Generally, a sparkline is positioned close to the data it represents, to have the greatest impact.

CREATING A SPARKLINE

You want to display the sparkline in cell O25, to the right of the profit margin row.

1

- Move to cell O25.

- Open the Insert tab.

- Click 〰 Line in the Sparklines group.

- Select cells B25 through M25.

- Click [OK].

- Increase the width of column O to 30, and the height of row 25 to 50.

Your screen should be similar to Figure 3.54

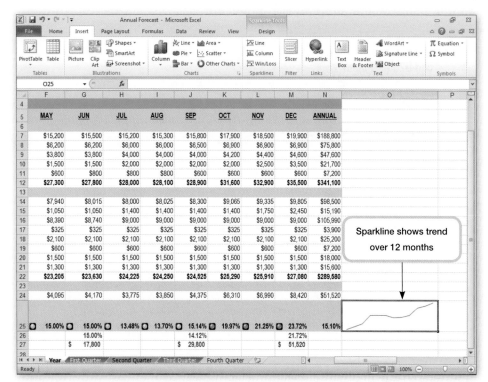

Figure 3.54

A simple line chart of the profit margin values clearly shows the increase in profit margin over the year.

ENHANCING A SPARKLINE

Next you want to improve the appearance of the sparkline by adding data markers and color. Then you will enter a descriptive label in the cell to clarify the meaning of the sparkline.

1

- If necessary, select cell O25 and open the Sparkline Tools Design tab.

- Choose Markers in the Show group.

- Open the Style gallery and choose Sparkline Style Colorful #1 (6th row, 1st column).

- Open the Home tab, click [icon] ▼ Fill Color, and choose Green, Accent 1, Lighter 80%.

- Type **Monthly Profit Margin** and press [Enter].

- Click [icon] Top Align in the Alignment group.

- Save the workbook.

Your screen should be similar to Figure 3.55

Figure 3.55

Additional Information

To delete a sparkline, select the cell containing the sparkline and choose [⊘ Clear ▼] in the Group group of the Sparkline Tools Design tab.

The addition of the sparkline helps clarify the profit margin trend for the year. Just like a chart, if the data in a referenced cell changes, the sparkline will automatically update to reflect the change.

Customizing Print Settings

Now you are ready to print the workbook. Just because your worksheet looks great on the screen, this does not mean it will look good when printed. Many times you will want to change the default print and layout settings to improve the appearance of the output. Customizing the print settings by controlling page breaks, changing the orientation of the page, centering the worksheet on the page, hiding gridlines, and adding custom header and footer information are just a few of the ways you can make your printed output look more professional.

CONTROLLING PAGE BREAKS

First you want to preview the Year sheet.

● Open the File tab and choose Print.

● Display page 2 of the worksheet.

Your screen should be similar to Figure 3.56

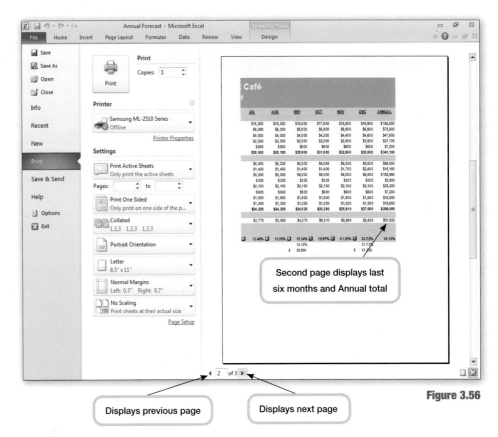

Second page displays last six months and Annual total

Displays previous page

Displays next page

Figure 3.56

The first page of the Year worksheet displays the first six months, and the second page, the remaining months and the annual total. The sparkline is by itself on a third page. Although you could change the orientation to landscape and use the Fit To feature to compress the worksheet to a single page, this would make the data small and difficult to read. Instead, you decide to fit the printout on two pages, with the sparkline on the second page.

To do this, you will change the location of the **page break**, the place where one printed page ends and another starts. Excel inserts automatic page breaks based on the paper size, margin settings, and orientation when the worksheet exceeds the width of a page. You can change the location of the automatic page break by inserting a manual page break location. To help you do this, Page Break Preview is used to adjust the location of page breaks.

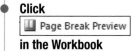

● **Open the View tab.**

● **Click** Page Break Preview **in the Workbook Views group.**

Another Method

You also could click in the status bar to change to Page Break Preview.

● **If a Welcome to Page Break Preview box appears, click** OK **.**

● **Change the zoom to 80% and scroll the window horizontally to see the entire sheet.**

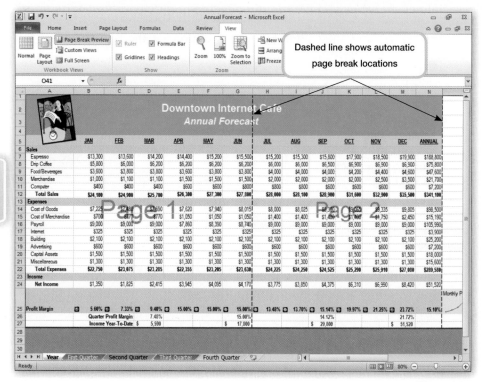

Figure 3.57

Your screen should be similar to Figure 3.57

Additional Information

You can work in Page Break Preview just like in Normal view.

Now you can easily see the page break locations. The dashed line indicates the location of the automatic page breaks. You can change the location by dragging the page break line. When you move an automatic page break location to another location, the page break line changes to a solid line, indicating it is a manual page break. To include the sparkline on page two, you will move the second page break to the right of column O.

Additionally, you realize that the worksheet title will be split between the two pages You will fix the title by unmerging the cells, moving the title to the left on page 1 and copying the title to page 2.

3 ● Point to the page break line after column N, and drag it to the right of column O.

Another Method

You also can insert page breaks by moving to the column location in the worksheet where you want the break inserted and using [Breaks icon] /Insert Page Break in the Page Layout tab.

● Select the two merged cells containing the titles.

● Open the Home tab.

● Open the [Merge & Center icon] Merge & Center drop-down menu and choose Unmerge Cells.

● Copy the contents of D2 through D3 to K2 through K3.

● Press [Esc] to clear the selection and move to cell K4.

Your screen should be similar to Figure 3.58

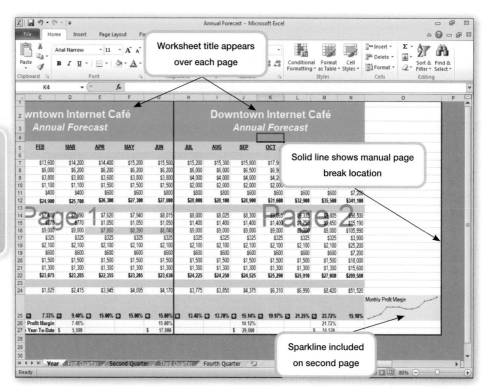

Figure 3.58

The entire worksheet will now print on two pages. Unmerging the cells split the merged cell into its original cells and moved the contents into the upper-left cell of the range of split cells. The center formatting was not removed. Now both pages of the worksheet printout will display a worksheet title.

ADDING A CUSTOM HEADER AND FOOTER

Additional Information

You also can add a custom footer by clicking in the footer area of the page.

You also would like to add a custom header to this worksheet. You will do this in Page Layout view because you can add the header simply by clicking on the header area of the page and typing the header text.

Switch to Page Layout view at 70% zoom.

Click on the left end of the header area of page 1.

Your screen should be similar to Figure 3.59

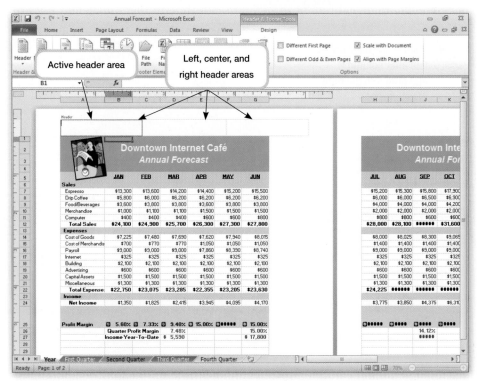

Figure 3.59

The header area is divided into three sections. The left section text box will display the text you enter aligned with the left margin; the center section will center the text; and the right section will right-align the text. You want to enter your name in the left section, class in the center, and the date in the right section. You will enter your name and class information by typing it directly in the box. You will enter the current date using the Current Date feature on the Header & Footer Tools Design tab.

2

- **Type** Created by Your Name

- **Press** Tab.

Another Method

You also could click on the section to move to it.

- **Enter the name of your class and the section or time.**

- **Press** Tab.

- **Click** in the Header & Footer Elements group.

Your screen should be similar to Figure 3.60

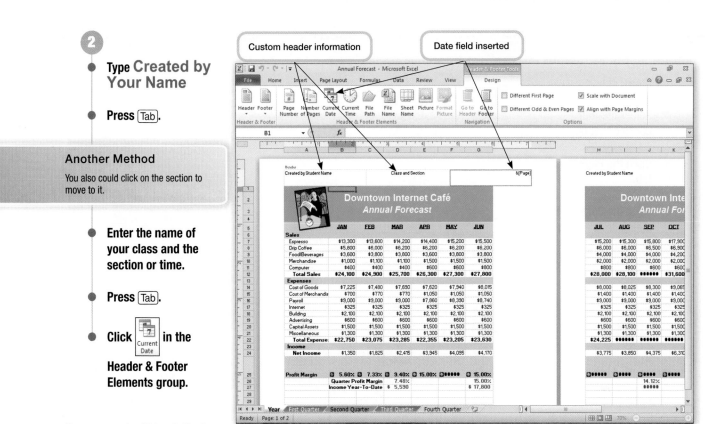

Figure 3.60

Additional Information

Be careful when making changes to multiple sheets as these changes may replace data on other sheets.

The Date field is entered in the header. It will enter the current date whenever the worksheet is opened. The actual date will display when you leave the header area.

Next, you want to add footers to the quarter sheets. It is faster to add the footer to all sheets at the same time. If you make changes to the active sheet when multiple sheets are selected, the changes are made to all other selected sheets.

3

- Display the First Quarter sheet.

- Select the four quarter sheets.

- Open the Page Layout tab.

- Open the Page Setup dialog box.

- Open the Header/ Footer tab.

- Click Custom Footer... .

Your screen should be similar to Figure 3.61

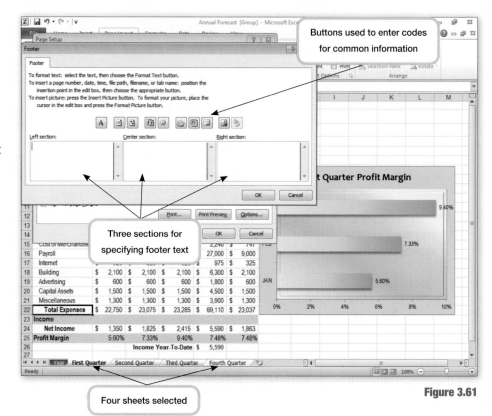

Figure 3.61

Four sheets selected

Additional Information

The quarter sheets are displayed in Normal view. The view you are using applies only to the individual sheet.

Just like in Page Layout view, the footer area consists of three sections. The buttons above the section boxes are used to enter the codes for common header and footer information. The cursor is currently positioned in the Left section text box.

You will enter your name in the left section, the file name in the middle section, and the date in the right section.

4

- **Type your name**

- **Press** Tab.

- **Click** **Insert File Name.**

- **Press** Tab.

- **Click** **Insert Date.**

Your screen should be similar to Figure 3.62

Figure 3.62

Next you will change the orientation of the four sheets to landscape, change the margins to 0.5 inch, and scale the sheets to fit the page. Then you want to make one final check to see how the worksheets will look before printing the workbook.

5

- Click OK .

- **Open the Page tab and choose Landscape.**

- **Choose Fit to, to scale the sheets to one page.**

- **Open the Margins tab and reduce the left and right margins to 0.5 inch.**

Having Trouble?

Use the scroll buttons to increase or decrease the margin size.

- Click Print Preview .

- **Look at the four sheets to confirm that the footer and orientation changes were added to all the quarter sheets.**

Your screen should be similar to Figure 3.63

Landscape orientation and scaled to fit

Footer added to quarter sheets

Figure 3.63

Additional Information

You also could drag the right or left border of the margin area in the ruler while in Page Layout view to adjust the size of the margins.

The footer as you entered it appears on all selected worksheets and the page layout changes were made as well.

PRINTING SELECTED SHEETS

You want to print the Year and Second Quarter worksheets only. Because the annual worksheet is large, you also feel the worksheet may be easier to read if the row and column gridlines were printed. Although gridlines are displayed in Page Layout View and Normal view, they do not print unless you turn on this feature.

1

- Open the Home tab.

- Right-click on a sheet tab and choose Ungroup Sheets.

- Make the Year sheet active.

- Open the Page Layout tab and choose Print in the Gridlines section of the Sheet Options group.

- Save the workbook again.

- Hold down `Ctrl` and click the Second Quarter sheet tab to add it to the selection of sheets to print.

- Open the File tab and choose Print.

- Preview the three pages and then print the worksheets.

> **Another Method**
>
> You also can print gridlines by choosing Gridlines from the Page Setup dialog box.

Your printed output should look like that shown in the Case Study at the beginning of the lab.

PRINTING SELECTED AREAS

You are finished printing the Year and Second Quarter sheets and you have the information Evan requested. However, you think Evan also would like a printout of the First Quarter worksheet without the chart displayed. To print a selected area, you first select the cell range that you want to print.

1

- Make the First Quarter sheet active.

- Select cells A1 through F26.

- Open the Page Layout tab.

- Click [Print Area] in the Page Setup group and choose Set Print Area.

Your screen should be similar to Figure 3.64

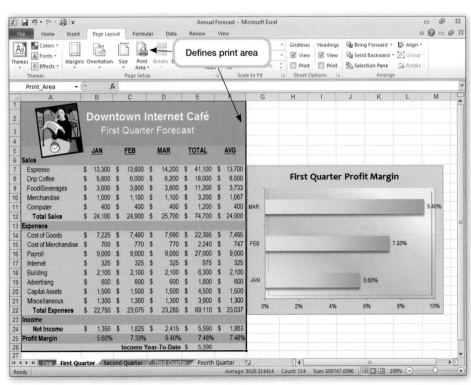

Figure 3.64

The area you selected, called the **print area**, is surrounded with a heavy line that identifies the area.

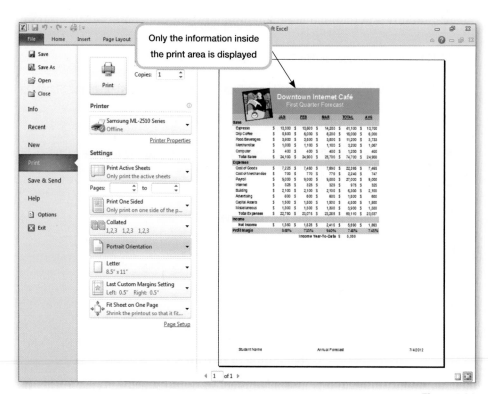

Open the File tab and choose Print.

Change the orientation to Portrait Orientation.

Your screen should be similar to Figure 3.65

Figure 3.65

The Preview displays only the information contained in the defined print area. The print area is saved with the worksheet and will be used automatically whenever you print the worksheet. It can be cleared using Clear Print Area in the menu.

3

- If necessary, specify any printer settings.

- Print the worksheet.

- Change to Normal view and move to cell A6 in the First Quarter sheet.

- Close and save the workbook and exit Excel.

FOCUS ON CAREERS

EXPLORE YOUR CAREER OPTIONS

Medical Sales Accountant

Medical sales accountants visit doctors and clinics to promote the pharmaceuticals and supplies made by the company they represent. The accountants usually specialize in a few pharmaceuticals or products so that they can help the doctor understand the benefits and risks associated with their products. Medical sales accountants must keep careful and complete records of the samples they have in inventory and what they have delivered to doctors. An Excel workbook is a useful tool to keep track of the many doctors and the deliveries made. A career as a medical sales accountant can start with a salary of $35,000 and go up to over $90,000 plus car and travel benefits.

Absolute Reference (EX3.10)

An absolute reference is a cell or range reference in a formula whose location does not change when the formula is copied.

Sheet Name (EX3.14)

Each sheet in a workbook can be assigned a descriptive sheet name to help identify the contents of the sheet.

AutoFill (EX3.17)

The AutoFill feature makes entering a series of headings easier by logically repeating and extending the series. AutoFill recognizes trends and automatically extends data and alphanumeric headings as far as you specify.

Sheet and 3-D References (EX3.19)

Sheet and 3-D references in formulas are used to refer to data from multiple sheets and to calculate new values based on this data.

Find and Replace (EX3.26)

The Find and Replace feature helps you quickly find specific information and automatically replace it with new information.

Split Window (EX3.34)

The split window feature allows you to divide a worksheet window into sections, making it easier to view different parts of the worksheet at the same time.

Freeze Panes (EX3.37)

Freezing panes prevents the data in the pane from scrolling as you move to different areas in a worksheet.

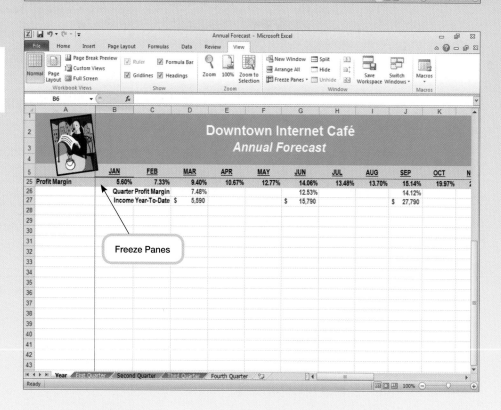

What-If Analysis (EX3.42)

What-if analysis is a technique used to evaluate the effects of changing selected factors in a worksheet.

Goal Seek (EX3.44)

The Goal Seek tool is used to find the value needed in one cell to attain a result you want in another cell.

Conditional Formatting (EX3.48)

Conditional formatting changes the appearance of a range of cells based on a condition that you specify.

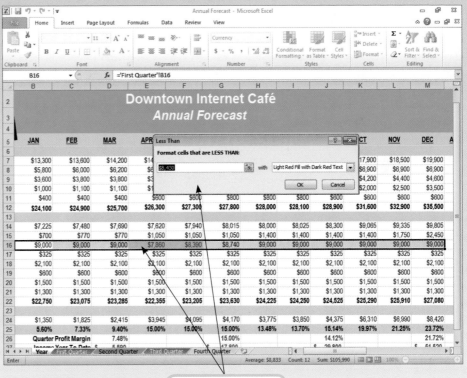

KEY TERMS

3-D reference EX3.19	page break EX3.57
absolute reference EX3.10	pane EX3.34
AutoFill EX3.17	print area EX3.66
conditional formatting EX3.48	sheet name EX3.14
Find and Replace EX3.26	sheet reference EX3.19
freeze panes EX3.37	sparkline EX3.54
Goal Seek EX3.44	split window EX3.34
mixed reference EX3.10	what-if analysis EX3.42

COMMAND SUMMARY

Command	Shortcut	Action
Home tab		
Styles group		
Conditional Formatting ▾		Applies Highlight Cells Rules, Top/Bottom Rules, Data Bars, Color Scales, and Icons Sets to selected cells based on criteria
Cells group		
Delete ▾ /Delete Sheet		Deletes entire sheet
Format ▾ /Rename Sheet		Renames sheet
Format ▾ /Move or Copy Sheet		Moves or copies selected sheet
Format ▾ /Tab Color		Changes color of sheet tabs
Editing group		
Find & Select ▾ /Find	Ctrl + F	Locates specified text, numbers, and/or formats
Find & Select ▾ /Replace	Ctrl + H	Locates specified characters or formats and replaces them with specified replacement characters or format
Find & Select ▾ /Go To	Ctrl + G	Goes to a specified cell location in worksheet
Insert tab		
Sparklines group		
Line		Inserts sparkline in the selected cell
Design Sparklines Tool tab		
Style group		
⟋⟍⟋		Applies pictured style to sparkline
Clear ▾		Removes sparkline

LAB REVIEW

COMMAND SUMMARY (CONTINUED)

Command	Shortcut	Action
Page Layout tab		
Page Setup group		
[Margins] /Narrow		Changes margin settings
[Margins] /Custom Margins/Horizontally		Centers worksheet horizontally on page
[Margins] /Custom Margins/Vertically		Centers worksheet vertically on page
[Print Area] /Set Print Area		Sets print area to selected cells
[Breaks] /Insert Page Break		Inserts page break at cell pointer location
[Breaks] /Remove Page Break		Removes page break at cell pointer location
[Breaks] /Reset all Page Breaks		Restores automatic page breaks
Scale to Fit group		
[Height:] /1 page		Scales worksheet vertically to fit one page
Sheet Options group		
Print Gridlines		Displays/hides gridlines for printing
Formulas tab		
Function Library group		
Σ AutoSum ▾		Enters Sum, Average, Minimum, Maximum, or Count function
Formula Auditing group		
Error Checking ▾		Checks worksheet for formula errors
[Watch Window]		Opens Watch Window toolbar

COMMAND SUMMARY (CONTINUED)

Command	Shortcut	Action
Data tab		
Data Tools group		
What-If Analysis ▾ /Goal Seek		Adjusts value in specified cell until a formula dependent on that cell reaches specified result
View tab		
Workbook Views group		
Normal		Changes worksheet view to Normal
Page Layout		Displays worksheet as it will appear when printed
Page Break Preview		Displays where pages will break when a worksheet is printed
Show group		
☑ Gridlines		Turns on/off display of gridlines
☑ Headings		Turns on/off display of row and column headings
Zoom group		
Zoom		Changes magnification of window
Window group		
Freeze Panes ▾ /Freeze Panes		Freezes top and/or leftmost panes
Freeze Panes ▾ /Unfreeze Panes		Unfreezes window panes
Split		Divides window into four panes at active cell or removes split

LAB EXERCISES

MATCHING

Match the lettered item on the right with the numbered item on the left.

1. panes   _____ a. technique used to evaluate the effects of changing selected factors in a worksheet

2. Goal Seek   _____ b. 3-D reference

3. Sheet1:Sheet3!H3:K5   _____ c. a what-if analysis tool

4. freezing panes   _____ d. mixed cell reference

5. M34   _____ e. applies formatting based on cell rules

6. 'Third Quarter'!A23   _____ f. pane that contains the cell selector

7. what-if analysis   _____ g. the sections of a divided window

8. conditional formatting   _____ h. sheet reference

9. sparkline   _____ i. absolute cell reference

10. #DIV/0!   _____ j. indicates division by zero error

11. $B12   _____ k. prevents data in pane from scrolling

12. active pane   _____ l. a tiny chart of worksheet data contained in a single cell

TRUE/FALSE

Circle the correct answer to the following questions.

1. The sheet reference consists of the name of the sheet separated from the cell reference by a question mark.   **True**   **False**

2. A sparkline is a miniature chart contained in a single cell.   **True**   **False**

3. To create two horizontal panes with the left pane frozen, move the cell selector in the top row of the window and select the column to the right of where you want the split to appear.   **True**   **False**

4. Dragging the sizing handle activates the AutoFill feature and recognizes the cell entry as one that can be incremented.   **True**   **False**

5. Icon Sets conditional formatting applies a two- or three-color graduated scale to compare values in a range.   **True**   **False**

6. You can freeze the information in the top and right panes of a window only.   **True**   **False**

7. The Trace Errors formula auditing command outlines the cell causing the error with a colored border   **True**   **False**

8. A relative reference is a cell or range reference in a formula whose location does not change when the formula is copied   **True**   **False**

9. B$7 is an absolute reference.   **True**   **False**

10. What-if analysis varies the value in the cell you specify until a formula that is dependent on that cell returns the desired result.   **True**   **False**

FILL-IN

Complete the following statements by filling in the blanks with the correct key terms.

1. A worksheet window can be divided into _____, either horizontal or vertical, through which different areas of the worksheet can be viewed at the same time.

2. A technique used to evaluate what effect changing one or more values in formulas has on other values in the worksheet is called _____.

3. A $ character in front of either the column or the row reference in a formula creates a(n) _____ reference.

4. A(n) _____ reference is created when the reference is to the same cell or range on multiple sheets in the same workbook.

5. The _____ feature logically repeats and extends a series.

6. _____ formatting changes the appearance of a range of cells based on a set of conditions you specify.

7. Use a(n) _____ to show the incremental change in data over time in one cell.

8. _____ consist of the name of the sheet enclosed in quotes, and are separated from the cell reference by an exclamation point.

9. When specified rows and columns are _____, they are fixed when you scroll.

10. The _____ tool is used to find the value needed in one cell to attain a result you want in another cell.

LAB EXERCISES

MULTIPLE CHOICE

Circle the correct response to the questions below.

1. A formula that contains references to cells in other sheets of a workbook is a(n) _____.
   a. Sheet formula
   b. Sparkline formula
   c. 3-D formula
   d. Average formula

2. The number 32534 displayed with the Currency style would appear as _____ in a cell.
   a. $32534
   b. 32,534
   c. $32,534
   d. $32,534.00

3. The _____ error value indicates that the wrong type of argument or operand was used.
   a. #####
   b. #DIV/0
   c. #N/A
   d. #VALUE!

4. The _____ function key will change a selected cell reference to absolute.
   a. F4
   b. F7
   c. F3
   d. F10

5. Which of the following is NOT a valid sheet name?
   a. Week 8–10
   b. Qtr 1
   c. 3/12/12
   d. Second Quarter

6. The _____ feature enters a series of headings by logically repeating and extending the series.
   a. ExtendSelect
   b. AutoFill
   c. AutoRepeat
   d. ExtendFill

7. The cell reference that will adjust row 8 without adjusting column E when it is copied is
   _____.
   a. E8
   b. E8
   c. $E8
   d. E$8

8. A cell or range reference in a formula whose location does not change when the formula is copied is a(n) _____.
   a. absolute reference
   b. frozen cell
   c. mixed reference
   d. relative reference

9. The information in the worksheet can be _____ in the top and left panes of a window only.
   a. fixed
   b. aligned
   c. frozen
   d. adjusted

10. _____ is used to evaluate the effects of changing selected factors in a worksheet.
    a. Value analysis
    b. AutoCalculate
    c. AutoFill
    d. What-if analysis

11. A division of the worksheet window that allows different areas of the worksheet to be viewed at the same time is called a _____.
    a. pane
    b. part
    c. window
    d. section

STEP-BY-STEP

GELATO SALES FORECAST ★

1. Leah Miller owns seven Gelato Fresco franchises. She has created a worksheet to record each store's first-quarter sales. Now she would like to create a second worksheet in the workbook to record the projected second-quarter sales for each store. The completed worksheets should be similar to the one shown here.

   a. Open the workbook ex03_Gelato Fresco.

   b. Calculate the total sales for each location and for each month. Adjust column widths as needed.

   c. Copy the worksheet data from Sheet1 to Sheet2 and maintain the column width settings. Check the height of the rows and adjust as needed to show text fully. Reposition the graphic as needed.

Student Name
10/16/2012

Gelato Fresco
Second Quarter Sales
(Projected)

Location	Apr	May	Jun	Total
Bellevue Square	$ 8,600	$ 9,460	$ 10,879	$ 28,939
Southcenter	$ 15,610	$ 17,171	$ 19,747	$ 52,528
The Galleria	$ 12,030	$ 13,233	$ 15,218	$ 40,481
Northgate	$ 9,580	$ 10,538	$ 12,119	$ 32,237
Alderwood	$ 6,740	$ 7,414	$ 8,526	$ 22,680
South Hill	$ 8,700	$ 9,570	$ 11,006	$ 29,276
Pacific Place	$ 10,980	$ 12,078	$ 13,890	$ 36,948
Total	**$ 72,240**	**$ 79,464**	**$ 91,384**	**$ 243,088**

Sales Year-To-Date $ 441,108

   d. Rename the Sheet1 tab **1st Quarter Sales** and the Sheet2 tab **2nd Quarter Sales**. Add color to the tabs. Delete Sheet3.

   e. In the 2nd Quarter Sales sheet, change the monthly labels to Apr, May, and Jun using AutoFill. Change the subtitle line to **Second Qtr Sales**. Enter and bold the heading **(Projected)** in cell A4. Merge and center the heading between columns A and E.

   f. Enter the following projected April sales figures:

Location	Number
Bellevue Square	8600
Southcenter	15610
The Galleria	12030
Northgate	9580
Alderwood	6740
South Hill	8700
Pacific Place	10980

   g. A new advertising campaign for May and June is expected to increase monthly sales. May sales for each location are expected to be 10 percent more than April sales, and June sales are expected to be 15 percent more than May sales. Enter formulas to calculate May and June sales for the "Bellevue Square" location and then copy these formulas into the other appropriate cells.

h. Select both sheets and make the following changes:
- Add a thick bottom border below the headings in row 5.
- Apply the Total cell style to the Total row heading and Total row values.
- Use the Find and Replace command to change "Qtr" to "Quarter."
- Reduce the font size of the subtitle line to 14 points.

i. In the Second Quarter sheet, enter, bold, italicize, and right-align the heading **Sales Year-To-Date:** in cell D14. In cell E14, enter a formula to calculate the total sales for the first six months by summing cells E13 on both sheets.

j. Document the workbook to include your name as the author.

k. In Page Layout view, add a custom header to both worksheets that displays your name and the date right-aligned on separate lines. Center the worksheet horizontally on the page.

l. Preview the workbook. Print the 2nd Quarter Sales worksheet.

m. Save the workbook as Gelato Fresco.

FORECASTING SALES ★★

2. The La Delice Cookies bakery has decided to add brownies to their offerings and wants to know the impact on sales. You are in the process of creating a worksheet of the cookie sales for the last six months. In addition, you want to add brownies to the items for sale and project how much of this item you would need to sell to increase the net income to $2,000 a month. Then, you want to set up a second sheet that you will use to enter the sales information for the second six months when it is available. When you are done, your completed worksheets should be similar to those shown here.

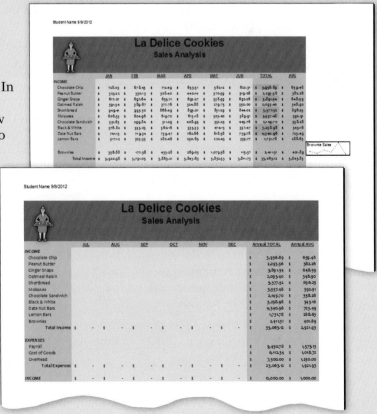

a. Open the workbook ex03_La Delice. Use AutoFill to complete the month headings. Save the workbook as La Delice.

b. Add a blank row below row 15 for brownies. Add the row heading **Brownies** in A16.

c. Edit the formula in B17 to include B16 and copy it across the row through column G.

d. Increase the cost of goods for each month by 12 percent to account for the added goods needed to make the brownies.

e. Enter the formulas to calculate the Total Expenses in row 23.

f. Correct all the formula errors in row 25.

g. Enter the functions to calculate the Total and Average values in row 6. Copy the functions down the columns through row 25. Clear the formulas from all cells that reference blank cells, except for row 16.

h. Freeze the window with the titles in column A and above row 5 frozen so you can scroll to see the Income values in row 25 while working on the brownie sales next.

i. Assuming other cookie sales remain the same, you want to know how much brownie sales would be necessary to generate a monthly net income of $2,000. Use Goal Seek to answer these questions and calculate the brownie sales figures. (Hint: Net income is displayed in row 25.)

j. Unfreeze the window.

k. Using conditional formatting, create a cell rule that will highlight those cookies that have total sales greater than $3,000. Use a highlight color of your choice.

l. You will soon be working on the sales figures for the second six months and want to set up a second sheet to hold this information when it is available. Copy the entire worksheet from Sheet1 to Sheet2, retaining the original column widths. Increase the row height of row 3 to 35.25 points and, if necessary, resize and move the graphic. Change the month headings using AutoFill for the second six months (JUL to DEC).

m. Rename Sheet1 to **January-June Sales**. Rename Sheet2 to **July-December Sales**. Add tab colors of your choice. Delete the extra sheet in the workbook.

n. In the July-December Sales sheet, delete the contents only in cells B6:G16 and B20:G22. In cell H6, enter a formula that adds the total from January through June with the monthly figures from July through December. Copy the formula down the column. Change the average formula to average the 12 months. Clear the formula from all cells that reference blank cells. Clear the conditional formatting from all cells in the July-December Sales sheet. Check the formulas by entering (and then removing) some sample data. Change the label in H4 to **Annual TOTAL** and I4 to **Annual AVG**. Best fit both columns.

o. In the January-June Sales sheet, add a line sparkline in cell J16 using the monthly sales numbers for brownies in row 16. Type **Brownie Sales** in the cell and top-align the text. Increase the row height and column width to show the sparkline. Display markers and choose a style of your choice. Add a thick box border to J16.

p. Use the Find and Replace command to change "bars" to "Bars" in both sheets. In Document Properties, type your name in the Author text box. Add a custom header with your name and the date left-aligned to both sheets.

q. Preview the workbook. Change the print orientation to landscape. Make the necessary adjustments to print each worksheet on a single page. Print both worksheets.

r. Add workbook documentation and save the workbook.

3. Colleen, a travel analyst for Adventure Travel Tours, is evaluating the profitability of a planned Italy Tour package. She has researched competing tours and has determined that a price of $5,000 is appropriate. Colleen has determined the following costs for the package.

Item	Cost
Air transport	$1,400 per person
Ground transportation	$460 per person
Lodging	$1,475 per person
Food	$900 per person
Tour guides	$3,000
Administrative	$1,200
Miscellaneous	$1,500

She has started a worksheet to evaluate the revenues and costs for the Italy Tour. She wants to know how many travelers are needed to break even (revenues equal costs), how many are needed to make $5,000, and how many are needed to make $10,000. When completed your Break Even and $10,000 Profit worksheets should be similar to those shown here.

a. Open the workbook ex03_Italy Tour. Notice that Colleen has already entered the tour price and an estimated number of travelers.

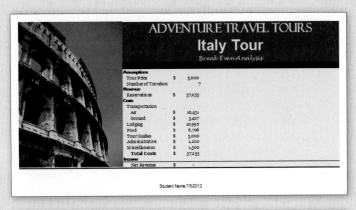

b. Revenue from reservations is calculated by multiplying the tour price times the number of travelers. Enter this formula into C9. Save the workbook as Italy Tour in a folder named Tour Analysis.

c. Based on Colleen's cost information, air transportation is $1,400 times the number of travelers. Enter this formula into C12. Enter formulas into C13, C14, and C15 for the other expenses (see table above) related to the number of travelers.

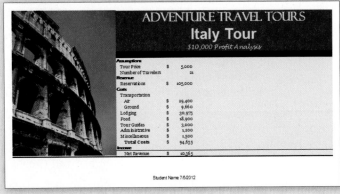

d. Enter the remaining expenses into cells C16, C17, and C18.

e. Calculate total costs in cell C19. Net revenue is the difference between revenue from reservations and total costs. Enter this formula into cell C21.

f. Format the currency values in the worksheet to Accounting with no decimal places.

g. Use Goal Seek to determine the number of travelers needed to just break even (net revenue equals zero).

h. Rename the Sheet1 tab to **Break Even**. Copy the data in the Break Even sheet to Sheet2, preserving column width settings. Rename the Sheet2 tab **$5,000**. Add color to both sheet tabs.

i. In the $5,000 sheet, change the title in B3 to **$5,000 Profit**. Use Goal Seek to determine the number of travelers needed to attain net revenues of $5,000.

j. Copy the $5,000 sheet data to Sheet3 and rename the tab of the copy **$10,000**. Change the tab color. Change the title in B3 to **$10,000 Profit**. Use Goal Seek to determine the number of travelers needed to attain net revenues of $10,000.

k. Use the Find and Replace command to change Trip Guides to Tour Guides in all sheets.

l. Select all three sheets and change the page layout to landscape. Change the left and right margins to 0.5 inch and scale the worksheet to fit on one printed page. Add a custom footer to the three sheets with your name and the date center-aligned.

m. Preview the worksheets. Adjust the picture size if needed.

n. Save the workbook. Print the Break Even sheet and the $10,000 sheet.

CALCULATING TOTAL POINTS AND GPA ★ ★ ★

4. George Lewis is a college student who has just completed the first two years of his undergraduate program as an architecture major. He has decided to create a worksheet that will calculate semester and cumulative totals and GPA for each semester. The completed Spring 2012 worksheet should be similar to the one shown here.

a. Open the workbook ex03_Grade Report. Look at the four sheets. Rename the sheet tabs **Fall 2010**, **Spring 2011**, **Fall 2011**, and **Spring 2012**. Add color to the tabs. Save the workbook as Grade Report in a folder named Grade Analysis.

b. You need to enter the formulas to calculate the Total Points and GPA for the four semesters. You will do this for all four sheets at the same time. Select the four sheets. In the Fall 2010 sheet, multiply the Grade by the Credits Earned to calculate Total Points for Collaborative Studio I. Copy that formula down the column. Sum the Credits Attempted, Credits Earned, and Total Points columns and display the results in the Semester Total row.

c. In cell G13, divide the Semester Total's Total Points by the Semester Total's Credits Earned to calculate the GPA for the semester. Format the GPA to two decimal places. Ungroup the sheets.

d. Use what-if analysis to see the grade George would have had to earn in Western Civilization to get an overall 3.0 GPA for the Fall 2010 semester. Change the grade back to a 2.

e. Look at each sheet to see that the formulas were entered and the calculations performed.

f. Go to cell D14 in the Fall 2010 sheet. Enter the reference formula =D13 to copy the Semester Total Credits Attempted number to the Cumulative Total row. Copy the formula to cells E14 and F14 to calculate Credits Earned and Total Points.

g. Go to the Spring 2011 sheet and calculate a Cumulative Total for Credits Attempted by summing the Spring 2011 and Fall 2010 Semester Totals. (Hint: You can use pointing to enter the Cumulative Totals formula.)

h. Copy that formula to the adjacent cells to calculate Cumulative Totals for Credits Earned and Total Points. Repeat this procedure on the Fall 2011 and Spring 2012 sheets.

i. Go to the Fall 2010 sheet. Select all four sheets. In cell G14, calculate the GPA for the Cumulative Total. Format the Cumulative Total GPA to display two decimals. Look at each sheet to see the cumulative GPA for each semester. (Hint: George's cumulative GPA at the end of the Spring 2012 semester is 3.03.)

j. In each sheet, you want to highlight the information in the grade earned column. In the Fall 2010 sheet, apply a Color Scale conditional formatting to the grade column. In the Spring 2011 sheet, apply Data Bars conditional formatting to the grade column. In the Fall 2011 sheet, apply the 5 Arrows (Colored) Icon Set to the grade column. In the Spring 2012 sheet, apply the 3 Symbols (Circled) Icon Set and a Data Bars conditional formatting to the grade column.

k. Add a custom header with your name left-aligned, the sheet name centered, and the date right-aligned to all sheets.

l. Save the workbook. Print the Spring 2012 sheet.

YEAR-TO-DATE SALES ANALYSIS ★ ★ ★

5. Mei Liao is the owner of the Doggie Day Care Center, which offers full- and half-day care for dogs as well as grooming and training services. She has been asked to prepare a report on the year-to-date accounting totals. She has already entered the figures for January through June. Next, she will create a worksheet for the July through December data and compile the year's totals. Your completed worksheet should be similar to that shown here.

a. Open the file ex03_Doggie Day Care. Adjust the zoom to display all the data. Correct the formula errors. Save the workbook as Doggie Day Care.

b. Enter formulas in cells H9 and H10 to calculate the services totals.

c. Enter the following formula in cell B12 to calculate the income from day care for January: =(B6*B32) + (B7*B33). Copy the formula across the row to calculate the Day Care income. Enter the appropriate formulas in the Total column to calculate the total income figures.

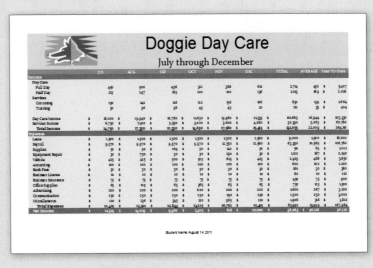

d. Enter formulas in cells H16 through H28 to calculate the total expenses. In cell H29, total the expenses.

e. In cell B30 enter a formula that subtracts the Total Expenses from the Total Income. Copy the formula across the row.

f. Enter the heading **AVERAGE** in cell I3. Adjust the formatting of the new column to match the other columns in the sheet. Enter a formula to calculate the average number of full-day dogs in cell I6. Copy the formula down the column. Delete the division by zero errors. Adjust the formatting of the sheet as needed.

g. Select the range A1:I30 and copy it to Sheet2, maintaining the original column widths. Adjust the graphic size and the row height to accommodate the graphic. Rename the new sheet **Jul-Dec**. Add tab colors to both sheets.

h. Change the title in the Jul-Dec sheet to **July through December**. Change the month heading in cell B3 to **JUL**. Use AutoFill to change the remaining month headings.

i. Adjust the references in the formulas of rows 12 and 13 by adding the sheet reference.

j. Select cells I14 and I30 and use Watch Window to view the changes made when you enter the following values in the specified cells:

	Jul	Aug	Sep	Oct	Nov	Dec
Full Day	450	500	436	321	386	402
Half Day	225	247	185	100	120	136
Grooming	130	142	116	122	156	166
Training	30	36	36	45	45	20

k. Delete the watch cells and close the Watch Window. Move to cell J3 and enter the heading **Year-to-Date**. In cell J6, enter a formula to compute the total full-day care in the first and second six-month periods. Copy the formula down the column to find the year-to-date totals for all of the rows. Adjust the formatting in column J to match the others in the sheet.

l. Delete Sheet3. Use Find and Replace to change the Marketing labels to **Advertising** in both sheets.

m. Use Goal Seek to calculate the number of full-day dogs needed to increase the Net Income for December to $10,000.

n. Add a custom footer with your name and the date to both sheets. Save the workbook.

o. Print the Jul-Dec sheet on one page.

ON YOUR OWN

EXPANDING BUDGET PROJECTIONS ★

1. In On Your Own exercise 2 of Lab 1, you created a Personal Budget workbook for a three-month budget. Extend the worksheet to add three more months for a total of six months. Add two additional sheets. One sheet will contain a budget for the next six months. The final sheet will present a full year's summary using 3-D references to the values in the appropriate sheets. You need to budget for a vacation. On a separate line below the total balance in the summary sheet, enter the amount you would need. Subtract this value from the total balance. If this value is negative, reevaluate your expenses and adjust them appropriately. Format the sheets using the features you have learned in the first three labs. Add your name in a custom header on all sheets. Preview, print, and save the workbook as Personal Budget2.

COMPANY EXPENSE COMPARISONS ★

2. Using the Internet or the library, obtain yearly income and expense data for three companies in a related business. In a workbook, record each company's data in a separate sheet. In a fourth sheet, calculate the total income, total expenses, and net income for each company. Also in this sheet, calculate the overall totals for income, expense, and net income. Format the sheets using the features you have learned in the first three labs. Add your name in a custom header on all sheets. Preview, print, and save the workbook as Company Expenses in a folder named Business.

HOUSE ANALYSIS ★ ★

3. Select three cities in which you would consider living after you graduate. Using the Internet or the library, select one price point of housing and determine each house's asking price, square footage, acreage, number of bedrooms, and number of bathrooms. In a workbook containing four sheets, record each city's housing prices and statistics in separate worksheets. In the fourth sheet, calculate the average, maximum and minimum for each city. Include a chart showing the average data for the three cities. Format the sheets using the features you have learned in the first three labs. Add your name in a custom header on all sheets. Preview, print, and save the workbook as House Analysis in a folder named Housing.

LAB EXERCISES

INVENTORY TRACKING ★ ★ ★

4. It's a good idea to have an inventory of your personal items for safe keeping. Design a worksheet that will keep track of your personal items divided by category; for example: living room, dining room, bedroom, and so forth. Each category may have as many detail lines as needed to represent the items. For example: sofa, vases, art, and so on. The worksheet should keep track of the number of items; the price paid for each item; the extended price (items * price), if applicable; and the replacement value. Determine the percentage increase in replacement value. Sum the price paid and replacement value in each category and the total value. Format the sheet using the features you have learned in the first three labs. Add your name in a custom header on all sheets. Change the worksheet orientation if necessary; preview, print, and save the workbook as Inventory Tracking.

START YOUR OWN BUSINESS ★ ★ ★

5. Owning and managing a small business is a dream of many college students. Do some research on the Web or in the library and choose a business that interests you. Create a projected worksheet for four quarters in separate worksheets. In a fifth sheet, show the total for the year. Include a year-to-date value in each quarterly sheet. In the last-quarter sheet, depending on the business you select, determine how many customers or sales you need in the last quarter to break even and to end the year with a 10 percent profit. Format the sheets using the features you have learned in the first three labs. Add your name in a custom header on all sheets. Preview, print, and save the workbook as My Business.

Working Together 1: Linking and Embedding between Word 2010 and Excel 2010

CASE STUDY

Downtown Internet Café

Your analysis of the sales data for the first quarter of operations for the Downtown Internet Café projects a small, steady increase in sales each month. If an advertising campaign promoting the new Internet aspect of the Café is mounted, you forecast that coffee and food sales in that quarter will increase sharply.

Evan, the Cafe owner, is still trying to decide if he should advertise and has asked you to send him a memo containing the worksheet data showing the expected sales without an advertising campaign and the chart showing the projected sales with an advertising campaign. Additionally, Evan wants a copy of the second-quarter forecast showing the 15-percent profit margins for each month. He also wants a copy of the workbook file so that he can play with the sales values to see their effects on the profit margin.

You will learn how to share information between applications while you create these memos. Your completed documents will look like those shown below.

NOTE **This lab assumes that you know how to use Word 2010 and that you have completed Labs 2 and 3 of Excel 2010.**

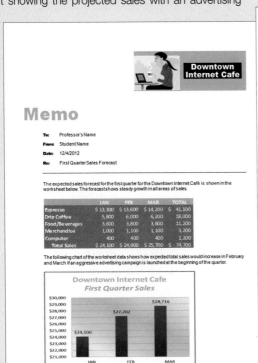

All Microsoft Office 2010 applications have a common user interface such as similar Ribbon commands and galleries. In addition to these obvious features, they have been designed to work together, making it easy to share and exchange information between applications. For example, the same commands and procedures to copy information within an Excel 2010 worksheet are used to copy information to other Office 2010 applications such as Word. The information can be pasted in many different formats such as a worksheet object, a bitmap, a picture, a linked object, or an embedded object. How you decide to paste the object depends on what you want to be able to do with the data once it is inserted in the Word document.

COPYING BETWEEN EXCEL AND WORD

The memo to Evan about the analysis of the sales data has already been created using Word 2010 and saved as a document file.

1

● **Start Word 2010 and open the document** exwt1_Sales Forecast Memo. docx**.**

● **In the memo header, replace Professor's Name with your instructor's name and Student Name with your name.**

● **Save the file as** Sales Forecast Memo **to your solution file location.**

Your screen should be similar to Figure 1

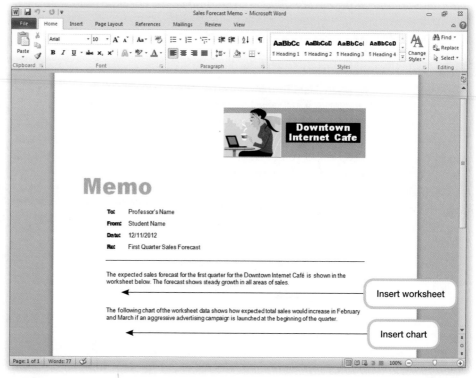

Figure 1

As you can see, you still need to add the Excel worksheet data and chart to the memo. To insert the information from the Excel workbook file into the Word memo, you need to open the workbook. You will then tile the two open application windows to make it easier to see and work with both files.

2

● **Start Excel and
open the workbook**
exwt1_Sales
Charts.

**Your screen should be similar to
Figure 2**

Figure 2

There are now two open applications, Word and Excel. You will insert the
worksheet data of the first-quarter sales forecast below the first paragraph.
Below the second paragraph, you will display the chart.

You will begin by copying the chart from Excel into the Word document.
While using Excel, you have learned how to use cut, copy, and paste to move
or copy information within and between worksheets. You also can perform
these operations between files in the same application and between files in different Office applications. You want to insert the chart as a picture object that
can be edited using the Picture Tools commands in Word.

3

- Select the column chart.

- Click 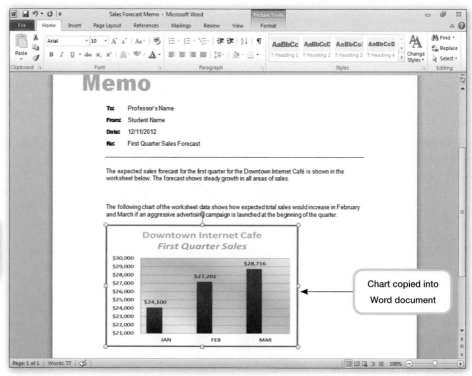 Copy to copy the selected chart object to the Clipboard.

- Switch to the Word document.

Having Trouble?

Click the Word document button in the taskbar.

- Move the cursor to the second blank line below the last paragraph of the memo.

- Click **Paste** to open the Paste menu and choose **Picture**.

- Click on the chart object to select it.

- Open the Picture Tools Format tab.

- Click **Wrap Text** and choose Top and Bottom.

- Adjust the size of the chart and position it as in Figure 3.

Your screen should be similar to Figure 3

Figure 3

A copy of the chart has been inserted as a picture object into the Word document. By changing the text wrapping to top and bottom, the picture object can be moved anywhere in the document and the text will always appear above and below the object. It can be formatted, sized, and moved like any other picture object.

Linking between Applications

Next, you want to copy the worksheet showing the sales trends to below the first paragraph in the memo. You will insert the worksheet into the memo as a **linked object**. Information created in one application also can be inserted as a linked object into a document created by another application. When an object is linked, the data is stored in the **source file** (the document in which it was created). A graphic representation or picture of the data is displayed in the **destination file** (the document in which the object is inserted). A connection between the information in the destination file to the source file is established by the creation of an **external reference**, also called a **link**. The link contains references to the location of the source file and the selection within the document that is linked to the destination file.

When changes are made in the source file that affect the linked object, the changes are reflected automatically in the destination file when it is opened. This is called a **live link**. When you create linked objects, the date and time on your computer should be accurate. This is because the program refers to the date of the source file to determine whether updates are needed when you open the destination file.

You will copy the worksheet as a linked object so that it will be updated automatically if the source file is edited. To make it easier to work with the two applications, you will display the two open application windows side-by-side.

1

- Right-click on a blank area of the taskbar and choose **Show Windows Side by Side** from the shortcut menu.

- Click in the Excel window and select cells A9 through E15.

- Click 🗐 Copy.

- Click in the Word document and move to the center blank line between the paragraphs of the memo.

- Open the Paste menu and choose Paste Special.

- Choose Paste link from the Paste Special dialog box.

Your screen should be similar to Figure 4

Figure 4

The Paste Special dialog box displays the type of object contained in the Clipboard and its location in the Source area. From the As list box, you select the type of format for the object you want inserted into the destination file. There are many different object types from which you can select. It is important to select the appropriate object format so that the link works correctly when inserted in the destination. In this case, you want to use the Microsoft Office Excel Worksheet Object format.

The Result area describes the effect of your selections. In this case, the object will be inserted as a picture, and a link will be created to the worksheet in the source file. Selecting the Display as Icon option changes the display of the object in the destination file from a picture to an icon. When inserted in this manner, double-clicking the icon displays the object picture.

2

● **Choose Microsoft Office Excel Worksheet Object.**

● **Click** OK **.**

Your screen should be similar to Figure 5

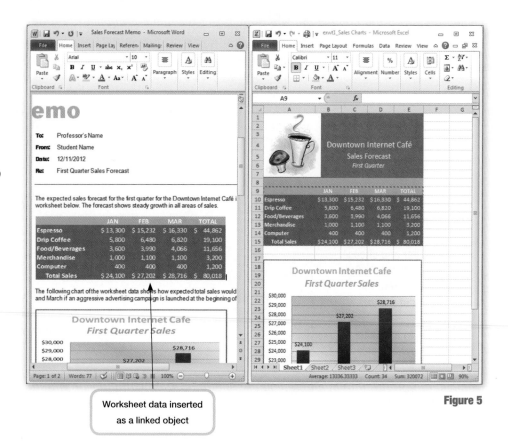

Worksheet data inserted as a linked object

Figure 5

The worksheet data has been copied into the Word document as a linked object that can be sized and moved like any other object.

UPDATING A LINKED OBJECT

Next, you want to return the sales data in the Excel worksheet to the original forecasted values assuming an aggressive marketing campaign is not mounted.

1

- Switch to the Excel window.

- Press $\boxed{\text{Esc}}$ to clear the moving border.

- Change the entry in C10 to **13600** (you are removing the formula).

- In the same manner, replace the formulas in the following cells with the values shown.

Cell	Value
D10	**14,200**
C11	**6,000**
D11	**6,200**
C12	**3,800**
D12	**3,800**

Your screen should be similar to Figure 6

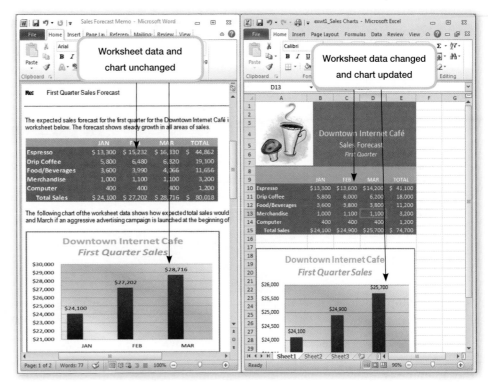

Figure 6

The Excel worksheet and chart have been updated; however, the worksheet data and chart in the Word document still reflect the original values. You will update the worksheet in the Word document next.

2

- Switch to the Word window.

- Select the worksheet object.

- Press $\boxed{\text{F9}}$ to update the linked object.

Another Method

You also can choose Update Link from the linked object's shortcut menu.

Your screen should be similar to Figure 7

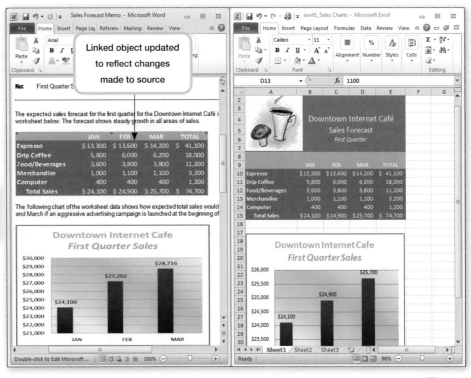

Figure 7

The linked worksheet object in the memo now reflects the changes you made in Excel for the sales data. This is because any changes you make in Excel will be reflected in the linked object in the Word document. Next, you will see if the chart has been updated also.

3

- If necessary, scroll the memo to see the entire chart.

- Click on the chart and press `F9`.

- Deselect the chart.

Additional Information

The chart may have moved to the next page when the worksheet data was inserted. If this happened, reduce the size of the chart object.

Your screen should be similar to Figure 8

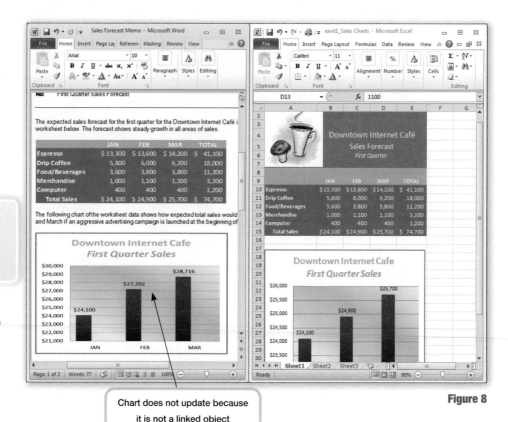

Chart does not update because it is not a linked object

Figure 8

Because the chart in the Word document is not a linked object, it does not update to reflect the changes in data that you made in Excel.

EDITING LINKS

When a document is opened that contains links, the application looks for the source file and automatically updates the linked objects. If the document contains many links, updating can take a lot of time. Additionally, if you move the source file to another location or perform other operations that may interfere with the link, your link will not work. To help with situations like these, you can edit the settings associated with links. You will look at the links to the worksheet data created in the Word document.

1

- Open the taskbar shortcut menu and choose Undo Show Side by Side.

- If necessary, maximize the Word window.

- If necessary, adjust the size of the chart to the same width as the worksheet object.

- Right-click the worksheet object and select Linked Worksheet Object.

- Choose Links from the submenu.

Your screen should be similar to Figure 9

Path to source of linked object

Figure 9

The Links dialog box displays the object path for all links in the document in the list box. The field code specifies the path and name of the source file, the range of linked cells or object name, the type of file, and the update status. Below the list box, the details for the selected link are displayed.

The other options in this dialog box are described in the table below.

Option	Effect
Automatic update	Updates the linked object whenever the destination document is opened or the source file changes. This is the default.
Manual update	The destination document is not automatically updated and you must use the Update Now command button to update the link.
Locked	Prevents a linked object from being updated.
Open Source	Opens the source document for the selected link.
Change Source	Used to modify the path to the source document.
Break Link	Breaks the connection between the source document and the active document.

The links in the Word document are to the exwt1_Sales Charts workbook file. Next, you will save the Excel workbook file using a new file name. Then you will recheck the link settings.

②

- Click OK .

- **Switch to the Excel window.**

- **If necessary, maximize the window.**

- **Save the Excel workbook as** Sales Charts Linked **to your solution file location.**

- **Close the workbook file (do not exit Excel).**

- **Switch to the Word window.**

Figure 10

Having Trouble?

Click the application taskbar button to switch between windows.

- **From the worksheet object's shortcut menu, select Linked Worksheet Object and choose Links.**

Your screen should be similar to Figure 10

You can now see that the link has been updated to reflect the new workbook file name.

③

- Click OK .

- **Open the File tab and choose the Print group.**

- **Check the layout of the document in the preview and if necessary return to the document and make any needed adjustments.**

- **Print and then close the document, saving any changes if needed.**

EMBEDDING AN OBJECT

Additional Information

The source data is stored in an Excel worksheet that is incorporated in the Word file.

The last thing you need to send Evan is a memo that describes and shows the second-quarter forecast. To do this, you will open the memo already created for you in Word and embed the worksheet containing the second-quarter data that Evan wants in the appropriate location. An **embedded object** is stored in the destination file and becomes part of that document. The entire file, not just the selection that is displayed in the destination file, becomes part of the document. This means that you can modify it without affecting the source document where the original object resides.

1

- **Open the Word document** exwt1_ Second Quarter Memo.docx.

- **In the memo header, replace Student Name with your name.**

- **Save the document as** Second Quarter Memo **to your solution file location.**

- **Switch to Excel and open the workbook file** exwt1_Second Quarter.

Your screen should be similar to Figure 11

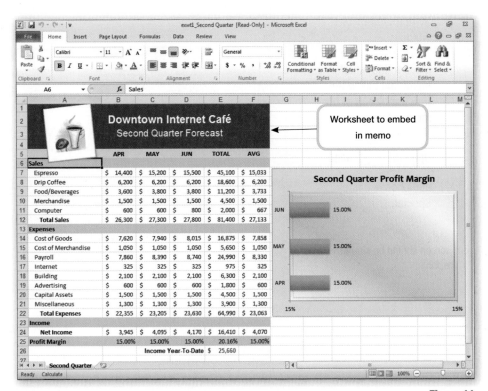

Figure 11

This workbook file contains a copy of the second-quarter worksheet from the Annual Forecast workbook. You will embed the second-quarter forecast worksheet in the Word document.

- **Copy the range A1 through F25.**

- **Switch to the Word window.**

- **Move to the middle blank line below the first paragraph of the memo.**

- **Open the** 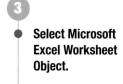 **menu and choose Paste Special.**

Your screen should be similar to Figure 12

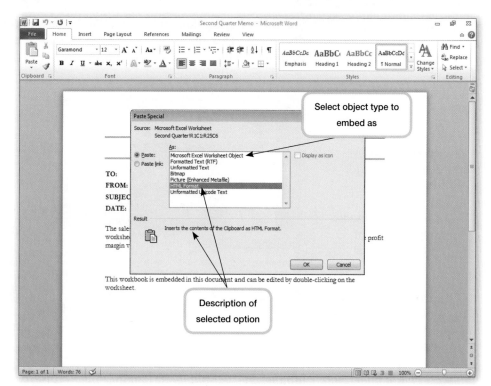

Figure 12

The Paste option inserts or embeds the Clipboard contents in the format you specify from the As list box. The default is to insert the Clipboard contents in HTML format. You want to embed the contents of the Clipboard into the document so it can be edited using the source program. To do this, you select the option that displays the source name, in this case Excel.

3

- **Select Microsoft Excel Worksheet Object.**

- **Click** OK **.**

Your screen should be similar to Figure 13

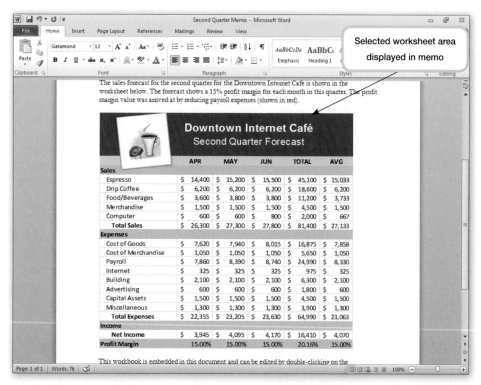

Figure 13

The selected portion of the worksheet is displayed in the memo at the location of the insertion point.

UPDATING AN EMBEDDED OBJECT

You want to add color to the payroll range of cells you adjusted to arrive at the 15 percent profit margin. Because the worksheet is embedded, you can do this from within the Word document. The source program is used to edit data in an embedded object. To open the source program and edit the worksheet, you double-click the embedded object.

● **Double-click the worksheet object in Word.**

Having Trouble?

If the worksheet does not fully display the numbers, click outside the worksheet to return to the document, make the worksheet object larger, and then open the source program again.

Your screen should be similar to Figure 14

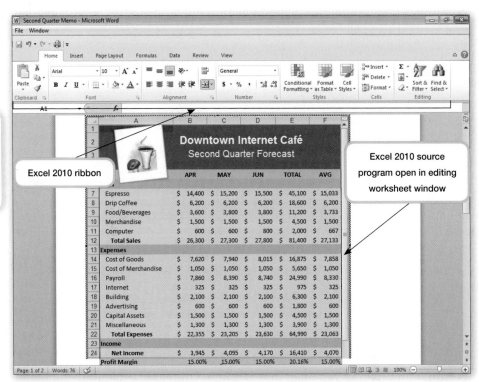

Figure 14

Additional Information

The source program must be installed on the computer system to be able to open and edit the embedded object.

The source program, in this case Excel 2010, is opened. The Excel Ribbon replaces the Word Ribbon and the embedded object is displayed in an editing worksheet window. Now you can use the source program commands to edit the object.

2

● Change the font color of cells B16 through D16 to the Red, Accent 2 theme color.

● Close the source program by clicking anywhere outside the object.

● Save the document.

Your screen should be similar to Figure 15

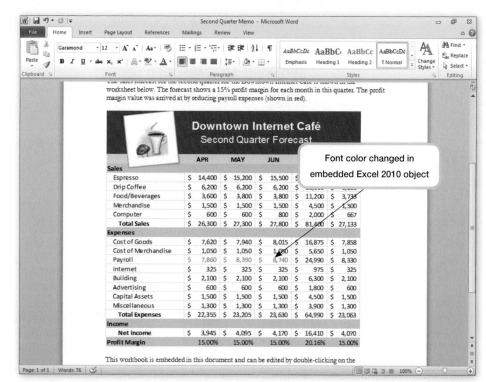

Figure 15

The embedded object in the memo is updated to reflect the changes you made. However, the Excel worksheet is unchanged.

3

● Preview and print the memo.

● Exit Word.

● Look at the Excel worksheet to confirm that the worksheet has not changed.

● Exit Excel.

Deciding When to Link or Embed Objects

Linking documents is a very handy feature, particularly in documents whose information is updated frequently. If you include a linked object in a document that you are giving to another person, make sure the user has access to the source file and application. Otherwise the links will not operate correctly.

Keep the following in mind when deciding whether to link or embed objects.

Use linking when:	Use embedding when:
File size is important.	File size is not important.
Users have access to the source file and application.	Users have access to the application but not to the source file.
The information is updated frequently.	The data changes infrequently.
	You do not want the source data to change.

KEY TERMS

destination file EXWT1.5
embedded object EXWT1.10
external reference EXWT1.5
link EXWT1.5

linked object EXWT1.4
live link EXWT1.5
source file EXWT1.4

COMMAND SUMMARY

Command	Shortcut	Action
Home tab		
Clipboard group		
/Paste Special/Paste		Inserts object as an embedded object
/Paste Special/Paste Link		Inserts object as a linked object
Linked Object shortcut menu (Word)		
Update Link	F9	Updates linked object
Linked Worksheet Object/Links		Modifies selected link

STEP-BY-STEP

RESCUE FOUNDATION INCOME MEMO ★ ★

1. The Animal Rescue Foundation's agency director has asked you to provide her with information about income for 2011. She is particularly interested in the two pet show fund-raising and membership drive events that are held in April and October. You will create a memo to her that will include a copy of the worksheet analysis of this data. Your completed memo will be similar to that shown here.

   a. Start Word and open the document exwt1_ Rescue Memo.docx.

   b. In the memo header, replace the From placeholder with your name.

   c. Start Excel and open the workbook exwt1_ Contributions.

   d. Insert both worksheets as Microsoft Excel Worksheet Object links below the first paragraph in the Word memo. Reduce the size of the worksheets until the memo fits on one page.

   e. You notice the April raffle ticket sales value looks low and after checking your records, you see it was entered incorrectly. In Excel, change the April raffle ticket sales income to $3,120.

   f. In the memo, update the linked worksheet.

   g. Save the Excel workbook as Contributions. Exit Excel.

   h. Save the Word document as Rescue Memo Linked. Preview and print the document.

Memo

To:	Barbara Wood, Director
From:	Student Name
CC:	Mark Wilson
Date:	6/27/2012
Re:	Income

Below is the completed income analysis for 2011. As you can see, the income for Fall/Winter is much higher due to corporate donations.

Animal Rescue Foundation

	March	April	May	June	July	August	Total
Annual Memberships	$9,200	$18,783	$8,595	$9,934	$5,684	$5,781	$57,977
Private Donations	$825	$1,400		$1,225			$3,250
Corporate Donations		$17,000	$15,000		$4,000	$9,000	$45,000
Raffle Tickets		$3,120					$3,120
Pet Show		$8,000					$8,000
Other	$3,000	$3,000	$3,000	$3,000	$3,000	$3,000	$18,000
Total	$12,825	$51,303	$26,595	$14,159	$12,684	$17,781	$135,347

Animal Rescue Foundation

	September	October	November	December	January	February	Total	Annual Total
Annual Memberships	$6,740	$23,723	$10,595	$22,134	$11,984	$10,781	$85,557	$143,534
Private Donations	$800	$2,200	$5,600	$79,900	$1,900	$3,000	$93,400	$96,650
Corporate Donations		$15,000		$312,000		$10,000	$337,000	$382,000
Raffle Tickets		$3,294					$3,294	$3,414
Pet Show		$11,000					$11,000	$19,000
Other	$3,000	$3,000	$3,000	$3,000	$3,000	$3,000	$18,000	$36,000
Total	$10,540	$58,217	$19,195	$417,034	$16,484	$26,781	$548,251	$680,596

Also, the pet show fundraising events have been very successful in boosting income during the slow periods of each year.

1

LAB EXERCISES

STUDENT RETENTION MEMO ★★

2. As part of your job at the State College, you keep track of the number of students who return each year and how many of those students graduate in four or five years. You record this data in a worksheet and are preparing to include the results for the class of 2012 in a department memo. Your completed memo will be similar to that shown here.

a. Start Word and open the exwt1_Student Retention.docx document. Replace Student Name with your name on the From line in the heading.

b. Start Excel and open the exwt1_College Student Retention workbook.

c. Copy the worksheet as a linked object to below the paragraph of the memo.

d. In Excel, enter the fourth-year graduation data for 2012 of **1495** in cell E11 and the fifth-year graduation rate for 2012 of **67** in E13.

e. Save the workbook as Student Retention to your solution file location. Exit Excel.

f. In Word, update the linked worksheet object.

g. Save the Word document as Student Retention Rates to your solution file location. Print the memo.

INTEROFFICE MEMORANDUM

TO:	STATE COLLEGE ADMISSIONS STAFF
FROM:	STUDENT NAME
SUBJECT:	STUDENT RETENTION RATES
DATE:	7/11/2012

The rate of student retention for the past four years is displayed in the worksheet below. The number of students who return to State College every year and finish their degrees in four years is laudable, but there is growing concern at the increasing number of students who either do not return for the fourth year, or don't graduate after four years. There is a meeting scheduled for next week to discuss this issue and possible ways to decrease the rate of change. Please review this information prior to the meeting.

State College
Student Retention Rates

	2009	2010	2011	2012	Average
Enrolled First Year Students	1537	1579	1670	1700	1622
Returning Second Year Students	1397	1433	1571	1598	1500
Returning Third Year Students	1285	1398	1520	1562	1441
Returning Fourth Year Students	1221	1324	1484	1555	1396
Graduating Fourth Year Students	1211	1312	1461	1495	1370
Percent Graduate In Four Years	79%	83%	87%	88%	84%
Graduating Fifth Year Students	44	55	62	67	57
Percent Graduate In Five Years	82%	87%	91%	92%	88%

3. Jennifer works in the marketing department for a local real estate company. She has recently researched the median home prices and number of days on the market over the last three years for existing homes in the local market area. She has created a worksheet and column charts of the data. Now Jennifer wants to send a memo containing the information to her supervisor. The completed memo will be similar to that shown here.

a. Start Word and open the document exwt1_Home Price Memo.docx.

b. In the header, replace the CC: placeholder information in brackets with your name.

c. Start Excel and open the workbook exwt1_Real Estate Prices. Embed the worksheet data including the charts below the paragraph in the Word memo. Exit Excel.

d. Open the embedded worksheet object in Word and scroll to see the column chart of the Average Price. Change the title to Median Price and the chart type to a clustered cylinder.

e. Change the Days on Market chart to a clustered bar in 3-D. Select a more colorful chart style.

f. Reduce the size of the embedded worksheet object until it is just large enough to display the Median Price chart only. (Hint: Drag the sizing handles of the editing worksheet window until only the chart is displayed.) Close the embedded object, leaving the chart displayed in the memo.

g. Save the Word document as Home Price Memo to your solution file location. Preview and print the document.

Memo

To:	Mel Stacker
From:	Jennifer Pizzaro
CC:	Student Name
Date:	July 11, 2012
Re:	Median Existing Home Prices

Below is a chart showing the median existing home prices over the past three years. As you can see, existing home sale prices increased slightly in 2011 and then jumped dramatically in 2012. Another dramatic change has been the decrease in the number of days on the market for homes since 2010 which shows a marked upturn in real estate market demand. This workbook is embedded in this memo and can be viewed in its entirety by double-clicking on the object.

1

Using Solver, Creating Templates, and Evaluating Scenarios

Objectives

After completing this lab, you will know how to:

1. Use Solver.

2. Create an Answer report.

3. Create customized templates.

4. Protect worksheets and workbooks.

5. Arrange workbook and worksheet windows.

6. Hide worksheets and workbooks.

7. Link workbooks.

8. Create, edit, and use scenarios.

9. Create a Scenario Summary report.

10. Create SmartArt.

Downtown Internet Café

After further discussion with Evan, the owner of the Downtown Internet Café, you continued to refine the forecast analysis. Based on Evan's input, you revised the third-quarter sales to show a 16 percent monthly profit margin. You also increased the fourth-quarter sales to show a 10 percent increase over third-quarter sales and increased the fourth-quarter payroll expenses.

Evan thinks these changes are more realistic but wants you to further refine the fourth-quarter analysis to show a fourth-quarter profit margin of 19 percent and an annual profit margin of 15 percent. You will use the Solver tool to help determine these values.

Once the annual forecast for 2013 is complete, Evan wants you to use the same procedure to create the forecast for the following year, 2014. You will use the next year annual forecast worksheet to create a template for the following year's forecast. Then you will use the template to create the first-quarter forecast for that year.

Additionally, you have been asked to create three different scenarios that will show the best, worst, and most likely scenarios for the first-quarter forecast for the following year. The completed scenario summary report is shown here.

Finally, Evan wants you to create a graphic that will illustrate how the five sales categories are related. You will use the SmartArt feature to create a drawing of a pyramid to show how the five sales categories are related.

Using Scenario Manager, you can analyze various possible outcomes to help plan for the future.

Creating links between workbooks allows changes you make in one workbook file to be automatically reflected in another workbook file.

Using Solver, you can quickly determine the effect of changing values in two or more cells on another cell.

EX4.3

Concept Preview

The following concepts will be introduced in this lab:

1 Solver Solver is a tool used to perform what-if analysis to determine the effect of changing values in two or more cells, called the adjustable cells, on another cell, called the objective.

2 Custom Template Custom templates are specialized template files containing settings that are used as a pattern for creating similar worksheets in new workbooks.

3 Protection The protection feature controls what information can be changed in a workbook. Excel includes two levels of protection: worksheet protection and workbook protection.

4 Window Arrangement The window arrangement feature displays all open workbook files in separate windows on the screen, making it easy to view and work with information in different workbooks.

5 Link A link, also called an external reference, creates a connection between files that automatically updates the linked data in one file whenever the data in the other file changes.

6 Scenario A scenario is a named set of input values that you can substitute in a worksheet to see the effects of a possible alternative course of action.

7 SmartArt A SmartArt graphic is used to create a visual representation of textual information

Analyzing the Worksheet

After seeing how the payroll values changed each month to achieve the higher second- and third-quarter profit margins, Evan would like you to do a similar analysis on the fourth quarter. First you want to look at the current total profit margin value for the fourth quarter.

1

- Start Excel 2010.

- Open the workbook file ex04_Revised Annual Forecast.

- Make the Fourth Quarter sheet active.

- Select cell E25.

Your screen should be similar to Figure 4.1

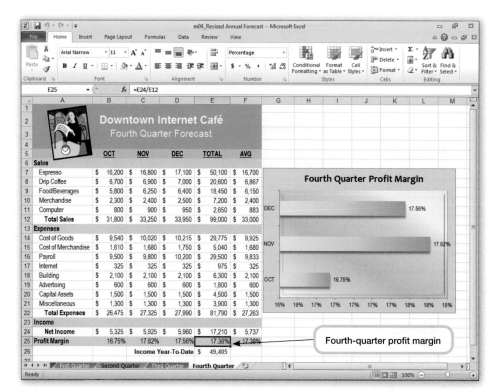

Figure 4.1

The current total profit margin for the fourth quarter is 17.38 percent. Evan would like to achieve a 19 percent quarterly profit margin. To do this, you will need to reduce the monthly payroll expenses. While you are making changes to the quarterly worksheet, you will display the Watch Window to see how the changes affect the annual profit margin.

- **Display the Year sheet.**

- **Select cell N25.**

- **Open the Watch Window.**

Having Trouble?

Click in the Formula Auditing group of the Formulas tab. Click and then to set the watch cell.

- **If necessary, select any existing watch cells in the Watch Window and click** Delete Watch **to delete them.**

- **Add cell N25 to the Watch Window.**

- **If necessary, size and position the Watch Window as in Figure 4.2.**

Your screen should be similar to Figure 4.2

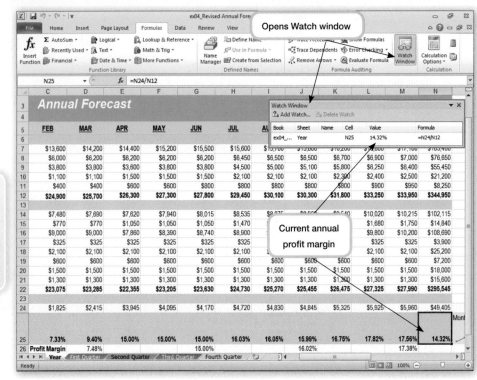

Figure 4.2

The annual profit margin is currently 14.32 percent. Evan also would like to see this value closer to 15 percent for the year.

USING SOLVER

Although you could manually perform a what-if analysis or use the Goal Seek feature to determine the desired profit margin value for the fourth quarter, it would be much quicker to use the Solver tool.

Concept 1 Solver

Solver is a tool used to perform what-if analysis to determine the effect of changing values in two or more cells, called the **variable cells,** on another cell, called the **objective cell.** Solver calculates a formula to achieve a given value by changing one of the variables that affect the formula. To do this, Solver works backward from the result of a formula to find the numbers. The cells you select must be related through formulas on the worksheet. If they are not related, changing one will not change the other. You also can include constraints to restrict the values Solver can use. The constraints can refer to other cells that affect the objective cell formula. Additionally, you need to select the solving method to be used: Generalized Reduced Gradient (GRG) Nonlinear for problems that are smooth nonlinear; LP Simplex for problems that are linear; and Evolutionary for problems that are non-smooth.

Solver also can produce three types of reports about the solution: Answer, Sensitivity, and Limits. In an Answer report, the original and final values of the objective cell and adjustable cells are listed along with any constraints and information about the constraints. Information about how sensitive the solution is to small changes in the objective cell formula or in the constraints is provided in a Sensitivity report. A Limits report includes the original and objective values of the objective cell and adjustable cells. It also lists the lower limit, or the smallest value that the adjustable cell can take while holding all other adjustable cells fixed and still satisfying the constraints, and upper or greatest value.

NOTE: Solver is an Excel Add-in tool that does not appear on the Ribbon until you install it. If <kbd>?➡ Solver</kbd> **is not displayed in the Analysis group of the Data tab (see Figure 4.3), you will need to install it according to the instructions in Step 1. Otherwise, skip to Step 2.**

You will use Solver to calculate the values needed to obtain a 19 percent profit margin for the fourth quarter.

1

- **Open the Data tab and continue with step 1 if** <kbd>?➡ Solver</kbd> **is not displayed in the Analysis group. Otherwise, skip to Step 2.**

- **Open the File tab, choose** <kbd>▤ Options</kbd> **and open the Add-Ins category.**

- **Select Excel Add-ins from the Manage box and click** <kbd>Go...</kbd>.

- **Select Solver Add-in from the Add-Ins available list box and click** <kbd>OK</kbd>.

- **Click** <kbd>Yes</kbd> **to install it.**

Additional Information

You may need the original install CD if you are using your own computer to load this add-in.

The configuration process to add this feature may take a few minutes. When complete, <kbd>?➡ Solver</kbd> appears in the Analysis group of the Data tab.

2

● **Display the Fourth Quarter sheet.**

● **If necessary, open the Data tab.**

● **Click** [? Solver] **in the Analysis group.**

● **Move the Solver Parameters dialog box to the bottom right side of the screen as in Figure 4.3.**

Your screen should be similar to Figure 4.3

Figure 4.3

In the Solver Parameters dialog box, you need to supply three items of information: the objective cell where the result will appear, the desired result value, and the cell or cells that will be changed to achieve the result.

The cell reference of the current cell containing the formula you want to solve is already correctly entered in the Set Objective text box. The number you want as the result of the formula needs to be entered in the To text box. You can set the number to be a maximum, a minimum, or an exact number. The maximum option sets the objective cell to the highest possible number, while the minimum option sets the objective cell to the lowest possible number.

The final information needed is the cell or cell range whose contents can be changed when the formula is computed. This range is entered in the By Changing Variable Cells text box.

In the Fourth Quarter sheet, you are looking for a profit margin value of 19 percent in cell E25 by changing the payroll values in the range of cells B16 through D16.

3

● If necessary, specify cell E25 as the Set Objective cell.

● Choose Value Of.

● Type .19 in the Value of text box.

● Specify the range B16 through D16 in the By Changing Variable Cells text box.

Having Trouble?

You can minimize the dialog box using the ⬚ Collapse Dialog button and select the range by highlighting it in the worksheet.

Your screen should be similar to Figure 4.4

Additional Information

Use Help for more information about the features and uses of Solver.

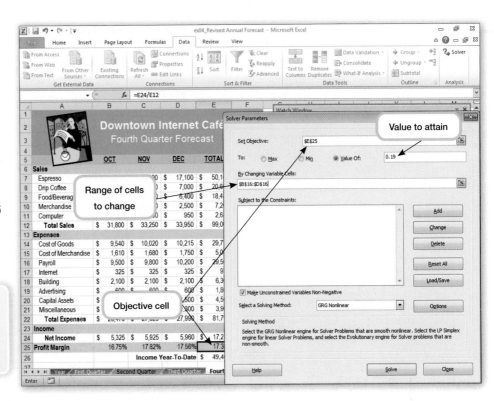

Figure 4.4

The option to make unconstrained variables non-negative remains selected because you are working with positive values. The solving method, GRG Nonlinear, is appropriate for your problem. Now you are ready to have Solver find the values to meet the parameters you specified.

4

● Click .

● Move the Solver Results box as necessary to see the payroll values as shown in Figure 4.5.

Your screen should be similar to Figure 4.5

Additional Information

Although the objective cell value of 19% is the same as in Figure 4.5, the values in your variable cells may be different. This is because Solver can use any number of formulas to modify the variable cells to achieve the objective. If you were to run Solver again using the same information, it is possible you would attain different results.

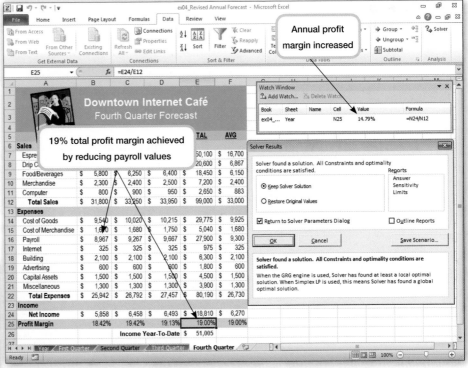

Figure 4.5

The Solver Results dialog box tells you that Solver found a solution. The new payroll numbers are entered in the worksheet range and the worksheet is automatically recalculated. By reducing the payroll expenses slightly each month, the total profit margin for the quarter is 19.0 percent. As you can see in the Watch Window, the profit margin for the year increased from 14.32 to 14.79 percent as a result of reducing payroll expenses in the fourth quarter.

You think the revised payroll values are reasonable. However, using these values does not attain the 15 percent annual profit margin that Evan wants. You decide to run Solver again and set the quarterly profit margin to 20 percent to see if this attains the desired annual profit margin.

From the Solver Results dialog box, you can choose whether to keep the solution or restore the original values. You will keep the proposed solution and run Solver again.

5

- If necessary, choose **Return to Solver Parameters Dialog**.

- Click **OK**.

- **Change the Value Of** to **.20 percent**.

- Click **Solve**.

- Move the Solver Results dialog box to see the new Payroll values.

Your screen should be similar to Figure 4.6

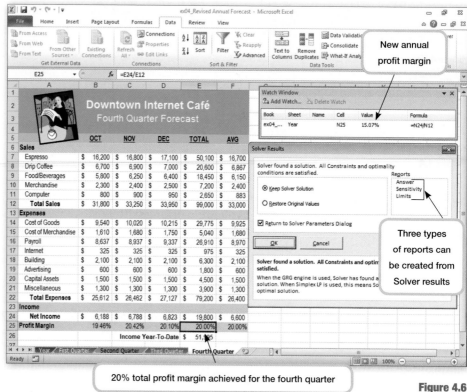

20% total profit margin achieved for the fourth quarter

Figure 4.6

This time the Solver solution increases the annual profit margin to 15.07 percent by reducing the payroll expenses for the fourth quarter.

CREATING AN ANSWER REPORT

In addition to generating Solver solutions, you can have Solver create Answer, Sensitivity, or Limits reports. Reports are created in a new sheet in the workbook.

Report Type	Report Content
Answer	Lists objective cell and adjustable cells with their original and final values
Sensitivity	Provides information about how sensitive the solution is to small changes in the formula in the Set Objective cell.
Limits	Lists objective cell and adjustable cells with their respective values, lower and upper limits, and objective values.

To show Evan the results of the analysis, you will keep the new solution and create an Answer report.

1

● **Clear the Return to Solver Parameters Dialog option.**

● **Choose Answer from the Reports list box.**

● **Click** OK **.**

● **Make the Answer Report 1 sheet active.**

Your screen should be similar to Figure 4.7

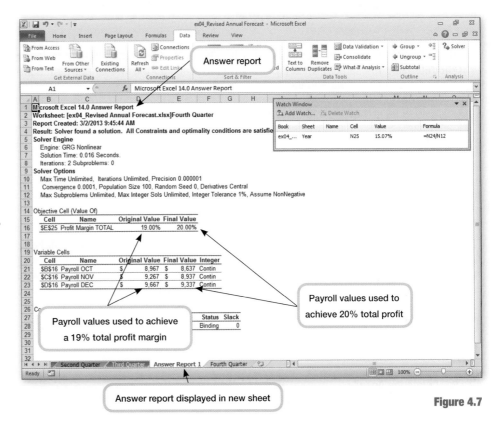

Answer report displayed in new sheet

Figure 4.7

The Answer Report 1 sheet displays the Answer report that was generated. The Objective Cell section of the report shows the original profit margin value of 19 percent and the final value of 20 percent. The Variable Cells area shows the Payroll values needed to achieve a 19 percent profit margin and, in the final values column, the payroll values needed to achieve the profit margin of 20 percent.

The forecast for 2013 is now complete.

2

● **Move the Answer Report 1 sheet after the Fourth Quarter sheet.**

● **Close the Watch Window.**

● **Make the Year sheet active.**

● **Move to cell A6 and save the workbook file as** 2013 Forecast.

Creating a Custom Template

After seeing the effects of your analyses on the Year sheet, Evan has found Solver to be a valuable tool for planning and managing operations. He has asked you to create a new workbook containing a forecast for the following year. You could create this new forecast workbook by starting all over again, specifying the formats and formulas. However, as the current workbook already contains this information, you decide to use it as a model or template for future forecasts.

Concept 2 Custom Template

Custom templates are specialized template files containing settings that are used as a pattern for creating similar worksheets in new workbooks. Custom templates are useful in applications where input and output are required using the same format. By not having to redesign the worksheet form each time the same information is needed, you save time and increase accuracy.

Many custom templates are included with Excel 2010 and more are available from the Microsoft Office Online Web site. They include templates that create different styles of balance sheets, expense statements, loan amortizations, sales invoices, and timecards, to name a few, and are designed to help you quickly create professional-looking workbooks. You also can design and save your own workbook templates or create a template from an existing workbook.

A well-designed template allows you to enter information into the appropriate locations while protecting formulas and basic formats. Since the basic workbook design you want to use for your template is already in place, you will modify the worksheets in the workbook to create the template. The first steps are to eliminate the Answer Report 1 sheet and to change the values in the quarter sheets to zeros.

1

● Delete the Answer Report 1 sheet.

● Select the First Quarter through Fourth Quarter sheets.

Having Trouble?

Hold down Shift to extend the sheet selection.

● Enter **0** in cells B7 through D11 and cells B16 through D21 in the First Quarter sheet.

● Move to cell B22.

Your screen should be similar to Figure 4.8

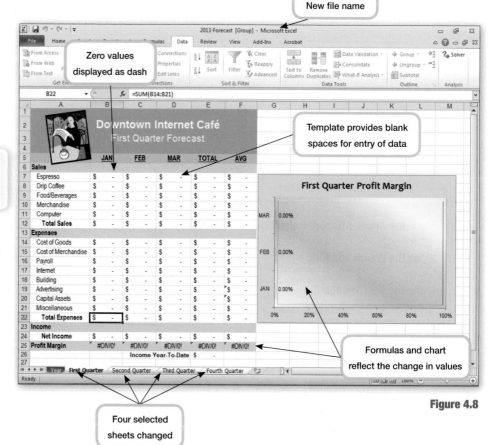

Figure 4.8

The cell format used in the quarter sheets displays cells containing zero values with a dash symbol. All other worksheet cells containing formulas as well as the chart reflect the change in the values.

2

● Look at each of the three other quarter sheets to verify that the values have been replaced.

● Make the Year sheet active and move to cell B7.

Your screen should be similar to Figure 4.9

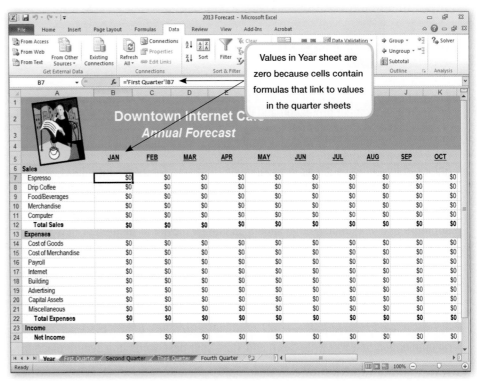

Figure 4.9

Because the Year sheet contains formulas that link to the values in the quarter sheets, this sheet also displays zero values. However, the cell format used in the Year sheet sets the display to show 0 rather than a dash.

Now, whenever you are creating another annual forecast, you will simply enter the new values in place of the blanks in the quarter sheets and the annual sheet will automatically be completed.

PROTECTING THE WORKSHEET

Now that all the values have been removed and the template is ready to use, you want to prevent unwanted changes to the worksheets that would cause headings and formulas to be altered or cleared. To do this, you can protect the worksheet.

Concept ③ Protection

The **protection** feature controls what information can be changed in a workbook. Excel includes two levels of protection: worksheet protection and workbook protection.

Worksheet protection prevents users from changing a worksheet's contents by protecting the entire worksheet, or elements of the worksheet such as specific cells. When a worksheet is protected, all cells and graphic objects on it are locked. The contents of a locked cell cannot be changed. If you want to leave some cells unlocked for editing such as in a worksheet that you use as an entry form, you can lock cells containing labels and formulas but unlock the entry fields so that other users can fill them in. This type of protection prevents you from entering or changing an entry in any locked cells.

Workbook-level protection prevents changes to an entire workbook in two ways. First, you can protect the structure of a workbook so that sheets cannot be moved or deleted or new sheets inserted. Second, you can protect a workbook's windows. This prevents changes to the size and position of windows and ensures that they appear the same way each time the workbook is opened.

In addition, you can include a **password** that prevents any unauthorized person from either viewing or saving changes to the workbook. Two separate passwords can be used: one to open and view the file and another to edit and save the file. Strong passwords combine uppercase and lowercase letters, numbers, and symbols and are at least eight characters in length. If you use a password, you must remember the password in order to use the workbook or worksheet or to turn protection off in the future. Because passwords cannot be retrieved, it is recommended that you write down and store your passwords in a secure place away from the information they protect or use a strong password that you can remember.

Initially all cells in a worksheet are locked. However, you can enter data in the cells because the worksheet protection feature is not on. When protection is turned on, all locked cells are protected. Therefore, before protecting this sheet, you need to unlock the areas in the worksheet where you want to allow users to make changes to information.

The only area of the Year sheet that needs to be unprotected is the subtitle where the year will be entered when the template is used. You will unlock the cell containing the subtitle and add protection to the rest of the worksheet.

- Move to cell D3 on the Year worksheet.

- Click [icon] in the Alignment group of the Home tab to open the Format Cells dialog box.

- Open the Protection tab.

- Clear the Locked option.

Your screen should be similar to Figure 4.10

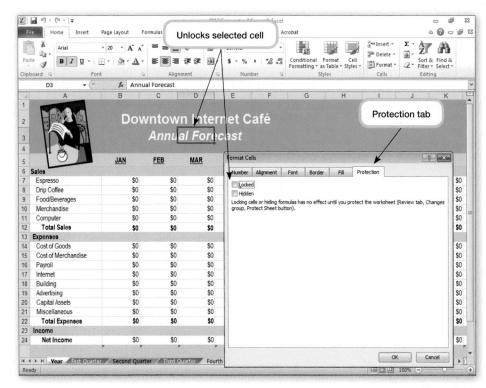

Figure 4.10

Once the cells you want to allow changes to in a worksheet are unlocked, you can add protection.

- Click [OK].

- Click [Format] in the Cells group and choose Protect Sheet.

Another Method

You also can use [Protect Sheet] on the Review tab.

Your screen should be similar to Figure 4.11

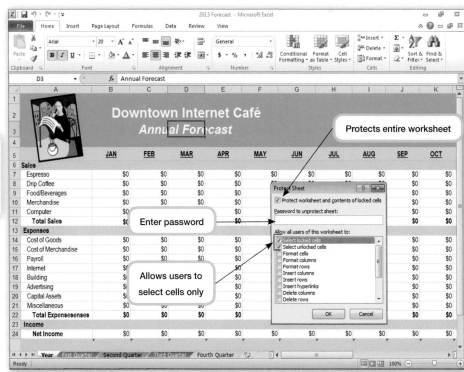

Figure 4.11

Creating a Custom Template   **EX4.15**

In the Protect Sheet dialog box, you can enter a password to prevent unauthorized people from removing protection from the sheet and specify the options that you want to enable for all users of the template. The Select Locked Cells and Select Unlocked Cells options are enabled by default. Leaving these selected and the others unselected provides complete protection for the worksheet. You will complete the command to protect this sheet and then you will unlock the data entry areas of the four quarter sheets using another method.

3

- Enter your name as the password for the sheet.

- Click [OK].

- Reenter the password.

Additional Information

Passwords are case sensitive and must be entered using the same capitalization.

- Click [OK].

- Select the First Quarter through Fourth Quarter sheets.

- Select cells B7 through D11 and B16 through D21.

Having Trouble?

Hold down Ctrl to select nonadjacent ranges.

- Click [Format ▼] and choose Lock Cell to unlock all cells in the selection.

Your screen should be similar to Figure 4.12

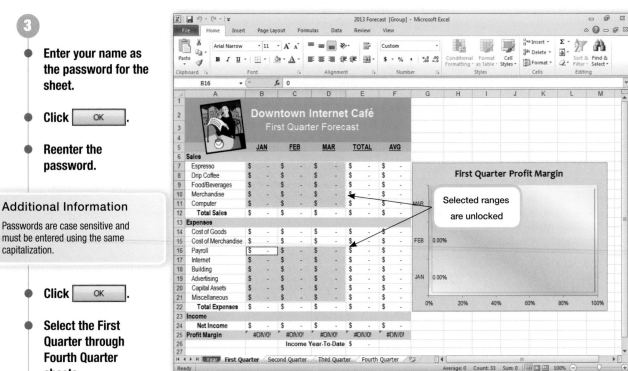

Figure 4.12

All selected cells in the four quarter sheets are unlocked. Next, you will protect the four quarter worksheets. When protecting worksheets, you must protect each sheet individually. You will ungroup the sheets and protect each sheet.

4

- **Choose Ungroup Sheets from the sheet tab shortcut menu.**

Another Method

You also can hold down ⟨Shift⟩ while clicking a sheet tab to ungroup sheets.

- **If necessary, make the First Quarter sheet active.**

- **Click [Format ▾] in the Cells group and choose Protect Sheet.**

- **Enter your password.**

- **Click [OK].**

- **In a similar manner protect the other three quarter sheets.**

Your screen should be similar to Figure 4.13

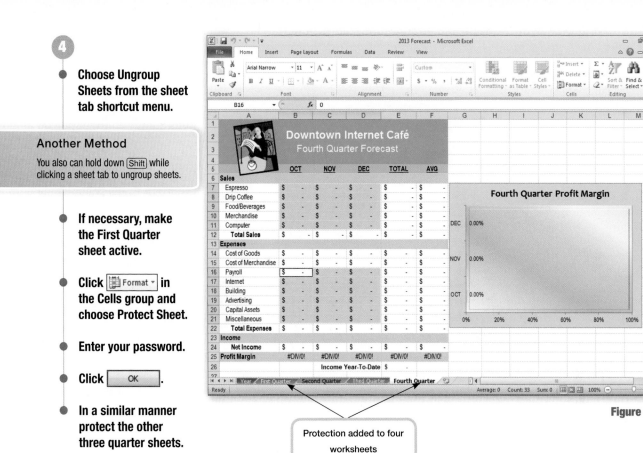

Protection added to four worksheets

Figure 4.13

Now all locked cells in the four quarter sheets are protected. Only those cells you unlocked prior to turning on protection can be changed. To test this out, you will try to make an entry in a protected cell.

5 Type any character in cell B5 of the Fourth Quarter sheet.

Your screen should be similar to Figure 4.14

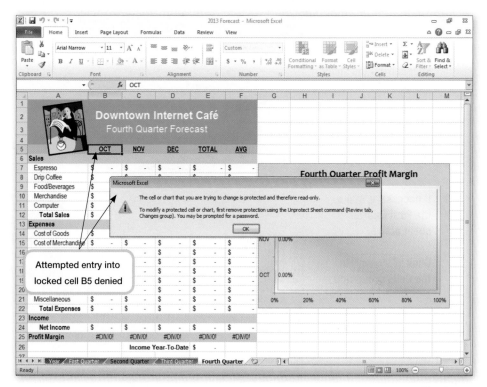

Attempted entry into locked cell B5 denied

Figure 4.14

The warning dialog box informs you that you cannot change entries in locked cells. Next, you will enter a value in an unlocked cell.

6 Click OK to clear the message.

Type **1250** in cell B7 and press [Enter].

Your screen should be similar to Figure 4.15

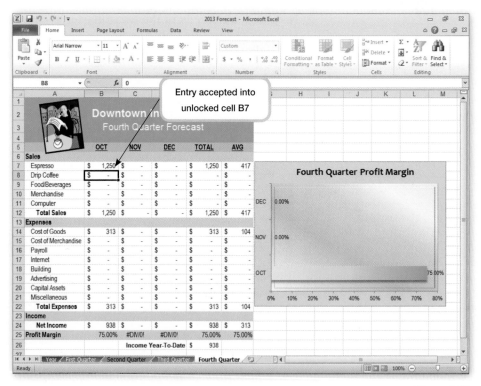

Entry accepted into unlocked cell B7

Figure 4.15

The entry is accepted because the cell was unlocked before protection was applied to the sheet.

PROTECTING THE WORKBOOK

In addition to protecting each worksheet, you can add protection to the work-book file. You will protect the structure of the file and include a password so that workbook protection cannot be changed by anyone who does not know the password.

● Click in the Changes group of the Review tab.

Your screen should be similar to Figure 4.16

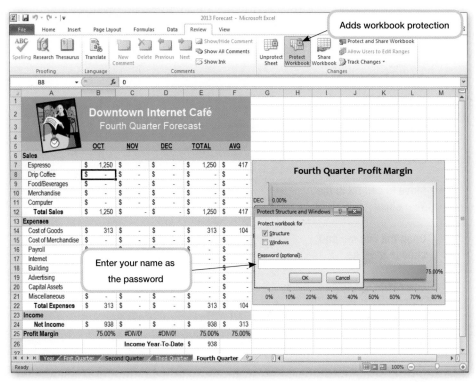

Figure 4.16

The default setting to protect the workbook structure is selected.

2

● Enter your name as the password.

● Click [OK].

● Reenter the password.

● Click [OK].

Notice that [Unprotect Sheet] is displayed in the Changes group. Worksheet protection can be turned off using this button and the appropriate password. Likewise, you can use [Protect Workbook] to turn off workbook protection.

SAVING THE TEMPLATE

Now that the sheets are protected, you will save this workbook as a template file. Excel saves a workbook template using a special file format with the file extension .xltx. Workbook templates are also stored in a special Templates folder.

First, you will clear the test entry and move the cell pointer to the location in the worksheet where you want it to appear when opened.

1

- Click ↺ Undo to remove the test entry.

- Move to cell B7 in each of the quarter sheets.

- Move to cell D3 in the Year sheet.

- Open the File tab and choose Save As.

- Enter Forecast Template in the File Name text box.

- From the Save As Type list box, choose Excel Template.

Figure 4.17

Additional Information

You cannot save a workbook as a template by typing the file extension .xltx in a file name. You must select the Excel Template file type from the Save As Type list box.

Templates are saved by default to the Templates folder on your computer. You can also save templates to other locations just like any other workbook file.

Your screen should be similar to Figure 4.17

2

- Click Save .

Having Trouble?

If a file already exists with this name, click [Yes] to replace it.

- Close the Forecast Template file.

The Forecast Template workbook is now ready to use.

Now you will use the Forecast Template file to create a new forecast workbook for the following year, 2014. To use a workbook template, you select the template file name from the My Templates section of the New window in Backstage view.

1

- **Open the File tab and choose New.**

- **Choose My Templates.**

Your screen should be similar to Figure 4.18

Figure 4.18

The Forecast Template file name appears in the Personal Templates tab of the New dialog box. You will open the template and change the subtitle in the Year sheet to display the year 2014. Then you will try to move one of the sheets to verify that workbook protection is on.

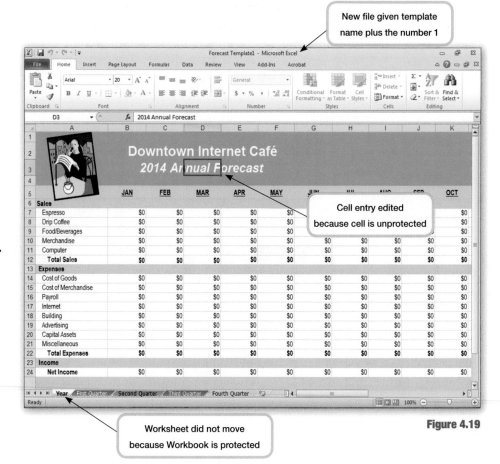

2

- Select the Forecast Template file.

- Click **OK**.

- Edit the subtitle in cell D3 of the Year sheet to **2014 Annual Forecast**.

- Try to move the Year worksheet after the Fourth Quarter sheet.

Your screen should be similar to Figure 4.19

New file given template name plus the number 1

Cell entry edited because cell is unprotected

Worksheet did not move because Workbook is protected

Figure 4.19

The subtitle was successfully changed to reflect the year; however, you were not able to move the sheet because that feature is restricted by workbook protection.

Before continuing, you want to save the revised template file as a new workbook file for use in entering the 2014 forecast data. Notice the file name in the title bar is Forecast Template1. Excel automatically adds a number to the file name when the template is opened to prevent you from accidentally overwriting the original template file when saving. Additionally, when using a template to create a new workbook file, even if you use the Save command, Excel automatically displays the Save As dialog box so that you can specify a new file name. It also changes the file type to an Excel workbook (.xlsx). This ensures that you do not unintentionally save over the template file.

3

- Click 🖫 **Save** in the **Quick Access Toolbar.**

- Enter the new name, **2014 Forecast,** in the File Name text box.

- **Change the Save In location to the appropriate location to save your files.**

- Click [Save] .

Your screen should be similar to Figure 4.20

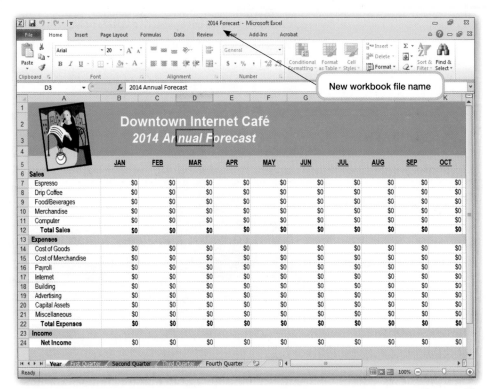

Figure 4.20

Working with Multiple Workbooks

Evan wants you to focus on the 2014 first-quarter forecast. Because he expects all sales and expenses to remain the same as the December 2013 values, you can obtain this data from the 2013 Forecast workbook. To do this, you want to copy the data from one workbook to the other. In Excel, you can open multiple workbook files at the same time. Each workbook is opened in its own window. The open windows can be arranged so that you can see them simultaneously to make it easy to work with data in multiple workbooks at the same time.

OPENING A SECOND WORKBOOK FILE

You will open the workbook file containing the 2013 forecast data you saved earlier.

- **Open the** 2013 Forecast **workbook file.**

- **Point to the Excel icon on the taskbar.**

Your screen should be similar to Figure 4.21

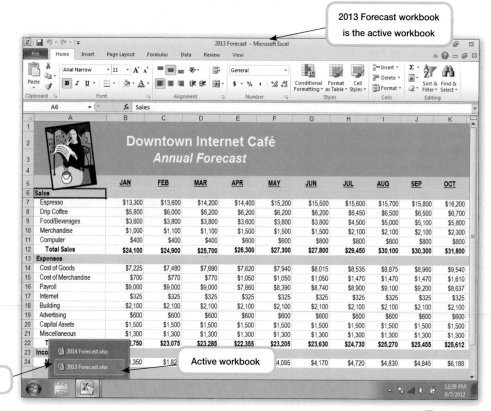

Figure 4.21

Now there are two opened workbook files. The 2013 Forecast workbook file window is open on top of the 2014 Forecast workbook file window. The newly opened file is the **active workbook** file. It is the file that will be affected by changes and the file that contains the cell selector.

ARRANGING WORKBOOK WINDOWS

The way the workbooks are currently displayed makes it difficult to work with both files simultaneously. To make it easier to work with both files at the same time, you can change the arrangement of the windows.

Concept 4 — Window Arrangement

The **window arrangement** feature displays all open workbook files in separate windows on the screen, making it easy to view and work with information in different workbooks. When new workbook windows are opened, they appear in the same size and on top of any other open windows. Open windows can be arranged in the following ways:

Tiled: The windows are displayed one after the other in succession, across and down the screen.

Horizontal: The windows are displayed one above the other.

Vertical: The windows are displayed side by side.

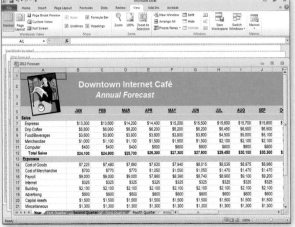

Cascade: The windows are displayed one on top of the other, cascading down from the top of the screen.

You decide that the easiest way to work with the two files is to tile them.

1

Open the View tab.

Click [Arrange All] **in the Window group.**

Additional Information

The Windows of Active Workbook option arranges the windows of only the active workbook.

If necessary, choose Tiled.

Click [OK].

Your screen should be similar to Figure 4.22

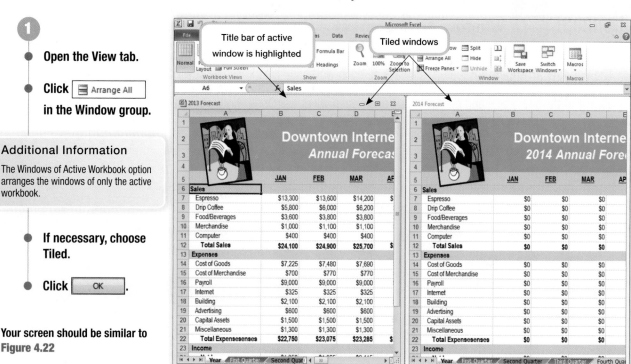

Figure 4.22

The two workbook windows appear side by side. The title bar of the active workbook file is highlighted and the window displays the cell pointer and scroll bar. You want to see the December values in the Fourth Quarter sheet of the 2013 Forecast and the First Quarter sheet from the 2014 Forecast.

2

Display the Fourth Quarter sheet in the 2013 Forecast workbook.

Click in the 2014 Forecast workbook window to make it active.

Another Method

You can also use [Switch Windows] in the Window group of the View tab.

Display the First Quarter sheet.

Your screen should be similar to Figure 4.23

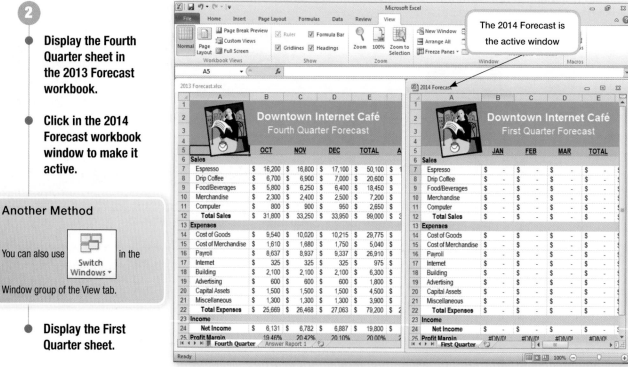

Figure 4.23

HIDING WORKBOOKS AND WORKSHEETS

When you are working with two workbooks that have similar data in them, you might easily confuse them. To help in situations like this, Excel allows you to hide the unnecessary worksheets or even an entire workbook. When you hide worksheets and workbooks, they remain in memory but are not visible to the user. However, the data in the hidden workbook can still be referenced by other workbooks.

You will hide the 2013 Forecast file while you work with the 2014 Forecast.

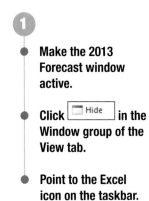

- **Make the 2013 Forecast window active.**

- **Click** Hide **in the Window group of the View tab.**

- **Point to the Excel icon on the taskbar.**

Your screen should be similar to Figure 4.24

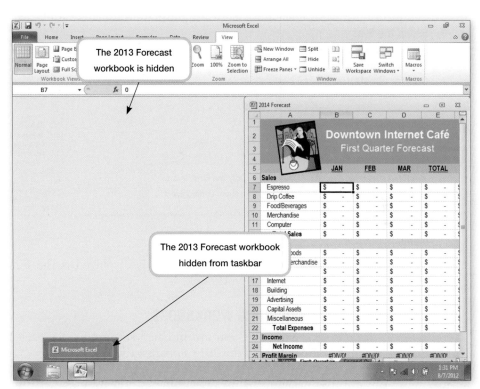

Figure 4.24

The 2013 Forecast workbook file is hidden and no longer appears on the workspace and the Excel icon in the taskbar displays a single file.

Now you want to hide all sheets except the First Quarter sheet in the 2014 Forecast workbook. To do this, you will first need to turn off workbook protection.

2

● Click in the Changes group of the Review tab.

● Enter your password and click OK.

● Select the Year, Second Quarter, Third Quarter, and Fourth Quarter sheets.

Having Trouble?

Hold down Ctrl while clicking the worksheet tabs to select them.

● Choose Hide from the sheet tab shortcut menu.

Your screen should be similar to Figure 4.25

Figure 4.25

The only worksheet that is displayed is the First Quarter sheet in the 2014 Forecast workbook.

UNHIDING WORKBOOKS

Now that you are finished setting up the 2014 Forecast workbook, you will redisplay the 2013 Forecast file.

1

● Click Unhide in the Window group of the View tab.

● If necessary, choose 2013 Forecast.

● Click OK.

● Hover over the Excel icon on the taskbar.

Your screen should be similar to Figure 4.26

The 2013 Forecast workbook now shows on the taskbar

Figure 4.26

The workbook that was hidden is redisplayed in the same window arrangement as before it was hidden and the taskbar button again shows that there are two open Excel workbooks.

LINKING WORKBOOKS

You will use the December data from the 2013 Forecast workbook as the data for January in the first quarter worksheet of the 2014 Forecast workbook. Additionally, you want the data in the 2014 forecast to update automatically if the data in the 2013 forecast changes. To do this, you will create a link between the two workbook files.

Concept 5 Link

A **link**, also called an **external reference,** creates a connection between files that automatically updates the linked data in one file whenever the data in the other file changes. When data in a linked cell changes, the workbook that is affected by this change is automatically updated when it is opened.

The link between the workbook files is formed by entering an **external reference formula** in one workbook that refers to a cell in another workbook. The formula is entered in the workbook that receives the data. This workbook file is called the **destination workbook.** The workbook that supplies the data is called the **source workbook.** The cell containing the external reference formula (the **destination cell**) refers to the cell (the **source cell**) in the source file that contains the data to be copied.

An external reference formula uses the following format:

$$= [\text{2013 Forecast}]\text{Fourth Quarter}!\$D\$8$$

[workbook file reference]sheet reference!cell reference

The file reference consists of the file name of the source workbook followed by the name of the worksheet. The cell reference of the cell or range of cells containing the numbers to be copied into the destination workbook follows the file reference. The two parts of the formula are separated by an exclamation point.

You will create a link between the two workbook files by entering external reference formulas in the 2014 First Quarter worksheet that reference the cells containing the values in the Fourth Quarter sheet of the 2013 Forecast workbook. The 2013 Forecast workbook is the source workbook, and the 2014 Forecast workbook is the destination workbook.

The first external reference formula you will enter will link the Espresso sales numbers. To create an external reference formula, you first select the cell or cells in which you want to create the link and begin by typing an = sign followed by an arithmetic operator if you want to perform a calculation using the linked data.

The source cell is cell D7 of the Fourth Quarter sheet in the 2013 Forecast workbook and the destination cell is cell B7 in the First Quarter sheet of the 2014 Forecast file.

1

- Move to cell B7 in the First Quarter sheet of the 2014 Forecast workbook.

- Type =.

- Make the 2013 Forecast workbook active.

- Move to cell D7.

- Press Enter.

- Move to cell B7 in the First Quarter sheet of the 2014 Forecast workbook.

Your screen should be similar to Figure 4.27

Figure 4.27

The link has been established and an external reference formula has been entered into the selected cell of the destination workbook. The formula is displayed in the formula bar, and the number in cell D7 of the source workbook is entered into the destination workbook and displayed in cell B7. Notice that Excel uses absolute references in the external reference formula.

Next, you want to create a link between the other December values in the source workbook. To do this quickly, you can copy the external reference formula down the column. However, you must first change the absolute cell reference, D7, in the external reference formula to a mixed reference of $D7 so that it will adjust appropriately as the formula is copied.

2

- In cell B7 of the 2014 Forecast workbook, change the absolute reference (D7) in the formula to $D7.

- Copy the external reference formula in cell B7 to cells B8 through B11 and B16 through B21.

- Click cell B21 to deselect the range.

Your screen should be similar to Figure 4.28

Figure 4.28

The data for January 2014 is now complete. It is the same as the December 2013 data. Because the data in the worksheets is linked, a change in the December 2013 worksheet values will automatically be reflected in the First Quarter 2014 worksheet.

UPDATING LINKED DATA

After reviewing your note regarding the payroll values needed to achieve a 20 percent profit margin, Evan has decided to use the payroll values that were generated using Solver for the 19 percent profit margin. You will rerun Solver to quickly revise the figures in the Fourth Quarter worksheet.

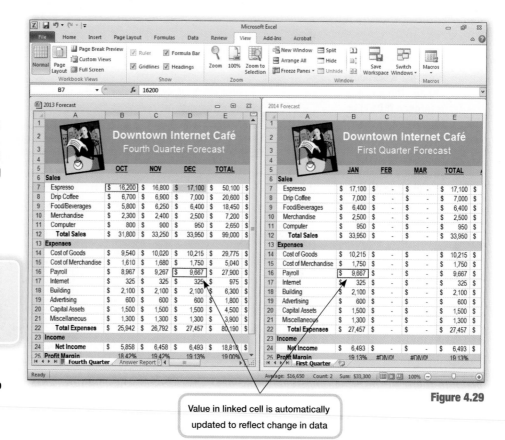

1

- Switch to the 2013 Forecast workbook window.

- Use Solver to obtain a 19 percent profit margin in the fourth quarter by adjusting the payroll values.

- Keep the Solver solution.

Additional Information

Do not be concerned if your solver solution is slightly different; this is a function of how solver rounds the new figures.

Your screen should be similar to Figure 4.29

Value in linked cell is automatically updated to reflect change in data

Figure 4.29

The Payroll value in the linked cell is updated and all affected formulas are recalculated. Because the workbooks are linked, the change in the 2013 Forecast is automatically reflected in the 2014 Forecast. Once an external reference formula is entered in a worksheet, whenever the data in the cell referenced in the source file changes, the dependent file is automatically updated if it is open.

If the dependent file is not open, it is not updated. To ensure that a dependent file gets updated when you open the source file, Excel displays an alert message asking if you want to update references to unopened documents. If you respond Yes, Excel checks the source documents and updates all references to them so that you will have the latest values from the source worksheet.

You do not need to obtain any further data from the 2013 Forecast workbook at this time. You will save it and enlarge the 2014 Forecast window to make it easier to work with.

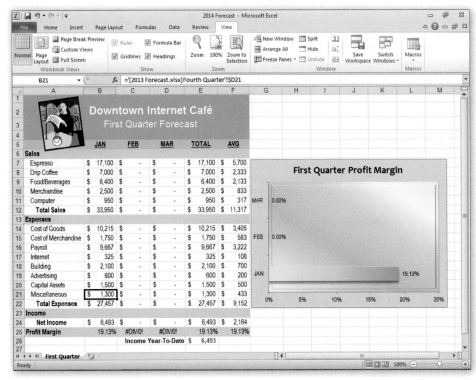

2

• Save and hide the 2013 Forecast file.

• Maximize the 2014 Forecast window.

• Save the 2014 Forecast file.

Your screen should be similar to Figure 4.30

Figure 4.30

Using Scenarios

Evan has reviewed the January 2014 projections and is comfortable with them. He predicts, however, that post-holiday sales in February and March will decline. He has asked you to complete the First Quarter forecast with the following data:

Sales and Expenses		February	March
Sales	Espresso	16,800	16,200
	Drip Coffee	6,900	6,700
	Food/Beverages	6,250	5,800
	Merchandise	2,200	2,000
	Computer	950	900
Expenses	Payroll	9,200	8,800
	Internet	325	325
	Building	2,100	2,100
	Advertising	600	600
	Capital Assets	1,500	1,500
	Miscellaneous	1,300	1,300

1

Enter the values shown in the table on the previous page to update the First Quarter forecast.

Your screen should be similar to Figure 4.31

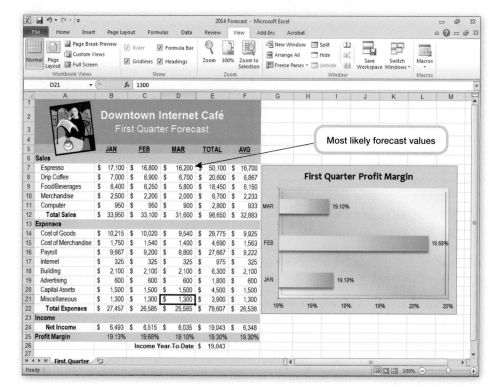

Most likely forecast values

Figure 4.31

While he realizes that sales and costs may be higher or lower than those presented, Evan believes the most likely **scenario,** or set of values, is reflected in the First Quarter worksheet. He has asked you to evaluate a best-case scenario and a worst-case scenario.

Concept 6 Scenario

A **scenario** is a named set of input values that you can substitute in a worksheet to see the effects of a possible alternative course of action. Scenarios are designed to help forecast the outcome of various possible actions. You can create and save different groups of scenario values on a worksheet and then switch to any of these scenarios to view the results.

For example, if you want to create a budget forecast based on various revenue values, you could define the potential values and then switch between the scenarios to perform what-if analyses. You also can create reports in separate sheets that summarize the scenarios you create.

The current data in the First Quarter worksheet reflects the most likely scenario. Evan has identified the best-case scenario as one where Espresso sales increase 25 percent above the current estimate in February and March and all other values remain unchanged. His worst-case scenario is if Espresso sales decrease 10 percent below the current estimate for the entire quarter and the building expenses in March increase to $2,500.

CREATING SCENARIOS

You will use the Scenario Manager tool to evaluate the alternative scenarios by changing the values for Espresso sales for January (cell B7), February (cell C7), and March (cell D7), and for March Building expense (cell D18). You could create separate worksheets to evaluate each scenario. However, using the Scenario Manager tool, you can create different scenarios and insert these scenarios directly into the workbook to see how each affects the worksheet.

- Open the Data tab.

- Click

  from the Data Tools group and choose Scenario Manager.

- Move the Scenario Manager dialog box to the right of column F, as shown in Figure 4.32.

Your screen should be similar to Figure 4.32

Figure 4.32

Additional Information

It is always a good idea to create a scenario of your original data as this will allow you to redisplay this information at any time.

The Scenario Manager dialog box is used to add, delete, and edit scenarios. There are no scenarios named yet. First, you will define the most likely scenario.

2 Click [Add...].

Your screen should be similar to Figure 4.33

Enter name of new scenario

Specify cells whose values will change

Add comments to clarify scenarios

Figure 4.33

In the Add Scenario dialog box, you enter a name for the first scenario and the range of cells that will contain the changing values.

3
- Type **Most Likely** in the Scenario name text box.

- Specify the range B7 through D7 and cell D18 as the changing cells in the Changing cells text box.

Having Trouble?

Click [icon] to reduce the dialog box and select the range from the worksheet. Hold down Ctrl while selecting nonadjacent cells.

Your screen should be similar to Figure 4.34

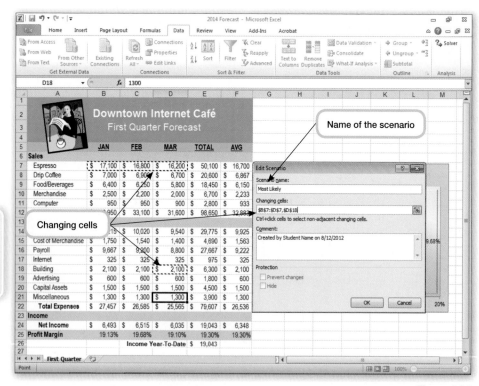

Name of the scenario

Changing cells

Figure 4.34

It is often helpful to add a comment to clarify the data included in the scenario. The default comment in the Comment text box is "Created by [name] on [date]." You will include additional information to clarify the meaning of the scenario.

4

- Click in the Comment text box.

- If necessary, replace the name with your name.

- Press [Enter] at the end of the date.

- Type **Expected first quarter sales and expenses.**

- Click .

- Click [OK] to accept that formulas will be replaced by values.

Your screen should be similar to Figure 4.35

Figure 4.35

The Scenario Values dialog box is used to enter the values to be varied for the different scenarios. The current worksheet values are displayed. These are the values you want to use for the Most Likely scenario.

5

- Click [OK].

Your screen should be similar to Figure 4.36

Figure 4.36

You are returned to the Scenario Manager dialog box and the name of the new scenario is displayed in the Scenarios list box.

Next, you will create the worst-case scenario. In this scenario, there would be a 10 percent decrease in Espresso sales and an increase in the Building expense.

6

- Click .

- In the Scenario name text box, type **Worst Case.**

- In the Comment text box, change the name if necessary and enter the following: **Espresso sales are 10% less than the most likely values and March building expense increases to $2,500.**

- Click OK .

- Click OK to accept that formulas will be replaced by values.

- Enter the following scenario values into the appropriate changing cells text boxes.

  B7   **15390**

  C7   **15120**

  D7   **14580**

  D18 **2500**

Your screen should be similar to Figure 4.37

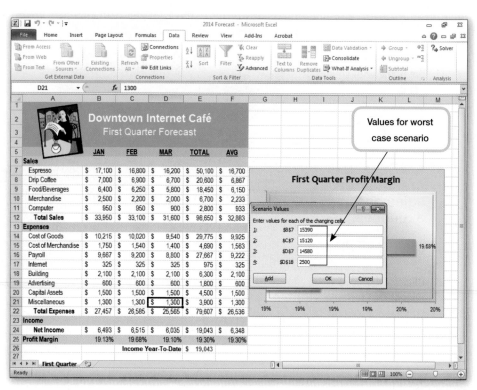

Figure 4.37

Next, you will create the best-case scenario. In this scenario, Evan anticipates that Espresso sales will increase 5 percent above the most-likely values and the March Building expense will remain the same. You could create the scenario in the same way by entering the new values in the changing cells. Another way is to use Solver to calculate the expected values for you and then create the scenario from the Solver result. You will need to provide the objective cell value in cell E7 of 52650 for Solver, which reflects a 5 percent increase in total espresso sales for the quarter. Because the objective cell (E7) is not unlocked, you will need to remove worksheet protection before using Solver.

7

- Click [OK].

- Click [Close].

- Save the workbook file.

- Click in the **Unprotect Sheet** **Changes group of the Review tab, enter your password, and click** [OK].

- Click [?ₐ Solver] in the **Analysis group on the Data tab.**

- **Set the objective cell as E7, the value equal to 52650, and the changing cells as B7:D7.**

- Click [Solve].

Your screen should be similar to Figure 4.38.

Figure 4.38

The Solver solution increases the Espresso sales for each month to attain the objective value. You will create the scenario from these results. You will not keep the Solver solution, as you want the original values maintained in the worksheet.

8

- Click [Save Scenario...].

- Enter the scenario name of **Best Case**.

- Click [OK].

- Choose **Restore Original Values**.

- Click [OK].

- **Save the** workbook file.

Your screen should be similar to Figure 4.39

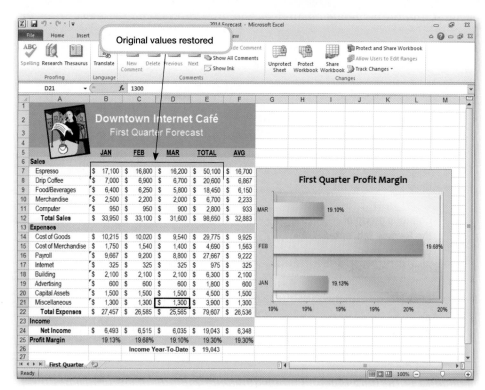

Figure 4.39

The original values are displayed in the worksheet again and the Solver results have been stored as a scenario.

SHOWING AND EDITING SCENARIOS

There are now three different scenarios in the worksheet. You want to see the effects of the worst-case and best-case scenarios.

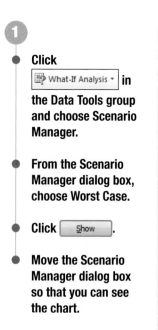

1

- Click [What-If Analysis] in the Data Tools group and choose Scenario Manager.

- From the Scenario Manager dialog box, choose Worst Case.

- Click [Show].

- Move the Scenario Manager dialog box so that you can see the chart.

Your screen should be similar to Figure 4.40

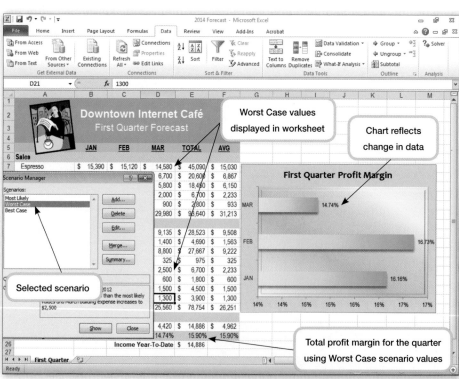

Figure 4.40

EX4.40   Lab 4: Using Solver, Creating Templates, and Evaluating Scenarios

WWW.MHHE.COM/OLEARY

The worksheet displays the worst-case values. These values result in a total profit margin of 15.90 percent. The chart reflects the change in monthly profit margins.

● **In a similar manner, display the Best Case scenario.**

Having Trouble?

If Excel did not update the chart, move the Scenario Manager box slightly to refresh the window.

Your screen should be similar to Figure 4.41

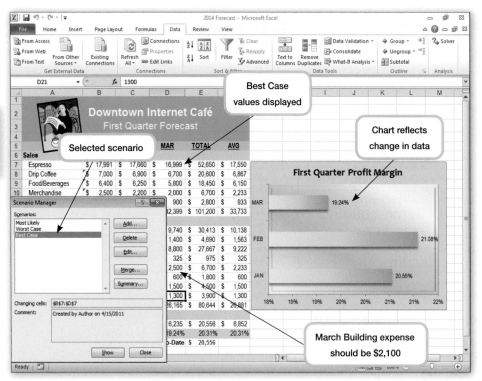

Figure 4.41

The best-case values are displayed in the worksheet. You notice, however, that the March Building expense value is the value that was last used in the Worst Case scenario. You need to edit the Best Case scenario to reset the March Building expense to $2,100. You also will add a comment to the scenario.

- Click [Edit...].

- Specify the Changing cells range as B7:D7 and cell D18.

- In the Comment text box, if necessary, change the name and enter the following: **Total Espresso sales increase 5% over the most likely values and March building expenses remain the same.**

- Click [OK].

- Enter **2100** as the value for D18.

- Click [OK].

- Click [Show].

Your screen should be similar to Figure 4.42

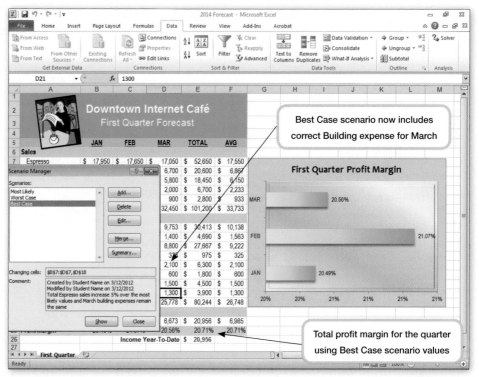

Figure 4.42

The Best Case scenario now shows a total profit margin of 20.71 percent.

CREATING A SCENARIO REPORT

Another way to evaluate the scenarios is to create a summary report that will display the effect on the profit margins for each scenario.

● Click .

● **Specify the Result cells range as B25 through E25 (containing the profit margin values) as the range of cells whose results you want summarized.**

● **Click [OK].**

Your screen should be similar to Figure 4.43

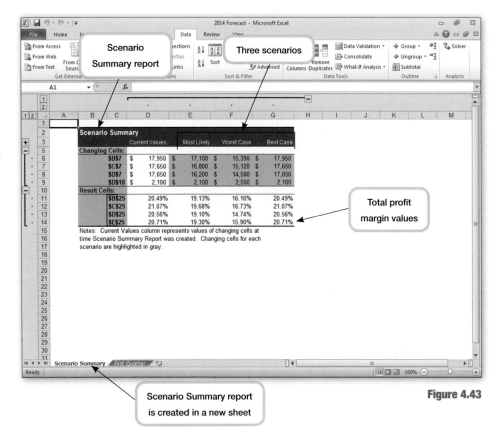

Scenario Summary report
is created in a new sheet

Figure 4.43

The Scenario Summary report is created and displayed in a separate sheet. It displays the values for the three scenarios and the profit margin results for each scenario. As you can see from the summary, the Most Likely scenario shows a total profit margin of 19.30 percent. The Best Case scenario yields higher profit margins, with a total profit margin of 20.71 percent for the quarter. The Worst Case scenario yields lower profit margins, with a total profit margin of 15.90 percent.

The report, however, is hard to understand because it uses cell references as the labels. To clarify the meaning of the report, you will edit the row labels.

2

Replace the cell references with the descriptive labels shown below:

Cell	Label	Cell	Label
C6	EspressoJAN	C11	ProfitMarginJAN
C7	EspressoFEB	C12	ProfitMarginFEB
C8	EspressoMAR	C13	ProfitMarginMAR
C9	BuildingMAR	C14	ProfitMarginTOTAL

AutoFit the width of column C to fit the column contents.

Save the workbook file.

Your screen should be similar to Figure 4.44

Figure 4.44

You have now completed best- and worst-case scenarios for the first quarter of 2014, as Evan requested.

Now that you have created the 2014 first-quarter forecast, Evan has asked you to create a drawing to illustrate the relationship between the four sales categories.

INSERTING A WORKSHEET

You will create the drawing on a separate worksheet. To do this, you will insert a new worksheet in the workbook and name it.

1

● **Click** [icon] **Insert Worksheet (next to the sheet tabs).**

Another Method

The keyboard shortcut is Shift + F11 or [icon] Insert ▾ /Insert Sheet in the Cells group of the Home tab.

● **Name the new sheet Sales Pyramid.**

Your screen should be similar to Figure 4.45

Figure 4.45

You now have a new blank worksheet in which to create the pyramid drawing that Evan requested.

ARRANGING WORKSHEET WINDOWS

You want to be able to see the data in the First Quarter worksheet while you create the graphic. To make it easier to work with two different parts of the same workbook, Excel allows you to open additional separate windows to display the different parts of the active workbook. Just like workbook windows, you can arrange displayed worksheets in the workspace. Then, you can specify the window arrangement.

- Click [New Window] in the Window group of the View tab.

- Click [Arrange All].

- Choose Windows of Active Workbook.

- Click [OK].

Your screen should be similar to Figure 4.46

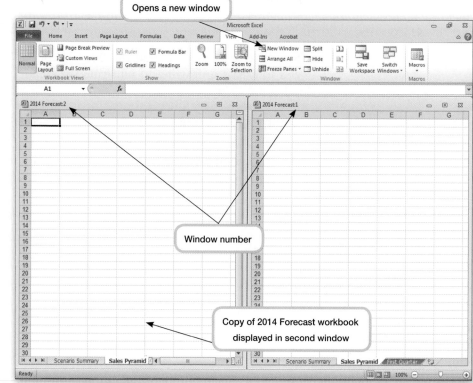

Opens a new window

Window number

Copy of 2014 Forecast workbook displayed in second window

Figure 4.46

A copy of the 2014 Forecast workbook is displayed in the second window. The window title bar displays the file name followed by the window number to help you identify the windows.

Now you will display the First Quarter sheet in the right window (window 1).

- Click on the 2014 Forecast:1 window to make it active.

- Display the First Quarter sheet.

Your screen should be similar to Figure 4.47

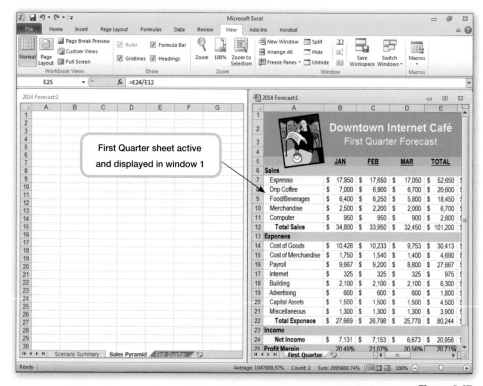

First Quarter sheet active and displayed in window 1

Figure 4.47

INSERTING A SMARTART GRAPHIC

You want to create a graphic that will display the importance of the four sales categories relative to each other. Excel includes several ready-made Smart-Art graphics that help you quickly create a drawing to show this type of information.

Concept 7 SmartArt

A **SmartArt graphic** is used to create a visual representation of textual information. The SmartArt graphics feature consists of predesigned diagrams whose purpose is to illustrate different concepts. There are eight types of SmartArt graphics you can use. The type of graphic you choose depends on the purpose of the graphic and the type of concept you want to illustrate. The table below describes the graphic types and uses.

	Type	Use
	List	Shows nonsequential information in a list
	Process	Shows steps in a process or timeline
	Cycle	Shows a process that has a continuous cycle
	Hierarchy	Shows an organization chart or decision tree that illustrates hierarchical relationships
	Relationship	Shows relationships of elements to a core element
	Matrix	Shows areas of overlap between and among elements
	Pyramid	Shows proportional relationships
	Picture	Shows a picture to convey a message

More SmartArt graphic layouts are available from the Office.com Web site.

Additionally, you can create flowcharts (or flow graphics) using a combination of shapes in the Drawing tools, including flowchart shapes and connectors. Flowcharts show a process that has a beginning and an end.

You will use the Pyramid SmartArt graphic type to illustrate how the four sales categories relate.

1

● **Click on the Sales Pyramid sheet in the 2014 Forecast:2 window to make it active.**

● **Click** SmartArt **in the Illustrations group of the Insert tab.**

Your screen should be similar to Figure 4.48

Figure 4.48

The complete gallery of SmartArt graphic designs is displayed. They are divided into categories by the type of graphic, such as Process, Cycle, or Hierarchy. Within each category are different layouts. When you select a layout, the dialog box displays an enlarged sample of the graphic and a brief description of its use.

2

- Choose the Pyramid category.

- Click .

- Click OK.

Your screen should be similar to Figure 4.49

Figure 4.49

A pyramid graphic consisting of three levels is created by default. The pyramid graphic is the selected graphic object and is surrounded with a selection rectangle. The SmartArt Tools Design and Format tabs also are displayed and contain buttons to add shapes, modify the layout, and enhance the graphic. Each level is a separate element of the graphic that can be selected and modified independently. Currently, the top-level element of the pyramid is selected.

ADDING SHAPES TO SMARTART

Because you want the graphic to represent the five sales categories, you first need to add two more levels to the pyramid for the fourth and fifth sales categories. Then you will display the Text pane in preparation for entering text in the SmartArt graphic.

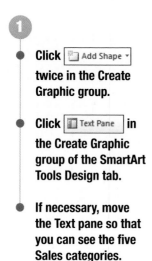

- **Click** ⬚ Add Shape ▾ twice in the Create Graphic group.

- **Click** ⬚ Text Pane in the Create Graphic group of the SmartArt Tools Design tab.

- **If necessary, move the Text pane so that you can see the five Sales categories.**

Your screen should be similar to Figure 4.50

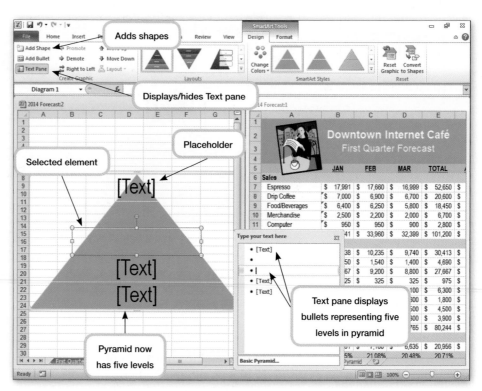

Figure 4.50

The pyramid shape now consists of five levels. The text pane is open and displays a bullet for each level in the pyramid. Sample text enclosed in brackets, called **placeholder text,** appears in the elements of the SmartArt graphic and in the corresponding bullet of the text pane.

ADDING TEXT TO A SMARTART GRAPHIC

Next, you want to add text to each segment of the pyramid. To add text, you can type in the Text pane or you can select the [Text] placeholder and type in it.

When an element is selected, it is surrounded by a solid border and sizing handles that are used to decrease or increase the size of the shape. While the element is selected like this, you can format the entire element. If you click on the element again, the border changes to a dashed border and a cursor appears. A dashed border indicates that you can enter, delete, select, and format text. If the element contains a [Text] placeholder, clicking directly on the placeholder displays a dashed border and cursor, ready for entry of text.

First you will add text to the bottom element, which will represent the largest sales category. As you can see from the First Quarter worksheet, this category is Espresso. The next largest sales category will be represented in the next level, and so forth.

Additional Information

You can also copy text from another worksheet or program and paste it into the Text pane.

1

- **Click on [Text] in the bottom level.**

- **Type Espresso.**

Your screen should be similar to Figure 4.51

Dashed border indicates you can enter, delete, select, and format text

Espresso is largest sales category

Placeholder replaced with text you typed

Text pane displays new text

Figure 4.51

The placeholder text was replaced with the text you entered. It is centered both horizontally and vertically in the pyramid segment. The text also appears in the lowest bullet in the Text pane. Using the First Quarter sheet as a reference, you will enter the remaining sales category names into the pyramid using the Text pane.

2

● Click on the second bullet from the bottom in the Text pane and type Drip Coffee.

● In a similar manner, add the text Food/ Beverages, Merchandise, and Computer to the other levels.

Your screen should be similar to Figure 4.52

Figure 4.52

As you typed in the Text pane, the SmartArt graphic was automatically updated and displays the entry you typed in the corresponding segment of the pyramid. The font size of the entries reduced as needed to fit within the shapes. All of the text in the other shapes reduced to the same size to keep the SmartArt graphic looking consistent.

FORMATTING THE SMARTART GRAPHIC

In this case, all the text has been sized to 18 points to match the size of the smallest label, Computer. You want to customize the text size of each segment to more closely fit the size of the segment.

1

- Double-click on the text in the top bullet of the Text pane to select it.

- Open the [18 ▾] Font Size list in the Mini toolbar and change the font size to 12.

- Select the Merchandise text in the second segment and decrease the font size to 18.

- Change the text size for the third segment to 20, the fourth to 32, and the bottom to 40.

- Click to the side of the pyramid to deselect the segment.

Your screen should be similar to Figure 4.53

Additional Information

The Format tab contains options for changing the color of each shape individually.

Figure 4.53

You also think the pyramid would look better if the segments were different colors that coordinate with the colors used in the worksheet. You could apply colors individually to each segment or you can use one of the preset color design schemes. You can then further enhance the appearance of the pyramid by applying a **SmartArt Style**, combinations of different formatting options such as edges, gradients, line styles, shadows, and three-dimensional effects. You can try different combinations of colors and styles until you find the one that suits you.

- Click [Text Pane] to close the Text pane.

- Click in the **Change Colors** SmartArt Styles group.

- Choose **Gradient Range – Accent 3**.

- Click [▾] to open the SmartArt Styles gallery.

- Point to several SmartArt Style designs to see the Live Preview.

- Choose **Cartoon (first row, third column under 3-D)**.

Your screen should be similar to Figure 4.54

Changes colors of graphic

Cartoon style selected

Opens SmartArt Style gallery

Figure 4.54

The selected colors and SmartArt Style greatly improve the appearance of the pyramid.

Additional Information

If, after making many formatting changes to a SmartArt graphic, you want to return to the original graphic design, use [Reset Graphic].

UNHIDING SHEETS

Now that you are finished working on the SmartArt graphic, you will close the 2014 Forecast:2 window and maximize the remaining window. Then you will redisplay the other sheets in the workbook.

1

- Click ⊠ in the window title bar to close the 2014 Forecast:2 window.

- Maximize the 2014 Forecast window.

- Click in the Cells group on the Home tab, select Hide & Unhide, and choose Unhide Sheet.

- Select the Year sheet from the Unhide dialog box and click OK.

- In a similar manner, unhide the three other sheets.

Your screen should be similar to Figure 4.55

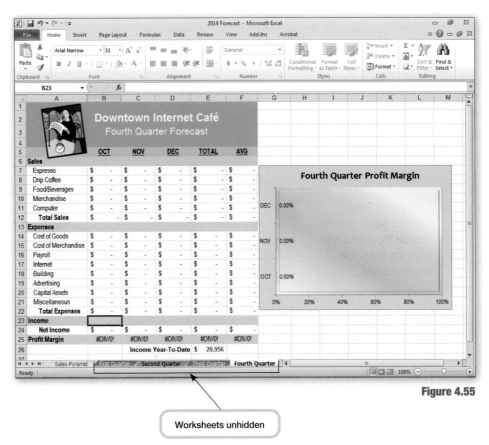

Worksheets unhidden

Figure 4.55

All the worksheets are displayed again. Finally, you want to include a copy of the Sales Pyramid sheet in the 2013 workbook file. You will redisplay this file, tile the workbook windows, and copy the sheet.

2

- Click [Unhide] in the Window group of the View tab.

- Select 2013 Forecast and click [OK].

- Click [Arrange All] in the Window group on the View tab.

- Clear the Windows of Active Workbook option and click [OK].

- Display the Sales Pyramid sheet and choose Move or Copy from the sheet tab shortcut menu.

- From the To Book list, choose 2013 Forecast.xlsx.

- From the Before Sheet list, choose (move to end).

- Choose Create a copy.

- Click [OK].

Your screen should be similar to Figure 4.56

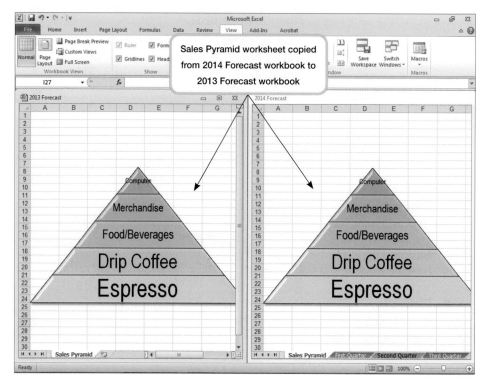

Sales Pyramid worksheet copied from 2014 Forecast workbook to 2013 Forecast workbook

Figure 4.56

Now both workbooks include the worksheet containing the pyramid SmartArt graphic.

3

- Save and close the 2013 Forecast **workbook file.**

- Maximize the 2014 Forecast **workbook window.**

- **Select the First Quarter, Scenario Summary and Sales Pyramid worksheets.**

- **Open the File tab and choose Print.**

- **Create a custom header to display your name, left-aligned, and the current date, right-aligned.**

- **Center the worksheets horizontally on the page.**

- **Print the worksheets.**

- **Protect the workbook, save the workbook, and exit Excel.**

Your printed output should be similar to that shown in the Case Study at the beginning of the lab.

FOCUS ON CAREERS

EXPLORE YOUR CAREER OPTIONS

Cage Cashier

Do you like to count money? Have you ever wondered who handles the money in a casino behind the scenes? Cage cashiers manage the cash, chips, and all the paperwork needed to track the large amounts of money that change hands every day. Some cage cashiers work to verify guests' financial records so they can open house credit lines. Other cashiers are primarily responsible for using computer spreadsheet programs to access and reconcile the books. Cage cashiers must have good math skills and experience with accounting or bookkeeping. Salary is dependent on experience, and cage cashiers typically make tips in addition to an hourly wage. The demand for cage cashiers is expected to increase as gaming expands beyond the traditional centers in Nevada and New Jersey.

Solver (EX4.7)

Solver is a tool used to perform what-if analysis to determine the effect of changing values in two or more cells, called the adjustable cells, on another cell, called the objective.

Custom Template (EX4.18)

Custom templates are specialized template files containing settings that are used as a pattern for creating similar worksheets in new workbooks.

Protection (EX4.11)

The protection feature controls what information can be changed in a workbook. Excel includes two levels of protection: worksheet protection and workbook protection.

Window Arrangement (EX4.22)

The window arrangement feature displays all open workbook files in separate windows on the screen, making it easy to view and work with information in different workbooks.

Link (EX4.27)

A link, also called an external reference, creates a connection between files that automatically updates the linked data in one file whenever the data in the other file changes.

Scenario (EX4.41)

A scenario is a named set of input values that you can substitute in a worksheet to see the effects of a possible alternative course of action.

SmartArt (EX4.54)

A SmartArt graphic is used to create a visual representation of textual information.

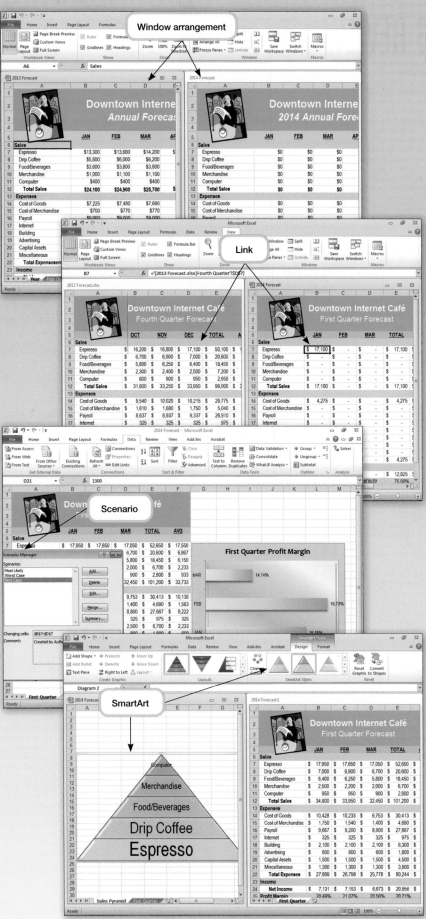

KEY TERMS

active workbook EX4.24
adjustable cell EX4.7
cascade EX4.25
custom template EX4.12
destination cell EX4.29
destination workbook EX4.29
external reference EX4.29
external reference formula EX4.29
horizontal EX4.25
link EX4.29
objective cell EX4.7

password EX4.14
protection EX4.14
scenario EX4.34
SmartArt graphic EX4.47
SmartArt style EX4.53
Solver EX4.7
source cell EX4.29
source workbook EX4.29
tiled EX4.25
vertical EX4.25
window arrangement EX4.25

COMMAND SUMMARY

Command	Shortcut	Action
File tab		
⊡ Options /Add-Ins/Excel Add-Ins/Solver Add-In		Adds Solver tool to Ribbon
New/My Templates		Applies custom template to workbook
Home tab		
Alignment group		
Wrap Text		Makes all content visible in a cell by displaying it on multiple lines
Cells group		
▤ Insert ▾ /Insert Sheet		Inserts a new worksheet into the workbook
▤ Format ▾ /Hide & Unhide/Hide Sheet		Hides selected sheets
▤ Format ▾ /Hide & Unhide/Unhide Sheet		Redisplays hidden sheets
▤ Format ▾ /Protect Sheet		Prevents unwanted changes to the data in a worksheet
▤ Format ▾ /Unprotect Sheet		Removes worksheet protection and allows modification of contents
▤ Format ▾ /Lock Cell		Toggles between locking and unlocking a cell
Insert tab		
Illustrations group		
▦ SmartArt		Inserts a SmartArt graphic to visually communicate information
SmartArt Tools Design tab		
Create Graphics group		
▦ Add Shape ▾		Adds a shape to an existing SmartArt graphic shape
SmartArt Styles group		
⦿ Change Colors ▾		Changes colors of selected SmartArt graphic

LAB REVIEW

COMMAND SUMMARY (CONTINUED)

Command	Shortcut	Action
▼ More		Opens SmartArt Styles gallery to select overall visual style for SmartArt graphic
Reset group		
Reset Graphic		Restores SmartArt graphic to original settings
Data tab		
Data Tools group		
What-If Analysis ▾ /Scenario Manager		Starts Scenario Manager tool to create sets of data for what-if analysis
Analysis group		
Solver		Starts Solver tool to perform what-if analysis
Review tab		
Changes group		
Protect Sheet		Prevents unwanted changes to the data in a worksheet
Unprotect Sheet		Removes worksheet protection
Protect Workbook		Prevents unwanted changes to the structure of the workbook
Protect Workbook		Removes workbook protection

COMMAND SUMMARY (CONTINUED)

Command	Shortcut	Action
View tab		
Window group		
New Window		Displays a new window
Arrange All		Arranges open windows vertically, horizontally, tiled, or cascaded
Hide		Hides current workbook
Unhide		Unhides selected workbook

LAB EXERCISES

MATCHING

Match the lettered item on the right with the numbered list on the left.

1. link   _____ a. prevents any unauthorized person from either viewing or saving changes to a workbook

2. workbook protection   _____ b. used as a pattern for creating new workbooks

3. external reference   _____ c. prevents changes to an entire workbook

4. password   _____ d. cell that contains data to be copied

5. objective cell   _____ e. creates a connection between files that automatically updates the data in one file when a change is made in another file

6. Solver   _____ f. named set of input values that you can substitute in a worksheet to see the effects of a possible alternative course of action

7. source cell   _____ g. tool used to perform what-if analysis

8. template   _____ h. cell affected by changes in other cells

9. scenario   _____ i. cell that contains the external reference formula

10. destination cell   _____ j. formula that links two workbooks

MULTIPLE CHOICE

Circle the correct response to the questions below.

1. A workbook _____ is a workbook file that contains predesigned worksheets that can be used as the basis for creating similar sheets in new workbooks.
   a. template
   b. model
   c. design
   d. pattern

2. The workbook that receives the data is called the _____.
   a. source workbook
   b. destination workbook
   c. recipient workbook
   d. target workbook

3. _____ calculate(s) a formula to achieve a given value.
   a. Source cells
   b. Solver
   c. Scenario Manager
   d. Target cells

4. _____ are designed to help forecast the outcome of various possible actions.
   a. Answer reports
   b. Scenarios
   c. Sensitivity reports
   d. Limit reports

5. In the external reference formula [Forecast.xls]Year!N8, Year is the _____.
   a. source file
   b. destination file
   c. active reference
   d. sheet reference

6. The _____ command removes the selected worksheet from the user view.
   a. Format/Sheet/Hide
   b. Format/Sheet/Remove
   c. Windows/Sheet/Hide
   d. Windows/Hide

7. _____ is a tool used for what-if analysis.
   a. Sheet Manager
   b. Solver
   c. Data tab
   d. Finder

8. A(n) _____ is entered in one worksheet to create a link to another worksheet.
   a. dependent value
   b. linking formula
   c. internal reference formula
   d. external reference formula

9. _____ prevents users from changing the contents of a worksheet.
   a. Locking cells
   b. Protecting a worksheet
   c. Unlocking cells
   d. A password

10. _____ are objects that can be used to illustrate concepts and enhance the workbook.
    a. Clip Art graphics
    b. Pictures
    c. SmartArt graphics
    d. Shapes

LAB EXERCISES

TRUE/FALSE

Circle the correct answer to the following questions.

1. A worksheet that is protected requires a password. **True   False**
2. A scenario report shows the results of all scenarios created for a worksheet. **True   False**
3. Cells you select as variables in Solver must be related through formulas on a worksheet. **True   False**
4. The vertical window arrangement displays windows side by side. **True   False**
5. Solver can produce a report about a solution. **True   False**
6. SmartArt graphics are normally used to display numerical data. **True   False**
7. Worksheet protection prevents unauthorized users from viewing or saving changes to a workbook. **True   False**
8. A password prevents unauthorized users from viewing or saving changes to a workbook. **True   False**
9. You can create a template file by typing the file extension .xltx when you save the file. **True   False**
10. Whenever data in an external reference formula is changed in the source workbook, data in the linked cell in the destination workbook is automatically changed as well. **True   False**

FILL-IN

Complete the following statements by filling in the blanks with the correct key terms.

1. The _____ tool lets you view the effect of varying values applied to a worksheet.

2. Once a(n) _____ formula is entered in a destination worksheet, the _____ file is automatically updated if it is open.

3. To arrange displayed worksheets in the workspace, each worksheet you want to arrange must be open in a separate _____.

4. The cells that contain the values to be changed when using Solver are called the _____.

5. To protect a worksheet from changes by an unauthorized person, you should include a _____.

6. The workbook that supplies data to another workbook is called the _____.

7. A(n) _____ is a named set of input values used to help forecast the outcome of various possible actions.

8. The cell containing a formula you want to solve is called the _____.

9. The _____ is the workbook that the next action you take affects.

10. _____ is a tool used to perform what-if analyses to determine the effect of changing values in two or more cells.

STEP-BY-STEP

IRONWORKS INCOME ANALYSIS ★

1. IronWorks creates unique wrought iron home accents. The accounting manager uses a six-month income worksheet that tracks the amount of income from different sources. The company would like to create a template that it can use each year to track the information. Your completed worksheets will be similar to the one shown here.

   a. Open the file ex04_IronWorks Income.

   b. Make a copy of Sheet1. Rename Sheet1 **First Six Months** and Sheet 1(2) **Second Six Months**. Delete Sheet2 and Sheet3.

   c. Modify the month column labels in the Second Six Months sheet to reflect the last six months of the year. Change the title of the sheet in cell A3 to **2nd Six Months**.

   d. Add the column label **Annual Total** in cell I4. Format this label to match the other column labels. AutoFit the column. Enter formulas in the Annual Total column to calculate the totals for the year.

   e. Extend the worksheet formatting to the new column. Recenter the worksheet titles.

   f. Select both sheets. Select cell A3 and cells B5 through G11 and unlock the cells. Deselect the selection. Ungroup the worksheets. Protect both worksheets.

   g. Move to cell B5 of the First Six Months sheet.

   h. Switch to Page Layout View. Enter your name and the current date in the header in both sheets.

   i. Change the orientation of both sheets to landscape. Center the worksheets horizontally. Fit each worksheet on a single page. Print the Second Six Months worksheet.

   j. Save the workbook as IronWorks Income1 to your solution file location.

   k. Delete the values in cells B5 through G11 on both worksheets. Save the workbook as a template with the name IronWorks Income Template to your solution file location. Close the workbooks.

ADVENTURE TRAVEL TOURS INCOME ANALYSIS ★★

2. Adventure Travel Tours has begun a new marketing campaign that emphasizes their airline packages. You have been asked to create a Scenario Summary that analyzes quarterly income in three scenarios. The company would also like to create a template to allow easy analysis of next year's performance. Your completed worksheets should be similar to the one shown here.

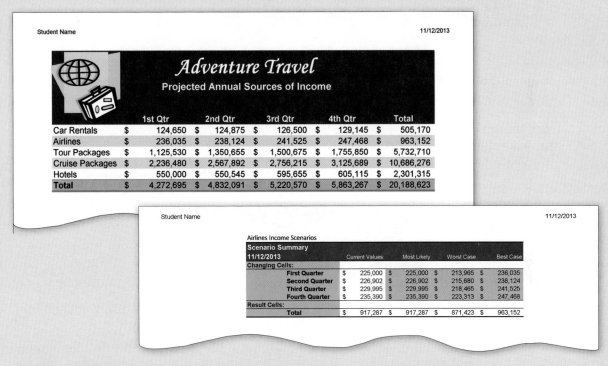

a. Open the file ex04_Travel Analysis.
b. Make a copy of Sheet1. Rename Sheet1(2) **Current Income** and Sheet1 **Projected Income**. Delete the other sheets.
c. Change the subtitle of the Projected Income sheet to **Projected Annual Sources of Income**. Change the subtitle of the Current Income Sheet to **Current Annual Sources of Income**.

After lengthy discussion regarding projected Airlines income, it has been determined that the most-likely case is that Total Airlines income will be unchanged from the current year, or $917,287. Further, it has been determined that the worst case would be a 5 percent decrease, or $871,423, and the best case would be a 5 percent increase, or $963,152.

d. Use the Projected Income sheet and Solver to calculate the quarterly income needed to achieve each of these Total Airlines income figures.
e. Create a scenario for each case using the values you found with Solver. Keep the original values after using Solver.
f. Create a Scenario Summary for the Total Airlines income with the results in cell F11. Replace the cell references with the names of the quarters (B11 = **First Quarter**). Increase column width as needed to fully display the labels. Delete the notes below the summary table. Add and format the worksheet title **Airlines Income Scenarios** in cell B1. Insert the current date in cell B3.

LAB EXERCISES

g. Move the Summary worksheet to the third tab position. Use the Scenario Manager to show the Best Case scenario on the Projected Income sheet.

h. Include your name and the date in a custom header on all sheets. Save the workbook as Airlines Income Analysis to your solution file location. Print the workbook with each sheet centered horizontally on one page in landscape orientation.

i. Delete the values in cells B5:E9 in the Current Income and Projected Income sheets. Delete the Scenario Summary sheet. Unlock the appropriate cells and protect the worksheets. Save the workbook as a template named Income Analysis Template to your solution file location.

DOGGIE FUN DAY CARE EXPENSE PROJECTIONS ★★

3. The owners of Doggie Fun Day Care have two facilities, East Side and West Side. They have collected some data on the operational costs for each facility for the current year. The owners would like to remodel the East Side day care facility and to open a new facility to be known as North Side. They are concerned, however, about the rising costs of utilities. You will help them evaluate next year's costs by creating a scenario summary similar to the example shown.

a. Open the file ex04_Day Care.

b. The owners are particularly concerned about the cost for next year's electricity. They would like

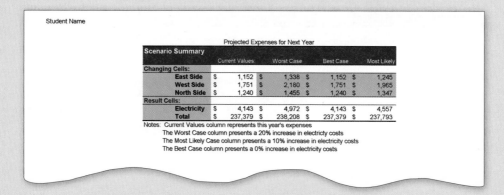

to evaluate a worst-case scenario in which electricity costs are 20 percent higher than the values in Sheet1. For example, the East Side's electricity would increase from $1,152 to $1,338. Use Solver to calculate the impact of this increase (keeping all other expenses unchanged) for each day care facility. Save the results as a scenario called **Worst Case** and restore the original values. (If Solver is not available to you, use Scenario Manager.)

c. The most-likely case would be for electricity to increase only 10 percent for each facility. Use Solver to determine the costs for each facility. Save the results as a scenario and restore the original values. (If Solver is not available to you, use Scenario Manager.)

d. Add a scenario using the original values as the best case. Save the workbook as Doggie Day Care to your solution file location.

e. Create a Scenario Summary for the electricity expenses. In cell B1, insert the title **Projected Expenses for Next Year**. Center this title over the table. Replace the cell references with the appropriate labels used in Sheet1. Size column C to fully display the labels. Replace the notes below the summary table with a short description of each scenario.

f. Hide Sheet2 and Sheet3. Rename Sheet1 **Budget**. Move the Scenario Summary sheet after the Budget sheet. Include your name in a custom header on both sheets.

g. Save the workbook and print the Scenario Summary centered horizontally in landscape orientation.

CARDS & GIFTS FINANCIAL PROJECTIONS ★ ★ ★

4. Dennis Ma owns and operates Ma's Cards & Gifts. He is reviewing his quarterly sales and is preparing his projections for the fourth quarter. He will need to review the previous year's totals to make his projections. Your completed sheets and scenario summary should be similar to those shown here.

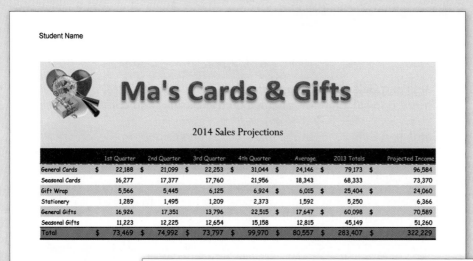

Student Name

Ma's Cards & Gifts

2014 Sales Projections

	1st Quarter	2nd Quarter	3rd Quarter	4th Quarter	Average	2013 Totals	Projected Income
General Cards	$ 22,188	$ 21,099	$ 22,253	$ 31,044	$ 24,146	$ 79,173	$ 96,584
Seasonal Cards	16,277	17,377	17,760	21,956	18,343	68,333	73,370
Gift Wrap	5,566	5,445	6,125	6,924	$ 6,015	$ 25,404	$ 24,060
Stationery	1,289	1,495	1,209	2,373	1,592	5,250	6,366
General Gifts	16,926	17,351	13,796	22,515	$ 17,647	$ 60,098	$ 70,589
Seasonal Gifts	11,223	12,225	12,654	15,158	12,815	45,149	51,260
Total	$ 73,469	$ 74,992	$ 73,797	$ 99,970	$ 80,557	$ 283,407	$ 322,229

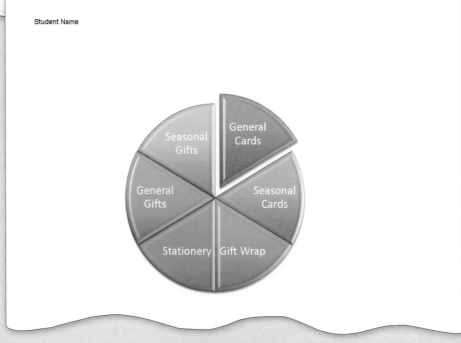

Student Name

Student Name

Scenario Summary 9/25/2013		Current Values:	Fourth Quarter Ideal
			Created by Student Name on 11/13/2013
Changing Cells:			
	General Cards	$ 38,106	$ 39,249
	Seasonal Cards	23,108	23,781
	Gift Wrap	5,130	5,284
	Stationery	2,373	2,444
	General Gifts	24,241	17,616
	Seasonal Gifts	17,103	17,103
Result Cells:			
	Total		

a. Open the file ex04_Cards and Gifts 2014. Change the name of Sheet1 to **2014**.

b. Insert formulas in column F to calculate the average quarterly sales and column H to calculate the 2014 totals.

c. Open the file ex04_Cards and Gifts 2013. In the ex04_Cards and Gifts 2014 file, create a formula to link column G with column G of the ex04_Cards and Gifts 2013 file. Save the workbook as Cards and Gifts 2014 to your solution file location. Close the ex04_Cards and Gifts 2013 file.

d. Dennis hopes to achieve a 3 percent increase in total sales for each category. For each category of sales, use Solver to determine what level of sales is needed in the fourth quarter of 2014 to achieve projected yearly sales 103 percent higher than the previous year. For example, use Solver to determine the fourth-quarter sales level for General Cards in 2014 to achieve projected total sales equal to $96,584 (103 percent of 93,771). Use Solver in a similar manner for the other categories using total sales equal to $73,370, $24,060, $6,366, $70,589, and $51,260. Keep these solutions.

e. Complete row 11 by entering the appropriate formulas in columns E through H.

f. Dennis is planning a new marketing campaign he hopes will increase fourth-quarter sales even more. Using the following fourth-quarter sales goals, create a scenario named **Fourth Quarter Ideal**.

General Cards	$39,249
Seasonal Cards	$23,781
Gift Wrap	$ 5,284
Stationery	$ 2,444
General Gifts	$24,968
Seasonal Gifts	$17,616

g. Create a Scenario Summary displaying the results for cell E11. Change the cell references to appropriate labels. Adjust column width to fully display labels. Delete the note below the summary report.

h. Insert the SmartArt Basic Pie from the Cycle category into Sheet2. Add three additional wedge shapes. For each wedge, enter the name of a sales category from sheet 2014. Apply the SmartArt style Inset and change the colors to Colorful Range – Accent Colors 2 to 3. Increase the size of the graphic.

i. Rename Sheet2 to **Sales Categories**. Delete Sheet3 and reorder the remaining sheets so that 2014 appears first, followed by Sales Categories, followed by Scenario Summary. Enter your name in the header of each sheet. Enter the current date in cell B3 of the Scenario Summary.

j. Save the workbook as 2014 Sales Projections.

k. Print the workbook with each sheet centered horizontally in portrait orientation.

l. Delete the Sales Categories and Scenario Summary sheets. Delete the values in cells B5 through E10 and G5 through G10. Unlock the same cells. Protect the sheet. Save the workbook as a template named Cards and Gifts Analysis Template to your solution file location.

ANIMAL RESCUE FOUNDATION CONTRIBUTIONS ★★★

5. The Animal Rescue Foundation, a nonprofit animal rescue agency, relies on donations to cover all its expenses. You would like to analyze and project the amount that will be needed for next year based on various scenarios. Your completed analysis will be similar to that shown here.

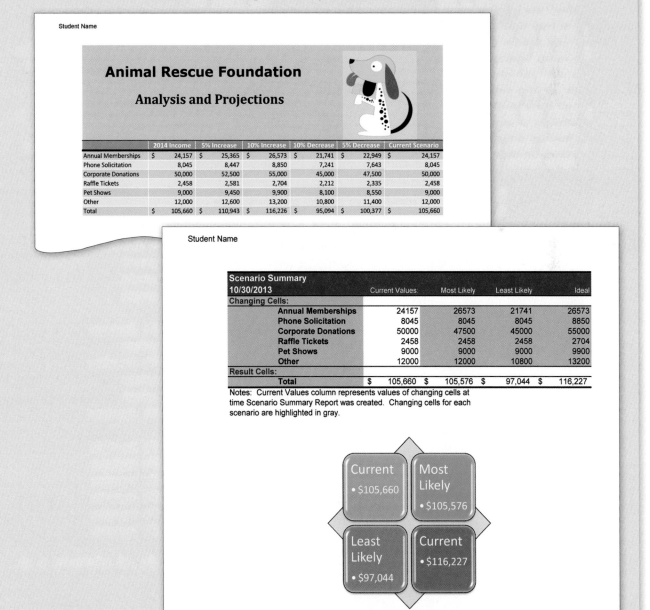

LAB EXERCISES

a. Open the file ex04_ARF Contributions to see last year's income. Save the file as ARF Contributions Reviewed to your solution file location.

b. Copy the Fall-Winter sheet to a new workbook. Rename the tab for the new sheet **Analysis**. Delete the extra sheets if necessary. Delete column H. Adjust the formatting as needed.

c. In cell A5, enter the subtitle **Analysis and Projections**.

d. In cells B9 through G9, enter the labels **2014 Income**, **5% Increase**, **10% Increase**, **10% Decrease**, **5% Decrease**, and **Current Scenario**. Adjust the size of the columns to fully display the labels.

e. In cell B10, enter a link to cell H10 of the Fall-Winter sheet in the ARF Contributions Reviewed file. In a similar manner, enter links in cells B11 through B15 to cells H11 through H15 of the Fall-Winter sheet in the ARF Contributions Reviewed file. Close the ARF Contributions Reviewed workbook.

f. Delete the values in cells C10 through G15.

g. Use the number in cell B10 to calculate the values for cells C10 through F15. Copy the formulas down the columns to row 15. (Hint: Cell C10 should contain the formula = B10*1.05, cell F10 should contain the formula = B10*.95.) Then copy the formulas in cells C10 through F10 to cells C11 through F15.

h. Copy and paste just the values from B10:B15 to G10:G15. Save the workbook as ARF Analysis to your solution file location.

i. Create three scenarios using cells G10 through G15 as the changing cells and the following scenario names and calculated values from the worksheet:

Scenario Name:	Most Likely	
Scenario Values:	Annual Memberships	10% increase
	Phone Solicitations	Current
	Corporate Donations	5% decrease
	Raffle Tickets	Current
	Pet Shows	Current
	Other	Current
Scenario Name:	Least Likely	
Scenario Values:	Annual Memberships	10% decrease
	Phone Solicitations	Current
	Corporate Donations	10% decrease
	Raffle Tickets	Current
	Pet Shows	Current
	Other	10% decrease
Scenario Name:	Ideal	
Scenario Values:	Annual Memberships	10% increase
	Phone Solicitations	10% increase
	Corporate Donations	10% increase
	Raffle Tickets	10% increase
	Pet Shows	10% increase
	Other	10% increase

j. Create a Scenario Summary displaying the results for cell G16. Change the cell references to appropriate labels and adjust the column width to fully display the labels.

k. Insert the Basic Matrix SmartArt graphic below the Scenario Summary. Adjust the size of the graphic as needed. Apply the SmartArt Intense Effect style and change the colors to Colorful Range – Accent Colors 3 to 4. Starting with the upper-left segment of the graphic, enter the labels **Current**, **Most Likely**, **Least Likely**, and **Ideal**. While in the Text Pane, add a bullet to each segment, then enter the total value for that segment in the bullet. For example, the Current segment would have the bullet $105,660.

l. Enter your name in the header of the Scenario Summary and Analysis sheets. Enter the current date in cell B3 of the Scenario Summary.

m. Print the Analysis sheet centered horizontally in landscape orientation. Print the Scenario Summary sheet centered horizontally in portrait orientation. Fit to one page.

n. Save the workbook.

o. Delete the Scenario Summary sheet. Delete the values in cells B10:B15 and G10:G15. Unlock the cells B10:B15 and G10:G15 and protect the sheet. Save the sheet as ARF Analysis Template to your solution file location.

ON YOUR OWN

GAMES GROWTH PROJECTIONS ★

1. You have been hired as a consultant by a video game manufacturer to help the company project expected growth over the next five years based on its research. Assume that the company currently has 42 percent of the market. The current number of customers is 320,500. Available research estimates an increase of 2 percent in year 1; 3 percent in year 2; 5 percent in year 3; 8 percent in year 4; and 13 percent in year 5 over the previous year. Create a worksheet that shows the current number of customers and the estimated numbers for the next five years. Use these numbers to create revenue figures based on a yearly profit of $225 per customer. Create scenarios with the calculated values as the most-likely case, a 3 percent decrease per year in customers as the worst case, and an increase of 5 percent per year as the best case. Create a Scenario Summary report. Enter your name and the current date in the header of all the worksheets. Protect your workbook and save the file as Video Game Projections to your solution file location. Print the worksheets.

SPRING BREAK SCENARIOS ★ ★

2. Now that your personal budget is complete, you have decided to do some analysis to determine whether a trip during spring semester break is possible. Use the budget you created in Lab 3, On Your Own exercise 1, and evaluate your yearly budget to determine whether you will have enough money to pay for a spring break trip next year. Use Solver to create an answer report indicating the number of hours you need to work to earn enough money for the trip in addition to the rest of your expenses. Create three scenarios: one showing the current values, a second showing a 7 percent decrease in entertainment expenses, and a third showing a decrease in one of your other expenses. Create a Scenario Summary. Enter your name and the current date in a header for all the worksheets. Save the file as Spring Break Analysis to your solution file location. Print the worksheets.

LAB EXERCISES

SMALL BUSINESS EXPANSION PROJECTIONS ★ ★

3. You believe the small business you created in Lab 3, On Your Own exercise 5 could see greater profits with an additional location. Use the information you gathered in the previous workbook and Solver to determine what variables would increase profits by 30 percent. Create an Answer report. Create three scenarios to determine the effects of a 5 percent, 10 percent, and 15 percent increase in profits in each quarter on the total yearly profits. Create a Scenario Summary. Protect the workbook and save your file as Expansion Projections to your solution file location. Print the summary.

STOCK PORTFOLIO ANALYSIS ★ ★ ★

4. You have been studying the stock market in your economics class and would like to evaluate a portfolio of four different stocks. Using the Web or other news source, choose four stocks listed on the New York Stock Exchange and enter the following information about each stock in separate sheets of a workbook: stock exchange number, cost per share, brokerage fee, total cost per share, price/earnings ratio, dividend return percentage, and week-ending price. Enter data for each stock using the previous month's values. Create scenarios of good, bad, and expected market changes in the current month-ending price over the next month. Enter your name and the current date in headers in the worksheets. Save the file as Stock Analysis to your solution file location. Print the workbook.

USING EXCEL TEMPLATES ★ ★ ★

5. You would like to analyze the costs of a new car loan. Use the Excel Loan Amortization template and conduct research into new car prices and loan rates. Insert a new sheet and do a cost comparison of several cars you have analyzed. Add a picture of the cars you are researching. Create scenarios for different loan rates and create a Scenario Summary using the techniques you learned in the lab. Save the file as New Car Loan to your solution file location. Print the workbook. Save your sheet as a template named Loan Analysis Template, with the values removed.

Using Data Tables, Using Lookup and IF Functions, and Designing Forms

Objectives

After completing this lab, you will know how to:

1. Use the PMT function.

2. Create a data table.

3. Create and modify shapes.

4. Use Lookup functions.

5. Create a form.

6. Name cell references.

7. Use the IF function.

8. Create a drop-down list.

9. Add cell comments.

10. Prepare a workbook for distribution.

Downtown Internet Café

Evan, the owner of the Downtown Internet Café, has been impressed by your use of Excel 2010 to forecast the café's future for the next two years. Now, he has two new projects that he wants you to complete.

First, he is considering the purchase of a new espresso machine to replace the current machine, which is leased. Evan plans to finance the purchase and would like you to evaluate several different loan options. You will create a loan analysis spreadsheet that incorporates Office Excel's PMT function and data table features.

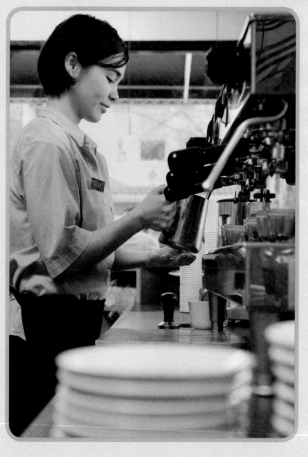

Next, Evan would like you to develop a spreadsheet to calculate and record customer Bonus Dollars. Bonus Dollars are awarded to customers based on their monthly expenditures at the café and can be applied to their bill for any purchase. They are an incentive for customers to keep coming back to the café and, of course, spend more money while they're there. You will create a form to calculate and record customer Bonus Dollars. The completed loan analysis and Bonus Dollars form are shown on the opposite page.

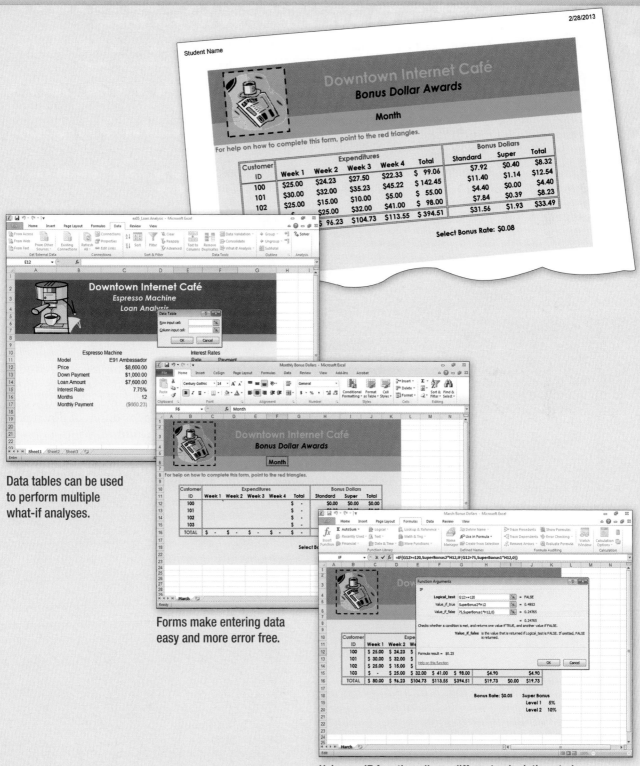

Data tables can be used to perform multiple what-if analyses.

Forms make entering data easy and more error free.

Using an IF function allows different calculations to be performed if certain conditions are met.

The following concepts will be introduced in this lab:

1 Data Table A data table is a range of cells that is used to quickly calculate multiple what-if versions in one operation and to show the results of all variations in the worksheet.

2 Lookup Functions Lookup functions permit you to use worksheet tables as sources of information for formulas and calculations in other parts of the worksheet.

3 Form A form is a formatted worksheet with blank spaces that can be filled in online on an individual computer or on a network, or printed and completed on paper.

4 Name A name is a description of a cell or range of cells that can be used in place of cell references.

5 IF Function The IF function checks to see if certain conditions are met and then takes action based on the results of the check.

6 Comment Comments are notes attached to cells that can be used to clarify the meaning of the cell contents, provide documentation, or ask a question.

Calculating a Loan Payment

Evan has read several reviews in the *Tea and Coffee Trade Journal* and looked at several different models of commercial espresso makers at restaurant supply stores. He is still undecided about the model to purchase and wants to see an analysis of what the monthly loan payments would be for different down payments, interest rates, and repayment periods for each kind.

Based on the information Evan has given you, you started a workbook for the loan analysis by entering some descriptive labels and formats in a worksheet. You will open the workbook file and continue to work on the loan analysis.

Start Office Excel 2010 and open the workbook file ex05_Loan Analysis.

If necessary, maximize the application and worksheet windows.

Your screen should be similar to Figure 5.1

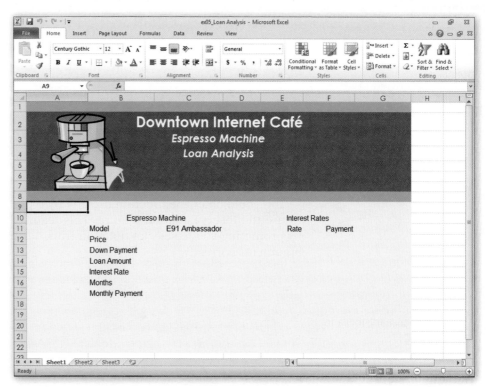

Figure 5.1

Much of the structure and formatting for the worksheet has already been completed. To continue to create the worksheet you will enter the price and down payment for the first espresso machine Evan is considering, the E91 Ambassador. Then, you need to enter a formula to calculate the loan amount. The amount of the loan is the price of the item minus the down payment. He wants to repay the loan in monthly payments over a one-year period.

First you will calculate loan payments using a 7.75 percent loan rate.

2

In cell C12 enter 8600.

In cell C13 enter 1000.

In cell C14 enter the formula = C12 − C13.

In cell C15 enter 7.75.

In cell C16 enter 12.

Your screen should be similar to Figure 5.2

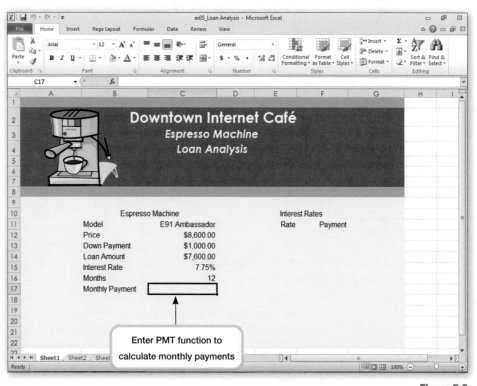

Enter PMT function to calculate monthly payments

Figure 5.2

Calculating a Loan Payment   **EX5.5**

USING THE PMT FUNCTION

Additional Information

When using the PMT function, it is important to use consistent units for specifying rate and nper.

Next you need to calculate the monthly payment using the PMT function. The **PMT function** calculates a periodic payment on a loan. The value returned includes the loan amount and interest but no taxes, reserve payments, or fees sometimes associated with loans. The PMT function uses the following syntax:

PMT(rate, nper, pv)

This function contains three arguments: rate, nper, and pv. The rate argument is the interest rate of the loan. The nper argument is the total number of payments for the loan. The pv argument is the amount of the loan, also referred to as the **principal** or present value.

You could enter the function directly by typing it. However, another way is to use the Insert Function feature. This feature simplifies entering functions by prompting you to select a function from a list and then helps you enter the arguments correctly.

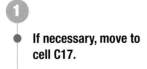

1

● If necessary, move to cell C17.

● Click f_x **Insert Function** in the formula bar.

Another Method

The Ribbon equivalent is f_x Insert Function in the Function Library group of the Formulas tab.

Your screen should be similar to Figure 5.3

Figure 5.3

The Most Recently Used category of the Insert Function dialog box displays a list of recently used functions. If the PMT function is not displayed in this list, you can locate a function by typing a description of what you want to do in the Search text box or by selecting a function category. You will select a category.

From the Or select a category drop-down list, choose Financial.

Scroll the Select a function list and choose PMT.

Click [OK]

Your screen should be similar to Figure 5.4

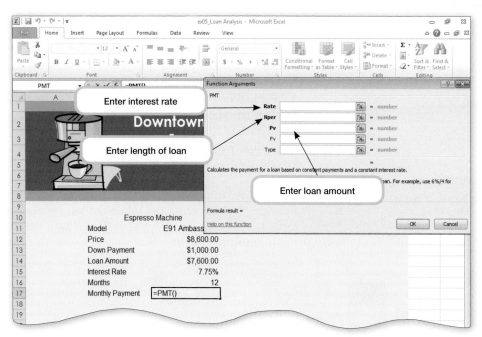

Figure 5.4

Additional Information

If the loan payment was in years, you would need to multiply the value by 12 to calculate the number of monthly payments.

Next, in the Function Arguments dialog box you enter the function arguments. The upper section of the dialog box contains text boxes for the possible arguments that may be used in the PMT function. The required arguments are in bold. The lower section provides information about the function and about the selected argument. The Rate is the monthly interest rate for the loan. In this case, it is the yearly interest rate (C15) divided by 12. This converts the yearly rate to a monthly rate. The nper argument is the length of the loan in months (C16). The pv argument is the loan amount in cell C14. As you specify the arguments in the dialog box, the function in the formula bar and in cell C17 displays the arguments.

Enter C15/12 as the Rate, C16 as the Nper, and C14 as the Pv.

Click [OK]

Your screen should be similar to Figure 5.5

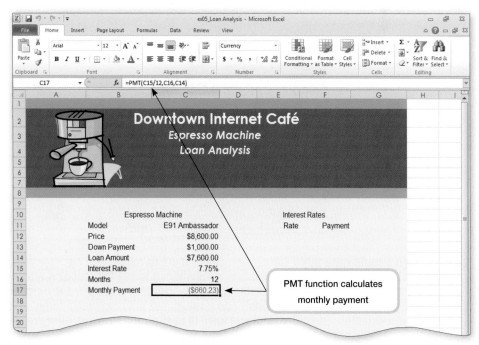

Figure 5.5

Excel calculates the monthly payment and displays it in cell C17 based on a 7.75 percent interest rate. Notice the payment value is displayed in red because a payment is a negative value.

Creating a Data Table

Next, you will expand the worksheet to evaluate the loan payments based on a range of possible loan rates. Evan has checked with a local bank for information on short-term, small-business loan rates. He found that for loans less than $25,000, the maximum interest rate must not exceed the prime rate plus 4.25% when maturity is less than seven years. Prime rate is the lowest rate of interest on loans that is available from a bank set at a given time.

Because interest rates will vary depending on which loan institution finances the purchase and when the loan is obtained, you want to set up a data table that shows the effect of different interest rates on the monthly loan payment amount.

Additional Information

The text will base the following loan analysis on a maximum loan rate of 8.75 percent (4.5 percent for prime plus a maximum of 4.25 percent).

Concept Data Table

A **data table** is a range of cells that is used to quickly calculate multiple what-if versions in one operation and to show the results of all variations in the worksheet. Data tables perform a type of what-if analysis in which one or more variables are changed to see the effect on the formulas that include these variables.

Espresso Machine

Model	ES1500 Royal
Price	$10,500.00
Down Payment	$1,000.00
Loan Amount	$9,500.00
Interest Rate	7.50%
Months	18
Monthly Payment	($559.67)

One-Variable Table
Varying Interest Rates Only

Rate	Payment
	($559.67)
6.25%	($554.28)
6.50%	($555.35)
6.75%	($556.43)
7.00%	($557.51)
7.25%	($558.59)
7.50%	($559.67)
7.75%	($560.75)
8.00%	($561.83)
8.25%	($562.92)

Two-Variable Table
Varying Interest Rates and Length of Loan

Rate	Months		
($559.67)	12	18	24
6.25%	($818.72)	($554.28)	($422.12)
6.50%	($819.82)	($555.35)	($423.19)
6.75%	($820.91)	($556.43)	($424.26)
7.00%	($822.00)	($557.51)	($425.34)
7.25%	($823.10)	($558.59)	($426.42)
7.50%	($824.20)	($559.67)	($427.50)
7.75%	($825.29)	($560.75)	($428.58)
8.00%	($826.39)	($561.83)	($429.66)
8.25%	($827.49)	($562.92)	($430.74)

A **one-variable data table** can contain one or more formulas, and each formula refers to one input cell. An **input cell** is a cell in which a list of values is substituted to see the resulting effect on the related formulas. Input values can be listed down a column (**column-oriented**) or across a row (**row-oriented**).

A **two-variable data table** uses only one formula that refers to two different input cells, one column-oriented and one row-oriented. The purpose of this table is to show the resulting effect on the formula when the values in both of these cells are changed.

SETTING UP THE DATA TABLE

Since you are interested in seeing the effects of changing the interest rate only, you will create a one-variable data table. When designing a one-variable data table, the input values and formulas must be in adjacent rows or columns. The title and column headings have already been entered in cells E10 through F11 of the worksheet for the data table. To create the data table, you will begin by entering a series of interest rate percentages.

1

● **In cell E13, enter 6.75% and in cell E14 enter 7.00%.**

● **Select the range E13 through E14 and drag the fill handle through cell E21.**

Your screen should be similar to Figure 5.6

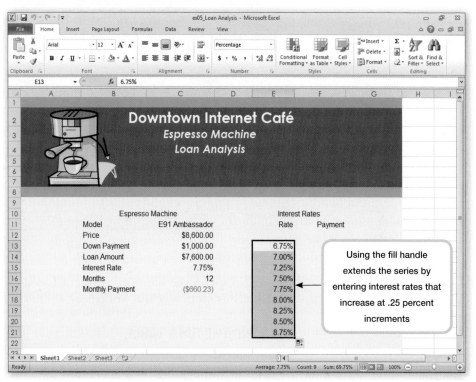

Figure 5.6

Cells E13 through E21 display interest rates that range from 6.75 percent to 8.75 percent in 0.25 percent increments. Dragging the fill handle to copy the selected range quickly filled column E with an increasing series of values that follows the same pattern as the data in the range.

Next, you enter the monthly payment formula to be used in calculating the various payments. The formula is always entered in the row above the first input value and one cell to the right of the column of values. In this case, you will enter the formula in cell F12. You could copy this formula from the monthly payment cell in the loan analysis section of the worksheet. Instead, you will define the new formula as equal to that cell. This way, the data table formula will be automatically updated if the original formula (the one in the loan analysis section of the worksheet) changes.

Additional Information

If the input values are listed across the row, the formula is entered in the column to the left of the first value and one cell below the row of values.

In cell F12, enter = C17.

Your screen should be similar to Figure 5.7

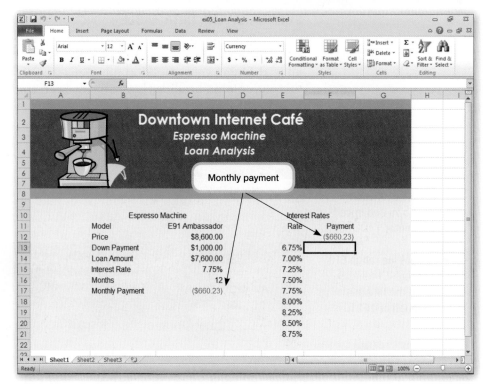

Figure 5.7

Cell F12 displays the monthly payment based on the interest rate used in the loan analysis section of the worksheet, in this case, 7.75 percent.

DEFINING THE DATA TABLE

Finally, you need to define the range of cells that comprise the data table. The data table range consists of all cells except the ones containing the title and headings.

Select the range E12 through F21.

Open the Data tab.

Click What-If Analysis **in the Data Tools group and choose Data Table.**

Your screen should be similar to Figure 5.8

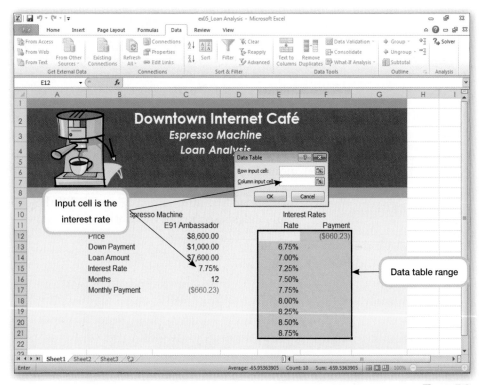

Figure 5.8

In the Data Table dialog box, you define the input cell in which values from the data table are substituted. Because the values in the data table are listed down a column, the input cell is entered as a Column input cell. In this case, the input cell is cell C15, the Interest Rate cell from the loan analysis section of the worksheet.

2

- Enter **C15** in the Column input cell text box.

Another Method

You also can define the input cell by reducing the dialog box and selecting the input cell in the worksheet.

- Click [OK].
- Deselect the table.

Your screen should be similar to Figure 5.9

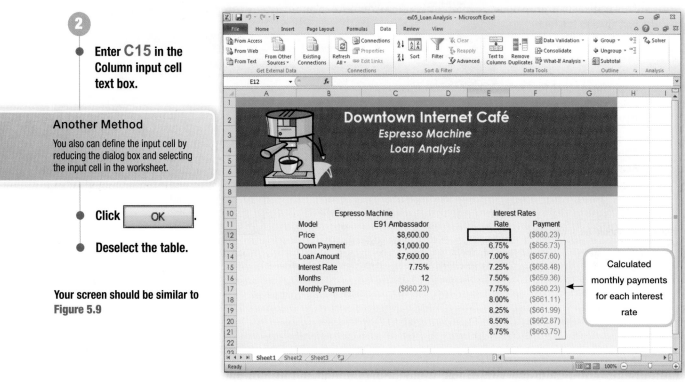

Figure 5.9

The data table shows the calculated monthly payments for each interest rate.

To quickly improve the appearance of the worksheet, you will format the data table and the loan analysis data.

3

- Apply a Heading 1 cell style to the titles in cells B10 and E10.

- Apply a Heading 2 cell style to the four column headings in row 11.

- Apply the Accent 1 cell style to the range B12:C17.

- Apply the 40% – Accent 1 cell style to the range E12:F21.

Your screen should be similar to Figure 5.10

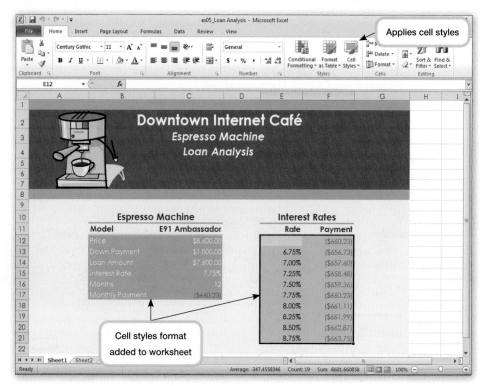

Figure 5.10

Adding Shapes

To clarify the meaning of the first payment value in the data table, you decide to add a descriptive note in a box with an arrow pointing to the value. To add these features to a worksheet, you first create the separate shape element and then add the descriptive text.

CREATING A TEXT BOX

The shape you will use to clarify the meaning of the first value in the data table is a text box shape. A **text box** is a graphic object that is a container for text or graphics. Because it is one of the most commonly used shapes, it has a separate button on the Ribbon.

- Open the Insert tab.

- Click in the Text group.

Another Method

You can also create a text box by selecting the Text Box shape from the Shapes ▾ gallery.

- Click in column G to the right of the data table.

- Type **Calculated Loan Payment**.

- Reduce the width of the text box to display the content on two lines.

Having Trouble?

Use the sizing handles to adjust the text box size.

Your screen should be similar to Figure 5.11

Additional Information

To start a new line inside a text box, press Enter.

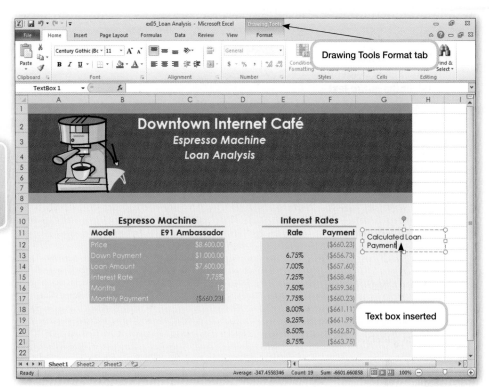

Figure 5.11

The content of the text box automatically wrapped to a second line as you reduced the width of the text box.

ADDING A SHAPE STYLE

The text box can be enhanced using many of the Drawing Tools. You will add a background fill color, border line color, and text color. You could format each item individually, but using the Shape Styles feature provides a quick way to apply formatting.

1

- If necessary, click on the text box border to select the entire text box object.

- Open the Drawing Tools Format tab.

- Click ▼ More in the Shape Styles group to open the Shape Styles gallery.

- Click [Abc] Moderate Effect, Brown, Accent 2 (fifth row, third column).

- Click [🔲 Shape Effects ▾] and select Shadow.

- Click [ ] Offset Diagonal Bottom Right in the Outer section.

- Size and position the text box as in Figure 5.12. Adjust the column width of column G as needed.

- Click outside the text box to deselect it.

Your screen should be similar to Figure 5.12

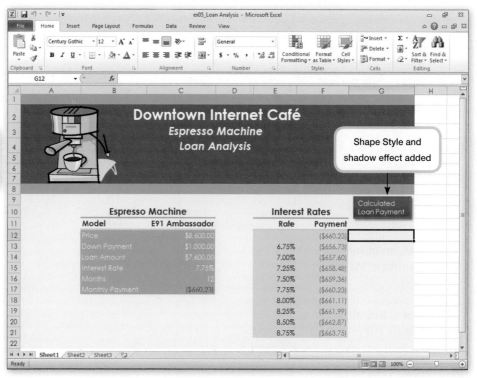

Figure 5.12

The selected Shape Style and shadow effects greatly improve the appearance of the text box.

CREATING AN ARROW SHAPE

Next, you will add an arrow from the text box to the value in cell F12.

1

- Open the Insert tab and click Shapes ▾ in the Illustrations group.

- Click ◥ Arrow in the Lines category.

- Draw an arrow by clicking on the bottom edge of the text box and dragging from the text box to the right edge of cell F12.

- Click ▾ More in the Shape Styles group and click ⬚ Moderate Line – Accent 2 style.

Your screen should be similar to Figure 5.13

Figure 5.13

Although you like how this combination of shapes looks, you decide to try another shape to see if you like it better. This shape will be a block arrow shape that contains text.

2

- Click ▾ More in the Insert Shapes group of the Drawing Tools Format tab and click ⇦ Left Arrow in the Block Arrows category.

- Click in column G below the text box to insert the shape.

- Type Calculated Loan Payment.

- Size the shape to display the text on two lines.

Your screen should be similar to Figure 5.14

Figure 5.14

The block arrow shape already includes some basic style effects. You like how this shape looks, but it is too large. You will decrease the font size and then reduce the size of the shape.

3

- Select the text in the shape and reduce the font size to 10 points using the Mini toolbar.

- Open the Shape Style gallery and click 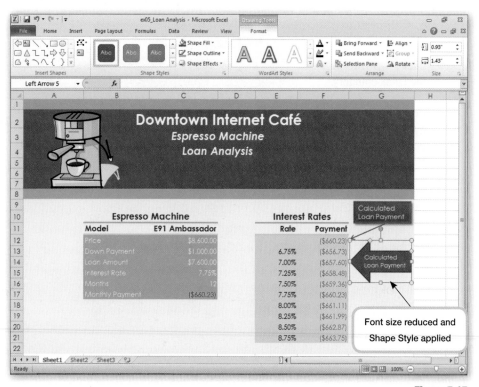Moderate Effect Brown, Accent 2.

- Size and position the arrow as shown in Figure 5.15.

Your screen should be similar to Figure 5.15

Figure 5.15

DELETING SHAPES

You decide to use the block arrow shape and delete the text box and arrow.

1

- Select the line arrow shape and press Delete.

- Delete the text box shape using the same method.

- Position the block arrow shape as in Figure 5.16.

- Click outside the shape to deselect it.

Your screen should be similar to Figure 5.16

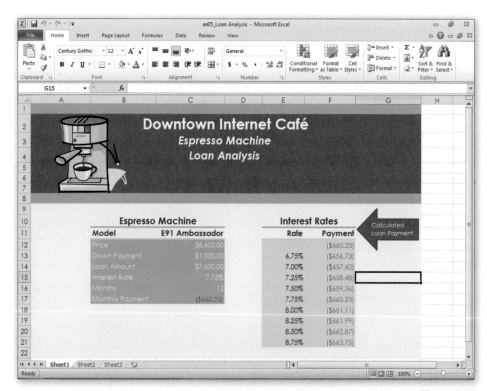

Figure 5.16

ROTATING OBJECTS AND SIZING ELEMENTS

Additional Information

You can restrict the rotation to 15 degree angles by holding down [Shift] as you rotate the object.

To add some more interest, you will rotate the shape so that it points to the value at an angle. Then you will make the arrow head element of the shape narrower. To rotate an object, click on the ● rotation handle at the top of the object and drag in the direction you want to rotate the object. To adjust the size of an element in an object, drag the ◇ located at the top of the object element.

1

- **Select the block arrow shape.**

- **Drag the ● rotation handle to the left to rotate the arrow as in Figure 5.17.**

Another Method

You can also use ⟨Rotate ▾⟩ in the Drawing Tools Format tab to rotate an object.

- **Drag the ◇ at the head of the arrow to the left slightly to decrease the size of the arrow head and reposition the arrow as in Figure 5.17.**

Additional Information

The mouse pointer appears as when you rotate the object and ▷ when you size the element.

- **Rename the Sheet1 tab** Analysis.

- **Move to cell A9 and save the workbook as** Loan Analysis **to your solution file location.**

Your screen should be similar to Figure 5.17

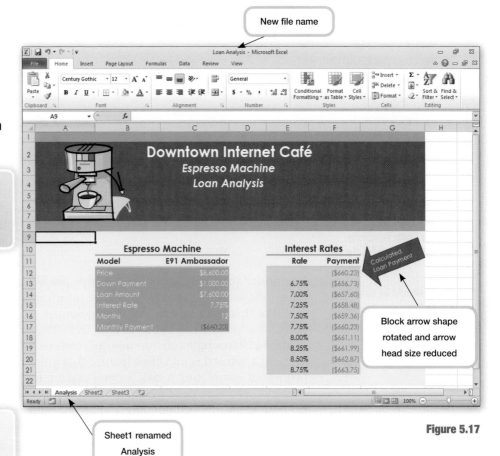

New file name

Calculated Loan Payment

Block arrow shape rotated and arrow head size reduced

Sheet1 renamed Analysis

Figure 5.17

You have completed the loan analysis for the E91 Ambassador model espresso machine that Evan requested. Evan can now easily see what the monthly payment would be for a range of possible interest rates.

SPLITTING CELL CONTENT

Evan is pleased with the worksheet you created and would like to see the same loan analysis applied to other espresso machines he is considering. He also wants to use the worksheet to evaluate other potential purchases.

Evan entered the product information for several espresso machines he is considering in a worksheet. You will copy this data into Sheet2 of the Loan Analysis workbook.

Open the workbook file ex05_Espresso Machines List.

Copy Sheet1 from the ex05_Espresso Machines List **workbook to a new sheet positioned before Sheet2 in the Loan Analysis workbook.**

Rename the tab of this new sheet in the Loan Analysis workbook Models.

Your screen should be similar to Figure 5.18

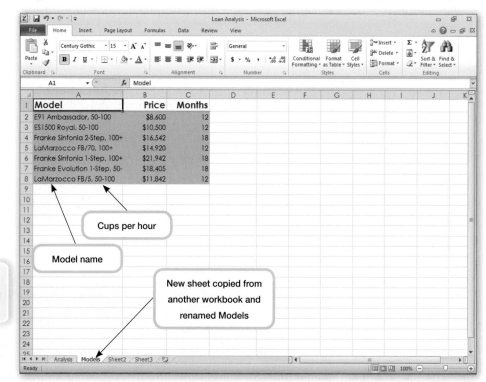

Cups per hour

Model name

New sheet copied from another workbook and renamed Models

Figure 5.18

You notice that Evan included the cups per hour that each machine can produce following the name and model information in column A. You want to separate this information into two columns, one for the model information and the other for the cups-per-hour information. You can quickly split text contained in a single cell into multiple cells using the Convert Text to Columns Wizard. A **wizard** is an Office feature that guides you step by step through the process of completing a task. In preparation for using this wizard to split cell contents, you first need to insert a blank column following column A. This is because when the cell content is split, the split content is entered in the column to the right of the existing column. Inserting a blank column prevents the existing content in column B from being overwritten by the data that is distributed.

- **Insert a blank column to the left of column B.**

- **Select A2:A8 to specify the range of cells containing the content to be split.**

- **Click** **in the Data Tools group of the Data tab.**

Your screen should be similar to Figure 5.19

Figure 5.19

The first wizard dialog box advises you that the wizard has determined that the data in the selected range is delimited. This is correct, as the cups-per-hour data is separated from the model information with a comma.

3

- **Click** [Next >] **to continue.**

Your screen should be similar to Figure 5.20

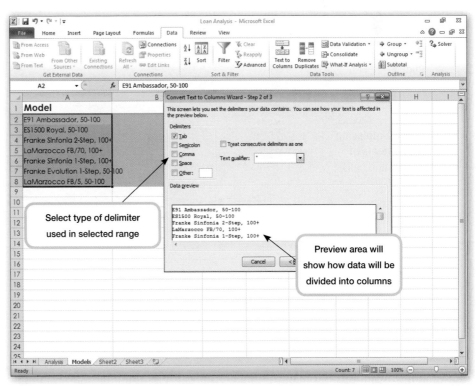

Figure 5.20

Next, you set the delimiters that are used. As you do, the preview area shows how the data will be divided into columns.

Choose Comma.

Deselect Tab.

Click Next > .

Your screen should be similar to Figure 5.21

Data will be split into two columns based on comma delimiter and formatted using General format

Figure 5.21

The final wizard step is used to set the format for each column. The General format is set appropriately for both columns.

Click Finish .

Click OK to confirm replacing the contents of destination cells.

Your screen should be similar to Figure 5.22

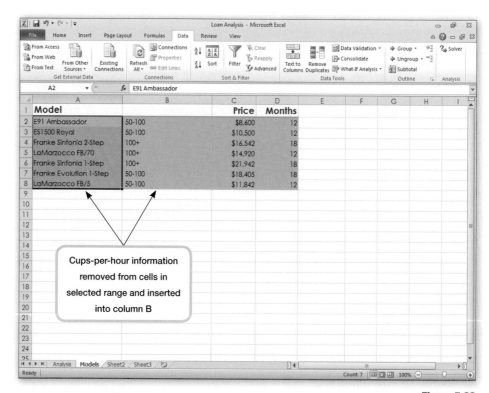

Cups-per-hour information removed from cells in selected range and inserted into column B

Figure 5.22

The cups-per-hour data has been removed from the cells in the selected range and inserted into adjacent cells in the column to the right.

Add the heading Cups/Hour in cell B1.

AutoFit column B.

Your screen should be similar to Figure 5.23

Figure 5.23

Now that you have information for several more espresso machines, you can use the loan analysis sheet to calculate the loan amounts for each. As you look at the information Evan has provided, you notice that he has changed the number of months for the loan to 18 months for the most expensive espresso machines. You also will need to reflect this change in the loan analysis for each machine.

Looking Up Values in a List

Each time you use the loan analysis worksheet, you need to enter the model data for each different espresso machine. Instead of entering the information each time, you will use a Lookup function to add the information from the list of data on the espresso machine models automatically for you. Then you can quickly generate the loan payment information for any model.

Lookup functions permit you to use worksheet tables as sources of information for formulas and calculations in other parts of the worksheet. There are two types of lookup functions: VLOOKUP is a vertical or columnar lookup and HLOOKUP is a horizontal or row-based lookup.

The **VLOOKUP function** searches for a value in the leftmost column of a table. It then returns a value in a cell you designate from the same row in a column you list in the table. The function is VLOOKUP(lookup_value, table_array, col_index_num, range_lookup).

The **HLOOKUP function** searches for a value in the top row of a table. It then returns a value in a cell you designate from the same column in a row that you list in the table. The function is HLOOKUP(lookup_value, table_array, row_index_num, range_lookup).

The arguments used in the lookup functions are explained in the following table.

Argument	Description
lookup_value	The value (number), reference, or text (in quotes) that you want to find
table_array	The range of cells to look in
col_index_num	The column of the table used to select the result
row_index_num	The row of the table used to select the result
range_lookup	A logical value that specifies whether you want the lookup function to find an exact match or an approximate match. TRUE returns the closest match and FALSE returns an exact match.

You will use the VLOOKUP function to add the model information to the loan analysis worksheet. To make it easier to see the model information as you enter and use the functions, you will copy the model data from the Models sheet to below the loan analysis data in the Analysis sheet.

● Copy A1:D8 from the Models sheet to cell B24 of the Analysis worksheet.

● Scroll the worksheet to see the entire table of model data.

Your screen should be similar to Figure 5.24

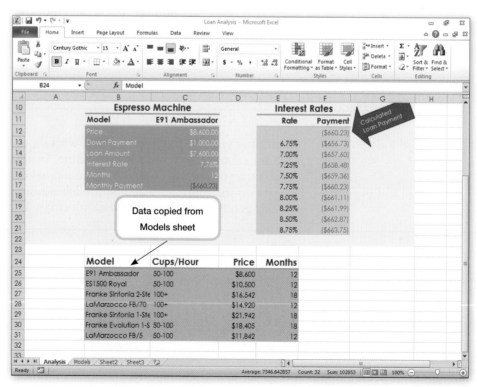

Figure 5.24

You want to calculate the loan payment for the ES1500 Royal next. You will enter the model name in cell C11 and then a VLOOKUP function in cell C12 to display the price of the machine. The VLOOKUP function you will enter is =VLOOKUP(C11, B24:E31, 3, FALSE). This function will search the first column in the range B24:D31 for an exact match (FALSE) to the data in cell C11 and return the price data in column 3.

2

- Enter **ES1500 Royal** in cell C11.

- Enter = **VLOOKUP (C11, B24:E31, 3, FALSE)** in cell C12.

- Move to cell C12.

Your screen should be similar to Figure 5.25

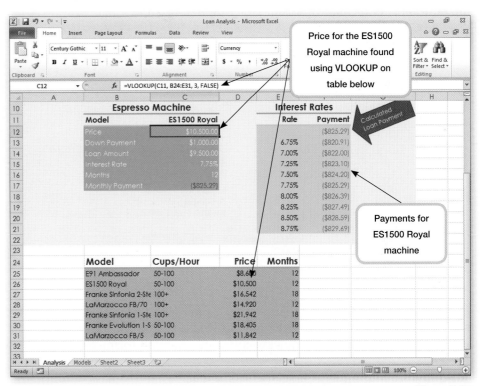

Figure 5.25

The price of the espresso machine, $10,500 from cell D26, is displayed in cell C12 and the new payments are displayed in cells F13 through F21.

Next, you will calculate the loan payment for the Franke Sinfonia 2-Step. Rather than typing the model name in cell C11, you will use a cell reference formula. Additionally, you notice that Evan wants to extend the term for this model to 18 months. Since this will occur with several models, you will enter a second VLOOKUP function to automatically add this data to the loan analysis.

3

- Enter **=B27** in cell C11.

- Best fit column C.

- Enter **=VLOOKUP (C11, B24:E31, 4, FALSE)** in cell C16.

Your screen should be similar to Figure 5.26

Figure 5.26

Using the cell reference to the model name in C11 ensures that the lookup function will find an exact match. Additionally, the second lookup function quickly enters the month information for each model.

4

- Delete the Models sheet.

- Print the Analysis worksheet in landscape orientation, with narrow margins, centered horizontally, and with your name and current date in the header.

- Save and close the workbook.

- Close the ex05_Espresso Machines List **workbook.**

Creating a Form

The Downtown Internet Café recently started a Café Club that provides perks to members such as an e-mail newsletter, coupons, and Bonus Dollars awards. Your second project is to create a spreadsheet that calculates the Bonus Dollars earned by each customer. Bonus Dollars are awarded to customers who belong to the Café Club based on their monthly expenditures and can be applied toward any future purchases at the Café. You will create a form to record and calculate this information.

Concept 3 Form

A **form** is a formatted worksheet with blank spaces that can be filled in online on an individual computer or on a network, or printed and completed on paper. The steps in creating a form are the same for both purposes. However, certain elements are more appropriate for one than for the other. For example, color and shading are more effective on online forms, while simplicity of design and layout is very important in printed forms. In addition, online forms can contain formulas that immediately calculate results such as totals, whereas printed forms would need to include blank spaces where the calculations would be entered manually.

The first step when creating a form is to decide what should appear on the form and what information will be entered into the form. When customers make a purchase, the cashier swipes their Café Club card and the total purchase amount is then recorded as part of the transaction. Obtaining expenditures for each customer is just a matter of checking the computer file. The Bonus Dollars form needs to be designed to accept input of customer expenditures and to calculate Bonus Dollars earned. Although Evan wants the form to be electronic, he also wants to be able to print it out for reference.

You have already started designing the form by entering much of the text, many of the formulas, some formatting to improve the appearance, and some sample data.

1

● Open the workbook file ex05_Bonus Dollars.

● If necessary, maximize the worksheet.

● Move to cell H12.

Your screen should be similar to Figure 5.27

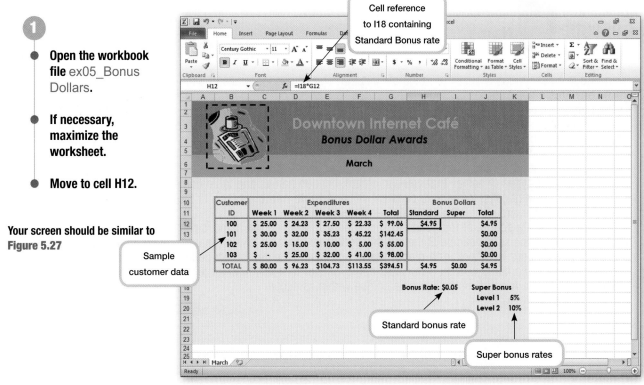

Figure 5.27

The worksheet displays identification numbers for four sample customers and their expenditures for each week in columns C through F.

The last three columns will be used to calculate and display customer Bonus Dollars. The Downtown Internet Café awards Bonus Dollars based on total monthly expenditures. A Standard Bonus is applied to every customer at a rate of $0.05 per dollar spent. An additional Super Bonus is awarded at two different levels for those customers who spend more. The bonus awards are explained in the following table.

Bonus	Award
Standard Bonus	All expenditures earn a standard bonus of $0.05 per dollar spent
Super Bonus Level 1	If total monthly expenditures are greater than $75 but less than $120, the Super Bonus is 5% of the Standard Bonus
Super Bonus Level 2	If total expenditures are greater than or equal to $120, the Super Bonus is 10% of the Standard Bonus.

Using Named Ranges

To complete the form, you need to enter the formulas to calculate the bonus awards. Many times, especially in a large worksheet, formulas are difficult to read and understand. This is because the cell references used in the formula do not identify the cell content. For example, the formula used in cell H12 references cell I18. To understand this formula, you would need to look at the worksheet to find out the content of cell I18. In this case, cell I18 contains the Standard Bonus rate amount of $0.05 per dollar.

To help clarify the meaning of a formula, you can name cells and ranges.

Concept 4 Name

A **name** is a description of a cell or range of cells that can be used in place of cell references. The name can be used any time a cell or range is requested as part of a command or in a formula or function. A name must begin with a letter, underscore (_), or backslash (\) and can be up to 255 characters long. It can include letters, numbers, underlines, periods, backslashes, and question marks. It cannot contain spaces. Names can contain upper- and lowercase characters. Excel displays the name as you enter it; however, it does not distinguish between names based on the case. Therefore, a cell name of *Bonus* is the same as *bonus* and Excel would prompt you to enter a unique name. A name that resembles a cell reference is not allowed.

There are two types of names that you can create: defined names and table names. A **defined name** represents a cell, range of cells, formula, or constant value. A **table name** represents the range of cells that stores an Excel data table. (You will learn about data tables in Lab 6.)

All names have a **scope**, or restriction to a location within which the name is recognized without qualification. A defined name scope can be limited to the worksheet in which it was created, called the **local worksheet level**, or to the entire workbook, or a **global workbook level**. The default scope is workbook level. This level is set by preceding the name with the worksheet name, similar to how you enter a formula that references data in another worksheet. A name must always be unique within its scope.

You will name several cells in this worksheet to make the formulas you will create easier to understand.

NAMING CELL REFERENCES

You will begin by naming cell I18, containing the Standard Bonus rate amount of $0.05 per dollar.

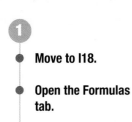

Move to I18.

Open the Formulas tab.

Click

Opens New Name dialog box to define cell name

Proposed name from adjacent cell

Absolute reference to active sheet and cell

Figure 5.28

Click 🗒 Define Name ▾

in the Defined Names group.

Your screen should be similar to Figure 5.28

Another Method

You could also create a name by typing the name in the Name box in the formula bar.

The New Name dialog box is used to name, modify, and delete cell names. In the Name text box, Excel has proposed the name Bonus_Rate. Excel automatically proposes a name for the cell or range using the contents of the active cell if it contains text, or the cell above or to the left of the active cell if the active cell does not contain text. If none of the proposed names is appropriate, you can type the name in the text box. In this case, the proposed name is the contents of the cell to the left of the active cell. Excel replaced the blank space between the words with an underscore character.

The Refers to text box displays the reference for the active cell. The reference includes the sheet name and cell reference. By default Excel makes named cell references absolute. In this case, both the name and the cell reference are acceptable.

Click OK.

Your screen should be similar to Figure 5.29

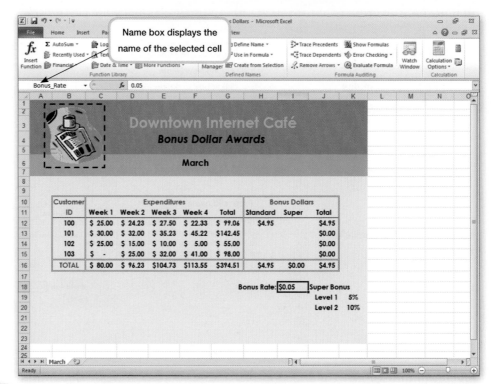

Name box displays the name of the selected cell

Figure 5.29

Additional Information

You can toggle between temporarily displaying the cell reference and the name by holding down the mouse button on the cell to display the cell reference and releasing it to display the name.

In place of the cell reference in the Name box of the formula bar, the name is displayed.

Now you need to replace the cell reference in the formula in cell H12 with the name.

Move to H12.

Change to Edit mode.

Select (highlight) the cell reference I18 in the formula.

Click f_x **Use in Formula ▼ in the Defined Names group.**

Choose Bonus_Rate.

Click ✓ **Enter.**

Your screen should be similar to Figure 5.30

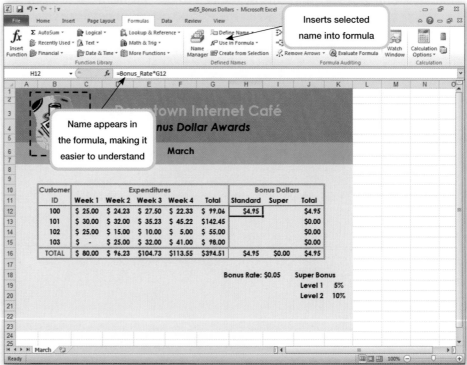

Inserts selected name into formula

Name appears in the formula, making it easier to understand

Figure 5.30

The selected name has replaced the reference to cell I18 in the formula. Using a name makes the formula easier to understand.

Next, you will name the Super Bonus levels in cells K19 and K20 that will be used in the formula to calculate the Super Bonus. You will name both cells at the same time using the labels in J19 and J20 as the names.

4
- Select J19 through K20.
- Click

   Create from Selection

  in the Defined Names group.

Your screen should be similar to Figure 5.31

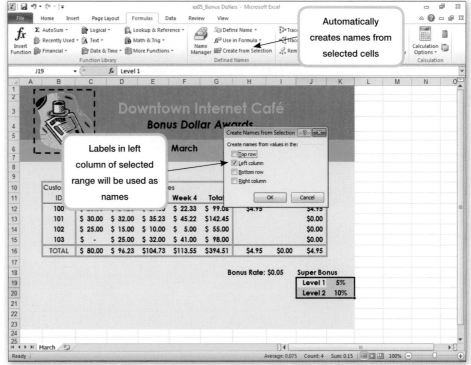

Figure 5.31

In the Create Names from Selection dialog box, you specify the location of the labels you want to use for names in relation to the cells to be named. In this case, you want to use the labels in the column to the left (J), which is the default. You will accept the default and then move to the cells to verify that the names have been created.

5
- Click [OK].
- Move to K19 and note that Level_1 is displayed in the Name box.
- Move to K20 and note that Level_2 is displayed in the Name box.
- Save the workbook as March Bonus Dollars to your solution file location.

USING NAME MANAGER

In a worksheet that has many named ranges, it is convenient to view and manage the named cells using the Name Manager feature.

● **Click** Name Manager **in the Defined Names group.**

Your screen should be similar to Figure 5.32

Figure 5.32

Additional Information

To delete a name, select it from the list and click **Delete** or press **Delete**. To add a name, click **New...** to access the New Name dialog box.

The Name Manager displays the name, values, and cell references for the three named cells. The scope of all three names is the current workbook. Using the Name Manager, you can create a new named range or edit or delete existing named ranges. You will edit the existing names.

If necessary, choose the Bonus_Rate name from the list.

Click Edit… .

Change the name to BonusRate and add the description Standard Bonus in the Comment box.

Click OK .

In a similar manner, change Level_1 to SuperBonus1 with a comment of Level 1 Bonus and Level_2 to SuperBonus2 with a comment of Level 2 Bonus.

Figure 5.33

Next, you will copy the standard bonus formula down the column.

Your screen should be similar to Figure 5.33

Click Close .

Move to cell H12.

Use the fill handle to copy the formula to cells H13:H15.

From the Auto Fill Options button menu, choose Fill Without Formatting.

Click cell H15 to deselect the range.

If necessary, Best Fit column H to fully display the cell borders.

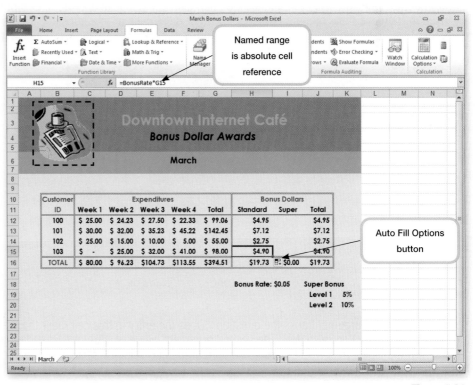

Figure 5.34

Your screen should be similar to Figure 5.34

Notice the formulas correctly adjusted to calculate the bonus rate using the appropriate total value. The named cell reference, BonusRate, did not adjust when copied because named cells are by default absolute references.

Using the IF Function

Now you want to enter a formula in cell I11 to calculate the Super Bonus. For any customer with more than $75 of expenditures, the Super Bonus is calculated using one of two levels. The highest level is for those with expenditures of $120 or more. Those customers receive a Super Bonus equal to 10 percent of their Standard Bonus. The other level is for those with expenditures less than $120 but more than $75. Those customers receive a Super Bonus equal to 5 percent of their Standard Bonus. You will use the IF function to calculate the Super Bonus.

Concept 5 IF Function

The **IF function** checks to see if certain conditions are met and then takes action based on the results of the check. IF functions are included in the logical function category because they use conditional logic to test whether conditions are true or false and make logical comparisons between expressions.
  The syntax for the IF function is

IF(logical_test,value_if_true,value_if_false)

This function contains three arguments: logical_test, value_if_true, and value_if_false. The logical_test argument is an expression that makes a comparison using logical operators. **Logical operators** are symbols used in formulas that compare numbers in two or more cells or to a constant. The result of the comparison is either true (the conditions are met) or false (the conditions are not met). The logical operators are

Symbol	Meaning
=	Equal to
<	Less than
>	Greater than
<=	Less than or equal to
>=	Greater than or equal to
<>	Not equal to
NOT	Logical NOT
AND	Logical AND
OR	Logical OR

The logical_test argument asks the question, "Does the entry in this cell meet the stated conditions?" The answer is either True (Yes) or False (No). The second argument, value_if_true, provides directions for the function to follow if the logical test result is true. The third argument, value_if_false, provides directions for the function to follow if the logical test result is false.

First you will enter the formula to calculate the bonus earned for monthly expenditures of $120 or more. Then you will modify the function to include the other conditions.

1

- Move to cell I12.

- Click 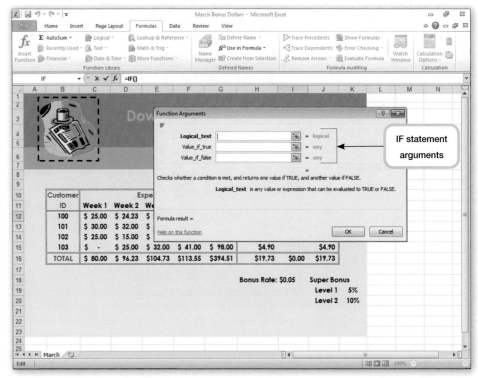 **Logical ▾** in the Function Library group on the Formulas tab.

- Choose IF.

Your screen should be similar to Figure 5.35

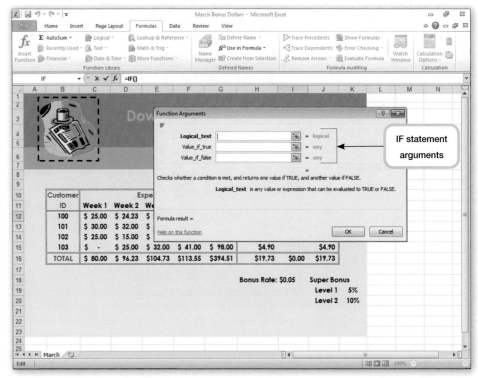

Figure 5.35

The Function Arguments dialog box is displayed to help you enter the parts of the function. The upper section of the dialog box contains three text boxes, one for each IF statement argument. The lower section provides information about the selected argument.

In this case, the logical test is whether the total expenditures for a customer are greater than or equal to $120. The value_if_true argument provides directions for what to do if the logical test is true. In this IF function, the value_if_true directions will be to multiply the value in cell H12 times the value in the cell named SuperBonus2.

2

- In the Logical_test text box, type **G12>=120**.

- Press **Tab**.

- In the Value_if_true text box, type **SuperBonus2* H12**.

Your screen should be similar to Figure 5.36

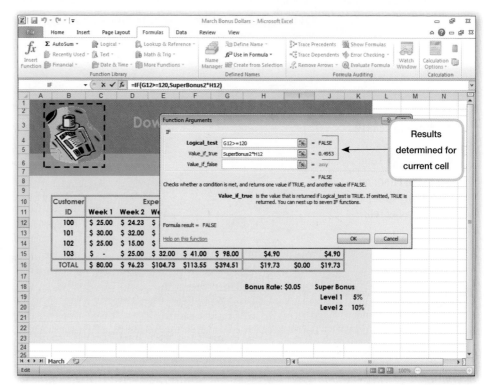

Figure 5.36

As you specify the arguments, to the right of the argument text box Excel has already determined whether the conditions are true or false for the current customer based on the values in the referenced cells. In this case, because the value in G12 is less than $120, the logical test result is False.

Next, you need to enter the value_if_false argument. It contains instructions that are executed if expenditures are less than $120. If the expenditures are greater than $75 but less than $120, then the Level 1 amount is used to calculate the Super Bonus. If the expenditures are less than or equal to $75 then the Super Bonus is 0. To enter this condition, you include a second IF statement that will apply the SuperBonus1 bonus. The arguments for the second IF statement are enclosed in their own set of parentheses. This is called a **nested function**.

3

● In the Value_if_false text box, type IF(G12>=75, SuperBonus1* H12,0).

Your screen should be similar to Figure 5.37

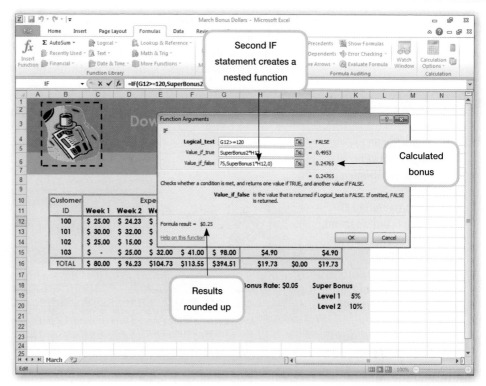

Figure 5.37

Now the calculated result is 0.24765 for the current customer. The formula result will be rounded up to $0.25.

4

● Click OK.

Your screen should be similar to Figure 5.38

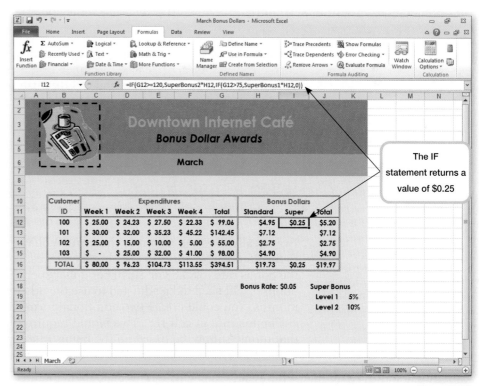

Figure 5.38

The Super Bonus for customer 100 is $0.25. The IF function determined that the number in cell G12 was less than 120 but greater than 75. Therefore, the bonus was calculated using SuperBonus1, or 5 percent. Next, you will enter formulas to make these same calculations for the other three customers.

5

- Using the fill handle, copy cell I12 to the range I13 through I15.

- From the Auto Fill Options button menu, choose Fill Without Formatting.

- Click cell I15 to deselect the range.

Your screen should be similar to Figure 5.39

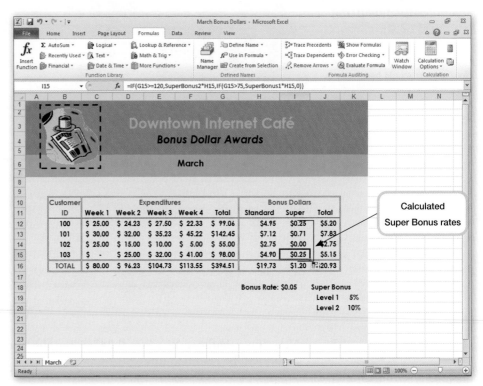

Figure 5.39

Because the named references in the copied formulas are absolute, they copied correctly. Customer 101 earned a Super Bonus award of 10 percent because the value in cell G13 is greater than $120. Customer 102 did not earn a Super Bonus because the value in cell G14 is less than $75. Customer 103 earned a Super Bonus award of 5 percent because the value in cell G15 was greater than $75 but less than $120.

Using a Drop-Down List

Evan really likes the layout of the form. A change needs to be made, however, to the Standard Bonus rate. During the slowest months, Evan plans to increase the bonus rate to $0.08 or $0.10 per dollar spent. The formulas to calculate the bonuses will need to be adjusted to use the other two bonus rates during those months. You could create two additional forms that would each have a different bonus rate in cell I18. This would require that the correct form used for that month's input be based on the bonus rate for that month.

A simpler way to deal with this problem is to create a drop-down list of the bonus rates that can be selected to set the bonus rate for the month. The cell containing a drop-down list displays an arrow. Clicking on the arrow opens the list of the items that can be selected.

CREATING A DROP-DOWN LIST

The first step in creating a drop-down list is to enter the items you want to appear in the drop-down list in a columnar range. You will enter the three bonus amounts as the items to appear in the list. Then you move to the cell where you want to create the drop-down list.

1

● **In cells H19 through H21, enter** .05, .08, **and** .10.

Additional Information

Cells H19:H21 are preformatted to Currency.

● **Move to cell I18.**

● **Click**

　🖽 Data Validation ▾

in the Data Tools group of the Data tab.

● **If necessary, open the Settings tab.**

Your screen should be similar to Figure 5.40

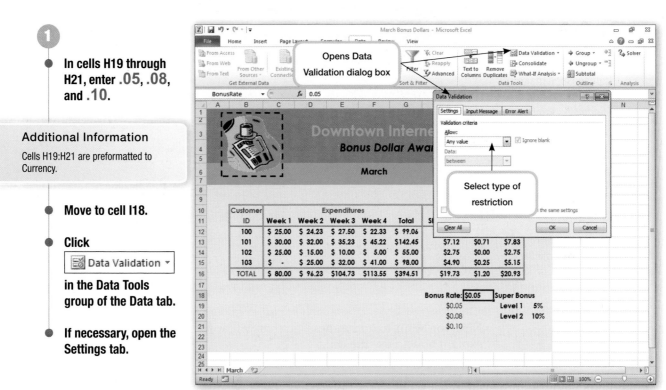

Figure 5.40

Additional Information

You will learn about other validation methods in Lab 6.

In the Settings tab, you specify the type of validation that you want to apply to the cell. **Validation** ensures that the data entered in a cell is acceptable or valid by placing restrictions on the data that can be entered. Initially, no restrictions are placed on entries that can be made in a cell. One way to restrict the data that can be entered is to limit the entries to those entries displayed in a drop-down list. Then you provide the location of the cells containing the list data.

2

Open the Allow drop-down menu and choose List.

Enter the range H19:H21 as the Source.

If necessary, make the source range an absolute reference.

Your screen should be similar to Figure 5.41

Figure 5.41

Next you want to add a message that will appear when the cell is selected to explain how to use the cell.

3

Open the Input Message tab.

If necessary, choose Show input message when cell is selected.

Type Select the bonus rate for the month. in the Input message text box.

Your screen should be similar to Figure 5.42

Figure 5.42

Finally, you want to include an error alert message that appears when an invalid entry is made in the cell. There are three error alert styles that can be selected: Stop, Warning, and Message. A Stop alert prevents entry of invalid data. Warning or Message alerts display a warning or information message but do not prevent entry of invalid data.

4
- Open the Error Alert tab.
- If necessary, choose Show error alert after invalid data is entered.
- If necessary, select the Stop style from the Style drop-down menu.
- Type **This entry is not allowed. Select an entry from the list.** in the Error message text box.

Your screen should be similar to Figure 5.43

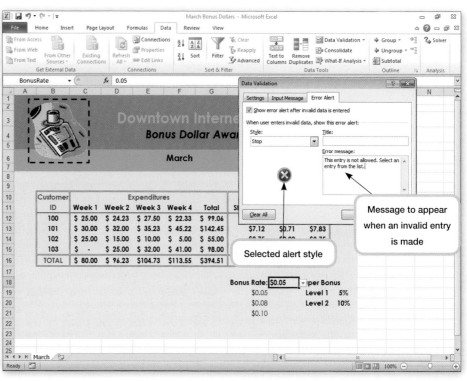

Figure 5.43

Additional Information

The title and text for the message can be up to 225 characters.

The error alert message will display the text you entered and the stop symbol in a dialog box if an invalid entry is made.

5
- Click OK .

Your screen should be similar to Figure 5.44

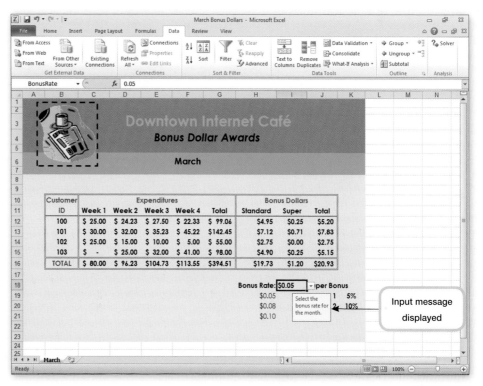

Figure 5.44

The process of creating and defining the validation settings for the drop-down list are now complete. Because cell I18 is selected, the input message you entered is displayed, providing directions on how to use the cell.

TESTING THE DROP-DOWN LIST

The next step is to test the drop-down list cell to make sure the validation settings are working correctly. First you will select a bonus rate from the list.

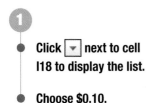

Click ▼ **next to cell I18 to display the list.**

Choose $0.10.

Your screen should be similar to Figure 5.45

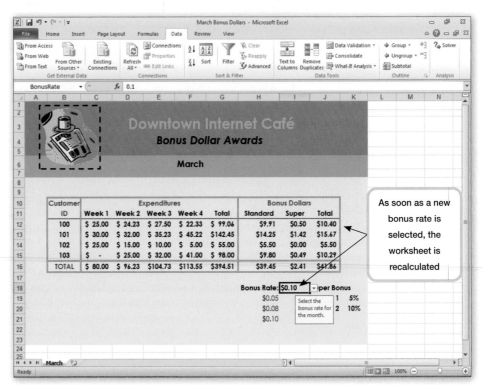

Figure 5.45

The selection you made from the drop-down list is entered in the Bonus Rate cell, I18, and the worksheet is recalculated using the new bonus rate.

Now you will test the data validation settings by entering an incorrect bonus amount.

Type 25 in cell I18 and press (Enter).

Your screen should be similar to
Figure 5.46

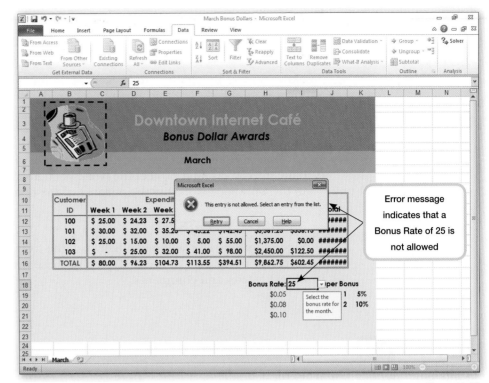

Figure 5.46

Because the value you entered was not a value on the list, the error message is displayed. You will type in a correct entry next.

Click [Retry].

Type .08 and press (Enter).

Change the label in cell H18 to Select Bonus Rate:.

Increase the width of column H slightly to display the cell borders.

Save the workbook.

Your screen should be similar to
Figure 5.47

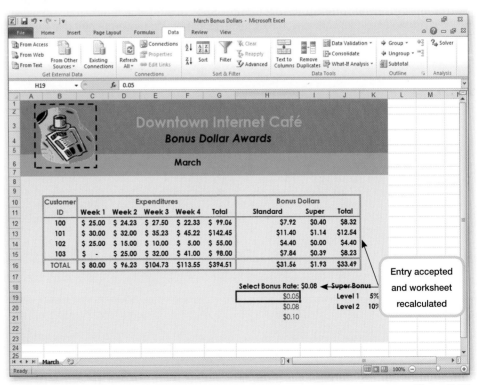

Figure 5.47

The entry is accepted because it is the same as one of the items in the list.

Finalizing the Form

Now you will prepare the form to be used for other months. A well-designed form is simple to use and uncluttered in design. To make the form easy to use, you will add comments and a command button to print the output. To simplify the design, you will hide nonessential items. Then you will prepare the workbook to be saved as a template to be used each month to record the customer's Bonus Dollar earnings. You will clear the sample data, unlock all data entry areas, and protect the worksheet. You also will add documentation to the workbook to clarify the purpose of the template.

ADDING COMMENTS

Since someone else will most likely use the form, it is a good idea to include instructions on how to use it. Typically, these instructions are a combination of text entries and comments.

Concept 6 Comment

A **comment** is a note attached to a cell that can be used to help clarify the meaning of the data, provide documentation, or ask a question. Using comments is a good method of adding instructions that do not interfere with the appearance of the worksheet.

A cell containing a comment displays a red indicator triangle in the upper-right corner. Pointing to a cell containing a comment displays the comment text in a comment box. You can move and resize a comment box just as you would any other type of graphic object. If you move the cell that contains a comment, the associated comment box moves with it.

You will add one text entry and three cell comments that will provide the instructions for this form.

1

● Move to cell A8.

● Enter For help on how to complete this form, point to the red triangles.

● Format the entry in cell A8 using a font color of red and bold.

Your screen should be similar to Figure 5.48

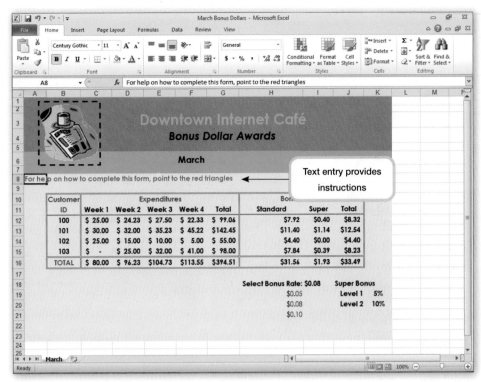

Figure 5.48

Next, you will add the cell comments using the Review tab. The first comment will appear in cell F6 and will direct users to update the month.

2

● Move to cell F6.

● Open the Review tab.

● Click in the Comments group.

Your screen should be similar to Figure 5.49

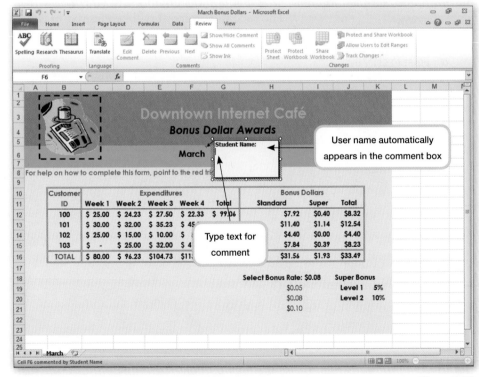

Figure 5.49

By default, the comment box includes the user name. You will delete the name and then enter the text for the comment.

3

- Select the user name and press Delete.

- Type **Enter the month.**

- Size the comment box to fit the text.

- Click on any cell to complete the comment.

Having Trouble?

If the comment box continues to display after moving to another cell, click

 Show All Comments in the

Comments group.

Having Trouble?

If the red triangle is not displayed, open the File tab, click

📄 Options , and

choose Indicators only, and comments on hover from the Display section of the Advanced category.

- Point to cell F6.

Your screen should be similar to Figure 5.50

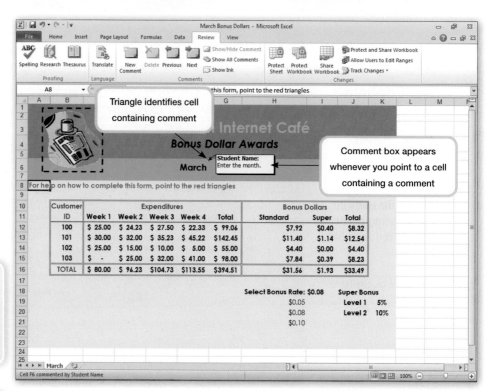

Figure 5.50

A red triangle appears in the upper-right corner of the cell containing the comment. When you point to a cell containing a comment, the comment text is displayed in a comment box. An arrow from the comment box points to the cell to which the comment is attached.

The second comment will be entered in cell C12.

4

● Add a comment to C12.

● Delete the user name and enter the text **Enter expenditures here.**

● Size the comment box to fit the text.

● Click on any cell to complete the comment.

● Point to cell C12 to display the comment.

Another Method

You also can move to a cell containing a comment and click to display and then hide the comment. The comment remains displayed until you hide it again.

Your screen should be similar to Figure 5.51

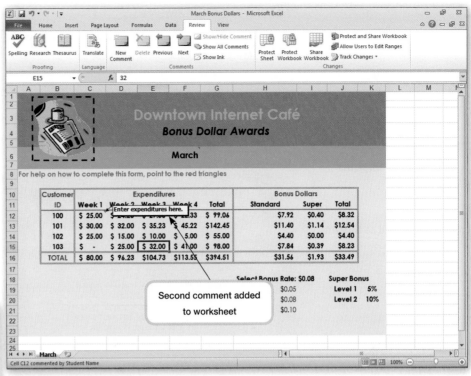

Figure 5.51

EDITING COMMENTS

You decide the comment is not descriptive enough and will edit the comment text.

1

● Move to cell C12 and click .

Another Method

You also can edit a comment using Edit Comment from the shortcut menu.

● Move the cursor before the word "expenditures" and type the word **weekly** followed by a space.

● Size the comment box to fit the text.

● Click on any cell to complete the comment.

● Display the comment.

Your screen should be similar to Figure 5.52

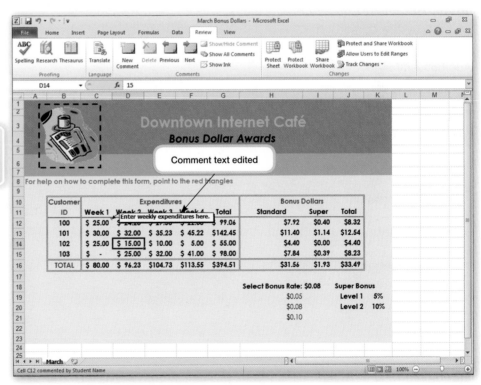

Figure 5.52

You have added two comments to the form to provide directions on how to use the form.

VIEWING ALL COMMENTS

To quickly check all comments, rather than displaying each comment individually, you can display all the comments at the same time.

Click

Show All Comments

in the Comments group.

Your screen should be similar to Figure 5.53

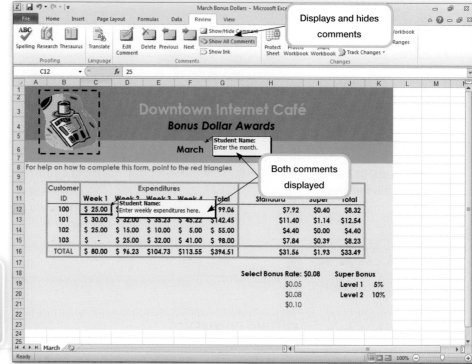

Figure 5.53

Another Method

You also can click 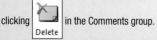 Next or Previous to cycle from one comment to the next.

Additional Information

You can delete a comment using Delete Comment from the shortcut menu or by clicking Delete in the Comments group.

Additional Information

You also can print comments where they appear on the worksheet or in a list at the end of the worksheet by selecting the appropriate option from the Sheet tab of the Page Setup dialog box.

The two comments you entered are displayed. If comments overlay one another, you can move them around just like any other graphic object. However, when you hide and redisplay the comments, they return to their original location.

Next, you will hide the comments again and then you will hide any nonessential information in the form to simplify its appearance.

Users of this form do not need to see the list of bonus rates and the two bonus levels. To simplify the form, you will hide this information.

Click

Show All Comments

to hide comments again.

- Move the contents of cells J18:K20 to J19.

- Reapply the fill color to the vacated cells.

- Select and hide rows 19 through 21.

- In cell I18, select .05.

- Save the workbook.

Your screen should be similar to Figure 5.54

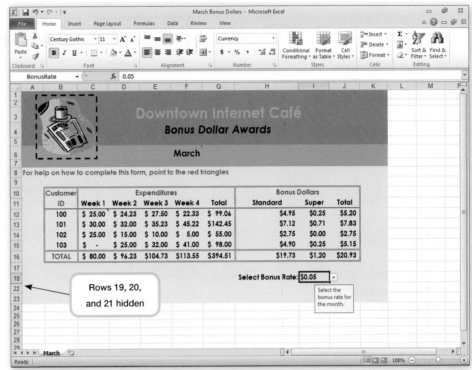

Figure 5.54

Now only the information that is necessary to complete the form is displayed.

Preparing the Workbook for Use

Each month, the form will be used to record the customer's Bonus Dollars earnings. Although the form needs to be expanded to include all the Club members, you will save the sample design as a template file for Evan to try out.

To prepare the form for use as a template, you need to first clear the sample data and unlock those cells for editing. Then you will include file documentation so that users of the template will understand the purpose of the file and perform several other steps to prepare the workbook for use by others. Finally, you will protect the worksheet.

PROTECTING WORKSHEET ELEMENTS

First, you will clear the contents of the entry areas and unlock these cells for editing.

- **Replace the contents of cell F6 with** Month.

- **Rename the March tab** Month.

- **Clear the contents only of cells C12 through F15.**

- **Unlock cell F6.**

Having Trouble?

Refer to Concept 3: Protection in Lab 4 to review worksheet protection.

- **Unlock cell I18.**

- **Unlock the cells for weekly expenditures (cells C12 through F15).**

Your screen should be similar to Figure 5.55

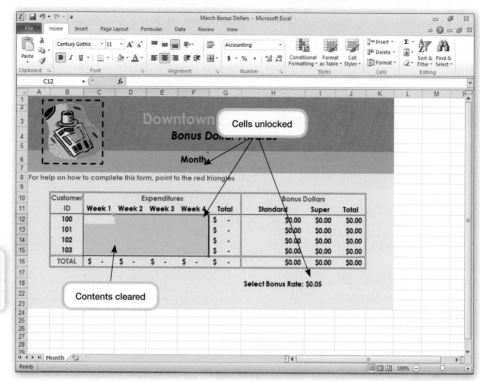

Figure 5.55

Next, you will enter basic documentation regarding the workbook file in the Properties section of the Info window and save the workbook.

2

- **Open the File tab and click** <u>Show All Properties</u> **on the Info page.**

- **Enter your name in the Author text box.**

- **Enter Monthly record of expenditures and bonuses in the Subject text box.**

- **In the Comments text box, type Point to the red triangles for instructions. Select the bonus amount for the month from the Bonus Rate drop-down list.**

Figure 5.56

You are now ready to save this generalized workbook.

Your screen should be similar to Figure 5.56

3

- **Click on the Home tab.**

- **Move to cell A9.**

- **Save the workbook as** Monthly Bonus Dollars **to your solution file location.**

CHECKING FOR PRIVATE INFORMATION

Before you give a file to another user, it is a good idea to check the document for hidden data or personal information that may be stored in the computer itself or in the document's properties (metadata) that you may not want to share. To help locate and remove this information, you use the Document Inspector.

Open the File tab,

click **on the**

Info page and choose Inspect Document.

If necessary, select [No] **in response to the prompt to save the file since the file has been recently saved.**

Your screen should be similar to Figure 5.57

Figure 5.57

Using the Document Inspector dialog box, you can specify the type of content you want inspected by checking each of the types described in the following table.

Type	Removes
Comments and Annotations	Comments, tracked changes revision marks, document version information, and ink annotations
Document Properties and Personal Information	All document properties, including statistical information, e-mail headers, routing slips, send-to-review information, document server properties, content type information, user name, template name
Custom XML Data	All custom XML data that was stored within the document
Headers and Footers	All information in headers and footers
Hidden Rows and Columns	All rows and columns that were hidden
Hidden worksheets	Any text that was formatted as hidden
Invisible Content	All content that has been formatted as invisible

You will inspect the workbook file for all types of information.

● **If necessary, select all seven types of content to check.**

● **Click** Inspect .

Your screen should be similar to Figure 5.58

Worksheet comments located

Document properties and named cell comments located

Hidden rows located

Figure 5.58

The inspector results identify three areas containing hidden data or personal information. These include comments and hidden rows as well as potentially private information in document properties. If you wanted to remove any of the located information, you would click Remove All next to each item in the list. In this case, you do not want to remove the comments or hidden rows, so you will close the inspector without making any changes.

● **Click** Close .

MARKING A WORKBOOK AS FINAL

Another feature you can use when sharing a workbook with others is to mark it as final. This feature makes the document read-only and thereby prevents changes to the document. However, this feature is not a security feature, as anyone using the file can easily remove the Mark as Final status from the file. You will try out this feature to see how it works as it may be useful in other situations. Then you will turn the feature off.

1

- Open the File tab.

- Click [Protect Workbook ▾] and choose Mark as Final.

- Click [OK] to authorize saving the file.

- Click [OK] in response to the informational message about marking the document as final.

- Click the Home tab.

- Move to cell F6 and try to type the month.

Your screen should be similar to Figure 5.59

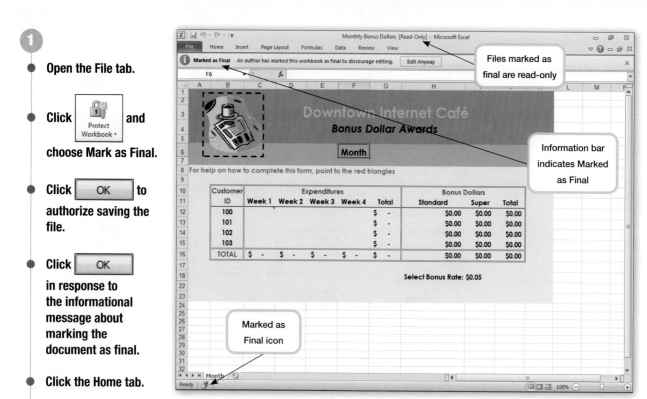

Figure 5.59

A Marked as Final information bar now appears below the Ribbon tabs indicating that this feature is on and that the file cannot be edited. The Ribbon is reduced to tabs only because the document cannot be edited. Also, the Marked as Final icon appears in the status bar. Since you may still want to make changes to the document, you will turn off this feature.

2

- Click [Edit Anyway] in the information bar.

Another Method

You also can choose the Mark as Final option again from the Info window to turn off this feature.

The read-only restriction is removed from the file and the Ribbon is fully displayed. Also, the information bar and Marked as Final icon are no longer displayed.

ADDING A DIGITAL SIGNATURE

Another feature that can be used when giving someone else a file to look at is a digital signature. This feature authenticates that the people and products are who and what they claim to be. A **digital signature** is an electronic encryption-based stamp of authentication that confirms the document originated from the signer and has not been changed. For the signature to be valid, it must be issued by a certificate authority (CA), a commercial organization that issues digital signatures.

Digital signatures can be visible in a document or invisible. A visible digital signature is displayed on a signature line in the document. An invisible signature is stored in the document file and recipients can verify that the document was digitally signed by viewing the document's digital signature or by looking at the Signatures icon in the status bar. You will add and then remove an invisible digital signature.

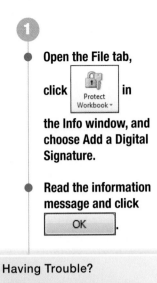

1

- Open the File tab,

  click in

  the Info window, and
  choose Add a Digital
  Signature.

- Read the information
  message and click

  [OK].

Having Trouble?

If prompted, choose Create your own

digital ID and click [OK].

Then enter your name in the Name box

and click [Create].

- Click [Sign]
  to add your digital
  signature.

- Click [OK]
  in response to
  the Signature
  Confirmation
  message.

- Open the Home tab to
  view the document.

- If necessary, click
   in the status
  bar to display the
  Signatures pane.

Additional Information

The default signature is the user name
on your computer.

Your screen should be similar to
Figure 5.60

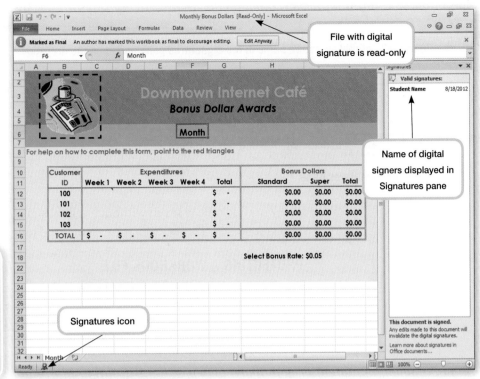

Figure 5.60

Again the Ribbon is reduced to tabs to discourage editing and the Marked as Final information bar is displayed. The file was saved as read-only. If you click [Edit Anyway] you can edit the worksheet; however, doing so immediately invalidates the digital signature and automatically removes the signature from the document. The status bar displays the 🖼 Signatures icon. Clicking on this button hides and displays the Signatures pane.

The Signatures pane displays the names of the digital signers. Again, because you want Evan to be able to make changes to the worksheet, you will turn off this feature.

2

- Point to the digital signature name in the Signatures pane and open the drop-down menu.

- Choose Remove Signature.

- Click | Yes | to permanently remove the signature.

- Click | OK | to acknowledge that the signature was removed.

- Close the Signatures pane.

The workbook file is saved without a digital signature and the read-only restriction is removed. The 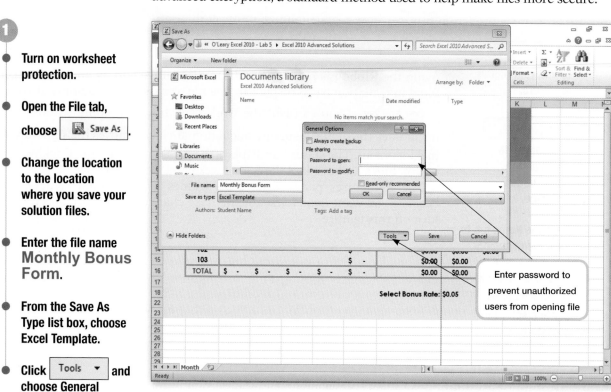 Signatures icon is no longer displayed in the status bar.

PROTECTING A WORKBOOK FILE

Finally, you are ready to protect the worksheet and save the workbook file as a template file type. To prevent any unauthorized users from opening the workbook file, you will also add a password to the file. Using password protection enables only those users who know the password to access the file. This feature uses advanced encryption, a standard method used to help make files more secure.

1

- Turn on worksheet protection.

- Open the File tab, choose | Save As |.

- Change the location to the location where you save your solution files.

- Enter the file name **Monthly Bonus Form**.

- From the Save As Type list box, choose Excel Template.

- Click | Tools ▼ | and choose General Options.

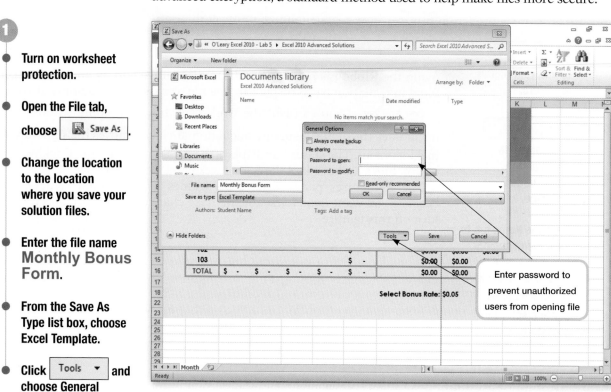

Enter password to prevent unauthorized users from opening file

Figure 5.61

Another Method

You also can save a file and change the file type using the Save and Send window of Backstage view.

You will add your password next.

Your screen should be similar to
Figure 5.61

2

- In the Password to open text box, enter your name and press [Enter].

- Reenter the password to confirm it and click [OK].

- Click [Save].

- Close the workbook.

Now, when you reopen this workbook file, you will be prompted to enter the password exactly as you entered it when it was created.

3

- Create a new workbook file using the Monthly Bonus Form template.

- Unprotect the worksheet and enter your name in cell A9.

- Protect the worksheet again.

- Enter the current month in cell F6, change the bonus rate to .08 and enter some sample data.

- Print the worksheet in landscape orientation, centered horizontally with your name and the current date in the header.

- Save the workbook with the file name Monthly Bonus Analysis to your solution file location.

- Exit Excel.

Your printed worksheet will be similar to that shown in the Case Study at the beginning of the lab.

FOCUS ON CAREERS

EXPLORE YOUR CAREER OPTIONS

Payroll Clerk

Have you ever wondered who makes sure you get your paycheck? Have you ever had to address inaccuracies on your paycheck with someone in payroll? Payroll clerks track employee hours and compute employee pay after making subtractions for taxes and insurance. Payroll clerks also add new employees to the system and prepare earnings statements employees use for filing taxes. They must have excellent math skills and good communication skills. Some offices use automated payroll systems, but in these situations payroll clerks are typically responsible for doing analysis and looking at trends using spreadsheet programs. Salary range is typically between $30,000 and $40,000, depending on experience. The demand for payroll clerks is expected to decrease slightly as many companies move toward automation.

Data Table (EX5.8)

A data table is a range of cells that is used to quickly calculate multiple what-if versions in one operation and to show the results of all variations in the worksheet.

Lookup Functions (EX5.22)

Lookup functions permit you to use worksheet tables as sources of information for formulas and calculations in other parts of the worksheet.

Form (EX5.24)

A form is a formatted worksheet with blank spaces that can be filled in online on an individual computer or on a network, or printed and completed on paper.

Name (EX5.26)

A name is a description of a cell or range of cells that can be used in place of cell references.

IF Function (EX5.32)

The IF function checks to see if certain conditions are met and then takes action based on the results of the check.

Comment (EX5.42)

A comment is a note attached to a cell that can be used to clarify the meaning of the cell contents, provide documentation, or ask a question.

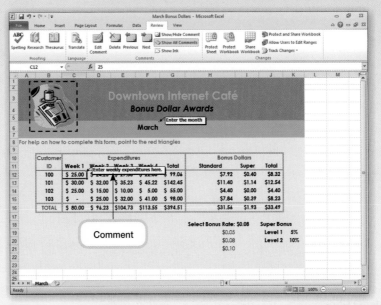

KEY TERMS

column-oriented EX5.8
comment EX5.42
data table EX5.8
defined name EX5.26
digital signature EX5.52
form EX5.25
global workbook level EX5.26
HLOOKUP function EX5.22
IF function EX5.32
input cell EX5.8
local worksheet level EX5.26
logical operator EX5.32
lookup function EX5.22

name EX5.26
nested function EX5.34
one-variable data table EX5.8
PMT function EX5.6
principal EX5.6
row-oriented EX5.8
scope EX5.26
table name EX5.26
text box EX5.12
two-variable data table EX5.8
validation EX5.37
VLOOKUP function EX5.22
Wizard EX5.18

COMMAND SUMMARY

Command	Shortcut	Action
File tab		
Info/Properties		Displays information about a file
Info/Check for Issues/Inspect Document		Starts Document Inspector to locate and remove hidden and private information
Info/Protect Workbook/Mark as Final		Marks file as final and changes it to read-only
Info/Protect Workbook/Add a Digital Signature		Adds a digital signature to a file
Save As/Tools/General Options		Adds a password to the workbook file
[Options] /Advanced/Display/ Indicators only, and comments on hover		Displays comment indicators and comments when you point to a cell
Insert tab		
Illustrations group		
[Shapes ▾]		Creates selected shape
Text group		
[Text Box]		Creates a text box
Formulas tab		
Function Library group		
[fx Insert Function]		Prompts you to select a function from a list and helps you enter the arguments correctly
[Logical ▾]		Creates a logical function
Defined Names group		
[Name Manager]		Creates, edits, and deletes cell and range names
[Define Name ▾]		Creates a range name using text in cells

LAB REVIEW

COMMAND SUMMARY (CONTINUED)

Command	Shortcut	Action
ƒ Use in Formula ▾		Places selected range name in formula bar or lists names in worksheet
Create from Selection		Automatically generates name from selected cells
Data tab		
Data Tools group		
Text to Columns		Separates information contained in one cell into two columns
Data Validation ▾ /Settings/List		Creates a drop-down list
What-If Analysis ▾ /Data Table		Creates a data table based on specified input values and formulas
Review tab		
Comments group		
New Comment		Inserts a new comment in selected cell
Edit Comment		Edits comment in selected cell
Delete		Deletes comment in selected cell
Show All Comments		Displays all comments
Next		Displays the next comment
Previous		Displays the previous comment

COMMAND SUMMARY (CONTINUED)

Command	Shortcut	Action
Drawing Tools Format tab		
Insert Shapes group		
⯆ More		Opens Shapes gallery to insert ready-made shapes
Shape Styles group		
⯆ More		Opens Shape Styles gallery to apply a visual style to a shape
Arrange group		
🔄 Rotate ▾		Rotates selected shape

LAB EXERCISES

MATCHING

Match the letter on the right to the item in the numbered list on the left.

1. name	____	a. ensures that the data entered in a cell is acceptable
2. data table	____	b. a note attached to a cell
3. IF	____	c. a formatted worksheet with blank spaces to be filled in
4. logical operators	____	d. a description of a cell or range that can be used in place of the cell or range reference
5. rotation handle		
	____	e. a function that checks to see if a condition is met and takes action based on that condition
6. digital signature		
	____	f. authentication that confirms the document's origination
7. lookup	____	g. a range of cells that is used to quickly calculate multiple what-if versions
8. comment		
	____	h. changes the angle of the selected object
9. form	____	i. compares numbers in two or more cells or to a constant
10. validation	____	j. functions that use worksheet tables as sources of information

MULTIPLE CHOICE

Circle the correct response to the questions below.

1. An IF statement is _____ if it contains one or more other IF statements as arguments.
   a. invalid
   b. circular
   c. nested
   d. incomplete

2. A _____ data table can be row- or column-oriented.
   a. multivariable
   b. one-variable
   c. single-variable
   d. two-variable

3. A(n) _____ is a formatted worksheet with blank spaces to be filled.
   a. cell form
   b. object
   c. template
   d. Wizard

4. _____ locates hidden and private information in a document.
   a. Finalizer
   b. Private Investigator
   c. Workbook Protector
   d. Document Inspector

5. The _____ function searches for a value in the top row of a table.
   a. IF
   b. HLOOKUP
   c. VLOOKUP
   d. PMT

6. An Excel form can contain _____.
   a. text
   b. cell comments
   c. graphics
   d. all of the above

7. A(n) _____ argument is an expression that makes a comparison using logical operators.
   a. if_then
   b. logical_test
   c. and_or
   d. logical_if

8. The _____ function calculates a periodic payment on a loan.
   a. RATE
   b. NPER
   c. PMT
   d. PV

9. _____ are used in formulas and functions that compare numbers in two or more cells.
   a. Relational operators
   b. Function arguments
   c. Conditional arguments
   d. Logical operators

10. A name assigned to a cell must start with _____.
    a. a backslash
    b. an underscore
    c. a letter
    d. any of the above

LAB EXERCISES

TRUE/FALSE

Circle the correct answer to the following questions.

1.	Dragging adjusts the size of an element in a shape.	**True**	**False**
2.	A digitally signed document is automatically read-only.	**True**	**False**
3.	A range name can only include letters.	**True**	**False**
4.	A comment cannot be attached to a formula.	**True**	**False**
5.	The Lookup_value is the range of cells to look in.	**True**	**False**
6.	The result of an IF argument is either true or false.	**True**	**False**
7.	The Stop warning does not prevent invalid entries.	**True**	**False**
8.	The IF function requires three arguments.	**True**	**False**
9.	A form created in Excel cannot be used online.	**True**	**False**
10.	A text box can be used to display graphics.	**True**	**False**

FILL-IN

Complete the following statements by filling in the blanks with the correct key terms.

1. There are two types of lookup functions: VLOOKUP and _____.

2. A(n) _____ name represents a cell, range of cells, formula, or constant value.

3. The PMT function contains three arguments: _____, nper, and pv.

4. A(n) _____ name represents the range of cells that stores an Excel data table.

5. The _____ function checks to see if certain conditions are met and takes actions based on the results.

6. A cell containing a comment displays a(n) _____ in the upper-right corner.

7. A(n) _____ permits you to use worksheet tables as sources of information for formulas and calculations in other parts of the worksheet.

8. All names have a(n) _____, or restriction to a location within which the name is recognized without qualification.

9. A(n) _____ is a formatted worksheet that is intended to be filled in by the user.

10. In a one-variable data table, a(n) _____ is a cell in which a list of values is substituted to see the resulting effect on the related formulas.

STEP-BY-STEP

EDEN'S GARDEN VOLUNTEER REWARDS PROGRAM ★

1. After viewing the revenue analysis you provided, Julia Richardson and the other Eden's Garden board members have begun the budget planning for the next year. They have realized that daily operation of the agency depends on the volunteers. To repay them for their time, the board has decided to implement a rewards program with some of the budget surpluses you have anticipated. You have been asked to create a worksheet to track the number of hours people have worked and determine their award level. Your completed worksheets should be similar to the one shown here.

   a. Open the workbook file ex05_ Edens Garden Volunteers.

   b. Enter formulas to calculate the average and total hours for the year in columns F and G. Copy the formulas down the columns.

   c. Enter the labels **Award Level** in cell I40 and **Hours** in cell J40, right-aligned. Enter the labels **Star Level 1**, **Star Level 2**, and **Star Level 3** right-aligned in cells I41 through I43. In cells J41 through J43, enter **300**, **200**, and **100** as the award levels.

   d. Apply formatting to enhance cells I40 through J43. Adjust the column widths and layout as necessary.

   e. Use the Create from Selection command to name the values for the three star levels.

   f. In cell H5 enter the following formula to calculate the award level for the volunteers: =IF(G5>=Star_ Level_1,1,IF(G5>=Star_Level_2, 2,IF(G5>=Star_Level_3,3,0))).

   g. Change the value in cell B5 to **450** and then to **0** to check the formula. Return the value to **45**. Copy the formula down the column.

   h. Add cell comments to the worksheet that explain the star system.

Student Name | 1/23/2013

"Growing food to feed our neighbors"

EDEN'S GARDEN VOLUNTEERS

	1st Qtr	2nd Qtr	3rd Qtr	4th Qtr	Average	Total	Level
Bell, Patricia	45	34	102	35	54	216	2
Carey, Ronnie	106	45	55	106	78	312	1
Carver, Kathi	30	83	3	3	29.75	119	3
Chorley, Besty	68	2	235	96	100.25	401	1
Clark, Jamel	51	30	28	58	41.75	167	3
Cody, Martin	28	66	6	45	36.25	145	3
Dickson, Diane	72	19	77	32	50	200	2
Edwards, Mike	12	20	61	28	30.25	121	3
Ferguson, Robby	99	12	0	43	38.5	154	3
Forester, Kimberly	32	66	34	30	40.5	162	3
Franklin, Stacey	57	98	93	80	82	328	1
Fulton, Anne	13	25	55	100	48.25	193	3
Garcia, Maria	5	23	61	36	31.25	125	3
Gatens, Chris	0	100	58	85	60.75	243	2
Henderson, James	9	76	51	60	49	196	3
Ingram, Helen	29	12	33	12	21.5	86	0
Isbell, Sonya	46	65	47	3	40.25	161	3
Johnson, Thaman	5	25	18	7	13.75	55	0
Jones, April	70	83	38	79	67.5	270	2
Kelly, William	13	78	52	88	57.75	231	2
Kettonhoeffer, Bill	4	59	57	8	32	128	3
Kullman, Rodney	28	30	35	16	27.25	109	3
La Paglia, Sally	39	10	12	134	48.75	195	3
Lee, Su	56	6	5	0	16.75	67	0
Legge, Cristan	3	81	73	34	47.75	191	3
López, Andrew	83	3	165	0	62.75	251	2
Marcus, Danielle	3	19	24	2	12	48	0
Merwin, Michael	44	9	95	37	46.25	185	3

i. Select the entire worksheet excluding the star values. Enter **your name** and the **current date** in a header. Then center the worksheet horizontally.

j. Print the selection in portrait orientation. Save the workbook as Volunteers to your solution file location

WILSON ELECTRONICS FINANCIAL ANALYSIS ★★

2. You have been hired as a salesperson for the Wilson Electronics Company. You want to be able to give your customers up-to-date and accurate information on the cost of high-end electronics you sell. To automate the process, you plan to use a data table containing the model information and a table to calculate the different payments at various loan interest rates. The completed worksheet will be similar to the one shown here.

a. Open the file ex05_Electronics Analyzer.

b. Instead of typing in the model and price of the item each time, you want to be able to enter a model number and choose it from a drop-down list that links to a data table. The information for the data table has already been created in cells D23 through E42. Enter the number **1** in cell B13. You will use the CHOOSE function to select the items in the data table based on the number entered in cell B13. In cell B12 enter **=CHOOSE(B13,D23,D24,D25, D26,D27,D28,D29,D30,D31,D32,D33,D34,D35,D36,D37,D38,D39,D40,D41,D42)**.

c. Create a similar CHOOSE function in cell B14 to display the price associated with each item. Format cells B14 and B15 as currency with two decimal places.

d. Enter the following sample data: **$500** for the down payment in cell B15, **2** for the years in cell B16, and **0.0725** for the interest rate in cell B17.

e. Enter the PMT function **=PMT(B17/12,B16*12,B14−B15)** in cell B18. To calculate the total amount of the loan, enter the formula **=B18*B16*12** in cell B19. To calculate the total cost, enter the formula **=-B15-B19** in cell B20.

f. Enter the numbers **1** to **20** in cells C23 to C42. Use the numbers in a drop-down list of model numbers for cell B13.

g. In cell G27:G32, enter **7.00%, 7.25%, 7.50%, 7.75%, 8.00%,** and **8.25%**.

h. Create a drop-down list in cell B17 presenting the alternative loan interest rates in cells G27:G32.

LAB EXERCISES

   i. In cell A10, type **To determine loan information, select the appropriate Model Number, Down Payment, and Interest Rate.** Format the text bold and red.

   j. Include cell comments to inform the user how to use the form.

   k. Hide rows 23 through 43.

   l. Unlock cells B13, B15:B17. Turn on sheet protection.

   m. Enter the following data into the workbook: model number **2**, down payment **$500**, number of years **3**, and interest rate of **7.00%**.

   n. Save the worksheet as Electronics Analyzer to your solution file location. Include your name and the current date in a header and print the worksheet centered horizontally in landscape orientation.

ADVENTURE TRAVEL TOURS PACKAGE ANALYSIS ★ ★

3. Adventure Travel Tours agents work hard to sell travel packages. To give their customers the best possible fares, ATT agents make reservations based on group rates. Because the rates are calculated as a percentage of the previous year's sales, you would like to create a worksheet that will show the effects of a change in sales ranging from −5 percent to 10 percent. The completed Adventure Travel Sales worksheet will be similar to the one shown here.

   a. Open the file ex05_ATT Sales.

   b. Enter functions to calculate the totals.

   c. Starting in cell K5, enter the values **−5%** to **+10%** at 1% increments.

   d. Using Data Validation, create a drop-down list that contains these values and display the list box in cell C13 with the input message **Select the assumed percentage change from the current year's sales from the drop-down list.** and the error message **You must select one of the values in the drop-down list box.**

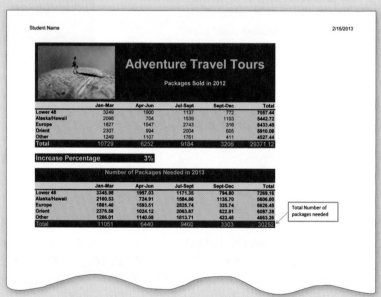

   e. Format cell C13 to display percentage with zero decimal places and surround the cell with a thick box border.

   f. Enter the formula **=C13** in cell J5.

   g. Enter the label **Increase Percentage** in cell A13.

   h. Copy cells A3 through F11 to cell A15. Change the title in row 15 to **Number of Packages Needed in 2013**.

   i. In cell B18 enter the formula **=B6*(1 + J6)**. Copy the formula through the cell range B18:E22. Format the selection as Number.

j. Enter comments to tell the user how to use the worksheet.

k. Hide columns J and K. Set the percentage change to 3%.

l. Add a text box and an arrow that points to the total number of packages needed.

m. Enter your name and the current date in a header, center the worksheet horizontally, and print the worksheet in landscape orientation.

n. Save the workbook as ATT Projected Sales to your solution file location.

HAYES FURNITURE SALES FORM ★ ★ ★

4. The sales staff at Hayes Furniture needs a quick way to let customers know how much they need to pay for sales tax and optional delivery. Your boss would like the form to be easy to modify if the tax rate and delivery charges change. You will finish the form that your boss started. The completed sales form will be similar to the one shown here.

a. Open the workbook file ex05_Furniture Sales.

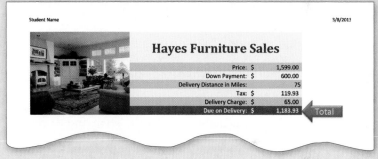

b. Name the values in cells G5 through G10 using the labels in column F. Name the value in cell G12 using the label in cell F12.

c. In cell C8 enter the IF function that calculates the delivery charge using the named range based on the number entered in cell C6. (Hint: The first IF is =IF(C6<=5,_0_to_5,IF(C6<=6,_6_to_11, IF. . .)).

d. In cell C7, calculate the tax due on the order using a 8.5% rate applied to the order price. In cell C9, enter the formula to calculate the payment due on delivery.

e. Test the worksheet by entering the following values.

Price: 750.00

Down Payment: 75.00

Delivery Distance: 25

The amount due on delivery should be $776.25.

f. Enter the following cell comments:

Cell	Comment
C4	Enter the amount of the total order before taxes
C5	Enter the down payment
C6	Enter the delivery distance in whole miles

g. Insert a block left arrow pointing to cell C9. Select a shape style of your choice. Add the text **Total**. Format the text with font size 20 and a color of your choice. Size and position the arrow appropriately.

h. Document the properties of the workbook by entering your name as the author, **Sales Associate** as the title, **Furniture Delivery Charges** as the subject, and **Point to the red triangles for instructions.** in the comments box.

i. Hide columns F and G.

j. Enter the following values:

Price: **$1,599.00**

Down Payment: **$600.00**

Delivery Distance: **75**

k. Enter your name and the current date in a header, center the worksheet horizontally, and print the worksheet in landscape orientation.

l. Save the workbook as Furniture Delivery to your solution file location.

m. Clear the values of the workbook. Unlock the cell contents of cells C4 through C6. Turn sheet protection on.

n. Move to cell C4 and save the workbook as a template named Furniture Delivery Form to your solution file location.

GRADE BOOK MAINTENANCE ★ ★ ★

5. You are a graduate assistant working for a university professor. A major part of your responsibilities is to record grades throughout the term and to calculate final grades. You have recorded the scores in a workbook and are now ready to calculate final grades. You have created a Summary sheet in the workbook and have entered the student identification numbers and names. You will use this sheet to determine final grades. Your completed Summary sheet should be similar to that shown here. You will use the completed workbook to create a form to be used next term.

a. Open the file ex05_Grades. The workbook contains five sheets. You will be using the first sheet, Summary, to calculate final grades. The other four sheets contain student scores for homework, projects, quizzes, and exams respectively.

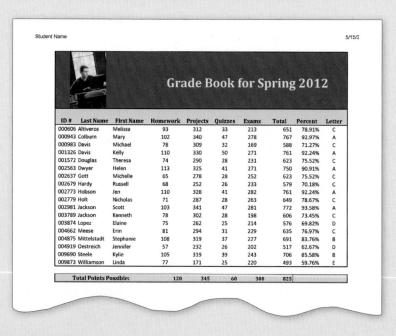

b. Enter a formula into cell D6 in the Summary sheet that will display the total number of homework points for the first student (Melissa Altiveros) from the Homework sheet.

c. In a similar manner, enter formulas to display the total projects, quizzes, and exam points for each student in the Summary sheet.

d. Enter formulas in column H of the Summary sheet to calculate the total points for each student.

e. Name cell H25 **PossiblePoints**. Enter the formula =H6/PossiblePoints in cell I6. Copy the formula down the column for the other students. Apply the percentage format with two decimal places.

f. Enter the following IF statement in cell J6: =IF(I6>0.899,"A", IF(I6>0.799,"B",IF(I6>0.699, "C",IF(I6>0.599,"D",IF(I6<0.599,"E"))))). You can use the Insert Function feature or type the IF statement directly into the cell. Copy the IF statement down the column for the other students.

g. Review the Summary worksheet and make any necessary formula and/or formatting changes.

h. In cell J5 enter a comment explaining how letter grades are determined.

i. Enter your name and the current date in a header, center horizontally, and print the Summary sheet in landscape orientation.

j. Save the workbook as Gradebook with a password that is your name to your solution file location.

k. Clear all the values of the workbook and save the workbook as a template named Gradebook Form to your solution file location.

l. Revise the Gradebook file to calculate the grade using a VLookup function instead of an IF statement. Save the workbook as Gradebook VLookup to your solution file location. Print the Summary sheet on one page.

ON YOUR OWN

CAR PURCHASE ANALYSIS ★

1. You have been shopping for a new car and have decided on a specific make and model of car. Three dealerships have the car in stock and each is offering a unique sales package combination of purchase price, down payment requirement, loan interest rate, and number of years to pay off the loan. These packages are shown below. Create a workbook to compare these different packages. Use the PMT function to calculate the monthly payment and the total cost of each car. Insert comments to explain how to use the worksheet. Insert a graphic to draw attention to the offer that you believe is the best. Save the workbook as Car Purchase Analysis and print with your name and current date in the header. Modify the worksheet to create an appropriate template named Car Payment Analysis Template. Print the template with your name and current date in the header.

	Dealerships		
	1	2	3
Purchase price	$18,900	$22,500	$25,000
Down payment	none	3,000	4,500
Interest rate	4.5%	3%	2%
Years to pay off	5	3	4

LAB EXERCISES

401(K) ANALYSIS ★ ★

2. The company you work for will contribute 12 percent of your gross pay to a 401(k) plan in your name. You can add up to another 10 percent of your gross pay to the same account, but the total contribution (the company's plus yours) cannot exceed $10,000. Create a worksheet with the following columns: Gross Pay, Employer Contribution, My Contribution, and Total Contribution. Enter a value for your gross pay and create a formula to calculate the company contribution. In a column to the right, enter the numbers 0 to 10. Format them as percentages. Create a list box that uses the percentages and calculates your contribution for the My Contribution column. Total the contributions. Use the combo box to see how much of your gross pay you can contribute to the IRA without exceeding the $10,000 limit. Select the value you think is most appropriate for you. Enter your name and the current date in the worksheet. Save the workbook as My 401K and print the worksheet.

SPEEDING FINE CALCULATOR ★ ★

3. You have been hired to work for a local traffic court. Create a worksheet that the clerks can use to calculate fines for speeding tickets. The worksheet should contain the following information: actual speed limit, speed the offender was traveling, and number of tickets the offender has received. The worksheet should calculate miles above the speed limit and additional charges for each ticket previously received ($100 for each offense after the first offense). Create a list box to enter the number of tickets the offender has received. Use this information to calculate the amount due the court. Enter your name and the current date centered in a header of the worksheet. Save the workbook as Speeding Fines and print the worksheet. Create an appropriate template named Speeding Fines Template. Print the template with your name and current date in the header.

Speed	Fine
Up to 5 mph over speed limit	$148
10 mph over speed limit	$178
15 mph over speed limit	$223
20 mph over speed limit	$268
25 mph over speed limit	$285
30 mph over speed limit	$285

GAMEHUT SALES INCENTIVES ★ ★

4. The GameHut is promoting a big sales push for the fourth quarter and has put together a sales incentive program to reward the sales staff for all their hard work. Create a form that tracks the monthly sales for each of your employees. Calculate the incentive based on the following monthly sales: $750 − $1000 = 3%, $1001−1500 = 4%, >$1500 = 5%. Add an extra 2% for any employee whose quarterly sales exceeded $4500. Save the file as GameHut Sales Incentives. Print the bonus calculations for the payroll department. Include your name and the current date in a header.

	October	November	December
Julie	$ 750	$1200	$2000
Tom	$1500	$1400	$1250
Sarah	$1000	$ 580	$2100
Connor	$ 500	$ 750	$ 100
Brandon	$1200	$1900	$2300

3D TELEVISION COMPARISON SHOPPING ★ ★ ★

5. You are interested in buying a new 50-inch 3D television. Use the Internet or newspaper advertisements to find prices for televisions with similar features manufactured by different companies. Using the features you learned in this lab, create a worksheet that allows you to compare multiple televisions on the same worksheet. Use a list box to select possible loan interest rates you have to pay for financing the purchase. Link the down payment, number of years, and interest rates to cells that can vary. Format the worksheet in an attractive manner. Enter your name and the current date in a header and print the worksheet. Save the worksheet as 3D Televisions to your solution file location. Modify the worksheet to create an appropriate template named 3D Television Template to your solution file location. Print the template with your name and current date in the header.

	Store 1	Store 2	Store 3
Purchase total	$13,785	$9,320	$10,470
Down payment	$ 2,500	$1,000	$ 1,500
Interest rate	7.5%	6.5%	15%

Creating and Working with Tables

Objectives

After completing this lab, you will know how to:

1. Create a table.

2. Enter records in a table.

3. Format a table.

4. Ensure data integrity.

5. Sort data.

6. Filter data.

7. Summarize data.

8. Outline, group, and subtotal data.

9. Create a PivotTable Report.

10. Create a PivotChart Report.

11. Create, edit, and use hyperlinks.

Downtown Internet Café

The form you created to track the Downtown Internet Café's customer expenditures and Bonus Dollar awards is working quite well. Evan would now like to have a separate worksheet that contains the café customers' contact information so that he can use it to send out the Bonus Dollars discount coupons. This type of information can be entered into a worksheet as a table. While using Excel to create the table, you will learn about locating,

modifying, sorting, and filtering records in the table. You also will learn how to analyze information in a table using totals and subtotals.

Now you have two workbooks containing data pertaining to the Downtown Internet Café customers. To make it easier to work with the two workbooks, you will create a hyperlink in one workbook to open the other workbook. A printout of a filtered table and a summary report are shown here.

WWW.MHHE.COM/OLEARY

Multilevel sorting is a powerful organizational tool.

PivotTables and PivotCharts are powerful analytical tools for analyzing long lists of figures and for comparing several facts about each figure.

Hyperlinks provide connections or links to files, Web pages, e-mail addresses, and more.

Concept Preview

The following concepts will be introduced in this lab:

1 **Table** A table is an organized collection of related information that is entered into a series of worksheet rows and columns.

2 **Hyperlink** A hyperlink is a connection or link to a destination location. The destination can be a location in the current file or another file, a Web page, or an e-mail address.

3 **Sort** You can sort or arrange data in a specified sequence: alphabetically, numerically, or by date.

4 **Filter** A filter is a restriction you place on records in a table to quickly isolate and display a subset of records.

5 **Grouping and Outlining** Grouping and outlining organizes data in a worksheet by showing and hiding different levels of detail for groups of related data.

6 **Subtotal** The Subtotal feature automatically takes data in a list, organizes it into groups, and includes subtotals for each group of data.

7 **PivotTable Report** A PivotTable report is an interactive table that can be used to summarize and manipulate worksheet data.

8 **PivotChart Report** A PivotChart report is an interactive chart that can be used to view and rearrange data.

Creating a Table

You want to create an Excel worksheet that will contain the café's customer contact information and monthly expenditures. So that you can manipulate the data the way you want, you decide to format this worksheet as a table.

Concept Table

A **table** is an organized collection of related information that is entered into a series of worksheet rows and columns. Each row contains a **record**, which is all the information about one person, thing, or place. Each column is a **field**, which is the smallest unit of information about a record.

The first row, called the **header row**, in a table must contain column labels that serve as field names. A **field name** is a descriptive label used to identify the data stored in the field. Field names must be text entries. All rows below the field names contain the records. The area containing the records is called the **table range**.

The data in a table is managed independently from the data in other rows and columns of the worksheet. A worksheet also can contain more than one table.

The main advantage to using a table is that it saves you time. This is because Excel does many things automatically for you that would otherwise take you a number of steps to do. For example, tables make it easy to sort and filter, to add special formatting, and to fill in formulas.

You have already entered many of the field names to create the structure for the table and have saved it in a workbook file named Customer Table.

● **Start Excel 2010 and open the workbook file** ex06_Customer Table.

Your screen should be similar to Figure 6.1

Figure 6.1

The worksheet titles are formatted using cell style headings associated with the current worksheet theme, Austin. Row 6 contains the field names for the customer information that will be entered in the table.

ADDING FIELD NAMES

You decide to change the Phone field to a field for each customer's e-mail address. Additionally, you still need to add field names for the months, which will be used to record the monthly expenditures for each customer. You also will change the format of these cells as Currency.

1

- Replace the entry in H6 with E-mail.

- Enter Jan in cell I6.

- Drag the fill handle of cell I6 to extend the range through December (cell T6).

- Format cells I7 to T7 as Currency with two decimals.

- Move to A6.

- Save the workbook as Customer Table to your solution file location.

Your screen should be similar to Figure 6.2

Figure 6.2

DEFINING THE TABLE RANGE

Next, you define the row containing the field names as the table range, the area where the records will be entered. Designating a range as a table lets you manage and analyze the data in the table independently of other data in the worksheet.

1

- Select the range A6 through T6.

- Open the Insert tab.

- Click [Table] in the Tables group.

- Choose My table has headers.

- Click OK.

- Move to A7.

Your screen should be similar to Figure 6.3

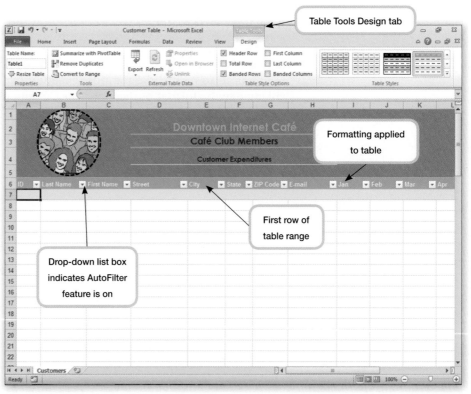

Figure 6.3

The header row of the table is formatted with a green fill color and white text color. This is the default formatting for a header row of a table that is associated with the Austin worksheet theme. The first blank row below the header row is the first row of the table range. This area is formatted using the Input cell color associated with the Austin theme. The first record of information will be entered in this row.

In addition, drop-down list buttons appear next to each field name in the header row. These buttons indicate the AutoFilter feature is on. The AutoFilter feature is used to filter and sort the data in the table. You will learn about these features shortly.

Additional Information

You could also define the table range after records have been entered by including the field name row and all rows containing records in the range.

Also, when any cell in the table range is selected, the Table Tools Design tab is displayed. It is used to modify settings associated with the design of the table. When you select a cell outside the table, the table becomes inactive and the tab is not displayed.

You are now ready to begin entering the information for the first record.

Adding and Editing Data in a Table

You will use the Café Club membership sign-up sheets containing the information for each customer as the source of information for the table. In addition, you have a printout of the monthly expenditures for these customers for the first two months of the year. You want to enter this information into the table next.

ENTERING RECORDS

When entering the data in a table, it is important that you enter it consistently. For example, if you abbreviate the word "Street" as "St.", it should be abbreviated in the same way for each record where it appears. Also, be careful not to include blank spaces before or after an entry as this can cause problems when trying to locate information in the table. The first record in the table must begin in the row immediately below the header row containing the field names.

1

● Enter the information shown here for the first record, using [Tab] to move from one field to the next.

ID	100
Last Name	Dwyer
First Name	Jack
Street	21 N. Navesink River Dr.
City	Red Bank
State	NJ
Zip	07730
E-mail	JD@email.com
Jan	77.34
Feb	81.98

Your screen should be similar to Figure 6.4

First record

Additional Information

The E-mail address is underlined and in a different font color because Excel recognized it as an E-mail address and formatted it to a hyperlink. You will learn about hyperlinks shortly.

Figure 6.4

The data for the first record is complete.

You need to add another row to the table for the next record. If you are at the end of the table row and press [Tab], a new row is added to the table. Alternatively, entering new record data into the row just below the last record in a table automatically expands the table range to include that row.

Having Trouble?

Do not be concerned that the leading zero in the Zip Code is missing. You will learn how to fix this shortly.

2

- Press Enter

- Press Home.

- Enter the information shown here for the second record.

ID	101
Last Name	Hamlin
First Name	Rose
Street	7 Church St.
City	Little Silver
State	NJ
Zip	07739
E-mail	RH@email.com
Jan	102.50
Feb	115.78

Your screen should be similar to Figure 6.5

Second record added to table and table range expanded

Figure 6.5

A new row was added to the table and the fill color from the selected table style is applied. The currency style is carried to the new row as well.

3

Finally, move to cell A9 and add the following information as the third record in the table.

ID	103
Last Name	Thomas
First Name	Grant
Street	159 Branch Ave., Apt 15B
City	Red Bank
State	NJ
Zip	07730
E-mail	GG@email.com
Jan	75.89
Feb	62.47

● AutoFit the Street column width so that the entries are fully displayed.

Your screen should be similar to Figure 6.6

Three records in table

Column width increased to fully display data

E-mail addresses are hyperlinks

Figure 6.6

The field information for the first three records is displayed in the table range.

USING SPECIAL CELL FORMATS

Now that you have entered several records, you notice that the ZIP Codes do not display the leading zero (07730 and 07739). This is because Excel drops leading zeros for numeric data. Since this field will not be used in calculations, you will change the cell format so that numeric entries will appear as entered.

1

- **Select the range G7 through G9.**

- **Click in the Number group of the Home tab to open the Format Cells dialog box.**

- **Choose Special from the Category list of the Number tab.**

- **Move the dialog box to see the ZIP Codes.**

Your screen should be similar to Figure 6.7

Figure 6.7

There are four special formats that are designed particularly for use in tables where numeric data is frequently entered but not used for calculations. You want to format the selection to the standard Zip Code format.

2

- **From the Type list box, if necessary, choose Zip Code.**

- **Click [OK].**

Your screen should be similar to Figure 6.8

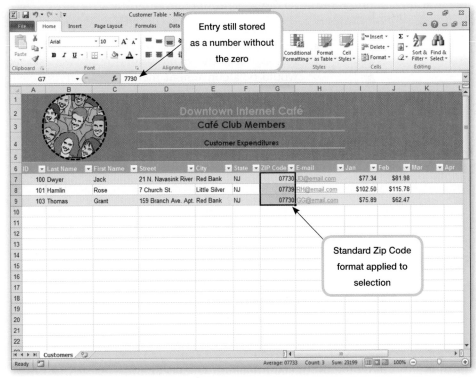

Figure 6.8

The number entries appear as they were entered because they are formatted as a special number entry. However, the entries are stored as numbers without the zero.

USING AND EDITING A HYPERLINK ENTRY

You've also noticed the addresses in the E-mail column are underlined and in dark orange. This is because they were automatically identified as an e-mail address and formatted as a hyperlink.

 Concept 2 Hyperlink

A **hyperlink** is a connection or link to a destination location. The destination can be a location in the current file or another file, a Web page, or an e-mail address. The hyperlink itself can be text or a picture. Clicking on a hyperlink allows the user to quickly navigate or jump to the destination location when viewing the document on the screen. The action that occurs when you click a hyperlink depends on the type of destination. For example, if the hyperlink destination is a Web page, clicking on the hyperlink starts a browser program and displays the specified Web page. If it is to an e-mail address, an e-mail program is started and a new message window that is preaddressed to the e-mail address hyperlink is opened.

When a hyperlink is created, it stores the information about the location of the destination as a **Uniform Resource Locator (URL)**. A URL is an address that specifies the location of the destination document.

The automatic identification of Internet or network paths and the conversion to hyperlinks is a feature common to all Office programs. Sometimes you may not want the item to be automatically formatted as a hyperlink. You can turn off this feature using File/ [Options] /Proofing/ [AutoCorrect Options...] and clearing the "Internet and network paths with hyperlinks" option in the AutoFormat As You Type tab. You also can remove the hyperlink autoformatting from an individual cell by selecting Remove Hyperlink from the shortcut menu.

In this case, clicking on the e-mail address hyperlink opens a new e-mail message window to allow you to send a message to the address. You think this would be a convenient method of notifying customers of special sales as well as their Bonus Dollars status.

Point to cell H7.

Additional Information

The mouse pointer changes to when you point to a hyperlink and a ScreenTip appears with instructions on how to follow a link.

Click on cell H7.

Your screen should be similar to Figure 6.9

Figure 6.9

The New Message window for the e-mail application on your system opens and is already addressed to the selected address.

If you want to select a cell containing a hyperlink without activating the hyperlink, click and hold down the mouse button until the mouse pointer changes to ✛. This indicates it will select the cell rather than jumping to the hyperlink destination.

Having Trouble?

Your New Message window may be different from that shown here if you are using a different e-mail application.

Click ⊠ **Close to close the New Message window.**

If necessary, click No **to discard the message.**

Click and hold down the mouse button on cell H7 until the mouse pointer changes to ✛, and then release the mouse button.

Your screen should be similar to Figure 6.10

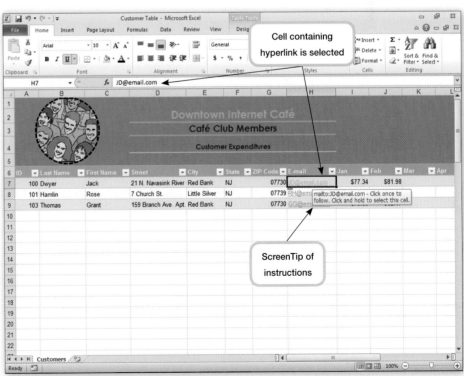

Figure 6.10

The cell containing the hyperlink is now selected and can be edited as needed. Notice that the color of the hyperlink that you clicked in cell H7 has changed. The color of the hyperlinks in the other cells is the default color of dark orange. The change in color indicates the link has been followed.

You notice that the e-mail address in cell H9 is incorrect. You can easily correct the mistake by simply editing the hyperlink text in the cell. You also can move to a cell containing a hyperlink without activating the link by using the directional keys.

- Press ↓ twice to move to cell H9.

- Press F2 to change to Edit mode.

- Edit the hyperlink text to GT@email .com and click ✓.

Another Method

You can also edit a hyperlink by choosing Edit Hyperlink from the shortcut menu and then editing the entry in both the Text to display and the E-mail address text boxes.

Your screen should be similar to Figure 6.11

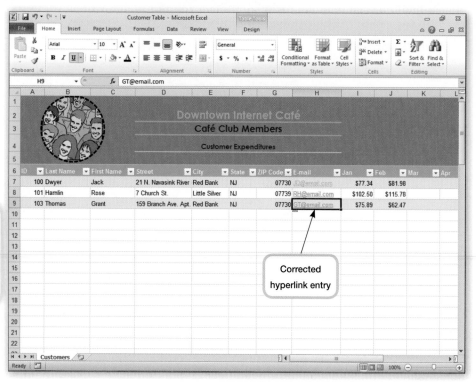

Figure 6.11

Modifying a Table

Evan would like to give each Bonus Dollars customer a special discount on their birthday. You need to modify the Customer Table to include a column for birth date. Additionally, you notice that you missed adding the record for customer number 102. You will need to insert a row to add the missing record in the correct location in the table.

INSERTING TABLE COLUMNS

You've decided to add the birth date column before the E-mail column and then enter the information for each of the records. A new column is inserted to the left of the selected column and the table range automatically expands to include the new column. The cell selector must be in the table range to insert a new table column. In this case, it is currently in the correct location to insert this column.

1

● Open the [Insert ▾] drop-down menu in the Cells group of the Home tab.

● Choose Insert Table Columns to the Left.

Another Method

You can also choose Insert/Table Columns to the Left from the shortcut menu.

Your screen should be similar to Figure 6.12

Figure 6.12

Additional Information

You can insert multiple columns by first selecting a range. The same number of columns as in the selected range are added to the table.

A new blank table column with a default column heading of Column1 was inserted to the left of the selected column. You will replace the default heading with a descriptive heading. Then you will add the data for the three records to the field.

2

● Edit cell H6 to display the heading **Birth Date**.

● Enter the birth dates shown below in column H for the three records.

Record	Birth Date
100	8/7/81
101	12/18/54
103	1/5/91

Your screen should be similar to Figure 6.13

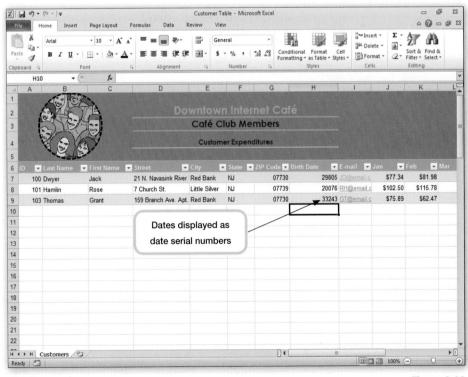

Figure 6.13

Excel recognized the entries as dates; however, unlike worksheet entries, in a table it displays the date serial number. You will change the cell format to display the date using the short date format.

3

● Select cells H7 through H9.

● Click

Special ▼

in the Home tab and choose Short Date.

● AutoFit the Birth Date, E-mail and Street columns.

Your screen should be similar to Figure 6.14

Figure 6.14

The serial numbers are now displayed using the short date format. New date entries in this column will automatically be displayed using this format.

INSERTING TABLE ROWS

Now you want to insert a row for the missing record. The process of inserting a row is similar to inserting a column. The row is inserted above the selected row.

Additional Information

You can insert multiple rows by first selecting a range. The same number of rows as in the range are added to the table.

1

● Right-click on any cell in row 9.

● Select Insert and choose Table Rows Above from the shortcut menu

Another Method

You also can use ▤ Insert ▾ in the Cells group of the Home tab and choose Insert Table Rows Above. If you are in the last row of the table, the Table Row Below option is also available.

● Enter the following information in the newly created table row.

ID	102
Last Name	Brown
First Name	Sara
Street	1005 First Ave.
City	Mt. Vernon
State	NY
Zip	10552
Birth Date	5/22/87
E-mail	SB@email.com
Jan	50.16
Feb	45.12

Your screen should be similar to Figure 6.15

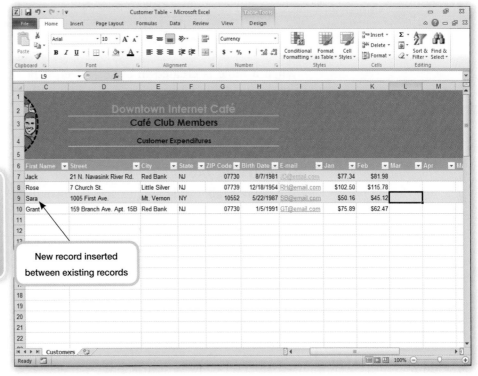

New record inserted between existing records

Figure 6.15

The record was inserted into the table between the existing records.

Formatting the Table

When a table is created in a worksheet, it is automatically formatted using the default table design style associated with the worksheet theme. You can change the formatting associated with any area of the table by manually applying many different formats to the cells. You can also quickly change the overall table style by selecting a different table quick style.

FORMATTING TABLE AREAS

The default table style applies special formatting to the header row and uses a banded row effect. However, if you don't like the default style, you can use the Table Style Option group to turn the formatting of any area of the table on and off. You would like to see how the table would look without some of these features.

1

- **Move to cell A9.**

- **Open the Table Tools Design tab.**

- **Choose**
  ☑ Header Row
  and
  ☑ Banded Rows
  in the Table Style Options group to turn off these features.

- **Choose**
  ☐ Banded Columns
  and
  ☐ First Column
  to turn on these features.

Your screen should be similar to Figure 6.16

Figure 6.16

Additional Information

The Table Styles gallery also reflects the changes in the style options.

The green color background was removed from the table header row and because the text is white, the field names are not visible. Bold text effect was added to the first column to emphasize the data. Finally, banded rows were removed and banded columns added. As you can see, the Table Style Options allow you to quickly emphasize different areas of the table. You prefer how the table looked before these changes and will restore these features.

2

- Choose ☑ First Column and ☑ Banded Columns to turn off these features.

- Choose ☐ Header Row and ☐ Banded Rows to restore these settings.

APPLYING TABLE STYLES

The quickest way to change the look of an entire table is to select a new table style from the Table Styles gallery. The Table Styles feature includes built-in combinations of formats that consist of different fill or background colors, patterns, borders, fonts, and alignment settings. You decide to find a table style that will change the overall look of the table.

1

- Click ▼ More to open the Table Styles gallery.

Your screen should be similar to Figure 6.17

Additional Information

If a custom style has been saved, it appears in a Custom styles area.

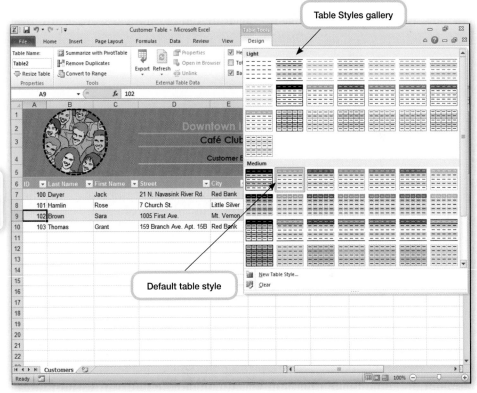

Figure 6.17

From the Table Styles gallery, you select the table design you want to use. There are 61 built-in styles that use colors associated with the selected theme. As you point to the style, the style name appears in a ScreenTip and Live Preview shows how it will look in the table.

Additional Information

Table Style Medium 2 is the default table style.

2

● Point to several styles and look at the Live Preview.

● Choose Table Style Light 11.

Your screen should be similar to Figure 6.18

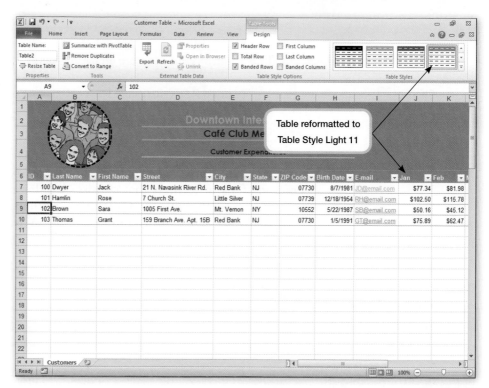

Figure 6.18

The table is reformatted to the new design. It includes a different color background for the heading row and orange row lines to separate the rows of data, replacing the banded rows of color. Using a table style was much faster than applying these features individually.

Ensuring Data Integrity

You asked one of your employees to add more records to the table including March expenditures. You will open the updated workbook file and continue working with the table.

1

● **Save and close the** Customer Table **workbook file.**

● **Open the workbook file** ex06_Customer Table2.

● **Enter the following information using your first and last names in row 43 as the last record in the table.**

ID	**999**
Last Name	**your last name**
First Name	**your first name**
Street	**999 Main St.**
City	**Anytown**
State	**NJ**
Zip	**07999**
Birth Date	**1/1/1990**
E-mail	**SN@email.com**
Jan	**110.42**
Feb	**170.89**
Mar	**140.19**

● **Move to the ID field of your record.**

Your screen should be similar to Figure 6.19

Figure 6.19

The table automatically grew in size to accommodate the new record. Notice also that when you scroll the table, the worksheet column letters are hidden and the table column headers are displayed instead so that you can continue to identify the columns.

Unfortunately, as you review the records, you discover several errors. For example, in the ID column, there are blank entries as well as four-digit and two-digit entries. Additionally, several state entries are inconsistent, with some spelled out and others abbreviated differently. As you are working on designing the customer table, you want to include features that will help make entry of data in the table as accurate as possible.

RESTRICTING DATA USING DATA VALIDATION

First, you want to prevent entry errors in the ID field. The Café Club ID number is assigned to each member when his or her information is entered into the table. It is a number that uniquely identifies each member. As each new member is added to the table, the next available sequential number is assigned. The first club member was assigned the number 100. To help ensure the validity of the data, you want to restrict the number of digits used in the ID field to three and to require that each new record include an ID number.

1

- Scroll to the top of the window and move to cell A1.

- Point to the top edge of the ID column header and click when the mouse pointer changes to ↓ to select all the entries in the column.

Additional Information

If you click the top edge of the header twice, it selects the entire table column, including the header.

- Click ⬚ Data Validation ▾ in the Data Tools group of the Data tab.

- Choose Whole Number from the Allow drop-down list in the Settings tab.

- Choose "between" from the Data drop-down list.

- Enter 100 as the minimum and 999 as the maximum.

- Choose Ignore blank to deselect this option.

- Open the Input Message tab and add the Input message Enter the three digit ID.

- Open the Error Alert tab and create a Stop style error alert with the error message of Only three digit numbers are allowed.

- Click [OK].

Your screen should be similar to Figure 6.20

Figure 6.20

The process of creating and defining the validation settings for the text-length data restriction is now complete. Because the ID column is selected, the input message you entered is displayed, providing directions on how to use the cell. Also, any entries that do not meet the new restrictions, including blank cells, are identified with a green triangle in the upper-left cell corner, showing that the validation restriction is working correctly.

TESTING DATA VALIDATION

Next, you will fix the identified errors and further test the data restriction to make sure it displays the error message and is working correctly.

1

- Move to cell A14.

- Click and choose Display Type Information.

Your screen should be similar to Figure 6.21

Figure 6.21

The Field Type Information dialog box describes the restrictions associated with this cell. First you will change the entry to another invalid entry to test the error message. Then you will enter valid ID numbers for the entries that contain invalid IDs.

2

- Click [OK] to close the dialog box.

- Attempt to change the entry in cell A14 to **10**.

- Click [Retry].

- Attempt to change the entry to **ten**.

- Click [Retry].

- Change the entry in cell A14 to **121**.

Your screen should be similar to Figure 6.22

Figure 6.22

The error alert message was displayed when you entered an invalid two-digit entry and a text entry. The three-digit entry was accepted as valid. Now, you will correct the remaining errors in the ID column.

Enter the following correct ID numbers.

Cell	ID
A16	120
A25	114
A29	105
A42	107

Next, you want to restrict the data in the State column.

4

- **Scroll to the top of the window.**

- **Select the State column of data and add the following validation restrictions:**

  - **Allow only a text length of two.**

  - **Include an input message of Enter 2-letter state abbreviation in uppercase.**

  - **Include a Stop style error alert and error message of Only 2-letter entries are allowed.**

- **Fix all identified errors and change any lowercase state abbreviations to uppercase.**

Figure 6.23

Although data validation helps ensure that only data meeting the restrictions is entered, it does not ensure that it is entered in the correct format. However, because the input message will always be visible to remind the user to enter uppercase letters only, fewer input errors should occur.

Currently, the records in the table are in the order in which they were entered. However, you want the table to be in ascending ID number order when it is first opened. This way it is easier to see what the last-used ID number is when assigning a number to a new member. To do this, you can sort the records in the table.

Concept 3 Sort

You can **sort** or arrange data in a specified sequence: alphabetically, numerically, or by date. Sorting data often helps you find specific information quickly. The data in a worksheet can be sorted into ascending (A to Z, 1 to 9, earliest date to most recent date) or descending (Z to A, 9 to 1, most recent date to earliest date) order. When you sort, Excel rearranges the rows, columns, fields, or individual cells according to the sort order you specify.

You also can sort by cell attributes such as font or cell color, or on conditional formatting such as an icon set. Most sorts are performed on a selected range of cells or on a table column. However, you also can sort on rows.

A single sort operation can be based on up to three columns or fields of data. When a sort is done on more than one column or field, it is called a **multilevel sort**. For example, if you wanted to rearrange a table of employee data to begin with those who have worked for the company the longest, you could sort it in ascending order by date and then by name.

The settings, or **criteria**, you specify for a sort on a table are saved with the workbook file. This allows you to quickly reapply the sort when you open the workbook. Sort settings are not saved for sorts using a worksheet range. This feature is especially helpful when you have created a complicated multilevel sort.

SORTING ON A SINGLE FIELD

For the first sort, you want the records arranged in ascending order by ID. The cell selector needs to be in any cell in the table column to be sorted.

1

- Scroll to the top of the window and move to cell A7.

- Click ⬇ Sort

  Smallest to Largest in the Sort & Filter group.

Another Method

You also can click Sort & Filter ▾ in the Editing group of the Home tab and choose Sort Smallest to Largest.

Your screen should be similar to Figure 6.24

All records in table rearranged in ascending numerical order

Figure 6.24

The records in the table range are rearranged to display in ascending numerical order. The ![AutoFilter] AutoFilter button in the column header has changed to a ![Sort] Sort button, which indicates the column is sorted and the direction of the sort.

This will make it easier to know the last-used ID number. When creating a table, if the order in which you enter records in a table is important, always include a field for a unique record number, such as the ID field in this table that identifies each customer. Then you can return to the entry order by sorting on the number field.

SORTING ON MULTIPLE FIELDS

Evan often asks for information in order by name. You will create this sort next.

1

● Open the AutoFilter menu for the Last Name column.

● Choose Sort A to Z.

Your screen should be similar to Figure 6.25

Figure 6.25

The records appear in ascending alphabetical order by last name. However, notice that although the records for Sara, Kurt, and Jill Brown are sorted correctly by last name, they are not sorted by first name. You want records that have the same last name to be further sorted by first name. To do this, you will perform a multilevel sort.

2

Click in the Sort & Filter group of the Data tab.

Another Method

You also can click **Sort & Filter ▾** in the Editing group of the Home tab and choose Custom Sort.

Your screen should be similar to Figure 6.26

Figure 6.26

A multilevel sort uses the first field name selected in the Sort By section of the dialog box as the primary sort field; all other fields are sorted in order after the primary sort is performed. The Sort by text box correctly displays the name of the field on which the primary sort will be performed. Additionally, because the default setting is the A to Z sort order, this option does not need to be changed. You need to add the First Name field as the secondary sort.

3

Click **Add Level**.

Choose First Name from the Column Then by drop-down list.

Your screen should be similar to Figure 6.27

Figure 6.27

When a sort is performed, Excel assumes that you want all data except the header row in the table range to be sorted. If your data did not include a header row as the first row in the range, you would need to choose the My data has headers option to change the setting to include this row in the sort. Since this worksheet includes field names in the first row, the My data has headers option is correctly specified already.

4

● Click [OK].

● Move to cell C13.

● Save the changes you have made to this workbook as Customer Table2 to your solution file location.

Your screen should be similar to Figure 6.28

> All records with the same last name are further sorted alphabetically by first name

Figure 6.28

The records are now in sorted order first by last name and second by first name within the same last names. As you can see, sorting is a fast, useful tool. The sort order remains in effect until you replace it with a new sort order.

SORTING ON CELL ATTRIBUTES

Another way to perform a sort is to sort on a cell attribute such as a font color that was applied manually to specific cells or by using conditional formatting. To show Evan those club members who qualified for the Super Bonus Level 2 awards in March, you will first apply a highlight cells rule conditional formatting to the March column and then sort it in descending order.

● **Select the Mar table column.**

● **Click** **in the Styles group of the Home tab.**

● **Select Highlight Cells Rules and choose Greater Than.**

● **Enter a value of 119.99 with Light Red Fill.**

● **Click** **.**

● **Open the AutoFilter menu for the Mar column and select Sort by Color.**

● **Choose the Light Red Fill color option.**

Your screen should be similar to Figure 6.29

Figure 6.29

Although all records that contain the selected cell format are sorted separately from the other data in the column, they are not in either ascending or descending sorted order. This is because there is no default cell color, font color, or icon sort order. The order must be specified for each sort using these criteria.

2 ● Choose Sort Largest to Smallest from the Mar AutoFilter menu.

Your screen should be similar to Figure 6.30

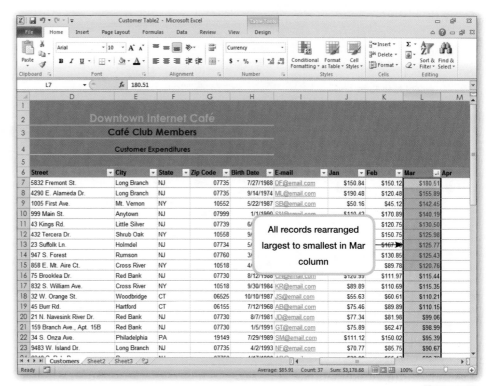

Figure 6.30

This sort clearly identifies the Super Bonus Level 2 customers; however, the other two levels are not identified. You decide to use an icon set conditional format next to identify the three levels and display them in descending sort order.

3

• Click , select Icon Sets, and choose the Three Traffic Lights (Rimmed) icon set.

• Click and choose Manage Rules.

• Choose the Icon Set rule and click Edit Rule....

• Change the Type to Number for both Value boxes.

• Edit the icon set to identity Super Bonus Level 2 (expenditures > 119.99) with the green light and to identify Super Bonus Level 1 (expenditures > 74.99) with the yellow light.

• Click OK twice.

• Open the AutoFilter menu for the Mar column, select Sort by Color, and choose the green icon option.

• Open the AutoFilter menu for the Mar column, select Sort by Color, and choose the yellow icon option.

• Choose Sort Largest to Smallest from the Mar AutoFilter menu.

Your screen should be similar to Figure 6.31

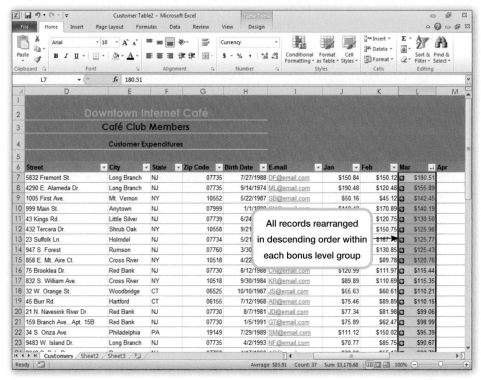

Figure 6.31

The records are now in descending sorted order by the March expenditure values within each bonus level group. Sorting the table data helps you better understand the table data by organizing it and helps you more quickly find the data you want.

Filtering Data

When you sort data, it simply takes all the data in the table and reorganizes it into the specified order. Consequently, there is often much more information than you want included in the displayed data. To display only those records that meet specific criteria, you can filter the table.

Concept Filter

A **filter** is a restriction you place on records in the table to quickly isolate and display a subset of records. Filtering a table helps you quickly find and display only the information you want to see. A filter is created by specifying criteria that you want records to meet in order to be displayed. Unlike the Sort feature, the Filter feature does not rearrange a table but temporarily hides rows that do not meet the specified criteria. A filter is ideal when you want to display the subset for only a brief time and then return immediately to the full set of records. All records are redisplayed when you remove the filter.

You can work with the data in a filtered table much like any other table data. However, only the displayed subset of data is affected. You can find, edit, format, chart, and print the filtered records to help you analyze the data in a table. Filters are also additive, meaning that each additional filter you add to a filtered table further reduces the subset of data.

You also can sort by cell attributes such as font or cell color, or on conditional formatting such as an icon set. Most sorts are performed on a selected range of cells or on a table column. However, you also can sort on rows.

When you first create a table, filtering is on by default and AutoFilter buttons are displayed in the table header row. You can turn off filtering by clicking

 in the Sort & Filter group of the Data tab. When filtering is off, AutoFilter

buttons are not displayed in the header row and filtering cannot be used.

FILTERING ON A SINGLE CRITERION

The Café is located in New Jersey, and consequently the majority of club members are residents of that state. However, because the town attracts many summer visitors and college students, there are many club members from out of state. You decide to first filter the table to display only New Jersey residents. To specify the criterion, you select the field value from the AutoFilter drop-down menu. This menu displays a list of the unique entries in the field.

Additional Information

Only the first 1,000 unique entries appear in the AutoFilter list.

Open the State AutoFilter menu.

Your screen should be similar to Figure 6.32

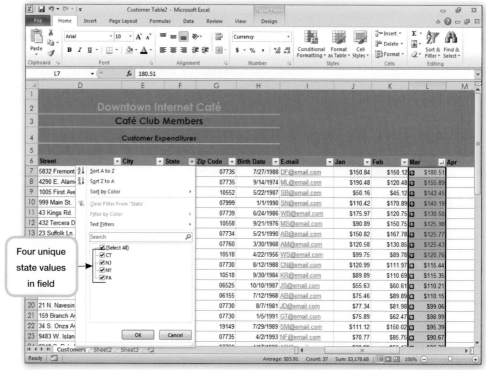

Four unique state values in field

Figure 6.32

The drop-down list displays the four unique state values in the field. Because the filter list of values is derived from the content of the column, it is important that data in a table be entered consistently. It is also important that data not include leading spaces. However, uniqueness is not affected by the case of the entry; for example, nj and NJ would not be considered unique entries. When there are different variations of the same information, the filter list displays each variation; for example, NJ and New Jersey would both appear on the list and both items would need to be selected to obtain the correct filter results.

All the values are selected; therefore, the table displays all records. The Select All option above the list of unique values is used to quickly select all values in the field or to deselect all the values.

Immediately above the list of values are three commands that are used to specify the filter criteria or to clear all filter settings. These options, described in the following table, vary depending upon the type of data contained in the column; for example, text, date, or numbers.

Option	Effect
Clear Filter	Removes the filter from the field
Filter by Color	Filters by fill or text color if applied
Text/Number/Date Filters	Applies custom filter based on the type of data

You want to set the filter criterion to display only records that have a state value of NJ.

2

- Clear the Select All check box.

- Choose NJ from the list.

- Click [OK].

- Move to G44.

Another Method

You could also specify the filter criterion by selecting a cell containing the data that is equal to the information you want displayed and then choosing the Filter by option from the cell's shortcut menu.

Your screen should be similar to Figure 6.33

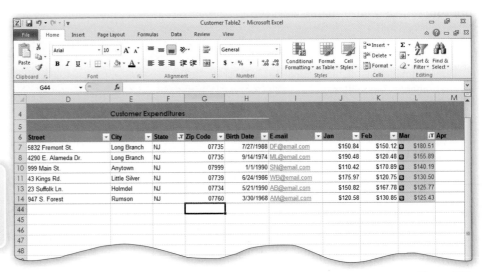

Figure 6.33

Only those records for customers whose state is NJ are displayed. The icon in the column heading displays a [▾] Filter button, which shows that the table is filtered on data in that column. A ScreenTip displays the type of filter when you point to the Filter button.

FILTERING ON MULTIPLE CRITERIA

Next, you decide to find out how many of the NJ customers are also in the Super Bonus Level 2 category for March.

- Open the Mar AutoFilter menu.

- Select Filter by Color and choose the green icon.

Additional Information

If the data in the column had been manually formatted, the format attributes would also be available in the Filter by Color list.

Your screen should be similar to Figure 6.34

Figure 6.34

Only those NJ customers whose March expenditures meet the Super Bonus Level 2 criteria are displayed. Finally, you want to know how many non–New Jersey customers met this expenditure level.

Open the State AutoFilter menu, choose Select All, and clear the NJ selection.

Click OK .

Your screen should be similar to Figure 6.35

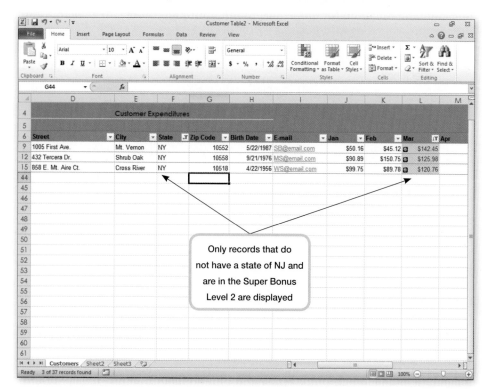

Only records that do not have a state of NJ and are in the Super Bonus Level 2 are displayed

Figure 6.35

Now the filtered table displays only those records that have a March value over $119.99 and do not include a state of New Jersey. Each time you added a new filter criterion, fewer records were displayed in the subset. Next, you will remove the filters and redisplay all the records.

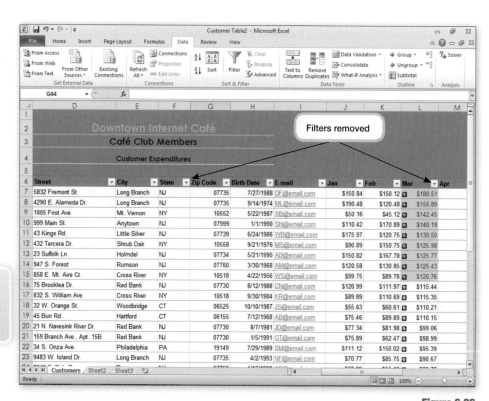

Filters removed

Figure 6.36

Open the Mar AutoFilter menu and choose Clear Filter from "Mar".

Open the State AutoFilter menu and choose Clear Filter from "State".

Scroll to the top of the window.

Another Method

You also could click ✖ Clear in the Sort & Filter group of the Data tab to remove all filters from the table.

Your screen should be similar to Figure 6.36

All filters are removed and all records are redisplayed.

CREATING A CUSTOM AUTOFILTER

Evan wants to send e-mails to all customers who have qualified for the Super Bonus Level awards for all three months, thanking them for their patronage and giving them a 50-percent-off espresso drink coupon. To accomplish this, you want to specify further criteria to filter out values less than $75 in the month fields.

1

- Open the Mar AutoFilter menu.

- Select Number Filters and choose Greater Than Or Equal To.

Additional Information

You also can select Number Filters/ Custom from the shortcut menu.

Your screen should be similar to Figure 6.37

Figure 6.37

The Custom AutoFilter dialog box is used to specify a filtering operation that makes comparisons between two values. The type of comparison to make is specified in the box on the left, and the value to compare to is specified in the box on the right. You can include a second set of criteria by selecting the And or Or option and specifying the settings in the lower row of boxes. The AND and OR operators are used to specify multiple conditions that must be met for the records to display in the filtered table. The AND operator narrows the search because a record must meet both conditions to be included. The OR operator broadens the search because any record meeting either condition is included in the output.

Because you selected "Is greater than or equal to" from the shortcut menu, the type of comparison is already filled in. You just need to specify the value.

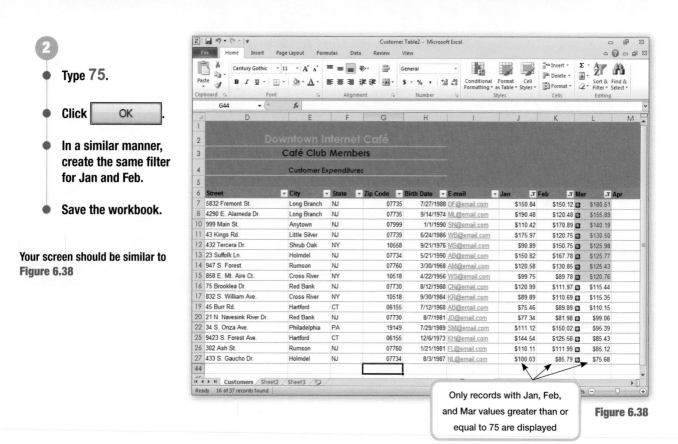

- **Type 75.**

- **Click** OK .

- **In a similar manner, create the same filter for Jan and Feb.**

- **Save the workbook.**

Your screen should be similar to Figure 6.38

Only records with Jan, Feb, and Mar values greater than or equal to 75 are displayed

Figure 6.38

Only the records that meet the specified criteria are displayed.

FILTERING FOR UNIQUE VALUES AND REMOVING DUPLICATES

Sometimes, when data is entered in a table, the same data can be inadvertently entered more than once. To check the data in a table or worksheet range, you can identify unique data and then remove duplicate data. Duplicate data is where all values in a row are an exact match of all values in another row. The duplicate data is determined by the displayed value, not the stored value, in the cell. For example, if the same values are stored in a cell, but formatted differently, they would be considered unique.

Before removing duplicate values, it is a good idea to filter to locate unique values first to confirm that the results are what you want before removing the duplicates.

1

- Click **Advanced**
  in the Sort & Filter
  group of the Data tab.

- If necessary, choose
  Filter the list, in-place.

- Choose **Unique
  Records only.**

Additional Information

The default range to filter is the entire
table range.

- Click **OK**.

**Your screen should be similar to
Figure 6.39**

Number of
unique records

Number of total
records

Figure 6.39

The status bar tells you that 34 unique records were found from the 37 total records. This means that there are three duplicate records. Also notice that the AutoFilter buttons are no longer displayed in the header row, indicating that the Filter feature was turned off.

Before removing the duplicate records, you will verify them by redisplaying all records and then sorting the ID column.

Click 🐾 Clear

in the Sort & Filter
group to remove the
filter from the table.

Another Method

You also can use [Sort & Filter icon] in the Editing
group on the Home tab and choose Clear.

**Sort the ID column in
ascending sort order.**

Having Trouble?

Move to the ID column and click [A↓].

Move to B7.

Figure 6.40

**Your screen should be similar to
Figure 6.40**

After reviewing the records, you note that there are three duplicate records:
106, 111, and 124. To remove the duplicate records, you could select each
record row and delete it individually or you can use the Remove Duplicates
feature. You will use both methods.

**Right-click on any cell
in row 14 of the table,
select Delete, and
choose Table Rows.**

Another Method

You also could use [Delete icon] Delete ▾
in the Cells group of the Home tab and
choose Delete Table Rows to delete the
selected table row.

**Your screen should be similar to
Figure 6.41**

Additional Information

Do not use the Delete Sheet Rows
command to delete a table row, as this
will delete the entire worksheet row and
any data in that row that is not part of
the table range.

Figure 6.41

The duplicate record for ID 106 has been deleted. To quickly remove the
remaining duplicates, you will use the Remove Duplicates feature.

4

● Click [Remove Duplicates] in the

Data Tools group.

Your screen should be similar to
Figure 6.42

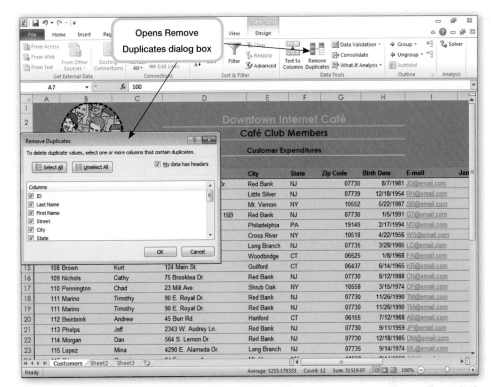

Figure 6.42

In the Remove Duplicates dialog box, you can specify the columns to be used to determine duplication. When all columns are selected, each entry in every column must exactly match those in another record. Selecting specific columns limits the match to data in those columns only. You want to find and remove records that contain duplicate information in all columns.

5

● If necessary, click [Select All] to select all columns.

● Click [OK] to complete the command.

● Click [OK] in response to the informational message about the number of duplicates found and deleted.

● Scroll the window to see record 124.

Your screen should be similar to
Figure 6.43

Figure 6.43

The last two duplicate records were removed. It is a good idea to check for duplicates before filtering data or analyzing the information in a table or worksheet to ensure that the results are as accurate as possible.

Summarizing Data

The next piece of information you want to gather from the table is a total amount for each state for the three months and a grand total of each month's expenditures. Additionally, you want to display a count of the number of records in the table. You can get this information easily by displaying a total row and inserting subtotals.

DISPLAYING A TOTAL ROW

To calculate statistics for all records in the table, you can display a total row and select the type of calculation you want performed on the data in a field. You will first use this feature to display a count of records in the table.

- Open the Table Tools Design tab.

- Click ☐ Total Row in the Table Style Options group.

Another Method

You could also select Table and choose Totals Row from the shortcut menu of any cell in the table.

Your screen should be similar to Figure 6.44

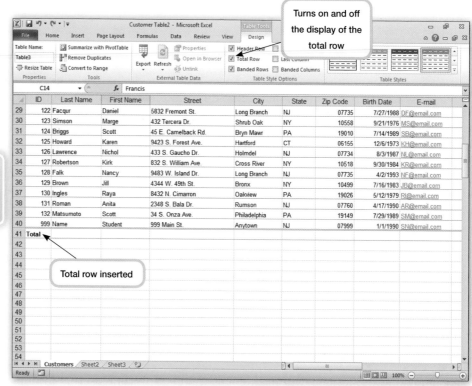

Figure 6.44

The worksheet window scrolls to display the bottom of the table where a total row is displayed.

The word "Total" appears in the left-most cell of the total row and an appropriate calculation is automatically entered in the right-most cell of the table (U41). Selecting any cell in the total row displays a ▾ drop-down list arrow that displays a list of function names from which you can select. You will use the Count function to display the number of records below the Last Name field column.

Additional Information

If you type a formula in a cell directly below a table that does not include a total row, the total row is displayed with the formula and without the word Total in the first cell.

2

- Click in the total row for the Last Name field.

- Click ⯆ to open the drop-down list and choose Count.

Your screen should be similar to Figure 6.45

Figure 6.45

A count of all entries in the Last Name field column is displayed. You also decide to calculate a total of the monthly expenditures.

3

- Open the Jan Total drop-down list and choose Sum.

- In a similar manner, display the sum for Feb and Mar.

Your screen should be similar to Figure 6.46

Figure 6.46

Notice the formula bar displays a Subtotal function instead of a Sum function. In tables, the Subtotal function is automatically used because it is the only function that can be used with filtered columns to correctly calculate the values of displayed data when rows are hidden. The number 109 in this function is the argument for Sum. Finally, the [Mar] entry in the formula is a **column name** that is automatically created for each column in a table. Column names are always surrounded with square brackets. It is similar to a named range and makes it easy to read and understand what data is being used in the formula.

You also can enter formulas in the total row that are not included in the drop-down list or type a text entry in a cell of this row. You will add a text entry in the E-mail column of the total row to describe the values to the right and then change the entry in the ID row to Count.

- Type **TOTAL:** in the E-mail column of the total row.

- Replace the entry in the ID column of the total row with **COUNT:**.

Your screen should be similar to Figure 6.47

Figure 6.47

Now, if you apply a filter to the table, because a Subtotal function was used, the calculated values in the total row change to reflect the amounts for the displayed records only.

⑤

If necessary, move to anywhere in the table to make it active.

Click in the Data tab to redisplay the AutoFilter buttons.

Filter the table to display only those records whose State is NJ.

Scroll the window to display all the filtered records and the Jan column.

Your screen should be similar to Figure 6.48

Turns on/off filtering and sorting

Filtered to display only records with NJ

	Last Name	First Name	Street	City	State	Zip Code	Birth Date	E-mail	Jan
7	Dwyer	Jack	21 N. Navesink River Dr.	Red Bank	NJ	07730	8/7/1981	JD@email.com	$77.34
8	Hamlin	Rose	7 Church St.	Little Silver	NJ	07739	12/18/1954	RH@email.com	$102.50
10	Thomas	Grant	159 Branch Ave., Apt. 15B	Red Bank	NJ	07730	1/5/1991	GT@email.com	$75.89
13	Chaplin	Lon	91 Monmouth Ave.	Long Branch	NJ	07735	3/28/1985	LC@email.com	$66.52
16	Nichols	Cathy	75 Brooklea Dr.	Red Bank	NJ	07730	8/12/1988	CN@email.com	$120.99
18	Marino	Timothy	90 E. Royal Dr.	Red Bank	NJ	07730	11/26/1990	TM@email.com	$90.77
20	Phelps	Jeff	2343 W. Audrey Ln.	Red Bank	NJ	07730	9/11/1959	JP@email.com	$35.69
21	Morgan	Dan	564 S. Lemon Dr.	Red Bank	NJ	07730	12/18/1985	DM@email.com	$65.99
22	Lopez	Mina	4290 E. Alameda Dr.	Long Branch	NJ	07735	9/14/1974	ML@email.com	$190.48
24	Merwin	Adda	947 S. Forest	Rumson	NJ	07760	3/30/1968	AM@email.com	$120.58
26	Bloomquist	William	43 Kings Rd.	Little Silver	NJ	07739	6/24/1986	WB@email.com	$175.97
27	Brett	Anna	23 Suffolk Ln.	Holmdel	NJ	07734	5/21/1990	AB@email.com	$150.82
28	Liston	Frank	302 Ash St.	Rumson	NJ	07760	1/21/1981	FL@email.com	$110.11
29	Facqur	Daniel	5832 Fremont St.	Long Branch	NJ	07735	7/27/1988	DF@email.com	$150.84
33	Lawrence	Nichol	433 S. Gaucho Dr.	Holmdel	NJ	07734	8/3/1987	NL@email.com	$100.03
35	Falk	Nancy	9483 W. Island Dr.	Long Branch	NJ	07735	4/2/1993	NF@email.com	$70.77
38	Roman	Anita	2348 S. Bala Dr.	Rumson	NJ	07760	4/17/1990	AR@email.com	$30.99
40	Name	Student	999 Main St.	Anytown	NJ	07999	1/1/1990	SN@email.com	$110.42
41	18							TOTAL:	$1,846.70

Count of records in NJ

Sum of Jan expenditures for NJ

Figure 6.48

Now the total row Count and Sum functions have been updated to calculate these values based on the displayed data in the table only.

⑥

Print the range A1:L41 in landscape orientation on one page with your name and the current date in a header.

CREATING A CALCULATED COLUMN

The last calculation you want to include is the average expenditures for each customer. You will enter a column label in cell V6 and the function to calculate the average in cell V7.

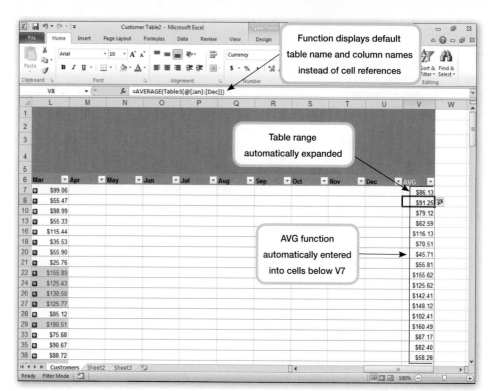

1

- Enter **AVG** in cell V6.

- Copy the format from U1 to V1 through V5.

- Enter an Average function in V7 to calculate the average of cells J7:U7.

- Save the workbook.

Your screen should be similar to Figure 6.49

Figure 6.49

When you typed the column heading in cell V6, the table range automatically expanded to include the new column. Because the Average function was entered in a table, it displays the default table name and the column names in place of the cell references. Additionally, the formula was automatically copied down the column to calculate the average for each displayed record in the table.

Grouping and Outlining Data

You have sorted and filtered the table to organize the data and used functions to analyze the information in the table. Now you want to further analyze the data by grouping related data and displaying subtotals for each group. You will use Excel's grouping and outlining tools to do this.

Concept **5** Grouping and Outlining

Grouping and outlining organizes data in a worksheet by showing and hiding different levels of detail for groups of related data. Grouping data has two functions: to collapse and expand rows or columns. Collapsing a group hides the rows within the group to display only the row with subtotals. After a group is collapsed, it can be expanded to redisplay the hidden rows. Worksheet data that is grouped also can be summarized using Summary functions.

Groups can be created for any level and location that you want on the worksheet. In contrast, outlines are based on a structured list or table. By sorting table data into categories first, you can then create groups that you can manipulate to show or hide rows within the group. For example, if you first sort the table by state, you can then create groups to manipulate the records within each state group.

GROUPING DATA

You decide grouping will be helpful in analyzing the data by state and city. First, you will create a group of the records with a state of CT. Before grouping data, you first need to sort the table so that the data you want grouped are together. You also will hide the total row.

1

- Clear the filter from the State column.

- Clear the Total Row option in the Table Style Options group on the Table Tools Design tab.

- Do a multilevel sort on the table data by State and then by City.

- Select the range A7:A11, which contains the IDs of the five individuals living in CT.

- Click **⇨ Group ▾** in the Outline group of the Data tab.

- Choose Rows and click **OK**.

Your screen should be similar to Figure 6.50

Figure 6.50

The outline levels are displayed in a column to the left of the table data. The numbers at the top of the column indicate the number of outline levels, with the higher number representing each inner level. The outline symbols are used to hide and show the detail information in a group. Because the CT group does not contain any sublevels, there are only two levels of data that can be displayed; level one hides the detail data and level two displays the detail data.

A level bar next to the group extends from the first row to the last row of data in the group and each bullet identifies a record in the group. The **+** and **−** outline symbols indicate if the group is expanded **−** and all levels are showing, or collapsed **+** and all levels are hidden. Clicking on these buttons hides and displays the data in the associated group.

Additional Information

You can create up to eight outline levels, one for each group.

Another Method

You also can use **Show Detail** or **Hide Detail** in the Outline group.

You will hide and display the data in the CT group and then you will define another level for the city of Woodbridge in the group.

2

- Click **–** to hide the data in the CT group.

- Click **+** to display the data in the group again.

Having Trouble?

When using the level numbers to hide and display levels, the cell selector must be in the group you want affected.

- Create a group using the range A10:A11, which contains the IDs of the two individuals living in Woodbridge.

Your screen should be similar to Figure 6.51

Figure 6.51

The City group is a sublevel group within the CT State group and a third level number is displayed. The bullet next to the two records in this group are indented one level to show that they are at a higher level.

3

- Click **2** to display only level-two records.

Your screen should be similar to Figure 6.52

Figure 6.52

Now the Woodbridge records are hidden. When a group contains several levels, using the ⊞ and ⊟ symbols hides and displays all records within the group and the level buttons control the levels within the group.

You decide that creating the sublevel by city within the group is not necessary and will remove it.

4

- Click ⊞ to display all the records.

- Select A10:A11 and click ⬅ Ungroup ▾.

- Choose Rows and click OK.

Your screen should be similar to Figure 6.53

Figure 6.53

The subgroup has been removed.

GROUPING DATA AND CALCULATING SUBTOTALS

In addition, you want to know how much money each group spends in each month. To do this, you need to add a summary row and the SUM Subtotal function to calculate a subtotal for the group.

Although you could continue to define groups and add summary rows, a faster way is to use the automatic Subtotal feature.

Concept **6** Subtotal

The Subtotal feature automatically takes data in a list, organizes it into groups, and includes subtotals for each group of data. A **list** is a series of rows that contain related data but are not defined as a table. Subtotals can be calculated on any column or columns you select that contain numbers. The SUM subtotal is the default calculation; however, you can change it to subtotal using other functions such as COUNT, MAX, and MIN. The SUBTOTAL function uses the syntax =SUBTOTAL(function_num, ref1, ref2 . . .) where the function_num tells the function the type of calculation to apply and ref refers to the range to subtotal.

When using the Subtotal feature, the data in the table needs to be in sorted order first so that the rows you want to subtotal are grouped together. The table data is already in sorted order as you want it. Additionally, because the Subtotal feature can only be used on a list of data, and not data defined as a table, you need to convert the table range to a normal range. You also will remove the current group from the table.

- Select A7:A11 and click **Ungroup**.

- **Choose Rows and click OK.**

- Open the Table Tools Design tab.

- Click anywhere in the table.

- Click **Convert to Range** in the Tools group.

- Click **Yes**.

- Open the Data tab.

- Click **Subtotal** in the Outline group.

Your screen should be similar to Figure 6.54

Figure 6.54

From the Subtotal dialog box, you first specify the field you want to display subtotals after each change in data. In this case, you want subtotals calculated after each change in State. Then you select the type of function you want to use to calculate the subtotals, such as Sum, Count, or Average. You want to calculate a sum. Finally, you select the fields that contain the values you want to subtotal. You will display subtotals for the three months of expenditures. You also can have an automatic page break after each subtotal and can have the subtotals displayed above the subtotaled rows instead of below.

2

- Choose **State** from the **At each change in** drop-down list.

- Click on **AVG** in the **Add subtotal to** list to remove the checkmark.

- Choose **Jan, Feb,** and **Mar** in the **Add subtotal to** list.

- Click [OK].

- Scroll to see the bottom of the range and the monthly expenditure data.

Your screen should be similar to Figure 6.55

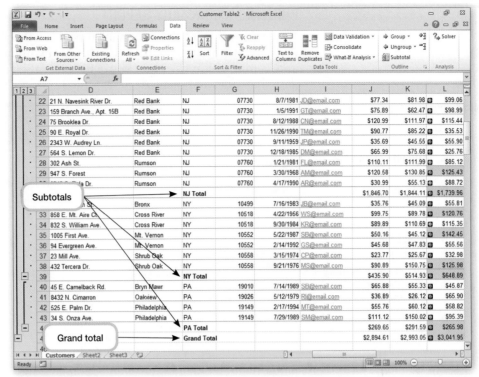

Figure 6.55

The worksheet now displays a subtotal for each change in state and a grand total for each month. Additionally, along the left side of the row numbers, the worksheet is outlined so you can see its structure.

You can create a summary report by clicking the numeric outline symbols 1, 2, 3 to display different levels of detail. Clicking 1 displays the grand total only, 2 the subtotals, and 3 all levels. You can also use + to display and − to hide the details within a group.

3

- Click 2.

- Scroll to the top of the window.

Your screen should be similar to Figure 6.56

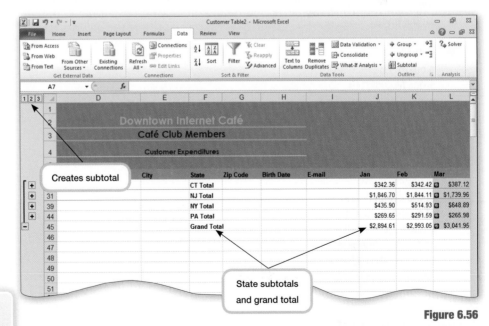

Figure 6.56

Additional Information

You also can create a chart of the visible data in a worksheet that contains subtotals.

The worksheet displays the subtotals and grand total values only.

PRINTING A SUMMARY REPORT

Next you will print the summary report for Evan showing the State and the three month columns only. To do this, you will hide the Zip Code, Birth Date, and E-mail columns. Then you will select the range of cells containing the data that you want printed.

1

- AutoFit column F.

- Hide columns G through I.

- Select the range containing the field names and summary statistics (F6:I45).

- Open the File tab and choose Print.

- If necessary, change the Print Active Sheets setting to Print Selection.

- If necessary, change the orientation to portrait and select the printer.

- Use the Page Setup dialog box to center the table horizontally on the page.

- In the left section of a custom header, enter Monthly Expenditures on the first line and Summary Statistics on the second.

- In the right section of a custom header, enter your name on the first line and the current date on the second.

Your screen should be similar to Figure 6.57

Figure 6.57

Only the selected range of the worksheet is displayed in the preview window. You will print the selection, unhide the columns, and then remove the subtotals.

- **Click** **to print the selection.**

- **Unhide Columns G through I.**

- **Click 3 to show all details.**

- **Click anywhere in the table range.**

- **Click** ▦ **Subtotal in the Data tab and click** Remove All **.**

- **Sort the worksheet in ascending order by ID.**

- **Move to cell A5 and save the workbook.**

Your screen should be similar to Figure 6.58

Columns unhidden and subtotals removed

ID	Last Name	First Name	Street	City	State	Zip Code	Birth Date	E-mail
100	Dwyer	Jack	21 N. Navesink River Dr.	Red Bank	NJ	07730	8/7/1981	JD@email.com
101	Hamlin	Rose	7 Church St.	Little Silver	NJ	07739	12/18/1954	RH@email.com
102	Brown	Sara	1005 First Ave.	Mt. Vernon	NY	10552	5/22/1987	SB@email.com
103	Thomas	Grant	159 Branch Ave., Apt. 15B	Red Bank	NJ	07730	1/5/1991	GT@email.com
104	Trent	Maria	525 E. Palm Dr.	Philadelphia	PA	19149	2/17/1994	MT@email.com
105	Shoemaker	Wendy	858 E. Mt. Aire Ct.	Cross River	NY	10518	4/22/1956	WS@email.com
106	Chaplin	Lon	91 Monmouth Ave.	Long Branch	NJ	07735	3/28/1985	LC@email.com
107	Amlin	Francis	6698 Chestnut St.	Woodbridge	CT	06525	1/8/1968	FA@email.com
108	Brown	Kurt	124 Main St.	Guilford	CT	06437	6/14/1965	KB@email.com
109	Nichols	Cathy	75 Brooklea Dr.	Red Bank	NJ	07730	8/12/1988	CN@email.com
110	Pennington	Chad	23 Mill Ave.	Shrub Oak	NY	10558	3/15/1974	CP@email.com
111	Marino	Timothy	90 E. Royal Dr.	Red Bank	NJ	07730	11/26/1990	TM@email.com
112	Beinbrink	Andrew	45 Burr Rd.	Hartford	CT	06155	7/12/1968	AB@email.com
113	Phelps	Jeff	2343 W. Audrey Ln.	Red Bank	NJ	07730	9/11/1959	JP@email.com
114	Morgan	Dan	564 S. Lemon Dr.	Red Bank	NJ	07730	12/18/1985	DM@email.com
115	Lopez	Mina	4290 E. Alameda Dr.	Long Branch	NJ	07735	9/14/1974	ML@email.com
116	Sitzman	Georgia	94 Evergreen Ave.	Mt. Vernon	NY	10552	2/14/1992	GS@email.com

All records sorted by ID number

Figure 6.58

The worksheet is in sorted order by ID number. Because the list has not been redefined as a table range, the AutoFilter buttons do not display in the header row.

Creating a PivotTable Report

Another way to analyze your worksheet data from different viewpoints is to create a PivotTable report.

Concept 7 PivotTable Report

A **PivotTable** report is an interactive, cross-tabulated table that summarizes and analyzes worksheet data. When a PivotTable report is created, Excel automatically sorts, subtotals, and totals the data. You can then expand and collapse levels of data to focus your results as you want. You can move rows to columns or columns to rows (or pivot) to see different data summaries. You also can filter, sort, group, and conditionally format the data to create a concise, attractive, and informative report. A PivotTable is most useful for when you want to analyze a long list of figures and you want to compare several facts about each figure.

The criteria to create a PivotTable report are that the worksheet data must be a data table or list, the columns and rows must contain unique labels, and there cannot be any blank rows or columns. In a PivotTable report, each column or field from the source data becomes a PivotTable field that summarizes multiple rows of information. A numeric field provides the values to be summarized. After a PivotTable is created, it is interactive, meaning that you can rearrange the data in many ways by adding or removing fields.

A typical PivotTable report pivots one column against another, with the intersection of the two columns serving as the area for the summary data. A PivotTable report can calculate the sum, count, average, maximum, minimum, standard deviation, and variance without the need for entering formulas.

You will create a PivotTable report of the data in the table.

1

- **Move to cell A7.**

- **Click** **in the Tables group of the Insert tab.**

Your screen should be similar to Figure 6.59

Figure 6.59

In the Create PivotTable dialog box, you specify the data to analyze and where to place the PivotTable. The default data selection is the current table, which is the one you want to analyze. The default location is a new worksheet, but you could specify a range of cells in which to place the PivotTable on the current worksheet. You decide to place the PivotTable on the existing blank Sheet2.

2

- **Choose Existing Worksheet.**

- **Click on cell A3 of Sheet2.**

- **Click** OK **.**

Your screen should be similar to Figure 6.60

Figure 6.60

A blank PivotTable report is displayed in a new sheet. In addition, the Pivot-Table Tools Options and Design tabs, and the PivotTable Field List pane are displayed. You would like the PivotTable report to summarize monthly expenditures by city and state. To set up this report layout, you need to select the fields from the Field List pane to add them to the blank report.

3

In the Choose fields to add to report list, choose City, State, Jan, Feb, and Mar.

Your screen should be similar to Figure 6.61

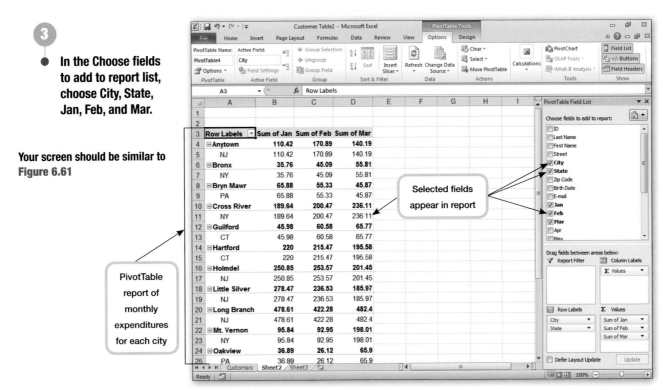

Figure 6.61

The PivotTable report displays a sum of the monthly expenditures in each month for each city as well as the grand total of their expenditures. The cities are listed in alphabetical order.

You decide that the data would be more meaningful without the city breakdown.

4

- Clear the checkmark from the City field.

- Name the worksheet **PivotTable Report**.

Your screen should be similar to Figure 6.62

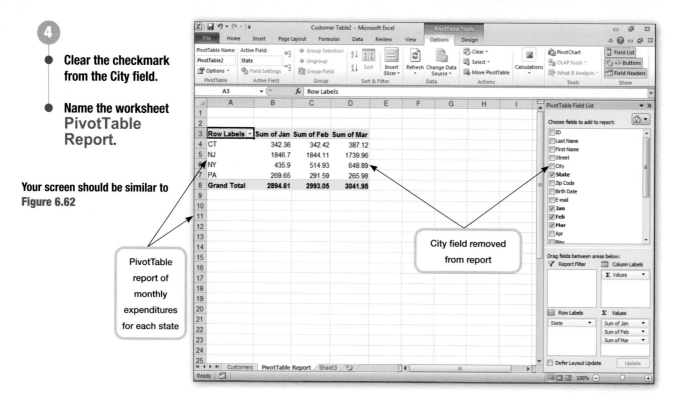

PivotTable report of monthly expenditures for each state

City field removed from report

Figure 6.62

The report now simply shows a summary of expenditures for each month by state. The report is formatted using the default PivotTable style. Just like a worksheet, you can change the style by selecting another from the PivotTables Styles gallery in the Pivot Table Tools Design tab.

Creating a PivotChart Report

Next, you want to see the state and monthly expenditure data graphed on a chart. To do this, you will create a PivotChart using the PivotTable you just created as the data source.

Concept ❽ **PivotChart Report**

A **PivotChart** report is an interactive chart that can be used to view and rearrange data. A PivotChart is most useful when you need to quickly change data views to see comparisons and trends in different ways.

A PivotChart report must have an associated PivotTable report in the same workbook. Both of these reports contain the same source data and, as in the PivotTable report, you can rearrange the data to see different views and display details. When you make changes to a PivotTable (such as removing a field from it), the associated PivotChart also changes, and vice versa.

1

- If necessary, click anywhere in the PivotTable.

- Click [⬛ PivotChart] in the Tools group of the PivotTable Tools Options tab.

- Choose [⬛] Clustered Column.

- Click [OK].

- Move the chart below the PivotTable.

- Move to cell A3.

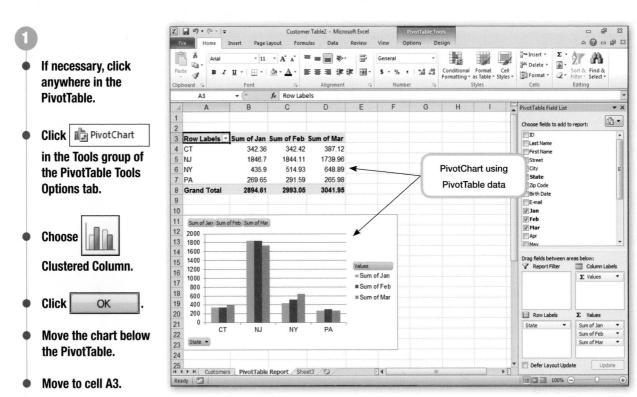

Figure 6.63

Your screen should be similar to Figure 6.63

The PivotChart has been automatically created using the PivotTable data. The row fields in the PivotTable become the category fields in the PivotChart, and the column fields in the PivotTable become the series fields in the PivotChart.

The PivotChart Filter pane can be used to apply filters to the data displayed in the fields. Any changes you make to the PivotChart are also reflected in the PivotTable report.

As with the PivotTable report, you can manipulate and reformat the Pivot-Chart to view the data in different ways. But remember, anything you do to the PivotChart fields will affect the associated PivotTable report fields.

2

- Print the Pivot Table Report worksheet with your name and the current date in the header.

- Save the workbook.

Hyperlinking Workbook Files

As you noticed earlier, when you type a URL or e-mail address, Excel will automatically convert the text into a hyperlink. You can also attach a hyperlink to any text, shape, or graphic using the Insert Hyperlink button. The last thing you want to do with this workbook is to create a hyperlink from the Customers worksheet to the Bonus Dollars workbook. Your plans are to include the Bonus Dollars worksheets for each month of the year in separate sheets of this workbook file.

CREATING A HYPERLINK TO ANOTHER WORKBOOK

Adding a hyperlink to this workbook file will make it easy to switch to the appropriate sheet in the Bonus Dollars workbook and copy the customers' total monthly expenditures into the Customers table. You will link to the Bonus Dollars workbook file and display the hyperlink in cell J4 above the expenditure columns of data.

● **Move to cell J4 of the Customers sheet.**

● **Click** **in the Links group of the Insert tab.**

Another Method

You also can select Hyperlink from a cell's shortcut menu.

Your screen should be similar to Figure 6.64

Figure 6.64

From the Insert Hyperlink dialog box, you first need to specify the type of link from the Link to bar. The four options are described below.

Option	Effect
Existing File or Web Page	Creates a link in an existing Web page or file
Place in This Document	Creates a link to a place in the active file
Create New Document	Creates a link to a file that you have not created yet.
E-mail Address	Creates a link that allows users to create an e-mail message with the correct address in the To line.

You want to create a link to a location in another workbook file. You also need to enter the text that the hyperlink will display in the worksheet. If you do not enter anything in the Text to display box, the hyperlink automatically displays the path of the linked file. Finally, you will add instructions that will appear in the hyperlink ScreenTip.

- If necessary, choose **Existing File or Web Page** from the Link to bar.

- Enter Monthly Expenditure Data in the Text to display text box.

- Change to your Excel data files location and choose ex06_Bonus Dollars from the file list.

- Click ScreenTip... .

- Type Click to open the worksheet.

- Click OK .

Your screen should be similar to Figure 6.65

Figure 6.65

In the future, as you record each month's Bonus Dollars awards using the Monthly Bonus Form template, you plan to maintain the completed monthly worksheets in a single workbook file. When the workbook contains many worksheets, you will want to make sure that the user is taken directly to the worksheet containing the data for the appropriate month. To do this, you create a bookmark to that location in the linked workbook file. A **bookmark** establishes a link to a specific worksheet location.

2

● **Click**

  Bookmark...

Your screen should be similar to
Figure 6.66

Figure 6.66

In the Select Place in Document dialog box, you select a specific location to which you want the user to be taken in the linked document. The list box displays a tree diagram showing the outline of the information in the workbook and named ranges. From the outline, you select the location to which you want to link. In this case, you want the cell pointer positioned on the first customer's total expenditures (G12).

3

- Choose **Month** in the Cell Reference list.

- In the **Type in the cell reference** text box, enter **G12**.

- Click to close the Select Place in Document dialog box.

- Click to close the Insert Hyperlink dialog box.

- Change the font color for the hyperlink to Light Green, Background 2.

- Point to cell J4 to see the ScreenTip.

Your screen should be similar to Figure 6.67

Figure 6.67

The text you entered for the hyperlink is displayed underlined in the cell. The ScreenTip displays the text you entered.

CHANGING THE HYPERLINK SCREENTIP

As you read the ScreenTip, you realize it does not provide enough information. You decide to change the ScreenTip text to include the worksheet name. Then you will use the hyperlink to open the worksheet.

- **Right-click cell J4.**

- **Choose Edit Hyperlink from the shortcut menu.**

Additional Information

You can edit the text of the hyperlink just like any other cell entry.

Another Method

When the cell containing a hyperlink is selected, you also can click [Hyperlink] in the Links group on the Insert tab to edit the hyperlink.

Figure 6.68

Your screen should be similar to Figure 6.68

The Edit Hyperlink dialog box displays the hyperlink destination. The Look in location identifies the location of the active workbook file. The Address box displays the destination workbook file name and cell location the link will follow. Notice the Address box does not include the drive location of the destination workbook file as part of the address. This is because it is a **relative link**, which means it will locate the destination workbook file relative to the location of the current workbook file. If you move both files to the same location, the link will continue to operate correctly because the relative positions of the files remain unchanged. If you move one of the files to another location, the link would not work. You would then need to edit the address to include the complete destination path location, making the address an **absolute link**.

You will edit the ScreenTip text to include the destination workbook file name.

2

● Click [ScreenTip...]

● Add the text **Bonus Dollars** before the word "worksheet".

● Click [OK].

● Click [OK].

● Change the font color for the hyperlink to Light Green, Background 2 again.

● Point to the hyperlink cell to see the ScreenTip.

Figure 6.69

Your screen should be similar to Figure 6.69

The revised ScreenTip is now much more descriptive of the purpose of the hyperlink. Now you will use the hyperlink.

3

● Click on the hyperlink.

Your screen should be similar to Figure 6.70

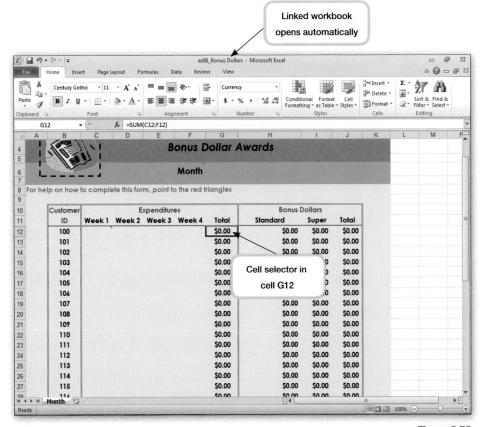

Figure 6.70

The Bonus Dollars workbook is open and the cell selector is in the location you specified as the bookmark. Now, assuming that the worksheet contained the data for the month, you could copy the customer monthly expenditure totals from the Bonus Dollars workbook to the Customers worksheet.

4

● **Close the** ex06_Bonus Dollars **workbook file.**

Restoring the Table

Now that you are finished using the Subtotal feature, you need to restore the range back to a table range.

1

● **Move to cell A6.**

● **Click** **on the Insert tab.**

● **If necessary, define the range as A6:V40.**

● **Click** ☐ OK ☐ **.**

● **Click anywhere in the table to clear the highlight.**

Your screen should be similar to Figure 6.71

Figure 6.71

The range is now again recognized as a table and the default table style is applied.

2

● **Save and close the workbook.**

FOCUS ON CAREERS

EXPLORE YOUR CAREER OPTIONS

Lodging Manager

Have you ever wondered who ensures you get excellent customer service and enjoy your stay at a hotel? Have you ever attended a convention in a hotel and wondered who made sure the equipment and resources the group needed were attended to? Lodging managers are responsible for making sure customers are satisfied and the establishment is profitable. Managers must use guidelines to allocate and disperse funds for needed improvements and maintenance. They must track income and manage overhead. Many use spreadsheet programs to handle these tasks. The salary range for lodging managers is typically between $35,000 and $60,000. College graduates with experience in the lodging industry will have a competitive advantage in this industry.

Table (EX6.4)

A table is an organized collection of related information that is entered into a series of worksheet rows and columns.

Table

Hyperlink (EX6.12)

A hyperlink is a connection or link to a destination location. The destination can be a location in the current file or another file, a Web page, or an e-mail address.

Hyperlink

Sort (EX6.26)

You can sort or arrange data in a specified sequence: alphabetically, numerically, or by date.

Filter (EX6.33)

A filter is a restriction you place on records in a table to quickly isolate and display a subset of records.

Grouping and Outlining (EX6.46)

Grouping and outlining organizes data in a worksheet by showing and hiding different levels of detail for groups of related data.

Subtotal (EX6.49)

The Subtotal feature automatically takes data in a list, organizes it into groups, and includes subtotals for each group of data.

PivotTable Report (EX6.53)

A PivotTable report is an interactive table that can be used to summarize and manipulate worksheet data.

PivotChart Report (EX6.56)

A PivotChart report is an interactive chart that can be used to view and rearrange data.

KEY TERMS

absolute link EX6.62
bookmark EX6.59
column name EX6.44
criteria EX6.26
field EX6.4
field name EX6.4
filter EX6.33
grouping and outlining EX6.46
header row EX6.4
hyperlink EX6.12
list EX6.49

multilevel sort EX6.26
PivotChart EX6.56
PivotTable EX6.53
record EX6.4
relative link EX6.62
sort EX6.26
table EX6.4
table range EX6.4
Uniform Resource Locator
(URL) EX6.12

COMMAND SUMMARY

Command	Shortcut	Action
File tab		
Options /Proofing/		
AutoCorrect Options... /AutoFormat As You Type/ Internet and network paths with hyperlinks		Automatically formats a hyperlink
Home tab		
Number group		
(icon)		Formats cells
Styles group		
Conditional Formatting ▾		Formats cells based on selected criteria
Cells group		
Insert ▾ /Insert Table Row Below	Tab	Adds a new row below the current row in a table
Format ▾ /Format Cells/Number/Special		Applies selected special format to number entries
Format ▾ /Hide & Unhide		Hides and unhides rows and/or columns
Editing group		
A↓Z /Sort A to Z		Sorts the table column in ascending alphabetical order
AZ/ZA Sort /Custom Sort		Performs a multilevel sort on the table column
AZ/ZY Sort & Filter ▾ /Filter		Turns AutoFilter on or off
Clear /Clear		Clears filters from a table

LAB REVIEW

COMMAND SUMMARY (CONTINUED)

Command	Shortcut	Action
Insert tab		
Tables group		
PivotTable		Inserts a PivotTable
Table		Converts a range of data into a table
Links group		
Hyperlink		Inserts a new hyperlink or modifies selected hyperlink
Data tab		
Sort & Filter group		
Sort Smallest to Largest		Sorts a column of data in ascending order
Sort		Arranges data alphabetically, numerically, or by date
Filter		Turns AutoFilter on or off
Clear		Redisplays all records
Advanced		Specifies complex criteria to limit records in a query result
Data Tools group		
Remove Duplicates		Deletes duplicate rows
Data Validation ▾		Prevents invalid data from being entered into a cell

COMMAND SUMMARY (CONTINUED)

Command	Shortcut	Action
Outline group		
➡ Group ▾		Ties range of cells so they can be collapsed or expanded
⬅ Ungroup ▾		Ungroups range of cells
▦ Subtotal		Displays totals for each change in a category
▦ Subtotal / Remove All		Removes subtotals from worksheet
Table Tools Design tab		
Tools group		
▦ Convert to Range		Converts table to normal range
Table Style Options group		
☑ Header Row		Formats the top row of the table
☐ Total Row		Adds a total row to the table
☑ Banded Rows		Formats even rows differently from odd rows
☑ First Column		Displays formatting for first column of the table
Table Styles group		
▾ More		Opens Table Styles gallery to apply a predefined format and colors to a table
PivotTable Tools Options tab		
Tools group		
▦ PivotChart		Inserts a chart based on the PivotTable data

LAB EXERCISES

MATCHING

Match the item on the left with the correct description on the right.

1. hyperlink   ____ a. Z to A order
2. record   ____ b. the label used to identify the data stored in a field
3. PivotTable   ____ c. a connection to a location in another file
4. field name   ____ d. organizes data in a specified sequence
5. field   ____ e. the smallest unit of information about a record
6. descending   ____ f. displays a subset of records according to specified criteria
7. sort   ____ g. a row of a table that contains a group of related fields
8. filter   ____ h. summarizes and manipulates worksheet data
9. table   ____ i. a sort on more than one column or field
10. multilevel   ____ j. an organized collection of related information

MULTIPLE CHOICE

Circle the correct response to the questions below.

1. _____ a group hides the rows within the group to display only the row with subtotals.
   a. Sorting
   b. Expanding
   c. Collapsing
   d. Pivoting

2. A _____ is one group of information in a table.
   a. field
   b. record
   c. sort
   d. database

3. You can _____ or arrange data in a specified sequence: alphabetically, numerically, or by date.
   a. sum
   b. sort
   c. filter
   d. pivot

4. _____ data has two functions: to collapse and expand rows or columns.
   a. Sorting
   b. Filtering
   c. Analyzing
   d. Grouping

5. A(n) _____ is a hyperlink to a specific location in a file.
    a. marker
    b. bookmark
    c. absolute link
    d. relative link

6. The single-level sort operation feature lets you sort on up to _____ column(s) or field(s) in a table at a time.
    a. 1
    b. 2
    c. 3
    d. 4

7. Use a _____ to quickly jump to another location in a file.
    a. Web page
    b. hyperlink
    c. browser
    d. filter

8. _____ can be used to summarize numbers in a table.
    a. Subtotals
    b. Graphics
    c. Sorts
    d. Filters

9. When a hyperlink is created, it stores the information about the location of the destination as a _____.
    a. URL
    b. sort
    c. filter
    d. HTML

10. The _____ feature temporarily hides rows that do not meet the specified criteria.
    a. sum
    b. sort
    c. filter
    d. pivot

LAB EXERCISES

TRUE/FALSE

Circle the correct answer to the following questions.

1. A filter rearranges data according to the criteria you specify.	**True**	**False**
2. An absolute link includes the complete destination path location.	**True**	**False**
3. Subtotals can be added above each category in the worksheet.	**True**	**False**
4. Changing the data in a PivotChart also changes the PivotTable.	**True**	**False**
5. Each column is a field, which is the smallest unit of information about a record.	**True**	**False**
6. Field names are entered in the first row of a table.	**True**	**False**
7. A hyperlink is a connection to a location in the current file or in another file, or to a Web site.	**True**	**False**
8. Changing data on a PivotChart does not affect the worksheet data.	**True**	**False**
9. A multilevel sort displays a subset of the records.	**True**	**False**
10. A bookmark establishes a link to a specific worksheet location.	**True**	**False**

FILL-IN

Complete the following statements by filling in the blanks with the correct terms.

1. A(n) _____ jumps you to a new location in a worksheet, workbook, document, or Web page.

2. When a sort is done on more than one column or field, it is called a(n) _____ sort.

3. A filter is created by specifying _____ that you want records to meet in order to be displayed.

4. A(n) _____ is an interactive table that can be used to summarize and manipulate worksheet data.

5. An organized collection of related information is called a(n) _____.

6. The group of related fields in a table is called a(n) _____.

7. A(n) _____ does not include the drive and folder location of the destination file as part of the address.

8. _____ a table to display records in a specified order.

9. Apply a _____ to a table to display a subset of records.

10. A(n) _____ is a descriptive label used to identify the data stored in the field.

STEP-BY-STEP

LIFESTYLE FITNESS CLUB EMPLOYEE DATABASE ★

1. You work in human resources at the Lifestyle Fitness Club. One of your duties includes maintaining an Excel database of employee information. Your supervisor requested some payroll information that will be used to determine pay raises. You have been asked to provide an analysis of jobs and pay rates. Your completed analysis will be similar to those shown here.

   a. Open the file ex06_LFC Employee List.

   b. Convert the range A6 through H32 to a table with headers. Apply a table style of your choice.

   c. Use Data Validation tools to restrict column A entries to only whole numbers between 1000 and 9999. Include an explanatory Input Message indicating that ID# must be four digits long.

   d. Enter a new record into the table. Use **your name** as the employee. Enter **9999** as your employee number, the **current date** as the hire date, **Sales Associate** as your job title, **13.00** as your pay rate, and **20** as your hours.

   e. Edit the entry for Kimberly Kieken. Her last name is now **Beinbrink**. Add your name and the current date to the header.

   f. Sort the table to display the records by pay rate first, job title second, and hire date third, all in ascending sort order. Print the table in portrait orientation, centered horizontally, fit to one page.

   g. Filter the table to exclude records with a pay rate of salary.

   h. Add a total row to the table. Use the subtotal functions to include a count of the total number of nonsalaried employees and the total number of hours worked.

   i. Print the table again in landscape orientation, centered horizontally with your name and the current date in the header.

   j. Save your completed workbook as LFC Analysis to your solution file location.

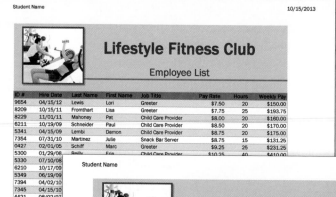

IRONWORKS DATABASE ★★

2. IronWorks creates unique wrought iron home accents. The accounting manager uses an Excel table to keep track of jobs for the year. They have asked you to do some analysis on the data so they can better see trends and make any needed adjustments. Your completed analysis of the table will be similar to the ones shown here.

a. Open the workbook file ex06_IronWorks Projects.

b. Convert the range A4:G27 to a table with headers. Apply a table style of your choice.

c. Use Data Validation tools to restrict column A entries to only five-digit-long whole numbers. Include an explanatory Error Message.

d. You have been given invoices for three new jobs. Enter the following three new records into the table:

Job Number	Date	Category	Site Address	Contact	Phone	Amounts
24025	04/23/12	Residential	2983 Club House Dr	Larson, Edward	(480) 555-1763	$58.50
24026	04/26/12	Residential	20234 Midway Ave	Wilson, Gary	(480) 555-0031	$400.00
24027	04/28/12	Commercial	467 Broadway Rd	enter your name	(480) 555-2763	$1,275.50

e. The Accounting department has requested a table of jobs whose amounts were more than $1,000. Filter the table to display these records only.

f. Display a total row that includes a count of the records in the Category field and a sum of the Permit Amounts.

g. Print the filtered table with your name and the date in the header, in landscape orientation, centered horizontally.

h. Remove the filter. Sort the table on Category. Use the Subtotal feature to group the data and calculate subtotals for the Amounts field.

i. Print all the fields of the table with your name and the current date in the header, in landscape orientation, centered horizontally on a single page. Adjust the top and bottom margins as needed.

j. Remove all subtotals. Convert the range back to a table. Save the workbook as IronWorks Projects Update to your solution file location.

MEGA MEDIA WAREHOUSE EMPLOYEE DATABASE ★ ★

3. Part of your job in the Personnel department at Mega Media Warehouse is to maintain the employee sales database. Recently, the company has been running a rewards program for the employees based on sales performance. In addition to the standard database maintenance, you have been asked to examine the employee database and determine the appropriate rewards. Your completed analysis and update of the database should be similar to those shown here.

a. Open the file ex06_Mega Media Employees.

b. Convert the range A5 through E44 to a table with headers. Apply a table style of your choice.

c. The employee data for several new employees has not been included in the database. Enter the records shown below.

Employee #	Last Name	First Name	Department	Total Sales
45925	Phillips	Jennifer	Game Systems	$752.98
08420	Schwartz	Grant	Small Appliances	$1,230.79
64301	Thurman	Andy	Electronics	$2,951.50
00345	Wood	Cyrus	Computers	$3,459.97

d. Sort the Last Name column alphabetically.

e. There have been some personnel changes since the last database update. Tony Patel and Eugene Radden are no longer with the company. Find and remove their records from the database. Joann Hancock recently got married. Find her record and change her last name to **Keifer**.

f. You have finished making the necessary changes to the database and can now begin your analysis. Use a multilevel sort to display the records first by department and then by last name.

g. Now that you have the data organized, you need to filter the records to determine which employees have earned rewards. There are two awards levels. Level 1 includes those who have sales from $2,000 up to sales less than $4,000. Use AutoFilter to determine these employees.

h. Copy this filtered sheet to a new sheet and name the new sheet **Bonus Level 1**. Replace the subtitle in cell C3 of this new sheet with **Level 1 Winners**.

i. Print this sheet without displaying the field Total Sales (adjust the width of column D as needed) with your name and the date in the header, in portrait orientation, centered horizontally.

j. Level 2 winners include those individuals with sales greater than or equal to $4,000. Create another sheet for these individuals. Name this sheet **Bonus Level 2** and edit the subtitle to **Level 2 Winners**.

k. Print this sheet without displaying the field Total Sales (adjust the width of column D as needed) with your name and the date in the header, in portrait orientation, centered horizontally.

l. Remove the filter from the Employee Sales sheet and save the workbook as Employee Rewards to your solution file location.

LAB EXERCISES

ANIMAL RESCUE FOUNDATION DONATION INVENTORY ★ ★ ★

4. The Animal Rescue Foundation relies on donations to furnish foster homes with needed supplies. They have started to record the donation information in an Excel workbook so they can keep an inventory of goods. You have been asked to update and maintain this inventory and furnish the board of directors with an inventory status report identifying those items with dangerously low inventory levels. Your completed worksheets should be similar to those shown here.

a. Open the file ex06_ARF Inventory.

b. The inventory consists of a table of items showing the quantity on hand and the desired quantity. You need to add a column that will identify whether a shortage or surplus exists for each item. Add a table column to the right of the Ideal Quantity column. Add the label **Status** in cell E9.

c. In order to indicate a need for an item, you will enter a formula that will calculate when an item's on-hand amount is less than half of the ideal amount, and display either "Stocked" or "Request" based on the determination. Enter the formula **=IF(C10<(D10/2), "Request", "Stocked")** in cell E10. If necessary, copy the formula to the rest of the cells in that column and center the text.

d. Add a table column to the right of the Status column and add the label **Quantity Requested** in cell F9. Adjust the formatting as needed. In cell F10, create a formula to calculate the difference between the Ideal Quantity and the Quantity On Hand.

e. Extend the background fill color in the title area to above the two new columns. Sort the table on Item Description.

f. You now have a table that displays which items need to be restocked and how many of each. Now you need to provide a table of low-stock items to the board. Create a PivotTable on a new worksheet that displays only the Item Description and Quantity Requested for those items with "Request" status. (Hint: Add the Item Description and Quantity Requested fields to the Row Labels box, add the Status field to the Report Filter box, and filter the list on "Request.") Hide the plus/minus buttons. (Hint: Click in the Show/Hide group on the PivotTable Tools Options tab.) Turn off subtotals. (Hint: Click [Subtotals] and then click in the

Layout group on the PivotTable Tools Design tab.) Turn off the grand total. (Hint: Click 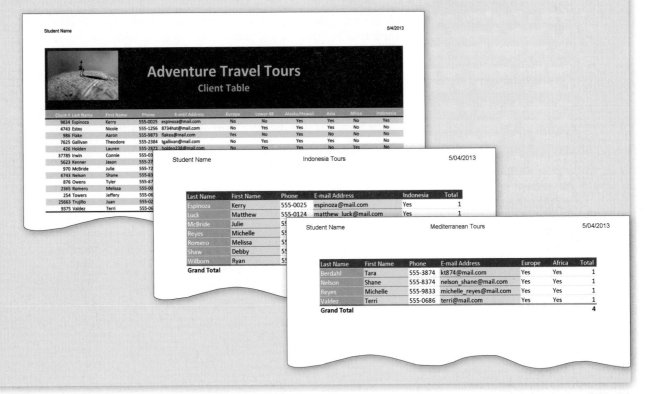 Grand Totals ▾

and then click ⊞ Off for Rows and Columns in the Layout group on the PivotTable Tools Design tab.)

Click ⊟ Report Layout ▾ and choose ⊟ Show in Tabular Form (in the Layout group on the PivotTable Tools Design tab).

g. Apply a PivotTable style of your choice. Rename the sheet **Inventory Request** and move it after the Supply Inventory sheet. Add your name and the current date to a custom header and print the sheet in portrait orientation centered horizontally.

h. Save your completed workbook as ARF Inventory to your solution file location. Print the stocked items only of the supply inventory worksheet with your name and the date in the header, in landscape orientation, centered horizontally.

ADVENTURE TRAVEL TOURS CLIENTS ★★★

5. As a travel agent at Adventure Travel Tours, you maintain an Excel table of your clients. You have recently created several new tour packages and would like to inform your clients about them. Your table includes information about where customers have traveled in the six areas your new packages cover. You would like to target those who have already traveled in the new areas of your packages. You decide to create PivotTables to break down the volume of customers into more manageable segments. Some of your completed PivotTables will be similar to those shown here.

LAB EXERCISES

a. Open the file ex06_ATT Client Table.

b. Merge and center the words **Client Table** under the company name at the top of the worksheet. Set the font to bold, size to 24, and color to light green.

c. Convert the client data to a table. Format the table and adjust column widths as needed.

d. One of the new packages is a cruise. You've been asked to put together a list of clients who've taken cruises in Alaska or Hawaii. Filter the list to show only these clients. Sort the list by Last Name. Insert your name and the current date in a header. Print the list in landscape orientation, centered horizontally and fit to one page.

e. One of your new packages is a tour of Indonesia. Insert a PivotTable in a new worksheet. Choose the Last Name, First Name, Phone, and E-mail Address fields for the report. Hide the plus/minus buttons. (Hint: Click [⊞ +/- Buttons] in the Show/Hide group on the PivotTable Tools Options tab.) Turn off subtotals. (Hint: Click [Subtotals] and then click [Do Not Show Subtotals] in the Layout group on the PivotTable Tools Design tab.)

f. Add the Indonesia field to the report. Filter the PivotTable to display those clients who have traveled to Indonesia in the past. Add the Client Number field to the report. Change the field settings to Count. (Hint: Click [▼] in the Values box and select Value Field Settings from the drop-down list. Then select Count.)

g. Click [Report Layout] in the Layout group on the PivotTable Tools Design tab and choose [Show in Tabular Form]. Change the contents of cell F3 to **Total** and AutoFit each of the columns.

h. Apply a PivotTable style of your choice. Insert your name, **Indonesia Tours**, and the current date in a header. Rename the sheet **Indonesia Tours** and move it to after the Client List sheet. Print the Indonesia Tours sheet in portrait orientation, centered horizontally.

i. You have another tour package that explores the Mediterranean and then ventures into Africa. Create a copy of the Indonesia Tours sheet and move it to the end.

j. Change the title of this new sheet to **Mediterranean Tours**. Uncheck the Indonesia field and clear the filter. Choose the Europe and Africa fields. Filter the Europe and Africa fields to show those clients who traveled to Europe and Africa.

k. Change the title in the header to **Mediterranean Tours**. Print the Mediterranean Tours sheet in portrait orientation, centered horizontally. Save the workbook as ATT Client Table 2 to your solution file location.

ON YOUR OWN

BRADFORD SUPPLIERS TABLE ★

1. Bradford Building Supply needs you to create a table to hold supplier information such as company name, location, sales representative, and product category (such as wood, hardware, hand tools, electric tools, and so on). Enter at least 20 records in an Excel table with the appropriate fields. Format the table in an attractive manner. Sort the table by the supplier's state. Print the sorted table with your name and the date in the header, in portrait orientation, centered horizontally. Filter the table to display suppliers of the same category of product. Enter a total row to count the number of records. Print the filtered table with your name and the date in the header, in portrait orientation, centered horizontally. Save the workbook as Bradford Suppliers to your solution file location.

SOCCER LEAGUE ROSTER ★★

2. You have a summer internship working in your town's community activities department. You have been asked to create a database of players enrolled in the spring soccer program in order to divide them into the various teams. Create a table that lists the players' names, addresses, phone numbers, ages, and positions. Format the table in an attractive manner. Enter 30 records in the table. Include your name as one of the records and a position of goalie. Sort the database by player name, position, and age. Print the sorted table with your name and the date in the header, in portrait orientation, centered horizontally. Filter the table to show only goalies. Print the filtered table with your name and the date in the header, in portrait orientation, centered horizontally. Save the workbook as Spring Soccer League to your solution file location.

KIDS EXPRESS INVENTORY ANALYSIS ★★

3. The Kids Express Toy Company needs help with its inventory. Create a table that has 20 inventory records. The records should contain a product identification number, description, wholesale distributor, wholesale price, retail price, and quantity on hand. Format the table in an attractive manner. Sort the records by distributor. Print the sorted table with your name and the date in the header, in portrait orientation, centered horizontally. Filter the records to display a selected distributor and total the quantity on hand for that distributor. Print the filtered table with your name and the date in the header, in portrait orientation, centered horizontally. Filter the table next to find all items with a retail price higher than a selected value. Print the filtered table with your name and the date in the header, in portrait orientation, centered horizontally. Save the workbook as Toy Inventory to your solution file location.

CLEANING SERVICE CUSTOMER LIST ★★★

4. Desert Rescue Cleaning wants to keep track of its customers with an Excel worksheet database. Create a worksheet database that includes customer ID number, cleaning address with suite or apartment number, contact name, phone number, and square footage. Format the worksheet in an attractive manner. Enter 15 records into the database. Enter your name as the contact for the first record. Sort the database by contact name. Filter the list to display only those records with a square footage larger than a specified value. Enter functions to display the minimum and

LAB EXERCISES

maximum square footage values. Include appropriate labels. Enter your name and the current date as a header to the worksheets. Print the filter results. Save the workbook as Cleaning Company Customers to your solution file location.

CHANGING HANDS INVENTORY PLANNING ★ ★ ★

5. The Changing Hands Bookstore has a challenge keeping track of its book inventory. To demonstrate how they might use Excel to maintain their inventory records and how to use those records for analysis, you have agreed to develop a demonstration workbook. Create a table that includes at least 25 titles. Include an inventory number, title, author, ISBN number, number of copies on hand, ideal number of copies to have on hand, and status. Status will be either "order" or "hold." Whenever actual inventory is less than the ideal, the table will indicate "order." Otherwise, the table will indicate "hold." Name this sheet **Store Inventory**. Create a PivotTable on a new worksheet that displays only the title and ISBN number for those items with "order" status. Format this table appropriately and apply a PivotTable style of your choice. Name this sheet **Analysis**. Print the workbook with your name and the date in the header, in portrait orientation, centered horizontally. Save the Inventory worksheet as CHB Inventory to your solution file location.

Working Together 2: Importing Access Data, Sharing Workbooks, and Creating a Web Page

CASE STUDY

Downtown Internet Café

On a weekly basis, you need to check the inventory on hand of certain items. If some items are overstocked, such as a certain type of coffee beans, you run a special on them to lower inventory. On the other hand, if certain items are low, you reorder the item from the vendor. The inventory information is maintained in an Access database table. You plan to import the table into Excel 2010 to quickly analyze the inventory numbers. Then you will share the Excel workbook of this information with Evan so he can make changes directly in the worksheet.

The second project you are working on is to make the bonus dollars award information available to customers on the Café's Web site so they can check their award status. To do this, you will convert the monthly bonus awards worksheet to a Web page.

Importing data from Access allows you to analyze the table information using Excel.

Using Web Page preview displays a worksheet in the browser so you can see how it will look before converting it to a Web page.

Importing Data

The inventory information is maintained in an Access database table. You have found, however, that it is easier to use Excel to analyze the inventory numbers. To do this, you will import the information in the Access database table into Excel 2010. **Importing** converts external data that has been saved in another format into a format that can be used by the application. **External data** is data such as a database or text file that is stored outside the application, in this case Excel.

IMPORTING ACCESS TABLE DATA TO EXCEL

You want to import the data from the Vendors table of the Café Supplies Access database to an Excel workbook so you can more easily analyze the inventory-on-hand data.

1

- **Start Excel 2010.**

- **Open the Data tab.**

- **Click** From Access **in the Get External Data group.**

- **Select** exwt2_Café Supplies.accdb **from your data file location.**

- **Click** Open .

Your screen should be similar to Figure 1

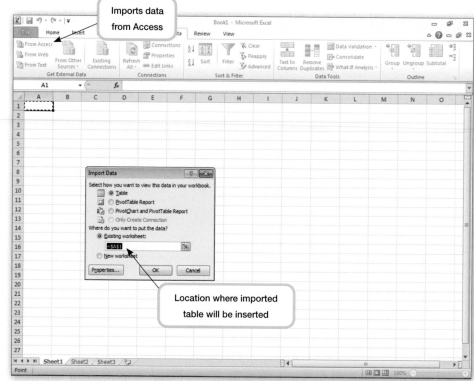

Figure 1

In the Import Data dialog box, you need to specify how you want the data displayed and where you want the data inserted. The default selections, as a table in cell A1 of the worksheet, is appropriate. When specifying the location, be careful to select an area that is empty below and to the right of the selected cell so that any existing data in the worksheet is not overwritten.

2

● If necessary, choose Table from the Import Data dialog box.

● Click [OK].

Your screen should be similar to Figure 2

Access database table imported into Excel worksheet as a table

	A	B	C	D	E	F	G	H	I	J
1	Item #	Description	# On Hand	Special Order	Vendor Name	Contact	Address	City	State	Zip Cod
2	1100	Stirrers	12	N	Basics Restaurant Supply	Mandy Swanson	13990 N. Central Ave.	Phoenix	AZ	84317-
3	1101	Coffee filters	45	N	Basics Restaurant Supply	Mandy Swanson	13990 N. Central Ave.	Phoenix	AZ	84317-
4	1102	Napkins	50	N	Basics Restaurant Supply	Mandy Swanson	13990 N. Central Ave.	Phoenix	AZ	84137-
5	1104	Cups-small	5	N	Basics Restaurant Supply	Mandy Swanson	13990 N. Central Ave.	Phoenix	AZ	84317-
6	1105	Cups-medium	80	N	Basics Restaurant Supply	Mandy Swanson	13990 N. Central Ave.	Phoenix	AZ	84317-
7	1106	Cups-large	67	N	Basics Restaurant Supply	Mandy Swanson	13990 N. Central Ave.	Phoenix	AZ	84317-
8	1108	Sugar	78	N	Basics Restaurant Supply	Mandy Swanson	13990 N. Central Ave.	Phoenix	AZ	84317-
9	1109	Sugar substitute	34	N	Basics Restaurant Supply	Mandy Swanson	13990 N. Central Ave.	Phoenix	AZ	84317-
10	1110	Powdered cream	123	N	Basics Restaurant Supply	Mandy Swanson	13990 N. Central Ave.	Phoenix	AZ	84317-
11	1720	Decaf Viennese	34	Y	Pure Processing	Nancy Young	1124 Mariner Rd.	Half Moon Bay	CA	94019
12	1721	Decaf Sumatra	56	N	Pure Processing	Nancy Young	1124 Mariner Rd.	Half Moon Bay	CA	94019
13	1722	Decaf Guatemala	83	N	Pure Processing	Nancy Young	1124 Mariner Rd.	Half Moon Bay	CA	94019
14	1723	Decaf Colombian	9	N	Pure Processing	Nancy Young	1124 Mariner Rd.	Half Moon Bay	CA	94019
15	1724	Decaf Dark	24	N	Pure Processing	Nancy Young	1124 Mariner Rd.	Half Moon Bay	CA	94019
16	2000	Business cards	6	Y	Pro Printing	Dan O'Dell	373 Hayden Rd.	Mesa	AZ	85205-
17	2343	Herbal teas	57	N	Tea Time	Sandy Price	3010 Washington St.	Napa	CA	94019
18	2575	Coffee mints	1	Y	Tasty Delights	Lorelei Tan	772 China Lane	Redwood City	CA	94065
19	2900	Brochures	23	N	Pro Printing	Dan O'Dell	373 Hayden Rd.	Mesa	AZ	85205-
20	2924	Coffee mugs	12	Y	Central Ceramics		772 Hayden Road	Scottsdale	AZ	85254
21	3520	Colombian coffee	57	N	Better Beverages, Inc.	Pat Lawry	212 Pinkton Rd.	Seattle	WA	73210-
22	3521	Kenya coffee	49	N	Better Beverages, Inc.	Pat Lawry	212 Pinkton Rd.	Seattle	WA	73210-
23	3522	Guatemala coffee	0	N	Better Beverages, Inc.	Pat Lawry	212 Pinkton Rd.	Seattle	WA	73210-
24	3523	Java coffee	38	N	Better Beverages, Inc.	Pat Lawry	212 Pinkton Rd.	Seattle	WA	73210-
25	3524	Arabian coffee	45	N	Better Beverages, Inc.	Pat Lawry	212 Pinkton Rd.	Seattle	WA	73210-
26	3525	Sumatra coffee	11	N	Better Beverages, Inc.	Pat Lawry	212 Pinkton Rd.	Seattle	WA	73210-
27	3526	Ethiopian coffee	2	Y	Better Beverages, Inc.	Pat Lawry	212 Pinkton Rd.	Seattle	WA	73210-

Sheet1 Sheet2 Sheet3

Figure 2

The database table is converted to an Excel table with the field names in the first row of the worksheet and the records beginning in row 2. The column heads and column widths are formatted as they appeared in the Access table.

ANALYZING THE TABLE

Now the data can be manipulated using Excel commands and features. You want to find out how much coffee is on hand to determine what coffee specials to offer next week. Because the data is set up as a table, you can filter the data and use Excel functions to calculate values.

1

- Change the table style to Medium 11.

- Filter the Vendor Name column to show only Better Beverages, Inc.

- Sort the # On Hand field in ascending sort order.

- Display a total row and enter a SUM function to calculate the total coffee on hand.

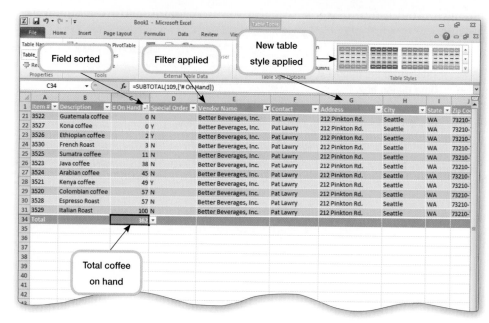

Figure 3

Your screen should be similar to Figure 3

You can now easily see that the Italian Roast coffee quantity on hand is very high and decide to offer a special on that item. At the same time, you need to order several coffees whose quantity is very low. Next, you will create a column to be used to specify the order amount so that Evan can confirm your ordering decisions.

2

- Right-click on any cell in the Special Order column.

- Select Insert and choose Table Columns to the Left.

- Enter Order Amt as the new column label.

- Best fit all columns.

- Move to cell D21.

Figure 4

Your screen should be similar to Figure 4

Collaborating on Workbook Data

Now you want to enter your suggested orders for Evan to review. Collaborating on documents, such as creating a travel brochure using Word 2010 or preparing a budget using Excel 2010, is a team effort. One person is typically responsible for assembling the document, but several people may be involved in reviewing the content. Office 2010 includes many features that make it easy to collaborate or work with others to complete a project. These features include the capability to circulate documents for review; to insert, view, and edit comments; and to track and accept or reject proposed changes.

To make online reviewing of documents easier, you can track changes made to a document. **Tracked changes** identify any insertion, deletion, or formatting change that is made to the document. Typically a document is sent out for review by several people. When it is returned to the author, a document that has been edited using tracked changes can then be quickly reviewed to evaluate the suggested changes. As the author reviews tracked changes, each change can be accepted or rejected as appropriate.

To show Evan what order amounts you are suggesting, you will use the Track Changes feature. However, before you can turn on this feature, the table needs to be converted to a range.

1

• Click **Convert to Range** and click **OK** in response to the advisory message.

• Click **Track Changes** in the Changes group of the Review tab and choose Highlight Changes.

• Choose Track changes while editing from the Highlight Changes dialog box.

• Click **OK**.

• If prompted, click **OK** to verify that you want to save the file.

• Save the workbook as Café Supplies to your solution file location.

Figure 5

When Track Changes is enabled, the workbook status is also changed to shared and [Shared] appears in the title bar. When a workbook status is shared, the workbook can be made available to others on a server and can be changed and manipulated simultaneously.

Your screen should be similar to Figure 5

Now you want to enter the order amounts. As you do so, the worksheet will display markup of the tracked changes.

2

● Click in the Data tab to turn on filtering.

● Filter the Vendor Name column to show only Better Beverages, Inc.

● If necessary, sort the # On Hand field in ascending sort order.

● Enter the following data in the Order Amt column for the specified items:

Guatemala	25
Kona	25
Ethiopian	25
French Roast	50

● Point to the last cell entry.

Your screen should be similar to Figure 6

Figure 6

A small blue triangle appears in the corner of each changed cell that indicates that the cell has been changed since the Track Changes feature was turned on. Additionally, a cell comment appears showing who made the change and when, and what information was changed.

As you look at the order amounts, you decide to increase the order for Guatemala coffee.

3

- Change the Guatemala coffee order amount to **30**.

- Point to the Guatemala order amount to see the updated comment.

Your screen should be similar to Figure 7

Figure 7

The comment displays updated information about the change made to the cell.

4

- Save and close the workbook.

The workbook is saved with the shared workbook status enabled. Next, you will provide a copy of the workbook to Evan via e-mail containing your proposed orders for him to review.

COMPARING AND MERGING DOCUMENTS

While checking your e-mail for new messages, you see that Evan has returned the workbook file you sent to him to review. As you requested, he saved it using a new file name. When you receive changes from multiple reviewers for the same file, the easiest way to review them is to combine or merge the documents together. This way you can review the changes from a single document.

You will first open the original document you sent to Evan. Then you will merge the file containing his changes with the original. When merging workbook files, the files must be in the same folder and the shared workbook file name must be unique from the original file name. You also may need to add the Compare and Merge Workbooks command to the Quick Access Toolbar.

If the 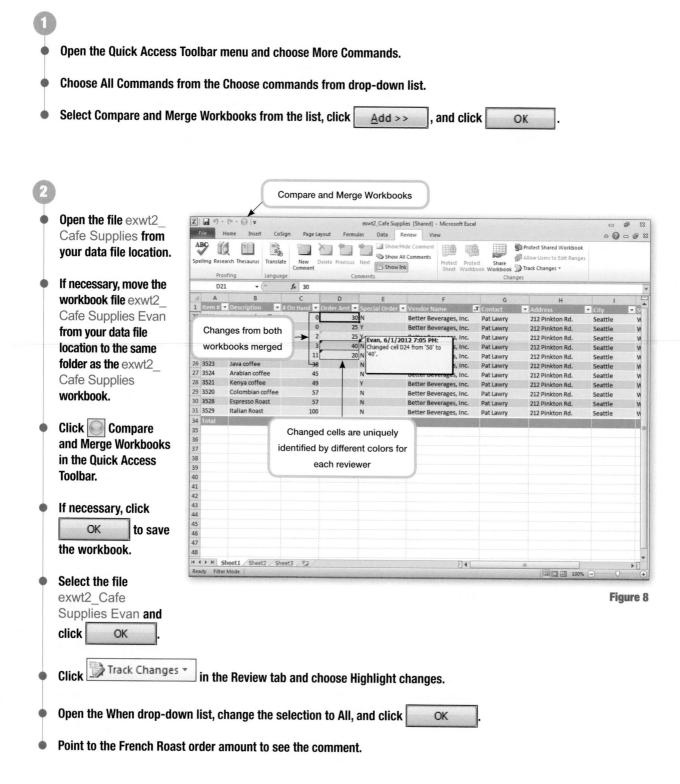 Compare and Merge Workbooks icon is not displayed in the Quick Access Toolbar, follow step 1; otherwise, skip to step 2.

1

● Open the Quick Access Toolbar menu and choose More Commands.

● Choose All Commands from the Choose commands from drop-down list.

● Select Compare and Merge Workbooks from the list, click ⟨ Add >> ⟩, and click ⟨ OK ⟩.

2

Compare and Merge Workbooks

● Open the file exwt2_ Cafe Supplies from your data file location.

● If necessary, move the workbook file exwt2_ Cafe Supplies Evan from your data file location to the same folder as the exwt2_ Cafe Supplies workbook.

Changes from both workbooks merged

Evan, 6/1/2012 7:05 PM: Changed cell D24 from '50' to '40'.

● Click ⊙ Compare and Merge Workbooks in the Quick Access Toolbar.

● If necessary, click ⟨ OK ⟩ to save the workbook.

Changed cells are uniquely identified by different colors for each reviewer

● Select the file exwt2_Cafe Supplies Evan and click ⟨ OK ⟩.

● Click ⟨ Track Changes ⟩ in the Review tab and choose Highlight changes.

● Open the When drop-down list, change the selection to All, and click ⟨ OK ⟩.

● Point to the French Roast order amount to see the comment.

Figure 8

Your screen should be similar to Figure 8

Having Trouble?

The colors used to identify the tracked changes may be different on your screen.

The changes from Evan's workbook have been combined with the original workbook. Excel automatically assigns unique colors to the tracked changes made by each reviewer. Evan made two changes to the worksheet: he revised the French Roast order amount and added an order for the Sumatra coffee.

ACCEPTING AND REJECTING CHANGES

Now you are ready to review the changes. In a document where many responses were received, it is helpful to use the Accept/Reject feature to quickly move from one tracked change to another and make a decision regarding whether to keep or reject the change.

1

● Click and choose Accept/Reject Changes.

● Click **OK** to accept the default settings in the Select Changes to Accept or Reject dialog box.

● If necessary, move the dialog box to see the Order Amt column.

Your screen should be similar to Figure 9

Figure 9

The first tracked change (based on the date and time associated with the change) made to the workbook is identified with a moving border. The dialog box displays the single change that was made in that cell. Since Evan did not change the Kona order, you will accept the change.

Click **Accept**.

Your screen should be similar to Figure 10

Figure 10

The number is accepted and the next tracked change is identified. If you do not want to accept a change, click **Reject** and the original value is reentered. You will try this feature by rejecting this change.

Click **Reject**.

Your screen should be similar to Figure 11

Figure 11

The order amount you entered is removed from the cell and the previous entry, a blank, is restored. The next tracked change shows both your order amount and Evan's. Frequently when reviewing tracked changes from multiple workbooks, there may be conflicting changes that need to be resolved. Selecting one of the suggested changes replaces the current entry in the worksheet. You need to select the change you want to use. In this case, you will accept Evan's change.

● Select Evan's change from the list.

● Click **Accept**.

Your screen should be similar to Figure 12

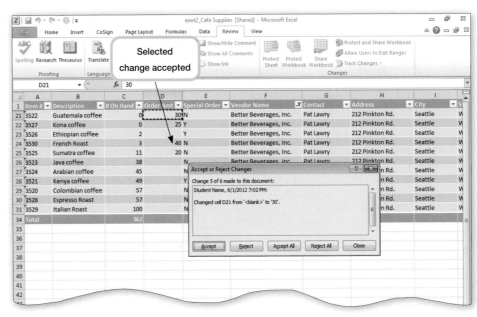

Figure 12

Because you know that all the remaining changes are correct, you will accept them all.

● Click **Accept All**.

● Enter **25** for the Ethiopian coffee order again.

● Click **Share Workbook** and clear the Allow changes option.

● Click **OK** and then click **Yes**.

● Save the workbook as Coffee Orders to your solution file location.

Your screen should be similar to Figure 13

Figure 13

The last project Evan has asked you to look into is to make the Bonus Dollars award information available to customers on the Café's Web site so they can check how much they earned each month. To do this, you will convert the Excel worksheet to a Web page.

Concept Web Page

A **Web page** is a document that can be used on the World Wide Web (WWW) and displayed in a browser. A **browser** is a program that connects to remote computers and displays the Web pages you request. The browser interprets the HTML commands that are included in the Web page in order to know how to display the page contents. **HTML** (Hypertext Markup Language) is a programming language used to create Web pages. HTML commands control the display of information on a page, such as font colors and sizes, and how an item will be processed. HTML also allows users to click on hyperlinks and jump to other locations on the same page, other pages in the same site, or other sites and locations on the WWW.

PREVIEWING THE WEB PAGE

NOTE This section assumes that a Web browser is installed on your computer. The figures show the use of Microsoft Internet Explorer 8.

Several changes needed to be made to the worksheet before it could be used on the Web. First you converted all the formulas to values and removed the weekly amounts and the Bonus Rate information. Then you removed the graphic and all cell comments. Finally, you removed and modified fill colors and text colors to match other pages on the Web site.

Close the Coffee Orders workbook.

Open the workbook file exwt2_March Bonus Dollars Web.

Your screen should be similar to Figure 14

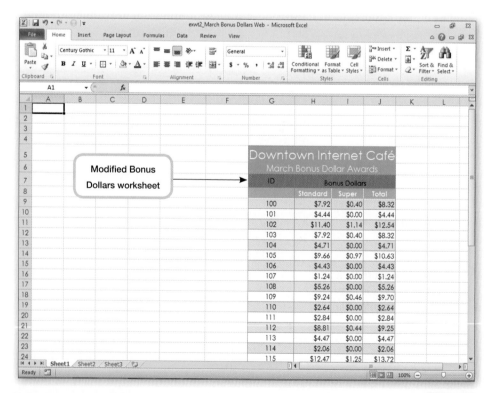

Figure 14

Now the only information that is included in the worksheet is the summary information for the month. Before you convert the worksheet to a Web page, you want to preview how it will look as a Web page first. To do this, you use the Web Page Preview command on the Quick Access Toolbar. If the Web Page Preview icon is not displayed in the Quick Access Toolbar, follow step 2; otherwise, skip to step 3.

2

- Open the Quick Access Toolbar menu and choose More Commands.

- Choose All Commands from the Choose commands from drop-down list.

- Select Web Page Preview from the list, click [Add >>], and click [OK].

3

- Click Web Page Preview in the Quick Access Toolbar.

- If necessary, maximize the browser window.

Your screen should be similar to Figure 15

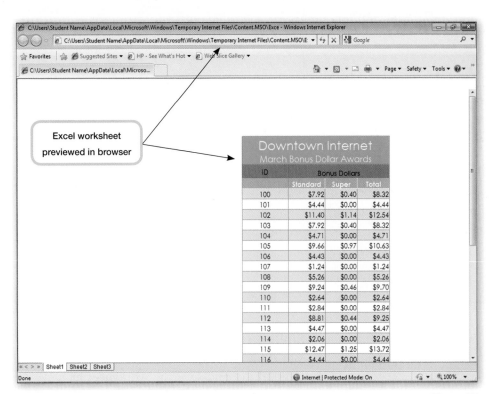

Figure 15

The browser on your system opens and displays the worksheet as it would appear when converted to a Web page. Although the information looks good, you decide to add a background image to make it more interesting.

ADDING A WORKSHEET BACKGROUND

A background is a graphic that is repeated to fill the viewing area of the sheet. You will add an image of a coffee cup with milk, coffee, and sugar being added behind the worksheet content. Adding an image to the background is similar to inserting a picture or clip art on the worksheet. Because background patterns are designed for viewing only, they do not print when you print the worksheet data.

1

- Close the browser application.

- Click 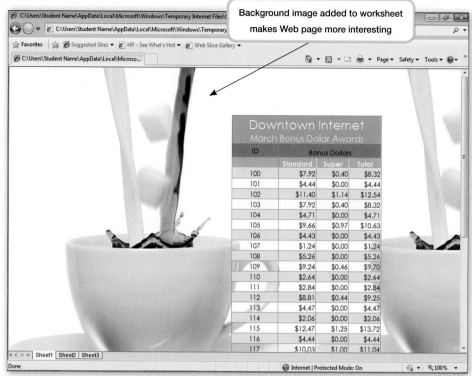 in the Page Setup group of the Page Layout tab.

- Choose exwt2_Cup from your data file location.

- Click **Insert**.

- Preview the Web page in your browser.

Your screen should be similar to Figure 16

Background image added to worksheet makes Web page more interesting

Figure 16

Additional Information

To remove a background, click 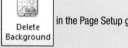 in the Page Setup group.

A repeated pattern of coffee cups appears behind the worksheet data.

SAVING THE WORKSHEET AS A WEB PAGE

You think the background makes the worksheet more interesting and decide to go ahead and save the worksheet as a Web page. You can save the entire workbook, a worksheet, or selected portions of a worksheet as a Web page. Additionally, the worksheet can be saved with or without interactivity. When it is saved with interactivity, users can manipulate data and formatting, switch between sheets, and change formulas while viewing the worksheet in the browser. When saved without interactivity, the data appears as it would in Excel, but users cannot change or interact with the data in the browser.

1

● Close the browser.

● Open the File menu and choose Save as.

● If necessary, select the location where you save your files.

● From the Save as type list box, choose Web Page.

Your screen should be similar to Figure 17

Figure 17

Saves workbook as a Web page file

Additional Information

You also can preselect a range to use as the area to save as a Web page.

In the Save As dialog box, you enter a name for the Web page file and specify whether you want the entire workbook or the current selection saved as your Web page contents. To retain the background image, you need to save the entire workbook as a Web page. You also can add a title that will appear centered over the selection and add interactivity to your Web page. You will save the entire workbook without interactivity as the contents for the Web page. Because the worksheet already contains its own title, you will not add a title.

2

● If necessary, choose Entire Workbook.

● Change the file name to March Bonus Dollars Web.

● Click [Save] and click [Yes] in response to the informational dialog box.

MAKING A WEB PAGE PUBLIC

Now that you have created a Web page, in order for others to see it, you need to make it available on the Internet. The steps that you take to make your pages public depend on how you want to share them. There are two main avenues: on your local network or intranet for limited access by people within an organization or on the Internet for access by anyone using the WWW. To make pages available to other people on your network, save your Web pages to a network location. To make your Web pages available on the WWW, you need to either install Web server software on your computer or locate an Internet service provider that allocates space for Web pages.

Adding a Watermark

Finally, you want to save the workbook again as an Excel file and include a Draft watermark to show that the file is not final. A **watermark** is text or pictures that appear behind text in a document. Unlike Word 2010, where a watermark is inserted directly in the document page, in Excel 2010, the graphic is inserted in the worksheet header or footer area. The graphic can be sized to fill the entire page. You also can modify the graphic's color to make it appear behind the worksheet text, mimicking how a watermark appears in a text document.

1

- **Save the workbook as an Excel workbook with the file name** March Bonus Dollars Web Draft **to your solution file location.**

- **Click** **in the Text group of the Insert tab.**

- **Click** [Picture] **in the Header & Footer Elements group of the Header & Footer Tools Design tab.**

- **Select** exwt2_Draft **from your data file location and click** Insert **.**

- **Click** Format Picture **and increase the Height Scale to 125%.**

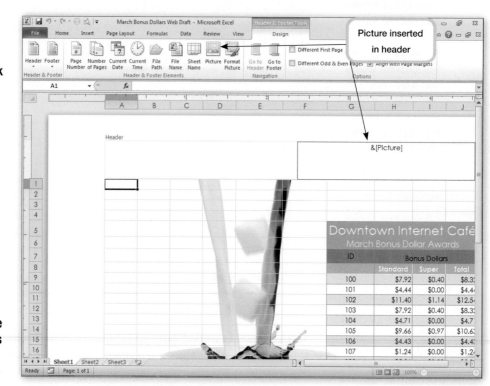

Figure 18

A picture placeholder is displayed in the header until you make the worksheet area active again. You will add your name and date to the header and then preview and print the worksheet in landscape orientation.

Additional Information

Both the height and width scales will change together because the Lock Aspect Ratio option is enabled.

- **Open the Picture tab in the Format Picture dialog box and choose Washout from the Color drop-down list.**

- **Click** OK **.**

Your screen should be similar to Figure 18

2

- Enter your name and the current date in the right header section.

- Click in the worksheet to make it the active area.

- Open the File menu and choose Print to view a preview of the draft.

Your screen should be similar to Figure 19

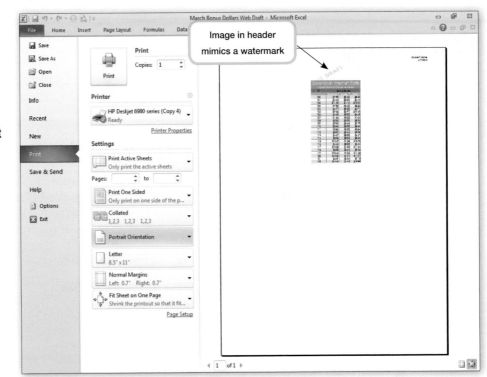

Figure 19

Notice the preview of the March Bonus Dollars worksheet does not include the cups background image. This is because background images are designed for viewing only and will not print.

3

- Print the worksheet.

- Save the workbook.

- Open the Quick Access Toolbar menu and choose More Commands.

- Click [Reset ▼] and choose Reset only Quick Access Toolbar.

- Click [Yes] and then click [OK].

- Exit Excel.

Additional Information

You also can individually remove commands from the Quick Access Toolbar by right-clicking them and selecting Remove from Quick Access Toolbar.

KEY TERMS

browser EXWT2.14	import EXWT2.2
export EXWT2.2	tracked changes EXWT2.5
external data EXWT2.2	watermark EXWT2.15
HTML EXWT2.14	Web page EXWT2.14

COMMAND SUMMARY

Command	Shortcut	Action
Quick Access Toolbar		
Compare and Merge Workbooks		Merges multiple shared workbook changes
Web Page Preview		Displays the worksheet in the browser
Page Layout tab		
Page Setup group		
Orientation		Changes orientation between Portrait and Landscape
Background		Displays an image as the background on a worksheet
Delete Background		Removes the background image from the worksheet
Data tab		
Get External Data group		
From Access		Imports data from Access into a worksheet
Review tab		
Changes group		
Share Workbook		Changes workbook status to shared to allow multiple people to work on it at the same time
Track Changes /Highlight		Identifies all changes made to the worksheet, including insertions, deletions, and formatting changes
Track Changes /Accept/Reject Changes		Cycles through all tracked changes and allows you to make a decision regarding whether to keep or reject the change

STEP-BY-STEP

MEGA MEDIA WAREHOUSE EMPLOYEE REWARDS WEB PAGE ★

1. The Mega Media Warehouse employee rewards program is running well now that you are tracking employee sales using the Excel table you recently set up. However, employees are always asking you for their latest sales information. Rather than have to look it up for each employee, you decide to share the information on the company's Web site. To do this, you will create a Web page using the information in the Mega Media Warehouse Employee Rewards workbook (Lab 6, Step-by-Step exercise 3).

   a. Open the workbook Employee Rewards. (If this file is not available, open exwt2_Employee Rewards).

   b. Sort the table by Employee Number.

   c. Convert the table to a range.

   d. Delete the graphic. Move the worksheet titles to the left into column A.

   e. Delete the last name and first name columns.

   f. Insert three columns at the beginning of the worksheet.

   g. Save the workbook as Employee Rewards Web Page.

   h. Add a page background using the exwt2_Awards image.

   i. Preview the worksheet as a Web page.

   j. Make any improvements to the layout and design you like.

   k. Save the worksheet changes you have made both as an Excel workbook and with the same name as a Web page.

CAROLINA COTTAGE RENTALS ★★

2. Alice works at Carolina Cottage Rentals. Her manager has informed her that they will be running a discount on cottage rentals in Atlantic Beach and Emerald Isle. Consequently she wants you to create an attractive flyer that can be sent to customers and agents so that they can see which properties are available. Alice has been tracking cottage availability in Access but decides that it would be easier to filter the data using Excel. Since she needs to find out which properties are available in these cities, she plans to use the information in the Access Gallery database file and analyze it using Excel.

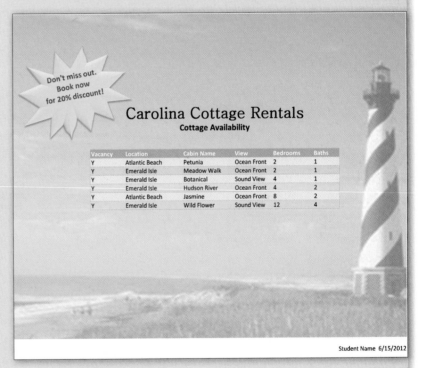

a. Open the workbook exwt2_Carolina Cottage Flyer.

b. Import the **Cottage Availability** table from the exwt2_Carolina Cottage Rentals Access database file to cell D12.

c. Add the subtitle **Cottage Availability** on row 10.

d. Delete column I.

e. Filter the Location column to show only the Emerald Isle and Atlantic Beach properties. Filter the Vacancy column to show only the available cottages.

f. Sort the list in ascending order by bedrooms available.

g. Switch to Page Layout view and add a footer with your name and today's date.

h. Insert file exwt2_coast.jpg as a watermark. Make the following changes to its formatting:

● Increase the scale to 350%.

● Change the color to Washout.

● Change the brightness to 70%.

● Change the contrast to 20%.

i. Make any changes you want to the formatting of the table. Appropriately size the columns.

j. Save the workbook as Cottage Availability.

k. Print the filtered list.

l. Close the file.

EXCEL 2010 COMMAND SUMMARY

COMMAND	SHORTCUT	ACTION
Excel Button		Starts Excel program
Quick Access Toolbar		
Save **Save**	Ctrl + **S**	Saves document using same file name
Undo	Ctrl + **Z**	Reverses last editing or formatting change
Redo	Ctrl + **Y**	Restores changes after using Undo
Compare and Merge Workbooks		Merges multiple shared workbook changes
Web Page Preview		Displays the worksheet in the browser
File Tab		
Save	Ctrl + **S**	Saves file using same file name
Save As	F12	Saves file using a new file name
Save As /Tools/General Options		Adds a password to the workbook file
Open	Ctrl + **O**	Opens an existing workbook file
Close	Ctrl + F4	Closes open workbook file
Info/Properties		Displays information about a file
Info/Check for Issues/Inspect Document		Starts Document Inspector to locate and remove hidden and private information
Info/Protect Workbook/Mark as Final		Marks file as final and changes it to read-only
Info/Protect Workbook/Add a Digital Signature		Adds a digital signature to a file
Print/ Orientation /Landscape		Changes page orientation to landscape
Print/ Scale: /Fit To		Scales the worksheet to fit a specified number of pages
Options		Displays and changes program settings
Options /Add-Ins/Excel Add-Ins/ Solver Add-In		Adds Solver tool to Ribbon

EXCEL 2010 COMMAND SUMMARY

COMMAND	SHORTCUT	ACTION
📄 Options /Advanced/Indicators only		Displays comment indicators and comments when you point to a cell
📄 Options /Proofing/ AutoCorrect Options... /AutoFormat As You Type/ Internet and network paths with hyperlinks		Automatically formats a hyperlink
⊠ Exit or ✕	Alt + F4	Exits Excel program

Home Tab

Clipboard Group

COMMAND	SHORTCUT	ACTION
📋 Paste	Ctrl + V	Pastes selections stored in system Clipboard
📋 Paste /Paste Special/Paste		Inserts object as an embedded object
📋 Paste /Paste Special/Paste Link		Inserts object as a linked object
✂ Cut	Ctrl + X	Cuts selected data from the worksheet
📋 Copy	Ctrl + C	Copies selected data to system Clipboard
🖌 Format Painter		Copies formatting from one place and applies it to another

Font Group

COMMAND	SHORTCUT	ACTION
Calibri ▾ Font		Changes text font
11 ▾ Font Size		Changes text size
B Bold	Ctrl + B	Bolds selected text
I Italic	Ctrl + I	Italicizes selected text
U ▾ Underline	Ctrl + U	Underlines selected text
⊞ ▾ Borders		Adds border to specified area of cell or range

COMMAND	SHORTCUT	ACTION
Fill Color		Adds color to cell background
Font Color		Adds color to text
Alignment Group		
Align Text Left		Left-aligns entry in cell space
Center		Center-aligns entry in cell space
Align Text Right		Right-aligns entry in cell space
Decrease Indent		Reduces the margin between the left cell border and cell entry
Increase Indent		Indents cell entry
Merge & Center		Combines selected cells into one cell and centers cell contents in new cell
Wrap Text		Makes all content visible in a cell by displaying it on multiple lines
Number Group		
General ▼ Number Format		Applies selected number formatting to selection
$ ▼ Accounting Number Format		Applies Accounting number format to selection
% Percent Style		Applies Percent Style format to selection
Increase Decimal		Increases number of decimal places
Decrease Decimal		Decreases number of decimal places
		Formats cells
Styles group		
Conditional Formatting ▼		Formats cells by applying Highlight Cells Rules, Top/Bottom Rules, Data Bars, Color Scales, and Icon Sets to selected cells based on selected criteria
Cell Styles ▼		Opens Cell Styles gallery to apply predefined combinations of colors, effects, and formats to selected cells

EXCEL 2010 COMMAND SUMMARY

COMMAND	SHORTCUT	ACTION
Cell Styles /Modify		Modifies existing cell style
Cells Group		
Insert /Insert Cells		Inserts blank cells, shifting existing cells down
Insert /Insert Cut Cells		Inserts cut row of data into new worksheet row, shifting existing rows down
Insert /Insert Copied Cells		Inserts copied row into new worksheet row, shifting existing rows down
Insert /Insert Sheet		Inserts a new worksheet into the workbook
Insert /Insert Sheet Rows		Inserts blank rows, shifting existing rows down
Insert /Insert Sheet Columns		Inserts blank columns, shifting existing columns right
Insert /Insert Table Row Below	Tab	Adds a new row below the current row in a table
Delete /Delete Sheet Rows		Deletes selected rows, shifting existing rows up
Delete /Delete Sheet Columns		Deletes selected columns, shifting existing columns left
Delete /Delete Sheet		Deletes entire sheet
Format /Row Height		Changes height of selected row
Format /AutoFit Row Height		Changes row height to match the tallest cell entry
Format /Column Width		Changes width of selected column
Format /AutoFit Column Width		Changes column width to match widest cell entry
Format /Default Width		Returns column width to default width
Format /Rename Sheet		Renames sheet
Format /Move or Copy Sheet		Moves or copies selected sheet
Format /Hide & Unhide		Hides and unhides rows and/or columns
Format /Hide & Unhide/Hide Sheet		Hides selected sheets
Format /Hide & Unhide/Unhide Sheet		Redisplays hidden sheets

EXCEL 2010 COMMAND SUMMARY

COMMAND	SHORTCUT	ACTION
Format ▾ /Tab Color		Changes color of sheet tabs
Format ▾ /Protect Sheet		Prevents unwanted changes to the data in a worksheet
Format ▾ /Unprotect Sheet		Removes worksheet protection and allows modification of contents
Format ▾ /Lock cell		Locks a cell to make a cell editable when protection is enabled. Toggles between locking and unlocking a cell
Format ▾ /Format Cells/Number/Special		Applies selected special format to number entries
Editing Group		
Σ ▾ Sum		Calculates the sum of the values in the selected cells
Σ ▾ Sum/Average		Calculates the average of the values in the selected range
Σ ▾ Sum/Max		Returns the largest of the values in the selected range
Σ ▾ Sum/Min		Returns the smallest of the values in the selected range
⬇ ▾ Fill/Right	Ctrl + R	Continues a pattern to adjacent cells to the right
✐ ▾ Clear		Removes both formats and contents from selected cells
✐ ▾ Clear/Clear Formats		Clears formats only from selected cells
✐ ▾ Clear/Clear Contents	Delete	Clears contents only from selected cells
Sort & Filter ▾ /Sort A to Z		Sorts the table column in ascending alphabetical order
Sort & Filter ▾ /Custom Sort		Performs a multilevel sort on the table column
Sort & Filter ▾ /Filter		Turns AutoFilter on or off

EXCEL 2010 COMMAND SUMMARY

COMMAND	SHORTCUT	ACTION
Sort & Filter /Clear		Clears filters from a table
Find & Select /Find	Ctrl + **F**	Locates specified text, numbers, and/or formats
Find & Select /Replace	Ctrl + **H**	Locates specified characters or formats and replaces them with specified replacement characters or format
Find & Select /Go To	Ctrl + **G**	Goes to a specified cell location in worksheet

Insert Tab

Tables Group

PivotTable		Inserts a PivotTable
Table		Converts a range of data into a table

Illustrations Group

Picture		Inserts a picture from a file
Shapes		Creates selected shape
SmartArt		Inserts a SmartArt graphic to visually communicate information

Charts Group

Column		Inserts a column chart
Pie		Inserts a pie chart

WWW.MHHE.COM/OLEARY

EXCEL 2010 COMMAND SUMMARY

COMMAND	SHORTCUT	ACTION
Sparklines Group		
Line		Inserts sparkline in the selected cell
Links Group		
Hyperlink		Inserts a new hyperlink or modifies selected hyperlink
Text Group		
Text Box		Creates a text box
Header & Footer		Adds header or footer to worksheet
Page Layout Tab		
Themes Group		
Themes		Applies selected theme to worksheet
Themes	/Save Current Theme	Saves modified theme settings as a custom theme
Page Setup Group		
Margins	/Narrow	Changes margin settings
Margins	/Custom Margins/Horizontally	Centers worksheet horizontally on page
Margins	/Custom Margins/Vertically	Centers worksheet vertically on page
Orientation		Changes orientation between Portrait and Landscape

EXCEL 2010 COMMAND SUMMARY

COMMAND	SHORTCUT	ACTION
Orientation /Landscape		Changes page orientation to landscape
Print Area /Set Print Area		Sets print area to selected cells
Breaks /Insert Page Break		Inserts page break at cell pointer location
Breaks /Remove Page Break		Removes page break at cell pointer location
Breaks /Reset All Page Breaks		Restores automatic page breaks
Background		Displays an image as the background on a worksheet
Delete Background		Removes the background image from the worksheet
Scale to Fit Group		
Width:		Scales worksheet width to specified number of pages
Height:		Scales worksheet height to specified number of pages
Height: /1 page		Scales worksheet vertically to fit one page
Scale:		Scales worksheet by entering a percentage
Scale: /Fit To		Scales the worksheet to fit a specified number of pages
Sheet Options Group		
Print Gridlines		Displays/hides gridlines for printing

EXCEL 2010 COMMAND SUMMARY

COMMAND	SHORTCUT	ACTION
Formulas Tab		
Function Library Group		
fx Insert Function		Prompts you to select a function from a list and helps you enter the arguments correctly
Σ AutoSum ▾		Enters Sum, Average, Minimum, Maximum, or Count function
Logical ▾		Creates a logical function
Defined Names Group		
Name Manager		Creates, edits, and deletes cell and range names
Define Name ▾		Creates a range name using text in cells
fx Use in Formula ▾		Places selected range name in formula bar or lists names in worksheet
Create from Selection		Automatically generates name from selected cells
Formula Auditing Group		
Show Formulas	Ctrl + `	Displays and hides worksheet formulas
Error Checking ▾		Checks worksheet for formula errors
Watch Window		Opens Watch Window toolbar
Data Tab		
Get External Data Group		
From Access		Imports data from Access into a worksheet
Sort & Filter Group		
A/Z ↓ Sort Smallest to Largest		Sorts a column of data in ascending order
▾↑		Arranges data alphabetically, numerically, or by date

EXCEL 2010 COMMAND SUMMARY

COMMAND	SHORTCUT	ACTION
Filter		Turns AutoFilter on or off
Clear		Redisplays all records
Advanced		Specifies complex criteria to limit records in a query result
Data Tools Group		
Text to Columns		Separates information contained in one cell into two columns
Remove Duplicates		Deletes duplicate rows
Data Validation		Prevents invalid data from being entered into a cell
Data Validation	/Settings/List	Creates a drop-down list
What-If Analysis	/Scenario Manager	Starts Scenario Manager tool to create sets of data for what-if analysis
What-If Analysis	/Goal Seek	Adjusts value in specified cell until a formula dependent on that cell reaches specified result
What-If Analysis	/Data Table	Creates a data table based on specified input values and formulas
Analysis Group		
Solver		Starts Solver tool to perform what-if analysis
Outline Group		
Group		Ties range of cells so they can be collapsed or expanded
Ungroup		Ungroups range of cells
Subtotal		Displays totals for each change in a category
Subtotal	/ Remove All	Removes subtotals from worksheet
Review Tab		
Proofing Group		
ABC Spelling	F7	Spell-checks worksheet

EXCEL 2010 COMMAND SUMMARY

COMMAND	SHORTCUT	ACTION
Thesaurus	Shift + F7	Opens the Thesaurus for the selected word in the Research task pane
Comments Group		
New Comment		Inserts a new comment in selected cell
Edit Comment		Edits comment in selected cell
Delete		Deletes comment in selected cell
Show All Comments		Displays all comments
Next		Displays the next comment
Previous		Displays the previous comment
Changes Group		
Protect Sheet		Prevents unwanted changes to the data in a worksheet
Unprotect Sheet		Removes worksheet protection
Protect Workbook		Prevents unwanted changes to the structure of the workbook; removes workbook protection
Share Workbook		Changes workbook status to shared to allow multiple people to work on it at the same time
Track Changes /Highlight		Identifies all changes made to the worksheet, including insertions, deletions, and formatting changes

EXCEL 2010 COMMAND SUMMARY

COMMAND	SHORTCUT	ACTION
Track Changes ▾ /Accept/Reject Changes		Cycles through all tracked changes and allows you to make a decision regarding whether to keep or reject the change

View Tab

Workbook Views Group

COMMAND	SHORTCUT	ACTION
Normal		Changes worksheet view to Normal
Page Layout		Displays worksheet as it will appear when printed
Page Break Preview		Displays where pages will break when a worksheet is printed

Show Group

COMMAND	SHORTCUT	ACTION
☑ Gridlines		Turns on/off display of gridlines
Delete		Turns on/off display of row and column headings

Zoom Group

COMMAND	SHORTCUT	ACTION
Zoom		Changes magnification of window

Window Group

COMMAND	SHORTCUT	ACTION
New Window		Displays a new window
Arrange All		Arranges open windows vertically, horizontally, tiled, or cascaded
Freeze Panes ▾ /Freeze Panes		Freezes top and/or leftmost panes
Freeze Panes ▾ /Unfreeze Panes		Unfreezes window panes
Split		Divides window into four panes at active cell or removes split
Hide		Hides current workbook
Unhide		Unhides selected workbook

EXCEL 2010 COMMAND SUMMARY

COMMAND	SHORTCUT	ACTION
Picture Tools Format Tab		
Picture Styles Group		
Picture Border ▾		Specifies color, width, and line style for outline of shape
Picture Effects ▾		Adds glow, shadow, and other effects to pictures
Picture Layout ▾		Changes the layout of a picture on the page
Chart Tools Design Tab		
Type Group		
Change Chart Type		Changes to a different type of chart
Data Group		
Switch Row/Column		Swaps the data over the axes
Select Data		Changes the data range included in chart
Location Group		
Move Chart		Moves chart to another sheet in the workbook
Chart Tools Layout Tab		
Labels Group		
Chart Title ▾		Adds, removes, or positions the chart title
Axis Titles ▾		Adds, removes, or positions the axis titles

EXCEL 2010 COMMAND SUMMARY

COMMAND	SHORTCUT	ACTION
Legend		Adds, removes, or positions the chart legend
Data Labels		Adds, removes, or positions the data labels
Background Group		
Chart Wall		Formats chart walls
Chart Tools Format Tab		
Current Selection Group		
Chart Area		Selects an element on the chart
Format Selection		Opens Format dialog box for selected element
Shape Styles Group		
More		Opens Shape Styles gallery
Shape Fill		Adds selected fill to shape
Shape Outline		Specifies color, weight, and type of outline
Shape Effects		Adds selected effect to shape
Design Sparklines Tool Tab		
Style Group		
		Applies pictured style to sparkline
Clear		Removes sparkline
SmartArt Tools Design Tab		
Create Graphics Group		
Add Shape		Adds a shape to an existing SmartArt graphic shape
SmartArt Styles Group		
Change Colors		Changes colors of selected SmartArt graphic

EXCEL 2010 COMMAND SUMMARY

COMMAND	SHORTCUT	ACTION
⯆ More		Opens SmartArt Styles gallery to select overall visual style for SmartArt graphic
Reset Group		
Reset Graphic		Restores SmartArt graphic to original settings
Drawing Tools Format Tab		
Insert Shapes Group		
⯆ More		Opens Shapes gallery to insert ready-made shapes
Shape Styles Group		
⯆ More		Opens Shape Styles gallery to apply a visual style to a shape
Arrange Group		
Rotate ▾		Rotates selected shape
Table Tools Design tab		
Tools Group		
Convert to Range		Converts table to normal range
Table Style Options Group		
☑ Header Row		Formats the top row of the table
☐ Total Row		Adds a total row to the table
☑ Banded Rows		Formats even rows differently from odd rows
☑ First Column		Displays formatting for first column of the table
Table Styles Group		
⯆ More		Opens Table Styles gallery to apply a predefined format and colors to a table
PivotTable Tools Options Tab		
Tools Group		
PivotChart		Inserts a chart based on the PivotTable data

b

Backstage view: Contains commands that allow you to work with your document, unlike the Ribbon that allows you to work in your document; contains commands that apply to the entire document.

Buttons: Graphical elements that perform the associated action when you click on them using the mouse.

c

Clipboard: Where a selection is stored when it is cut or copied.

Commands: Options that carry out a selected action.

Context menu: Also called a shortcut menu; opened by right-clicking on an item on the screen.

Contextual tabs: Also called on-demand tabs; tabs that are displayed only as needed. For example, when you are working with a picture, the Picture Tools tab appears.

Cursor: The blinking vertical bar that marks your location in the document and indicates where text you type will appear; also called the insertion point.

d

Database: A collection of related data.

Default: The standard options used by Office 2010.

Destination: The new location into which a selection that is moved from its original location is inserted.

Dialog box launcher: A button that is displayed in the lower-right corner of a tab group if more commands are available; clicking opens a dialog box or task pane of additional options.

Document window: The large center area of the program window where open application files are displayed.

e

Edit: To revise a document by changing the parts that need to be modified.

Enhanced ScreenTip: Displayed by pointing to a button in the Ribbon; shows the name of the button and the keyboard shortcut.

f

Field: The smallest unit of information about a record; a column in a table.

Font: Type style; also called typeface.

Font size: Size of typeface, given in points.

Format: The appearance of a document.

g

Groups: Part of a tab that contains related items.

h

Hyperlink: Connection to information located in a separate location, such as on a Web site.

i

Insertion point: Also called the cursor; the blinking vertical bar that marks your location in a document and indicates where text you type will appear.

k

Keyboard shortcut: A combination of keys that can be used to execute a command in place of clicking a button.

Keyword: A descriptive word that is associated with the file and can be used to locate a file using a search.

l

Live Preview: A feature that shows you how selected text in a document will appear if a formatting option is chosen.

m

Metadata: Details about the document that describe or identify it, such as title, author name, subject, and keywords; also called document properties.

Mini toolbar: Appears automatically when you select text; displays command buttons for often-used commands from the Font and Paragraph groups that are used to format a document.

o

Office Clipboard: Can store up to 24 items that have been cut or copied.

On-demand tabs: Also called contextual tabs; tabs that are displayed only as needed.

p

Paste Preview: Shows how a Paste Option will affect a selection.

Properties: Shown in a panel along the right side of the Info tab, divided into four groups; information such as author, keywords, document size, number of words, and number of pages.

q

Quick Access Toolbar: Located to the right of the Window button; provides quick access to frequently used commands such as Save, Undo, and Redo.

r

Records: The information about one person, thing, or place; contained in a row of a table.

Ribbon: Below the title bar; provides a centralized location of commands that are used to work in your document.

s

ScreenTip: Also called a tooltip; appears with the command name and the keyboard shortcut.

Scroll bar: Horizontal or vertical, it is used with a mouse to bring additional information into view in a window.

Selection cursor: Cursor that allows you to select an object.

Shortcut menu: A context-sensitive menu, meaning it displays only those commands relevant to the item or screen location; also called a context menu, it is opened by right-clicking on an item on the screen.

Slide: An individual page of a presentation.

Slide shows: Onscreen electronic presentations.

Source: The original location of a selection that is inserted in a new location.

Status bar: At the bottom of the application window; displays information about the open file and features that help you view the file.

t

Tables: A database object consisting of columns and rows.

Tabs: Used to divide the Ribbon into major activity areas.

Tag: A descriptive word that is associated with the file and can be used to locate a file using a search; also called a keyword.

Task pane: A list of additional options opened by clicking the dialog box launcher; also called a dialog box.

Text effects: Enhancements such as bold, italic, and color that are applied to selected text.

Tooltip: Also called a ScreenTip; appears displaying a command name and the keyboard shortcut.

Typeface: A set of characters with a specific design; also commonly referred to as a font.

u

User interface: A set of graphical elements that are designed to help you interact with the program and provide instructions for the actions you want to perform.

v

View buttons: Used to change how the information in the document window is displayed.

w

Worksheet: An electronic spreadsheet, or work-sheet, that is used to organize, manipulate, and graph numeric data.

z

Zoom slider: Located at the far-right end of the status bar; used to change the amount of information displayed in the document window by "zooming in" to get a close-up view or "zooming out" to see more of the document at a reduced view.

3-D Reference: A formula that contains references to cells in other sheets of a workbook; allows you to use data from multiple sheets and to calculate new values based on this data.

a

Absolute Link: An address that includes the complete destination path location.

Absolute Reference: A cell or range reference in a formula whose location does not change when the formula is copied.

Active Cell: The cell your next entry or procedure affects, indicated by a black outline.

Active Sheet: The sheet in which you can work, the name of which appears bold.

Active Workbook: The file that will be affected by changes you make.

Adjacent Range: A rectangular block of adjoining cells.

Adjustable Cell: Cells that can be altered in a what-if analysis.

Alignment: The settings that allow you to change the horizontal and vertical placement and the orientation of an entry in a cell.

Antonym: Words with an opposite meaning.

Area Chart: Shows the magnitude of change over time by emphasizing the area under the curve created by each data series.

Argument: The data a function uses to perform a calculation.

AutoCorrect: A feature that makes some basic assumptions about the text you are typing and, based on these assumptions, automatically corrects the entry.

AutoFill: A feature that makes entering a series of headings easier by logically repeating and extending the series. AutoFill recognizes trends and automatically extends data and alphanumeric headings as far as you specify.

AutoFit: Automatically adjusts the width of the columns to fit the column contents.

AutoRecover: A feature that, when enabled, will automatically save your work and can recover data if the program unexpectedly closes.

b

Bar Chart: Displays data as evenly spaced bars. The categories are displayed along the Y axis and the values are displayed horizontally, placing more emphasis on comparisons and less on time.

Bookmark: A link to a specific worksheet location.

Browser: A program that connects to remote computers and displays requested Web pages.

Bubble Chart: Compares sets of three values. They are similar to a scatter chart with the third value determining the size of the bubble markers.

c

Cascade: The windows are displayed one on top of the other

Category Axis: The X axis, usually the horizontal axis; contains categories.

Category-Axis Title: Clearly describes the information on and/or the format of the X axis.

Cell: The intersection of a row and a column.

Cell Reference: The column letter and row number of the active cell (e.g., A1).

Cell Selector: The black border that surrounds the active cell.

Cell Style: A defined theme-based combination of formats that have been named and that can be quickly applied to a selection.

Character Effect: Font formatting, such as color, used to enhance the appearance of the document.

Chart: A visual representation of data in a worksheet.

Chart Gridlines: Lines extending from the axis line across the plot area that make it easier to read the chart data.

Chart Layout: A predefined set of chart elements that can be quickly applied to a chart. The elements include chart titles, a legend, a data table, or data labels.

Chart Object: A graphic object that is created using charting features. An object can be inserted into a worksheet or into a special chart sheet.

Chart Style: A predefined set of chart formats that can be quickly applied to a chart.

Chart Title: A descriptive label displayed above the charted data that explains the contents of the chart.

Clip Art: Simple drawings.

Column: The vertical stacks of cells in a workbook.

Column Chart: Displays data as evenly spaced bars. They are similar to bar charts, except that categories are organized horizontally and values vertically to emphasize variation over time.

Column Letter: Located across the top of the workbook window; identifies each worksheet column.

Column Name: Full name used to identify a column.

Column-Oriented: When values are listed down a column.

Comment: A note attached to a cell that can be used to help clarify the meaning of the data, provide documentation, or ask a question.

Conditional Formatting: Changes the appearance of a range of cells based on a condition that you specify.

Constant: A value that does not begin with an equal sign and does not change unless you change it directly by typing in another entry.

Copy Area: Range of data to be copied and pasted.

Criteria: The settings a user specifies for a sort on a table.

Custom Dictionary: In the spelling checker, holds words you commonly use but that are not included in the main dictionary.

Custom Template: Specialized template files containing settings that are used as a pattern for creating similar worksheets in new workbooks.

d

Data Label: Labels that correspond to the headings for the worksheet data that is plotted along the X axis.

Data Marker: A bar, area, dot, slice, or other symbol in a chart, representing a single data point or value that originates from a worksheet cell.

Data Series: Related data markers in a chart.

Data Table: A range of cells that is used to quickly calculate multiple what-if versions in one operation and to show the results of all variations in the worksheet.

Default: Predefined settings, used on new blank workbooks.

Defined Name: A name that represents a cell, range of cells, formula, or constant value.

Depth Axis: The Z axis; a third axis, in a 3-D column, 3-D cone, or 3-D pyramid chart; allows data to be plotted along the depth of a chart.

Destination Cell: Cell containing the reference formula in a destination workbook.

Destination File: The document into which an object is inserted

Destination Workbook: The workbook that receives data.

Digital Signature: An electronic encryption-based stamp of authentication that confirms the document originated from the signer and has not been changed.

Doughnut Chart: Similar to pie charts except that they can show more than one data series.

Drawing Object: A graphic element.

e

Embedded Chart: Chart that is inserted into a worksheet; it becomes part of the sheet in which it is inserted and is saved as part of the worksheet when you save the workbook file.

Embedded Object: An object, such as a graphic, created from another program and inserted in the worksheet, becoming part of the sheet in which it is inserted; it is saved as part of the worksheet.

Explode: Separation between the slices of a pie chart to emphasize the data in the categories.

Export: Saving data in another format so that it can be used in an application other than the application in which it was created.

External Data: Data such as a database or text file that is stored outside the application.

External Reference: References the location of a source file and the selection within a document that is linked to the destination file.

External Reference Formula: The formula that links between the source cells and destination cells.

f

Field: The smallest unit of information about a record.

Field Name: A descriptive label used to identify the data stored in the field.

Fill Handle: The black box in the lower-right corner of a selection.

Filter: A restriction placed on records in the table to quickly isolate and display a subset of records.

Find and Replace: A feature that helps you quickly find specific information and automatically replaces it with new information.

Footer: Provides information that appears at the bottom of each page; commonly includes information such as the date and page number.

Form: A formatted worksheet with blank spaces that can be filled in online on an individual computer or on a network, or printed and completed on paper.

Formula: An equation that performs a calculation on data contained in a worksheet. A formula always begins with an equal sign (=) and uses arithmetic operators.

Formula Bar: Below the Ribbon; displays entries as they are made and edited in the workbook window.

Freeze Panes: Prevents the data in the pane from scrolling as you move to different areas in a worksheet.

Function: A prewritten formula that performs certain types of calculations automatically.

g

Global Workbook Level: The level of scope that includes the entire workbook.

Goal Seek: A tool used to find the value needed in one cell to attain a result you want in another cell.

Gradient: A fill option consisting of a gradual progression of colors and shades that can be from one color to another or from one shade to another of the same color.

Graphic: A nontext element or object such as a drawing or picture that can be added to a document.

Group: Two or more objects that behave as a single object when moved or sized. A chart is a group that consists of many separate objects.

Grouping and Outlining: Tools that organize data in a worksheet by showing and hiding different levels of detail for groups of related data.

h

Header: Information appearing at the top of each page.

Header Row: The first row in a table that typically contains column labels.

Heading: Entries that are used to create the structure of the worksheet and describe other worksheet entries.

HLOOKUP Function: A function that searches for a value in the top row of a table, then returns a value in a cell you designate.

Horizontal: A window arrangement where the windows are displayed side-by-side.

HTML: A programming language used to create Web pages.

Hyperlink: A connection or link to a destination location.

i

IF Function: A function that checks to see if certain conditions are met and then takes action based on the results of the check.

Import: Converting external data that has been saved in another format into a format that can be used by the application.

Input Cell: A cell in which a list of values is substituted to see the resulting effect on the related formulas.

k

Keyword: Descriptive term associated with a graphic.

l

Legend: A box that identifies the chart data series and data markers.

Line Chart: Displays data along a line; used to show changes in data over time, emphasizing time and rate of change rather than the amount of change.

Link: Contains references to the location of a source file and the selection within a document that is linked to the destination file.

Linked Object: Information created in one application that is inserted into a document created by another application.

List: A series of rows that contain related data but are not defined as a table.

Live Link: A link that updates the linked object when changes are made to the source file.

Local Worksheet Level: The level of scope that is limited to the worksheet.

Logical Operator: Symbols used in formulas that compare numbers in two or more cells or to a constant.

Lookup Function: Functions that permit you to use worksheet tables as sources of information for formulas and calculations in other parts of the worksheet.

m

Main Dictionary: The dictionary that is supplied with the spelling checker program.

Margin: The blank space outside the printing area around the edges of the paper.

Merged Cell: Two or more cells combined into one.

Mixed Reference: In a formula, either the column letter or the row number is preceded with the $. This makes only the row or column absolute. When a formula containing a mixed cell reference is copied to another location in the worksheet, only the part of the cell reference that is not absolute changes relative to its new location in the worksheet.

Multilevel Sort: A sort done on more than one column or field.

n

Name: A description of a cell or range of cells that can be used in place of cell references.

Name Box: Displays the cell reference.

Nested Function: A function that contains a second or more additional functions enclosed in their own parentheses.

Nonadjacent Range: Two or more selected cells or ranges that are not adjoining.

Number: The digits 0 to 9.

Number Format: Changes the appearance of numbers onscreen and when printed, without changing the way the number is stored or used in calculations.

o

Object: An element that is added to a document.

Objective Cell: The cell that shows the output of numbers in the adjustable cells.

One-Variable Data Table: A table that can contain one or more formulas, and each formula refers to one input cell.

Operand: The values on which a numeric formula performs a calculation, consisting of numbers or cell references.

Operator: A symbol that specifies the type of numeric operation to perform, such as + (addition), − (subtraction), / (division),* (multiplication), % (percent), and ^ (exponentiation).

Order of Precedence: In a formula that contains more than one operator, Excel calculates the formula from left to right and performs the calculation in the following order: percent, exponentiation, multiplication and division, and addition and subtraction.

p

Page Break: The place where one printed page ends and another starts.

Pane: The sections of the window when using the split window feature.

Password: A user-generated code that prevents any unauthorized person from either viewing or saving changes to the workbook.

Picture: A graphic element.

Picture Style: Adds a border around a graphic object that consists of combinations of line, shadow, color, and shape effects.

Pie Chart: Displays data as slices of a circle or pie; shows the relationship of each value in a data series to the series as a whole. Each slice of the pie represents a single value in the series.

PivotChart: An interactive chart that can be used to view and rearrange data.

PivotTable: An interactive table that can be used to summarize and manipulate worksheet data.

Placeholder: A graphic element that is designed to contain specific types of information.

Plot Area: The area within the X- and Y-axis boundaries where the chart appears.

PMT Function: A function that calculates a periodic payment on a loan.

Principle: The amount of a loan.

Print Area: The area you selected for printing; surrounded by a heavy line that identifies the area.

Protection: The feature that controls what information can be changed in a workbook.

r

Radar Chart: Displays a line or area chart wrapped around a central point. Each axis represents a set of data points.

Range: A selection consisting of two or more cells on a worksheet.

Range Reference: Identifies the cells in a range.

Recalculation: When a number in a referenced cell in a formula changes, Excel automatically recalculates all formulas that are dependent upon the changed value.

Record: All the information about one person, thing, or place.

Relative Link: A link that will locate the destination workbook file relative to the location of the current workbook file.

Relative Reference: A cell or range reference in a formula whose location is interpreted in relation to the position of the cell that contains the formula.

Row: Horizontal strings of cells in a workbook.

Row Number: Along the left side of the workbook window; identifies each worksheet row.

Row-Oriented: When values are listed across a row.

s

Sans Serif: Fonts that do not have a flare at the base of each letter, such as Arial and Helvetica.

Scaling: Reducing or enlarging the worksheet contents by a percentage or to fit it to a specific number of pages by height and width.

Scenario: A named set of input values that you can substitute in a worksheet to see the effects of a possible alternative course of action.

Scope: A name's restriction to a location within which the name is recognized without qualification.

Selection Rectangle: Box that surrounds a selected object, indicating that it is a selected object and can now be deleted, sized, moved, or modified.

Serial Value: Data stored as consecutively assigned numbers, such as dates where each day is numbered from the beginning of the 20th century. The date serial values begin with 1.

Series Axis: The Z axis; a third axis, in a 3-D column, 3-D cone, or 3-D pyramid chart; allows data to be plotted along the depth of a chart.

Series Formula: Links a chart object to the source worksheet.

Serif: Fonts that have a flare at the base of each letter that visually leads the reader to the next letter. Two common serif fonts are Roman and Times New Roman.

Sheet: Used to display different types of information, such as financial data or charts.

Sheet Name: Descriptive name that can be assigned to each sheet in a workbook. A sheet name helps identify the contents of the sheet.

Sheet Reference: The name of the sheet, followed by an exclamation point and the cell or range reference, in a formula.

Sheet Tab: Where the name of each sheet in a workbook is displayed, shown at the bottom of the workbook window.

Size: The width of a column.

Sizing Handle: Eight squares and circles located on the selection rectangle that allow the object to be resized.

SmartArt Graphic: A graphic used to create a visual representation of textual information.

SmartArt Style: The way to apply combinations of different formatting options such as edges, gradients, line styles, shadows, and three-dimensional effects.

Solver: A tool used to perform what-if analysis to determine the effect of changing values in two or more cells, called the adjustable cells, on another cell, called the objective.

Sort: To arrange data in a specified sequence: alphabetically, numerically, or by date.

Source Cell: Cell that contains the data to be copied or referenced.

Source File: The document that houses information that is referenced elsewhere.

Source Program: The program in which an object was created.

Source Workbook: Workbook that contains the data to be copied or referenced.

Sparkline: A tiny chart of worksheet data contained in the background of a single cell.

Spelling Checker: Locates misspelled words, duplicate words, and capitalization irregularities in the active worksheet and proposes the correct spelling.

Split Window: A feature that allows you to divide a worksheet window into sections, making it easier to view different parts of the worksheet at the same time.

Spreadsheet: A worksheet; a rectangular grid of rows and columns used to enter data.

Stacked-Column Chart: Displays data as evenly spaced bars; this type of chart also shows the proportion of each category to the total.

Stock Chart: Illustrates fluctuations in stock prices or scientific data; requires three to five data series that must be arranged in a specific order.

Stops (Gradient Stops): Specific points where the blending of two adjacent colors in the gradient ends.

Surface Chart: Displays values in a form similar to a rubber sheet stretched over a 3-D column chart. These are useful for finding the best combination between sets of data.

Synonyms: Words with a similar meaning.

Syntax: Rules of structure for entering all functions.

t

Table: An organized collection of related information that is entered into a series of worksheet rows and columns.

Table Name: Name that represents the range of cells that stores an Excel data table.

Table Range: The area in a table that contains the records.

Tab Scroll Buttons: Located in the sheet tab area; used to scroll tabs right or left when there are more sheet tabs than can be seen.

Template: A file that contains settings that are used as the basis for a new file you are creating.

Text: Any combination of letters, numbers, spaces, and any other special characters.

Text Box: A graphic object that is a container for text or graphics.

Theme: A predefined set of formatting choices that can be applied to an entire worksheet in one simple step.

Thesaurus: A reference tool that provides synonyms, antonyms, and related words for a selected word or phrase.

Thumbnail: Miniature representations of graphic objects.

Tiled: Window arrangement in which the windows are displayed one after the other in succession across and down the screen.

Tracked Changes: Notes that identify any insertion, deletion, or formatting change that is made to the document.

Two-Variable Data Table: A table that uses only one formula that refers to two different input cells, one column-oriented and one row-oriented.

U

Uniform Resource Locator (URL): An address that specifies the location of the destination document.

V

Validation: Action that ensures that the data entered in a cell is acceptable or valid by placing restrictions on the data that can be entered.

Value Axis: The Y axis, usually the vertical axis; contains data.

Value-Axis Title: Describes the information on and/or the format of the Y axis.

Variable: A value that can change if the data it depends on changes.

Vertical: Window arrangement in which the windows are displayed one above the other.

VLOOKUP Function: Function that searches for a value in the leftmost column of a table, then returns a value in a cell you designate.

W

Watermark: Text or pictures that appear behind text in a document.

Web Page: A document that can be used on the World Wide Web (WWW) and displayed in a browser.

What-If Analysis: A technique used to evaluate the effects of changing selected factors in a worksheet.

Window Arrangement: A feature that displays all open workbook files in separate windows on the screen, making it easy to view and work with information in different workbooks.

Wizard: An Office feature that guides you step by step through the process of completing a task.

Workbook: An Excel file that stores the information you enter using the program.

Workbook Window: The large center area of the program window.

Worksheet: Also commonly referred to as a spreadsheet; a rectangular grid of rows and columns used to enter data.

X

X Axis: Also called the category axis; is usually the horizontal axis and contains categories.

XY (Scatter) Chart: Used to show the relationship between two ranges of numeric data.

Y

Y Axis: Also called the value axis; usually the vertical axis and contains data.

Z

Z Axis: Also called the depth axis or series axis; a third axis, in a 3-D column, 3-D cone, or 3-D pyramid chart; allows data to be plotted along the depth of a chart.

LOWER, EX1.41
LP Simplex, EX4.7

M

Magnification, IO.33
Main dictionary, EX1.25
Major concepts. *See* Concept
Manual page break, EX3.57, EX3.58
Margin, EX2.71, EX2.72
Mark as Final, EX5.51–EX5.52
Marked as Final icon, EX5.52
Marked as Final information bar, EX5.52
Math & Trig functions, EX1.41
Matrix SmartArt graphic, EX4.47
MAX, EX1.41
.mdb, IO.54
Medical sales accountant, EX3.67
Merge Across, EX1.56
Merge & Center, EX1.55, EX1.56
Merge Cells, EX1.56
Merge menu, EX1.56
Merging cells, EX1.55–EX1.56
Message alert, EX5.39
Metadata, IO.51
Microsoft Clip Organizer, EX2.9
Microsoft Help system, IO.60–IO.65
MIN, EX1.41
Mini toolbar, IO.39, IO.41–IO.43, EX1.59
Minimize button, IO.14
Minimize/expand ribbon, IO.24
Mixed reference, EX3.10
Mode indicator, EX1.13, EX1.15, EX1.45
Month headings, EX3.18
Mouse actions, IO.31, IO.37
Mouse pointer, IO.14, EX1.5
Move, IO.47–IO.48
Moving around the worksheet, EX1.8–EX1.11
Multilevel sort, EX6.26, EX6.27–EX6.29
Multiple workbooks, EX4.23–EX4.33

N

#N/A, EX3.6
Name, EX5.26
#NAME?, EX3.6
Name box, EX1.5, EX3.33
Name Manager, EX5.30, EX5.31
Named range, EX5.26–EX5.32
Naming cell references, EX5.26–EX5.29
Navigation keys, IO.31, IO.35, EX1.9
Nested function, EX5.34
New folder, EX3.30–EX3.31
New Formatting Rule dialog box, EX3.50
New Message window, EX6.13
New Name dialog box, EX5.27
New tab, IO.26
New worksheet, EX3.12–EX3.18
Nonadjacent range, EX1.31
NOT, EX1.41, EX5.32
NOW, EX1.41
nper, EX5.6
#NULL!, EX3.6
#NUM!, EX3.6
Number cell style, EX2.23–EX2.24
Number entries, EX1.12, EX1.20
Number format, EX1.61–EX1.64
Number format styles, EX2.23
Number group, EX1.82, EX6.69, EXCS.3

O

Object, EX2.5
Objective cell, EX4.7
Office 2010 programs, IO.2
Office clipboard, IO.45
Office.com Web site, EX4.47
Office help, IO.60–IO.65
Office Online clip art, EX2.9
Office theme, EX2.16
On-demand tabs, IO.20
One-variable data table, EX5.8
OneNote 2010, IO.2
Open, EX1.24
Open dialog box, IO.28
Open options, IO.29
Opening a file, IO.28–IO.30
Operand, EX1.37
Operator, EX1.37
OR, EX1.41, EX5.32
Order of precedence, EX1.37
Orientation, EX1.76
Other charts button, EX2.27
Outline group, EX6.71, EXCS.10
Outline levels, EX6.47
Outline symbols, EX6.47, EX6.49
Outlook 2010, IO.2
Overview (application programs). *See* Application programs
  (overview)

P

Page break, EX3.57–EX3.58
Page Break Preview, EX3.57–EX3.58
Page Layout tab, EX2.77–EX2.78, EX3.74, EXWT2.19,
  EXCS.7–EXCS.8
Page Layout view, EX2.65
Page orientation, EX1.76
Page Setup dialog box, EX2.70, EX3.62, EX3.63
Page Setup group, EX3.74, EXWT2.19, EXCS.7–EXCS.8
Pane, EX3.34
Paragraph dialog box, IO.23
Parentheses, EX1.37
Password, EX4.13, EX5.54, EX5.55
Paste, IO.45, IO.46, IO.48, EX1.29–EX1.30, EX1.32
Paste button, EX1.29
Paste Options, IO.46
Paste Options menu, EX1.30
Paste Preview, IO.46
Paste Special dialog box, EXWT1.5, EXWT1.12
Payroll clerk, EX5.55
.pcx, EX2.6
Percent data label, EX2.51
Percent style, EX2.23, EX3.12
Photograph, EX2.5
Picture, EX2.5. *See also* Graphics
Picture Border, EX2.14
Picture Effects, EX2.14
Picture Layout, EX2.14
Picture SmartArt graphic, EX4.47
Picture style, EX2.13–EX2.15
Picture Styles group, EX2.78, EXCS.13
Picture Tools Format tab, EX2.7, EX2.78, EXCS.13
Pie chart, EX2.27, EX2.54–EX2.64
  color, EX2.62–EX2.63
  exploding/rotating the pie, EX2.58–EX2.60
  selecting data, EX2.55
  texture, EX2.61
  titles/data labels, EX2.55–EX2.58, EX2.60

X

X axis, EX2.25, EX2.29
.xls, EX1.23, IO.54
.xlsm, IO.54
.xlsx, IO.54, EX1.23, EX4.22
.xltx, IO.54, EX4.20
.xps, IO.54
XY (scatter) chart, EX2.27

Y

Y axis, EX2.25, EX2.29
Year-to-date total, EX3.18–EX3.20

Z

Z axis, EX2.25
Zip code, EX6.10, EX6.11
Zoom, IO.33–IO.34
Zoom dialog box, IO.33, IO.34, EX3.32
Zoom feature, EX1.6
Zoom group, IO.67, EX2.79, EX3.75, EXCS.12
Zoom percentage, EX2.65
Zoom slider, IO.14, IO.15, IO.33